German Unification
— *in the* —
European Context

German Unification
—— *in the* ——
European Context

Peter H. Merkl

With a Contribution by Gert-Joachim Glaessner

The Pennsylvania State University Press
University Park, Pennsylvania

Library of Congress Cataloging-in-Publication Data

Merkl, Peter H.
    German unification in the European context / by Peter H. Merkl;
with a contribution by Gert-Joachim Glaessner.
        p.   cm.
    Includes bibliographical references and index.
    ISBN 0-271-00921-7 (alk. paper). — ISBN 0-271-00922-5 (pbk.)
    1. Germany—History—Unification, 1990.   2. Germany—Relations
—Europe.   3. Europe—Relations—Germany.   I. Glaessner, Gert-
Joachim, 1944–   II. Title.
DD289.M47   1993
943.087′9—dc20   92-31665
                                                                                    CIP

Published by The Pennsylvania State University Press, Suite C, Barbara Building,
University Park, PA 16802-1003

Printed in the United States of America

It is the policy of The Pennsylvania State University Press to use acid-free paper
for the first printing of all clothbound books. Publications on uncoated stock
satisfy the minimum requirements of American National Standard for Information Sciences—Permanence of Paper for Printed Library Materials, ANSI
Z39.48–1984.

Contents

Preface

This study was occasioned by the collapse of the communist GDR and
the coming about of German unification in 1989/90. Since I was scheduled to be a visiting professor at the University of Göttingen in 1990, at
first I was planning only to write an account of this process along the
lines of my *Origin of the West German Republic* (1963): that is, a
political history of the genesis of the German Basic Law and the establishment of the Federal Republic in 1948/49. But, in the midst of discussions
with German colleagues and with associates at the Mannheim Institute
of Electoral Research, the project quickly grew and became a full-scale
inquiry into at least the most salient factors: the international aspects
(the historical German question, the collapse of East European communism, and the Two-Plus-Four Treaty negotiations); the political and
institutional transformation from the old FRG and GDR; the economic
problems of unifying a communist system with a capitalist economy;
and the changing sense of German national identity emerging from this
upheaval. While holding the Shephard Stone Chair Professorship at the
Free University of Berlin the following year (1991), I had the opportunity
to co-opt a well-known West German expert on the GDR and the
problems of unification, Gert-Joachim Glaessner, to write a chapter on

the GDR (Chapter Three). Originally we had also planned to do a chapter on the social dimensions of unification such as the integration of East German teachers and professionals into the united German staff. We decided against including this topic because it is very large and not as important to an American or British audience as, say, the economic dimensions, which have an immediate impact on the financing of the U.S. deficit, East European recovery, and the future of the European community.

At the heart of this book is a generational analysis of German attitudes, East and West, toward unification, the German sense of national identity, and the German past and future, accomplished with the help of the opinion polls archive of the Mannheim Institute and with the advice of its principal staff such as Prof. Dr. Dieter Roth, Wolfgang Gibowski, and Prof. Dr. Max Kaase. Let me summarize my findings: German unification was supported most heavily by those over fifty, particularly the generations of Chancellor Kohl and World War II. The younger generations, especially those under twenty-five, were at best lukewarm toward it. They are, however, emphatically anti-Nazi, only mildly nationalistic, and rather pacifistic and environmentally oriented in their politics. The all-German parliamentary elections of December 2, 1990 (I returned to observe them *in situ*) was a generational showdown in which the older generation carried the day.

The bulk of my attention was focused on analyzing the transformation of West and East German politics, from 1989 to the united Germany of the first half of 1991, with regard to a) the elections and party system, b) the institutional system, and c) the economic system. The principal findings were as follows. The East German additions have confused and destabilized the old West German party system. East German voters have not only proven fickle but are evidently not even identifiable by class and occupation: unlike in the West, the CDU voters turned out to be predominantly working-class, the communist PDS voters white-collar and civil service. The parliamentary elections routed the Greens (at least temporarily) and greatly diminished the SPD following. There is a confused neo-Nazi element, many of them the "brown sons of red fathers," that is, the children of communist officialdom. Nevertheless, the future points to equal strength between the SPD and the CDU/CSU in the united political system. Moreover, unification has brought a new federalism, greater power (and blame) to the chancellor, extraordinary economic leverage to the Treuhand agency, a complex mix of property law and relationships, a new capital in Berlin, and a different support base for issues such as first-trimester abortion and political asylum. It will take several years of adjustment before the institutional system may settle down, quite possibly only after major constitutional reforms.

The fervently desired currency union at a rate of 1:1 had a disastrous impact on the East German industrial economy (on top of its many flaws and liabilities), and the exorbitant cost of rehabilitating, privatizing, and modernizing East Germany may yet topple Chancellor Kohl and keep West Germany from fulfilling its role as the economic locomotive of European integration and East European economic growth. Kohl and the unifiers, to be sure, under the circumstances, had little choice in the matter of currency reform. Last but not least important has been the international context of German unification, both as a causative factor of great importance and as the recipient of the widening impact of unification. Here my findings were that German unification greatly upset the balance among the neighboring nations, with some more than with others. Their fears of a united Germany and its interest in Eastern Europe can be contained, however, by a continued U.S. presence in Europe. German unification has also accelerated European integration by propelling Germany toward efforts to merge German economic and political might (via EPC and ECSC) with the "deepened" and "broadening" European Community. United Germany is, however, still as reluctant to move toward European monetary union as it is hesitant to agree to "out-of-theater" military operations.

This is no library dissertation. My principal research source (other than a reliance on the polls archive of the Mannheim Institute), of course, was BEING THERE, as I was teaching at the University of Göttingen (1990) and at the Free University of Berlin (1991), where Glaessner also teaches, in the midst of the events themselves: privy not only to the full range of European press and official statements and of West and East German television (which is infinitely more political than our commercial TV), but also to the opinions of German colleagues, politicians, students, and people in the street. A subject such as the enormous changes of the last two years, moreover, cannot be studied like some long-past event or long-dead literary figure. There are few reliable books out as yet, even in German, and we used most of them. The analysis of such a subject required a solid grasp of public opinion as it was being formed by and as it influenced people, preferably by sophisticated examination of public opinion polls and the news media. A look at the footnotes should be tempered with an awareness of all the other sources available to a researcher on location.

Some aspects of German unification are still sorting themselves out as this manuscript goes to the publisher, in particular the economics of it and the complex international relationships on which it has a major impact. Some of the details related in this book stand the risk of being drastically revised by scholarly research and with the disclosure of additional information. The pressing need to explain the world we live in to English-speaking students and contemporaries, nevertheless, suggested we present a coherent picture of what is already known as soon as possible, and this in spite of the continually changing situation in an important theater of the world.

In this endeavor, I had a good deal of help from various people whom I would like to thank. Among these, of course, is Prof. Gert-Joachim Glaessner of the Otto-Suhr-Institute at the Free University of Berlin. I also thank Jennifer Knerr of Westview Press; the German government's Center of Excellence program at the University of California, which covered some of my research expenses; and Dr. Renate Friedemann, of the German Consulate General in Los Angeles, who furnished such materials as the texts of the two unification treaties and other official statements. Particular gratitude for generous assistance and advice should go also to Prof. Dieter Roth of the Forschungsgruppe Wahlen, Mannheim, who made the public opinion polls of his institute available. I also benefited from the courtesy of representatives from all the major German parties, who furnished material or were willing to talk to me, as well as from the youth study and relevant remarks of Dr. Joachim Hoffmann-Göttig. Profs. Glaessner, Gerhard Zwahr (Leipzig), Ferdinand Müller-Rommel (Lüneburg), Hans-Adolf Jacobsen (Bonn), Michael Minkenberg (Göttingen), and my research assistant, Sabine Hübner, also helped with comments and advice on various aspects of my undertaking. Ms. Hübner also saw the manuscript through various versions and revisions on the word processor. Finally, I owe an immense debt of gratitude and appreciation to the person who inevitably suffered the greatest burden of patience and forbearance while I was engaged in this consuming effort: my wife, Lisa.

Introduction

November 9, 1989—it was a people's revolution, an avalanche of discontent loosened in weeks of ever larger demonstrations and protest gatherings before government buildings: some 500,000 in Leipzig on a Monday night, 60,000 in Halle, 50,000 in Karl-Marx-Stadt (since renamed Chemnitz), 80,000 at the Domplatz in Erfurt, 20,000 in Schwerin, 10,000 each in Gera and Cottbus, and more than half a million at Alexanderplatz in East Berlin half a week before *it* happened. The new East German communist leader Egon Krenz still had massive police forces and barricades out to block the way to the Wall two days before the big Alexanderplatz rally on November 4. He called on East Germans to be thoughtful (*besonnen*) and even promised to lift restrictions on East German travel to the West. But the authority of the communist state and party was unraveling so fast that no soothing words could stop it.[1] The newly appointed Central Committee Information Secretary, Günter Schabowski, one of the reformers in the East German Politbureau, said in a

---

1. A month earlier, the government of Erich Honecker had still played with the thought of stopping the unrest with violent repression, Tiananmen Square style. There is still a lot of controversy over who called off the violence against peaceful demonstrators.

televised press conference at about 7:00 P.M. on November 9 that "from this minute (*ab sofort*), citizens of the East German republic can travel to the West without any problems, without [the excuse of] relatives there, without giving a reason, just as they please. The authorities have been instructed to issue visas quickly and unbureaucratically."

Whether this statement was premature or found the East German border guards unprepared, it took nearly three hours to ignite the spark on that gloomy November day among the suspicious East Berliners. By ten o'clock crowds began to gather at the border crossings. People stuck their ID cards through the bars and demanded to be let through into West Berlin. The surly border guards at first held fast and insisted, everyone had to go and get a visa from the People's Police (*Volkspolizei*). But the crowds would not go home and rumors that the border was about to open began to spread like wildfire. Half an hour later they simply pushed their way through upon the most cursory examination of their personal identification. People began to flood across from the West as well, and together they simply overran the concrete and fortified battlements of twenty-eight years. Queues of "Trabis" (East German Trabant cars) formed at the crossings Heinrich-Heine-Strasse, Bornholmer Strasse, and Invalidenstrasse, patiently waiting their turn to take possession of the other half of the streets of their city. Some border policemen were handed flowers and some managed a smile amidst the enormous wave of jubilation. Within minutes, West and East Berliners were dancing on top of the Wall, champagne corks of East German *Rotkäppchensekt* and West German brands were popping all over, and tipsy revelers began to sing and to embrace each other with tears streaming down their cheeks. Foreign journalists later reported they had never seen so many grown men cry and laugh at the same time. With beaming, happy faces, strangers from East and West were hugging and exchanging drinks, fraternizing as if they had not been separated by deliberate design for two generations. "The miracle was accomplished by the people of the [communist] German Democratic Republic, without arms or violence. Pushed by Mikhail Gorbachev and inspired by the elimination of the Iron Curtain in Hungary,[2] it started an avalanche . . ." the West German newsmagazine *Der Spiegel* editorialized. "And for the first time in German postwar history, with the flying speed of change in East Berlin, [German] reunification seems thinkable and not just utopian."[3]

2. The reference is to the preceding summer's decision of the Hungarian government not to stop tens of thousands of East German tourists from crossing the Hungarian border into Austria, a decision that ran counter to agreements with East Germany but was in accordance with the Helsinki Agreements signed by most European governments, West and East.

3. *Der Spiegel* 43, no. 44, Nov. 13, 1989, pp. 18–21.

Few were the people that failed to be moved when the Berlin Wall was breached on November 3, 1989. The event symbolized to many minds the rebirth of freedom that was taking place throughout Eastern Europe in that turbulent year of 1989 when communist dictators were falling like dominoes to popular demonstrations and the fresh wind from Moscow.

But if nearly everyone cheered at the penetration of the Wall, this was far less true when prospects of the unification of East and West Germany developed soon afterward and the unification efforts got under way and gathered speed. Deep emotions surfaced in opposition to German union, and controversies erupted over issues both relevant and tangential to the German question. Even in the [East] German Democratic Republic (GDR) and the [West] German Federal Republic (FRG), the longed-for "reunification" was by no means universally approved. Younger Germans, say the generations under forty-five, rarely shared the enthusiasm of their elders for unification. When one high-level West German dignitary gushed on the Day of German Unity (October 3, 1990) that this was "the happiest day in my life and that of many Germans," a thirty-five-year-old was overheard muttering: *"Der hat doch nicht alle Tassen im Schrank"* (he ought to have his head examined). Yet many Germans, sixty or older, cried with deep emotion. German opposition to unification ranged from East German dissident groups and demonstrators who desired a reform communist regime in a separate state to factions of the West German opposition parties (and much of the public) who were alarmed at what union might cost them in disruption and distortion of their agenda for a better society. As one Leipzig demonstrator put it in February 1990, "we really just wanted a little democracy, a little more personal liberty, a little freedom to travel, just a little and nothing else. . . . I have been coming to [these Monday-night demonstrations] since last September. I don't know how this reunification business got in. It's out of our hands now."[4]

Opposition and Support from Abroad

Weighty and vociferous opposition came also from abroad where it had never been true that, to quote a prestigious American business weekly, "for nearly half a lifetime, the Western world schemed . . . to achieve this

4. Quoted by Horst D. Schlosser, "Ein nur scheinbar bundesdeutscher Wahlkampf," *Deutschland Archiv* 23, no. 4 (Apr. 1990), 520–524, esp. 521.

outcome [reunification]." It is closer to the truth to view the FRG and GDR of the last forty years as products of the international parallelogram of forces. German public opinion had always sensed a lack of support, even among German allies, for the perennial German postwar goal of unification. Actually, German perceptions of public opinion on this subject among the Western allies were much worse than the reality of such opinion. To be sure, the daily press and many a prominent politician among Germany's neighbors had left no doubt on this score. One prominent Italian Christian Democrat, Giulio Andreotti, in fact was quoted only a few years ago as repeating the old French saw that "he liked Germany so much he'd rather there were two of them." But the West German public clearly underestimated the support that public opinion in France (68% pro, 16% against), Italy (66% vs. 18%), the Netherlands (62% vs. 21%), Sweden (71% vs. 17%), and the United States (67% vs. 16%) gave to German reunification.[5] Only in Britain were there majorities opposed to German union (41% pro vs. 49% against), and even there 59% of the adult population had no doubt that reunification would occur.

British feelings were highlighted further with the Ridley affair of mid-1990. British Trade and Industry Secretary Nicholas Ridley, one of the closest advisers to Prime Minister Margaret Thatcher for the past decade, forcefully expressed his opposition to German economic and financial dominance in the process of European unification in an interview with the arch-conservative weekly *The Spectator*: "this is all a German racket designed to take over the whole of Europe," he said, and he likened giving parts of British sovereignty to a European Community agency to giving it "to Adolf Hitler, frankly." When asked whether Helmut Kohl was not preferable to Hitler, he added, "I'm not sure I wouldn't rather have the shelters [of World War II] and the chance to fight back." Britain, he felt, needed to maintain the balance of power in Europe now more than ever, "with Germany so uppity."[6] The significance of this flap lay in the widespread assumption that Nicholas Ridley was speaking for Mrs. Thatcher herself, and this impression was deepened further with the disclosure that the prime minister had earlier convened a small seminar at Chequers to brief her on the many undesirable attributes of the

5. The quotation is from *Business Week*, Apr. 2, 1990, p. 47. Public opinion polls in West Germany noted years ago that the Germans expected only 15% of the French and 14% of the British to endorse German unification, with 53% and 41%, respectively, opposed. See Wolfgang Bergsdorf, "Wer will die Deutsche Einheit?" *Die politische Meinung* 35 (Jan./Feb. 1990), 13–19, esp. 18. The information on the United States stems from a survey of the Social Research Center of the University of Michigan.

6. Quoted in *Manchester Guardian Weekly*, Jul. 22, 1990, pp. 1–4.

"German character" before she had to meet West German Chancellor Kohl for an official visit.[7] The Chequers memorandum and the remarks of the loose-lipped Mr. Ridley provoked considerable criticism in Britain and abroad,[8] even though the prime minister's feelings on the subject of German unification had been no secret. Whatever one may think of the outmoded concept of national character, there was no doubt that Secretary Ridley had expressed the feelings of many Britons. In his defense and Mrs. Thatcher's, it must be emphasized that both were well over sixty (as were many other members of her cabinet) and obviously represented a British wartime generation that had to dig in and, with all determination, defend their country in its darkest hour against the German assault. Thatcher and Ridley must have been in their early twenties when the bombs had rained down on British cities and Britain barely escaped being invaded by "the hun." However, their war-born sentiments were hardly appropriate for dealing with more recent German generations that have reestablished democratic and constitutional government in the Federal Republic and have lived in peace with their neighbors since 1949. Secretary Ridley had to resign in the wake of the embarrassing affair while the Thatcher government issued soothing statements, in principle endorsing both European cooperation and German union.

American Opinion on a United Germany

In the United States, too, there were undercurrents of criticism while the Bush administration was generally supportive of West German goals. As early as December 4, 1989, and following his Malta summit meeting with the Soviet President, Mikhail Gorbachev, President Bush told NATO members that his administration supported German unification "in the context of continued commitment to NATO [and] an increasingly integrated European community." Meeting with the foreign ministers of NATO and Warsaw Pact countries two months later, the United States agreed to the "two-plus-four" formula of convening the original four

7. According to a copy of the memorandum leaked to the press, the March 24 seminar included top politicians and a few academics, such as Hugh Trevor-Roper, Fritz Stern, and Timothy Garton Ash, who have since dissociated themselves from it. The latter compiled, among other things, a list of German "attributes" in alphabetical order, nimbly fingered in the dictionary: "aggressiveness, angst, assertiveness, bullying, egotism, inferiority complex, sentimentality . . . a capacity for excess . . . a tendency to over-estimate their own strengths and capabilities."

8. See, for example, *Le Monde*, Jul. 14, 1990.

major World War II allies (Britain, France, the Soviet Union, and the United States) and the governments of East and West Germany to work out the "external aspects" of a German unification process of which the "internal" ones were to be left to the Germans. "External aspects" referred to all matters involving the borders of a united Germany, to European security arrangements and Germany's connection with NATO, the Warsaw Pact, or new arrangements of European collective security, and to other aspects pertaining to a peace settlement following World War II (see Chapter Eight), since the outbreak of the Cold War had prevented a peace treaty from being negotiated.

Official American support and endorsement of German union by many a newspaper editorial were accompanied also by some strong and, at times, emotional opposition which, for lack of better arguments, eagerly fastened upon a number of controversies of passing import. One was the Polish border issue of the Oder-Neisse line. In 1945 about one-fourth of German prewar territory had been detached, after driving out the German inhabitants, and given to Poland as compensation for eastern Poland. The eastern half of Poland had been annexed by the Soviet Union as part of its spoils from the Nazi-Soviet pact of 1939[9] and not returned after 1945. The cession of the Oder-Neisse area, now that nearly all the German residents had fled or been expelled, was finally recognized *de facto* by the West German government of Willy Brandt (SPD) in the early seventies and again with the Helsinki Agreements of 1975 after decades of challenges by Oder-Neisse refugees and expellees that had settled in the Federal Republic.

Under leaders like Chancellor Konrad Adenauer (1949–1963), the West German Christian Democrats (CDU/CSU) had always been able to attract most of the German refugee voters from this and other East European areas, a segment amounting to about one-fifth of all voters of the Federal Republic, with token expressions of sympathy for their desire to return "home." In late 1989, when German unification became a distinct possibility, Chancellor Helmut Kohl (CDU) once more tried the old ploy in a vain effort to stall refugee politicians and, in particular, the new right-wing Republican party which had made significant inroads into the voting support of the CDU and its Bavarian affiliate, the CSU.[10] It is

9. This pact, also known as the Ribbentrop-Stalin pact, gave Nazi Germany a free hand with western Poland and thus removed the last barrier to the onset of World War II. The Soviet's share included a part of Romania and a free hand with Lithuania, Latvia, and Estonia. All of Poland, as a result of earlier annexations, had been under the domination of the Russian, Austrian, and German empires until the end of World War I, when the long struggle for Polish national liberation finally culminated in the establishment of a Polish nation-state.

10. The Republicans did particularly well in the south, especially in Bavaria where they

extremely doubtful that the refugee voters believed Kohl's pretense of reluctance to accept the Oder-Neisse border—any hope of Soviet, East European, West European, and American agreement to German unification was known to be contingent on the acceptance of this border. But the alarm signals went up nevertheless from Warsaw and Paris to the U.S. Congress and to the editorial columns of American newspapers. It was as if American journalists had never come across a case of moderately conservative politicians fishing for the votes of the extreme right. One American cartoonist even depicted Kohl as a tall, overweight Hitler ready to launch World War III. This issue was finally settled with joint resolutions in the West German and East German parliaments reiterating the German acceptance of the Polish border. Two months later, American newspaper editorials and columns once more attacked Kohl for his "brusque refusal" to accede to the request of the last communist prime minister of East Germany, Hans Modrow, for 16 billion marks in emergency funds to stabilize his bankrupt government—and this two weeks before the East German parliamentary elections which were sure to sweep the communist state party, the SED/PDS, out of power. A lot of emotional opposition seized upon a rather improbable issue to express itself and to assail Chancellor Kohl, whom many people still have not forgiven for the Bitburg flap of 1985[11] and for other infelicities. Many a column in the *New York Times* and other prominent American periodicals simply declared their strong anti-German feelings without presenting any particular argument about the pros and cons of German union.

Other foreign opinions tended to be balanced between positive and negative reactions, for example in Eastern Europe, in France, and even in Israel, which has had a special relationship with the Federal Republic

---

had originated with several prominent defectors from the CSU. See Merkl's review essay in the *Newsletter* of the Conference Group on German Politics, Nov. 1989, pp. 2–5, and below, Chapter Four.

11. In 1985, President Reagan and Chancellor Kohl, as a gesture of American-German reconciliation, visited a military World War II cemetery in Bitburg where, unbeknownst to them or American and German officialdom, 27 members of the Waffen-SS lay buried among 2,000 German soldiers. Unlike the dreaded SS, which has been condemned as a criminal organization by the Nuremberg War Crimes Tribunal, the Waffen-SS were crack divisions into which, from 1943, soldiers were simply drafted. The Nuremburg tribunal specifically exempted Waffen-SS recruits of 1943 and later from its edict of criminalization of the SS. To make sense of the Bitburg affair, therefore, the ages of the Waffen-SS members buried there would have been a crucial piece of evidence, but this was never clarified. It should be mentioned also that German custom tends to forgive even the worst offender once he is dead and to give the benefit of the doubt to people "too young" to know what they are getting involved in. A poll of West German adults disclosed that three-fourths supported the Bitburg visit. See David Conradt, *The German Polity*, 3rd. ed. (New York: Longman, 1986), p. 50.

since the compensation agreements of 1952 between the Adenauer government and Israel.[12] While the conservative Premier Itzak Shamir, for example, fulminated against a German union, his predecessor of the Labor party, Shimon Peres, saw no problem with it so long as a united Germany would remain as reliably democratic as the Federal Republic had been for forty years. President Vaclav Havel of Czechoslovakia said exactly the same thing, and this endorsement was echoed also by some of the comments from France and England and by several spokespersons for American Jewish organizations.

Military Keynesianism

Underlying the strong emotions arrayed against German unification at this time were also a number of rather controversial issues of which at least some will be addressed in this introduction. Some of them are questions of enduring significance for our understanding of the whole twentieth century, such as the role of nationalism and the nation-state system, fascism, imperial power politics, pacifism and racial prejudice, ideologies like communism and socialism, political economy, and the responsibility of a people for horrendous crimes committed in its name. Some raise partisan emotions in this country, such as U.S. foreign and defense policies under Reagan or the German refusal to fight in the Gulf War. While we cannot promise to arrive at ultimate answers to each of these questions, they need to be brought out into the open where reasonable people can discuss them further.

The first of the issues relevant to German union is, in comparison to most of the others, a lightweight concern and yet, in the short run, it greatly complicates thinking about the great changes of liberalization and democratization triggered by President Gorbachev throughout Eastern Europe, including the German Democratic Republic. It is impossible for a new European security order to replace forty-odd years of armed camps—which faced off at the Iron Curtain dividing East from West Germany—if Western and ex-Soviet leaders do not really believe the threat is gone. In fact, the ex-Soviet and East European fears of the NATO military threat may return with a vengeance if German union within NATO is presented with the rhetoric that "we have won the Cold War and are now the only superpower left in the ring," just as we were in the decade and a half following World War II.[13] For to the ears of the ex-

12. See also the essay by Lily Gardner Feldman in Merkl, ed., *The Federal Republic of Germany at Forty* (New York: New York University Press, 1989), pp. 442–463.

13. Such formulations, in various versions, have appeared in syndicated columns by Ben

Soviet and East European military, and the public in those countries, such Western braggadocio obviously appears threatening and confirms the hard-line argumentation of some of their own disgruntled generals: Who lost East Germany? How did we [the Soviets] lose our dominant position throughout Eastern Europe? Maybe we had better not yet withdraw the hundreds of thousands of Soviet soldiers still stationed with full battle equipment in East Germany and elsewhere. We must stop making so many concessions in arms-reduction agreements and end the erosion of our position vis-à-vis our arch-enemy, the United States.

Some of the urge to proclaim and exploit a presumable Western victory is psychological and reflects the unfulfilled yearnings of nationalism. Some of the same attributes that Mrs. Thatcher's Chequers seminar on German national character found in German history between 1871 and 1945, the angst-ridden need to assert the national honor, the tendency to bully small antagonists, the inferiority complex, and the overestimation of one's own strength have been alive and well in recent years in the United States and Britain, and wherever else a wounded national pride may be present. Many people responded eagerly to the nationalistic appeals of President Reagan and Prime Minister Thatcher and rallied to the violent assertion of national pride at the Falklands, in Grenada, Nicaragua and Panama, and most recently in Iraq. None of this, of course, approaches even remotely the nationalistic slaughter of World War II, but our point is that national pride everywhere can lead to belligerent and jingoistic behavior perpetrated with the utmost self-righteousness.[14] As recently as October 1992, for example, the military commander of the Commonwealth of Independent States, Yevgeny I. Shaposhnikov, indicated that Russian nuclear missiles are still pointed at the United States (despite official statements to the contrary) and that he thought Russia should resume nuclear tests as long as the West did not stop conducting them. Without mutual trust between East and West and an overriding desire for peace and cooperation, the prerequisites for mending the rift in the center of divided Europe may still be lacking.

A large part of the obstacle to making genuine peace with the Russians also has been the result of the military-industrial and economic policies

---

Wattenberg and other conservative voices in Britain and the United States, not to mention military opinion in both countries.

14. There is a curious contrast between the contempt for and violations of international law by the Reagan-Bush administration in Central America, on the one hand, and the propagandistic appeals, for example, to human rights against the Soviet Union, on the other. Or between the hostility of the same administration to the United Nations, culminating in nonpayment of dues to the organization, and then the championing of U.N. collective security against Iraqi aggression.

of both superpowers, in particular the great defense buildup in the Soviet Union in the sixties and seventies, and in the United States in the eighties. After many decades of Soviet paranoia about "capitalist encirclement" and the presumed need to pour the lion's share of the country's resources into defense, the Soviet Union has long served the military-industrial "monkey on its back," and the military privileges and priorities still hold back the development of private enterprise.[15] Behind the Reagan rhetoric of the "evil empire"—which at the time was under the leadership of three dying men in succession, Brezhnev, Andropov and Chernenko, and rapidly slipping into its terminal crisis rather than being a real threat to the West—stood an all-out effort to counteract inflation, stagnation, and recession with massive military spending. The American defense buildup of the eighties was so large, and never matched with the corresponding tax revenues, that it alone accounts for most of the enormous increase in the public debt and for the continuing annual deficits of the federal government, including the huge amounts needed to service the debt. Related monetary policies (high-interest) tied military spending and the record deficit also to the ensuing negative trade balance and made the United States the biggest debtor nation in the world. Worse yet, they made the United States dependent on the willingness of foreign investors—including Germany, which would rather invest in its own, unified economic development now—to buy up our treasury bonds and valuable assets. To keep these crutches of our sluggish economy from being withdrawn, we seem to be compelled to adopt the posture of a great, invincible military power. The cycle from military buildup to imperial extortion of our allies so we can keep up the military posture is complete.

The great defense buildup, at any rate, created a Frankenstein monster of a military-industrial complex in this country as well that insists on being fed regardless of the country's ability to pay or the real need for its bloated services. The original idea of curing problems of lagging economic growth in industrialized nations by deficit spending, or by "priming the pump," of course goes back to the problems of the thirties and forties and to the solutions proposed by British economist John Maynard Keynes. Until the economic crises of the seventies, Keynesianism was the panacea of economic policies throughout the Western world. But priming the pump with massive military spending, "military Keynesianism," is another matter—even when it provides jobs and new industrial activity in the short run, as it did under Presidents John F. Kennedy and Ronald Reagan. Unlike public investment in the private sector, it does not

15. Hedrick Smith gives many examples of these misplaced priorities in *The New Russians* (New York: Random House, 1990), pt. 3, chaps. 10–13.

stimulate the circulation of goods and services but mostly creates products, armaments that will never be used, *or so we hope*.[16] Cold War, or the threat of war, are the lifeblood of demand of military Keynesianism. Neither the bloated Pentagon of today, nor the largely useless defense industries, nor the unemployed of our defense industries want to hear of the winding down of the Cold War and of the peaceful intentions of longtime adversaries. Worse yet, there is a danger of rampant militarism in our thinking which understands the "new world order" as one of military posturing instead of economic competition.

Similar thoughts have come from the Soviet military-industrial complex despite President Gorbachev and now Russian President Yeltsin. Both sides would much prefer to think that the "evil empire" or "capitalist encirclement" are about to return and that, therefore, the massive disarmament desired by continental Europeans—the British government has followed in the footsteps of American military Keynesians—may be unwise or, at the very least, premature. Hence, leading voices in the major Western powers and in the Soviet Union have tended to oppose the radical arms reductions, restructuring of NATO, and disbanding of the Warsaw Pact that are prerequisites of peaceful union in the center of Europe.[17] Without peace and disarmament between the military blocs that created and maintained the German division, there can be no German unification and new "European peace order."[18] At the height of the buildup of Desert Storm in Saudi Arabia, the conservative Soviet military establishment eyed the Western strike forces with great suspicion, fearing an attack on the motherland at a moment of great Soviet weakness and disarray. In fact, the Soviet Union withheld its signature on the Two-Plus-Four Treaty governing German unification until March 1991 to make sure a unified Germany would not join Desert Storm at this crucial moment. And, indeed, the Germans stayed out of the military alliance except for some

16. In an eerie echo of this kind of thinking, an American economist and former cabinet secretary, Charles Schulz, insisted that the massive use of bombs and ordinance in the Gulf War "did not cost us anything because it only used up what we had been stockpiling for decades" against the Soviets. "MacNeil-Lehrer Newshour," Feb. 24, 1991.

17. A good example of these sentiments are the statements of U.S. Defense Secretary Dick Cheney and of conservative columnists like Patrick J. Buchanan, who have warned us apropos of the invasion of Kuwait by Iraq to beware of "unconsidered defense cuts," not to mention the expectation that military equipment used up in the Gulf should be replaced so that we would be ready for the next encounter.

18. See also Robert Kuttner's argument tying together the military and the economic logic of the Cold War, as well as to America's economic decline and struggle to maintain military hegemony. *The End of Laissez-Faire: National Purpose and the Global Economy After the Cold War* (New York: Knopf, 1990).

token gestures and massive financial concessions, although it would have been an exaggeration to describe them as eager to become involved.

It is not possible to discuss these matters without getting into the thick of partisan controversy about them, and possibly triggering the urge toward partisan censorship of views critical of "patriotic" arms buildups, arms sales, and the Bush administration's secret support for Iraq up until its invasion of Kuwait. The Gulf War against Saddam Hussein was hardly over when the American defense industries, loath to accept the inevitable cutbacks from the heights of defense spending under Reagan, pushed for massive arms sales to such allies as Saudi Arabia, Kuwait, the United Emirates, and Egypt. President Bush, in his triumphal speech at the end of the war, had just called it "tragic" if the nations of the Middle East and Persian Gulf were to embark on another arms race, although he could hardly escape the logic of "regional defense cooperation" and "balance" that had armed Iraq for its long war against Iran with advanced weapons from the Soviet Union, the United States, France, Britain, and West Germany, among others. Over sixty German firms, including such well-known giants as Daimler-Benz (partner of Messerschmidt-Bölkow-Blohm) and Siemens had exported military-related equipment to the Middle East in the last decade, helping among other projects to build chemical weapons plants in Libya and Iraq in spite of elaborate export requirements with which the Bonn government presumably attempted to stop such arms exports to "crisis areas." Through close relations with key members in the Kohl government and partnerships with French and other European firms, German companies circumvented the export controls, much as American exporters usually got their permits for highly questionable arms exports with the help of friends in the Reagan-Bush administrations, friends in Congress, or over the protests at Defense and State from the export-minded Commerce Department. Among other things, German companies supplied Saddam with the makings of the lethal sarin and tabun gases—originally developed by I. G. Farben for the Nazis, and possibly also acquired from Iraq's Soviet allies who took over Nazi World War II stockpiles—with which he threatened to wipe out half of Israel.[19]

Many German, French, and British defense-related firms were partly owned by Iraqi and other Middle Eastern holding companies. The new German government has now tightened the export-licensing controls but is unlikely to stop the "export of death" completely. To assuage its guilt

---

19. See especially the new book by Hans Leyendecker and Richard Rickelmann, *Exporteure des Todes: Deutscher Rüstungsskandal in Nahost* (Göttingen: Steidl Verlag, 1991). Also see *The Economist*, Feb. 16, 1991, pp. 39–40.

feelings during the war, in fact, Germany also furnished Israel with batteries of Patriot missiles to protect Israeli nuclear arms facilities in the Negev desert and after the war offered to supply it with another 1 billion marks (about $700 million) in arms. German chemical-weapons detector tanks went to several Middle Eastern allies, most recently to Egypt. In the crazy world of arms exports, strange forms of logic prevail, so long as the cash register jingles; and rationalizations readily crop up, such as "promoting exports" or "balancing" advanced arms sales to one country because its rival has acquired dangerous arms. American arms manufacturers, too, are happy to point a finger at those dastardly Germans or government-subsidized Europeans exporting arms in order to "compete" with them. In spring 1991, in fact, this argument won an Export-Import Bank guarantee of $1 billion for them. The arms race between the antagonists of the Cold War has thus become an arms exporters' race—with appropriately patriotic hoopla—to arm the next Iran-Iraq war or the next Saddam Hussein.[20]

Continental Pacifism

Military Keynesianism, the belief that "a war will pick up the sluggish economy," and the insatiable demands of the bloated American "military-industrial complex," to speak with the late President Dwight D. Eisenhower, have also brought about a growing transatlantic alienation on matters of NATO and defense policy because many Germans in and out of government, by degrees, are opposed to it. Early in the eighties, a huge European peace movement had gathered hundreds of thousands of followers from many walks of life, and especially among the churches in Germany, to mobilize against the modernization of NATO intermediate-range nuclear forces (INF) to counter the buildup of Soviet SS-20s, a gift of the Soviet military-industrial complex under Brezhnev. This missile refurbishment had still been agreed on by President Jimmy Carter and Chancellor Helmut Schmidt (SPD) in 1979 (the NATO "double decision"), but by 1983 the latter found himself ostracized within his own party for supporting it.[21] After the Reykjavík summit, in any case, the

20. German semilegal exports of military-related equipment and matériel also have enjoyed government credit guarantees for their contracts since the beginnings of the export-minded FRG. *Kölner Stadtanzeiger*, Feb. 16, 1991. The old GDR, too, was a major arms exporter.
21. The Soviet missile buildup during the years of détente (1960s and 1970s) was very real and was directed at the NATO forces in West Germany—also at China. Thus it was not at all absurd to counter the Soviet SS-20s with new cruise missiles and Pershing 2s,

INF missiles were phased out by both sides. In spring of 1988, half a decade after the big peace demonstrations, Schmidt's successor, Helmut Kohl, who had still been solidly behind refurbishing the INF missiles in 1983, balked at modernizing the remaining NATO short-range nuclear forces in West Germany with American Lance missiles, and was bitterly assailed for it by both the American and the British military establishment, who were ready to defend NATO against the "evil empire" to the last German. The peace movement and the Green party had evidently made large parts of the West German public very much aware of and nervous about the vast stockpiles of nuclear missiles, huge conventionally armed garrisons, U.S. poison gas depots, and other hazards in their small country—pointing out among other things that such objects in one's backyard would inevitably place one's neighborhood on a Soviet missile target map, even if some of them did not simply explode by accident. Scuttlebutt had it that "the worst case scenario is, of course, a Soviet attack on us [Germans] but the worst-worst scenario is that our NATO allies would then defend us, until no German, east or west, is alive."

NATO field commanders, especially in the air force and including West German Bundeswehr officers, routinely aggravated the rising climate of antimilitary feeling with their insensitivity to civilian complaints about NATO air shows in which crashing planes killed scores of spectators on the ground, frequent low-altitude training flights over inhabited areas, civilian lake resorts and recreational areas, and other dubious military display. Major NATO maneuvers had to be postponed or canceled amidst popular protests. In spring of 1990, two Canadian NATO jets collided in a low-level training flight over densely settled parts of Karlsruhe, raining large fragments of their craft upon schools and suburban neighborhoods. No civilians were killed, but the very pro-Western and liberal magazine *Der Stern*, for one, described the scene by showing a picture of a parked car, its roof smashed in by parts of a jet engine. The magazine pointed out that, normally, a mother and her child were in that car and that the child could have been killed by that falling metal: "It could have been YOUR CHILD." People in the street refer to the "damn cowboys" of NATO, and one can hear at least some young Germans stubbornly refer to the American NATO allies as "occupation troops" that have long overstayed their welcome. Polls show a sharply rising number of Germans who want all foreign troops out of Germany. After forty years of being

except that this was done against a background of such immense "overkill capacity" on both sides that it seemed a pointless exercise or worse. See Geir Lundestad, *East, West, North, South: Major Developments in International Politics, 1945–1986* (Oslo: Norwegian University Press, 1986), pp. 163–168, 173–175.

defended by NATO allies, many Germans also tended to look for the *self-serving* reasons why American and other troops are still there, such as that it must be very good for American (defense) business and not motivated by love of the Germans.

What does all this have to do with German unification? Well, a funny thing happened to German unification on the way to its formal completion, the formation of a duly elected coalition government in mid-January 1991. The Persian Gulf War, a looming if largely ignored presence in German political awareness since the preceding summer months, had sprung into raging flames. Germany's principal allies were demanding from a most reluctant, flustered Kohl government that it should send combat troops to fight as part of the American and allied military juggernaut against the Iraqi dictator who had raped Kuwait. This once more brought basic disagreements to the surface, along with major doubts about the role of a united Germany in the world and the future purpose of the NATO alliance. "NATO Fumbles a Chance to Find a Post–Cold War Role," headlined an article in the *Los Angeles Times*,[22] now that "the classic Cold War threat of a massive ground attack from the Soviet Union and its East European allies no longer seems credible." Individual European NATO members (and non–NATO member France) were quite willing to support the American blockade and boycott against Iraq but, except for Britain and the United States, there was no intention of changing NATO's original mission of keeping the peace in Europe. There was particular resistance to turning NATO into an instrument for fighting Third World antagonists of American or British imperial policies.

We often forget that continental Europeans were not very supportive of Britain in the Falklands War either. To the West Germans, in particular, who pledged in their constitution not to sent troops outside of Europe for military action,[23] the very idea of searching for a full-fledged post–Cold War NATO role outside Europe appeared to be the height of absurdity. Precisely because half a century ago and earlier they were smitten by militarism and disastrous aggressions, today they want to keep down and reduce their military posture and that of the NATO alliance. They warmly welcomed the waning of the threat from the Warsaw Pact and the Soviet Union as a chance at drastically cutting down the burdensome presence and vastly wasteful expense of the military in

22. Aug. 18, 1990.

23. The constitutional prohibition has not yet been tested before the Federal Constitutional Court. It specifically exempts the territory of Turkey and actions to "defend German interests." But there are also clauses subjecting domestic law to international law and obligations to international collective security organizations. See articles 24–26 of the Basic Law of Germany.

their backyard (see Chapters Four and Eight). Nearly halving the combined military forces of East and West Germany (as agreed between Kohl and Gorbachev), destroying the old remaining nuclear missiles, and seeing NATO become more of a political organization suited them perfectly—if anything, they were impatient to get on with it. Some of the Greens and Young Socialists even dream of abolishing the German army. For all these reasons, of course, Germans also found it difficult to comprehend that some of their neighbors still saw them as a potential *military* threat, once they were united again. This perception met its most embarrassing moment when British opinion switched from Nicholas Ridley's fears of German aggression to complaints about German "cowardice" and unwillingness to fight in the Gulf.[24]

German Demonstrations Against the Gulf War

When at last the standoff of American military might with Saddam came down to an ultimatum and then to the unleashed fury of the aerial assault on Iraq, the long-dormant German peace movement came back to life with demonstrations to rival the East German ones of the previous year:[25] 200,000 mostly young people, but also church-related and professional people, in seventy cities rallied on the Sunday (January 12) before the ultimatum ran out, extremely critical of the ultimatum as a negotiating device and quite aware that the Bush administration had no intention of giving Iraq a reasonable chance to respond (a trick repeated with the start of the ground war). In Berlin, where 50,000 rallied, there was minor violence and ten demonstrators were arrested. There were rallies all over Western Europe as well, even including the capitals of allies participating in the war, for example, in Paris and Rome. Vigils at NATO offices in Stuttgart, at U.S. missions in large cities, and at the Rhine-Main Air Base waited through the night, especially on the night of the ultimatum, and

24. At the height of the conflict, it was striking indeed to read in the *Manchester Guardian* and elsewhere references to the British "warrior nation," the very term used by Thomas Mann to define why the German "warrior nation" in World War I was fighting the British "nation of greengrocers." It was hardly surprising, however, after a decade of Thatcherite jingoism. But see also Ian Aitken, "Thank God the Germans Don't Want to Fight," *Manchester Guardian Weekly*, Feb. 3, 1991, p. 4.

25. There was such a substantial presence of high school and college students in the vigils, rallies, and demonstrations that we may well speak of another cohort of politically mobilized youth, an activist generation to follow the quiet second half of the eighties. Its rebellious motives may well include their awareness of the great East German and East European protests of 1989/90.

responded with howls and anguish to the news of the aerial bombardment. Large crowds of young people milled about, bearing signs "We Are Afraid," quite a contrast to the obsession of some Americans not to be considered "wimps." Ecologically minded protesters warned about the dangers of oil wells catching fire (long before they did), conjuring up visions of something like a nuclear winter caused by the smoke blocking the rays of the sun. Feminists derided the machismo of war. The feuilleton pages of newspapers talked about the priceless archaeological treasures that might be destroyed by massive bombing of Iraq. Anarchist groups organized minor violence. Terrorists shot out the windows of the American Embassy in Bonn, a city where the mother of demonstrations was about to unfold, ten days into the war, and where sprees of panic buying of food and gas masks were also reported. Some 200,000 demonstrators gathered in Bonn (January 26), many of them brought by twenty-eight trains from all parts of Germany. Speakers from the trade unions and major opposition parties, clergymen, and prominent writers and journalists all tried valiantly to undo the obvious anti-American overtones of the earlier rallies, acting on the conviction that the United States had in fact acted to stop unbridled aggression by a ruthless tyrant, and had even done so within the context of the alliance and the United Nations. They all spoke of the yearning for a better world, one without war and violence, without economic megalomania, the poisoning of nature, the exploitation of the Third World, without militarism and arms exports, without the oppression of women, minorities, and children.[26] They also called for boycotting the arms manufacturers and death merchants in their midst.

From that moment on, there has been a sharp and painful split in the German news media and in public discussions of the Gulf War that shows the depth and breadth of German sentiment far beyond the peace movement. No German, of course, shared the American patriotic enthusiasm and hyperbole about exorcising the "Vietnam syndrome" that marked the end of the ground war. "Imagine the reaction in countries like France, the Netherlands, or Belgium, if Germany's first act as a sovereign country were to reestablish itself as a military power," Bundestag President Rita Süssmuth (CDU) was quoted as saying. What indeed would their reaction have been if the Germans were longing to exorcise their "World War I and II syndrome," the legacy of two lost wars? Most Germans today, whether in East or West Germany, simply do not share

26. See *Die Zeit*, no. 5, Feb. 1, 1991, pp. 8–10; *Der Stern*, Jan. 24, 1991, pp. 33A–33F; and *Der Spiegel* 45, no. 5, Jan. 28, 1991, pp. 28–31. Some of the demonstrators pointedly likened the onset of the bombardment to the attack on Panama, "another lashing out at a villain built up by the U.S."

the popular American (and British) attitudes toward war as a self-affirmation of the nation, as a good patriotic show (see Conclusion). At best, they may agonize over pragmatic considerations of when wars may become unavoidable. Soon after the Gulf War, substantial German opinion emerged, including prominent politicians and intellectuals who argued that Germany should indeed have supported the allies more directly and with troops. Among them were government politicians who stressed the importance of being considered reliable allies by the West and of thinking in the context of multilateral collective security action by a future European security organization or the United Nations. Some Green politicians such as Petra Kelly and intellectuals such as the writer Hans Magnus Enzensberger[27] claimed to see great similarities between Adolf Hitler and Saddam Hussein. Others, more to the point, expressed their shock at Iraqi missiles exploding in Tel Aviv and Haifa and at those Germans—meanwhile being tried in court—who helped Saddam to develop poison gas, a grisly reminder of the holocaust of European Jews at German hands. Indeed, on the level of public opinion polls in West Germany in late January 1991, the fear of Israel being pulled into the war was the biggest (62% agreed) of eight concerns laid before the respondents as valid reasons for getting into the war.[28]

While it is not exactly clear how a German military participation would have kept Israel from being "pulled in" by Saddam, this was the same issue that divided the Left in other European countries. In France, it induced the ruling party, Mitterrand's Socialists, and many "68ers" to join the allied action in the Gulf, while the Old Left, especially the communists (PCF), and the National Front and New Right (not to mention many Arabs in France) were against it as "a product of U.S. imperialism." In Spain, an unlikely alliance of the Catholic church, intellectuals, and the communist party (PCE)—with the support of 51.6% of the adult population—opposed the socialist (PSE) government's decision to dispatch warships to the Gulf (supported by only 41.5%), while as many as 71.5% believed the war to be "unjust." Only 9% bought President Bush's claim that it was "a just war," and there may have been similar doubts on the minds of many German, French, and

27. For an extended German version of his frequently reprinted column, see "Hitlers Wiedergänger," *Der Spiegel* 45, no. 6, Feb. 4, 1991, pp. 26–28. Other notables for the Gulf War were Wolf Biermann and Jürgen Habermas.

28. Next in importance was the environmental pollution caused by burning oil fields (59%), followed by "terrorist attacks in Germany" and a possible Iraqi attack on Turkey which would have involved Germany under its NATO obligations in the Gulf War. See *Der Spiegel* 45, no. 5, Jan. 28, 1991, pp. 32–38.

Italian Catholics for whom a "just war" is a well-defined term and not political hyperbole.[29] Priests and theologians of the European Catholic, Greek Orthodox, and Protestant churches, not to mention the pope himself, were generally quite far from the position of certain American Protestant leaders who never saw an American war they did not like. On the other hand, there was the spectacular turnabout of the Israeli peace movement, which for obvious reasons embraced this war, as did many conservative Sunni mullahs in the Gulf and in Egypt.

To understand properly the German aversion to participation in this and most other wars—and without attributing too much to misleading labels such as "anti-Americanism" or "wimpishness"—we need to dig further into the phenomenon than the peace movement which, by the way, already marched against West German rearmament and "atomic death" in the fifties. Historically, the post-1945 German sense of national identity meant a final departure from a fifty-year obsession with militarism and warlike aggrandizement at the expense of Germany's neighbors—a struggle for "a place in the sun," for world power status befitting German delusions of national superiority and grandeur. For half a century, two nationalistic generations of Germans had sacrificed the flower of the nation's youth and, in the process, killed millions among their neighbors and devastated their lands.

When it was all over, the German survivors were encouraged by the allied victors in the late forties, especially by American "reeducation" policies, to return to a normal, peaceful state of mind, to live and let live among their European neighbors. Even their NATO role during the Cold War was understood by the German NATO soldiers as one of deterrence: to be well armed and well prepared so that the *casus belli* would never occur—among other reasons because, unlike the United States, Germany and the Germans would have been destroyed in a real war. Fortunately, the Soviets and other Europeans, West and East, have always shared this basic aversion to going beyond threats and pressures in Europe. The sudden change from the safety of the deterrent posture to the call to arms, "the Germans to the front," caused no fewer than 22,000 army recruits and reservists to seek refuge in conscientious objector status in January 1991.[30] Before the final showdown, in November, about half of

29. A war does not become "just" simply because its target is a widely acknowledged villain and a multilateral police force, or because a single, self-appointed world policeman decides to punish the aggressor. It has to be a war of defense, and all remedies short of war have to be exhausted first. See also the *Los Angeles Times*, Feb. 15, 1991.

30. To aggravate the German dissension, NATO Secretary General Manfred Wörner, a former West German defense minister, hawkishly promised that German troops would indeed defend Turkey, an "automatic nexus" the government and Bundestag leaders were

the West German adult public simply denied that "the Gulf crisis endangered peace in Europe" (47.4%); they wanted "to keep out of war" (45.9%) and "leave Kuwait to Iraq" (49.9%). A week after the aerial bombardment had started, two-thirds agreed that military intervention had become necessary, and slightly fewer (57%) said that the United States and its allies could have waited no longer to attack. But an irreducible body of opinion still insisted that the sanctions should have been allowed more time to take effect (28–38%),[31] that President Bush was coresponsible (24%) or solely responsible (4%) for the Gulf War, and that the German peace demonstrations were a positive thing (31%).

Behind these views, furthermore, there was a widely shared German distrust of American ulterior motives in the Gulf War, and in the pursuit of Middle Eastern peace and the "new world order" to follow. During the eighties, many Germans had developed a new and critical image of the United States as a military "Rambo" compensating for its long-term economic decline and its unwillingness to address economic problems. The end of the Cold War, the opening up of Eastern Europe, and the intended consolidation and eventual expansion of the European Community hinted at the advent of a very different kind of new order than was apparently on the mind of President Bush. The bloody Soviet crackdown in the Baltic states, just as the clock was ticking toward the Gulf ultimatum, and the threat of a Soviet military dictatorship—not to mention the transparent Soviet maneuvers to backpedal on disarmament agreements with the West[32]—deeply disturbed Poland, Czechoslovakia, and, of course, the newly united Germans, who after all still had 360,000 heavily armed Soviet troops stationed on their soil. The Germans were particularly worried about how the Soviet hard-liners would view Germany if its troops joined what some Soviet generals were known to

---

anxious to avoid. See the discussion and interviews with military figures in *Der Spiegel* 45, no. 7, Feb. 11, 1991, pp. 18–30, including the controversies in the SPD where antiwar *Moralos* such as Oskar Lafontaine and his following clashed with *Realos*, who supported German participation under the U.N. flag but never on an automatic basis. Also Helmut Schmidt, "Jammern allein hilft nicht," *Die Zeit*, no. 5, Feb. 1, 1991, p. 3.

31. 38% of the respondents were opting for sanctions; among SPD supporters it was 54% and angry Green supporters 59%. See *Der Spiegel* 45, no. 5, Jan. 28, 1991, pp. 32–38.

32. The Soviet Union attempted to lessen the impact of its own agreements to reduce forces by shifting some army divisions to Asian Russia and some over to the Soviet navy, neither of which was covered by the disarmament treaties. This subterfuge was probably inspired by the Soviet military, which was suspicious of American motives in the Gulf, fearing a possible attack on the Soviet Union. This may also have been behind Soviet peace initiatives during the Gulf War, together with hopes to salvage Soviet influence as well as equipment in Iraq.

regard as an American military plan to attack a weakened Soviet Union from the south. It did not help matters to notice the indifference to East European fears in Washington, where the Bush administration was preoccupied with the maintenance of the Gulf War coalition and willing to accept Soviet as well as Chinese peccadillos so as not to endanger support for the U.N. action.[33] German public opinion polls in late January revealed that a good one-third (36% vs. 51% who did not) expected the Soviet Union to "become a military dictatorship," with unforeseeable dangers from the Soviet troops inside East Germany. Of the respondents, 37% thought a Soviet civil war a distinct possibility (only 20% did not), and two-thirds (65%) were sure the Soviet Union would lose some of its union republics (35% did not). And all this was going on while U.S. attention and most of the NATO troops were engaged down in the Gulf. In fact, the allies wanted to draw German troops away from where they might be needed in a continental crisis.

The upshot of all this for the future of U.S.-German relations is still to come. There was a noticeable drop in the German popularity of George Bush just as his U.S. popularity was soaring to unprecedented heights (88%) as a result of his great martial triumph in the Gulf. At the same time, anti-American sentiment in Germany rose to levels never encountered before: between one-fourth and one-third of the German public described itself as in sympathy with the "anti-American mood," doubted "the ability of the U.S. to cope responsibly with world problems," and ascribed little or no importance to the presence of U.S. troops for German security.[34] They were obviously unimpressed by such criticism as that of U.S. Senator Robert Byrd, who referred to their policy to buy their way out with financial contributions and war matériel as "a monstrous shame"; or by Henry Kissinger's complaint about how they "could do this to us" after our strong support for reunification; or by the repeated press assertion that "they owed us gratitude for forty years of protection."[35] In their uncertain search for a new global role, the united

33. President Bush was even reported to have said at the outbreak of the ground war that he resented the bloody Soviet crackdown in Lithuania a lot less than he did Gorbachev's attempt to stop the ground war with a Soviet peace initiative.

34. See the *Spiegel*/EMNID polls in *Der Spiegel* 45, no. 5, Jan. 28, 1991, p. 37, and no. 6, Feb. 4, 1991, pp. 40–47. The doubts about our ability were high also in the eighties and, in this case, should be contrasted with American polls attributing greater ability to handle foreign affairs to the Republicans.

35. They were stung even more by a widely quoted editorial in the *Jerusalem Post*, which said, among other things, that the German "peace demonstrations were obscene and really pro-Saddam," and also by reports of hostile posters greeting Foreign Ministers Hans-Dietrich Genscher in Tel Aviv. As a German-Israeli historian, Michael Wolfsohn, put it, "German youth never again wants to become murderers and Israelis never again want to be victims."

Germans have begun to accept the necessity of their playing a military role in the world and in regional collective security arrangements, but evidently there is to be *no participation without representation*. They are reconsidering their earlier rejection of a permanent seat on the U.N. Security Council—the Soviets made a proposal in this regard in September 1990—and, if successful, such a step might help them to overcome their fears of American and British unilateralism in U.N. enforcement actions.

The Heavy Weight of the Past

The biggest liability of a united Germany and the chief cause of opposition to it has been the historical legacy of German conduct in the years from about 1900 to 1945, in particular during World Wars I and II, although it is true that the great nationalist and ideological battles of this bloodstained century left few people with the objectivity to identify good and evil in their own deeds. The First World War already became the stage for moral mass delusion and monstrous wrongs committed against individuals and nations. Even without adopting the simpleminded view that World War I was "started" by the Germans alone—historians have more complex explanations, with plenty of responsibility to go around for all sides—the Germans clearly shared a major part of the responsibility in their nationalist mania to fight the British and the French for the status of a true world power.[36] Worse yet, their conduct of the war was ruthless and left legions of innocent victims, beginning with neutral Belgium, which was overrun and brutalized in the course of the Schlieffen Plan of surprise attack on the French. They showed no pity to anyone, except themselves once they found they were losing the war and had to endure the harsh settlement of the victorious allies in the Peace Treaty of Versailles. We can also dig deeper for the causes of the great confrontation and its bitter end: the erosion of legitimacy within the Hapsburg, German-Prussian, Ottoman, and tsarist empires, indeed of residual feudalism before the urban-industrial age; the challenge of the socialist parties and trade unions to the capitalist regime; the cultural crisis of Western civilization; and, most of all, the German fixation on taking their own road to modernization, a *Sonderweg*, which led Germany to

36. Recent German historical research has actually weighed the side of German responsibility more heavily than conservative historians have admitted, as several disciples of Fritz Fischer, among others, have shown. See Fritz Fischer, *German Aims in the First World War* [Griff nach der Weltmacht] (New York: Norton, 1967).

spurn the liberal-democratic ways of the West and, in fact, to confront it in all-out struggle.

The original "German question" (Chapter One) from which many of the problems of today's unification stem was buried by the collapse of these old empires and then reemerged a more hideous threat to everyone than ever before. All war is in itself horrible and stupid; and the human propensity to rationalize engaging in "just wars" rarely lends any redeeming significance except for passing moments of atavistic delusion. The German excuse for self-righteously engaging in World War I was no exception, and the rhetoric of national honor and destiny no exoneration. Worse yet, having let out all stops and then losing the war disastrously only fixated the Germans more intensely on their mistaken path. The constitutional democracy of Weimar was quickly overcome by its own deep divisions—not everybody was a diehard nationalist bent on revenge—and by the old nationalist mania to renew the struggle and this time win. Back in the fifties, the German historian Ludwig Dehio pointed out the significance of the all-consuming German passion during those fateful years to fight for European hegemony and empire whatever the costs.[37] It subordinated everything of value in Germany, even the personal pursuit of happiness and liberty, to considerations of military effectiveness and final national victory, distorting the normal processes of human society and producing human killing machines instead of ordinary people. The twisting of human norms and values was particularly striking among the German bourgeoisie, which had once been a guardian of civilized morality and progressive ideas and now became capable of raising such human monsters as concentration camp doctors performing grisly experiments and SS captains with academic degrees, not to mention legions of educated apologists for rank barbarism. But it was not just the German bourgeoisie, but all Germans ready to hate and destroy anyone, whether for reasons of national origin, ethnicity, political conviction, or sexual preference, who did not suit the Nazi vision of a greater German racial empire.

Can we hold the Germans as a whole responsible for the horrors of the Third Reich, World War II, and the holocaust of 6 million Jews and huge numbers of other victims? This was one of the questions before the Nuremberg War Crimes Tribunal and other such courts, including those of denazification in occupied Germany during the late forties, after

37. Dehio, *Deutschland und die Weltpolitik im 20. Jahrhundert* (Munich: Oldenbourg, 1955). While there was and is nothing inherently sacrosanct about the pre–World War I order, dominated by the British and French empires and, especially, by British command of the high seas and of world trade, this was no justification for unleashing an immensely murderous and destructive war.

the great slaughter of the war came to an end. It was also a question on
the minds of important German postwar figures, philosophers, writers,
and politicians. There was a range of answers, according to how angry
the Allied spokespersons were, how soon after the war they spoke—after
the outbreak of East-West tensions in 1946/47, public opinion in Western
countries became much less vindictive toward the Germans—and how
strong their political views were.[38] No one doubted that Nazi activists
and their helpmates deserved to be punished and that care had to be
taken to spare the many victims and the democratic opposition to Hitler,
distinctions that often raised additional and difficult problems with
alleged borderline cases.[39]

But were not the whole German people guilty of letting Hitler and the
Nazi party come to power and of supporting or not opposing him, the
war effort, and genocide? If they had not given him well over a third of
the vote in 1933 (Hitler never won more than 37.2% in a democratic
election), he would not have been appointed chancellor and might never
have established his dictatorship and started the war. But can one
condemn voters for their misguided judgment, six years before the
outbreak of war and genocidal persecution? Can we hold individuals
responsible for not having resorted to acts of resistance and defiance
while suspended in a world of rather imperfect communication and
between degrees of ignorance—say, on the extent of the holocaust—and
a barrage of Nazi propaganda? Anglo-Saxon common law, Roman law,
and most reputable legal systems do not recognize a collective guilt of
nations or ethnic groups. Only the Nazis believed in such collective
condemnations[40] and, of course, tried the accused in a kangaroo court

38. Both among Allied occupation personnel and among the Germans, right-wingers
were more accepting, while left-wingers wanted to severely punish ex-Nazis and those who
had supported the Nazi government. Right-wing opinion also tended to blame, in a curious
reversal of approaches, social and economic circumstances rather than the individual Nazi
or Third Reich profiteer.

39. There is a large literature on denazification, ranging from first reports to much more
recent reassessments. An example of the first is Carl J. Friedrich, "Denazification," in
Friedrich, ed., *American Experiences in Military Government in World War II* (New York:
Rinehart & Co., 1948), pp. 253–275; and of the second, Ulrich Borsdorf and Lutz
Niethammer, eds., *Zwischen Befreiung und Besatzung* (Wuppertal: P. Hammer, 1976) and
other writings by Niethammer.

40. Actually there are other, similar examples of nationalist or fascist collective condemnations, more often implied by genocidal action rather than spelled out in legal phrases or
in a political philosophy: if someone were to set out to kill all Germans, it must be because
he thinks the whole people is evil and *deserves* to die. Communist regimes, too, at times
believed in the collective guilt of entire social classes, and they proceeded to try to punish
them for being landlords or capitalists or whatever.

made up of their own prejudiced minds. This is hardly a model to emulate.

On the other hand, some postwar German spokesmen (notably Theodor Heuss) came up with the formula that while there may be no such thing as objective "collective guilt," there certainly ought to be a subjective sense of "collective shame" after all that was done to people in the name of Germany and the Germans. This is an attractive concept, but it is not without its problems. One of these is the well-known fact that if we rely on subjective guilt feelings alone, it will invariably be those who have not engaged in any culpable actions themselves who will express shame and guilt, while the objectively guilty will show a sociopathic resistance to feeling responsible and will never run out of excuses to exonerate themselves. Back in the days of denazification, this was certainly the case. From 1946 to the early fifties, when the World War II (and Nazi) generation was still the overwhelming majority, one-half to two-thirds of adult respondents in polls were calling national socialism "a good idea badly carried out."[41] Forty years later, when that generation had nearly passed from the scene, such views commanded only a small minority. The sense of collective shame, of course, has also been lessened by time, and indifference has grown. It is important to see the changing nature of German politics in the framework of passing generations (Chapter One). And yet there is no mistaking the presence of subjective guilt feelings, particularly on the left and among many of the young.

A comparison between East and West Germany at the beginning of the unification process is instructive in this respect. After decades of GDR support for the Palestine Liberation Organization and other Palestinian terrorist groups against Israel, which it had not recognized, the result is hardly surprising. It makes for poor understanding of the phenomenon to interpret fascism, to quote the Israeli writer Amos Elon, "as if the holocaust somehow culminated in capitalists cornering the market in slave labor or something"—in other words, as a synonym for advanced capitalism and the capitalists. And it makes the Federal Republic—notwithstanding the Chequers memorandum—by comparison seem very sensitive to other peoples' feelings. In 1988 Bundestag President Philipp

41. The "bad execution" of Nazi ideals, the respondents confirmed, referred especially to the persecution of the Jews. This was an occupation-era survey carried out among adults in the American Zone only: 47% in 1945/46, 55% in 1947, and 68% in the early fifties agreed to this dubious formula. Anna J. Merrit and Richard L. Merrit, eds., *Public Opinion in Occupied Germany: The OMGUS Surveys, 1945–1949* (Urbana: University of Illinois Press, 1970), pp. 31, 99–100. By the early eighties, three-fourths of West German adults were condemning the Nazi regime without reservation. See Lewis J. Edinger, *West German Politics* (New York: Columbia University Press, 1986), p. 87.

Jenninger (CDU) was forced to resign after he gave a well-intentioned, if poorly worded, speech apropos of Kristallnacht.[42] The West German politicians present, however, turned out to be more sensitive to imagined slights than several Israeli and German Jewish representatives, who were quite willing to forgive Herr Jenninger's faux pas.

The Likely Future

The Chequers memorandum ends by exonerating the present set of German political leaders—"be nice to the Germans"—but raises the question as to what changes may be in the offing fifteen or twenty years from now, with a new set of leaders in control. At first glance, this is a silly question that might be asked just as well of every country on earth. On second thought, however, it may be worth speculating about possible scenarios because certain structural parts of the future are knowable in this case. For example, Konrad Adenauer, the founding father of the Federal Republic and its first chancellor, already strove quite successfully to tie his country intimately to the West by such devices as his special relationship with France, by European integration, and by rearmament, strictly under NATO control,[43] the organization often said to have been designed to "keep the United States in [Western Europe], the Russians out, and the Germans down" (see Chapter Seven, below). Chancellor Kohl was clearly following in the footsteps of his revered role model when he rejected any kind of isolation, or *Sonderweg*, for his country. He and other German and European leaders also intended to tie a united Germany firmly into the European Community, which was itself committed to a process of establishing a closer union after 1992. Finally, Kohl exerted great effort to make a deal with Gorbachev to permit a united Germany to remain in NATO. The NATO alliance, of course, would change very considerably, we assume, in the direction of scaled-down

42. *Kristallnacht*, or the "night of broken crystal," was November 9, 1938, when the Nazis organized a major pogrom throughout the Third Reich which resulted in the destruction of many synagogues and in the beatings and arrests of many German-Jewish citizens.

43. European integration, originally in the form of the European Coal and Steel Community (ECSC), was meant to tie up the German coal and steel resources under a supranational authority so they could not be used for a German defense effort as in past wars. Rearmament under NATO command left the Germans no national army of their own and was accompanied by prohibitions of certain kinds of arms. The Germans added of their own free will a ban on deploying their troops outside Europe, a limitation recently debated with regard to Iraq.

armaments and more political coordination and, in fact, with at least some Soviet participation. A Europeanized and Atlanticized Germany, rather than a powerful, centrally located nation-state neutral vis-à-vis the blocs,[44] would continue on the reliably Western, liberal-democratic path, tied firmly into these two organizations and their common purposes.

The sheer size and strategic location of a united Germany complicate the European scenario because Germany is bound to play a dominant role. As the more perceptive commentators observed from the beginning, the problem seems to be the size and not the intent. After four decades of a meek, cooperative Germany we have learned to take its low profile for granted, but that profile may not always be. There is little likelihood of military muscle-flexing on the part of a united Germany but, given a few years' transition, we will probably see the vast economic influence and coercion of which Nicholas Ridley was afraid. Germany's central location also makes it an influential and attractive economic partner for the new East European regimes, including what is left of the Soviet Union, which will give it additional clout among the West European EC countries (see Chapter Seven). To avoid becoming individually dependent on Germany, the East European countries should perhaps band together, forming an association if they cannot join the European Community directly. Thus envelopment in European unification may not, by itself, necessarily keep the Germans in check. In NATO, on the other hand, the presence of the United States will be a powerful counterweight to a united Germany and, for that reason, a guarantee to suspicious European neighbors that everything is under control. It would be a great disaster for Europe and, by implication, for the German role there if the United States ever decided to return to "fortress America" (see Chapter Eight).

There are other structural factors that may make the future of a united Germany in Europe more predictable. One is the barring of nuclear weapons on German soil, West and East, and very likely in Scandinavia, the Benelux countries, and parts of Eastern Europe as well. The July 1990 agreement between Chancellor Kohl and President Gorbachev in Zhelezdnovodsk in the Caucasus included the renunciation by Bonn of all ABC weapons—atomic, biological, and chemical—along with a voluntary ceiling on united German troops, 370,000.[45] These concessions

44. Armed neutralism between East and West must not be confused with a disarmed united Germany, which would form a power vacuum and constitute an invitation for other powers like France or the Soviet Union to move in. An armed but neutral, or nonaligned, Germany would probably return to the policies of Bismarck and Gustav Stresemann, playing East and West against one another and remaining committed to neither.

45. A lead article in *The Atlantic*, Aug. 1990, by John Mearsheimer, "Why We Will Soon Miss the Cold War," oddly predicts no fewer than three scenarios replete with nuclear weapons in various hands and, while warning the world about a German return to

were already well known half a year earlier, when Bonn was still casting about for easy ways to demonstrate its peaceful intentions. In the form of peace movement manifestos, Green party platform planks, and agreements between the West German SPD and the East German SED on a nuclear-free zone from Scandinavia down to Central Europe, they date back nearly a decade. Chemical weapons, too, have attracted a lot of negative attention among West Germans, culminating in popular protests from time to time. In 1990, when the U.S. Army in the FRG made public its plans to remove the American stockpiles of poison gas from West Germany, there were protests because German groups and local authorities were not satisfied with the safety precautions for moving such dangerous cargo through inhabited areas.

Another structural constraint is the considerable degree of decentralization both within Germany and among the members, present and future, of the European Community (Chapter Eight). German federalism in a united Germany is likely to amount to a considerable check on the policymaking capacity of the united German federal government. By the same token, the decentralization of authority in the European Community is a very potent antidote to whatever economic dominance Germany may achieve in it. Even the regime of 1993, when the rest of the barriers to a common internal market are expected to fall, will still be far from the centralization that Ridley feared. Reluctant members such as Great Britain will probably slow down and modify the process and structures to suit themselves.

Finally, there is the question of a new generation of Germans who may have grown up by that time, fifteen to twenty years from now, when the remainder of the Nazi/World War II generation will be under the ground. It is anyone's guess what will then be on the minds of the young voters who are still children today. It is rather unlikely to be nationalism, racism, or militarism: the trend has been moving away from these all over Western Europe, if not all of Eastern Europe, since 1945 when the great hegemonial and imperial passion of the Germans had spent itself. There is, however, the growing alienation of many young Germans who, since the seventies, have been living in the never-never land of counterculture life and political protest of various hues of red and green. It is not yet clear whether this alienated life is becoming a new youth moratorium which remains stable while successive waves of young adults pass through on their way to maturity. But the counterculture is far too antithetical to militarism, imperialism, nationalism, and jingoism, not to mention "hypernationalism," to develop in this direction.

"hypernationalism," perversely concludes that we will soon wish we were back with the East-West nuclear standoff.

Since these are young people who resist being taught anything, they are (and perhaps will be) in great need to be enlightened about the recent past of Germany, the mistakes of their grandparents and great-grandparents, so that they will not repeat them. They will of course make mistakes of their own, as would anyone, but we can at least hope that those mistakes will not harm anyone else.

The Outline of This Book

Ours is a subject of such extraordinary complexity that we cannot simply follow a chronological outline. Instead, we shall concentrate on a few salient topics and pursue them in some detail. We shall begin with the historical configuration of the so-called German question, old and new (Chapter One), since the problems of founding or refounding a German nation-state are not at all new. There have long been several "solutions" around, in fact, some of which were disastrous to the Germans and to neighboring nations. The temporal dimensions of the German question need to be highlighted with reference to the succession of German political generations that have inclined to the various "solutions." Although the earlier generations (born in the late 1850s and early 1860s) who as young men and women founded the Bismarckian nation-state and supplied some of World War I's generals are long dead, their legacy of militarism and expansive nationalism lived on.[46] More recent generations that are alive in German politics today include the ones that grew up in the Third Reich and fought in World War II. Now in their mid-sixties and older, this World War II generation has gone through a great many changes since its Nazi and warlike period of formation.[47] This generation and those slightly older (together, born 1902–1927) still represent a certain nationalistic undercurrent whenever issues of national symbolism and identity, or *national reunification*, have come up. In this

46. After that generation (always labeled by the era that formed their minds when they were young adults), the "founders' generation," came another one that was formed by the economic and political development of the late 1880s and the 1890s and that supplied most of the chancellors of the Weimar Republic. It included Konrad Adenauer (born 1876) who nearly became a Reich chancellor of Weimar and, like no other German figure, put his stamp on the Federal Republic. See also Merkl, "Forty Years and Seven Generations," in Merkl, ed., *The Federal Republic at Forty*, pp. 1–16.
47. There was also a World War I generation (mostly born between 1896 and 1901), which supplied many of the Nazi leaders besides Hitler (born 1889) and some East and West German post-1945 politicians of the early decades, such as Ludwig Erhard, Kurt Schumacher, and Walter Ulbricht (GDR).

respect they are quite distinguishable from all the German postwar
generations (born 1928 and later) that followed and that will be discussed
in this book.

Chapter Two relates the dramatic breakup of the Soviet bloc and
empire, placing the East German revolution in the context of those in
other countries. Chapter Three will examine the East German communist
dictatorship that was there before 1990, the party state, its repressive
apparatus, its planned economy, its relation to the Soviet Union, and its
disintegration in 1989/90. In Chapter Four, we shall analyze the West
German response to the sudden opportunity to carry out what had been
advocated for forty years, national unification: the slow, cautious beginnings, the political and economic initiatives of the first five months of
1990 and, after a noticeable faltering of resolve in May and June, the
determined thrust to consummate the union formally. The chapter ends
with an electoral analysis of the first all-German elections (December 2)
and the cabinet formation that followed.

The last four chapters explore the most important aspects of the
unification process. Chapter Five describes the constitutional evolution
of the United Germany, the options before the parties, the emerging
federal system, and the agenda of issues for the new government. Chapter
Six delves into the murky depths of the economics of unification, the
enormous problems of "turning the fish soup" of a communist economic
system, as East Europeans like to put it, "back into an aquarium of live
fish" swimming around in a market economy. Questions of ruined
infrastructure, privatization of public enterprises, the vast problems of
East German agriculture and, last but not least, the best kept secret of
1990, the cost of unification will all demand our attention. Chapters
Seven and Eight, finally, tackle the crucial international entanglements of
German unification, their descent from Allied occupation rights and the
opposing military alliances of NATO and the Warsaw Pact, the evolving
European unification process, and the formation of a "new European
security order." The concluding chapter sets the emerging sense of
German identity in the context of how Germans expect to see themselves
in the year 2000.

Chapter ONE

The German Question, Old and New

Before we can go into the complex ramifications of the union of the two Germanys amidst the restructuring of East-West relations and the transformation of the system of European states, it is important to note that the questions of German national unity are not a new set of problems. They have been with us in varying forms at least since the days when the French Revolution and Napoleon I's campaigns inspired national movements and ambitions all over modern Europe. As in other European countries, conquest and occupation by the Napoleonic armies and the popular wars of liberation against France triggered a fervid nationalism and rekindled the intellectual debate about a unified nation-state in place of the memory of the moribund Holy Roman Empire of the German Nation which Napoleon had dissolved in 1803/1806. Unlike many other national movements that eventually created their own nation-states, German national ambitions collided from the start with a number of major obstacles and divisions of opinion that stood in the way of realizing the national dream.

Cultural Particularism or National Assertion?

To begin with, the German lands were in the hands of numerous small and larger potenta⁺es, ranging from independent knights and imperial cities to the kings of Prussia and Bavaria, not to mention the Hapsburg emperors who had been the nominal rulers of the Holy Roman Empire before 1806. These small and middle-size states not only prized the sovereign autonomy they had acquired at the end of the Thirty Years' War (1618–1648) with the Peace Treaty of Westphalia, but they gloried in the rich cultural life of their particularism and showed little desire to grow into one national culture. The German historian Friedrich Meinecke has tellingly described the discussion between the advocates of a nationalist will to power, perhaps seeking national unification under a Machiavellian prince, and those prizing cultural particularism and cosmopolitanism more.[1] As it happened, the German national movement was effectively bottled up by the 1815 Congress of Vienna and the Holy Alliance of reactionary Russia, Prussia, and Austria, thus obscuring the fundamental dilemma of the German national question for the first half of the nineteenth century. As new nations went, the German one was huge and largely undefined in parts of its membership and ethnic boundaries. Substantial numbers of German ethnics lived in certain parts of Russia and Eastern Europe. Large Germanophone states such as the Netherlands, German Switzerland and, eventually, German Austria were quite content to be on their own.

In the great revolutionary upheaval of 1848, however, which staggered most of the particularistic powers of the German Confederation of 1815–1866, the question of German national identity and unity asserted itself most forcefully before the Frankfurt National Assembly, which attempted to frame a democratic constitution for a German nation-state. The Frankfurt deputies not only had to define the relationship of their would-be German nation-state to the national ambitions of the Danes and the Poles at their borders; they also found themselves deeply divided between advocates of a "Greater German (*grossdeutsch*) solution," which would have included Austria and the Hapsburgs (including also substantial non-German populations) in their nation-state, and advocates of a "Small German (*kleindeutsch*) solution" excluding Austria. The

1. See his *Weltbürgertum und Nationalstaat* (Munich: Oldenbourg, 1908). Meinecke did not view these two principles as mutually exclusive and is often quoted by opponents of national unification because, to him, being a *Kulturnation* did not necessarily require political unity. See also Robert A. Pois, *Friedrich Meinecke and German Politics in the Twentieth Century* (Berkeley and Los Angeles: University of California Press, 1972).

Small German solution meant domination of the future German nation-state by Prussia, which was likely to lend its own brand of authoritarianism, militarism, Protestantism, and a head start in social and economic modernization to the union. The Frankfurt National Assembly voted for the Small German solution and vainly offered the imperial crown of the new nation-state to the king of Prussia, who refused it as "a gift from the gutter" while the revolutionary assembly fell victim to its own dissension and military intervention. In the midst of the unification process of 1990, German newspapers once more recalled the heady days of 1848/49, when Germans first tried to establish a national constitution and a bill of rights—and failed.

Bismarck's Small German Empire

Twenty years later, after several unsuccessful attempts to negotiate national unification, Prime Minister Otto von Bismarck made the Small German solution under a Prussian kaiser a reality. He had to fight no fewer than three wars to this end: one against Denmark (1864); one to fight off Austria, which was in league with several southern German states (1866); and one against France (1870). There was a chorus of criticism not only from friends of Austria and the Catholic and European traditions within Germany but even more poignantly from abroad, where defeated France, Great Britain, and other European neighbors reacted with alarm to the prospect of a powerful hegemonial German nation-state in the geopolitical center of Europe. One long-forgotten domestic critic, Constantin Frantz, painted the future scenario of Bismarck's new nation-state in great detail. He predicted that the geographic position and potential military and economic power of the unified national state would, sooner or later, tempt Germany to establish hegemony over its continental neighbors and lead it into a disastrous confrontation with another grand alliance of powers, like the ones that had gathered to defeat the hegemonial ambitions of Napoleon I and Louis XIV in centuries past.

An apprehensive Bismarck and the jubilant German masses thought they could ignore these critics. They received abundant support from the German Liberal parties, the same Liberals he had fought so bitterly in the Prussian constitutional conflict of the 1860s. Having achieved his goal of a Prussian-dominated Small Germany, nevertheless, the Iron Chancellor henceforth pursued a cautious policy in Europe and in the world, avoiding conflict with the major powers over such questions as colonies, trade, and a navy and refraining from any further policy of German aggrandizement. Fearing that France and tsarist Russia, in particular, might combine their forces against Germany—his *cauchemar des coalitions* (nightmare of a hostile coalition)—and bring down his new nation-state with a two-front war, Bismarck carefully cultivated German relations with Russia, and also with Austria and Italy. Unfortunately, his successors lacked both his prudence and his diplomatic skills and permitted Germany to lapse increasingly into isolation, particularly from Russia. Bismarck's policies, too, preoccupied media pundits during the unification debates of 1989/90 although, unlike Adenauer, no one has yet likened Helmut Kohl to Bismarck in a convincing fashion.

At the same time, extraordinary industrial growth and social modernization in Germany began to outgrow the authoritarian and semifeudal political structure that Bismarck had reinforced so solidly while Great Britain and France were becoming notably more democratic. By the end of the first decade of this century, Germany's national leadership had made the country's political backwardness in combination with industrial strength into a virtue, a distinctively separate German path, or *Sonderweg*, to modernization and felt ready to challenge the West in every way: in the acquisition of colonies, in regard to the naval buildup, on the world markets, and in major diplomatic confrontations. Reich Chancellor von Bülow (1900–1909) coined the phrase that the country wanted "a place in the sun" and the status of a world power. In 1914, on the side of the disintegrating Hapsburg empire, Germany blundered into the presumable war for national greatness and confidently believed it would win in less than a year against the gathering grand alliance of its enemies,[2] eventually including the United States. By the end of 1918, the Small German solution to the German national question had led to decisive defeat, the collapse of kaiser and kingdoms, and there was worse to come.

A Greater German Empire

The long drawn-out struggle, to be sure, had brought the various regional elements of the Small German nation closer together, and there were many testimonials to the newfound sense of national solidarity in spite of increasing social conflict.[3] But it had also awakened both an acute

2. See L. L. Farrar, Jr., *The Short War Illusion: A Study of German Policy, Strategy, and Domestic Affairs, August–December, 1914* (Santa Barbara, Calif.: ABC-Clio, 1973). Also see Koppel S. Pinson, *Modern Germany: Its History and Civilization*, 2nd ed. (New York: Macmillan, 1966), chaps. 12–13.

3. See Hajo Holborn, *A History of Modern Germany, 1840–1945* (Princeton, N.J.:

sense of identity in the Germans and, in their adversary neighbors, a bitter anti-German hostility that drove many a German residing abroad back home, among his conationals. Germans living and working in overseas colonies streamed back when those colonies were taken over by other imperial powers. The collapse of the Hapsburg, Prussian, and Russian empires and the establishment of various successor states left large German ethnic populations, which had lived there for centuries, under new Polish, Czechoslovak, Yugoslav, and other governments and frequently in the midst of complex, ethnic rivalries among the new ruling majorities and various minorities. In the Austrian case, it left behind a German-Austrian rump state, which at the end of World War I was, at least at first, eager to be joined to Germany, although the victorious allies would not permit it. From all these ethnically contentious sources a witches' brew of prewar groups such as the Pan-Germans—who wanted to bring all ethnic Germans under one empire—small anti-Semitic parties, and *völkisch*[4] writers cropped up. And after World War I, legions of veterans were on the march, seething to fight the war over and in particular to attack the communists and socialists, who had allegedly "stabbed the army in the back." Thus, in the wake of the collapsing German and Austrian empires there grew a virulent popular movement led by an Austrian expatriate of great political ambition, Adolf Hitler.

Hitler, like many Germans, wanted to undo the defeat and surrender of 1918 and to renew the great national crusade for European hegemony. But by this time it had also become a quest to reestablish the once dominant positions of German ethnics, a superior race in his opinion, over the Poles, Czechs, and other allegedly inferior breeds in one Pan-Germanic racial empire. Once he had established his dictatorship, Hitler began with the *Anschluss* (annexation) of the rump state of Austria (1938), proceeded to the takeover of the ethnic German Sudetenland, seized the rest of Czechoslovakia (1939), and then launched the attack on Poland, which both began World War II and completed the Greater Germany solution of 1848. There followed invasions of the Benelux countries (1939), France, parts of Scandinavia (1940), the Balkans, North Africa, and finally the Soviet Union (1941). Hitler's solution to the old German question not only carried the old idea of Greater Germany to absurd lengths, it attracted ethnic Germans from all over and even lured

---

Princeton University Press, 1969), pp. 428–431, and, on the undertones of social conflict, Ulrich Wehler, *The German Empire 1817–1918* (Lemington Spa/Dover: Berg, 1985), pp. 213–216 et passim.

4. *Völkisch* denoted a populist literature characterized also by nationalism, anti-Semitism, and xenophobia. See Merkl, *The Making of a Stormtrooper* (Princeton, N.J.: Princeton University Press, 1980), on the varied origins of the Nazi movement.

other, "unredeemed" nationalities, such as anticommunist Ukrainians, Balts, Croats, and others who deluded themselves about their nation's fate in his racial empire. Worst of all, Hitler's campaign was accompanied by vast destruction and human slaughter on a scale that defies the imagination: the holocaust of nearly 6 million Jews, the death of more than 25 million Russians, millions of Poles, hundreds of thousands of others, and most of this neither in combat nor under the necessities of war.

The End of the Nationalist Quest

When the Third Reich was finally brought down by yet another grand alliance in which the United States, as in World War I, played a decisive role, this seemed to be the end of all German questions. The German armies were utterly defeated, and vast numbers of German prisoners of war (about 11 million) were kept for years (in the Russian case, as long as eleven years) in forced labor for the victorious powers. Many never came home again. German cities were destroyed by air raids, the economy had collapsed, and for years the civilian population suffered from a catastrophic lack of food and shelter. An estimated 12 million or more German ethnics all over Eastern Europe fled or were expelled forcibly and with considerable violence and death, also meted out to women and children—this was the ultimate result of the Pan-German quest. Ten million of these ethnic German refugees eventually trekked into East and West Germany, mostly just ahead of the Red Army, which particularly terrorized German civilians in East Prussia and what soon became the Oder-Neisse area, perhaps to cause them all to leave and make room for the intended shifts of populations and borders (see Table 1.1).

In its advance through Eastern Europe, the victorious Russian army not only drove out the German troops and their satellite regimes; it also conducted purges and installed friendly, increasingly communist governments in one East European country after another. Since Stalin had divided Poland with Hitler under the Hitler-Stalin pact of 1939, and had no intention to return eastern Poland to its rightful owners in 1945, he devised a clever swap of territory (see below, Chapter Seven). He took the German areas east of the rivers Oder and Neisse, about one-fourth of Germany's prewar territory, and gave it to Poland as compensation for eastern Poland. Poland also received half of German East Prussia; the other half went to the Soviet Union. The Oder-Neisse area was swept

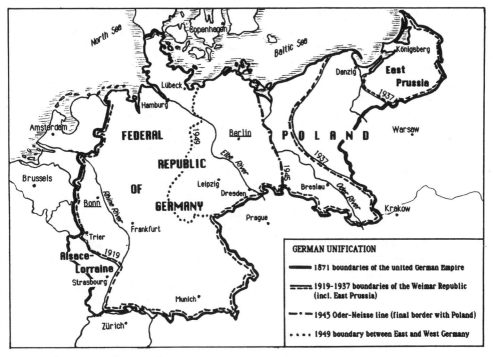

Fig. 1.1. German unification, 1871–1990.

nearly clean of its German population and, in the intervening decades, has been repopulated by Poles. The psychological effect on Polish loyalty to the Soviet Union has been profound. Fearing that some day a strengthened Germany might demand the return of these lands, Polish governments have had to swallow their distrust of Moscow and rely on its political and military support. The revived controversy over the Oder-Neisse border in early 1990[5] even induced the Polish government to request that Russian troops not be withdrawn from Poland until a unified Germany might offer ironclad guarantees of the sanctity of the Polish western border.

In 1945, the Red Army had also battled its way through East Germany and taken Berlin in a final heroic assault while Hitler took his life in the Reich Chancellery. Subsequently, the Soviet Military Administration took

5. As described earlier, Chancellor Kohl made a play for the votes of ethnic refugees and the right-wing Republicans by a show of reluctance to accept the present German-Polish border. International pressures and criticism from his own coalition partner (the FDP) and from others persuaded him to abandon this stratagem.

Table 1.1. German Refugees and Expellees, 1941–1946 (in thousands)

	1945 Population	Dates of Flight (F) or Expulsion (X)	Losses by Death; Forced Labor
From outside pre-1938 borders			
Sudetenland (CSR)	3,000	May 1945 (X)	230
Rest of CSR	450	Oct./Nov. 1944 (F); May 1945 (X)	35
Hungary	600	Oct./Nov. 1944 (F); Jan. 1946 (X)	55
Romania	750	Aug.–Oct. 1944 (F)	80
Yugoslavia	550	Aug.–Sept. 1944 (F); May 1945 (X)	135
Baltic states	123	Jan.–March 1945 (F and X)	20
Danzig and Memel area	480	Aug. 1944–Jan. 1945 (F); Apr. 1945 (X)	90
Soviet Union*	1,500	Jul.–Oct. 1941, Jan.–Jul. 1944 (F)	30–100 est. deaths; 50 forced labor in camps
From inside pre-1938 borders			
East Prussia	2,385	Oct. 1944 (F); March 1945 (X)	280
East Pomerania-Brandenburg	2,430	Jan. 1945 (F); Apr. 1945 (X)	600
Poland (esp. Oder-Neisse area)	1,300	June–Sept. 1944 (F); March 1945 (X)	185
Silesia	4,500	Jan. 1945 (F); Apr. 1945 (X)	450

SOURCES: Statistisches Bundesamt, *Die deutschen Vertreibungsverluste*; G. C. Behrmann et al., *Aussiedler* (Bonn: Bundeszentrale für Politische Bildung, 1988).

NOTE: These are estimates. At least 2 million ethnic Germans remained in their home areas. CSR = Czechoslovak Socialist Republic.

*Relocated within USSR.

6. The Soviet and communist idea of who was a Nazi and what was a Nazi crime, however, tended also to pillory former capitalists and bourgeois "class enemies." See Wolfgang Benz, *Potsdam 1945. Besatzungsherrschaft und Neuaufbau im Vierzonen-*

charge of the occupation zone agreed upon among the Allies and carried out there such measures as it saw fit, including denazification, land reform, and the expropriation of the East Elbian Junkers.[6] The geographic configuration of this occupation zone, plus the Russian part of quadripartite Berlin, later became the territory of the GDR. In 1948/49, when the cooperation between the four Allies in Berlin and on the Allied Control Council for Germany broke down and the Soviets refused to go along with major Western plans for currency reform and the Marshall Plan, not to mention the establishment of the Federal Republic in the three Western zones, the Soviets decided to establish the German Democratic Republic. From this point on, for the next forty years, Germany was divided into West and East Germany, a division that has only now been overcome.

Today's Scaled-Down Unification

We should note, however, that this unification, or reunification, is hardly of the geographic magnitude of either the Small German or the Greater German unity plan of the nineteenth century, not to mention that of the Third Reich to which some American press commentators have compared it. By American standards, in fact, the newly united Germany is not very large: if we were to place it inside the state of California, there would still be room for Massachusetts, Connecticut, and nearly all of New Hampshire. Today's German unification no longer raises the questions of an Austrian *Anschluss* (with or without the vast Polish, Czechoslovak, Yugoslav, and Italian territories once under Hapsburg control), nor those of the Polish areas once part of pre-1914 Prussia, nor indeed those of the Oder-Neisse area or East Prussia, not to mention other East European areas that once held substantial German minorities. As we shall see in Chapter Seven, nevertheless, the implications of the sheer size of the united German nation, its economic potential, and its geopolitical position at the center of Europe have not changed very much in the eyes of Germany's European neighbors.

6. The Soviet and communist idea of who was a Nazi and what was a Nazi crime, however, tended also to pillory former capitalists and bourgeois "class enemies." See Wolfgang Benz, *Potsdam 1945. Besatzungsherrschaft und Neuaufbau im Vierzonen-Deutschland* (Munich: DTV, 1986), pp. 157–182. Also see David Childs, *The GDR: Moscow's German Ally* (London: Allen & Unwin, 1983), pp. 1–33.

A Different Generation of Germans

On the other hand, we have to see the cataclysmic changes of twentieth-century German history also in the light of the succession of generations that shaped and were shaped by the historical epochs before us. Forty-odd years of steadfast democratic conduct and loyalty from the Federal Republic, vis-à-vis the Western alliance and West European cooperation, have persuaded many observers that the Germans of the 1990s are quite a different breed from those who, in World War II, carried their nationalistic quests to horrifying extremes. Indeed, most of today's Germans are of different political generations from those who participated in the war and in the cruel dictatorship of the Third Reich. Sociologists define a political generation not according to the years in which they were born, but rather according to the period in which they went through politically formative experiences such as a war, a great depression, a revolution, or at least a dramatic election campaign in a democratic country. Such experiences usually take place when a person is between fifteen and twenty-five years of age.

Thus, the World War II generation ended roughly when the last birth cohort was drafted to serve in the war. We count also those of the same age who for various reasons may not have served and experienced the worst of it, wives, sweethearts and sisters, and coevals excused for other reasons. The last birth cohort drafted in Germany was born in 1928 and was sixteen or seventeen in 1945, when the Third Reich was scraping the bottom of the barrel. Only those Germans born in 1928 or earlier could have shared in the formative experience of the nationalistic quest for glory and aggrandizement. In 1989, only 21% of the German population of the Federal Republic, and a slightly lesser percentage of the united German population—the West German population is older than that of East Germany—was old enough to be of the World War II and Nazi generation (or older),[7] because their cohorts among the living, especially the males, were reduced greatly by the war and by the expulsion of ethnic Germans in 1945/46. These older West Germans of the war generation

7. This is merely a summary attempt to account for the political socialization of the largest numbers of Germans, ignoring the large numbers of opponents and victims of the regime. The impact of the formative experience also must have varied among individuals and groups and, very likely, with the declining fortunes of war after the debacle of Stalingrad in early 1943, after which the German armies reeled from defeat to defeat and began to retreat while the civilians back home suffered massive air raids and deprivations. Perhaps the first birth cohorts formed by war and national-socialist enthusiasm are more likely to be found among Germans born in 1925/26 and earlier, about 18% of the total population in 1989 and nearly two-thirds female. See Statistisches Bundesamt, *Datenreport 1989*.

still differ in significant ways from those under sixty, especially with regard to their sense of national identity. When asked if they felt "proud to be German," despite everything, nearly nine out of ten said yes (87.9% as compared to 70.2% of all respondents). Three out of four said they "liked the sight of the [West] German flag" (74.4% as compared to 50.4% of all). Significantly higher percentages of the senior respondents also supported German reunification (83.9% as compared to 76.2%) and were reluctant to accept the Oder-Neisse line as the final German border with Poland (25.1% as compared to 17.2% of all). Indeed, among the older refugees from the Oder-Neisse area, nearly half of the seniors (43% as compared to 17% of all Oder-Neisse refugees) still do not accept the border. This hard-bitten generation is also considerably less charitable than younger Germans toward foreigners seeking political asylum or wanting to vote in Germany. On the other hand, they express a high degree of satisfaction with West German democracy and great confidence in its political institutions.[8]

When, for example, A. M. Rosenthal in the *New York Times* expressed the misgivings of the "blitzkrieged nations" and "slaughtered peoples" about German reunification, he rather touchingly exempted those "too young to be personally guilty," perhaps not realizing that he was speaking about four-fifths of today's Germans, including most of the present politicians and other elites of both Germanys. He also slighted the abundant evidence for remorse and atonement concerning the holocaust—including massive support for restitution to survivors and to the state of Israel[9]—among those older 21%. The genuinely incorrigible and

Zahlen und Fakten über die BRD. There is also a large political science literature on the concept of generations and generational conflict, much of it inspired by the generational upheaval of the late sixties in the United States and Western Europe.

8. Only 5.8% (average 13.3%) said they were "not proud of being German," and 23.4% (average 40.5%) that the sight of the flag left them indifferent. East German seniors have even higher rates of national pride (88.8%) and enthusiasm for German unification (95.3%), which they share with those aged fifty to fifty-nine (97.8%), the first postwar generation. Institut für praxisorientierte Sozialforschung (IPOS), *Einstellungen zu aktuellen Fragen der Innenpolitik in der BRD und der DDR*, May–June 1990: IPOS/BRD, pp. 36, 45, 107–109, 114, 137, 150–159; IPOS/DDR, pp. 52–59.

9. Public opinion polls conducted by the American occupation authority among representative samples of adults in its zone, at a time when the war and Nazi generation was still the vast majority, 1945–1949, put these statements in perspective. While 15–18% of the respondents held hard-core Nazi views and as many as 52% believed that "territories like Danzig, Sudetenland, Austria should be part of Germany proper," there was the realization among a majority of that generation, even then, that the greatest wrong of the Nazi regime had been the "persecution of Jews and other minorities." Some 29% of the respondents consequently expressed their desire to right the wrongs committed; a few years later, 26% specifically endorsed the Adenauer administration's 1952 bill proposing restitution to the state of Israel (49% opposed it). The growing weight of the postwar

unrepentant Germans on this score are few in number. On the other hand, it is true that Germany has hardly begun to make restitution to the Russians, Poles, and many others who suffered so cruelly under German conquest and occupation in those days.

The First Postwar Generation

The four out of five West Germans of the postwar generations need to be further subdivided into several distinctive political generations in order to understand *their* greatly differing formative experiences then and their resulting political attitudes today. One such scheme of interpretation distinguishes three postwar generations, beginning with the immediate postwar decade as a period of such "formative political experiences" as ruins and Allied occupation, the legions of the halt and the lame of the war, millions of refugees, denazification and democratization, but also the struggle to overcome widespread destruction and economic collapse and to build a stable and prosperous ("economic miracle") West German rump state.[10] This generation also experienced the efforts at democratic reeducation by the Western occupying powers as well as the great fear of the vengeful Soviet armies—the 1945 mass rapes and depredations in East Germany were well known—the Cold War, and the necessity to seek protection with the United States and NATO. Anticommunism and fear of a Nazi revival—neofascists and communists alike were legally suppressed in the fifties—were paired in the minds of this generation, Helmut Kohl's generation, with its great infatuation with American civilization, its ill-understood politics, and its social life-style and economic institutions. While there was a good deal of German diffidence and a political inferiority complex vis-à-vis the democratic West with which this generation had come to identify, they were quite proud of what they had accomplished in contrast to the militaristic, authoritarian, and racist Third Reich. Under Adenauer, they had rehabilitated themselves within the community of nations and joined the West by means of a network of treaties.

This was the generation which supported such genuinely democratic

<hr />

generations eventually improved this support level. See Anna J. Merritt and Richard L. Merritt, eds., *Public Opinion in Occupied Germany: The OMGUS Surveys, 1945–1949* (Urbana: University of Illinois Press, 1970), pp. 31, 99–100, and its sequel, *Public Opinion in Semisovereign Germany* (Urbana: University of Illinois Press, 1980), pp. 8–10, 198–199.

10. See Merkl, "Forty Years and Seven Generations," in Merkl, ed., *The Federal Republic at Forty* (New York: New York University Press, 1989), pp. 1–16.

leaders as Chancellor Konrad Adenauer and Ludwig Erhard, or opposition leader Kurt Schumacher—all of these leaders, of course, belonging to older generations but clearly not Nazi-influenced—who began the program of restitution to Israel and Jewish survivors (1952), integration into the Western Alliance and European unification (1951, 1955, and 1957), and the constitutional democracy of Bonn (1949–1990). The older generation of current West and East German politicians, including Chancellor Helmut Kohl and the East German Premier, Lothar de Maizière, belongs to this staunchly democratic, pro-Israel, and pro-Western first postwar generation.

To this first postwar generation, the pain of the German division was as immediate and deep—perhaps surpassed only by their more nationalistic predecessor generations—as the strength of their commitment to German democracy and peaceful cooperation among nations. During their formative years they witnessed the division and the struggle to build a democratic West Germany. They found it very hard to accept a divided Germany and continued to hope for reunification via a range of perhaps not very realistic avenues: Konrad Adenauer's "policy of strength" in alliance with the West against the communist East; détente and rapprochement with Soviet and East European leaders, as in the Eastern treaties of *Ostpolitik* during the early seventies; or simply by a miracle. It is easy today to understand the feelings of this first postwar generation about the opening of the Berlin Wall and the sudden opportunity to reunite the country. Disproportionate numbers of this and the older generation still identify with the Christian Democrats (CDU/CSU) today, and it is no accident that Chancellor Kohl (born 1930) considers himself the "heir of Adenauer."[11] We should not be surprised about their seeming eagerness, even haste, to complete the process of unification regardless of cost.

Their East German counterparts certainly shared their desire to unify the divided nation as fast as possible, even though their socializing experiences during the immediate postwar decade were profoundly different (see Chapter Three) from those of the West Germans. They not only witnessed the harsh Soviet occupation, which left mass graves behind, but saw the dark night of totalitarian oppression descend a second time upon their area. A small minority quickly accommodated itself to the communist dictatorship and

11. Adenauer himself, born 1876, belonged to the same generation as many Weimar chancellors, while Erhard and Schumacher (and East German communist leader Walter Ulbricht) were of the World War I generation. Other notable older democratic leaders, such as ex-Chancellors Willy Brandt (born 1913) and Helmut Schmidt (born 1918), also were in the World War II and older generation without having become Nazis. Generational analysis paints with a broad brush, which should not obscure the fact that different groups and subcultures may deviate in important ways.

took up various functions in its vast apparatus, while the majority either were passive or became victims of its coercive might. Today, a lifetime later, this majority of the first postwar generation has only just awakened to the new political environment, like Rip Van Winkle from his deep sleep. During the East German demonstrations of 1989, their enthusiasm for *"Deutschland, einig Vaterland"* (Germany, a united fatherland)[12] had a curiously old-fashioned ring to it. Their appetite for sharing in the consumer heaven of West Germany was rather naive and easily manipulated by West German politicians and entrepreneurs. Many in this generation never really identified with the GDR and were bitter that the regime kept them from enjoying the life of Germans in the West and from having real elections and real democracy instead of the mockery and hypocrisy of the communist system.[13] The majority of apparatchiks and members of the SED, and its tentacles through-out East German mass organizations, were never delighted with German unification—which has meant the end of a separate East German state and all its benefits for them—but were ready to accommodate in any way possible: by quitting the party and pretending to have been "in secret opposition" all along; by sticking with its successor party, the SED/PDS (Party of Democratic Socialism), and fighting some of the consequences of its fall from grace;[14] and by fishing shamelessly for new assignments with the new democratic East German government.

The Critical Generation of 1968

A second postwar generation of West Germans includes the many young people who associated themselves, in one way or another, with the

12. This phrase comes from the East German national hymn by Johannes R. Becher, who inserted the emphasis on German unity at the request of GDR President Wilhelm Pieck. The slogan *Deutschland einig Vaterland*, after the earlier emphasis on communist reforms, was increasingly heard in the demonstrations. The elections of March 19, 1990, finally confirmed and turned it into a mandate.

13. Among East Germans, this generation tended to be much closer to the war generation, with respect to its attitudes toward unification and related symbolic issues, than to the younger generations. IPOS/DDR, pp. 10, 52–59. See also Childs, *The GDR*, p. 317. There was a minority of idealistic young socialists in the FDJ (Free German Youth—i.e., communist state youth), the "Wische generation," who fervently believed they were the pioneers of a new society, until their utopia died in the disillusionment of the sixties.

14. For example, the decision of the newly elected East German government to review the vast properties of the SED/PDS, and possibly to expropriate them and the other "bloc parties" (i.e., SED satellite parties masquerading behind a multiparty façade), brought forth a fierce reaction on the part of PDS members of the People's Chamber.

political upheavals of the late sixties and early seventies. Unlike their rather withdrawn predecessors, this generation was highly politicized and activist. Born roughly between the early forties and the mid-fifties, these "68ers" grew up in stability and prosperity and promptly began to question and belittle most of the verities of the establishment, beginning with its ritualistic anticommunism, automatic loyalty to the Cold War posture of the United States, and hostility to the Soviet Union and GDR. This "critical generation" even questioned the depth of the democratic commitment of the previous generation, calling it "liberal-authoritarian" and, in some cases, accusing their elders of holding fascist views. It pushed for a thorough "democratization" of German schools and universities, of the German home and family—particularly in the direction of female equality and young people's freedom—and of the political parties of the Federal Republic. At their most dramatic, these young rebels marched and fought against the Emergency Laws of 1968, against press lord Axel Springer's newspapers, and against authoritarian university settings.[15] It was mostly a student revolt, though not without influence on young people beyond the halls of academe.

The rebels of their generation also challenged the policies of the Western capitalist democracies, including the FRG, toward the poor nations of the Third World and the waste of precious resources on defense and military posturing. In the seventies, they were joined by a tidal wave of local citizen movements (*Bürgerinitiativen*)—not limited to "68ers" or students—protesting against bureaucratic planning and authoritarian decisions regarding such things as urban development, large public projects (roads and bridges), nuclear plants, children's playgrounds, and historic preservation, to name some of the issues.[16] Many "68ers" would become leaders of such reform movements as the femi-

15. Many of the views of the German "68ers" have been shown to be part of a broad generational revolt and value change toward "postmaterialism" throughout Western industrial societies. See especially Ronald Inglehart, *The Silent Revolution: Changing Values and Political Styles Among Western Publics* (Princeton, N.J.: Princeton University Press, 1977) and his more recent writings. See also Samuel H. Barnes et al., *Political Action: Mass Participation in Five Western Democracies* (Beverly Hills, Calif.: Sage, 1979), which explores the new dimension of political action since the sixties. There were considerable differences between German university youth, which spearheaded the rebellion, and non-university youth.

16. See Jutta Helm, "Citizen Lobbies in West Germany," in Merkl, ed., *Western European Party Systems: Trends and Prospects* (New York: Free Press/Macmillan, 1980), pp. 576–596. Also see Russell J. Dalton, *Citizen Politics in Western Democracies* (Chatham, N.J.: Chatham House, 1988), where the public opinion and political behavior of this generation in the United States, Britain, Germany, and France are discussed, as well as the burgeoning literature on the pacifist and ecological protest movements of the last few decades.

nists, pacifists, and Greens of the next decade. The GDR counterpart of the 1968 generation—there was no student revolt like that of Western Europe—includes many of the leaders of the new parties and movements emerging from the collapse of the old regime: Wolfgang Berghofer, former vice-chair of the SED/PDS (born 1943); Gregor Gysi, chief of the same party (1948); Bärbel Bohley, cofounder of New Forum (1947), Gerd Poppe, cofounder of the Initiative for Peace and Human Rights (IFM) (1942); Konrad Weiss, cofounder of Democracy Now (1942); Angelika Barbe (1952), Ibrahim Böhme (1944), and Markus Meckel (1952), all three SPD; Rainer Eppelmann, cofounder of Democratic Awakening (1943) and GDR defense minister; Peter Michael Diestel (1952), the controversial DSU interior minister; and Martin Kirchner, general secretary of the CDU (1949).

It is interesting to contrast this set of new elites against the older generation of East German leaders. CDU Premier Lothar de Maizière (1940) was closer to the first postwar generation, even though he is ten years younger than Kohl (1930). Hans-Wilhelm Ebeling (1934), former chair of the DSU, is also of this cohort, and so is Günther Maleuda (1931), chair of the Farmers' party (DBD). Of the last communist leaders of the GDR, Egon Krenz (1937) is also first postwar generation, while Hans Modrow (1928) is on the borderline with the war/Nazi generation (he served as an antiaircraft helper) which, of course, included victims and dissidents as well. The old guard ousted along with Erich Honecker (1912), SED general secretary and president of the State Council—for example, Stasi chief Erich Mielke (1907) and Hermann Axen (1916), Politbureau member and former editor of the official GDR daily *Neues Deutschland*, or Willi Stoph (1914), Politbureau member and former premier—generally became active in the communist party (KPD) during the Weimar Republic or the early Nazi years. Günter Mittag (1926), longtime economic adviser in the Politbureau and second only to Honecker, is of the war generation. He, too, served as an antiaircraft assistant.

The politics of West Germany in the seventies were dominated by the polarization between the "68ers" and their elders. In 1989, when the Brandt administration came into power, the student and left-wing rebels joined the Young Socialists (*Jusos*) and Young Democrats (*Judos*) of the new government parties, the SPD and FDP, and some of their leaders came to occupy important government positions from which, for example, they could attempt to mold educational policy in Hessian public secondary schools. "Working within the system" no doubt moderated the radical thrust of this youthful rebellion as the "critical generation" became older. Nevertheless, there remained a deep-seated hostility between them, on the one hand, and their defensive elders and large numbers of similarly mobilized, right-of-center German youth, on the other hand, far from the metropolitan and university breeding grounds of the critical generation. Throughout the seventies, the battle was joined by these two camps over issues of educational policy, civil rights, warfare, and the new women's agitation over abortion rights. It reached heights of stridency over the panicky official German responses to Baader-Meinhof terrorism when right-wing exponents such as Franz-Josef Strauss sought to identify the "terrorist sympathizers" with the entire Left, while the latter attempted to defend the civil rights of people accused of collaboration with the terrorists. The radicals among the *Jusos* and *Judos* also had their problems with their own parties, and many left in disappointment to join other groupings more to their liking. The most important of these new rival groups were the predecessors of the Green party which began to assemble in the late seventies and, by 1983, had entered the West German Bundestag. Another strong attraction for the alienated "second postwar generation" was the broadly supported peace and antimissile movement of the early eighties. By this time, of course, the typical "68er" was in his or her thirties, and many of the young recruits of the Greens and the pacifist revival belonged to a third or even a fourth generation, born after 1955 and in the late sixties, respectively. The "68ers" still stood out among the leaders of the Greens and the pacifists, and even among the younger generations of the SPD in the big cities.

Nowadays, the first representatives of this second postwar generation have been vying for the highest political posts, including SPD chancellor candidate Oskar Lafontaine and other prominent opposition figures, not to mention outstanding female politicians, such as Antje Vollmer and Petra Kelly of the Greens, and even a few prominent Christian Democrats such as Horst Teltschik, the foreign policy adviser of Chancellor Kohl, and Günther Krause, the GDR negotiator of the unification treaties. These newcomers to the political scene make Kohl (1930), Brandt (1913), or Genscher (1927), the longtime foreign minister, seem old by comparison. The attitudes of this second postwar generation toward German reunification, moreover, tend to be rather free of old-fashioned nationalism and of concern with national prestige and power. Instead of a headlong rush into national unity, they would have preferred social reforms to secure individual economic well-being, a sound environment, and democracy for East Germans who were as fearful as the West Germans of the ultimate costs of unity.

A Third Postwar Generation in East and West

A third postwar generation (born after 1955) has since grown up and formed its political views amidst the oil crises of the seventies and the shocks of the eighties, many of its members embracing the mental worlds characteristic of the new social movements mentioned above. Although perhaps lacking the cohesiveness of their predecessors, their unifying experience is that of "limits to growth," the discovery that economic growth, industrial development without strong environmental safeguards, national power—in short, the vision of secular progress—cannot sustain future generations. To this should be added a renewed pacifism and concern about the insane levels of armaments located until recently in Germany alone: nuclear, chemical, and conventional weapons sufficient to kill every European a thousand times over. Add to this the ecology of our poisoned environment, faulty nuclear plants, chemical additives in our food, the waste of fossil fuels and energy, and the fixation of many Germans with "bigger and better," albeit inhumane, machinery and power. Last but not least important is the oppression of women, children, and various minorities in a society of patriarchal traditions and vivid memories of prejudice and racial persecution. The young Germans of this generation clearly missed out, then, on the ebullient mood of the eighties, when President Reagan proclaimed it to be "morning (again) in America." Theirs was a mood of pervasive economic and military insecurity, some of it in fact related to the same military Keynesianism that made Americans feel so ebullient.

This third postwar political generation is quite distinctive also in East Germany, where it had fueled illegal peace movements[17] and, with the support of church groups, human rights opposition under the communist dictatorship.[18] In 1989, this generation became the mainstay of the demonstrations and citizen movements against the hard-line Honecker regime and was instrumental in breaking its final resistance. As Erich Honecker gave way to Egon Krenz, and Krenz to the reform communist Hans Modrow, the bulk of these young rebel groups and movements

17. Official communist ideology has always championed "world peace" but has generally refrained from criticizing Soviet and East German militarism or Soviet armaments and adventures in power politics. The "illegal pacifists" were therefore prosecuted, and sometimes expelled to the West, while the dictatorship lasted.

18. On the role of the churches, see James R. Edwards, "The Fall and Rise of East Germany," *Christianity Today*, Apr. 23, 1990, pp. 17–18, and John P. Burgess, "Church-State Relations in East Germany: The Church as a Religious and Political Force," *Journal of Church and State* 32 (Winter 1990), 17–35. Also see Wilhelm Drühe, "Beruf Pfarrer," *Die politische Meinung* 35 (March/Apr. 1990), 74–81.

characteristically wanted to reform East German government and society, not simply to integrate with West Germany on West German terms.

This generation's attitude toward national unification, both among West and East Germans, is conditional upon major domestic reforms which they consider more pressing than mere unity, even though they of course welcome the liberation of East Germany from brutal dictatorship and ecological mismanagement on a grand scale. From their point of view, the whole enterprise of national unification has unfortunately run away under pressure from East German majorities who opted for quick economic and currency unification rather than for the internal reform agenda of the original East German opposition groups. German nationalism per se means nothing positive, but evokes in them horrid memories of the Third Reich and the war. The East German elections of March 18, 1990, gave the nod to the initiatives of Chancellor Kohl and the East German coalition government of right-wing and left-wing parties, with mildly nationalistic overtones: *Deutschland einig Vaterland* was the motto of the parties who won. The original opposition and its predominantly young clientele were appalled at this turn of events.

National Unity Less Important Today

After the third postwar generation there may well be a distinct fourth generation, whose cohorts were born after 1968 and who have barely begun to vote. The polling categories of the public opinion institutes correspond poorly to this group—there is one comprising eighteen- to twenty-four-year-olds—which barely includes the very young anti–Gulf War activists of today. We know that they vote disproportionately for the Greens (11%) and the Reps (2.8%), and that they gave only a modest fraction of their vote (37.9%) to the CDU/CSU. Particularly among young East Germans of this age group, Lafontaine was very popular (40.1%). While in May 1990 only one in twenty was actually against unification or expressed indifference, this left only 88.5% who were for it (as compared to 96.6% of those age fifty or older). And they expressed more worry than joy about the unification (57% vs. 43%) and seemed more inclined in 1990 to blame the Bonn government or the democratically elected GDR government for the bad economic turn there than older groups. In fact, 38.5% of them thought the unification had turned out worse than expected (as compared to 26.7% of all age groups). They described themselves as only "somewhat" or "hardly" interested in politics (61.9% vs. 45.7% of all groups). Yet these are the groups, at

least in West Germany, among which most of the peace demonstrators
of January 1990 could be found.[19] They are rather dissatisfied with West
German democracy (22.6%), but not particularly "proud of being German" (only 56.1% are, as compared to 70.2% of all age groups). They
are far more tolerant of foreign workers and are inclined to give them
voting rights. German unification moves them a great deal less than it
does their elders, and it would not be wrong to characterize them as
exhibiting little national feeling.

19. See also *Politbarometer*, November 1990, p. 5, where only 25% of the 18–24-year-
olds expressed a preference for the CDU/CSU. IPOS/BRD, p. 109, 150; IPOS/DDR, pp. 10,
59; *Bundestagswahl 1990*, p. 38; and *Politbarometer Ost*, Oct./Nov. 1990, pp. 50, 81–83,
86, 102.

Chapter TWO

The Communist Empire Opens Up

While there is no doubt about the oft-expressed German desire for reunification, it would be difficult indeed to find sufficient and initial evidence for the dramatic developments of 1989 and 1990 in Germany alone. On the contrary, there is every reason to believe that the Germans were taken as much by surprise as anyone (see below, Chapter Four). Europeans and Americans, however, tend to differ on the nature of the prime mover in this process. "In the beginning," to hear West Europeans tell it, "there was Gorby," Mikhail Sergeyevich Gorbachev, successor to three dying Soviet leaders and, by 1988, more popular among West Germans even than U.S. President Reagan. Of course, many Americans disagree, believing instead that the inspired formula of a presidential speech writer—"Mr. Gorbachev, tear down this wall"—delivered by President Reagan long ago (1987) during a ceremonial visit at the Berlin Wall "made him do it" or that the defense buildup of the Reagan years compelled the Soviets to "cry uncle" because they could no longer keep up the arms race at such a pace. Close examination of the process reveals, however, that the first of these answers is only half true and the second not at all.[1] The problems of the Soviet empire had long been generating

1. It is a sad testimonial to our gullibility and partisanship in this matter that any

relative decline from imperial overextension and economic weaknesses. It remained for CPSU General Secretary Gorbachev to sum up the results of the Brezhnev "years of stagnation" and to propose a radical "restructuring" of the Soviet economy and, eventually, of the political system as well. In any case, Gorbachev's *perestroika* (restructuring) and his new openness (*glasnost*) were initially understood as being principally concerned with domestic reforms and not with cutting back on the empire.[2] It was only after prolonged efforts at coping with domestic problems, in particular the threat of secessions on the Soviet periphery, and especially during the extraordinary year of 1989 that the revolutionary implications for the Soviet's East European satellites became clear. "Since the fall of 1989," to quote Coit D. Blacker, ". . . events have overtaken Moscow's carefully constructed plan for Europe, resulting in a kind of policy 'free fall.' "[3] The startling results, among other things, also imperiled Gorbachev's own position between impatient reformers and the reactionaries in the army and the KGB and brought about his ouster by the end of 1991.

The Old Soviet Empire

Let us first sketch the features of that once mighty Cold War empire of the Soviets so as to highlight the changes. World War II had left the Soviet Union a great military power, if not on a par with the United States. Its

---

analyst would even consider media-intended statements and photo opportunities in lieu of the complex decision process of political reality. As for the economic argument, this has not been demonstrated either. Aside from military Keynesianism and, perhaps, a desire to have the blessings of Reagan's "Opportunity Society" benefit the defense industry, in the short run the American defense buildup mostly damaged America's economic health and competitiveness vis-à-vis new challengers, such as Japan and the European Community, hastening American economic decline. By hastening deterioration and reform in the long run, however, it may have "benefited" his successors more than it did his administration.

2. See especially Paul Kennedy, *The Rise and Fall of the Great Powers* (New York: Vintage Books, 1987), pp. 488–514. The remarks of Foreign Minister Shevardnadze since his resignation have shown that there is a strong reaction among army, party, and KGB against the decline of the Soviet empire and a profound desire to roll back the decline. Kennedy, however, warns the West that Russian tradition has made it unlikely that the Soviet empire "could ever accept imperial decline gracefully" and to expect a "great power war" as the only way to make the Soviets give in to the inevitable (p. 514). On *perestroika* see also Padim Desai, *Perestroika in Perspective: The Design and Dilemmas of Soviet Reform* (Princeton, N.J.: Princeton University Press, 1989), chap. 7.

3. Blacker, "The Collapse of Soviet Power in Europe," *Foreign Affairs* 70, no. 1 (1991), 88–102.

victorious Red Army had not only liberated but had taken virtual possession of Romania, Bulgaria, Albania, Hungary, Czechoslovakia, Poland, East Germany, and North Korea.[4] It just barely failed to establish similar dominion in Yugoslavia—Tito's partisan army had already liberated their country before the Red Army got there, although the decisive break did not occur until 1948—and in Greece, where the Soviet-supported communists lost a bitter civil war against U.S.-supported loyalists. The Soviets at first permitted free elections and parliamentary coalitions as the baseline of the cat-and-mouse game by which, in a few years, they installed communist governments in most of the countries named (see Fig. 2.1). Then the takeover usually proceeded from a rather

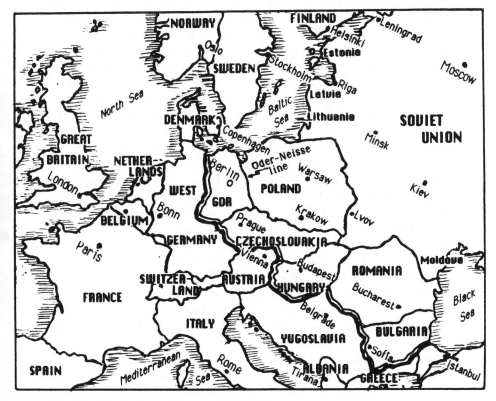

Fig. 2.1. The Soviet satellite empire in the West.

4. For a while, they also occupied parts of northern Iran, had designs on northern Turkey, and shared in the occupation of Austria. A few years later, communism also triumphed in China, although this was not the result of Soviet efforts.

small electoral base, but with key positions (Defense, Interior) in the coalition cabinets, and was accomplished by means of a coup taking place in the proximity of the Red Army.[5] There followed the establishment of politicoeconomic systems that resembled the Soviet system, although most East European countries had strong national traditions and, with the exception of Bulgaria and East Germany, viewed the Russians with great suspicion. The passage of time had not wiped out the historical memory of tsarist Russian imperialism.

The engineered takeover in Eastern Europe was motivated by the desire to create a *cordon sanitaire* of friendly governments between the Soviet Union and defeated Germany. Henceforth, the Soviet Union controlled these countries by various means: militarily through threats and, from 1955, through the Warsaw Pact (WTO), a military alliance similar to NATO, which had just incorporated a rearmed West Germany; economically through an elaborate network of trade and economic plans that tried to assign complementary supply functions to different satellites, coordinated by COMECON (CMEA); and politically through the international organization of the party, the Cominform, a revived Comintern, which subordinated the various communist party states to the CPSU. Communist theory accorded the satellites only the name "people's democracies" or "people's republics" as a mark of their incomplete transformation in the direction of communism, far from the communist near-perfection of the Soviet Union itself. Of the various East European satellites, East Germany was the most subdued and pliant, not only because it had been directly conquered and had suffered the greatest interventions through long years of Soviet occupation, but because German national pride and identity had been completely discredited by association with the Nazi regime, leaving the GDR the lowest in the communist pecking order. Even when its degree of industrial and agricultural development had raised it above all the other communist states in living standards, including the Soviet Union, East Germany was despised by all of them as somehow still afflicted with the mark of Cain while desperately trying to be more communist than any of them.

This Soviet empire was run with an iron fist, which manifested itself with recurring internal blood purges in the early years of each satellite and, later, with the repression by Soviet tanks of any disobedience. There were a number of rebellions, most of them not against communism per se but only against the governments of the day. Stalin's death in March

5. See especially R. V. Burks, "Eastern Europe," in Cyril E. Black and Thomas P. Thornton, eds., *Communism and Revolution: The Strategic Uses of Political Violence* (Princeton, N.J.: Princeton University Press, 1964), pp. 77–116.

1953 caused ripples of rebellion in several satellites. One of the first (June 15–17, 1953) was the German workers' uprising against harsh exploitation.[6] Rising in East Berlin and in more than 250 other towns of the GDR, it began as the equivalent of a labor dispute in a country with free unions and—in part through misunderstandings and in part from pre-GDR traditions of German labor solidarity—it escalated until some 300,000–400,000 workers were involved and the communist government could no longer count on its own police to keep it from being toppled. By the early morning of June 17, however, Soviet troops had already occupied railway stations and post offices in the larger towns, in harbors on the Baltic, and at the uranium mines of the Erzgebirge to frustrate any coordination of the local strike efforts. A state of emergency was declared by the government while huge crowds were still rallying and demonstrating—until Soviet tanks and infantry appeared. The tanks and soldiers proceeded with caution and mostly fired into the air, so that in the entire GDR only 21 people were killed on this occasion. Even at the Brandenburg Gate, where a handful of youths pulled down the Red flag, three companies of Soviet soldiers stationed there merely fired warning shots into the air. Expectations of Western intervention were disappointed and the uprising collapsed, to be followed by a campaign of purges that included the expulsion of Wilhelm Zaisser, the minister of state security, Rudolf Herrnstadt, the editor of the party newspaper, *Neues Deutschland*, and other high party officials of their dissident faction. More than 1,000 East Germans went to prison in the ensuing purges and seven were sentenced to death.[7] Czechoslovak unrest that same year was quelled by the communist government and its security forces.

A second wave of revolt followed upon the famous speech by Soviet leader Nikita Khrushchev, before the 20th Congress of the CPSU, denouncing the misdeeds of Stalin (February 1956) and followed by the dissolution of the Cominform (April 1956). In June, workers rebelled in Poznan (Poland) against the grim economic conditions and the administered high prices and low wages. The Soviets chose not to intervene there while an erstwhile dissident communist, Wladyslaw Gomulka, whom

6. Much of the industrial workers' dissatisfaction originated from the collective agreements of 1951 and the communist state unions (FDGB) that drew them up. An increase in the mandatory production quotas (*Soll*), in January 1953, triggered the actual revolt. See Arnulf Baring, *Uprising in East Germany, June 17, 1953* (Ithaca, N.Y.: Cornell University Press, 1972), pp. 30–49.

7. Ibid., pp. 52–116. There had been a series of halfhearted attempts at liberalization, in particular the New Course announced on June 9, a by-product of the changes in the Kremlin since the death of Josef Stalin. See also David Childs, *The GDR: Moscow's German Ally* (London: Allen & Unwin, 1983), pp. 31–33.

they regarded with distrust, became the new leader of the communist state party (PUWP). A year earlier, Khrushchev had shown unexpected tolerance when he tried in vain to woo Tito to join the Soviet empire. Now a Hungarian challenge to communist orthodoxy put this new Soviet tolerance to the test. In July 1956 the Soviets helped Hungarian dissident communists to oust Mátyás Rákosi, perhaps the worst of the East European dictators before Nicolae Ceauşescu's reign in Romania. But the Hungarian communist party remained deeply divided and, in the last days of October, newly appointed Premier Imre Nagy permitted, under pressure from opposition groups, the reestablishment of a multiparty system. Worse yet, Nagy announced Hungary's withdrawal from the Warsaw Pact and future neutrality. On November 4 the Red Army, which had withdrawn temporarily from Budapest, returned in full force and smashed the rebellion with great violence in only a few days. Khrushchev's policy of relative liberalization throughout the Soviet empire had failed and was replaced with a tightening of the reins. At the same time, a growing estrangement set in with the People's Republic of China, which had been under considerable Soviet influence during its first decade of existence until border disputes and ideological disagreement nearly brought the two countries to the edge of war.[8] Khrushchev was not able to maintain the authority of the Soviet Union over its empire and allies in quite the same fashion as Stalin.

The Cuban Missile Crisis of 1962, paradoxically, ushered in a period of détente and attempts at peaceful coexistence between East and West, even though Khrushchev's successor, Leonid Brezhnev, soon began to build up Russian military strength again at the same time that he pursued better relations with the West. East European countries also felt free to go after trade and cultural contacts with the West, and Hungary, for one, embarked on a course of domestic cultural and economic liberalization that placed it in the forefront of the Eastern bloc of nations. Romania pursued an independent foreign policy while maintaining orthodoxy at home. East Germany, on the other hand, the satellite that was politically, militarily, and economically the most dependent on Moscow, after a series of major crises and East-West confrontations over Berlin,[9] had

8. The estrangement began in the late fifties and intensified during the Great Leap Forward of 1958, when Mao Zedong's agricultural-industrial commune movement seemed to mock Russian communism, and in the early sixties, when the Soviets and Chinese denounced each other as "dogmatists" and "revisionists," respectively. By the close of the sixties, there were border clashes of increasing ferocity.

9. Among other conflicts, there were Soviet ultimatums and threats to conclude a separate Soviet–East German peace treaty which would turn the controversial Western access routes to isolated West Berlin over to the GDR. See Childs, *The GDR*, pp. 59–65.

started the decade with a continuing drain of East German refugees, of whom as many as a thousand were arriving day after day in West Berlin or West Germany. As it did twenty-seven years later, in 1989/90, the hemorrhage of East Germany's population to the West, especially of its younger and well-trained citizens, became intolerable to the communist government and its economy.[10] In mid-1961 rumors of the imminent closing of the border only increased the flow through the zonal border in Berlin, where it was hardest to control: each working day, on foot, by subway, streetcar or train, about 12,000 West Berliners and 60,000 East Berliners crossed the line between the Soviet and the three Western sectors; it was easy for East German refugees, who had access to East Berlin, to come across so long as they did not carry conspicuous luggage. So, a little after midnight on August 13, 1961, when most people slept or were away on vacation—it was a weekend and Western policymakers in Bonn and Washington were caught by surprise—GDR security forces closed off 193 streets and 74 official crossings throughout the city. Soon after that they built the infamous Wall, razing a wide strip of buildings along the Eastern side and setting up a "death strip" with dogs and armed border patrols, ready to shoot without asking questions. To the Western nations, the Berlin Wall became a symbol of the lack of freedom behind the Iron Curtain, the jailhouse door of communist dictatorship.

Once the borders of the GDR were sealed for all effects and purposes, Walter Ulbricht believed he could seriously pursue the goal of a model communist economy and society. Physical control over the exit of people became the foundation of GDR legitimacy. The sixties were indeed a period of ambitious economic, agricultural, and educational reconstruction for his country, consolidating communist rule and giving the GDR its first taste of foreign successes in trade and diplomatic expansion.[11] The building of the Wall and sealing of the borders undoubtedly reflected the desire of the Soviet Union, too, to give its East German satellite the stability it craved. Moscow may even have watched East Germany's rising economic success with pleasure, perceiving it as a tribute to communist

10. Over 200,000 East German refugees made it to the West in 1961, 155,000 of them alone, before the building of the Wall. Between the birth date of the GDR (1949) and 1961, over 2.7 million had left the GDR, almost one out of every six residents. During the following two decades, another 400,000 left, half of them older people (over age sixty-five) who were let go in order to save on their old-age pensions. Hundreds planned escapes every year and many were caught or killed in the attempt, well over a hundred at the Wall alone.

11. See Merkl, *German Foreign Policies, West and East* (Santa Barbara, Calif.: ABC-Clio, 1974), pp. 92–94, and Hans-Adolf Jacobsen, Wolfgang Mallmann, and Christian Meier, eds., *Drei Jahrzehnte Aussenpolitik der DDR* (Munich and Vienna: Oldenbourg, 1979).

economics. It is only now that we fully realize the glaring weaknesses and imperfections of the GDR economy. The Soviets may also have had second thoughts when they noticed that the economic achievements of the GDR, not to mention its prowess in international sports competition, began to top theirs.[12] We shall return to Soviet treatment of the GDR.

If the role of Soviet tanks, in this case, involved protecting a satellite, confronting American tanks eyeball to eyeball at Checkpoint Charlie in Berlin, it soon became evident that there continued to be a mailed fist as well behind all the glad-handing of détente during the sixties. Czechoslovakia, too, had begun to liberalize its economy in the early sixties, this time to make up for economic stagnation. Western trade offers and overtures met the country's desires halfway, but the Czechs were very conscious of the lessons of 1956: liberalization had to be partial, and there could be no questioning of membership in the Warsaw Pact or of the internal monopoly of the communist party. Nevertheless, in early 1968, they replaced their dictator of fifteen years, Antonin Novotny, with the liberal communist, Alexander Dubček, and the "Prague Spring" of free speech, free press, and freedom of the arts began to blossom. They even permitted independent new political figures and opposition parties, so long as they accepted the leadership of the communist party. The Soviet empire found this intolerable, however, and, on August 20, the Red Army plunged into Czechoslovakia, supported by Warsaw Pact units from Poland, East Germany, Hungary, and Bulgaria. To the dismay of Ulbricht's East German army units, Czechs painted swastikas on their rolling stock and flaunted signs with questions such as "Haven't we seen you here before, thirty years ago?" (the Nazis invaded Czechoslovakia in 1938). But all the bravery was to no avail, and the Prague Spring was frozen out by the frost of brutal repression. Soviet tanks had won once again and Brezhnev issued his new doctrine: any deviation from "the socialist form of government"[13] would bring on armed intervention by other members of the Warsaw Pact.

12. Drawn from a population of only 16 million, GDR athletes in recent Olympic competitions frequently topped the performance of the athletes of the Soviet Union, with a population twenty times as large. The secret of their success was a combination of early selection and scientifically refined sports training facilities that have now become accessible to Western observers. Recent disclosures about the use of drugs to increase athletic performance have lessened the achievement in the eyes of the West, although Western athletes have not been innocent in this respect.

13. The use of the word "socialist" in place of "communist," of course, is part of the communist game of word-mongering, a kind of linguistic imperialism like the communist use of the word "democratic," as in German Democratic Republic. The true socialist parties of France, Italy, Greece, Spain, and other Western countries, are democratic parties in the

Ostpolitik *in Lieu of Reunification*

East German leader Ulbricht and Polish leader Gomulka who, behind the scenes, had both been among the strongest advocates of the Czechoslovak invasion, received their comeuppance within a few years. In 1970 Gomulka was replaced with the more liberal Edward Gierek, who tried to end the Polish economic doldrums with imports of Western technology and, for a few years, did manage to turn the economy around. Ulbricht's fate was more ominous in that he was sacrificed to the Soviet desire to make a deal with West Germany. In 1968, his scheming against Prague still reflected his opposition to Dubček's liberalization and, among other things, to big West German trade overtures which he and others interpreted as political in motivation and potential impact. Less than two years later, however, the new government of Willy Brandt (SPD) renewed West German efforts to extend trade and diplomatic contacts to Eastern Europe. But this time, the West Germans launched their *Ostpolitik* (Eastern policy) by first talking to the Soviet Union and offering a series of mutual-renunciation-of-force treaties which implicitly recognized all the eastern borders left in the wake of the Red Army in World War II, including the Oder-Neisse line and the German-Czech border.[14] The Soviet Union, Poland, and Czechoslovakia found this acceptable and, after additional offers of trade and compensation (to Poland), signed the three treaties. This left the German Democratic Republic in a very uncomfortable position, which was intolerably worsened by the conclusion of four-power agreements on Berlin and Western access to the city in 1971.[15] Chancellor Brandt, the former mayor of West Berlin, had cleverly made ratification of the mutual-renunciation-of-force treaties by Bonn dependent on Russian cooperation in securing the status of his city.

To the GDR government, this rapprochement between Bonn and Moscow was an outrageous development, and the aging Ulbricht fought with all his might behind the scenes against the Soviet concessions to the Federal Republic. GDR Premier Willi Stoph, at a meeting with Brandt in March 1970, in Erfurt (GDR), demanded diplomatic recognition of the GDR and 100 billion deutschmarks in "reparations" for the pre-1961 loss of East German refugees and for the economic discrimination

---

Western sense just like the Social Democrats of Sweden (SD) or of Germany (SPD), and they are bitter rivals of the communist parties in these democracies.

14. The Czech border had been modified by the cession of the ethnic German Sudeten area in the Munich Agreements of 1938, which had been sanctioned by England and France and never officially rectified, even though at the end of the war most Sudeten Germans had been expelled and the *de facto* border restored to its pre-1938 location.

15. See Merkl, *German Foreign Policies, West and East*, chaps. 5 and 6.

suffered at West German hands under the Hallstein Doctrine.[16] He also rejected any remaining Western allied occupation rights over East Berlin and the territory of the GDR over which the newly negotiated access routes to West Berlin had to go. East Berlin had become the GDR capital—though West Berlin was not permitted to be part of the Federal Republic—and not just a zone of the quadripartite Allied *Komandatura* as before 1949.

The East German prime minister referred to the building of the Berlin Wall, the "death strip" at the border, and the killing of escaping refugees there as "a humanitarian act." Stoph also expressed East German dissatisfaction with Brandt's theory that the GDR was only one of "two states within one nation" and hence that it did not merit diplomatic recognition. The usual well-drilled official demonstrations of communist stage management, with shouted slogans and with banners praising the GDR and attacking the "revanchist Federal Republic," almost broke down at the Erfurt meeting at one point. Thousands of common people surged through the police lines to greet Willy Brandt, just as thousands had earlier stood by the railroad tracks for a glimpse of the first West German chancellor to come to the GDR. They held up signs bearing the letter *y* to show that their cheers were meant for Will*y* Brandt, not Will*i* Stoph.[17]

But the Soviet leaders obviously were not about to press the East German demands upon the Bonn negotiators. The agreement with the Western allies to assert their residual occupation rights and provide a Berlin settlement to Bonn's liking was a severe setback for GDR autonomy and pride. The East German leaders knew they were being led down the garden path and not to the altar. This was their equivalent of Bismarck's *cauchemar des coalitions*, an alliance of Bonn and Moscow, and it was Ulbricht's final downfall. The tough old communist was one of the few remaining leaders in the communist world who had personally

16. Longtime Adenauer adviser Walter Hallstein (CDU) had introduced the idea that since the Federal Republic claimed to be the *sole representative* of German interests in the world, any Third World nation (also Yugoslavia in 1957) that recognized the GDR would lose West German recognition and trade contacts. This doctrine and the claim to "sole representation" were dropped at this point as one of the few concessions to the GDR—after they had already become weakened when some Third World nations recognized the GDR anyway.

17. A return meeting two months later in Kassel turned into a huge melee of West German communists (DKP), neofascists (NPD), and right-wing youth groups, including refugee groups and the Young Union (CDU). The police were unable to stop the right-wing demonstrators from tearing down the GDR flag and defacing a wreath placed by Brandt and Stoph at a monument to the victims of fascism. The official SED newspaper *Neues Deutschland* spoke of "unheard-of provocations." Only the lower-level agreements to cooperate in postal and transportation matters survived the Kassel debacle.

known Lenin and many of the old Bolsheviks of the Russian Revolution. Once before, in 1964, he had opposed Khrushchev's initiatives toward better relations with Bonn, which caused the Soviet leader to refer to him and Mao Zedong as "warmongers." But then Khrushchev was deposed from within the Soviet system and East Berlin had its way. This time Ulbricht was not so lucky. He was made to resign and his protégé and deputy Erich Honecker took over, accepting the painful compromises imposed on the GDR and continuing Ulbricht's efforts to shield the GDR from West German inroads and establish its separate identity further,[18] insofar as this was possible in the face of penetration by West German television, which four of five East Germans have been able to receive for many years.

The Brandt administration of 1969–1974, for its part, broke resolutely with twenty years of ritual incantations—from Adenauer's "policy of strength" to Hallstein's doctrine of the "sole right of the FRG to the diplomatic representation of East Germans"—which had expressed faith in eventual German reunification. Chancellor Brandt and his team proposed to cleave this Gordian knot with an elaborate policy of détente and mutual renunciation of the use of force among all the major Central European and East European countries, *beginning* with the Soviet Union. Within this framework and with the support of the Soviets and Germany's eastern neighbors, the GDR became the object of Brandt's "embracing strategy"[19] of rapprochement. Brandt's government refused the long-desired diplomatic recognition of the GDR, but recognized it as one of "two states within one nation," in the realization that *de facto* international recognition would soon be granted by other Western governments and in particular by the United Nations, which eventually admitted both German states as sovereign entities.

For the GDR, Brandt's *Ostpolitik* meant a barefaced attempt at subversion of communist rule and principles by the agent of imperialism: "*Wandel durch Annäherung*" (domestic change in the GDR by means of rapprochement) and the "policy of small steps" was the formula by

18. There was a series of attempts to rename every organization or institution that referred to a common German nationality. The Deutschlandsender radio became the "Voice of the GDR," and the German Union of Journalists that "of the GDR." In 1972, the People's Chamber dropped all clauses of the 1968 Constitution that referred to a "German nation," "German states," or "reunification." See Jonathan Steele, *Inside East Germany: The State That Came in from the Cold* (New York: Urizen Books, 1977), pp. 208–210.

19. This embracing tactic (*Umarmungsstrategie*) had already been used ten years earlier in the Bad Godesberg reforms of the SPD, which "embraced" West German business, the churches, agriculture, and the military so lovingly that they were supposed to give up their hostility to the new "people's party," which had also diluted its Marxist ideology with humanism and Christianity as philosophical bases.

which the Bonn government intended to liberalize the GDR against its
will so as "to make life easier for the East Germans" in lieu of reunification. There followed, indeed, a series of cooperative agreements on traffic
and other intercourse between the two Germanys. And, not to be
overlooked, successive West German governments, including Christian
Democratic as well as SPD leaders, soon henceforth exhibited a willingness to conciliate and accommodate the SED regime that would embarrass them later on.[20]

A New Climate of Opinion

The era of détente created a new climate of opinion in West Germany
that was viewed with suspicion by American policymakers in Washington.[21] West German defense elites became far less convinced that military
strength was important to German security than were their American (or
French) counterparts, whose attitudes became ever tougher during the
early eighties.[22] West Germans felt so heartened by their new relationship
with the Soviet Union and the East European states that they have believed
ever since the seventies that they could negotiate their way out of any
crisis—rather than rely on nuclear threat and military bullying à la Cold
War. Nuclear deterrence for them thus became a political device under
which they could live in peace and prosperity so long as a rough balance
of armed power was maintained between East and West. To aggravate
the growing security dissension between Germany and the United States,
the pacifist struggle against refurbishment of NATO missiles to counter
the Soviet SS-20s in the early eighties brought out the fact that any actual
East-West confrontation, nuclear or conventional, would take place on
German soil and kill millions of Germans.[23] This was hardly a vision to
inspire West Germans to fight in NATO ranks or anywhere else.

20. Among such actions were friendly visits and contacts, major loans secured by Franz-
Josef Strauss (CSU) for the GDR, and the willingness of the SPD government in Bonn to
sweep communist misdeeds, which had been collected in an archive of refugee complaints
in Salzgitter, under the rug.
21. See Melvin Croan, "Dilemmas of Ostpolitik," in Merkl, ed., *West German Foreign
Policy: Dilemmas and Directions* (Chicago: Council on Foreign Relations, 1983), p. 35ff.
22. On the American views, see Tom W. Smith, "The Polls: American Attitudes Toward
the Soviet Union and Communism," *Public Opinion Quarterly* 47, no. 2 (1983), 277ff.;
on the German elite views, Peter Schmidt's RAND Corporation paper, "Public Opinion
and Security in West Germany," Sept. 1984.
23. West Germans have always been far more inclined than Americans to avoid nuclear
war at all costs. In 1981, 48% of West Germans expressed this view as compared to 32%

Substantial numbers of West Germans were also looking to a united Europe, the Council for Security and Cooperation in Europe, or at least the present European Community for their security in the eighties. As many as one-fourth of the respondents in a 1979 poll, moreover, expressed the desire to include the Soviet Union and Eastern Europe in a united Europe, an early harbinger of the difficulties of placing the united Germany of 1990/91 into a strict East-West alignment in Europe.[24] Indeed, West Germans who perceived a Soviet threat declined from a level of two-thirds of the population in the early fifties—when only 15% denied there was such a threat—to 28% in 1971, when 46% felt unthreatened. The number of West Germans who favored some cooperation with the Soviet Union also rose from 20% in the fifties to 50% in 1970 and then declined again.[25]

The turbulent seventies led West Germans once again to perceive a greater Soviet threat, given the disappointment of *Ostpolitik* and the Soviet invasion of Afghanistan, but even then four out of five (vs. 9%) said that "Europe and especially Germany should continue détente . . . and that the West [should] use all the means at its disposal to prevent a return to the Cold War."[26] Behind the insistence on détente, however, there still was a realistic perception of Soviet intentions as well as a rather exaggerated idea of Western weakness: in 1977, for example, 53% of West Germans attributed to Leonid Brezhnev a desire for domination of Europe "rather than for peaceful cooperation with the West." But a good one-third (29–37%) believed throughout the seventies that "we together with NATO" *could not* "defend ourselves against a serious Russian attack." In particular the West German mood of the years from 1976 to 1981 was characterized by a perception of "the East as more powerful" (46–57% thought so) than the West, which enjoyed the confidence of only 5–7% of the population in its defense capabilities.[27] Under a

---

of Americans in 1982. See *Public Opinion* for Aug./Sept. 1981 and Apr./May 1983. Peter Schmidt also found American and French security elites more willing to consider the use of nuclear weapons than their West German counterparts.

24. See Elisabeth Noelle-Neumann, ed., *The Germans: Public Opinion Polls 1967–1980*, rev. ed. (Westport, Conn.: Greenwood Press, 1981), p. 438, and Peter Schmidt, "Europeanization of Defense: Prospect of Consensus?" RAND Corporation paper, Dec. 7, 1984.

25. There was some fluctuation in this perception during the seventies, when the numbers of those expressing fear went from 25% (1977) to 61% (Jan. 1980) in response to the Soviet invasion of Afghanistan.

26. See Noelle-Neumann, ed., *The Germans*, pp. 477 and 466, and EMNID, "Verteidigungsklima 1972–1983."

27. See Noelle-Neumann, ed., *The Germans*, pp. 431, 433, 436–437. See also Peter Schmidt and Matthias Jung in Dietmar Schoessler, ed., *Militär und Politik* (Koblenz: Bernard & Graefe, 1983), esp. tables 8–11. Schmidt and Jung distinguish between

succession of moribund leaders, the Soviets never took advantage of their supposed strength.

The West finally rose to the challenge with the 1979 NATO defense "double decision" of Chancellor Schmidt and President Carter to oppose the Soviet SS-20 missiles pointed at Central Europe. They decided to replace the aging NATO missile armory with new cruise missiles and Pershing 2s, most of them to be located in West Germany. But the actual deployment of the new NATO missiles, at the same time as a new administration in Washington spoke glibly of Armageddon with the "evil empire" and of the "survivability of a nuclear war," produced a massive public reaction among young Germans, who were evidently not so sure that they and their families and friends could survive a nuclear holocaust in the center of Europe.[28] From 1981 to 1983, hundreds of thousands of mostly young Germans, but also church- and trade-union-related paci- fists, marched and rallied, raising the consciousness of all Germans regarding the extraordinary geographic concentration of lethal missiles and other sources of destruction in their small country.[29] During the same period, the assessment of President Reagan's "political actions all in all" as "too hard" rose from 25% (vs. 2%) to 47% (vs. 4%) toward the end of 1982. West Germans also perceived him as a likable man (36%), but not so many called him "good for Germany" (27%), just as the perceived likability of Americans as a people (42–51% yes) has always fallen short of the percentage (around 80%) that has consistently favored German international cooperation with the United States and NATO.[30]

Likes or dislikes aside, the West German public appeared to have a realistic grasp of the essential conditions of the international security of

aggressive, offensive, and defensive elite images of the Soviets and contrast the changing images of Soviet "aggressiveness" with the real threat configurations.

28. See also Merkl, "Pacifism in West Germany," SAIS Review, no. 4 (Summer 1982), 81–91, and Rüdiger Schmitt, "From 'Old Politics' to 'New Politics': Three Decades of Peace Protest in West Germany," in John R. Gibbins, ed., Contemporary Political Culture: Politics in a Postmodern Age (London: Sage, 1989), pp. 174–198.

29. The Green party had a chilling campaign poster that, without comment or slogans, simply showed every missile site—a stationary missile site, of course, placed the entire region on Soviet target maps—NATO base, chemical weapons deposit, and nuclear plant on a map of the FRG.

30. Noelle-Neumann, ed., The Germans, pp. 420–421, 426. By mid-1983, after President Reagan had visited Berlin and Bonn in the midst of demonstrations, majorities of two to one (45–51% vs. 18–24%) expressed disapproval. President Carter had done no better, following his election in 1976: 40% found him likable, but only 24% thought he was "good for Germany." Gebhard Schweigler, "Anti-Americanism in German Public Opin- ion," in Dieter Dettke, ed., America's Image in Germany and Europe (Washington, D.C.: Friedrich-Ebert-Stiftung, 1985), pp. 8–33.

the FRG. In 1981, only 1% of the respondents favored cooperating more closely with the presumably strong Soviet Union, while 56% wanted West Germany to work more closely with the United States. One-third (33%), however, hedged their bets by advocating that Bonn cooperate "equally" with the United States and the USSR. It was not quite clear whether "equal cooperation" was meant to denote an active national foreign policy between the two blocs or a pacifistic neutralism, as in the proposals for a nuclear-free zone in Central and Northern Europe, or possibly dropping out of NATO.[31] Neutralism, however, conjured up old West German fears about becoming "isolated" and either a pushover for the Soviets or tempted by the chimera of assertive nationalism. Hence, broad majorities of two-thirds opted for the Western alliance in polls taken in 1981 and 1984—among the supporters of the opposition SPD, the West barely prevailed (55% vs. 45% neutralists), and among the Greens it lost out to a majority of 73% neutralists.[32] In August 1983, at the height of the antimissile campaign, 72% of all the respondents and 68% (vs. 12%) of SPD adherents wanted the FRG to stay in NATO, while half the Greens (51% vs. 28%) wanted it to drop out.[33] (See Table 2.1.)

Eventually, the new NATO missiles were installed in spite of the pacifist

Table 2.1. West German Perceptions of a Soviet Menace, 1952–1980 (in %)

	1952	1964	1971	1979	1980
Perceive a Soviet menace	66	39	28	35	44
Do not see a menace	15	37	46	46	22
Undecided	19	24	26	19	34

SOURCE: Elisabeth Noelle-Neumann, ed., The Germans: Public Opinion Polls, 1967–1980, rev. ed. (Westport, Conn.: Greenwood Press, 1981), p. 430.

NOTE: Threat perceptions rose considerably in 1968 (invasion of Czechoslovakia) and 1980 (Afghanistan).

31. Whereas in 1954 only 20% (vs. 66% who did not) thought "peaceful coexistence" between the blocs possible, in 1976 it was 49.5%; in 1977, 56%; and in 1981, 51%. Noelle-Neumann, ed., The Germans, p. 416.

32. Among CDU/CSU and FDP supporters, more than three-fourths opted for the West. EMNID data cited by Schweigler, "Anti-Americanism," p. 26.

33. The neutralist option was linked to reunification in one 1979 poll, which ascertained that 49% (vs. 26%) would welcome a combination of withdrawal of both Germanys from NATO and the Warsaw Pact and reunification under international guarantees. However, only 17% considered this a probable outcome, while 64% did not. See also Gerhard Herdegen and Elisabeth Noelle-Neumann, "Protest Howls Belied by Opinion Polls," Die politische Meinung 212 (1984), 10–15.

resistance, and confidence in the United States recovered from its low point in the early eighties.[34] Suddenly NATO was again considered "strong enough to hold back Warsaw Pact aggression" (50% [vs. 40%] in 1985 and 58% in 1986), and more West Germans than ever (85–88% vs. 7–8%) endorsed Bonn's remaining a member of NATO. Three-fourths (76–77%) considered the presence of U.S. troops in the FRG "essential" to West German security. But now there were also 22–23% who thought the presence of U.S. troops was "unimportant" or even "damaging," a reflection not only of the antimissile agitation but also of a rising impatience with the military, which had habitually turned a deaf ear to civilian complaints about maneuver damage to roads and fields and to the constant irritant of military training flights over civilian communities and recreation areas. Most significant, the popular perception of a Soviet threat had dropped to 35% in 1986, when 64% of West Germans agreed that there was no longer any serious threat emanating from the USSR.[35] Although there had not been any particularly friendly overtures toward the FRG from the Kremlin, the sensitive antennae of the West German news media had evidently picked up a new tune from the new communist general secretary of the Soviet Union, Mikhail Gorbachev: *perestroika* instead of the pursuit of Soviet empire.

The Empire Opens Up

Gorbachev had not intended to preside over the collapse of the Soviet empire, whose long-standing economic and political weaknesses he became more aware of every day. But at age fifty-four, in 1984, a man of the first postwar generation, he did not share the war-hardened attitudes of his predecessors—Konstantin Chernenko was twenty years his senior—or of most of the sixty- and seventy-year-olds on the Politbureau. The Soviet nuclear-arms modernization campaign of Leonid Brezhnev and Yuri Andropov had ended with futile maneuvers to stop the West,

34. In May 1981, West German respondents were asked, "How confident are you that the U.S. is capable of taking a wise leadership role today?" Only 42% (vs. 47%) answered in the affirmative. By October 1984, the affirmative responses had climbed to 55% (vs. 44%). See Noelle-Neumann, ed., *The Germans*, p. 420, and Schweigler, "Anti-Americanism," p. 26. See also Merkl, "West German Public Opinion on Détente Since 1970," in Wolfram F. Hanrieder, ed., *Arms Control, the FRG, and the Future of East-West Relations* (Boulder, Colo.: Westview, 1987), pp. 29–49.

35. See the polls cited in *Bundeswehr Aktuell*, Oct. 29, 1986. The number of respondents who thought that the U.S. military presence in the FRG was "damaging" more than doubled from 5% in 1980 to 11–12% in 1985 and 1986, respectively.

one way or another, from modernizing its intermediate-range missiles as well. The Chinese border confrontations alone, according to Eduard Shevardnadze, had cost 200 billion rubles for military infrastructure. The war in Afghanistan swallowed another 60 billion. Maintaining Cuba for thirty years must have cost at least 100 billion. Who knows how many billions went for the last two decades of the Cold War—700? In 1985 the new CPSU general secretary was ready to return to the INF and Strategic Arms Reduction Talks (START) and was prepared to abandon the hidebound positions of the Soviet Cold Warriors one by one. Instead of maintaining control over Eastern Europe at all costs, he wanted to restructure the NATO–Warsaw Pact relationship and, in a series of meetings from 1986 to 1989, sought to lower arms levels drastically on both sides of the Iron Curtain.[36] At the same time, Gorbachev's (perhaps somewhat clumsy) efforts to encourage peaceful evolutionary change, or *perestroika*, among the satellite countries of Eastern Europe appear to have gone far beyond the target. Instead of moderate liberalization under firm, albeit enlightened, communist control, Gorbachev's encouragement generated popular revolutions from Gdansk to Bucharest. Frequently, the increasing oppressiveness of hard-line dictatorships merely served to destroy them all the more thoroughly.

The widespread impression that the great changes in Eastern Europe all happened in 1989 is not quite correct. The captious statement that "Poland took ten years, Hungary ten months, East Germany ten weeks, Czechoslovakia ten days, and Romania ten hours" (Timothy Garton Ash) reveals the underlying reality much better, even if we concede its minor inaccuracies. It was basically a thawing-out process which, over a period of time and with obvious acceleration during 1989, overcame the *political obstacles* to internal reform: the former Soviet Union is still in the thick of it, held back by its own conservatives, and may also take ten years from Gorbachev's advent to power[37] to get to where at least the first four

36. The estimates were cited by Shevardnadze in his essay in *Der Spiegel*, no. 22, May 27, 1991, pp. 172–187. The first of Gorbachev's conferences was the 1986 Conference on European Confidence and Security-Building Measures in Stockholm. Then came the revival of the old Mutual and Balanced Force Reduction (MBFR) negotiations in the so-called Mandate Talks of 1987–1989. Before the United Nations in December 1988, Gorbachev announced a unilateral reduction of half a million Soviet troops. Thus the Conventional Forces in Europe Talks in Vienna (March 1989) already witnessed a very different Soviet defense posture.

37. At the 27th CPSU Congress in February 1986, Gorbachev's political report presented, among other things, the main line of his new approach to Soviet foreign policy after the most controversial aspect—the withdrawal from Afghanistan—had been removed by unnamed Politbureau members, according to Shevardnadze. Gorbachev seems to have realized quite clearly, at the 28th CPSU Congress in 1988, that the power monopoly of the state party was a liability and an obstacle to reform; but the party continued to be by far

countries named above were by 1990. *Economic deterioration* alone, while obviously a major underlying trend of the eighties, had usually lacked the saliency and compelling power of organized political rebellion or political resistance. The political obstacles to reform in the East European satellite countries were, in order, 1) the external compulsions of the Warsaw Pact and of East-West tensions, 2) the monopoly on power of the communist state party, 3) the coercive apparatus of the KGB, Stasi, Securitate, or whatever the secret police was called, and 4) the stranglehold of communist control on mass organizations, in particular the labor and farmers' organizations in these industrializing countries. A fifth obstacle was communist control of the media which, in the process of reform or revolution, either fell victim to the peaceful advent of free speech and free press or was fought over and seized by determined rebel groups. Ousting the old leadership was important only where it had secured a considerable personal following.

Poland was the first communist party state to come undone and it did so in unique fashion, beginning with the extraordinary challenge of an independent 10-million-member trade union, Lech Walesa's Solidarity, which spawned an independent farmers' association as well, Rural Solidarity, in place of the usual communist state organizations. Among the many illusions held by Western observers has often been the naive assumption that a communist dictatorship would free the workers from oppression and exploitation. Polish workers knew better when they joined Solidarity, the illegal trade union that demonstrated it is possible to destabilize a communist dictatorship from within and in spite of all the political obstacles mentioned above. To be sure, the Polish rebellion had a number of advantages on its side when it first set out to upset the applecart. There was a tradition of labor unrest, which had brought on major domestic conflict as recently as 1976 and did so again just before the formation of Solidarity. There was also the fact that communism had never quite penetrated the socioeconomic fabric—e.g., agriculture had not been collectivized as it was in other satellite countries—and so Poland retained its precommunist cohesiveness thanks to Catholicism, the family, and a truculent nationalism that resisted communism as a Russian import. Poland also possesses an ancient tradition of rebellion against authority, whether that of foreign troops, empires, or its own government—a tradition that stood it in good stead during the "Red" decades.

Still, the political obstacles of a satellite existence continued to vitiate the mushroom growth of Solidarity in 1980/81 with the fear of an

---

the strongest political organization present, and it was under the control of conservative communists and other enemies of *perestroika*.

imminent Russian invasion. Even when the communist party (Polish United Workers—PUWP) practically caved in with massive defections to Solidarity and with internal demands from its local groups for democracy, Solidarity and Rural Solidarity, despite the millions of Poles behind them, never dared challenge the monopoly of the PUWP, no matter how discredited it was in the eyes of the people, until the late eighties. Instead, a military dictatorship loyal to the Warsaw Pact moved into the vacuum left by the tottering communist party state, and General Wojciech Jaruzelski became both the PUWP general secretary and the dictator in charge of the "state of war" of December 1981. Solidarity, too, went into a tailspin until its resurgence of self-confidence and public support in the late eighties.[38]

The Dominoes Are Falling

Early in 1989, the Polish government invited Solidarity and representatives of the church for roundtable talks. In April they agreed to legalize Solidarity and to hold June elections, which Solidarity won handily. A month later, Solidarity leaders had the satisfaction of turning down a communist invitation to form a government coalition, fearing they would be blamed for the preceding decades of economic mismanagement. One Solidarity leader, however, Tadeusz Mazowiecki, became prime minister in August 1989, and a year or so later Lech Walesa became president of the republic.

Hungary had been the leader of East European liberalization for a number of years, after János Kádár changed from postrevolutionary enforcer of Soviet repression into a benign reformer in the seventies and eighties, again well before Gorbachev. At the beginning of 1989, the Hungarian parliament passed a law permitting independent parties to compete with the communist state party. May 2 was the memorable day Hungarian soldiers began to dismantle the Iron Curtain by taking down parts of the wire fence separating their country from Austria, the signal that launched the great East German exodus toward the West. The opening of the border was a clear violation of Hungarian agreements with the GDR, though in conformity with the thirty-four-nation Helsinki

38. See the large body of literature on the 1980/81 rebellion, especially Zwi Gitelman, "The Limits of Organization and Enthusiasm: The Double Failure of the Solidarity Movement and the Polish United Workers' Party," in Kay Lawson and Peter Merkl, eds., *When Parties Fail: Emerging Alternative Organizations* (Princeton, N.J.: Princeton University Press, 1988), pp. 421–446.

Agreements that both countries had signed and that forbade such barriers as the Berlin Wall and the "death strips" of the GDR. Later in the month, the Hungarians ousted Kádár and engaged in a bit of *glasnost* when they declared the execution of pre-1956 President Imre Nagy at the time of the Soviet invasion "illegal." In September, Hungary voided its agreement with the GDR and dropped the rest of its border restrictions, after the GDR had stopped issuing exit permits for Hungarian vacations for East German citizens—57,000 had escaped by then. But the mass exodus continued, with many East German refugees going instead to Czechoslovakia and slipping illegally across the border to Hungary. In October, a majority of the party convention of the Hungarian communist party renamed itself the Hungarian socialist party and, under the leadership of Imre Poszgay, committed itself to a path of radical reform. But by the time of the parliamentary elections, the following spring, this party proved no match for the democratic opposition. Here, too, the threat of Soviet or Warsaw Pact invasion had evidently evaporated. Since the Reykjavík summit meeting, the abandonment of Cold War belligerency on the part of Gorbachev's Soviet Union had found a willing chorus in Washington, which until then, for reasons of its own, had missed no opportunity to stoke the fires confronting the dying "evil empire."

If the communist party's resistance to reform had been minor in Poland and Hungary, it was a major obstacle in post-1968 Czechoslovakia, whose regime (both party and political police force) clung with determination to the mandate it had received from Brezhnev's tanks and doctrine: "When forces hostile to socialism seek to reverse the [communist] development of any socialist country whatsoever . . . this becomes the concern of all socialist countries." Nevertheless, in mid-August of 1989, when East German refugees began to gather by the thousands at the West German Embassy in Prague (and simultaneously in East Berlin and Budapest), the hard-line Czechoslovak regime slowly came around to a decision to let them flee to the West. Instead of permitting them simply to cross the border into Bavaria, however, it was decided to ship them on trains through the GDR to the West. It is not clear whether the purpose was to embarrass the GDR government (a participant in the 1968 invasion of Czechoslovakia) or to dare them to stop the refugees after having consented to their departure. But the passage of the trains through Dresden in early October caused some 15,000 East Germans to gather at the railroad station with the intention of jumping on the slow-moving, crowded "freedom trains." It also led Honecker to order a vicious assault on these crowds by units of his people's police (*Vopo*) and people's army (NVA). This was the last straw in his downfall: after further assaults on demonstrators in Leipzig and East Berlin (October 7 and 8), and hints of his preference for a "Chinese solution" to the rebellion, Honecker himself was ousted (October 18) and replaced with Egon Krenz.

If anyone had misinterpreted the Czechoslovak decision to help East German refugees flee from the GDR as a sign of softening, they were soon corrected when Communist General Secretary Milos Jakes turned loose his police force with long white clubs, tear gas, and plastic shields against some 15,000 student demonstrators in Prague toward the end of November. Many were injured and about 100 were arrested. By this time, Honecker and Kádár had fallen, the Wall was down, and Krenz had begun to sing the praises of *perestroika*. Even in Bulgaria, longtime strongman Todor Zhivkov had already been ousted, and in Sofia 50,000 demonstrators were demanding that he be put on trial for his misdeeds. His reform communist successor, Peter Mladenov, called for free elections and a democratic parliament. Gorbachev himself had declared the Brezhnev Doctrine dead a month earlier and, like the governments of Poland and Hungary, condemned the 1968 Warsaw Pact invasion of Czechoslovakia. "We are getting a situation," quipped the Czech human rights leader and playwright Vaclav Havel, "in which only the occupied are still defending their own occupation."

At this point, Jakes's police brutality turned into a fiasco.[39] It triggered eight nights of ever larger public demonstrations, at the end of which Jakes and the entire Politbureau resigned. The ousted 1968 leader of the Prague Spring, Alexander Dubček, appeared once more from obscurity. By the end of the first week of December 1989, the communist government had abolished the "leading role" of the party and pledged to bring noncommunists into the cabinet. It also denounced the 1968 invasion as a "mistake," removed the requirement of "Marxist-Leninist social science" at the university, and relaxed censorship and travel restrictions. But the democratic opposition, once awakened, wanted more. They insisted on the resignation of President Gustav Husák, who had been in charge since the Warsaw Pact invaders had thrown out Dubček and his "socialism with a human face." They set a deadline of December 10 and demanded complete freedom of the press and of assembly as well as a commitment to determine proper procedures for free elections to replace the communist parliament. Finally, they wanted the release of all political

39. When the student demonstrators were attacked by riot squads, "antiterrorist commandos," and the secret police on November 17, the story of a student's death at the hands of the police was picked up by, among other media, the Voice of America, which gave it maximum exposure. The image of the martyred student probably helped to build up the demonstrations (as many as 200,000 on November 20) and to bring down the government, although in the end the story turned out to be false. There were also rumors that the Soviets themselves had dissuaded the Prague police from violent repression.

prisoners, the abolition of the people's militia, and the promise of a free market economy. A two-hour general strike signified their power over popular opinion. The principal opposition group, the Civic Forum, moreover, demanded half of the cabinet seats in the government while President Husák resigned, followed by the new reform communist Prime Minister Ladislav Adamec. The "velvet revolution" had won, in only a week and a few days, although the election of a new parliament and interim president would not take place until the following spring. Havel became president and, as in Poland, Hungary, and East Germany, the communists were overwhelmed by their democratic opposition. There was no stopping the dominoes of democratic revolution.

This was the setting and the time frame of the East German rebellion, although we need to recall also the instances of rebellion with a different outcome. In communist China, years of economic liberalization had finally triggered the student demonstrations in Beijing and other important centers. Buoyed by their own success, or by the absence of serious repression, the demonstrations grew into a nearly permanent presence in Tiananmen Square, especially during May 1989, when the contagion of rebellion began to spread to other social classes and ways of life in the city.[40] On that fateful night from June 3 to 4, 1989, when tanks and soldiers penetrated the makeshift barriers and massacred the small numbers of remaining holdouts around the "goddess of democracy," a replica of the Statue of Liberty, they killed an estimated 2,600 people in cold blood. The bloodbath was followed by a wave of arrests, beatings, torture, executions, and jail sentences that have etched the names Deng Xiaoping, Li Peng, and Yang Shankun forever into the book of inhumanity.[41] To the hard-liners of Eastern Europe the Chinese set a brutal example which people like Honecker and Ceauşescu briefly mistook to be a real option for defending their positions. The Romanian dictator even appealed to Beijing for an expression of moral support and comradeship in the battle against "counterrevolutionary elements."

Romania offers another example of a different outcome, although a final assessment has not yet emerged. A benign view of the successor

40. The anniversary of the Science and Democracy movement of 1919 and the official visit of Gorbachev obviously helped to raise the reform fever among the students, although the presence of the Soviet leader and the student appeals to him may also have enraged the Chinese hosts and induced them to take out their embarrassment on the students.

41. It is hardly a consolation that Chinese communism in its forty years in power had already set standards of mass execution and cruelty of such vast proportions as to dwarf the outrages committed at Tiananmen Square. See especially Alexander Dallin and George Breslauer, *Political Terror in Communist Systems* (Stanford, Calif.: Stanford University Press, 1970), pp. 49–62, 68–73 et passim.

regime of Ion Iliescu might just lump it together with Mladenov's Bulgaria as examples of communist dissidents replacing reigning dictators with their own brands of reform communism, though hardly with democracy. On the other hand, suspicions have been voiced that the entire popular and very violent Romanian revolution was merely a surface phenomenon, behind which Iliescu pulled off a carefully prepared palace coup.[42] Both new strongmen meanwhile have received popular legitimation by way of elections in which the true democratic opposition proved incapable of mobilizing the countryside against the old but well-lubricated communist political machine. In both cases, the opposition could not even manage to awaken an understanding of the issues among the politically naive and untutored peasantry. Iliescu's resort to brutal goon squads—miners rewarded with huge wage increases—to pummel the opposition bore a striking resemblance to how, in his day, Panama strongman Manuel Noriega had his vigilantes deal with political opposition, or how Benito Mussolini in the mid-twenties turned his Blackshirts loose on political opponents. In postwar Eastern Europe, communist and fascist methods have not always been easy to tell apart, and many a communist leader could easily be mistaken for a fascist *duce* or *Führer*.

During this dramatic upheaval throughout Eastern Europe, the Soviet government obviously played a minor role behind the scenes, encouraging reform movements and refusing to support or rescue the embattled hardline communist regimes. Gorbachev's own visits in 1989—e.g., at the fortieth anniversary of the GDR—sometimes became the final straws on the backs of the communist-satellite camels, adding their weight to years of calls for *perestroika* among the native citizenry. But already in late 1989, the counterforces were gathering in the Soviet Union, according to ex-Foreign Minister Shevardnadze, demanding that the popular rebellions, and in particular the threat of German reunification, be stopped by force. In August of that year, the foreign minister had still succeeded in persuading his government not to intervene in popular demonstrations within the GDR. The opening of the Wall, however, triggered massive pressures to "pull the emergency brake" (Valentin Falin) and close the border with the help of the Soviet forces stationed there. The opposition's failure to do so only intensified its efforts to blame the "new thinking" and *perestroika* for separatist movements and nationality conflicts in the several union republics, for the loss of the East European *cordon sanitaire* of the Soviet Union and, worst of all, for the loss of East Germany by

42. According to some reports in the European press, the popular uprising and street fighting between army detachments and Ceauşescu's dreaded Securitate surprised the plotters and the dictator, but could not stop the former from executing their plans.

means of German unification. The assault continued at the February
plenary session of the Central Committee, and it intensified especially at
the CPSU convention in July while the foreign minister found himself
beset with such underhanded intrigues as the transfer of armed units
slated for disarmament to the Asian parts of the Soviet Union. Between
September and December 1990, it became clear that Shevardnadze would
be forced to resign, as indeed he was on December 20, 1990. But he did
not leave without a parting shot concerning the imminent danger of
dictatorship, a warning clearly meant to expose the ultras in the Soviet
army and the communist party, and not his old comrade-in-arms Gorbachev. In any case it appears that German unification, if it had been
much delayed, if it had not been attempted until 1991 or later, might not
have been accomplished at all. The West and East German negotiators
and the Kohl government certainly could not foresee events in early 1990
as we know them now.

In mid-August of 1991, while President Gorbachev and his family were
vacationing in a resort on the Crimea, Shevardnadze's worst predictions
seemed to come true for a traumatic sixty-two hours, as a "gang of
eight" hard-liners—including Gorbachev's Vice-President Gennady I.
Yanayev, Prime Minister Valentin S. Pavlov, the ministers of defense and
of the interior, the chiefs of the KGB and of the Association of State
Enterprises, and the chief of the Soviet Peasant Union—seized power in
the style of "tank communism" made fashionable by the Chinese, the
[Serbian] Yugoslav army,[43] and the KGB's special troops (OMON) in the
Baltic states. They put Gorbachev and his family under arrest and
attempted to extort his acquiescence while the tanks were rolling against
the Baltic states and the Russian parliament, where the democratically
elected president of the Russian Federation, Boris Yeltsin, met their
challenge with a display of defiant personal courage extraordinary in any
communist-bred system. The West was stunned and the NATO Council
and EC leaders scrambled for emergency meetings—worrying, among
other things, about who controlled the Soviet nuclear arsenal and whether
the 273,000 Soviet troops in East Germany would begin to fight each
other or attempt to seize, say, the city of Berlin as a hostage—while
Czechoslovak troops were massed at the Soviet border.[44] With one stroke,

43. In early 1991, the Yugoslav Federal Army, commanded mostly by Serbian communists and out of the control of civilian authority, had loosed its tanks against Slovenian and
Croatian civilians and their elected governments, in a curiously novel combination of
hegemonic Serbian nationalism and communism, and usually assisted by irregular squads
of Serbian nationalists terrorizing the civil population of disputed areas. They have
continued their rampages in Bosnia-Herzegovina. Tens of thousands of deaths, many more
injured, and more than a million refugees have marked their path.

44. Poland too, where 50,000 Soviet troops were still stationed, must have been
apprehensive, and the same could be said of Hungary.

the barely achieved reign of peace and neighborly cooperation in Eastern Europe seemed in jeopardy, a rude reminder to West Europeans that it was not yet time to disarm NATO and to concentrate on peaceful pursuits. For the newly united Germany, which had committed an estimated 35 billion deutschmarks in aid, loans, and trade to Soviet *perestroika*, the crisis was as disturbing economically as it was militarily: the DAX index at the Frankfurt Stock Exchange tumbled 10% in a day. Fortunately, the coups fizzled because of popular opposition, resistance in the military ranks, and an evident failure of resolve on the part of the conspirators. The coup attempt was triggered by the pending ratification of the new Union Treaty for a true federation of the Soviet republics and probably—in spite of its destructive potential vis-à-vis democratization and economic restructuring in the Soviet Union—would have been unable to turn the tide in Eastern Europe, least of all in East Germany, which had long since scurried under the NATO umbrella.

Chapter THREE

The Rise and Decline of "Realistic Socialism" in the GDR

It is not easy to translate the German *"der reale* (or *real existierende) Sozialismus"* into meaningful English, certainly not as "the real socialism," which would make light of "unreal" visions of it as if they had been misleading rather than the utopian lodestars of an idealistic tradition. "Realistic socialism" or "the system of socialist realities" may better render a certain disillusionment, along with a certain assertiveness, much as "a realistic Christian life" would imply only partial conformity to the ideal, with a good deal of sinning and all-too-human frailty thrown in.

—P. H. Merkl

Back in 1989/90, when the Wall came down and especially after the currency union and political unification had actually transpired, why could not East and West Germans simply get together and live happily ever after? The answer to that question has several parts, some of which will be addressed in this chapter and some later (Chapter Six and Conclusion). Here we particularly want to show the profound differences of the GDR both from the Federal Republic that East Germans were taught to loathe and from the old Germany that they were made to reject for most of four decades. The late Milton Mayer once characterized the delusions of ordinary supporters of the Nazi regime with the words (in a book of the same name) "They thought they were free." For decades, the East Germans, more or less, believed they would live in a "workers' paradise on earth," a Germany better than any that had preceded them or any that coexisted across the border as an American satellite. To bring this about and maintain it, they accepted the dialectical view of the realities of the century of war and violent revolution described by Marx,

This chapter was written by Gert-Joachim Glaessner of the Free University of Berlin and translated and slightly edited by Peter Merkl.

Engels, and Lenin—the threesome whose statues graced public squares all over the GDR and other parts of the postwar Soviet empire. You were either for or against the great proletarian revolution defined in Moscow. They also accepted the communist party state, its repressive apparatus, and its never-resting propaganda. In its East German heyday, the SED (Socialist Unity party) was like a religious crusade, drawing behind it a legion of enthusiastic youth ready to sacrifice all in their quest for the Holy Grail.

But in the long run, and especially after the crusading idealism began to flag, the evolving system of the GDR became more and more an immensely centralized—under SED leadership—and sclerotic bureaucratic nightmare. It turned out to be really unable to reform its dysfunctional structure because of the party's unwillingness to give up its monopoly on power. Contemporary analyses by public administration specialists give us glimpses of the incredibly different Germany that was growing up here east of the Elbe River, showing traditional German strains only in such things as the survival of pre-Nazi working-class culture and authoritarianism. Until the sixties (ironically the time of the building of the Wall), it was still a closed-up world of aging socialist pseudoreligion, if sometimes stretching to compete with the pesky rival images of the burgeoning consumer heaven of West Berlin and the Federal Republic. As long as the faith was strong, we need to remind ourselves, the baubles of consumerism had far less appeal than they did in the consumer societies of the West.

A very different situation, however, arose after many more years of "irreligious" communist mismanagement, and especially after the waves of protest of the last years even though, in the final analysis, the brave protest movements of 1989/90 found themselves spurned by history and by the East German people: now the consumer appetite came back with a vengeance and East Germans were desperate to catch up with their Western cousins, which turned out to be a more difficult process than either ever expected (Chapter Six). And, make no mistake, the great ideological hangover of many former "true believers" in East Germany is no more amenable to freedom and consumer blandishments than a reforming drug addict can be helped by giving him freedom and an unlimited bank account.

If we could compare the degree of well-inculcated popular communist belief and conformity in the GDR of 1989/90 with the ideological hangover of Nazi Germany in 1945, the GDR would win hands down—the Nazis ruled for a much shorter time, and their indoctrination efforts were hopelessly entangled with the all-out war effort and disasters, leaving behind mostly a vague pre-Nazi nationalism and imperialism in that generation (see below, Conclusion). The SED left behind a well-established if flawed system of forty years and millions of people who had been raised and spent their lives in conformity with communism. The screening processes of ex-teachers and public employees of every kind have been convulsing posttotalitarian East Germany for years now, another subject of study we hope will be researched by someone else, since it simply exceeds the limits of our effort.

Back to the enormous European and eventually global drama from which the faith and the system of the GDR sprang. The twentieth century, Lenin said, is a century of wars and revolutions. There have been two world wars and a Cold War, not to mention smaller wars such as Korea and Vietnam. There has been the revolutionary upheaval of 1917, a veritable start of a new epoch, beginning with civil war and terror in Russia and elsewhere on an unimaginably violent scale even though, in the Soviet Union, it lasted only seventy-odd years. As Hannah Arendt wrote in *On Revolution*: "The aim of revolution was, and has always been, freedom. . . . In contrast to revolution, the aim of war was only in rare cases bound up with the notion of freedom. . . . Wars have turned so easily into revolutions and revolutions have shown this ominous inclination to unleash wars."[1]

Revolution from Above?

The great revolutions of the twentieth century, in Russia and in China, to a large extent were consequences of wars. Except for Yugoslavia, the establishment of socialist systems in East-Central and Southeastern Europe was a direct result of the rise of the Soviet Union to world power status. The Soviet Union not only created a political and military *cordon sanitaire*, as great powers like to do, but refashioned the societies of these countries in its own image. In none of these countries, least of all in East Germany, was the legitimacy of communist party government derived from a triumphant revolution. Nevertheless, there were social and political revolutions brought about by the Soviet Union and from above by a self-appointed, partisan vanguard of communists. In an 1949 essay entitled "The International Civil War," Sigmund Neumann described the revolutions of his day as a "sweeping, fundamental change in political

1. Hannah Arendt, *On Revolution* (London: Faber & Faber, 1963), pp. 2, 7, 9. Also see Carl Joachim Friedrich, ed., *Revolution* (New York: Atherton, 1966) and Michael S. Kimmel, *Revolution: A Sociological Interpretation* (Cambridge, Mass.: Polity Press, 1990).

organization, social structure, economic property control and the predominant myth of order," a fundamental break with the prevailing
order.[2] According to this definition, the developments in the Soviet Zone
of Occupation and, after 1949, in the GDR were a revolution indeed.

The changes left no part of the old order intact even though, as we shall
see below, certain elements of traditional authoritarianism survived in
different ideological garb. The social structure was thoroughly revamped,
old elites replaced with new ones, and the stratification of bourgeois
society eliminated by political means. Within a few years, property-
holding patterns were drastically changed. By the time the GDR was
founded, there was no private capital left to speak of and no private farm
above 125 acres (50 hectares). A new, party-directed bureaucracy (also
of pre-1949 vintage) controlled the new "people's property" and cooperative agricultural property. Step by step the ideology of Marxism-
Leninism replaced traditional views of the social order. The decisive steps
had been accomplished, even though the process of creating a society
according to Soviet-style socialism was still years short of the goal.

In her influential book *States and Social Revolutions*, Theda Skocpol
separated social revolutions from political rebellions, revolts, and revolutions, describing the former as "rapid, basic transformations of a
society's state and class structures . . . accompanied and in part carried
through by class-based revolts from below."[3] Using the French, Russian,
and Chinese revolutions as an empirical base, she argued that a social
revolution requires that the transformation of the polity and social
structure be the result of a massive class uprising and not just the revolt
of a small elite.[4] The upshot of the GDR takeover by a small elite after
1945, however—whether socialist revolutions succeeded through a putsch
as in Czechoslovakia (and not a political mass revolution), through
elimination of the hitherto legitimate representatives of the nation as in
Poland, or on behalf of the occupation as in the Soviet Zone of Germany—was a complete revolution of the old society. It was a continuation of the "revolution from above" just as it had been demonstrated at
the end of the twenties in the young Soviet Union itself. It was a new type
of revolution, by a self-appointed vanguard that pretended to be acting
in the interest of the revolutionary majority of the population, the
working class.[5] The final product of the political, social, and cultural

2. In *World Politics* 3, no. 1 (1949), 333ff.
3. New York: Cambridge University Press, 1979, p. 4.
4. This appears to be merely a mystification so long as the small elite has unrestricted
power to carry out whatever social change it wants.
5. For greater detail, see Gert-Joachim Glaessner, *Herrschaft durch Kader. Leitung der
Gesellschaft und Kaderpolitik in der DDR am Beispiel des Staatsapparates* (Opladen:
Westdeutscher Verlag, 1977), p. 37ff.

upheaval that was triggered and directed by this vanguard was a new society with a birth defect that proved fatal in the end: it was founded on violence, and the political elite never managed to achieve legitimacy before the majority of the subjects.[6]

Party Patrimonialism in Crisis

Contrary to Marx's prognoses, the original socialist revolutions were not rebellions of the working class against the capitalists of developed countries of Central and Western Europe but took place in rather underdeveloped states. The Stalinist model of development by which the Soviet Union in two decades rose to the rank of second-biggest world power— albeit at enormous human and social cost and with unprecedented terror—failed to bring much progress to the East-Central European countries on which it was imposed. In these countries, Stalinism interrupted the development of a rational kind of authority or, at least, caused it to regress toward the political structures of "sultanism," to speak with Max Weber. By this term Weber meant a tendency of traditional authority to incline toward patrimonialism and "a kind of [patrimonial] rule that exercises untrammeled, arbitrary, administrative power, though within the bounds of tradition"; it is not "rational in an objective sense but entertains its sphere of arbitrary power and grace to the extreme, thus differing from any rational form of authority."[7] Specifically applying this to the communist party state, we get the concept of "party patrimonialism" rather than the party acting in the public interest.[8]

Stalinism thus established patrimonial bureaucracies of a new type in the socialist states. The patrimonial administrators, or party cadres, in charge of all the important directive and policymaking functions were obliged to serve legally and exclusively the charismatic leader, the vanguard party, and the dominant ideology. The loyal service of the cadres

6. Cf. Juan Linz, "Totalitarian and Authoritarian Regimes," in Nelson Polsby and Fred Greenstein, eds., *Handbook of Political Science* (Reading, Mass.: Addison-Wesley, 1975), vol. 3, pp. 175–482.

7. Max Weber, *Wirtschaft und Gesellschaft. Grundrisse der verstehenden Soziologie*, 5th rev. ed. (Tübingen: J.C.B. Mohr, 1972), p. 233ff. Patrimonialism is a kind of rule in which the ruler acts as if he owned the realm *and the subjects* in the same way as one owns property. The opposite is a system that defines some of its relationships in terms of the public interest and public law.

8. See Gert-Joachim Glaessner, "Ende der Reformen? Bedingungen und Grenzen der Handlungsfähigkeit sowjet-sozialistischer Systeme am Beispiel der DDR." *Deutschland Archiv* 15, no. 2 (1982), 700–709.

was not that of civil servants to their office, but rather that of a partisan servant. It derived its legitimacy not from a belief in the legality of duly passed laws and ordinances, but from personal dedication to party and leader. Its violation called for social ostracism and, in the worst case, physical liquidation. Party and state had only one goal: to build a communist society. To oppose this made you an "enemy" or, as they said in the age of Stalinism, a "parasite" that had to be eliminated before it could do more damage. Little remained of the humanitarian ideals of Marxism. Whether or not we call these systems in their advanced phase "totalitarian,"[9] they turned out to be extremely authoritarian and thus held their ground, regardless of some changes, against all attempts at internal reform.

The social and political crisis of the GDR was part of a general crisis of post-Stalinist socialism in the countries that, after 1945, had the socioeconomic and political system of the Soviet Union imposed on them. The conditions and factors that led up to their systemic crises were a cluster of economic, political, social, and cultural causes. Next to the economic inefficiencies[10] and growing technological backwardness, as compared to the more competitive industries of the Western world, there was an ever more obvious desire for social emancipation from the monopoly on guidance of the communist party, which was bent on unifying society and on creating the new "socialist man." In fact, however, cultural social change overtook the GDR as it had other socialist countries. Similar to developments in the Western industrial societies, the social structure became more differentiated, new value systems and modes of behavior cropped up, and it became ever harder to keep out the international cultural and social influences, as had been done in the early sixties when the government tried to block the reception of Western radio programs. Knowledge of the evolving Western world made it all the harder to be kept from it by means of the Wall and the border fortifications. The SED ignored these expressions of discontent and responded rather inadequately. Once everybody realized how the Soviet guarantee

9. On the concept of totalitarianism see Gert-Joachim Glaessner, *Sozialistische Systeme. Einführung in die Kommunismus- und DDR-Forschung* (Opladen: Westdeutscher Verlag, 1983), 44ff.

10. The serious economic downturn of the GDR appears to have begun with the energy crises of the seventies, especially the second one (1979), which had a major impact on the ability of the entire Eastern trading bloc (CMEA) to continue paying for their imports which, in turn, hit the GDR as a major supplier particularly hard. To save or conserve its inflow of hard foreign currency, the GDR took to exporting everything it could spare and, on top of that, invested in a number of long-shot enterprises that never paid off, at the same time starving many sectors that might have saved the country from the progressive erosion of its few economic strengths and opportunities.

of the system began to crumble, "the people" seized the opportunity to knock down the whole edifice.

The GDR Revolution Begins

The great change followed the classic model of other revolutions, and yet there was also a new quality to it. With the exception of Romania, the upheavals no longer seemed to require a causal nexus between revolution and violence, leading some observers of the events of 1989/90 in the GDR to question whether there had really been a revolution. From the point of view of the old communist elites, who had feared this outcome of their social and political experiment all along, this was a *counterrevolution*, the restoration of the old capitalist order. The first freely elected premier of the GDR, Lothar de Maizière, addressed this question in his government declaration. He said that the great change in the GDR was

> part of a revolutionary process of renewal throughout Eastern Europe . . . which is at once also a European and worldwide process of change. . . . Some people may feel that, in the last analysis, it is counterrevolutionary. But after 70 years of "realistic socialism," the word "counter," or "against," is a necessity of nature. When someone thinks that socialism can be realized only with a brutal party dictatorship, by taking away the autonomy of society, by nationalizing the means of production, and by subjecting the economy to central planning and *dirigisme*; when that someone thus hopes to create a more just social order, he is so thoroughly wrong that we can only present him with a resolute "counter."[11]

As late as November 1989, the dean of GDR social science, Jürgen Kuczynski, spoke of a conservative revolution that would preserve and renew socialism.[12] As it soon turned out, this was an illusion. The writers Christa Wolf, Stefan Heym, and many others who addressed the crowds gathered on November 4, 1989, at Alexanderplatz, Berlin, were also hoping for a revolutionary renewal of socialism.

Perhaps it is best to speak of a "restoring"[13] and at the same time a

11. *Neues Deutschland*, Apr. 20, 1990, p. 3.
12. "Konservative Revolution," *Neues Deutschland*, Nov. 8, 1989, p. 4.
13. Jürgen Habermas speaks of a "catch-up" or "reverse-gear" revolution. See his *Die nachholende Revolution* (Frankfurt: Suhrkamp, 1990).

"broken-off" revolution which was meant to end an extreme form of authoritarian government, "realistic socialism," and to catch up with the libertarian tradition of the West, as its Eastern neighbors did. But it also wanted to take a major step forward—at least during its heyday at the end of 1989 and the beginning of 1990—namely, to reconcile the betrayed ideal of social justice with personal freedom. The GDR revolution was a broken-off endeavor because the question of national unification, as earlier in German history, won out prematurely over the question of political and social reform, leaving no room for an autonomous development of the GDR.

The collapse of the communist systems was a big surprise to all, even though many of the causes responsible for the implosion of a seemingly impregnable social and political system had long been described quite accurately by Western observers. Perhaps we lacked the imagination to picture a situation that we had expected only toward the end of a long process of East-West rapprochement. From 1985, from the beginning of *glasnost* and *perestroika* in the Soviet Union, nevertheless, it had become ever clearer that a world-historical change was occurring. Without a war, there had never been such a transition of a hegemonial dictatorship toward an enlightened authoritarianism and, potentially, toward democracy. This could not but have a deep impact upon the countries that once formed the "socialist camp." The rapid and (sometimes) very abrupt ideological and sociopolitical changes emanating from the Soviets shattered the social order of the countries and, in 1989, broke up the socialist bloc of states. The dissolution of this bloc into many individual, national, and hardly comparable communities is fundamentally changing the political landscape of Europe.

Earlier Waves of Communist Reform

Two main factors determined the collapse of the Soviet-type systems, as indicated before: the readiness of the Soviets to give up their *cordon sanitaire* and the internal weakness of these regimes, which had never succeeded in shaking off the Stalinist legacy. In the sixties, for a short while, Soviet-type socialism actually appeared to be willing and able to reform. From the early sixties on in the GDR, there had been several attempts to drop the Stalinist baggage and to emphasize the autonomy of this second German state. The New Economic System for Planning and Directing the Economy (NÖS), for example, had been started in 1963 as a pilot program for other socialist countries. The allusion to Lenin's New

Economic Policy of the twenties was no coincidence. But the experiment had to be modified after Khrushchev's fall in 1964 and was abandoned at the time of the next crisis in 1968/69. The space for experimentation tolerated by the Soviets had become narrower and narrower.

Under different conditions, NÖS could have become a model for a technocratic reform of the socialist systems. In the mid-sixties, Walter Ulbricht's government also developed autonomous policy ideas in a variety of areas, independent of Soviet positions and no longer on the utopian premise that communism was just around the corner. The idea of a "socialist human community," a conflict-free socialist society, took the place of utopian expectations. On closer inspection, the attempt to replace utopian, ideologically defined goals—which could be reached only by force—with new goals reachable during the lifetime of the living was a means to deny the existence of the real conflict and contradictions of society. The SED was certain that it could build up a "developed socialist system" with the help of scientific methods derived from cybernetics and systems theory. The building of socialism appeared to be the task of technocrats and specialists, and not of ideologues or of Lenin's "professional revolutionaries."[14] There were Western parallels to this line of thinking: for example, in the writings of the West German sociologist Helmut Schelsky. He announced the obsolescence of democracy in the wake of the technical inventions for "steering" a modern society,[15] while the GDR's Georg Klaus presented a cybernetic model of socialist society which no longer required the "leading role" of a Marxist-Leninist party.[16] The party soon caught on to this fatal flaw of the cybernetic discussion and put an end to these "spooky goings-on."

Aside from the technocratic reflections, however, few voices in the GDR of the sixties—unlike in Poland, Hungary, and Czechoslovakia—demanded political change. One of the few, and most vehement, was Robert Havemann in a series of lectures at Humboldt University in East Berlin.[17] The violent suppression of the "Prague Spring" and the termination of Khrushchev's reforms in the Soviet Union (1968/69) put an end

14. This problematic was reflected also in China, where Maoists insisted that it was far more important to be "Red than expert" and where "bourgeois revisionists" held the opposite opinion.

15. See Schelsky, *Der Mensch in der wissenschaftlichen Zivilisation* (Cologne and Opladen: Westdeutscher Verlag, 1961).

16. Klaus, *Kybernetik und Gesellschaft* (East Berlin: Deutscher Verlag der Wissenschaften, 1964 [3rd ed. 1973]), and *Kybernetik—eine neue Universalphilosophie der Gesellschaft?* (East Berlin: Akademie-Verlag, 1973).

17. Havemann, *Dialektik ohne Dogma. Naturwissenschaften und Weltanschauung* (Reinbek: Rowohlt, 1964).

to all experimentation and returned socialism in the GDR to another two decades of the old, centralist political control.[18]

For the GDR, Ulbricht's fall and replacement with Erich Honecker in 1971 was the end of the experiment, even though it opened the doors to a realistic cooperation of the SED with the West. It also created the preconditions for basic changes in economic and social policy that, again, had unmistakably independent features. The SED succeeded, in the early seventies, in setting new accents on its economic and social policy and again increased respect among its people for the new paternalism.[19] Unfortunately, the worldwide energy crisis of the seventies knocked the bottom out from under the ambitious plans for a "unified economic and social policy." It is easy to forget, also in retrospect, that the SED managed a remarkably independent foreign policy during the Brezhnev years and that this gave it more legitimacy at home and recognition abroad.[20] The SED also managed, in the middle of the escalating East-West conflict of the Reagan years, to salvage relations between the two Germanys for their mutual benefit. In the area of cultural policy, the SED quest for greater legitimacy vacillated between liberalization and an improved cultural climate at home.[21]

In striking contrast to these accomplishments, the SED regime proved helpless and without real understanding in the face of the value changes and new social movements that permeated GDR youth with new issues such as environmentalism, pacifism, and the quest for individual autonomy. There had long been a need for reforms; but now, in the last years before the fall of the Wall, many informal groups and associations emerged that are active today.[22] Under Ulbricht such attempts at forming

18. See Andrzej Korbonski, "The Politics of Economic Reforms in Eastern Europe: The Last Thirty Years," *Soviet Studies* 41, no. 1 (1989), 11.

19. Details in Sigrid Meuschel, *Legitimation und Parteiherrschaft. Zum Wandel der Legitimitätsansprüche der SED, 1945–1989* (Ph.D. diss., Freie Universität Berlin, 1991).

20. The *Ostpolitik* of Willy Brandt involved a trade-off for the GDR in that the East German regime traded painful concessions on many points, particularly on the travel restrictions of West Germans and on the status of Berlin, for a West German concession to drop the insistence on being the "sole representative" of all Germans. The upshot for the GDR was a gain in diplomatic recognition by other states (not the Federal Republic) and admission to the United Nations.

21. See Ian Wallace, "Die Kulturpolitik der DDR 1971–1990," in Gert-Joachim Glaessner, ed., *Eine deutsche Revolution. Der Umbruch in der DDR, seine Ursachen und Folgen* (Frankfurt and New York: Peter Lang, 1991), pp. 108–125.

22. A telling example of SED helplessness in the face of the new quest of GDR youth for autonomy is the regime's response to the punker phenomenon of the early eighties. The party and security apparatus became so alarmed at signs of youthful alienation and punished nonconformists so severely as to drive them into the hands of radical right-wing groups of various description that are active and very violent today. See *Jugend und*

autonomous groups would have been squelched from the start. Yet these internal developments by themselves would never have led to the over-throw of the SED regime had not the Soviet Union, unlike on earlier occasions of crisis, simply failed to stop the developments by force. It is too early to find out the motives of the Soviet leadership for not opposing the process or to untangle the varied external and internal factors of the terminal crisis of "realistic socialism," just as we still cannot fully account for the diversity of the paths taken by the different socialist systems in the first place.

Structural Defects of the Political System

Let us take a closer look at the structural defects of Soviet-type socialism and the politico-cultural legacy of the regime. In the understanding of the ruling communist parties, politics was definitely separate from the elec-toral or parliamentary process. Politics was a unified, organized process by which the goals and the will of the ruling class were transmitted to the entire society. It was based on the preformed insights of Marxism-Leninism, in particular concerning the laws of social development.[23] "Scientific communism," its political theory, spoke of the "political organization of socialist society" or the "political system" synony-mously.[24] That some policy fields might be autonomous from others was as unacceptable to the party as the constitutional separation of powers. For the first time in human history, went the ideological justification—since the abolition of private ownership of the means of production also removed the causes of antagonistic class struggle—there was real "popu-lar sovereignty" manifested in a fusion of powers, designed to realize the sociopolitical goals of communism by means of one centralized, unitary policy process. There were, of course, functional divisions within the party and among the branches of the state, between the state institutions and "social organizations" and the hierarchical levels of jurisdiction from the district (*Bezirk*) to the commune levels. But no one questioned the prerogative of the party to intervene at any point of the process:

Rechtsextremismus in Berlin-Ost, Fakten und Gegenstrategien (Berlin: Magistratsverwal-tung für Jugend, Familie und Sport, 1990).

23. See *Kleines politisches Wörterbuch*, 4th ed. (East Berlin: Dietz, 1983), p. 737ff.

24. Akademie für Staats- und Rechtswissenschaft der DDR, *Einführung in die marxi-stisch-leninistische Staats- und Rechtslehre*, 2nd ed. (East Berlin: Staatsverlag, 1986), p. 60, n. 2.

The political organization of socialist society is a complex of state and nonstate organizations and institutions (people's representative assemblies, the state apparatus, friendly [bloc] parties, the mass organizations and other social organizations, the work collectives) under the leadership of the Marxist-Leninist party of the working class, the political and juridical norms, the norms of socialist morality and ethics, the political tradition of the working class and other expressions of socialist state and legal culture (*Staats- und Rechtsbewusstsein*). With their help, the working class exercises political power and, deliberately and by way of planning, forms the social conditions according to the objective requirements of a socialist society.[25]

The parts of the "political organization of GDR socialism" were, in the official literature:

1. *The SED,* "the politico-organizational center of society"[26] that directs all the other parts. The preamble of the SED statute said: "As the highest form of the sociopolitical organization of the working class, and its battle-proven vanguard, the SED is the leading force of socialist society, of all working-class organizations, and of state and social organization."[27]
2. *The state* is the chief instrument of the working-class-led workers in the formation of a developed socialist society.[28] As a form of the "dictatorship of the proletariat" it also embodies the specific thinking of the SED about democracy.
3. *The law,* i.e., "the totality of the laws created and sanctioned by the socialist state and other legal ordinances." SED-formulated social norms (of the "socialist morality" or "way of life") were further instruments for the regulation of social relationships and were considered an "indispensable precondition for the functioning of the political system."
4. *The four [bloc] parties* "friendly" to the SED—the CDU, Democratic Peasant party (DBD), Liberal Democrats (LDPD), and National Democrats (NDPD)—recognized the leadership role of the SED "without reservations" and had "made their decision for

25. Ibid., p. 59ff.
26. *DDR. Gesellschaft Staat Bürger,* 2nd ed. (East Berlin: Staatsverlag, 1978), p. 26.
27. *Statut der Sozialistischen Einheitspartei Deutschlands* (East Berlin: Dietz, 1976), p. 5.
28. ASR–DDR, *Einführung in die marxistisch-leninistische Staats- und Rechtslehre,* p. 62.

socialism." Next to the SED and the associations represented in the people's assemblies, they were part of the "Democratic Bloc of Parties and Mass Organizations" (hence the name "bloc parties").

5. *The "social organizations,"* or mass organizations, were to realize the "special interests" of their members "in accord with the goals and tasks of the socialist social order." They included, next to the communist trade unions (FDGB), the Free Democratic Youth (FDJ), and the Democratic Women's Association (DFB), professional associations, such as the Society for Sports and Technique (GST), the Chamber of Technology (KdT), artists' associations, the Association of Small Gardeners, Settlers, and Small Animal Breeders (VdKSK). Their place in the political system stemmed from the comprehensive directive mission of the party, which pressed even seemingly unpolitical groups into service for its goals. Freedom of association was mentioned in the GDR Constitution (art. 29),[29] but in practice the SED maintained a monopoly on it. There were only associations that had been approved and controlled by the party, the only *de facto* exception being the churches. The Protestant church, in particular, was the closest thing the GDR had to an independent association.

6. *The National Front* of the GDR included all parties and social organizations and, in particular, organized the "elections." It also was in charge of mobilizing the citizenry in residential areas and for the solution of communal problems.

7. *The workers' collectives* of "people's own factories" (VEBs) and cooperatives were also part of the political system and, in fact, were its all-embracing basis in society. Working in the collective was more than gainful employment. It was always meant to be "social activity," participation in the officially formulated economic and social tasks.

The SED Monopoly on Power

This organizational complex that embraced all social areas was the expression of a mechanistic conception of politics which Stalin had trenchantly put in the paradigmatic formula "The cadres decide every-

---

29. "The citizens of the GDR have the right to associate in order to realize their interests by means of coordinated action in parties, social organizations, associations, and collectives *in accordance with the principles and goals of the Constitution*" (emphasis added).

thing." In spite of occasional efforts to reorient itself rationally with the help of modern organization theories, Marxist-Leninist organizational thinking never outgrew its origins in the conspirational underground under tsarist and other autocracies.[30]

Communist parties in power have always used the power of the state to realize their sociopolitical goals, even though this contradicted the Marxist-Leninist theory of revolution that was aimed at abolishing the state as an instrument of oppression. After the October Revolution in Russia, there had been advocates of turning over the functions of steering and regulating society to independent organizations, such as the trade unions. But the Soviet-style "dictatorship of the proletariat" in Eastern Europe was a dictatorship of the party and anything but a step toward the "withering away" of the state. On the contrary, the party built up strong, powerful, and centralistic states that set out to carry through its goals of a social transformation—in the Soviet Union before, and in East Central Europe after, World War II. The SED formulated its ideological program of 1976 as follows:[31] "It is the policy of the Socialist Unity party of Germany in every respect to strengthen the socialist state of workers and peasants as a form of the dictatorship of the proletariat that represents the interest of the whole people of the GDR. It is the main instrument of the working-class-led workers in the formation of a developed socialist society[32] and on the way to communism."[33]

The all-encompassing leadership claim of the party led to an artificial unification of GDR society and to a centralized political structure. Politics, economics, and administration were subjected to the same uniform principle: namely, "democratic centralism."[34] With the help of this principle, party leaders imposed their will both within the party and toward the wider society. This was the "structural principle of the entire

30. Peter Christian Ludz, in his book *Parteielite im Wandel. Funktionsaufbau, Sozialstruktur und Ideologie der SED-Führung. Eine empirisch-systematische Untersuchung*, 3rd ed. (Cologne and Opladen: Westdeutscher Verlag, 1970), p. 25ff., pointed to these origins.

31. *Programm der Sozialistischen Einheitspartei*, p. 55ff.

32. The term "developed socialist society," as applied to the Soviet Union by Brezhnev, is reminiscent of the old Soviet-bloc pecking order according to which the Soviet Union was most advanced toward communism whereas the satellites could only call themselves people's democracies at their present stage of development.

33. See Bálint Balla, *Kaderverwaltung. Versuch zur Idealtypisierung der "Bürokratie" sowjetisch-volksdemokratischen Typs* (Stuttgart: Enke, 1972), p. 267.

34. "Democratic centralism" denotes a system which carries on democratic discussion at only the local level and which does not permit the local groups to be connected with each other or to deliberate together. Higher levels of the hierarchic organization are each elected by the next lower level, but in order to be "elected" the candidates for this "election" are selected by the higher levels.

society" and determined the relationship between state and society, the relations between social groups and strata, and the direction of the "class coalition" by the vanguard party. At the end of World War I, Max Weber pointed out in a lecture that socialism—at least the contemporary notion of it in industrial societies—had grown from the cooperative "discipline of the factory."[35] The Leninist concept of socialism, in particular, reflects a fascination with solutions typical of large industries or large organizations, factorylike discipline, quasi-military obedience, centralized decisionmaking, and compartmentalized decisions, all part and parcel of democratic centralism. And if there was still a tension between an organization based on the division of labor and strict hierarchy under Lenin, his successor Stalin reduced it to a dogmatic form of democratic centralism. In the conspiratorial traditions of the Bolsheviks and similar secret societies, as Hannah Arendt has described so tellingly, the hierarchic "onion structure" depends on degrees of being "in the know," of knowing the "secrets." Concealment of the secrets together with ideological distortion and only stepwise "revelation of reality" produce the conspiratorial nature of all secret societies and their dichotomized view of the world as "good" and "evil."[36]

The Rear Guard of Socialism

Stalinist democratic centralism perpetuated the dichotomous structure of communist society. The party and its leading role were juxtaposed to the citizenry, and the leadership to the party members. At the same time, there was the hierarchy, which placed the party and its apparatus above the other organizations and institutions. This was the structural consequence of its vanguard position, which "instrumentalized" the state and the social organizations, progressively turning them into the rear guard of society. In the post-Stalinist age, this became a fatal structural flaw of communist systems suspended between the leadership of the party and the requirements of a highly complex, industrialized, socialist society that was unable to function without structural differentiation, rational and effective planning and direction, and at least minimal citizens' participation in the social process. The chasm between the two became ever larger and impossible to overcome so long as there was no room for

35. Weber, "Der Sozialismus. Rede zur allgemeinen Orientierung von österreichischen Offizieren in Wien 1918." In Weber, *Gesammelte Reden und Aufsätze zur Soziologie und Sozialpolitik* (Tübingen: J. B. Mohr (UTB), [1942] 1988), pp. 492–518.
36. Ludz, *Parteielite*, p. 25.

social emancipation from the party in communist thinking: structural differentiation and diversification in the flow of information and control could occur only within the straitjacket of existing institutions or by means of a revolutionary rupture.

This is also the origin of misunderstandings by Western social scientists ever since the beginning of the seventies, when they expected the principles of rational administration to prevail in communist systems. They postulated a process of specialization and rationalization that by necessity would in time overcome the paradigms of Marxist-Leninist rule.[37] A look at Max Weber's *Economy and Society* could have spared them the embarrassment, for he pointed out that "the objective indispensability and impersonal nature of the apparatus, once established, permits it to be used very easily—in contrast to social systems based on feudalism or personal piety—by anyone who succeeded in winning control over it."[38] Socialist theories viewed bureaucracy as a necessary, if ambiguous, aspect of capitalism. They expected its despotic character to be overcome by the proletarian revolution and its direction gradually to fall to society at large. Weber, however, thought that socialism would aggravate the despotism of bureaucracy, and this was precisely the reason for his rejection of socialism: the fear of a bureaucracy that regulates all questions of social life according to its unified will, that imprisons society in a "cage of psychological dependency," and that replaces the resolution of conflicts and consensus formation among competing, political bureaucracies with the instructions of an all-powerful center. Whereas in capitalist society "the state and private bureaucracies (cartels, banks, giant corporations) were separate bodies standing side by side and one could control economic power with political power," he argued elsewhere,[39] under socialism "the two bureaucracies would form a single body with one solitary interest and become uncontrollable."

It is difficult to deny that this dire prediction had indeed come true in Soviet-style socialist countries—as distinct from such democratic-socialist countries as the mixed economies of Scandinavia and continental Europe—where state ownership of the means of production and state bureaucracy created a system without countervailing powers. The ownership and disposition function were in the hands of the political leadership which, in spite of hierarchic and functional differentiation, was neither open to demands for social participation nor subject to control.[40]

37. See, for example, Ludz, *Parteielite*; H. Gordon Skilling and Franklyn Griffiths, eds., *Interest Groups in Soviet Politics* (Princeton, N.J.: Princeton University Press, 1971); Glaessner, *Sozialistische Systeme*.
38. Weber, *Wirtschaft und Gesellschaft*, p. 578.
39. Weber, "Der Sozialismus," p. 504.
40. See Andreas Hegedüs, *Sozialismus und Bürokratie* (Reinbek: Rowohlt, 1981), p. 77.

For decades, extreme centralization and the lack of democracy were justified with the claim that this was the only way to construct an economically viable and socially just socialist society. In recent years, however, it became obvious that "realistic socialism" was getting to be progressively less capable of modernizing economy and society.

Arterial Hardening in Stalinist Systems

The weakness of the post-Stalinist steering apparatus went beyond the excess of centralization and the paucity of participation. It was caused also by the mutual blockage of the giant administration's individual pillars, which limited each other's freedom of action. A hopeless thicket of instructions and ordinances, redundant control and directive mechanisms which threatened political interventions into personnel decisions, and uncoordinated policy changes by the party inhibited and stymied rational sociopolitical planning by the state and by the economic planning apparatus.

Helmut Klages has developed a model of the "arterial hardening" (*Verholzung*) of the implementation of political decisions that is worth emulating:[41] The GDR Politbureau and, derivatively, the People's Chamber, the Council of State, and Council of Ministers produced such a growing flood of laws and ordinances that the central state agencies, especially those concerned with economic planning and administration, developed a defensive "secondary reassurance mentality" which led them to "complete" the already overwhelming glut of laws with their own directives and ordinances. The subordinate agencies were afraid to use the leeway that still existed and, as insurance against citizen complaints, referred to the directions received from above, which was easy because there was no need to explain their reasons to anyone. The GDR had no administrative courts. The citizenry felt so helpless and alienated that it hardly used its few opportunities for participation and, instead, withdrew into the remaining niches of freedom in society. The control agencies so common in the West were nonexistent in the East. Policy changes could only be suggested by organizations such as the trade unions and had to be initiated and implemented by the party. Zigzags in the party line, interventions into current processes, and constant party control of one's activities increased the tendency to seek reassurance and to anticipate

41. See Klages, *Überlasteter Staat—verdrossene Bürger? Zu den Dissonanzen der Wohlfahrtsgesellschaft* (Frankfurt and New York: Campus, 1981), p. 149ff.

eventual corrections in the decisionmaking process. Structural principles such as democratic centralism and double responsibility moved the locus of responsibility downward, which again encouraged central regulation—an escalating spiral.[42]

Even the most dynamic factor of this process, the SED, could work only through these sclerotic structures. And since the SED wanted to retain its influence and its opportunity to correct a course it had itself chosen, it produced mostly immobility, rigidity, a fear of making decisions, and the tendency to move even small and insignificant decisions to higher levels. The halfheartedness of a party that was afraid of losing its monopoly of control squelched all attempts to encourage initiative and responsibility at lower levels. Decisions to stick with outmoded ideas and to increase political repression were a disastrous, if typical, mistake under these circumstances. As in the other socialist countries that went through revolutionary upheavals in 1989, the Soviet-style system in the GDR made it impossible to reform the system. All attempts in this direction either foundered in their earliest stages or were violently suppressed.

There are many reasons why we cannot go into in detail about how the GDR collapsed, but they all boil down to the basic contradiction: "realistic socialism" was a closed, monistic system based on a secular eschatology. The communist goals of salvation seemed reachable only if all members of society followed without reservation the leadership of the party, which claimed to be the executor of historical laws. Any attempt to modernize a part of this closed system appeared to be resistance against the great historical goal. Partial solutions or the self-regulation of a social subsystem were quite unacceptable. This monism was the doom of Soviet-style socialism. It is simply not possible to steer a modern society according to a uniform master plan, and neither is there a blueprint for the planned course of history. Communist ideology was stuck in the illusions of the great historical designs of the nineteenth century instead of coming to grips with the present.

An Ambiguous Political Culture

The political traditions of the GDR presented a manifest contradiction between an authoritarian system and its appeals to democratic traditions

42. Among the strange results of this process were such Politbureau decisions of the sixties as between city planning concepts for the district (*Bezirk*) towns. As Egon Krenz disclosed, the Politbureau even decided whether or not a house of culture should be built in Halle.

that had never been able to prevail in German history. In 1945/46, the SED strove to represent historical, political, and social movements that had fought for an end to the exploitation, oppression, social misery, and political paternalism of German history: poor peasants since the Peasants' Wars of the early sixteenth century, the German Jacobins and radical bourgeois democrats of the 1848 revolution, and the German workers' movement whose legacy the SED had claimed. In the few years of its existence, the SED believed, the GDR had done more for a better and more meaningful life, a higher material and cultural level of its citizenry, than had been accomplished in centuries.[43] In the eyes of the old Federal Republic, however, the "Soviet Zone of Occupation" (SBZ)—as the GDR was called far into the sixties—the German communist system, was beyond all humanistic traditions, a totally alien thing, and a secular challenge to a culture rooted in occidental, Christian traditions. The West Germans long ignored the Enlightenment roots of communism (not its only roots as we have seen) and its unfulfilled secular promises.[44]

If we define culture as the all-encompassing expression of the circumstances and behavior of a people, then it is a process that is transmitted (and transmuted) by society itself. Political culture is to the political system as culture is to society and, furthermore, is embedded in the broader cultural framework of society. Subjective political attitudes and the collective behavior of the citizenry with respect to politics are at the heart of the political culture of a given system.[45] Political cultures, however, especially in nondemocratic settings, never feature only one "ruling culture" but include several more or less distinctive subcultures.[46] Differing sets of traditional views may fill the lacunae of the sway of central power and offer determined resistance to its demands of modernization and its political and social changes. In all societies, different social strata have their own norms and value systems. Those who are socially disadvantaged or excluded from political power frequently develop a remarkable stubbornness and subculture of their own.[47]

43. See Erich Honecker, "Würdiges Jubiläum Berlins, das heute den Namen 'Stadt des Friedens' trägt," in *Konstituierung des Komitees der Deutschen Demokratischen Republik zum 750jährigen Bestehen von Berlin am 7. Februar 1985* (East Berlin: Dietz, 1985), p. 8.

44. See Richard Löwenthal, *World Communism: The Disintegration of a Secular Faith* (New York: Oxford University Press, 1964).

45. See Sidney Verba, "The Remaking of Political Culture," in Lucian Pye and Sidney Verba, eds., *Political Culture and Political Development* (Princeton, N.J.: Princeton University Press, 1965).

46. Barbara Jancar, "Political Culture and Political Change," *Studies in Comparative Communism* 17, no. 1 (1984), 69–82; Lowell Dittmer, "Comparative Communist Political Culture," *Studies in Comparative Communism* 16, nos. 1–2 (1983), 9–24.

47. See Oskar Negt and Alexander Kluge, *Geschichte und Eigensinn* (Frankfurt: Zweitausendeins, 1981).

The political culture of the GDR, as seen by its political elite, was one of "socialist democracy" and the "socialist way of life." The latter meant the totality of views and modes of behavior of people in all walks of GDR life, at work and at leisure, in public and within the family, in politics and among friends.[48] Central beliefs of the SED regarding society and politics determined the official political culture, including

1. the leading role of the working class and of its Marxist-Leninist party in state and society;
2. the right of the SED to direct and develop society in its totality according to its will and plan;
3. the belief that socialist society is capable of gradually equalizing the life chances of all people and that this must be reflected in their individual and collective behavior;
4. the central role of work as the expression of all human life activities;
5. the planned raising of the "material and intellectual-cultural level" of life as the goal of the policy of party and state;
6. the political participation and activation of the citizens under the conditions of "democratic centralism"; and
7. the linkage between SED military policy and the "protection of the socialist homeland" on the one hand and a socialist way of life on the other.[49]

Defining the Self from the Alter Ego

In 1949, when the two German states were born with very different ideas of socioeconomic and political order, they were both faced with the task of creating a new political culture. The GDR took the path of an "antifascist democratic revolution" after 1945 and thus brought about a radical break with the German political past. There were profound social and economic changes such as the land reform, the expropriation of large industries, and the transformation of education, to name a few, and they created the preconditions for launching a new era of development toward a socialist society, one oriented toward the Soviet model. "Learning from the Soviet Union," the relevant slogan went, "means learning how to win." The radical rupture with the past concealed the extent to which the

48. *Lebensweise und Lebensniveau im Sozialismus* (East Berlin: Wirtschaft, 1977).
49. Autorenkollektiv, *Wörterbuch des wissenschaftlichen Kommunismus* (East Berlin: Dietz, 1973), p. 352.

"revolution from above" failed to eliminate many a link to traditional German political culture. There were essentially four links of German tradition upon which the GDR was founded:

1. There was a specific version of traditional authoritarian elements that had taken a distinctive form in Germany.
2. The political system of the GDR included elements of the old workers' culture which became part of the dominant culture.
3. The SED claimed to bring a cultural revolution that would eventually realize the goal of a communist society.
4. The political culture of the GDR was always determined by special national conditions and hence differed considerably from other countries of the "socialist camp."

Other elements of significant confrontation were the cultural and political ideas of the "new social movements" of the West, each derived from different historical movements of the past and considered variously antiprogress, petit bourgeois, romantic, or radical-left by the SED. These ideas had a decisive influence on the rise of a protest movement in the GDR.

German political culture had long been shaped by such authoritarian elements as the principle of separation between state and society; the assumption of the "neutrality of the state," which was not the product of a social contract but the highest expression of public authority, an independent agent with its own, underived power; the image of the *Beamter* (civil servant), who is neutral with regard to partisan interests; as well as the political virtues of the subjects, their readiness to follow, obedience, and political absenteeism.[50] In March 1990, when the GDR citizenry went to their first free elections, the most recent free elections had taken place nearly sixty years earlier. Only eighty-year-olds could have had any memories of their own of political democracy. The political culture had been shaped by an almost seamless transition from one antidemocratic dictatorship to another, no matter how different. The great change of 1989 could not hide the extent to which the people in the GDR had internalized authoritarian thinking and behavior. As two Soviet journalists in West and East Berlin put it a year later: "In the GDR, thinking was a most dangerous activity. This came evidently from slipping smoothly from one totalitarian system to the next. This state of

50. See Martin Greiffenhagen, "Vom Obrigkeitsstaat zur Demokratie. Die politische Kultur in der Bundesrepublik Deutschland," in Peter Reichel, ed., *Politische Kultur in Westeuropa. Bürger und Staaten in der Europäischen Gemeinschaft* (Frankfurt and New York: Campus, 1984), p. 52ff.

affairs has prevailed now for a good three generations, and much that is
natural and taken for granted in a free society is simply missing. . . . The
whole society here has been infected with the virus of clicking heels and
carrying out orders at any price."[51]

After 1945, there was only a brief phase, if any, when the restitution
of democracy seemed possible. The formation of the Socialist Unity party
(SED), from a forced merger of KPD (communists) and SPD in the spring
of 1946 clearly signaled the coming of a new dictatorship.[52] By 1948, at
the latest, when it had become a "party of a new type," the SED had cut
the umbilical cord to the German Social Democratic tradition. It declared
itself to be the leading power in the state; and this state, far from being
neutral, was its instrument. Its power derived from the historic mission
of the party to build up socialism/communism. Its *Beamte* were not
neutral but were cadres of the party who served its interest in the
administration. The citizenry, for its part, was enjoined to help with all
its might in the construction of socialist society.

Three central pillars of the authoritarian state remained intact, nevertheless, and were put into the service of the Marxist-Leninist party. The
origins and justification of state authority were not based on the consent
and compact of the governed. State and society remained united, but the
citizens had no voice in the determination of the goals of either one. This
never diminished the role of the state as the highest authority vis-à-vis the
citizenry, nor did the fact of its being an instrument of the party. Political
absenteeism, however, was not seen as a virtue but as a violation of the
moral code of a socialist society. In its place, there arose the mobilization
(not participation) of the citizens for the goals of party and state, and
criticism of the latter inevitably led to punishment. To a remarkable
degree, Prussian-authoritarian, traditional modes of behavior rather than
socialist ones patterned the political and social system. As Rolf Henrich
wrote in his book, with the telltale title *The Tutelage State*, "It is still
considered morally reliable conduct for a person to carry out his duties,
if necessary, without a word and against his own, inner convictions. They
are still enthusiastic about the perfect organization, Prussian-style obedience, etc. without seeing the dangers of the world of organization and
the lack of personality. State socialism unscrupulously exploits for its

51. *Tageszeitung* (taz), Sept. 30, 1990, p. 15.
52. The Soviet occupation, after permitting democratic parties to form and being the
first to allow competitive elections in their zone in 1945, decided to force the German SPD
to merge with the communist party (KPD) and helped the latter to emerge in a dominant
position from the merger, as the SED.

social order all these aspects of the German social character which come from the Prussianization of Germany."[53]

The Authoritarian Character of Scientific Socialism

The political and social structures of the GDR and of other socialist countries (despite national differences) reflected the conviction that it was possible to plan a society "scientifically," according to the principles of Marxism-Leninism, and that there was a privileged group, the vanguard party, whose knowledge about the historical laws of social development gave it the absolute authority to carry them out. Hannah Arendt has pointed out the recurring contradictions between these goals and reality. They stem from the utter certainty in the minds of a group of people about the final goal, she explained, and their determination to trample the laws of nature, society, freedom, and human dignity underfoot and to rob humans of their social relationships. Arendt spoke of "an atomization [of society] by which human beings lost not only their place in society, but the entire sphere of communal relationships in whose framework *common sense* makes sense" (emphasis added). Only when common sense has lost its sense can totalitarian propaganda hit home.[54]

Because they proclaimed alleged certainties, these ideas offered people points of identification and found acceptance even in pluralist democracies, alien though they were to them. Today, after our historical experience and the obvious failure of the socialist regimes, such ideas have lost their spell. Like the other socialist countries, the GDR was a teleological political culture which had lost its telos over the years. After years of dynamic social and political development, it had finally arrived at the problem of maintaining and securing its achievements. Everyday life was characterized by new political attitudes and modes of social behavior that were no longer patterned by utopian socialism and the goal of communism, but rather by "realistic socialism." Both the political leadership and the citizenry had settled down to living in the here and now.

This was unlikely to succeed in the long run, however, because the old institutional structures got in the way of the newly developing life-style. The sociopolitical structures for planning and directing the system (and

53. Henrich, *Der vormundschaftliche Staat. Vom Versagen des real existierenden Sozialismus* (Reinbek: Rowohlt, 1989), p. 92.
54. See Arendt, *The Origins of Totalitarianism* (San Diego: Harcourt Brace Jovanovich, [1951] 1973), p. 352.

the ideological legitimation of the movement) remained and continued to impose their goals authoritatively from above, with the help of the state and its enforcers. They had survived the death of the utopian faith. The SED never liked the idea of an active *citoyen* as a part of the developed socialist system. Its hierarchical, authoritarian ideas of society placed narrow limits on the self-realization and autonomy of individuals and social groups. It insisted that people understand their own life experience according to the official templates of interpretation. Citizens' everyday experiences, attitudes, feelings, and insights, however, were more and more in conflict with the official political culture and procedures of Marxism-Leninism.

When the old faith dies, the naked authoritarian power of the system becomes painfully visible to all, not just to its victims. State security organizations modeled on the revolutionary Cheka of Lenin and Feliks Dzerzhinski and its successors (NKVD, NKGB, KGB) were present and played a decisive role in securing the power of the communist party in all communist states.[55] In their self-image, they were the "shield and the sword" of the party, and these symbols appear on the seals of both the Soviet KGB and the East German Stasi (Ministry for State Security). In the words of Stasi chief Erich Mielke, they were "the special organ of the dictatorship of the proletariat, which is in a position and has all the means, under the leadership of the party and together with all the other state organs and armed units and in close relations to the workers. . . . to protect the workers-and-peasants power and its revolutionary development reliably against any counterrevolutionary activity of enemies, foreign and domestic, as well as to guarantee in every respect internal security and order."[56]

The Stasi was one of the most important devices of the power of the SED and yet, as with other such systems throughout history, there was the constant problem for the rulers of how to keep the lions *under* the throne—or, in this case, the vipers in the grass—and not to permit them undue influence over the government. It was a comprehensive, highly differentiated and specialized bureaucracy and, at the same time, an influential pressure group with significant leverage in political and personnel decisions. The party strove to curb the Stasi tendency toward being a state by tying its leadership into the SED Central Committee and Politbureau, particularly with the rise of Honecker in 1971, when Stasi

55. See especially Alexander Dallin and George W. Breslauer, *Political Terror in Communist Systems* (Stanford, Calif.: Stanford University Press, 1970), pp. 1–23.

56. Mielke, "Mit hoher Verantwortung für den zuverlässigen Schutz des Sozialismus," *Einheit* 30 (1975), 44.

Minister Mielke was brought into the Politbureau. A Central Committee section on security attempted to guide and control what the West German press in 1989/90 came to call "the *Krake*" (octopus) with general guidelines, cadre political instructions, and an SED network throughout the Stasi organization. The SED, for example, subordinated all local Stasi activities to the supervision of the SED district secretaries, the office that Hans Modrow had held in Dresden before becoming GDR prime minister in December 1989. The Stasi had some 80,000 full-time employees, many occupied with opening mail, monitoring telephone calls in post office exchanges, and personal surveillance of "suspicious" characters. A vast army of perhaps as many as 700,000 "unofficial agents" (IMs) were pressed into part-time or occasional cooperation which reached into every nook and cranny of GDR society—for example, by bending the relations between attorneys and clients, doctors and patients, teachers and students, coaches and athletes, and priests and parishioners to its hideous purposes. The Stasi could destroy a career, deny any kind of license, and refuse a person's admission to university or other specialized training,[57] and this on top of its capacity for surveillance, harassment, and physical violence and detainment.

For the 1980s, the Stasi had made plans for huge concentration camps to hold several hundred thousand persons of "hostile-negative attitudes" and, even in its death-rattle of 1990, it still managed to derail (by means of carefully aimed indiscretions about earlier IM activities of prominent East German politicians) dozens of posttotalitarian political careers in a unified Germany. Stasi IM backgrounds of members of the newly elected East German *Landtage* (diets) and *Land* cabinets still fed major scandals in 1991, not to mention local imbroglios of the most varied sort. Finally, the Stasi legacy included the vast files that agents and IMs had compiled over the years on 5 million East Germans—more than one out of four of the entire population, including children—and 2 million West Germans. The democratic revolutionaries of 1989/90 fought for control over these enormous files and strove, with varied results, to keep SED officials from purging files of incriminating material. Some prominent democratic leaders would have preferred to burn the whole lot, while others wanted to save everything so the innocent could prove their victimization and the guilty could be prosecuted. The West German Federal Intelligence Service (BND) and Constitutional Protection Office would have loved to get their

57. See especially the *Spiegel* exposés reprinted in *Der Spiegel-Spezial* 2 (1990) and Karl W. Fricke, "Entmachtung und Erblast des MfS," *Deutschland Archiv* 23, no. 12 (Dec. 1990), 1881–1890, which gives organizational details. See also Fricke's earlier book, *Die DDR Staatssicherheit* (Cologne: Wissenschaft & Politik, 1982).

hands on these mountains of documents. In the end, though, the remaining files were retained by the *Land* authorities which permitted individuals to petition for seeing their own files, but not to learn the names of persons who had denounced or implicated them in "political crimes."[58]

Did the Stasi information methods, and especially its octopus network of hundreds of thousands of IMs, enable the regime to develop accurate knowledge about GDR social problems, the political "mood" of the moment, and potential centers of unrest? Western analysts assumed that the Stasi was an effective SED early-warning system against such threats as the citizens' groups of 1989. Reading the relevant reports with the benefit of hindsight, however, raises some doubts in this respect. To be sure, the summer 1989 reports to the Politbureau accurately describe the activities of such groups, but there is a perceptual wall of ideological stereotypes that obscured the real motives of the followers of these initiative groups. The security doctrines of the SED admitted only unconditional loyalty and ascribed even cautious criticism to the workings of "hostile-negative forces," thus preventing any realistic interpretation of information gathered on opposition groups.[59] This seems all the more surprising since, for years, the Stasi had successfully and systematically infiltrated all oppositional circles as well as the church-sponsored pacifist and environmental groups. Let us look at an example of the discrepancy between detailed inside knowledge of the life of an opposition group and the Stasi's ideologically distorted perception, as seen in an internal memo from the District of Potsdam, dated May 1989: "As has been demonstrated repeatedly in recent times, hostile-negative forces have increased their activities in the GDR, including the District of Potsdam, in order to organize politically negative, insecure, and misled GDR citizens under the cover of the churches and with the help of church-related persons, and to provoke them into utterances and actions against the socialist order of society and the social strategy of the party."[60]

To squelch the organization of resistance from the outset, the SED in the eighties strove to develop the security apparatus in a systematic way. It had no political strategy against the spreading of new cultural and

58. The utter complexity and explosiveness of such information and its ramifications recalls the Nazi legacy and the problems of denazification. The subject of punishment for Stasi and other regime criminality is too complicated to be treated here.

59. See Armin Mitter and Stefan Wolle, eds., *Ich liebe euch doch alle! Befehle und Lageberichte des MfS* (Berlin: Basis-Druck, 1990), 208ff.

60. Reinhard Meinel and Thomas Wernicke, eds., *Mit tschekistischem Gruss. Berichte der Bezirksverwaltung für Staatssicherheit Potsdam 1989* (Potsdam: Edition Babelturm, 1991), p. 54.

political attitudes, only repressive stratagems such as a 1976 guideline which, among other things, proposed tricks for demoralizing the opposition in any way possible: by systematic destruction of personal reputations, "by systematic arrangements for professional and social failures so as to undermine the self-confidence of particular individuals," by sowing distrust and mutual suspicions, by taking advantage of personal rivalries and weaknesses, and by any other means.[61] The Nazis of 1933/34 could not have said it any better, if they had drawn up a how-to manual of the loathsome tricks by which they defeated political rivals in their local takeovers and, eventually, their takeover of the highest army command. The buildup of the surveillance and repression system formed a striking contrast to the state's growing inability to put it to its intended use and to accomplish its goals. In the fifties and sixties, the spread of autonomous social groups had been inconceivable, and critical statements of SED individuals would have drawn the harshest punishment. The reason for the relaxation of repression since then was not a liberalization of the regime, but rather a gradual emancipation of the population from the communist party state and a lessening of the formerly all-pervasive fear. The security doctrine of the SED, which could never hide its Soviet historical origins in the twenties and thirties, simply began to miss its mark.

Discussion in Berlin newspapers and among social scientists in early 1991 threw a final ironic light upon the role of the Stasi in the democratic upheaval of late 1989. Since the omnipresent Stasi had completely infiltrated all the opposition groups and, in fact, was goading some of them into the confrontations and massive demonstrations—perhaps to incriminate them for later prosecution—and since it failed to use the means at its disposal to stop them, observers reasoned, was it not plausible to suggest that the Stasi was behind this revolution? Citing the example of the reforms of Mikhail Gorbachev, a longtime protégé of KGB chief Yuri Andropov, and of other *perestroika* advocates with a KGB background, why should we not expect reformist forces among the Stasi, just as they had surfaced among SED leaders? But then who was the target of their manipulated rebellion, their own police state? Such idle speculations were also encouraged by accounts of individual Stasi careers which revealed how a Stasi "Saul" often turned into an activist "St. Paul" of the democratic opposition, with equal moral conviction.

61. See Bürgerkomitee Leipzig, ed. *Stasi intern. Macht und Banalität* (Leipzig: Forum Verlag, 1991).

German Working-Class Culture

The culture of the workers' movement, the second traditional element of GDR political culture, had its roots in preindustrial, peasant, handicraft, and urban-plebeian traditions. It was patterned by the manifold efforts at organization of the workers' movement which included not only its political and social organization in parties and trade unions, but also its welter of leisure and sports organizations—singing clubs, nature societies, the different sports associations, cultural and educational undertakings—cooperatives, and mutual aid or self-help associations. The importance of the world of regional, parochial, and religious traditions for developing and consolidating an autonomous workers' culture has only recently found scholarly appreciation.[62]

From this perspective, the traditional workers' culture was a subculture with strong oppositional or alternative-cultural elements. It was the answer to a proletarian way of life, an attempt to improve one's life and condition in the midst of a hostile environment. It was the culture of a movement inspired by the conviction that capitalist society had outlived its historical role and that the future belonged to socialism. The SED, however, took up only certain aspects of this line of tradition. While the Social Democratic branch of the workers' movement increasingly lost the sense of certainty of such a future after 1945, the communists (KPD) and their successor, the SED, considered themselves the guarantors and executors of these "historical laws of development." They directed the working class, in whose name the SED thought it acted, to pursue the goals put forth by the party. The workers themselves had no role in their formulation. On the other hand, old forms of workers' solidarity survived in the GDR, such as had been developed during their long struggle for social and political rights, particularly in the world of factory work. Many of the rules of labor law, the stress on the workers' ethos, and the significance of traditions of work were carefully cultivated; later, the regime attempted to develop them further and adapt them to the different social conditions. For instance, "workers' honor" was a politically narrow and instrumentalized concept in the forties and fifties. Later it meant a new self-image of the "leading class" in a technical, scientifically informed socialist society.

For over two decades, the regime stressed the role of the scientific-

62. See Gerhard A. Ritter, ed., *Arbeiterkultur* (Königstein/Ts.: Anton Hain, 1979) and Albrecht Lehmann, *Studien zur Arbeiterkultur. Beiträge der 2. Arbeitstagung der Kommission "Arbeiterkultur" in der Deutschen Gesellschaft für Volkskunde in Hamburg vom 8. bis 22. Mai 1983* (Münster: F. Coppenrath, 1984).

technical intelligentsia, and there was the hope that the working class might progressively turn into such a technical intelligentsia. Rationalization and automation were expected to free more and more workers from physical drudgery and monotonous work. When this turned out to be an unreachable goal, it signified another painful loss of legitimacy for the SED. The workers had lost yet another individual and collective hope, that of rising socially by means of education and occupational qualifications. How was a person to find his place in a society with the slogan "Your workplace is your fighting place for socialism" when no improvement of the daily misery was in sight?

The GDR saw itself squarely in the tracks of the communist world revolution, the traditions of the Leninist cultural revolution. Not just a revolution of the socioeconomic system but of the existing culture as well. To the extent that they had been realized, however, communist revolutions had been minority revolutions, by a revolutionary elite whose ideas about the future were shared by the majority only in exceptional and passing moments. To realize the revolution, nevertheless, an educational dictatorship was required to overcome the traditional state of mind of the masses. Education, not experience, had to create the new socialist man (or woman). In the seventy years after the Russian October Revolution, and in forty-odd years of the GDR (and Soviet occupation), the elite's time horizon had approached that of the citizenry. They still talked about achieving the communist society as a distant goal, but the day-to-day struggle was over mastering the many economic, social, and cultural problems—not to mention internal and external security from the forces of counterrevolution—for which the party could no longer offer ready solutions. The SED hid more and more behind the ritual incantations of the great goals and ideals of socialism without pointing a way out of the escalating economic, ecological, social, and cultural crisis. In spite of the propaganda efforts of many an ideological tailor, it became more and more obvious that the emperor of socialism was naked.

Unlike other socialist countries, the political culture of the GDR was patterned by the special national situation of a Germany divided between East and West. Its very emphasis on being a very different kind of Germany separated by ideology and politics from the FRG—the presumable hotbed of fascism, capitalism, and Western NATO imperialism—tended to highlight the standards of comparison between the two. Everyday life and politics of the GDR's citizens were determined, even deformed, by the perpetual comparison with the FRG. The leadership never tired of stressing the social security in which GDR citizens could live in contrast to the unemployment, material want,[63] and other problems of

63. Anecdotes can illustrate the difficulties of this approach. In one case, GDR television

capitalist society, such as crime and drugs. Many GDR citizens were forever comparing their situation with that of the FRG—especially after the opening of the borders to West German visitors in the early seventies. They rarely compared themselves to other Western countries, and most had no opportunity to see Western life for themselves until after the fall of the Wall, when practically everyone felt a compulsion to visit West Germany at least once. As public opinion polls have shown, younger East Germans went again and again to look and even to buy a few things, and practically all the seniors had to satisfy their craving for the truth at least once. Until then, their comparison rested on West German television, receivable in most of the GDR, and on the accounts of Western visitors, and they probably believed only a part of this so long as official propaganda told them otherwise. Imagine the collective shock when, after November 8, 1989, they saw the other promised land, prosperous, clean, and orderly, and without political fear.

The New Political Culture of Revolt

Observers of the political and social developments in the GDR had long noticed the growing contradiction between the official political culture, with its tired rituals and slogans, and the everyday culture of the people.[64] The first West German representative in the GDR, Günter Gaus, invented the phrase "society of niches" to describe how individuals had withdrawn from the impositions of the regime to the few private spaces they could create among friends, family, and nonpolitical groups.[65] From the beginning of the 1980s, more and more people sought the niche spaces of the churches and there became engaged in various new causes.[66] It is impor-

---

reportedly prepared a special on a feeding of the poor by a New York welfare agency, but it could not be shown because the American poor were given bananas for dessert, a rare luxury in the GDR.

64. See Irma Hanke, *Alltag und Politik. Zur politischen Kultur einer unpolitischen Gesellschaft. Eine Untersuchung zur erzählenden Gegenwartsliteratur in der DDR in den 70er Jahren* (Opladen: Westdeutscher Verlag, 1987); Helmut Hanke, "Kulturelle Traditionen des Sozialismus," *Zeitschrift für Geschichtswissenschaft* 33, no. 7 (1985), 589ff.; and Helmut Meier and Walter Schmidt, *Erbe und Tradition in der DDR. Die Diskussion der Historiker* (East Berlin: Akademie-Verlag, 1988).

65. See, for example, Gaus's *Wo Deutschland liegt. Eine Ortsbestimmung* (Hamburg: Hoffmann & Campe, 1983).

66. See Reinhard Henkys, "Thesen zum Wandel der gesellschaftlichen und politischen Rolle der Kirchen in der DDR in den siebziger und achtziger Jahren," in Gert-Joachim Glaessner, ed., *Die DDR in der Ära Honecker. Politik–Kultur–Gesellschaft* (Opladen: Westdeutscher Verlag, 1988), pp. 332–353; Detlef Pollack, ed., *Die Legitimität der Freiheit.*

tant to be aware, however, of the marginal position of these groups in GDR society up until the summer of 1989 and of their decline to marginality within six months after the great explosion. For decades, the SED had worked at politicizing all of social life in the GDR in a never-ending campaign of production and harvest battles and organized competitions within. To believe the official propaganda, the policy of the party was a perpetual spur to daily positive action, as many examples could show. The workers of the petrochemical *Kombinat* of Schwedt on the Oder assured the SED General Secretary Erich Honecker in 1986, for instance,

> that the continuity and the forward-looking scientific leadership style of the Central Committee of the SED and your personal example shine an extraordinary beacon upon our desire to achieve success, upon the initiative and the creativity of the workers here. The profound harmony between the advantages of socialism experienced every day and the life interests of the workers and their families has proven to be an inexhaustible source of strength in this *Kombinat*, as in others, and it enables us to master . . . our strategic tasks.[67]

This kind of feedback illustrates both why the leadership wanted nothing more than to continue and how the workers and the public must have gotten tired of the constant attempts to politicize everyday life. Under the surface of a thoroughly politicized society, therefore, there grew "the political culture of an unpolitical society," a curious form of depoliticization, as it were.[68]

This politico-cultural system had developed for decades before it began to break up within a few weeks or months in the summer and early fall of 1989, spurred by the great exodus of people. In its place, for a short time, there arose a massive culture of political resistance. The acceleration of the flight in summer had been a reaction to the accumulation of social

---

Politisch alternative Gruppen in der DDR unter dem Dach der Kirche (Frankfurt: Peter Lang, 1990); and Jörg Swoboda, ed., *Die Revolution der Kerzen. Christen in der Umwälzung der DDR* (Wuppertal and Kassel: Onkenverlag, 1990).

67. "In hohem Masse strahlen die Kontinuität und der vorausschauende wissenschaftliche Leitungsstil des Zentralkomitees der SED und Dein persönliches Vorbild auf die Leistungsbereitschaft, Initiative, und das Schöpfertum der Werktätigen aus. Die tiefe Übereinstimmung der täglich erlebten Vorzüge des Sozialismus mit den Lebensinteressen der Werktätigen und ihrer Familien erweist sich auch in unserem Kombinat als unversiegbarer Kraftquell, mit dem es gelingt, strategische Aufgaben . . . zu meistern." *Neues Deutschland*, Jan. 27, 1986, p. 2.

68. See Hanke, *Alltag und Politik*.

and political problems.[69] It triggered the political and social eruption that
brought down the GDR within a few months. The, in part, paniclike
exodus vividly demonstrated the instability of the situation and encouraged many to speak up in public, loud and clear. As the East German
writer Stefan Heym put it in the great Berlin demonstration of November
4, 1989: "It was as if someone had pushed the windows open after all
the years of greyness and bad air *(Dumpfheit und Mief)*, of big phrases
and bureaucratic arbitrariness, of official blindness and deafness."[70] The
battering by the weekly Monday-night demonstrations in front of Leipzig's St. Nicolai Church, the massive "demos" in Dresden and other
cities, and the hundreds of thousands (estimates run from 500,000 to 1
million) on November 4 in Berlin had their effect on the SED party rank
and file, thousands of which appeared almost daily to press their demands in front of the mighty party headquarters. The action had passed
into the hands of the street demonstrators of the GDR. To speak with
Albert O. Hirschman, the challenges of both "exit" and "voice" and the
rapid erosion of "loyalty" spelled the doom of the once almighty SED
regime.

The massive "demos" exhibited a surprising degree of political maturity and imagination; witness some of the self-made banners: "Egon
[Krenz], what do you say about China [the Tiananmen Square massacre]
now?"[71] "For 40 years you preached water [to us] and drank wine
[yourself]"; "We are no longer talking bananas, now we want the cake
(jetzt geht es um die Wurst)"; "My proposal for the first of May [Labor
Day parade]: let the government pass before the people"; "40 years of
frustration are not bought off with four weeks of dialogue"; and "Everyone should get his passport papers, the government its walking papers."
In the revolutionary euphoria of fall 1989, many believed they saw the
seeds of an entirely new political culture sprouting.

The Citizen Movements

"GDR society stopped being a monolithic collective, united by the SED
leadership. The centrifugal forces of the economy, the international

69. Not the least of the triggers was the massive electoral fraud perpetrated by the SED
leadership in the communal elections of spring 1989. It was in some ways the quite
unnecessary straw that broke the camel's back. On the exodus, see especially Siegfried
Grundmann, "Aussen- und Binnenmigration der DDR 1989. Versuch einer Bilanz,"
Deutschland Archiv 22, no. 9 (1990), pp. 1422–32. Also see Siegfried Grundmann and
Ines Schmidt, *Wanderungsbewegung in der DDR 1989*, Berliner Arbeitshefte und Berichte
zur sozialwissenschaftlichen Forschung no. 30 (1990).

70. Quoted in various German newspapers.

71. Honecker and his successor, Krenz, had still toyed with a "Chinese solution" to civil
disobedience but were forced to yield to the sheer size of the public discontent.

developments, and the social contradictions had brought terrible distortions into the system. The tightly woven organizational fabric lost its power to socialize and integrate." This was the description of the situation of spring 1989 by one of the leading thinkers of the opposition, Ehrhart Neubert.[72] Before then, there had been no "opposition" to speak of, which rather distinguished the GDR from the other socialist countries. To be sure, there had been various informal groups from the late seventies which usually worked in the protected space of the churches—and which were not immune to penetration by the Stasi, as we have learned since. Since about the mid-eighties there emerged a "second public" represented by various forms of semilegal and illegal publications, but there was no organized opposition comparable to Charter 77 in the CSR or Solidarity in Poland. Neither were there personal or ideological links to opposition figures of the first three decades of the GDR,[73] perhaps a manifestation of pervasive Stasi control and isolation from the GDR diaspora in the West. While the earlier opposition attempts, following the destruction of the bourgeois forces, had come from dissidents in the party, the new informal groups tended to be characterized by subcultural orientations and an avoidance of formal organization.

Often there were links to "life reform" or cultural revolution movements from the beginning of the century or the twenties of which the principals were unaware. They simply found the prevailing political system and ideology oppressive but did not counterpose a finished ideology to it. What gave their political and cultural ideas such explosive power was their rejection of the party's monopoly on societal regulation, against which they claimed rights of privacy. As had the earlier life reform movement and the Western new social movement, they postulated the autonomy of private circles of friends, and of living communities of religious and secular beliefs, against the claims of the whole society.[74] The power of human communities—and, Hannah Arendt would have added, their common sense and decency rather than opposing ideologies, such as previous dissidents had developed[75]—overcame the party-centered

72. Neubert, "Die Opposition in der demokratischen Revolution der DDR, Beobachtungen und Thesen," in Pollack, ed., *Die Legitimität der Freiheit*, p. 209.
73. On the origins, see Hubertus Knabe, "Politische Opposition in der DDR. Ursprünge, Programmatik, Perspektiven," *Aus Politik und Zeitgeschichte*, B1–2/90, Jan. 5, 1990, pp. 21–32; and Helmut Müller-Enbergs, "Die Rolle der Bürgerbewegungen in der Volkskammer," in Gert-Joachim Glaessner, ed., *Eine deutsche Revolution*, pp. 94–107.
74. See Gert-Joachim Glaessner and Klaus-Jürgen Scherer, *Auszug aus der Gesellschaft. Gemeinschaften zwischen Utopie, Reform und Reaktion* (Berlin: Verlag Europäische Perspektiven, 1986).
75. For example: Havemann, *Dialektik ohne Dogma*, and Rudolf Bahro, *Die Alternative. Zur Kritik des real existierenden Sozialismus* (Cologne and Frankfurt: Bund Verlag, 1977).

political and social system. One could sharpen this thesis further by saying that the external events, the breakdown and transformation of Eastern socialist systems, forced individuals and groups to emerge from their respective niches and to organize themselves deliberately as a political opposition:

> They reached a breakthrough from a socially marginal position with the call to boycott the [communal] elections of spring 1989. The patent electoral fraud of the SED then sped up the erosion of loyalty—in this way, the groups contributed decisively to the revolutionary upheaval. Furthermore, we can say that the ecological, human rights, and peace groups as well as the growing commitment of church representatives and groups undermined the cultural hegemony [of the party] with the introduction of new and competing values and a reinterpretation of party dogma.[76]

Another important difference from the other socialist countries was that socialist ideas and concepts still played a decisive role in the democratic opposition of the GDR. There had long been discussion in small groups about the necessity for a fundamental reform of socialism. Voices rejecting it as the guiding principle were rare. And once the system had fallen, there emerged the paradox that the most determined critics of SED-type socialism were the most loyal advocates of socialism, presumably beyond "realistic socialism." As Neubert put it, "Others may have stuck with socialism for reasons of pure opportunism, often the same people who later did somersaults of immoderate criticism of socialism. Nevertheless, there was a consensus far into the year 1989 that the roots of socialism in our cultural history, its part in fighting fascism, its interest in peace, and especially the protection of values of equality in a political utopia would remain among the elements forming a European polity."[77] This judgment accurately marks the point of departure of the groups that set out to make history in the summer of 1989.

By the revolutionary fall of that year, these small groups of the opposition had become the vehicle of hope for a democratic renewal. The people in the streets demanded democracy, free elections, and legalization of the New Forum. Who were these groups?

76. Sigrid Meuschel, "Wandel durch Auflehnung. Thesen zum Verfall bürokratischer Herrschaft in der DDR," in Rainer Deppe, Helmut Dubiela, and Ulrich Rödel, eds., *Demokratischer Umbruch in Osteuropa* (Frankfurt: Suhrkamp, 1991), p. 41ff.
77. Ehrhart Neubert, *Eine protestantische Revolution* (Osnabrück: Edition Kontext, 1990), p. 12.

What the Opposition Wanted

Months before October 1989, strengthened by the scandals of the electoral fraud of May, some five hundred basic initiative groups which had found shelter in the churches had to decide whether and when to set the process of change in motion. The massive exodus of late summer forced them to take a clear position. On July 1, the members of a pacifist circle and the initiative group "No to the Practice and Principle of *Abgrenzung* [isolation]"[78] published an open letter that broached certain far-reaching political demands. Incensed by the fraudulent local elections, they demanded a reform of electoral law that would really provide a secret ballot and give the citizens real influence on the composition of representative assemblies. They further demanded the admission of "independent communities of interest" as guaranteed in the Constitution: "There has to be an end to the constant isolation of the governing group from criticism by the citizenry. The issues of society are a concern to us all and must be clarified in public discussion. The guaranteed right of the citizen to express an opinion freely and openly breeds responsibility in the individual and thus creates a basis for the necessary democratization of our society."[79]

It was no accident that, in October/November of that fateful year, the New Forum (NF) had become the symbol of change and rebellion. The NF was the strongest opposition group in numbers, having been founded on September 9, 1989, by thirty representatives of various, mostly church-related groups. Among the founders were the painter Bärbel Bohley, Robert Havemann's widow, Katja, the attorney Rolf Henrich, who had been expelled from the SED and written a critical book, *The Tutelage State*, the physicist Sebastian Pflugbeil, and the molecular biology professor Jens Reich. Within a short time more than 200,000 people signed the NF manifesto of October 1989. The NF thought of itself as a pluralistic receptacle of regime opposition and as a forum for "democratic dialogue" over issues of concern to the whole society. Their founding manifesto said, among other things, that in order

> to recognize all these contradictions, to hear out opinions and
> arguments about them, and come to a conclusion, distinguishing

78. The word literally means "demarcation" and formerly referred to the long-standing government policy of isolating GDR citizens and social activities from Western (especially West German) influences. The initiative, however, meant to attack the isolation of the governing circles from the complaining public.

79. "Wie viele müssen noch gehen . . . Offener Brief an Christen und Nichtchristen in der DDR," *Die Tageszeitung*, Aug. 18, 1989, p. 3.

the public from the special interests, a democratic dialogue is needed regarding the tasks of constitutional government [the *Rechtsstaat*], economy, and culture. We need to think and talk about these questions together and all over the country. . . . Therefore we are forming a common political platform for the entire GDR which will enable people from all occupations, circles, parties, and groups to participate in the discussion and work on the truly important social problems of this country. We shall call such a comprehensive initiative the New Forum.[80]

On September 12, twelve people published a "Call to Intervene on Our Own Behalf" which, since GDR state socialism showed no willingness to entertain reforms in the face of an acute crisis—and in the face of calls for *perestroika* and *glasnost* all around—proposed a coalition of all people interested in reform: "We invite all who want to participate in a dialogue on the principles and concepts of a democratic transformation of our country."[81] Among the founders of Democracy Now (DJ) was a cofounder of the group Women for Peace, Ulrike Poppe, the church historian Wolfgang Ullmann, the physicist Hans-Jürgen Fischbeck, and the movie director Konrad Weiss. The call of the citizens' initiative DJ was issued in only a few copies—duplicating equipment was as carefully controlled, perhaps more so in communist dictatorships, as dynamite— and recipients were asked to "please copy and pass on." Appended to the call were "Proposals for a Democratic Transformation of the GDR," with this introduction:[82]

> The goal of our proposals is to win the inner peace of our country and thus to serve external peace as well. We want to help create a society in solidarity and to democratize all facets of life. At the same time we must find a new relation of partnership with our natural environment. We would like to see socialist development carried beyond the state socialist stage in which it has bogged down. We want to prepare a future for it. Instead of a tutelage, party-dominated state, which without a social mandate appointed itself the director and schoolmaster of the people, we want a state

80. "Aufbruch 89. Neues Forum," in *Oktober 1989. Wider den Schlaf der Vernunft* (Berlin: Neues Leben/Elefanten Press, 1990), p. 18ff.
81. "Aufruf zur Einmischung in eigener Sache," reprinted in *Demokratie Jetzt. Dokumentation des Arbeitsbereichs DDR-Forschung und Archiv*, ed. Helmut Müller-Enbergs, Berliner Arbeitshefte und Berichte zur sozialwissenschaftlichen Forschung no. 19 (Berlin: Jan. 1990), doc. 26.
82. "Thesen für eine demokratische Umgestaltung der DDR," ibid., doc. 27.

that is founded upon the basic consensus of the society, is responsible to it, and hence becomes the public business *(res publica)* of mature *(mündige)* citizens, male and female. Social achievements *(Errungenschaften)*[83] that have proven themselves must not be sacrificed with a reform program.

Democracy Now (DJ) grew from two opposition groups: the initiative group Peace and Human Rights (the *Abgrenzung* initiative mentioned earlier) and some East Berlin intellectuals. Personal frictions had led to the separate organization of DJ even though its opinions on most subjects were the same as those of the NF. A third opposition group that was important in the early phase of the upheaval was Democratic Start *(Aufbruch)*–Social and Ecological (DA). The initiative group of mostly church-related principals had begun in June. Its cofounders included the Rostock attorney Wolfgang Schnur—who was later found guilty of cooperation with the State Security Service (Stasi)—Rainer Eppelmann, a minister and later, after the democratic elections, GDR defense minister, the Weimar theologian Edelbert Richter, and Ehrhart Neubert, a scientific adviser of the GDR church association. The founding assembly of DA was interrupted by the police (October 2, 1989), but the group formally constituted itself as a political party only four weeks later and was the first open competitor to the SED and its "friendly" bloc parties, or *Blockflöten*.[84] The reason for this step was dissatisfaction with the lack of formal structure among the opposition: Eppelmann explained that it was time to move from spontaneity to a permanent commitment and firm structures.[85] A party convention of DA in mid-December, however, was marked by serious clashes between a right and a left wing, in particular over economic policy and reunification. There was a split and many prominent members left DA for the Social Democrats (SDP, soon renamed SPD).

The Stasi Looked On

The citizen initiative groups originated at a time when every political activity in the GDR outside the routines of "socialist democracy" was

83. In the sixties, the phrase "social achievements" was a staple of German discussion about whether the socialist "achievements" of the GDR should be retained in event of reunification.

84. The word denotes a musical instrument, a wooden recorder, and has connotations of "faggots" in regard to the SED.

85. *Tageszeitung (taz)*, Oct. 18, 1989.

hindered and suppressed by the state. Reports of the Ministry of State Security (MfS), the Stasi agency, have been published meanwhile and, for the fall of 1989, they show concern about the growing influence of these groups on the population. One MfS report to the SED leadership (June 1989) describes the persistent attempts to rally and organize by "such persons, who aim at social softening up, disintegration, and political destabilization to the point of changing the social relationships in the GDR." The report names about a hundred and fifty church-related "base groups" (pacifist, environmental, ecological, women's issues, human rights, etc.) and ten personal circles such as the Working Circle Solidarity Church, the Church from Below, the Ecological network, the Ark, and the Initiative for Peace and Human Rights. The "total potential" of these groups was estimated at about 2,500 persons. Some 600 were said to be in leadership committees, while about 60 of them, "a hard core, a relatively small number of fanatical, mostly unteachable enemies of socialism, are driven by a so-called missionary consciousness and political vanity (Profilierungssucht)." Eppelmann, Poppe, Bohley, Werner Fischer, and others were named.[86] The MfS reports also show that these groups were under systematic Stasi surveillance,[87] mostly by informants inside the citizen groups who had previously been blackmailed into cooperation with the Stasi. It could have been worse if the Stasi "octopus" had gotten around to hauling them off to the dungeons and torture chambers, such as the Stasi jails in Potsdam and many other places, or had committed them to mental death in the psychiatric clinics of the regime.[88]

The citizen initiative groups were mostly intended to be forums for public discussion. They wanted to start public debates on the many social problems of the GDR which had accumulated in decades of the dictatorship of bureaucratic socialism. They saw in this the principal precondition for the emergence of a "civil society." Demanding a broad and unregulated dialogue in a closed society like the GDR is, of course, a sacrilege

86. "Informationen über beachtenswerte Aspekte des aktuellen Wirksamwerdens innerer feindlicher und anderer negativer Kräfte in personellen Zusammenschlüssen," in *Ich liebe euch doch alle! Befehle und Lageberichte des MfS Januar–November 1989*, ed. Mitter and Wolle, *Ich liebe euch doch alle!* p. 46ff.

87. See "Informationen über die weitere Formierung DDR-weiter oppositioneller Sammlungsbewegungen," in *Ich liebe euch doch alle!* p. 208ff.

88. Eyewitnesses have described the grim Stasi jails, with their special chambers and torments. There is irony in the protests of Stasi chief Erich Mielke, who in 1991 complained about the lack of windows when he was detained in one of his own jail cells after the collapse of the GDR. The regime also used to put opponents in mental clinics, where cooperating psychiatrists administered psychomedication and other mental tortures to induce the very results they had put down in their advance diagnosis.

that would have violated the party's monopoly on information. The groups had their own informal communication structure within which critical questions could be asked and problems identified. The hope of the new groups that their forums would permanently satisfy the need of the whole society for critical discourse was soon overtaken by the pressing need to face the issue of German unification. They had served their time as "representatives of the people" all too briefly, however, when they were pushed aside by mass demonstrations and the newly founded rival parties to the SED.

By way of an example of the disappointment of the citizen movements, let us turn to the *Leipziger Volkszeitung*, which late in 1989 published an editorial entitled "Reunification?" the new slogan that had become more and more prominent in recent demonstrations as the initiative passed to the demonstrators:[89]

> Why did we go into the streets:
> • to disempower the SED regime
> • for democracy and self-government
> • for an economic reform so that our work pays off
> • for the freedom to travel, to express opinions, and to form organizations
> • for democratic reforms and a new society.
> He who is dreaming of reunification today, a Mercedes car tomorrow, and Majorca vacations the day after will soon wake up. Life is different and we know it, in the old FRG and here too.[90]
>
> This is what we want: a democratic and bloc-free [neutralist] Germany in the European House, where borders no longer separate but bring people together. A Germany with an ecologically sound economy and responsible consumption levels of living in West and East, and with responsibility for the "two-thirds [Third] world."

The editorial mentions as steps toward the inevitable unification a "contractual community" (Modrow) and later "confederation" (Kohl). This was evidently the first contribution from the opposition in the SED district *(Bereich)* newspaper, which offered some space at the insistence

89. "Wiedervereinigung?" *Leipziger Volkszeitung*, Dec. 10, 1989, p. 13.
90. The honest writer of this editorial probably did not imagine the number of old SED functionaries who would manage to profit from the changeover or who had already, by way of corruption, feathered their nests with material acquisitions, such that they were often among the newly rich of the postcommunist GDR. Many raised their own pay and were still in command of factory management boards when half the workers were laid off.

of the Round Table. It was a joint production of DA, the NF, and the SDP (SPD) and marked the range of public discussion in the GDR as well as the incompatibility of the goals. But it clearly shows how far, even then, at the end of 1989, the utopian goals of the initiative groups had fallen *behind* the demands of "the people." Thus, already in December, while observers had not yet noticed—and while the SED eagerly placed their representatives at the Round Table—the opposition movements were marginalized by the pace of political developments.

The Need to Move On

It is striking that, unlike in other Soviet-style socialist countries, the GDR opposition "swam on the crest of the wave of revolutionary unrest so that it appeared as if it were leading the movement."[91] The dynamic of the events made it necessary to create new and democratically legitimized institutions—especially a freely elected parliament, the Volkskammer— in order to stave off the collapse of the social order and of the economy, so that attempts to ward off the very real SED maneuvers to recapture power[92] could be shunted aside. The critique of the old system became a casualty of events as the citizens' groups were forced prematurely to decide whether they wanted to become political parties or remain social movements—an often-favored choice that implied certain modes of organization and decisionmaking procedures and that condemned most of them to relative impotence among the big party machines competing for the Volkskammer elections. The NF, DJ, and the Initiative for Peace and Human Rights refused to become parties, a decision that reflects the historical experience of earlier social movements, especially the working-class movement, which lost control over their political representatives after becoming parties. The new social movements in the West have harbored similar fears, although the Greens have shown that movements can participate successfully in elections. In the case of the GDR's citizen initiative movements, however, not becoming parties seems to have weakened their influence early on.

91. Meuschel, "Wandel durch Auflehnung," p. 43.
92. There can be no doubt about the capability and desire of the MfS to snuff out the revolt of the brave citizens' initiatives if only the massive demonstrations had gone away and not turned on the Stasi headquarters and its centers throughout the land. Premier Hans Modrow's transparent attempt in December to save the Stasi from abolition by the Round Table, along with his order to destroy records implicating his own role and that of others, shows the unwillingness of the dictatorial regime to yield to gentle reasoning by well-meaning opponents.

There is a danger now that myths are being fabricated, such as that the "GDR revolution was betrayed" by various villains of the mythmaker's choice. This is obviously not true, even though high hopes for an entirely new political culture were disappointed, a culture that would be governed by "the desire for justice, democracy, peace, and the protection and preservation of nature" (NF).[93] Or one that would result from "thinking together about our future, about a society in solidarity, in which social justice, freedom, and human dignity are assured for all" (DJ).[94] But the "people of the GDR" which crowded the streets from fall 1989 to the elections of March 1990 in massive demonstrations were never united except in rejecting the old system. Visions of what was to come after the GDR were diffuse and certainly did not conform to the intellectual dream of a better and more democratic *socialist* future. Revolutionary upheavals have their own logic. The experiences with Soviet-style socialism have ruined socialism as a positive utopia and have discredited it for the foreseeable future.

93. "Gründungsaufruf. Eine politische Plattform für die ganze DDR," in Gerhard Rein, ed., *Die Opposition in der DDR. Entwürfe für einen anderen Sozialismus* (Berlin: Wichern, 1989), p. 14.
94. "Aufruf zur Einmischung in eigener Sache," in Rein, ed., *Die Opposition*, p. 59.

Chapter FOUR

The West German Response to the Challenge

The public and the news media in the Federal Republic had followed the dramatic events in the East with rapt attention, but also with a certain skepticism born of forty years of living with the German division. The public opinion polls on reunification accurately reflected West German views when they paired the simplistic question of whether the respondents were "for reunification"—around 80% always were—with a reality test: "Do you believe that within a foreseeable timespan a reunification of the FRG and the GDR will come about?" Over the last two decades, fewer and fewer would reply yes: 13% in 1968, 5% in 1984, and 3% in 1987. Most of the respondents thought real unification improbable or uncertain: In 1987, 25% believed it to be uncertain and 72% unlikely.[1] Active engagement or calls for "tearing down the Wall" or for thoughtfully commemorating the East German workers' uprising of June 17, 1953— long an annual holiday called "Day of German Unity"—had become the stuff of right-wing propaganda and of graffiti on public walls.[2] Before

1. In 1972, 45% still thought it uncertain and only 41% unlikely. Anne Köhler and Richard Hilmer, *Die Deutschen und ihr Vaterland*, quoted in *The Economist*, Oct. 28, 1989, p. 9.
2. On West German university campuses, typically, a small number of Christian

1989, reunification was a disembodied issue of nearly universal popularity, high ideological symbolism, and no policy content whatsoever except in the transmuted form of Willy Brandt's *Ostpolitik* measures of détente (see Chapter Two). As the reader will recall, there was also a diminishing perception of the Soviet threat and, in the early eighties, a virulent peace movement.

The Great Surprise of 1989

This then was the frame of mind of the West German public in the fateful year 1989. They had gradually begun to overcome their fear of the Soviet threat of the fifties and sixties[3] by first getting thoroughly involved with the Western alliance—with some neutralist reservations—and then with the careful reconciliation of the East *(Ostpolitik)*. One of the big concessions along the way had been the *de facto* recognition by the Brandt administration of the Oder-Neisse line as the German-Polish border.[4] Another was dropping the nasty habit of referring to the GDR as "the Eastern Zone" as if it were still Soviet-occupied or a mere appendage to the FRG.[5] By the mid-seventies, furthermore, increasing numbers of the younger generation (under age thirty), in other words the "68ers," showed a pronounced tendency to accept the German division as a given fact rather than as a festering wound.[6] At the same time, the geographic

Democratic students (RCDS) would face off every June 17 against a strong left-wing minority and a vast, indifferent majority over this issue. Newspapers like *Die Welt* or *Bild* would pontificate and an occasional far-right periodical, such as *Deutsche Nationalzeitung*, would editorially call upon the government to take action.

3. In 1952 and 1954, when asked what was more important to them, "security from the Russians" or reunification, they typically opted for security (51% and 59%, respectively, vs. 33% and 27%). But they responded with obvious pain when asked in 1963 whether they considered the German division "an intolerable situation" (53%) or had "gradually gotten used to it" (32%). *Jahrbuch der öffentlichen Meinung* (Allensbach: Institut für Demoskopie), 1947–1955 vol., p. 315; 1958–1964 vol., p. 486; 1965–1967 vol., p. 389; and 1968–1973 vol., p. 506 (hereafter *JöM* with the years covered).

4. In 1953, 66% of West Germans still insisted that, one day, "Pomerania, Silesia, and East Prussia would again belong to Germany" and "not be lost forever" (11% thought they were lost). In 1951, 80% still said "we should not resign ourselves to the Oder-Neisse border" (vs. 8% yes). *JöM 1947–1955*, p. 313. See also *JöM 1958–1964*, pp. 482–483.

5. Whereas in 1966, 57% preferred "Eastern Zone" or "the Zone" to "GDR" (11%), in 1970 it was only 37% vs. 37%, respectively. By 1980, "GDR" had won out with 61% over 19% who probably belonged disproportionately to the older generations. Elisabeth Noelle-Neumann, ed., *The Germans: Public Opinion Polls 1967–1980*, rev. ed. (Westport, Conn.: Greenwood Press, 1981), p. 125.

6. In 1976, substantially higher percentages of respondents under age thirty agreed

flaw in the German sense of identity seemed to become transmuted into low national self-esteem, guilt feelings about Germany having started World War II, and a majority negative response to the very word "patriotism" (reaching even into the West German army). Among the young, the sense of *identité manquée* became so deep that it was doubtful whether a mere reunification of East and West Germany was capable of healing it.[7] We need to delve more deeply into German identity to understand the nature of this wound.

As luck would have it, *Der Spiegel* magazine commissioned one of its frequent EMNID surveys early in 1989, this time about German historical identity, a subject brought on by the recent rise of yet another neo-Nazi party, the Republicans (Reps). While it has declined again in the meantime, the Republican upsurge had generated widespread public discussion of the German past, in part because its smooth-talking leader, the former TV host Franz Schönhuber, began his political career with candid revelations about his Waffen-SS past in the war.[8] The Reps did well by luring away CDU/CSU votes in *Land* elections (Berlin, Hesse, Bavaria) and in the European elections of 1989, when they won 7.1% of the vote and six seats. Prominent among Republican leaders were CDU/CSU dissidents and sympathizers such as the "Stahlhelm faction," notable pillars of the academic New Right, and recruits from the NPD and other neofascist groups. All of these were partial to such populist themes as anti-immigrant and -refugee sentiment and a *Schlusstrich* (bottom line) with respect to reckoning with the German past, especially under some American-sponsored German "reeducation."[9]

The *Spiegel* poll picked up the *Schlusstrich* issue and asked all West German respondents to pick a value between 1 (definitely disagree) and

that "East and West Germany would never be reunited" (73% as compared to the average of 65%) and that "this was not so important" to the respondent (52% vs. 36%). Ibid., pp. 119 and 126. In 1967, the numbers who found the German division "intolerable" had already tumbled to 31%, while 54% had "gotten used to it." *JöM 1968–1973*, p. 505.

7. See Merkl, "Politico-Cultural Restraints on West German Foreign Policy: Sense of Trust, Identity, and Agency," *Comparative Political Studies* 3, no. 4 (1971), 443–467, esp. 450–453.

8. See also the review of Schönhuber's several books by Gordon Craig in the *New York Review of Books*, June 18, 1989. Schönhuber once had a television show that invited ordinary people to speak their minds on political and cultural matters. See also Glaus Leggewie, *Die Republikaner. Phantombild der Neuen Rechten* (Berlin: Rotbuch, 1989) and Kurt Hirsch and Hans Sarkowtiz, *Schönhuber, der Politiker und seine Kreise* (Frankfurt: Eichborn, 1989).

9. They also favor German neutrality between the power blocs, a "Europe of nations" rather than any further integration, law and order, and a populist environmentalism. Rep members and voters tend to be quite young, "postfascistic," and frequently from law enforcement, public service, and the working class.

6 (wholeheartedly agree) to the following statements. First: "We ought to put forth a final bottom line concerning our past—What happened among other nations was just as bad." Respondents from most parties voiced mild agreement with this sentence—except for Green supporters, who rejected it. Republican adherents, of course, agreed wholeheartedly, followed at a considerable distance by Christian Democrats. A second question brought almost identical results: "When foreigners are always talking about the past German guilt, this often reflects envy of the proficiency and well-being of the Germans." The responses were slightly less positive, barely above a neutral response. Still less positive, but with Christian Democrats on the mildly affirmative side (and Reps strongly so) was the response to the sentence "Many people here do not dare express their real opinion about the Jews." This time, all the other partisans mildly disagreed, possibly well aware that since the invasion of Lebanon in 1982 the German news media have frequently been critical of the policies of the Likud government in Israel. There was solid disagreement, except for Republican supporters, with several other statements, such as the alleged suppression of "national elements" in the FRG or that Germans ought to "look for a strong leader" and keep themselves "pure."[10] These, of course, are continuing preoccupations with the German past, another species of German *identité manquée* that happens to run counter to any assertive nationalism.

Inevitably, the goal of German reunification and other consequences of the lost war were made part of this last survey before the waters of revolution spilled across Eastern Europe and the GDR. The question "Should reunification remain a goal?" was juxtaposed to its having become a dead issue: 56% of West Germans (vs. 44%) said "it should remain a goal"—but this time there was no reality test. Some 66% of CDU/CSU supporters (vs. 34%) voiced their approval, a result topped only by the Reps (68%). SPD and FDP adherents were split down the middle—SPD 51% (vs. 48%) and FDP 45% (vs. 52%)—while the Greens presented the exact opposite of the CDU/CSU (34% for and 65% against). It is worth noting that these partisan alignments are very similar to what actually happened, once reunification took on reality and the campaign for control of a united Germany got under way. Only the SPD

10. Other questions elicited positive (47%), neutral (33%), or negative (18%) attitudes toward Jews living in the FRG and about whether national socialism had "only bad" (16%) "mostly bad" (38%), "good and bad" (43%), or "more good than bad" aspects (3%). Regarding Hitler as a historical figure on a ten-point scale, 36% gave him the worst (-5) and 27% the next to worst (-3 and -4) rating, while 11% were mildly negative, 12% undecided, and 14% scattered from $+1$ to $+5$. *Der Spiegel* 43, no. 15, Apr. 10, 1989, pp. 150–160.

voters seemed somewhat more committed to German unity as a goal than they were later under Oskar Lafontaine's leadership in the campaign. And the FDP, too, took a far more positive stance during the campaign, under the leadership of Count Otto Lambsdorff and Hans-Dietrich Genscher, than party supporters had in mind at this time. The reality test, by the way, would come in October 1989, just before the fall of the Wall, when a telephone poll claimed that only 24% of West German respondents expected to see reunification "within the next ten years." Two-thirds expressed their disbelief at this point.[11]

The earlier *Spiegel* poll raised another issue, the Oder-Neisse line, which became very salient for a few weeks toward the end of 1989: "Should we resign ourselves to the present German-Polish border, the Oder-Neisse line, or should we not accept it?" Among West Germans, 65% (vs. 34%) were ready to accept it, including only 55% of CDU/CSU voters but 72% of SPD supporters, 74% of FDP adherents, and 81% of the Greens. Only the Reps had a majority against acceptance (62%), which was probably the chief reason Kohl made a play for their votes the following December. Finally, there were two related questions: one involving President Weizsäcker's forthcoming visit to Warsaw on the fiftieth anniversary (Sept. 1, 1939) of the German invasion of Poland; the other a previous visit there by Chancellor Brandt (1970), who had knelt in front of the Warsaw Ghetto memorial to pay homage to the thousands of Jews slaughtered there by German troops. Weizsäcker's visit enjoyed majority support (58% vs. 41%) from all but the Reps. Brandt's (at the time) controversial gesture of atonement also did well (57% vs. 42%). However, the CDU/CSU supporters, while supporting their (CDU) federal president, considered Brandt's 1970 gesture "exaggerated" (56% vs. 43% who considered it "appropriate"). The SPD and FDP, who had supported Brandt's *Ostpolitik* in the early seventies, both gave it large majorities—SPD 69% (vs. 30%) and FDP 66% (vs. 34%)—as an "appropriate" signal. They also endorsed the Weizsäcker visit, albeit with more modest majorities of 62% and 59%, respectively. The Greens topped them on both occasions, three to one, while the Reps split one to three the other way, their exact mirror image.[12]

11. The poll was conducted by the public opinion institute Sample. See Wolfgang Bergsdorf, "Wer will die deutsche Einheit?" *Die politische Meinung* 35, no. 248 (Jan./Feb. 1990), 13–19.

12. *Der Spiegel* 43, no. 15, Apr. 10, 1989, pp. 150–160. The survey also asked respondents to rate on a six-point scale their "pride in being German." At the highest level, 27% of West Germans made their mark, as compared to 49% of the Reps and 8% of Green supporters. At level two, it was another 28% of West Germans against 34% Reps and 13% Greens. At level three, another 24% of West Germans contrasted with 7% Reps and 21% of Green adherents, the majority of whom preferred the lower values (4–6). Cf.

The West German Government Response

The fall of the Berlin Wall precipitated both the cautious ten-point program of Chancellor Kohl and major changes in West German public opinion. Kohl's proposal of November 28, 1989, included a common governing committee for political consultation and coordination, joint topical committees, and a common assembly, all to be located in Berlin. It represented the widely shared view that, given the major international constraints, the German question could be addressed only on the basis of gradual integration between two separate states. Kohl picked up the proposed "contractual community" of the new Modrow government (November 13) and chose to ignore the Monday demonstrators in Leipzig who on November 22 began to shout for the first time, "We are *one* people" instead of "*We* are the people." He proposed increasing cooperation on all levels between the two German states, with the goal of achieving a "confederative arrangement" (which would protect East German sovereignty and the SED dictatorship), and saw German governmental unity as a distant vision. The ten-point program sought to reassure the Soviets as well as the Western allies that the German initiative would be based on the extant German states and would be placed into the multilateral contexts of European and Atlantic cooperation, East-West disarmament, and the Conference of Security and Cooperation in Europe (the Helsinki Group).

As in twenty years of *Ostpolitik* designed to accommodate Soviet and East European security concerns, Kohl's proposal combined the effort to promote and protect the human and political rights of East Germans with an emphasis on détente and recognition of the legitimacy of all the East European regimes involved. In spite of the cautious formulations, however, there was a chorus of protest from every Western capital and the news media, complaining that the allies had not been consulted, another sign of the extent to which the FRG and the united Germany to emerge were universally understood to be products of the international constellation of forces and not just of what the Germans may have wanted

---

Institut für praxisorientierte Sozialforschung (IPOS), *Einstellungen zu aktuellen Fragen der Innenpolitik* (1989), p. 141, a poll of April/May 1989 which elicited this expression of pride in being German from 69.9% of West Germans (vs. 12.1% who were not proud). but there was also a striking range among age groups: respondents sixty years and older were proudest (85% vs. 4.3%); those over thirty expressed national pride above the two-thirds level; of those under twenty-five years, on the other hand, only 42.4% expressed pride (vs. 29.5%) and 28.1% said they "did not know," the highest number of indifferents for any group.

for themselves (see Chapters Seven and Eight).[13] Soviet Foreign Minister Eduard Shevardnadze was quoted as saying: "No European neighbor will fail to see this as a threat to security." Even Kohl's vice-chancellor and foreign secretary, Genscher (FDP), said he had not been consulted. There were also many personal attacks upon Kohl in the news media, depicting him as a bumbling provincial politician "plotting to become the first all-German chancellor."

Other West German parties and politicians reacted to the momentous fall of the Wall with stunned silence, obviously surprised by this turn of events and quite unprepared to see in it the great opportunity after forty years that it turned out to be. Only Willy Brandt, the former Berlin lord mayor and West German chancellor, said, while witnessing the mass enthusiasm on November 10 in Berlin, that "what belongs together will once more grow into one." The West German public was polled in November 1989 by the Institut für Demoskopie, which found perceptions of the reality of reunification substantially changed, though still far from what, in retrospect, we would have expected. Instead of the 3% in 1987 who "expected to see it in the foreseeable future," there were now 30% who believed "it would occur within their lifetime" while 46% still did not think so,[14] evidently not attributing the same significance to the momentous events in East Germany and East Berlin as the chancellery in Bonn. Obviously no one would have guessed that actual unity was but a year away. The modest response to the reality test still fell far short of the latest measurement of the desire for reunification, in another telephone poll by the Sample Institute in September 1989, when 88% expressed their preference for unification and 70% even agreed they would tend "to vote for politicians who actively promoted reunification."[15]

It should be mentioned also that, at this crucial moment, East German majorities, according to the first (and probably inaccurate) polls of EMNID and the Mannheim Institute election researchers, still opposed reunification in principle, probably preferring "socialism with a human face" in the GDR to union with a capitalist West Germany. At this point,

13. See also Karl Kaiser, "Germany's Unification," *Foreign Affairs* 70, no. 1 (1991), 179–205. The West German chancellor worked out detailed plans to address the complicated international constraints with bilateral and multilateral initiatives.

14. Among young respondents, 40% expected it to occur within their lifetime. A December 1986 poll by the same institute had found only 7% who expected reunification in their lifetime and 74% who did not. The 3% are cited from another poll (see n. 1, above). See Bergsdorf, "Wer will die deutsche Einheit?" p. 15.

15. The German wording was "*sich nachdrücklich für die Wiedervereinigung einsetzen*" (ibid). In 1986, 66% had even called reunification "an illusion" (*Wunschvorstellung*). See also Michael Mertes and Norbert J. Prill, "Die deutsche Einheit," *Die politische Meinung* 47, no. 2 (Nov./Dec. 1989), 4–15.

in fact, a group of thirty East German intellectuals and writers headed by Stefan Heym drew up a manifesto for a socialist alternative to the FRG.[16] Heym accused Kohl of trying to "take over the GDR," and the manifesto even bore the signature of Egon Krenz. A dissident SED group, the United Left, called for an antiunification demonstration in East Berlin. The democratic opposition in the GDR felt upstaged by the sudden appearance of unification slogans and flags in the Monday-night Leipzig demonstrations—"*Deutschland, einig Vaterland*"—and the East German SDP (SPD) leader Stephan Hilsberg refused a public appearance together with Willy Brandt and U. S. Senator Ted Kennedy for fear of giving the wrong signal.

Chancellor Kohl and his advisers explained the reasoning behind his ten-point proposal before the CDU Presidium[17] and the Bundestag. He sketched out the vision of a united Germany in a "European peace order" with the appropriate assurances to everyone. He referred to Modrow's "contractual community" but was really describing a confederation as a step on the way to federal union. Kohl insisted that the Bundestag should either "show national responsibility and give the Germans a vision of a united future" or dampen "the enthusiasm for unification in the country." The SPD at first reacted with confusion, as Johannes Rau, its 1987 chancellor candidate, and his 1983 predecessor, Hans-Jochen Vogel, expressed the old ingrained social democratic fears of a wave of nationalism that would come and pass them by: "We do not want to be the last to say no to unification." A group consisting of the 1990 chancellor candidate, Lafontaine,[18] "Red Heidi" Wieczoreck-Zeul, Norbert Gansel,

16. For the text, see *Der Spiegel* 43, no. 49, Dec. 4, 1989, p. 230. In a poll of early December 1989 (with a sample skewed in favor of the northern GDR and SED members), a majority of 71.4% expressed its preference for a sovereign GDR, while only 26.8% wanted reunification. Forschungsgruppe Wahlen, Mannheim (FGW), *Meinungen der Bürger der DDR. Dezember 1989*, p. 119.

17. According to *Der Spiegel*, he was worried that the SPD, notably Willy Brandt, might beat him to the punch in advocating unity, but was also concerned about the Republican challenge from the right. Hence he thought it inopportune to give up the Oder-Neisse territories and thus hand his right-wing competitors a potent appeal to the refugees from there. Staff members explained that Kohl was quite aware of the danger of reinforcing the German division and GDR legitimacy (at a moment of great instability in the East) with "confederative arrangements" but that he felt he needed to calm the apprehensions of the Soviets, of GDR officialdom, and of the democratic opposition in East Germany. At the EC summit in mid-November, Kohl had been careful to avoid the word "reunification" and had talked instead of the self-determination of the GDR.

18. Lafontaine called the ten points "a feuilletonistically inflated collection (*Sammelsurium*) of commonplace generalities supplemented with demands that *we* made long ago." He also warned against "bleeding the social security system of both, the GDR and the FRG," and suggested instead to retain a separate GDR citizenship so that its citizens would

and Horst Ehmke, however, wanted to make SPD consent contingent on Bonn's recognition of the Oder-Neisse line, on a ban on the modernization and stationing of short-range missiles in Germany, and on continued aid to Berlin. In the end, the SPD, under the leadership of Vogel and Karsten Voigt, endorsed the ten points; even the GDR's Modrow and Krenz believed them worthy of further discussion.[19] Federal President Weizsäcker (CDU) expressed his support for "a confederacy under a common European roof" but drew the line at a closer, federal union. Kohl's carefully calculated opening gambit seemed to be well designed to capture domestic endorsements before tackling the forbidding international obstacles (see Chapters Seven and Eight) one by one.

By this time, the SPD also began to show initiative beyond its self-imposed regard for the free will of East German government and opposition groups. There were plans to introduce an "Emergency Economic Program" for the GDR at the impending SPD meeting on December 18–20, a program that was to include aid for the development of East German infrastructure, environmental protection, transport, and tourism. The convention approved a new comprehensive SPD program, the first since the Bad Godesberg program of 1959, and containing a declaration of unification policy that echoed many of Kohl's points. This declaration called for a "speedy confederation," following Modrow's "contractual community" and without lifting the two countries' membership in NATO and the Warsaw Pact. As Vogel pointed out, a "step-by-step" demilitarization of both blocs and drastic disarmament of conventional and nuclear weapons would have to precede German unity. The designated chancellor candidate Oskar Lafontaine also intended to submit an "equalization of burdens" program—similar to the FRG's *Lastenausgleich*, which in the fifties had taxed native West Germans for the benefit of ethnic German refugees—in order to give an incentive to East

---

not be able to claim West German pension rights or take West German or West Berlin jobs while living in the East.

19. In an interview with *Der Spiegel*, Modrow interpreted his "contractual community" as a preconfederate phase and pointed to the discussions in the fifties of a possible East-West German confederacy. Back in those days, however, confederation had been a slogan to counter Western insistence on free democratic elections in the GDR which were sure to turn the SED out of power. Confederation then would not only have protected the communist dictatorship from its own people, but would have been based on the principle of sovereign equality of the two unequal states within a common confederate assembly. See the Ulbricht quote in *Der Spiegel* 43, no. 51, Dec. 18, 1989, p. 16. The fifties' proposal, by the GDR, also had been a part of the Soviet scheme to prevent the FRG from rearmament within the NATO alliance. Modrow now rejected a unification beyond confederation and refused to answer questions about the long years, until 1974, when the GDR still supported German unification. *Der Spiegel* 43, no. 49, Dec. 4, 1989, p. 34ff.

Germans to stay in the GDR. This new equalization plan had been developed by H. V. Pfeiffer and would annually have raised 15 billion marks in the FRG for a period of ten years.

The government developed a program to give each East German refugee 1,000 marks on top of social assistance and unemployment benefits for up to twelve months with the opening of the borders, but this measure was in jeopardy even before its official commencement on January 1. East Germans now could claim their money, return to the GDR, and then go again to claim more. West German working-class and lower-middle-class complaints about the alleged greed of East German refugees obviously began to color some of the SPD arguments, especially those of Lafontaine, who hoped to take advantage of the popular resentments toward East German and other refugees. The opposition candidate wanted to stop the onrushing flood of refugees (350,000 by January 1990) or at least to protect West German jobs and scarce housing—against considerable resistance on the part of SPD liberals such as Vogel, Björn Engholm, and Erhard Eppler. Lafontaine, however, could point to the public opinion polls: 81% of West German respondents expected the East German exodus to aggravate the existing housing shortages, and 57% believed it would add substantially to unemployment.[20]

By mid-December, as *Der Spiegel* editor Rudolf Augstein was still fatuously wondering at which point West German opinion about the state of the GDR might be considered "intolerable intervention into the affairs of the people of the GDR," Kohl and Genscher were busily trying to contain the rising distrust of Germany's neighbors and the victors of World War II, with significant assistance from Willy Brandt, who used his authority as a senior international statesman to criticize the reactions of Mitterrand, Thatcher, and Italian Prime Minister Giulio Andreotti (a Christian Democrat). In the face of continuing unrest, Modrow was quoted as threatening Soviet or East German army (NVA) intervention if demonstrators in the GDR tried to unify the country. Kohl and his team indeed feared such an escalation now, although the citizen committees of the GDR were preoccupied everywhere with storming the Stasi offices and demanding action in the direction of economic union. One of the democratic opposition groups, Democracy Now, proposed three simple steps: the election of a national assembly, a plebiscite on confederation, and one on a federal union. Conservative West German deputy Alfred Dregger, of the right-wing CDU Stahlhelm faction, opined: "We don't ask anymore whether, but when and how." Others were far more cautious and wary of alarming Germany's European neighbors. Genscher man-

20. *Der Spiegel* 43, no. 47, Nov. 20, 1989, pp. 16–17.

aged to inject the word "stability" twenty-one times into a single speech in Saarbrücken. President Weizsäcker, in an oblique slap at Kohl during an interview on GDR teleivsion, called for proceeding "with circumspection." It was under these circumstances, on December 19, that Kohl met with Modrow in Dresden to arrange for negotiations on the details of the "contractual community" suggested by the new East German premier.[21] No one expected the GDR government to break down as soon as it did. The implicit or explicit assumption about the GDR's future was instead that it might have democratic elections in May 1990, perhaps draw up a new constitution for itself after that and, as a democratically legitimated state, hold a plebiscite in late 1990 about whether to join an all-German confederation which would guarantee its sovereign equality with and immunity from the larger, West German state.

The Shift to Unification

Two crucial changes in public opinion West and East occurred almost simultaneously during January while the great flood of East German refugees continued. First, while the political leadership in government and opposition prepared plans of action during the crucial months of December and January, West German support for the East German exodus began to plummet. The two-thirds of respondents who had welcomed the refugees up to the fall of the Wall—74% also endorsed aid to the GDR *so long as it did not increase West German taxes*—dropped to one-fourth in January, according to data from the Mannheim Institute of Electoral Research, and fell to one-tenth by April 1990. At the same time, one-half and more of the West German respondents began to

21. It is worth noting also that Kohl's popularity in the GDR at about the time of this first meeting with Modrow stood at a modest 31% (57% took a dim view of him and his politics), far behind Berlin Mayor Walter Momper and President Weizsäcker (both 83%), Brandt (78%), Genscher (69%), and Vogel (68%)—and even behind Bohley (45%), Rainer Eppelmann (35%), and de Maizière (33%), not to mention Modrow himself (91%). *Der Spiegel* 43, no. 51, Dec. 18, 1989, pp. 86–89. On the other hand, ordinary workers in the GDR often were as distrustful of the ministers and chic intellectuals and artists of the democratic opposition as they were of the SED/PDS functionaries and bureaucrats of their state. They were more inclined toward reunification than they were toward finding ways to protect the sovereignty of the GDR. Ibid., p. 53ff. See also, in the early December poll, the very low opinion that East Germans then had of the West German CDU/CSU and of Kohl—especially as compared to the West German SPD: 79.6% of the East German respondents would have preferred an SPD government in Bonn over the existing CDU/CSU government, which only 13.8% favored. FGW, *Meinungen*, pp. 128, 131–135, 139.

clamor for a reduction or elimination of the benefits that seemed to attract the East Germans. The desire to "keep 'em there," of course, might still support Western programs to shore up the East German economy and society and speed up economic union before political unification.

The second crucial turning point came in January with the collapse of both the East German economy and the last props of the communist regime, especially the Stasi.[22] While West and East German intellectuals were ponderously debating in the news media whether and in what form German unification should occur, if at all, a frightened Modrow government sought counsel with Moscow and emerged with what amounted to its own death sentence. Already under siege from Kohl's shuttle diplomacy, a reluctant Gorbachev agreed "in principle" to German unification (January 30) while emphasizing the many international roadblocks still ahead.[23]

Upon his return from Moscow, Modrow, among other things, also reported that Gorbachev would like to see an international referendum held among Germany's European neighbors and World War II antagonists on the subject of German unification, but Chancellor Kohl immediately rejected the idea. The Germans, first of all, ought to vote on their own future; then German politicians could negotiate with other European powers. The date of the first free elections in the GDR had already been advanced from May 6 to March 18, and parties in both East and West were straining every organizational muscle in the pending election campaign for the Volkskammer. Once that crucial election had confirmed the East German intent to form a union, there would be a legitimate GDR government capable of deciding and implementing all further steps in the direction of unity. A Leipzig polling institute had now learned, in early February, that 75% of East Germans were in favor of unification—a far cry from December, when Premier Modrow had claimed that 80% were against. Even the PDS was now for reunification, if in somewhat different form from that envisaged by everyone else.[24]

22. See the account of East German disintegration by Ilse Spittmann, "Deutschland einig Vaterland," in *Deutschland Archiv* 23, no. 2 (Feb. 1990), 187–190. For details of Western economic plans, see Chapter Six, below.

23. After persistent efforts at the Round Table meetings to gain support from the democratic opposition groups, Modrow finally (January 29) persuaded them to form a coalition under the name "Government of National Responsibility." Uwe Thaysen, "Der runde Tisch. Oder: Wer war das Volk?" *Zeitschrift für Parlamentsfragen* 21, no. 1 (Apr. 1990), 99–100.

24. As reported just before the March elections, the percentage of GDR respondents "very much for unification" rose from 16% in November to 40% in January/February and 44% in February/March. Those "rather for" unification increased from 32% to 39% and 40%, respectively. Respondents "very much against" or "rather against" dropped from

A Plebiscite for Kohl's FRG?

The March 1990 elections were intrinsically bound up with unification, even though there were still predictions placing the actual event far into the future. The East German ADN news agency, for example, expected unification to be at least two to three years away. A former U.S. ambassador to Germany, George McGee, spoke of five years and everyone liked to quote an old prediction by ex-Chancellor Schmidt that it would happen "only in the next century, or millennium." The East German parties campaigning for the March elections arrayed themselves on the subject as follows. The CDU, DA, and DSU (Alliance for Germany) were for unity as quickly as possible and in accord with article 23 of the Basic Law.[25] The LDP/FDP wanted unity at "a moderate pace." These parties all enjoyed the direct support and advice of the West German government CDU/CSU and FDP. The East German SPD (formerly SDP) was for "federal unity" in the framework of European unification and according to article 146 of the Basic Law which called for a national constitutional convention. The democratic opposition in Bündnis 90 (New Forum, Democracy Now, and the Initiative for Peace and Human Rights) preferred unification, though "not as fast as possible but as good as possible" and "not a mere annexation" of the GDR. The PDS proposed a "gradual transition to a confederacy" within the framework of European unification. Smaller groups wanted a confederacy with "reforms on both sides" or a sovereign GDR in cooperation with the FRG. The unexpected landslide[26] of the Alliance for Germany clearly determined the direction of unification from here on.

There was no lack of last-minute fumbles and uncertainties on the way to the crucial decision. It was rather unlikely, for example, that the old "bloc parties" of the GDR would live down their reputation as toadies of the SED dictatorship and win out over such groupings as the SPD and Bündnis 90, which had earned their spurs in the struggle against the regime. Last-minute leaks from Stasi files stopped several candidacies and cast a most undignified shadow over others, including that of de Maizière. Chancellor Kohl, as a critical press never tired of pointing out, had put the cause of unification into an embarrassing bind with his past

---

52% in November to 21% and 16%, respectively, according to the Leipzig-based institute. *Der Spiegel* 44, no. 11, March 12, 1990, p. 40.

25. This article of the FRG Constitution, or Basic Law, permits accession by the new *Länder* and would not have involved further changes in the Constitution. See Chapter Five, below.

26. As late as a week before the election, the polls of the Leipzig Institute for Youth Research still gave the Alliance only 30% and the SPD, which had polled 54% earlier, a plurality of 34%. *Der Spiegel* 44, no. 11, March 12, 1990, p. 15.

public vacillation over the Oder-Neisse line with Poland.[27] And, finally, the chancellor had flip-flopped on the question of the best constitutional basis for union, having still spoken of a constitutional assembly and an entirely new constitution not too long ago.[28]

In the GDR, the elections were approached by the voters with considerable fear and trepidation about the imminent loss of identity (albeit tempered by hope for economic salvation) of the GDR. Even for the election researchers, the lack of the usual guideposts of past electoral behavior made this a difficult election to predict from polls: not only were there no previous democratic election results but, despite the very high turnout (93%), large numbers of voters were still undecided in the last weeks. The link to pre-Hitler partisan alignments was too far away—six decades—to have survived. There were hardly any clues from socioeconomic groupings, well-established party programs, or personalities. The old leadership, including the bloc parties, was likely to be associated with the frauds and crimes of the dictatorship, and the new leaders of the democratic opposition were neither well known nor all that popular among the working-class population.[29] Even the principal contenders, such as the Alliance for Germany or Bündnis 90, were not quite consolidated enough to give the voters clear choices.[30] The issues, too, pressing problems to be solved, were in limbo between the disintegrating authoritarianism and paternalism of the old regime and the democratic self-government about to emerge in the midst of crisis and confusion. In this volatile scene, it appears, the role of the West German parties was inflated far beyond their considerable actual assistance and participation in the GDR campaign. After all, with West German television accessible for decades, the East German voters knew better what the Western CDU/CSU, the FDP, the SPD, and even the Greens and their respective leaders stood for than they knew what their own parties and noncommunist leaders represented.[31] Thus

27. Polish Prime Minister Mazowiecki reportedly was not even satisfied with the Bundestag resolution on this subject and demanded a role in the "two-plus-four" group of World War II victors in order to satisfy Polish security concerns. *Der Spiegel* 44, no. 11, March 12, 1990, pp. 171–173.

28. As several papers pointed out, the choice of article 23 would give the FRG and its incumbent chancellor continuity—the GDR would disappear—whereas a constituent assembly would end the FRG as well and break the continuity of Kohl's tenure.

29. For a discussion of these problems of interpretation, see especially Dieter Roth, "Die Wahlen zur Volkskammer in der DDR," *Politische Vierteljahresschrift* 31, no. 3 (1990), 369–393, and Wolfgang Gibowski, "Demokratischer Neubeginn in der DDR. Dokumentation und Analyse der Wahl vom 18. März 1990," *Zeitschrift für Parlamentsfragen* 21, no. 1 (May 1990), 5–22.

30. See Ferdinand Müller-Rommel, "The Beginning of a New Germany? The GDR Elections of 18 March 1990," *West European Politics* 14, no. 1 (Jan. 1991), 139–144, where the electoral law and campaign financing are discussed as well.

31. West German leaders such as Genscher, Lafontaine, Vogel, Kohl, and Lambsdorff were far more popular in the GDR than in the FRG. Considerable mystery still surrounds the high popularity of Hans Modrow, who had destroyed Stasi files and attempted to save

the voters' image of their own CDU bloc party was probably strongly colored by Kohl, Weizsäcker, and other Western politicians—in the case of the FDP's Genscher this is even more obvious—and by confidence in what they would do. Since the great underlying issue on everybody's mind was unification as the key to a freer and better life in the future, the elections were bound to be a plebiscite on unification—though, naturally, one with options as to the governing personnel and the pace.

The Mannheim Institute pinpointed the importance of this issue in its survey on the pace of unification, done just before the elections which were won so clearly by the Alliance (CDU, DA, DSU) with 48% of the vote (Table 4.1).[32] As we see, not only was there overwhelming support (91%) for unification, but the parties' supporters are in neat alignment on this issue—from the Alliance (96.6%) to PDS voters (77.3%). As for the pace of unification, even though a majority wanted the GDR to take its time, again support for the Alliance and for proceeding with all deliberate speed are highly correlated: 75% of those in a hurry voted for the Alliance; only 15% voted SPD and none for the PDS.[33] Some 92% of East German voters

Table 4.1. A GDR Plebiscite on Unification and Its Pace (in %)

	Alliance Supporters	Liberals	SPD	Bündnis 90	Greens/ Women	PDS	Total
Unification							
For	96.6	96.9	93.6	88.3	84.2	77.3	91.0
Against or indifferent	2.9	1.9	6.4	8.7	15.8	21.5	8.4
Pace*							
Fast	57.5	36.0	26.0	13.2	6.6	2.2	35.3
Take time	39.0	69.9	67.4	75.1	77.6	75.1	55.5

SOURCES: Dieter Roth, "Die Wahlen zur Volkskammer in der DDR," *Politische Viertel-jahresschrift* 31, no. 3 (1990), 383; Forschungsgruppe Wahlen, *Umfrage DDR* (March 1990). For slightly different figures, see Wolfgang Gibowski, "Demokratischer Neubeginn in der DDR. Dokumentation und Analyse der Wahl vom 18. März 1990," *Zeitschrift für Parlamentsfragen* 21, no. 1 (May 1990), 18.

*Includes only respondents who were for unification.

---

the Stasi itself while he was in command: clearly that popularity did not translate into votes for the PDS/SED.

32. If the Alliance picked up about 20% from a week earlier, when the SPD was still expected to receive 54% of the popular vote, there was a second dramatic swing in the polls following the March elections while the public debate was raging over the exchange rate between Eastern and Western marks. Again, nearly 20% of the Alliance supporters shifted to the SPD and then back again.

33. See also the tables on whether respondents expected unification to bring more

welcomed the prospect of a currency union, including as many as 98% of the Alliance voters and 69% of the PDS voters. Most revealing, 30.2% of Alliance voters expected advantages to accrue from unification even in the short run, as compared to only 7% of PDS voters and 12.6% of Bündnis 90 voters. Still, 16% of Alliance voters expected disadvantages, as did 54.3% of the PDS and 38.6% of the Bündnis 90 voters. Nearly all of the voters said they expected both advantages and disadvantages in the short run. The anticipated long-run advantages of union were much higher (58.4%) and more evenly distributed across partisan voter groups.[34]

The Alliance was also credited with a significant edge (34.7%) in having the competence to solve the problems of the GDR following the elections—a grand coalition of the Alliance with the SPD would have added another 28.8%. Since these two and the Liberals did form just such a coalition in the end, under de Maizière (CDU), the combined popular vote of confidence added up to 90.3%. There can be little doubt that this competence was popularly expected to be assisted by the proven sister parties of West Germany.[35] As Wolfgang Gibowski of the Mannheim Institute wrote, "The election result in the GDR was a plebiscite for the path of unification proposed by Chancellor Kohl and the CDU/CSU of the Federal Republic." He projected from this the likelihood that, at least for a while, the CDU would continue to dominate elections in East Germany.[36]

A New Identity for East Germany

There were more visible signs that the sense of identity of the East Germans had faded. The pollsters had asked, before the elections, whether the respondents subjectively felt themselves to be "GDR citizens" or

advantages or disadvantages, over the short run or the long run, in Roth, "Die Wahlen zur Volkskammer," pp. 383–385. In the long run, everyone expected more advantages—even the PDS voters. Only 4.3% of the respondents expected more disadvantages in the long run, as compared to 27% for the short run.

34. See Gibowski, "Demokratischer Neubeginn," pp. 19–20. The same poll also asked who should become minister president of the new GDR government. Only 57.5% had any answer to this question and 35.5% picked Modrow, a sad demonstration of the legacy of authoritarianism.

35. Only a handful of diehards denied that the Alliance and SPD, together or separately, possessed such a competence: 21.2% of the PDS adherents, 10% of the Greens/Women, and 16.7% of Bündnis 90. Roth, "Die Wahlen zur Volkskammer," pp. 384–385.

36. See Gibowski, "Demokratischer Neubeginn," pp. 21–22. It should be noted also that in spite of the fact that twenty-three parties graced the ballot, a party system much closer to the West German one had actually emerged.

"Germans." The answer of the majority was "Germans," 60.8% to 37.4%, and again the supporters of those parties analogous to the parties of the FRG (Alliance, Liberals, and SPD) shared or outdid (Alliance 78.2%) this result, while the PDS had the exact opposite showing: 83.3% of its followers considered themselves "GDR citizens." Already in December, when asked whether they thought the GDR was being "taken over" (vereinnahmt) by an economically superior FRG, 44.9% of East Germans agreed, while only a bare majority of 52.1% rejected such an interpretation. A second set of questions inquired whether respondents thought "a great deal of," "set some store by," or "thought hardly anything or nothing of" socialism, which presumably was the old identity of the GDR: 30.1% responded "a great deal" (in March 25.6%, including 72.4% of the PDS voters); 41.2% "set some store by" socialism (in March only 28.9%, including 17.1% of PDS supporters and pluralities of around 40% for the other, smaller groups); 27.9% thought "hardly anything or nothing" of socialism (in March 45.2%, including 63.6% of the Alliance and 55.4% of the Liberal adherents). We could say that, in the subjective feelings of GDR citizens, nearly half of the old identity, GDR citizenship and socialism, were gone. Finally, the respondents were also asked what they thought of "democracy, as it prevails in the FRG": 51.4% held democracy in "high esteem," including nearly 70% of the Alliance supporters and 62.5% of the Liberals, but only 17.4% of the PDS; 39.3% had "some respect" for it, including majorities of Bündnis 90 (54.8%),[37] the PDS (53.3%), and the Greens/Women (74.1%). Only 7.9% thought "little or nothing" of democracy, including 29.1% among the PDS communists.[38]

There was also a pointed question as to whether respondents liked the appearance of FRG politicians in the GDR campaign: 55.1% said yes, including three-fourths each of the adherents of the Alliance and the Liberals, the worst offenders in this respect. Only 44% thought it was a bad thing, including 88.5% of PDS and Greens/Women followers, but also two-thirds of Bündnis 90.[39] All of this is overwhelming evidence that

37. That Bündnis 90, the democratic opposition, contributed only 40.7% to the category of "high esteem" is probably more reflective of a critical attitude toward capitalist West Germany than toward democracy.

38. Of those that regarded this whole business as a "takeover," one out of four (and one-third of those over age sixty) regarded such a takeover as a good thing. Thinking highly or rather highly of socialism had surprisingly little effect on whether or not East Germans spoke of a "takeover," but it correlated strongly with the expectation that the GDR would retain its sovereignty or that it would enter a confederate union with the FRG, not a complete one. FGW, Meinungen, pp. 1, 122–123, 126. In German the categories for both socialism and democracy are simply labeled "Halten Sie 1) sehr viel, viel," 2) "wenig," or 3) "kaum, gar nichts von . . . ?"

39. The SPD followers were evenly split, which may indicate resentment against the

the East Germans at this point in time had already made the great mental move into a united Germany, albeit against some bitter rearguard sentiments on the part of the PDS, the Greens/Women, and Bündnis 90.

A sidelight on the same syndrome of East Germans imagining themselves already in a (West German–dominated) united Germany was provided also by the question, in May 1990, concerning which of the West German parties the East Germans liked best: the result was 47% SPD, only 36% CDU and CSU, 10% FDP, and 3.5% Greens. For lack of choice, the PDS followers must all have designated the SPD as their second-best choice, which it may well become once the PDS fails to surmount the "5% minimum" hurdle of the electoral law likely to prevail after unification. In May, at any rate, East Germans were preoccupied with the overwhelming economic problems in their agricultural sector and with their general competitiveness in the European Community. The GDR local elections on May 6, consequently, gave the Farmers' party (DBD) a respectable 3.7% of the popular vote while the CDU dropped from 40.8% in the March elections to 34.4%, still a plurality of the vote. Soon the DBD, DA, and DSU were to merge with the CDU. One West German television commentator exulted that only now could democracy be regarded as having arrived in the GDR's local communities, where SED mayors and city council members had been holding forth since the fraudulent elections of the previous year.

Hesitating in Sight of the Goal

Once the basic decision had been made to unify with all deliberate speed, and the currency and economic union had been agreed upon and scheduled (see Chapter Six), there was a noticeable slowdown and stocktaking in the Kohl administration. Not only was the condition of GDR society and economy so much worse than had been realized up to the March elections, but even such objects of earlier admiration as the East German system of egalitarian education, public health, and universally available child care were found to be disasters.[40] The resistance to unification

likes of Willy Brandt, Lafontaine, and other Western SPD visitors. Roth, "Die Wahlen zur Volkskammer," pp. 388–389.

40. The physical plant and operating equipment of schools, universities, and hospitals were shamefully broken down, obsolete, and neglected; much of the staff had fled or was politically implicated. Even the network of kindergartens and child care centers—*Krippen, Horte, Kindergärten*, 1.2 million places for preschoolers—was in a desolate condition. See *Der Spiegel* 44, no. 12, March 19, 1990, pp. 20–57.

measures, both from outside and inside Germany, especially in the FRG, was also enough to give anyone pause. Further progress along the road to unity obviously required a great deal of flexibility and a willingness to accommodate the fears and insecurities of East Germans as well as the partisan squabbles about unification-related subjects in the FRG, where the opposition was already gearing up for the great all-German electoral contest of December. It would be a big mistake to overlook the partisan animus that colored so much of the internal criticism of Kohl's and Genscher's policies of unification—for example, the criticism of the particulars of the First State Treaty (a.k.a. Currency, Economic, and Social Unity Treaty) that took effect on July 1, 1990.[41] Even within the CDU/CSU, it was a necessity for East German CDU leaders every now and then to assert themselves against Kohl's policies so as to avoid the embarrassment of appearing now to be a "bloc party" connected to the West German Christian Democratic leadership, as it had once been connected to the SED dictatorship.

While the government paused to take a deep breath in its pursuit of unification, a mood of uneasiness and hesitation permeated public responses as well. A public opinion poll in May, after the details of the currency union had become public knowledge, asked West German adults if they were "prepared to bear personal financial sacrifices for German unification." Only 28% said yes, whereas in March there had still been a positive majority response of 61%. Now 58% insisted that the Bonn government had, since the opening of the borders, "put the emphasis of its work too much on the GDR and thereby neglected policies for the benefit of the West Germans." Evidently well aware that billions would have to be invested for GDR aid, overwhelming majorities of West Germans rejected financing this from increased income taxes (79% against) or value-added taxes (80% against).[42] Fortunately, this did not come as a surprise to the East Germans, of whom two-thirds (66%) already knew that they could not expect a willingness for financial sacrifice from their West German countrymen. West German sentiments of this kind have long been expressed against ethnic German and other refugees and foreign workers; when in concentrated form, they have been

41. For an account of the attempt of the opposition chancellor candidate, Lafontaine, to make the currency union an issue, see *Der Spiegel* 44, no. 22, May 28, 1990, pp. 21–31.

42. The choices before them included taxing higher incomes or businesses—they split down the middle on these options—cutting defense expenditures, or eliminating the subsidies to Berlin and zonal border areas (along the former Iron Curtain). Only these last two choices proved acceptable. See the *Spiegel*/EMNID poll results in *Der Spiegel* 44, no. 22, May 28, 1990, pp. 34–44, and Chapter Six, below.

called *"Wohlstandspatriotismus"* (patriotism of prosperity) and have
been fuel for radical right-wing movements.

West German respondents also expressed rising fears about the stability of their currency, a fear implicitly related to their fear of jeopardizing
the right social order and personal security. Probably in response to the
anticipated drain on the deutschmark, majorities expressed this concern,
beginning in March (52% vs. 47%) and rising to a peak in April (60%
vs. 39%) and May (52% vs. 41%). The East Germans, at the same time,
had no such fears: 80% (vs. 19%) believed in the stability of the West
German mark, and 68% expressed satisfaction with the promised exchange rate for their savings accounts, come July. The satisfaction was
particularly high among CDU supporters (87%) and among respondents
under forty-five years of age. It was no surprise that, by May, the
preference for unification was much higher in the GDR (94%, including
84% of PDS supporters) than in West Germany (76%, but only 51% of
the Reps and 58% of the Greens). Only among East Germans under age
thirty was the appreciation of the importance of unification a little
lower—in fact, only half as high as among seniors sixty years and older.[43]
Whereas two-thirds of the seniors considered it "very important," only
one-third of those under thirty did.

The low point in public support for the Kohl government team and its
policies coincided with their poor showing in the *Land* elections of North
Rhine Westphalia and Lower Saxony[44] and with the near-fatal assassination attempt on Oskar Lafontaine by a mentally disturbed woman in late
April. Most significant for the final showdown in the all-German elections, Lafontaine now won a clear edge of 50% to 44% over Chancellor
Kohl in the West German polls. In April it had only been 50% to 46%, a
margin that could have been explained away by sampling error or
sympathy for the severely wounded candidate. In the GDR, 53% thought
Lafontaine would make the better chancellor. The challenger had every
reason to believe that the time had come for a major bid and that the
electorate had not been carried away by the issue of German unification.
On the other hand, supposing German unification continued to be a
strong priority, nearly two-thirds of the respondents still regarded the
CDU/CSU more competent to carry out this assignment.

43. IPOS; *Einstellungen zu aktuellen Fragen der Innenpolitik in der BRD und in der
DDR* (Mannheim: 1990), pp. 57, 68–70. GDR respondents were just as sanguine (62% vs.
29% in the FRG) about the long-run advantages to come from unification. See also IPOS/
DDR, May–June 1990, p. 10.

44. The SPD gained modestly in both state elections at the expense of the CDU/CSU,
with the result that the SPD not only retained power in the first but won it in the second of
the two *Länder*. Taking over Lower Saxony also meant that the SPD had won a majority in
the federal upper house where each *Land* has representation.

"Rarely have optimistic expectations, fears and apprehensions lain so close to each other in such contradictory mixtures as they did a good half year . . . before . . . the first all-German elections," wrote Hans-Joachim Veen of the Adenauer Foundation about this period. He attributed the "open and unstable climate of opinion" to an extraordinary ambivalence among the West German population regarding German unification, an issue that seemingly overpowered all others and dominated the formation of opinions in regard to them. Among voters over forty-five years of age, the German division was often a matter of personal and painful experience, and many had relatives or friends in the GDR.[45] Younger Germans, on the other hand, rarely saw German unity "as a value in itself or as a national task of absolute priority." Where 76.2% of all West Germans had declared themselves "for unification" (9.6% against and 13.9% indifferent), respondents under thirty could muster only 64% for it. Another 18.3% were against it and 17.8% really did not care, for a total of 36.1% opposed or indifferent.[46] Being good neighbors and free to move seemed more important, and France and Italy were seen to be as close as the GDR. Veen thought that the unstable mixture of opinions in the early summer campaigns could just as easily be stampeded by manipulation of fears as by a long-range concept of German unity that presented a coherent scheme of economic and international integration for the German nation in a European context. Otherwise, many voters had hardly any clue regarding the goal, pace, and form of the unification process. The "systematic SPD campaigns to spread a sense of insecurity and envy" in regard both to refugees and the cost of unity were the reason for the electoral defeats of the CDU/CSU, especially since *Länder* like North Rhine Westphalia and Saarland could boast well-established SPD leaders.

What the CDU/CSU coalition needed to do now, according to Veen, was to forge ahead with determination toward the Second State Treaty (the final unification treaty between the two Germanys), after which the gathering momentum would be unstoppable regardless of doubts and objections. After all, he argued, well over 60% of West Germans endorsed the goal of a united Germany, and even among voters under forty-five

45. In a 1953 poll, 44% of West Germans and West Berliners claimed to have relatives or friends *"drüben"* (over there), and the same figure emerged in a 1970 poll. *JöM 1947–1955*, p. 313; *JöM 1968–1973*, p. 515. In the December 1989 poll, a good 78.6% of East Germans claimed to have personal ties to West Germans, including 29.1% who claimed family relatives. *JöM 1968–1973*, p. 179.

46. Respondents over age fifty, and over sixty, were a notch above the average in their eagerness for unification (81.3% for those in their fifties; 83.9% for those in their sixties, with only 4.5% against unification). IPOS/BRD, May–June 1990, no. 680, p. 114.

years the pro and con groups were rather evenly split. Among those over forty-five—who form a majority of about 53%—two-thirds wanted unification. A large majority of West Germans clearly favored pursuing unification regardless of cost and associated it with peace, greater European security, an opening to Eastern Europe, and increasing respect for the Germans globally.[47] Whatever the current ambiguities and uncertainties of the election campaign ahead—Veen expected the "two-plus-four" negotiations with the outside powers to play a considerable role—the evaluation suggested that the government parties should seize the initiative and impose their *Gesamtkonzept* (total concept) of a united Germany and a European future—including their internal, economic, social, environmental, and EC-related order—upon their countrymen. Veen emphasized also the popular image of greater Christian Democratic competence, both in European integration and in such reunification measures as the rebuilding of the East German economy. Given the slight edge in May of the CDU/CSU (40–42%) and the FDP (7–8%) over the SPD (37–39%) and the Greens (7–8%), the government parties stood a good chance of succeeding in December.

Full Speed Ahead

The developments of the months ahead proved Hans-Joachim Veen right. Chancellor Kohl and his team forced the pace of unification. They plunged into the implementation of the currency and economic union, speeded up the preparation of the Second State Treaty (see Chapter Five), and made significant headway with the "two-plus-four" negotiations, particularly in the Caucasus meeting between Kohl and Gorbachev (see Chapter Seven). And, lo and behold, the public opinion polls on Kohl and his adversary, Lafontaine, began to change dramatically. The *Spiegel/ EMNID* popularity polls of August had Kohl neck and neck with Lafontaine, at 61% for each politician.[48] More important still, what at

47. Hans-Joachim Veen, "Die schwankenden Westdeutschen. Ein vorläufiges Meinungsbild zur Einigung," *Die politische Meinung* 35, no. 250 (May/June 1990), 15–22. Veen also contrasted the expectation of long-range economic prosperity to the short-range anticipation of housing shortages (over 90%), tax increases (66%), and reduced social benefits. There are some differences in Veen's percentages, which come from the Adenauer Foundation or from the Institut für Demoskopie, and the Mannheim data quoted above.

48. The actual question in this recurring popularity poll is: "Which of these politicians [there is a list of twenty names that are subject to change] would you like to see playing an important role in the years to come?" Genscher invariably heads the preferences of his people, this time with 88%; and Bundestag President Rita Süssmuth (CDU/CSU), with

first, in June and July, had looked like a temporary recovery of Kohl as the choice for all-German chancellor was now confirmed as a steady and widening edge: Kohl was preferred by 49% in August, as in July, against 43% for his rival (45% in July). In like fashion, the government parties, CDU/CSU and FDP, were seen by 71% (72% in July) as "winning the election" as compared to only 26% who still thought the SPD and the Greens would take the race.[49] There could be little doubt that the actual arrival of the currency and economic union of July 1—contrary to Lafontaine's expectations—had benefited the fortunes of Kohl and his team, who were seen as brave, conquering heroes in the midst of the dismal East German economic scene.[50] In September, East Germans gave Kohl an even better edge as their choice for all-German chancellor (55% vs. 42% for Lafontaine), while West Germans chose 49% for Kohl and 41% for Lafontaine. Among the East Germans, 59% attributed to Kohl "competence in solving the difficult problems of unification," versus 36% for Lafontaine (West Germans: 53% vs. 40%).[51]

All during this decisive surge in Kohl's electoral fortunes, the issue of unification did not show any surprising change in the minds of Germans, up or down. Since November 1989, the unification issue had begun to outweigh by far all other issues—including environmental protection, unemployment, foreign migrants and, yes, from August 2, the Gulf War— that had motivated the electorate. Nevertheless, 29% of West Germans in a September 1990 poll by EMNID still were "against" or "somewhat against" unification. Three-fourths were "very much for" (25%), "in

75%, and Johannes Rau (SPD), with 65%, were well ahead of the chancellor candidates. De Maizière, with 43%, was the most popular GDR entry. *Der Spiegel* 44, no. 35, Aug. 27, 1990, pp. 40–50.

49. The recurrent question asks: "Who do you think will win the all-German Bundestag elections in December?" In June, the government parties were seen as likely victors by only 54%, versus 43% who bet on the opposition. See also the curve of respondents' preferences for the chancellor in *Bundestagswahl 1990*, p. 57, where Kohl continues to rise to nearly 60% of the respondents (October) while Lafontaine bottoms out at 34%.

50. Among East and West Germans, 81% called the economic situation in the GDR "bad" or "very bad." See also the additional judgments concerning various aspects of their economic fortunes (Leipzig Institute and others). *Der Spiegel* 44, no. 35, Aug. 27, 1990, pp. 40–41, 46–47, 50.

51. The image of Kohl's competence in matters of unification also emerges overwhelmingly in the *Politbarometer* polls of October and November, when Kohl was preferred by 47.7% (October) and 46.3% (November) over Lafontaine (22.1% in October and 24.5% in November). Another one-fourth of West Germans perceived "no difference." See *Politbarometer*, Nov. 1990, p. 25. More specifically, 59.2% of West Germans thought "the present CDU/CSU–FDP government" capable of rapid economic improvement in the GDR, while only 23.4% credited an SPD government with such competence. A similar endorsement of 57% (vs. 25.9% for the SPD) believed the present government would be able to avoid a downturn in West Germany. Ibid., p. 41.

favor of" (23%), or "somewhat for" (23%) unification. But only 38% of West Germans (31% of East Germans) thought in September that the West Germans were "prepared to make financial sacrifices for it," even though 67% (77% of East Germans) believed such sacrifices to be necessary.[52] This was a measure of the drawing power of Lafontaine's opposition to the cost of unification and his emphasis on who would have to pay for it. Undiminished by such important quibbles, which continued into the election itself, the unification issue and its impact on almost all other issues continued to dominate the field at least as late as the unity celebrations of October 3, 1990.

As if to mock Lafontaine, who had always challenged the hypocritical assurances of the government that no tax increases were necessary to pay for German unification, *Politbarometer* polls in November also provided a glimpse of the pragmatic realism of the West German voters. Asked if they considered tax increases necessary for financing unification, two-thirds (65.9%), including a majority of CDU/CSU supporters and three-fourths of FDP adherents, replied in the affirmative and only 30.8% in the negative. And a majority (52.7%) said they were "not in agreement" with such a tax hike, while only 45.6% said they were (including majorities of CDU/CSU and FDP supporters).[53] This did not do the challenger any good. In fact, three-fourths (74.5%) of all Germans felt that, at least for the first four months after the currency union, unification had proceeded "as well as expected" or "better than expected," a judgment challenged by only a minority of SPD (28.3%), Green (39.6%), or even PDS (35.6%) supporters. The answers to this question were about the same in the former GDR, right down to the partisan responses. In East Germany also, opinions were almost evenly divided on whether unification had brought "more joy" (about the end of the German

52. In regard to the difficulties of reforming the GDR economy, 76% of the West German respondents (67% of the East Germans) blamed the forty years of SED government, and 10% blamed the present GDR cabinet (18% of East Germans). Another 11% thought this was "the only way to introduce a market economy" (10% of East Germans), and only 5% (4% of East Germans) blamed "mistakes of the Bonn government," as Lafontaine had suggested. *Der Spiegel* 44, no. 38, Sept. 17, 1990, pp. 30–31.

53. These percentages had been different in October, when 77.2% (vs. 20.1%) recognized the need for a tax increase and willingness to bear it. *Politbarometer*, Nov. 1990, p. 49. Three-fourths of CDU/CSU supporters, in fact, had then, acknowledged the need for a tax hike, possibly reflecting the proposal to introduce an "environmental levy" to raise revenue. This did not stop majorities in the polls and during the Hessian *Land* elections of January 1991 from insisting that Kohl's government had "lied" about the tax increases needed to pay for unification, the so-called *Steuerlüge*. Forschungsgruppe Wahlen, Mannheim, *Blitzumfrage zur Landtagswahl 1991 in Hessen*, pp. 162–163, and *Wahltagsbefragung Landtagswahl in Hessen*, Jan. 20, 1991, pp. 185–189.

division) or "more worries" (about problems of unification), with CDU supporters being more joyful and PDS (91.7%) and SPD and Greens (61.3% and 56.7%, respectively) duly more worried. But, if anything, East Germans placed even less faith in the competence of an SPD government (15.6%, against 59.6% for a CDU/CSU–FDP government) to keep the economy sound. For this reason, 49.2% of the East Germans backed Kohl for German unification, compared to only 22.2% who backed the SPD; indeed, the Kohl backers included a majority of SPD supporters, the only such majority from any partisan group.[54] It was a discouraging verdict for Lafontaine and quite close to the actual election outcome in the East German contest of December.

The Significance of the December Elections

The all-German parliamentary elections for the unified German state were a significant climax to the process of unification in more than one sense. Formally, they signified the popular legitimation of a united Germany by a unified people, who thus gave their mandate to the newly elected Bundestag and to the chancellor and cabinet the Bundestag would support. But at the same time, these elections also constituted a popular verdict on the unification itself. Most West Germans had not had a formal opportunity to express their approval, and some—especially the adherents of the opposition candidate Lafontaine (SPD), the Greens, Bündnis 90, and the PDS—were known to have their doubts about unification, or at least about its cost to the West German taxpayer and consumer. East Germans who were originally for it might also have gotten cold feet since March 18 or at least since the currency union of July 1 and its economic consequences. Their 144 Volkskammer representatives in the Bundestag since October 3, 1990, also had not been elected specifically to represent them in the Bundestag.[55] In any case, the Volkskammer and the East German negotiators of the two state treaties between the GDR and the FRG had made far too many crucial decisions on their own not to require popular reendorsement at this point.[56]

54. *Politbarometer*, Nov. 1990, pp. 48, 72–74, 94; *Allensbacher Berichte 1990*, no. 25.

55. See below, Chapter Five.

56. Passing up the opportunity to have a constituent assembly write a new constitution and then have it popularly ratified (art. 146), and instead choosing to join the FRG *Land* by *Land* under article 23 of the Basic Law, placed heightened emphasis on popular legitimation of the unified state.

The all-German elections of December 2, 1990, also gave the newly unified people an opportunity to express their sense of who they were, their identity as Germans within the continuities of their common history and as they began to face a common future as one nation. Just what did it mean that German unification also signified overcoming the division of Europe into East and West? How could the newly unified colossus in the middle of Europe make sure these unifications would result in "a Europeanized Germany" and not in "a Germanized Europe" (Genscher)? Would it accept, or reject, or modify its obligations as a member of the community of European nations, and of the United Nations, once it was on its own?[57]

Finally, the elections also provided a penetrating glimpse of how well East German politics, political parties and voters, political elites and organized interests had really become integrated with the parties, groups, and elites of West Germany over the course of five to nine months. At the beginning of the campaign for the March 18 elections to the Volkskammer, the first democratic election in East Germany in fifty-eight years, the inexperience and lack of organization of the noncommunist parties might have doomed their takeover had it not been for the massive election assistance and postelection advice supplied by the West German parties. Eight and a half months later, East German parties and voters—except in East Berlin—had been seasoned by no fewer than three partisan contests at the Volkskammer, local, and *Länder* levels. Still, the election results of December 2 suggested plenty of differences and autonomous political life.

The International Context

The campaign for the all-German parliamentary elections and the elections themselves took place under the gathering clouds of international war and worldwide recession. Saddam Hussein had invaded Kuwait in early August and had shown no willingness to yield to the repeated demands of the U.N. Security Council and the United States to withdraw. A very substantial military force composed of U.S. troops and contingents of other U.N. members stopped any further Iraqi advance and threatened eventually to expel the invaders from Kuwait. At the same

57. This question had become salient from early August of 1990 when Saddam Hussein of Iraq invaded Kuwait and the U.N. allies insisted that West Germany ought to play a role in the grand military alliance against Saddam.

time, a deepening recession took hold in the economies of the United States, Britain, and more and more countries in Europe and around the world.

Germany during the process of unification had thus far avoided both war and recession, pleading constitutional limitations upon dispatching German troops beyond the European NATO area. Under mounting criticism, especially in the United States, the Kohl government eventually sent a flotilla of minesweepers to the eastern Mediterranean, presumably to replace American NATO naval forces that were sent to the Persian Gulf. Bonn also sent several hundred million marks in aid to nations impacted by the standoff in the Gulf, among them Israel, Egypt, and Turkey—to which country it also dispatched a defensive fighter squadron of aging Alpha jet planes. Even this carefully limited assistance to the U.N. effort caused storms of protest in the German press and in the Bundestag, where the SPD opposition demanded in one instance that the Alpha fighters be withdrawn. The Greens never tired of assailing the government for effectively failing to stop the exportation of illegal arms and of technology for Saddam's production of nuclear and chemical weapons. Far from the warlike mood in the United States and Britain, West Germans in mid-November 1990 refused to be distracted by the threat of war from their peaceful preoccupation with their own affairs, German unification, and the great upheaval in Eastern Europe. Barely half the respondents (50.9%) admitted that there was a real danger to peace in Europe.[58] Majorities among the adherents of all the important West German parties were prepared to abandon Kuwait to Saddam Hussein rather than compel him by means of war to leave. Some 45.9% believed Germany should "keep out of" a possible U.N. action, and another 33.8% favored "only monetary contributions." Only 17.2% were prepared to send German troops.[59]

German isolationism with regard to the U.N. Gulf action—the ultimatum and actual outbreak of the war in January brought huge peace demonstrations in German cities—needs to be contrasted with the German willingness at the time to become involved in a massive assistance

58. Another 47.4% said there was no danger to peace in Europe. There was a significant difference between adherents of the government parties, CDU/CSU and FDP, and those of the opposition SPD and Greens: while over 53% of the latter agreed that "European peace was in jeopardy," only about 47% of government supporters agreed. *Politbarometer*, Nov. 1990, p. 45.

59. Some 49.9% favored abandonment of Kuwait over war, which was preferred by only 34.1% of West Germans. Even among the government parties' supporters, 44–45% (vs. 39–40%) were in favor of abandonment, a choice preferred by 55.1% (vs. 29.9%) of the SPD and 69.1% (vs. 20.7%) of the Greens. Ibid., pp. 46–47.

effort for the Soviet Union that practically stole the limelight from the elections. In the weeks before and during the all-German elections, a wave of individuals, groups, and newspapers organized and helped finance the transport of food and medicine to the needy in the big Soviet cities where mismanagement, hoarding, and organized crime had prevented the normal distribution of native-grown supplies: close to 1 billion marks' worth of food was sent to the Soviet Union. West Germans had engaged in major charity drives before, most notably sending care packages to Poland, Armenia, and Romania—but nothing of this magnitude, nor ever before with such an explicitly political intent as "helping Gorbi" overcome his domestic nemesis.[60] From the conservative *Bildzeitung* ("A Heart for Russia") to a long list of semipublic and private aid organizations, the Red Cross, and the churches' charity groups, Germans opened their hearts and unzipped their pocketbooks.[61]

Special care was taken to avoid the many traps of the unwary, the bureaucratic snags and delays, the transport bottlenecks, the greed and rampant corruption of Soviet officialdom. Kohl had sent his foreign policy adviser, Horst Teltschick, to enlist local help in identifying worthy recipients, such as orphanages, old folks' homes, churches, and hospitals. Television also promoted the campaign and reported on its progress, for example, with pictures of pensioners contributing enthusiastically from their meager pension checks for the "poor starving Russians."[62] Aside from the sincere intentions of German groups and individuals—especially from the World War II generation, perhaps even from rueful veterans of the murderous Russian campaigns—there appeared to be the same political motive at work as in the earlier instances of Kohl's wooing of Gorbachev (e.g., the 13 billion marks for the repatriation of Soviet soldiers stationed in East Germany). The Germans were attempting to buy Soviet goodwill as insurance against a possible reversal of Gorbachev's fortunes in his own land, perhaps even in anticipation of a possible

60. At the CSCE summit meeting in Paris, on November 19, 1990, Chancellor Kohl promised President Gorbachev a private aid program involving food and medicine and, with the details awaiting clarification, up to 700 million marks worth of the iron food reserve of Berlin. *Süddeutsche Zeitung*, Nov. 20–21, 1990, p. 1.

61. Hamburg citizens alone sent 70,000 care packages to their sister city Leningrad, the city that German soldiers tried to starve into submission in World War II. See *Der Spiegel* 44, no. 48, Nov. 36, 1990, pp. 23, 195–203, and no. 49, Dec. 3, 1990, pp. 166–169.

62. Some Soviet agencies and aged beneficiaries were rather embarrassed to accept such largesse from former enemies and protested that the alleged Soviet food shortages did not really exist. The well-meant outpouring of aid for getting through the Russian winter, moreover, ran into major problems. By June 1991, only one-fourth of 138 million marks in cash donations had actually been distributed (see below, Conclusion).

Soviet military coup and its implications for East German and East European freedom. Last but not least important was the thought that the Gulf War had shifted much of NATO's forces and weaponry—except for those of West Germany—away at a crucial time, leaving Eastern and Central Europe nearly unprotected except for these psychological barriers to Soviet military aggressiveness.

The Tussle Over the Electoral Law

Among the suddenly flaring controversies that were dividing East Germans and West Germans alike and causing dissension in the GDR government, one of the more important was over the electoral law and the date of the all-German elections. The West German electoral law was a modified system of proportional representation,[63] with a minimum hurdle of 5% that a party had to clear in order to be represented at all. The controversy over the all-German elections began in July, when the East German SPD and the Liberals moved in the Volkskammer to resolve formal accession of the GDR *before the elections* so that the electoral law would apply to a united Germany as the base of the 5% hurdle. This would have had the effect of making any success by the PDS or by the democratic opposition groups (later united in Bündnis 90/Greens) rather unlikely. These parties therefore opposed the motion—preferring formal unification *after the elections*—and so did the CDU/DA and the DSU, precipitating a walkout of the Liberals (LDPD/FDP) and a similar threat by the SPD to leave the GDR cabinet.

Behind the high-sounding constitutional law and moral arguments of the CDU/DA and the other two, but also those of the SPD and Liberals, there were obvious political stratagems. The SPD and the Liberals simply wanted to inherit the votes of the PDS and Bündnis 90, neither of which could surmount a national 5% hurdle, and the CDU and CSU wanted to keep them from doing so. The DSU, as the sister party of the Bavarian CSU, played a role despite its internal dissensions because the CSU had to anticipate a diminished national role with German unification. Finally, in the Volkskammer and Bundestag, the Committees on German Unity agreed on an election date, December 2, *after* unification and also agreed

63. The modification consisted in providing for two ballots, of which only the second vote was among parties on a list. The first vote was for a particular candidate (with partisan affiliation) in a single-member district, along Anglo-American lines. Each vote determined half the composition of the Bundestag, but the overall proportionality of seats to the popular vote depended on the second vote only.

on the desirability of a common electoral law, which would be the subject of an election treaty between the two states.[64] The CDU, East and West, favored a 5% or lower hurdle to be applied separately to East and West Germany and the CSU and DSU—which was strong only in Saxony and Thuringia—with a minimum based on each *Land*. A 5% clause nationwide was estimated to require 23.8% of the popular vote in East Germany, or 2.5 million votes, an impossible hurdle for all but the Eastern CDU and SPD. When the West German parties began to negotiate, the CDU/CSU, FDP, and eventually the SPD agreed on a nationwide 5% hurdle, with the proviso that *parties which did not compete with each other*, such as the CSU and the DSU, could form a common list subject to the 5% clause. The PDS counted on its ability to win three direct (first ballot) mandates—a loophole in the old electoral law for regional minorities—or a 3% clause, which might have permitted its entry into the Bundestag. Bündnis 90/Greens were to be left in the cold, even though they had been the leaders of the democratic forces that toppled the communist GDR dictatorship. There was also a tug of war over CDU plans to advance the elections to October 14 so that the dire economic consequences of hasty union might not affect the outcome as much as they might by December. The SPD, on the other hand, was counting on East German mass unemployment to help it in the election.[65]

Neither the press nor the public welcomed these transparent political maneuvers. When *Der Spiegel* magazine became aware that the Green party planned to bring suit against the election treaty before the Federal Constitutional Court, it sent reporters to interview a prominent constitutional lawyer and specialist on election law, Frankfurt University professor Hans Meyer. The law professor was confident that the court would question the intent of the joint list of CSU and DSU as an attempt to subvert the purpose of the 5% hurdle and a violation of the principle of equal opportunity for all parties. He thought it quite likely that the court might lower the minimum hurdle to redress this inequity. The Greens' constitutional complaint indeed focused on the violation of equal opportunity for all parties and was joined also by the right-wing Republicans[66]

64. *Deutschland Archiv* 23, no. 8 (Aug. 1990), 1172.

65. See *The Economist*, Jul. 28, 1990, p. 37. In the Volkskammer debate (August 8 and 9), the election treaty failed to win the required two-thirds. A coalition of the SPD, PDS, and Bündnis 90/Greens also voted down de Maizière's proposal to advance the all-German election date to October 14, when the *Länder* in the former GDR would elect their respective parliaments. *Deutschland Archiv* 23, no. 9 (Sept. 1990), 1323–1324.

66. Another constitutional expert, Dietrich Murswieck of the University of Göttingen, also found the joint list discriminatory. An attorney for the Republicans pointed out that they had not even been legalized in the GDR until mid-August and hence were unable to organize there. *Der Spiegel* 44, no. 36, Sept. 3, 1990, p. 33, and no. 39, Sept. 24, 1990, pp. 63–68.

and the PDS/United Left party in the hope of getting at least a court injunction to suspend the 5% clause on election day. Meyer felt that the election treaty favored the CSU and forced the Greens to postpone their forming of a united party. By this time, the Liberals (FDP, including the NDPD), the CDU (including the Farmers' party), and the SPD had already united nationwide.

The Federal Constitutional Court hastened to take up the case in late September while its decision would still have a major effect on the outcome. It threw out the new election law on grounds of discrimination against some of the small parties, as predicted. A new *ad hoc* electoral law, applicable only on December 2, 1990, was passed by Parliament, which required of the parties a minimum of 5%, but only in the former GDR or the FRG, respectively. This placed the threshold for the PDS and Bündnis 90/Greens in the East at only about half a million votes, depending on the turnout, and thus assured the PDS of representation in the first united Bundestag. As it turned out, Bündnis 90/Greens made it, too, but the DSU no longer had a chance.

Unification and the Generations

The reader will recall our discussion of the political generations that have been shaped by Germany's cataclysmic history and that in turn are shaping its postwar development: the Third Reich and World War II generation (born 1928 and earlier); Kohl's first postwar generation (born between 1929 and 1940); the second postwar, or "68er," generation (typically born between 1941 and 1955); and a third (born between 1956 and 1970) and fourth (born since 1971) generation. They are each profoundly different from one another and have telling parallels in other countries (see Chapter One).[67]

German unification dramatically brought out the conflict between the first and second postwar generations, or rather between most Germans over age forty-five, certainly over fifty, and the voters below this level. It

---

67. West German electoral statistics and public opinion polls have always accounted for age groups. Since 1969 they have shown a considerable swing of voters under thirty to the SPD, and from 1980 to the Greens. See especially Joachim Hoffman-Göttig, "Die jungen Wähler. Zur Interpretation der Jungwählerdaten der Repräsentativen Wahlstatistik für Bundestag, Landtage und Europaparlament, 1953–1984" (Frankfurt, 1984) and *Die Mehrheit steht links—die jungen Wähler in der BRD* (Bonn: SPD-Parteivorstand, 1989). Also see Ulrich Eith, "Alters- und geschlechtsspezifisches Wahlverhalten," *Der Bürger im Staat* 40, no. 3 (Sept. 1990), 166–170.

was not anything so simple as that those younger than forty-five were against unification, but rather that they were noticeably less moved by it, frequently to degrees of indifference. "Who are these East Germans?" many young West Germans were quoted by the news media, "I don't want to badmouth them, but they are no different to me than the Czechs, or the Swiss." The implication was that there was no particular reason, therefore, to share scarce jobs or housing with them, or to pay more in taxes because of German unification. Neither was there any reason to abandon other political priorities, such as environmental protection or the reduction of unemployment, and to place unity ahead of them. In May 1990, in fact, several public opinion polls ascertained the rank order of policy goals among West Germans: unification ended up in about tenth or eleventh place, behind such goals as environmental protection, fighting unemployment or drug abuse, and various other social issues.[68]

The election campaign became personified in the contest between Chancellor Kohl, whose team could show nearly a year of concrete steps toward unification, and the SPD chancellor candidate[69] Oskar Lafontaine (age forty-seven), who was widely perceived as the candidate of the younger generation. Lafontaine's posters featured the catchphrase "The New Path" and usually showed him surrounded by young people, who were also reported to show up at rallies where he often criticized the hectic, unplanned pace and the likely high cost of unification *à la* Kohl. The chancellor, for his part, was billed as "Chancellor for Germany" on his posters, and he campaigned with slogans such as "Together we'll make it," stressing his image of competence rather than discussing facts and figures with his challenger.

Chancellor Kohl, of course, tried to ignore Lafontaine and his charges as much as possible and never actually called upon members of his own, first postwar generation or older generations to back him up with their superior numbers—53% were forty-five or older—against the self-styled champion of the younger generations. But the Kohl campaign exuded

68. An EMNID-*Spiegel* poll had unification and unification-related issues in tenth and eleventh place. An IPOS (Mannheim) poll conducted in West Germany gave it eleventh place; but the very same poll among East Germans gave unity second place (82%), after drug enforcement (83%) and before pensions (81%) and the environment (79%). IPOS/ DDR, May–June 1990, p. 55.

69. Since Germany has a parliamentary system, the voters vote only for candidates to the Bundestag, which then selects a chancellor with its majority. But it is customary for the parties inside and outside the Bundestag to pick and promote two likely contenders, and for the voters to understand their choice, among other things, as a choice between the two, in this case also including an incumbent chancellor.

pride and confidence in the West German political and economic system and made all the right appeals with a virtuosity that comes from long incumbency. There had already occurred in West German public opinion a remarkable 13% rise in "satisfaction with democracy in the FRG," from a level of 72% in 1989, an increase that probably reflected the inevitable comparisons with the sorry state of politics and the economy in the GDR.[70] Some observers close to Lafontaine even perceived a veritable "euphoria of pride in the FRG state," a sense of vindication over the critical generation and its critique of Bonn democracy twenty years ago: "We were right then, and today's developments[71] prove it." They saw in the voters' rejection of Lafontaine and his younger following "the revenge of the older generation."[72]

Needless to point out, such a claim on the loyalty of the younger generation was itself a highly political matter and was vigorously disputed by conservative voices. They pointed out, for example, that young German voters voted differently in East and West and that the SPD could boast only a narrow majority of West German voters aged eighteen to thirty-nine, clearest perhaps among those between twenty-five and thirty-nine, while the youngest (eighteen to twenty-four) had actually favored the CDU/CSU. In the former GDR, the CDU had carried the youth vote with an edge of at least 12% over the SPD. On the other hand, East German voters under forty gave Lafontaine (as distinguished from the SPD) a disproportionate share of their sympathies in October/November polls, especially if we compare these percentages with the modest vote the SPD received in the former GDR.[73] The reason for this conclusion lies

70. For the earlier levels, see IPOS, 1989, pp. 48–49, where the satisfaction level of 72% was exceeded only by those over fifty (76%) and by government party supporters (89–90%). Even among SPD supporters, those expressing satisfaction with democracy in the FRG jumped from 72% in 1989 to 83%; the Green adherents' level of satisfaction had risen from 38–42% in 1984/86 to 62% in 1990. IPOS/BRD, May–June 1990, pp. 21–23. Between August and October of 1990, in particular, West German satisfaction with "our democracy, our whole political system" surged from 71% to 82–83% (even among SPD supporters, where it went from 71% to 76%). Politbarometer, Jan. 1991, pp. 10, 41. The extent of East German dissatisfaction, however, brought the all-German level back to 71.5% by the following January.

71. The allusion was variously to the East German decision to adopt the West German system by joining under article 23 or simply to the collapse of communism in the East.

72. The argument was made from many quarters close to the SPD and the Greens, but nowhere clearer than in a presentation by Joachim Hoffmann-Göttig, of the Saarland representation in Bonn, to a group of American professors observing the election campaign. Lafontaine himself and Horst Ehmke (SPD), a senior Bundestag deputy from Bonn, repeated the claim on the loyalty of German youth on election night and made rosy predictions for the future of the SPD.

73. For the conservative interpretation, see Kurt Reumann in Frankfurter Allgemeine Zeitung, Dec. 4, 1990. But see also the data in Politbarometer Ost, Oct./Nov. 1990, p. 50,

in the fact that, of the two candidates, Lafontaine was heavily favored also by the PDS and Bündnis 90, not just by the SPD. The empirical evidence is a little more complicated than the conservative interpretation, since we are more interested in showing trends than in identifying the "majority" of a generational cohort: well-established party loyalties and other social-structural factors (family, occupation, place of residence) very likely kept most CDU voters of the younger age group in question from switching to Lafontaine. We also have to consider the presence of other parties in the East and West. Election analysts have pointed out that the Western Greens as well as the Eastern PDS had disproportionate shares of voters under forty, notably voters between twenty-nine and thirty-nine (PDS, mostly men) who liked Lafontaine better. The CDU/CSU, on the other hand, stood out among those over age fifty, both West and East. The coalition partner of the CDU/CSU, the FDP, also had more than its share of the voters between forty and sixty.[74]

Where does this leave the SPD, which received an estimated 600,000 second ballots from Green voters (a major reason why the Greens would lose their representation in the Bundestag) who were evidently worried about Lafontaine's electoral fortunes? To begin with, there were the claims of a CDU/CSU "majority" among the youngest West German voters, aged eighteen to twenty-four—37.9% indeed seems larger than the 35.5% of the SPD—but we have to compare these figures to the shares of the two parties in the West German popular vote: 44.6% CDU/CSU and 35.7% SPD. The CDU/CSU share of the young is only 85% of the share of its popular vote, while the comparable SPD share is close to its share of the popular vote. Among those aged twenty-five to twenty-nine the SPD received 118% of its share of the popular vote; among the thirty- to thirty-nine-year-olds, 112%. These are significant margins, even though the Greens and the PDS indeed had twice their respective shares of the popular vote. In the 1987 West German Bundestag elections, the SPD did particularly well among voters between the ages of thirty and fifty-nine, but had to share those aged twenty-five to twenty-nine with the Greens.[75] The East German SPD exhibited no such age differentials

where Lafontaine's 35–42% of eighteen- to thirty-nine-year-olds should be compared to an average of 33.2% for him, or to the 24% of actual votes for the SPD, and not to Kohl's majorities.

74. See *Bundestagswahl 1990*, p. 29. The Republican voters were mostly male and under 25. The CDU/CSU also had proportionately more voters from communities under 20,000 inhabitants than did SPD, FDP, Greens, or the PDS.

75. See IPOS, May–June 1990, no. 680, p. 180, and Peter H. Merkl, "The SPD After Brandt: Problems of Integration in an Urban Society," *West European Politics 11* (Jan. 1988), 44 and the sources cited there.

except for a small advantage among those over fifty, which may reflect the otherwise forgotten SPD tradition in industrial areas of the immediate post–World War II era and earlier. The West German CDU/CSU clearly shows its edge among those aged fifty to fifty-nine (114% of the CDU/CSU share of the popular vote) and among those over sixty (125%); and this is true also among East German CDU voters, of whom the fifty- to fifty-nine-year-olds are 111% and those over sixty are 116% of their popular share.[76] The generational factor in the elections was obviously stronger than the CDU/CSU and FDP would like to admit, producing results that favored the sentiments of Germans older than forty-five, the first postwar and older generations, over those of the "68er" and younger generations.

Is there further empirical evidence to support the linkage of the generations and German unification? Among East Germans, those expressing "worries" rather than "joy over unification" enjoy clear majorities among the eighteen- to thirty-nine-year-olds, while the older respondents tended to be filled with joy. Those who were worried also tended to feel that unification had gone "worse than expected" and to favor Lafontaine over Kohl.[77] Early on, there was a lot of curiosity about differences in attitude between East and West Germans and, in May/June 1990, IPOS concentrated on this question. Nearly all issues of public policy in the former GDR have been somehow related to unification. Yet the pollsters found that unification itself was only half as important to East Germans under thirty as it was to those over sixty: 65.5% of those over sixty thought it "very important," a judgment made only by a third of those under thirty. A good 95–98% of East Germans over fifty said they were "for unification," while only 88.5% of those under twenty-five shared this opinion. West Germans under age thirty were significantly less in favor of unification—only 64% instead of the average 76.2%—were nearly twice as likely to be in outright opposition (18.2%), and were much more likely to be "indifferent to union" (17.8%) than the average (13.9%). Among those over fifty, and especially those over sixty, by the same token, between 81% and 84% endorsed unification and only a very few opposed it.[78] The older refugee generations in both areas

76. The cohort aged between forty and forty-nine is close to the popular shares of both parties and in both parts of Germany. In the West we take this to indicate a rough balance between the tendencies of those under and those over forty-five, where we would expect to find the generational split. See *Bundestagswahl 1990*, pp. 29–38. The all-German voting statistics show the same differences in slightly diluted form.

77. *Politbarometer Ost*, Oct./Nov. 1990, pp. 83–89. Disproportionate numbers of those under age thirty favor Lafontaine's approach to unification, and a similarly disproportionate share of those between forty and sixty went for Kohl's unification policy.

78. IPOS/BRD, May–June 1990, p. 57. In the West, 76% of all respondents were for

were also less prepared to accept the Oder-Neisse line than their descend-
ants:[79] 25% of all West Germans over age sixty refused to recognize the
Polish western border (15% of East Germans of that age); among the
original refugee generation in West Germany, a bare majority of 56%
(vs. 43% against) did recognize it.[80]

Further probing reveals the depths of the generational difference on
many related questions. Asked whether they were "very satisfied," "rather
satisfied," or "rather dissatisfied" with the state of West German democracy, the respondents under thirty were almost twice as dissatisfied as the
average, while those over fifty were substantially more often "very
satisfied." Those over age forty, and especially over sixty, also exhibited
a lot more confidence in particular public institutions than the average
German, beginning with great trust in the police.[81] Those over age fifty
also said in much greater numbers that they "like the sight of the West
German (and now all-German) flag"—the respondents in their fifties split
two to one between "liking" and indifference; those over age sixty, three
to one—compared to the average, among whom liking the flag (56.4%)
is barely ahead of "*ist mir egal*" (indifference), the response of 40.5%.
And when asked whether they were "proud of being German," 87.9% of
those over sixty and 77.5% of those in their fifties replied "yes," while
among those between twenty-five and twenty-nine only 51.6%, and
between thirty and thirty-nine only 57.7%, felt such pride.[82] To sum up,
national pride, elation over German unification, and a preference for
Kohl's policies were clearly stronger among those over age fifty, while

---

unification (vs. 10% against and 14% indifferent), while 95% of East Germans (vs. 3%
against and 2% indifferent) shared this attitude. IPOS/DDR, May–June 1990, pp. 68–69.
    79. IPOS, May–June 1990, no. 680, p. 114; IPOS/DDR, May–June 1990, pp. 10, 59.
Of the West German population, 22.7% are German ethnic refugees from 1945 to 1947
(30.7% of East Germans) or their children and grandchildren.
    80. IPOS/BRD, May–June 1990, p. 87. Four out of five West Germans recognized the
Oder-Neisse border in 1990 while 17.2% were opposed. IPOS, May–June 1990, no. 680,
p. 137.
    81. As did Americans, West Germans went through a prolonged crisis of confidence in
nearly all institutions during the seventies, a crisis from which they have recovered only
gradually. The young still exhibit the highest levels of alienation from the system. IPOS,
May–June 1990, no. 680, pp. 36, 45.
    82. Ibid., pp. 107–109. Up to age twenty-four, 56.1% were proud to be Germans. The
average stood at 70.1%. This should be contrasted perhaps to the famous 1959 question in
the "civic culture" survey which asked respondents from five nations about what aspects of
their nation, they were proud. Among the West German respondents, 36% mentioned
alleged national characteristics of their people, more than the other nationals. See Gabriel
A. Almond and Sidney Verba, *The Civic Culture: Political Attitudes and Democracy in Five
Nations* (Princeton, N.J.: Princeton University Press, 1963).

those under forty preferred Lafontaine and were rather lukewarm on issues of pride and unity.[83]

The Elections of December

The all-German election campaign, and the election results, essentially demonstrated how a major, politically realigning issue can overcome the best-laid plans. Not only were the SPD and its candidate ahead of the CDU/CSU, or at least neck and neck with the incumbents in West Germany for much of the period since the last parliamentary elections, but they had a good program to offer. From September 1987, the SPD outdid the CDU/CSU in the polls by considerable margins, sometimes by nearly 10% (especially in early 1989) which created the impression that not even the votes of the FDP, Kohl's coalition partner, would be able to stop the Social Democrats. The personal popularity of the challenger, Oskar Lafontaine, remained well ahead of that of Chancellor Kohl from 1987 up until September 1990. Once Lafontaine was formally designated as the chancellor candidate of his party, and had provoked some opposition in his own party—e.g., from Helmut Schmidt, who resentfully recalled Lafontaine's obstruction and lack of support for him back when he was chancellor—he began to stumble over the unexpected turn of events of early 1990.[84]

The SPD had developed a program of issues that stressed the points that voters, according to the polls, really cared about: Lafontaine's "new path" was to be founded on a combined dedication to the solution of environmental problems,[85] the maintenance of the social welfare net, and

83. See also Joachim Hoffmann-Göttig, "Jungwählerverhalten," Feb. 1, 1991, a manuscript for a symposium volume to be edited by Wilhelm Heitmeyer. Hoffmann-Göttig rests his argument on the preelection *Politbarometer* values for both chancellor candidates and the actual edge of Kohl's party among older voters.

84. The popularity of the SPD remained above the 40% mark through most of this period, while that of Lafontaine was outdone only by the perennial favorite, Hans-Dietrich Genscher (FDP). But his margin of popularity over Kohl as chancellor candidate began to drop and, in June 1990—after a brief "sympathy respite" following his near assassination in April—Lafontaine fell clearly behind Kohl. Forschungsgruppe Wahlen (FGW), *Vorwahlbericht. Daten zur Bundestagswahl und der Wahl zum Berliner Abgeordnetenhaus am 2. Dezember 1990* (hereafter *Vorwahlbericht . . . 1990*), pp. 12–14.

85. In the last two parliamentary elections, the lukewarm endorsement of some ecological concerns had cost the SPD a vital margin of voters who went to the Greens instead. See, for example, Donald Schoonmaker, "The Greens and the Federal Elections of 1980 and 1983: Is the Ostpolitik Waxing?" Ferdinand Müller-Rommel, "The Social

the continuance of economic strength. German voters are far more issue-oriented than, say, those of the United States and are not so easily distracted by personalities and media manipulation. As formalized in the party's "Government Program for 1990–1994" at the SPD convention of September 28, 1990, the ecological commitment involved the ecological reconstruction of industrial society by means of energy policy incentives—also the end of nuclear power in Germany—and other environmental regulations (e.g., in agriculture and transportation). Within the social policy sphere, the program promised the creation of more jobs, shorter hours, and better opportunities for training, as well as housing programs, pensions, and a new approach to gender equality and the compatibility of career and child-rearing—including the right to an abortion during the first three months of pregnancy. The economic part focused particularly on jobs and infrastructure in the new *Länder* of a united Germany.[86] Yet there could be little doubt that German unification and its requirements had upstaged Lafontaine and his party. There were belated efforts to claim credit for alleged improvements in the unification treaties[87] and further appeals to women voters and to youth, particularly in regard to training and job opportunities.[88]

All this was to no avail against the triumphant Chancellor Kohl, whose often-cited "train of German unity" also induced many a member of the old guard SPD leadership, such as Brandt, Vogel, and Rau, to jump on the bandwagon. Beginning in June 1990, Kohl moved ahead so dramatically in the public opinion polls that by October/November he was ahead of his challenger by more than 20%. Indeed, 57.7% of the respondents named him as their choice to be chancellor, against a mere 35.8% for

---

Democratic Party: The Campaigns and Election Outcomes of 1980 and 1987," and Karl H. Cerny, "The Campaign and the 1987 Election outcome," in Karl H. Cerny, ed., *Germany at the Polls: The Bundestag Elections of the 1980s* (Durham, N.C.: Duke University Press, 1990), chaps. 4, 6, and 10.

86. All of these points were related to such acute and widely felt problems as the need for 250,000 new dwellings a year in West Germany alone, one-third of them low-income housing. See *Regierungsprogramm 1990–1994. Der Neue Weg: ökologisch, sozial, wirtschaftlich stark, beschlossen vom SPD-Parteitag in Berlin am 28. September 1990*. There were also planks relating to the end of the East-West conflict, the uniting of Europe—a "United States of Europe"—and concern for the well-being of the Third World.

87. One election leaflet claimed successes on the abortion issues (see Chapter Five, below), in addressing the ill-gotten wealth of the PDS and the bloc parties, and on labor issues. Another tied disarmament issues, such as reductions in the term of military service and in the size of the Federal Army, to German unity. Still a third one specifically addressed the problems of unemployment and job creation in the former GDR.

88. For this purpose, the SPD handed out the September 1988 issue of the party newsletter *Politik*, no. 13, containing a resolution on youth questions from the SPD convention of August 30–September 2, 1988.

Lafontaine. It was an amazing feat for a chancellor who had always suffered a bad press and lackluster polls.[89] Worse yet, Kohl carried with him the governing parties (CDU/CSU and FDP) so that, by November 1990, 88.2% of the respondents in all of Germany expressed an expectation that the governing coalition would win (as against 7.6% who were still betting on the opposition).[90] Two weeks before the actual elections, two-thirds of the supporters of the SPD expected the government parties to win. Imminent defeat had turned into a rout.

In the final weeks before the December elections, even the customary optimism of the challenger was wearing thin. Lafontaine no longer employed the triumphant formulas of the summer when he had proclaimed that "Kohl fell into the trap" of disastrous miscalculations regarding German unification. In November, just as Kohl and Finance Minister Waigel had to announce the first new "environment levies" *(Abgaben)*—by January the Gulf War had become the excuse for raising taxes after all—Lafontaine's vindicated charges about the premature currency union and the real cost of unification had begun to sound like played-out clichés.

Among the Greens, the other important West German opposition party, the electoral disaster to come was still veiled by what turned out to be wildly inaccurate election predictions by every major German polling institute. INFAS had predicted 8.5%, Allensbach 8.9%, EMNID 7%, even the cautious Mannheim group with 6.5%—all were well above the 5% hurdle for representation. The Greens had studiously avoided the subject of German unification altogether and concentrated instead on their usual ecological, pacifist, and feminist concerns. In the end, it may have been precisely the predicted success at the polls that induced an estimated half-million Green voters (INFAS) at the last minute to give their second ballot to the SPD, not realizing that their own party would be left with only 4.8% of the popular vote in West Germany and would be shut out from the Bundestag.[91] After a decade of ecological consciousness-raising, the major parties had undergone a considerable "greening-

89. See Dieter Roth, "Der ungeliebte Kanzler," in Reinhard Appel, ed., *Helmut Kohl im Spiegel seiner Macht* (Bonn: Aktuell, 1990), pp. 285–299.

90. See FGW, *Vorwahlbericht . . . 1990*, pp. 14–15, and the *Spiegel*/EMNID poll cited in *Der Spiegel* 44, no. 48, Nov. 26, 1990, p. 34. Also see FGW, *Bundestagswahl 1987*, pp. 50–51. The SPD chancellor candidate of 1987, Johannes Rau, also had been considerably ahead of Kohl in the polls until the surge of government supporters overtook him. Ibid., pp. 6–11 and 33–37.

91. Their allies in East Germany, Bündnis 90/Greens, received 6% in that area and thus won entrance to the national parliament. If the two had formed a party and competed under the nationwide 5% clause of the old (and, very likely, the future) electoral law, they would have achieved 5.1% of the national vote.

up" process that lured back SPD and CDU/CSU voters who had strayed to the Greens in 1983 and 1987. There were further reasons for the Green debacle in the West that one should not ignore. Among the large number of new, small parties contesting the elections in the West, there were at least five that drew on the traditional Western Green clientele: Bündnis 90/Greens (13,000 second ballots); the Greys, senior citizens (312,287); two ecological parties (ÖDP 190,924 and Öko-Union 4,681); and the Women's party (12,110)—for a total of 533,002 second-ballot voters, or 1.4% of the West German popular vote. Some of these competitors represented secessions from the factional infighting of the Greens. If the Greens had managed to keep just one out of six of these dissidents from going their own way—or if the election had been held six weeks later, when the Gulf War began and the German peace movement resurfaced—they would still be in parliament today.

The election brought the expected victory for Kohl's governing coalition of CDU/CSU–FDP, although voter turnout had dropped to 77.8% from its West German high in the low 90s or high 80s.[92] The great winner of the elections was Genscher's FDP, which achieved one of its best results ever: 11% (see Table 4.2). The FDP won 12.9% in East Germany alone and achieved spectacular results in Saxony-Anhalt and Thuringia. Though proclaiming its triumph the loudest, Kohl's CDU/CSU (with 43.8%) remained somewhat below the last West German parliamentary elections (44.3%) and, in fact, below its 37-year record since the second West German Bundestag (1953). On closer examination, however, the CDU/CSU did not lose any ground in West Germany as compared to its 1987 showing, and this despite a considerable drop in the CSU vote in Bavaria (−3.3% in Bavaria and down from 9.8% in the FRG to 7.1% in united Germany) where the death of Franz-Josef Strauss evidently still weighed heavily upon Christian Democratic fortunes. In fact, Kohl's CDU alone received a whole percentage point more of the West German vote (from 34.5% in 1987 to 35.5%) and he, for the first time, carried his own electoral district in Ludwigshafen on the first ballot. The CDU also carried West Berlin with 47.7%, a ten-point gain over the last elections. Most gratifying, the CDU (with 41.8%) did very well in East Germany and scored sizable gains in Brandenburg (+6.9%) and Mecklenburg-Vorpommern over the Landtag elections of October 1990, although it was not able to repeat its victory in Saxony (−4.9%).

92. In 1983, the turnout had still been 89.1% of those eligible to vote, but in 1987 it had already sunk to 84.3%, in part because of severe winter weather. For comparison, see also Peter H. Merkl, "Adenauer's Heirs Reclaim Power: The CDU and CSU in 1980–83," in Karl H. Cerny, ed., *Germany at the Polls*, pp. 58–87, where the rise of Kohl and the comeback of the CDU/CSU in 1982 are described.

Table 4.2. Results of the First All-German Bundestag Elections, Second Ballot, December 2, 1990

| | All-German | | West Germany* | | East Germany* | |
	% Vote	Seats	% Vote	Seats	% Vote	Seats
CDU/CSU	43.8	319	44.3	24()	41.8	61
FDP	11.0	79	10.6	55	12.9	16
SPD	33.5	239	35.7	202	24.3	30
Greens	3.9	0	4.8	0	0.1	0
PDS/Left List	2.4	17	0.3	1	11.1	16
Bündnis 90/Greens	1.2	8	0	0	6.0	7
DSU	0.2	0	0	0	1.0	0
Greys	0.8	0	0.8	0	0.8	0
Reps	2.1	0	2.3	0	1.3	0
NPD	0.3	0	0.3	0	0.3	0
ÖDP	0.4	0	0.5	0	0.2	0
Others	0.3	0	0.3	0	1.3	0

SOURCE: *Bundestagswahl 1990*, pp. 7–11, 17.

*Not including Berlin, where 12 CDU, 9 SPD, 3 FDP, 1 Bündnis 90/Greens, and 3 PDS/ Left List candidates were elected.

The SPD losses brought the chief opposition, with 33.5% nationwide, to its lowest point since the late fifties, when the party's enthusiasm for German unification was still frequently motivated, among other things, by the expectation of great electoral gains in traditionally (pre-1933) social democratic East Germany. Its showing of only 24.3% in that area alone points to the significant presence of the PDS (11.1%), whose voters would have boosted the East German SPD strength to the West German level (35.7%) and might still do so at the next national elections. But the SPD also lost substantial ground in West Germany, and especially in West Berlin, Bremen, Lower Saxony, and North Rhine Westphalia, including the Ruhr area.[93] Only in Saarland, where Lafontaine is the minister president, was there a gain: 7.6% of the popular vote over 1987. Every third Green party supporter of the previous election voted for the SPD this time, which compensated the latter party a bit for its losses to the CDU/CSU and FDP.[94] In East Germany, the SPD also gained votes

93. In the Ruhr, the SPD dropped 3.3% while the FDP picked up 2.9%. See *Bundestagswahl 1990*, p. 13. The FDP also gained in such SPD loss areas as West Berlin and Bremen.

94. Some Green voters also switched to CDU and FDP. For an overview of the complex shifts among the parties, see *Bundestagswahl 1990*, pp. 52–55. Generally speaking, voter loyalty has been high (above 80%) among CDU/CSU and SPD voters; among the current FDP voters, however, only one-third had voted for this party before. The Greens and smaller parties can rely even less on party loyalty.

from the shrinking PDS. The PDS received about 1 million votes (11.1%
of East German voters), disproportionately from younger East Germans,
and won seventeen seats, including a first-ballot mandate in East Berlin.
Bündnis 90/Greens, thanks again to the change in the electoral law,
obtained 6% of the Eastern popular vote and eight Bundestag seats.[95]

It is easy to demonstrate the superficial similarity of the voting results
East and West, except for the temporary survival of the legacies of the
communist dictatorship, the PDS, and its brave democratic opponents,
Bündnis 90/Greens. But underneath the surface resemblance there was a
world of difference. A simple comparison of the occupational composition of the vote of the three major parties, East and West, shows how
little the CDU/CSU electorates, or those of the other parties, have in
common across the former Iron Curtain (see Table 4.3). The Eastern
CDU, according to this comparison, is a veritable blue-collar workers'
party, and even the FDP of the former GDR has a percentage of workers'
votes three times greater than the Western FDP has. The PDS, legatee of
the dictatorship of the proletariat, by the way, has fewer workers than the
FDP and more white-collar employees, executives, and civil servants,
figures resembling those of the Bündnis 90/Greens of the East. By the
same token, neither the CDU nor the FDP shows the dominance of
independents that can be found among their Western cousins.

The Formation of the New Cabinet

The first all-German elections thus gave Chancellor Kohl an ample
mandate of 54.1% of the popular vote—and, under the modified proportional representation system, a similar majority (60%) of Bundestag

95. The split ballot also permits a glimpse of the affinity relationships among the
partisan electorate. According to exit polls, over 90% of the voters who gave their second
ballot to the CDU/CSU or SPD also voted for the local candidate of their respective parties
on the first ballot. This was true only of about 70% of the FDP voters and 58% of the
Greens. In East Germany, the PDS voters exhibited a consistency similar to that in the two
major parties—which may reflect both their relative isolation and the expectation of
winning direct mandates (they received one), a rare achievement for the smaller parties
under this system. Many FDP voters who split their vote gave their first ballot to a local
CDU/CSU candidate, while many Green voters favored a local SPD candidate. Republican
voters surprisingly often (around 70%) gave their first ballots to Republican local candidates who had no chance of winning, a measure perhaps of their distance from all the other
parties. Those who chose non-Republican candidates scattered their first-ballot votes
randomly, with a modest edge for a local CDU/CSU candidate. *Bundestagswahl 1990*,
pp. 25–29.

Table 4.3. Occupational Groups in Major Parties, East and West Germany (in %)

	FRG Pop.	CDU/CSU (West)	CDU (East)	GDR Pop.	SPD (East)	SPD (West)	FDP (West)	FDP (East)	PDS (East)
Workers	17.5	15.1	42.3	36.4	36.9	23.6	9.3	29.5	23.5
White-collar	36.0	34.3	34.4	39.7	40.8	37.3	39.0	43.9	48.5
Executives/civil servants	8.2	8.4	5.4	6.7	6.6	7.5	9.3	9.5	10.7
Independents	9.0	11.3	5.0	4.3	2.8	4.6	14.6	6.8	2.3
Students/trainees	6.1	4.3	1.2	2.9	2.8	5.9	6.5	2.6	5.9
TOTAL	76.8	73.4	88.2	90.0	89.9	78.9	78.7	92.3	90.9

SOURCE: Exit polls reported in *Bundestagswahl 1990*, pp. 30–35.

seats. But the cheering and self-congratulation had barely come to an end when partisan and personal jealousies within the government coalition began to erupt. The triumphant FDP wanted more cabinet seats. Then there was the Bavarian CSU, at whose expense such an increase of FDP posts would have to come—and whose thorough dislike for FDP leaders stretched like a red thread from the decades of the late Franz-Josef Strauss to Theodor Waigel and other current CSU chiefs. The CSU leadership threatened to dissolve its coalition of forty years with the CDU and to stay out of the government, depriving it of its hard-won majority, if its representation in the cabinet were reduced. The East Germans were concerned that their CDU and FDP might not be properly represented in the all-German government,[96] especially after the fall of CDU leader Lothar de Maizière on charges of involvement with the Stasi. There were also substantive issues, explicit or implied, connected with the personnel claims, such as the FDP insistence on special tax incentives in the former GDR for both investment and personal income. Count Lambsdorff was still holding out for an East German personal income tax exemption of 4,800 marks in mid-January 1991, but he finally settled for a compromise 600 marks.

The final choices of cabinet members and issues emerged after twenty-seven days of haggling and represented a compromise package that moved no one to any great display of enthusiasm. The coalition builders carefully avoided such issues as abortion, German participation in U.N. enforcement actions—the Gulf War had broken out in the meantime, finding the new government caught between the pressures of a pacifist revival at home and their belligerent and very critical allies abroad—or the financing of German unification. Three East Germans graced the new cabinet, including one CDU and one FDP male politician and a CDU woman (Angela Merkel, Youth and Women).[97] Among them, the indefatigable GDR negotiator of the details of unification, Günter Krause (CDU), was given the Transport Ministry, which was taken away from the CSU. Yet he had to tolerate the imposition of a CSU parliamentary state secretary in addition to his ministerial (civil service) state secretary. The meager representation of the five new *Länder* (all three were from

96. The East German representation in the transitional all-German cabinet, from October 3, 1990, to the swearing in of the new government, had consisted of four ministers without portfolio (for special assignments): ex-Premier de Maizière (CDU); Volkskammer President Sabine Bergmann-Pohl (CDU); the DSU chair; and the FDP vice-chair, Rainer Ortleb.

97. The old Ministry of Family Affairs, Youth, Women, and Health was split in three. Another part, Family Affairs and Seniors, was given to Hannelore Rönsch (CDU, Hesse) and a third part, Health, to Gerda Hasselfeldt (CSU).

Mecklenburg-Vorpommern) also signified Kohl's abandonment of the rule of regional proportionality, which in most earlier cabinets had given each *Land* some representation.[98] The modest stature of the East German ministries—the third one was Education, an area still largely reserved to *Land* jurisdiction—also fell short of the promises to give a major ministry to the "Ossies."[99]

The long-anticipated tax increase for unification—the Kohl administration had run the elections on promises that there would be no new taxes—now came under the guise of paying Germany's multibillion-dollar contribution for the U.N. effort in the Gulf War. It had already surfaced as an "environmental levy" in the months just before the elections. The impending *Land* elections in Hesse may have contributed to the duplicitous game with the taxes. The CSU lost another of its six cabinet posts but retained such key posts as Finance (Waigel) and Agriculture (Ignaz Kiechle). Still, the Bavarians were not at all pleased about their losses, although the decrease reflects not only the CSU's electoral losses but also its relative loss of political clout as a result of the addition of five new *Länder*. For Kohl, whose chief rivals, among them Lothar Späth, Wolfgang Schäuble, and Heiner Geissler, have all faded from the race,[100] it was the height of solitary power (see Table 4.4). He no longer seemed to need political allies or to attach himself to anyone else's strength.

It should be clear by now that East Germany and its five new *Länder* received a good deal less than a proportional share in the all-German political system. East German voters and *Bundestag* seats did not receive their due in cabinet ministries or in parliamentary state secretaries (four out of thirty). The new *Länder* were given proportionality neither in the cabinet nor among the parliamentary state secretaries, of whom three are from Saxony and one is from Berlin, the only representation of the nominal new capital city in the parliamentary executive.[101] Eventually,

98. Now there were also three cabinet members from Hesse and only one each from North Rhine Westphalia, the most populous *Land*, and from Baden-Württemberg.

99. According to *Der Spiegel* 45, no. 4, Jan. 21, 1990, pp. 21–25, eight of the East German members of the Berlin CDU abstained in the final vote on the cabinet formation, presumably to signal their disappointment. A seventy-six-page coalition agreement signed by the chairs of the CDU, CSU, and FDP spelled out a government program for the legislative term ahead, but also contained details of financing for unification that were unlikely to survive the first year's shortfall.

100. Späth was discredited in a major scandal, Schäuble was struck down by a would-be assassin—he is now confined to a wheelchair—and Geissler fell in a power struggle with Kohl even before the onset of the upheaval in the East. Geissler has now rejoined the field as a CDU parliamentary leader, and another once-expelled rival, Kurt Biedenkopf, became the minister president of Saxony.

101. It would be absurd to count West German politicians such as Genscher, who was

Table 4.4. Bundestag (BT) Seats and Cabinet Posts, January 1991

	Seats	(%)	Posts	(%)
Partisan composition*				
CDU	268	(67.3)	11	(55)
CSU	51	(12.8)	4	(20)
FDP	79	(19.8)	5	(25)
East-West composition†				
Former FRG (without Berlin)	306	(76.9)	17	(85)
Former GDR (without Berlin)	77	(19.3)	3	(15)
Berlin	15	(3.8)	0	(0)
Gender composition				
M (entire BT)	530	(80.0)	16	(80)
F (entire BT)	132	(20.0)	4	(20)
Entire Bundestag	662		20	

SOURCE: Compiled and calculated from newspaper accounts.

NOTE: Only the ministerial seats of the government coalition are shown here. There are also 30 parliamentary state secretaries (4 from East Germany), mostly CDU/CSU and frequently of the "68er" generation. One of these parliamentary state secretaries is Sabine Bergmann-Pohl, the former Volkskammer president.

*Posts include the chancellor and the ministers of the interior, finance, agriculture, foreign affairs, economy, and justice.

†All important posts are included.

the CDU Ossies in the *Bundestag* scored one small triumph when they insisted on the election of Maria Michalk (Saxony) as vice-president of the parliamentary CDU. Other parameters in Table 4.4 show that, in the partisan coalition game, the smaller parties are very much at an advantage while the senior partner receives far fewer posts than its parliamentary seats would warrant. With respect to gender composition (using the composition of the entire Bundestag), the women's share of posts equals their share of seats, but their cabinet posts are hardly the most influential.

The age balance, finally, comes close to an even break between those of the first postwar (Kohl's) generation, and older, and those of the second postwar ("68er") generation and younger.[102] In the new cabinet,

---

born in Halle but made his entire career in the West, as part of the East German contingent. The newly elected East German deputies and some of the *Land* politicians have complained both about their treatment and about the neglect of East German problems, but to no avail.

102. Since 1949, the average age of the Bundestag members has fluctuated, with few exceptions, between forty-seven and fifty, which is close to the present generational break that we have assumed. Cabinet members, of course, have been a little older, even when they did not have an octogenarian like Adenauer among them.

the older set predominates, but only about twelve to eight. Thus, the alleged "revenge of the older generation" cannot be said to be more than a slight or modest margin. As for Kohl's personal comeback and success in becoming the first all-German chancellor since Hitler or Karl Dönitz,[103] there could be no doubt that he had achieved his goal. In spite of the persistence of his critics, and as the self-styled heir of Konrad Adenauer, he had at last managed to place himself as close to the historic pedestal of great figures in German political history as it was possible to do for a sitting chancellor.[104] He had accomplished most of what he had hoped to do and, barring major lapses in his remaining years in office, could retire to the pages of the history books at any time.

103. Admiral Dönitz, the German naval commander during World War II, was personally chosen by Adolf Hitler. Having announced the death of the *Führer* on May 1, 1945, he was taken into custody a week later for trial at Nuremberg.

104. Adenauer's rank as a historic figure in the minds of his compatriots began to rise steeply only after he left office. See Merkl, "La función legitimadora del líder. Konrad Adenauer, 1949–1976," *Revista de Estudios Políticos*, no. 21 (May/June 1981), 7–25.

Chapter FIVE

Toward an All-German Constitution

"Just as much as the founders of a republic or a kingdom deserve praise, those who establish a tyranny ought to be detested." So wrote Niccolò Machiavelli in the *Discourses*, his sixteenth-century fountain of insights about either form of government. German unification in 1990 has brought together, at one level of a complex process, a democratic republic or constitutional democracy, the Federal Republic, with what used to be, at least until October 1989, a grim tyranny. But if we delve into the process by which both were founded in 1949 and take a look at the founders, praiseworthy or detestable, we find that the founding leaders of the Federal Republic and especially those of the GDR were working under a great deal of outside pressure. In fact, the foundation of the GDR, as the reader will recall, took place under alienating conditions so severe that the country was barely able to shape its own kind of dictatorship until the building of the Berlin Wall. What came after that was not exactly a social paradise either, but the population by all accounts did begin to develop a sense of state identity as well as a sense of identification with its repressive government. Some East Germans even became proud of their economic performance and social welfare state, and perhaps of their growing international role as well. The West Germans, according to the famous Almond and Verba survey of 1959, likewise expressed more pride in their economic performance than in their democratic politics.

The East Germans had less reason to take pride in their constitutions: The 1949 Constitution of the GDR was simply the old Weimar Constitution with modifications of no more significance than the politically rather unimportant document itself. Neither its bill of rights[1] nor the word "democracy" in it and in the adopted name of the country were worth anything. The adoption of the 1968 Constitution presumably meant that the GDR had become a "developed socialist democracy" in the sense of Brezhnev's categories of communist development. "Guaranteed" rights of free speech and political assembly were negated even in the language of the document (not to mention in practice) whenever their exercise challenged the goals and the "leading role" of the SED. The 1974 Constitution, finally, was mostly an effort to assert GDR identity as against the embrace of West Germany's *Ostpolitik*: it dropped all references to a common German identity and described the GDR as a "socialist state of workers and peasants" which was "eternally and irreversibly" tied to the USSR. Small wonder that the postcommunist GDR made no effort to carry over any of this constitutional heritage—or the SED old guard—into the union with the Federal Republic.

Far more important to the present state of Germany is the constitutional background of the Federal Republic and the legacy of its founders, and this for obvious reasons. First of all, the West German Basic Law was adopted in 1990 by the East German *Länder* with almost no modification. Second, the Parliamentary Council of Bonn, the founders of the Basic Law, was largely able to shape this provisional document in the light of their German constitutional traditions,[2] although they were certainly not free from the political impact of the political polarization of the Cold War, the ubiquitous signs of a catastrophic German defeat, and the overwhelming need, after Germany's moral and spiritual bankruptcy under the Nazi regime, to seek moral support from the great democratic civilizations of the West. These basic facts of 1948/49 simply cannot be emphasized enough in the face of the legends and myths that are likely to

1. Article 6 of the 1949 document puts expressions of "opposition to the new order" under criminal penalties. Certainly the Constitution never stopped the wholesale expropriations or the abolition of federalism in 1952. Nor did the replacement of its ceremonial presidency with a state council in 1961 bring any significant change.

2. See Merkl, *The Origin of the West German Republic* (New York: Oxford University Press, 1963), pp. 114–127. The oft-alleged influence of the occupying powers consisted of very limited and generally unsuccessful attempts at intervention.

originate and to be spread with German unification[3] among the willful and the ignorant.

A third reason has to do precisely with the stress on provisionality in the Basic Law, which literally looked forward to its own replacement by "a constitution adopted by a free decision of the German people" (art. 146), after a "transitional period" and "by free self-determination"; such a constitution was to be enacted also "on behalf of those Germans to whom participation was denied" (preamble). The Basic Law was never submitted for popular ratification because of this provisional character which the framers felt so keenly. It was submitted only to the *Länder* diets, which had selected the members of the Parliamentary Council to begin with. All this modest constitution-making, in any event, seems to have endeared the Basic Law to the West Germans, who also found it a reasonably useful and suitable constitution[4] and who have kept it largely intact for forty-one years. The East Germans similarly have confidence in it, and so it came to pass that it may yet serve a united Germany for many more years.

This is not to say that the Basic Law was so perfect that it never required adjustment. A modern constitution is a very complex system in which the official rules and structures of constitutional law must be firmly wedded to the living organizations and processes of politics. Such a marriage indeed occurred and has long since been consummated in the Federal Republic but, as the couple grew older, there had to be a number of modifications, large and small, in the oral contract or understandings of their marriage over the years. Donald P. Kommers has counted the many amendments, including those meant merely to fill gaps or elaborate on the original design. In the first two and a half decades alone, some sixty changes were adopted by the required majorities in parliament. Thirty-two new articles and twenty-three new paragraphs were also added, and five articles stricken. Major waves of amendment came with West German rearmament in NATO (1956), the final passage of defense

3. Already in 1963, the late Carl J. Friedrich complained about the legend of the "imposition" of the Basic Law by the occupation regime. Ibid., p. xvii. Today, and probably even more so tomorrow, there is heightened danger that a latent, right or left, German nationalism will seek to reassert German identity behind vast reinterpretations of German history, including a kind of symbolic emancipation from a once deeply felt moral dependency on America and the West. See also Andrei S. Markovits, "Anti-Americanism and the Struggle for a West German Identity," in Merkl, ed., *The Federal Republic of Germany at Forty* (New York: New York University Press, 1989), pp. 35–54.

4. But see the thesis of Peter J. Katzenstein, who has suggested that its federal constraints inhibit the capacity of its rather centralized parties and parastatal organizations to steer the economy and society of the country. *Policy and Politics in West Germany: The Growth of a Semi-Sovereign State* (Philadelphia: Temple University Press, 1987), chap. 1.

and emergency legislation (1968), and a major reform of federal–state relations with regard to finances and planning (1969).[5] In the seventies, moreover, the Bundestag set up an *Enquête* Commission on Constitutional Reform which, after spending six years considering various proposals for revision, finally issued a report of some seven hundred pages rejecting all but minor, fine-tuning kinds of amendment to strengthen the Basic Law.

Issues for Constitutional Reform

Those who would have preferred German unification via a constituent assembly drawing up a new constitution according to article 146 naturally had specific ideas either of reforming the West German Basic Law or of rescuing some of the social protections of GDR life for the united German future. Among these were, for example, the right to a job, the right of political asylum, and the right to an abortion. The "right to work" in the sense of a right to a job[6] had been in the GDR constitutions of 1968 and 1974 and, indeed, there had been no significant unemployment for forty years in the East German republic, only what the newspapers in 1990 began to call "mass unemployment at the place of work," that is, extremes of featherbedding.[7]

Critics of German unification contrast the pre-1990 near absence of unemployment with the imminent wave of as much as 25–33% unemployment of 1991, not counting the large number of early retirements and of women "voluntarily" quitting the labor market. Economists and especially Westerners speak of the deceptive illusion that communism had overcome one of the chief flaws of capitalism, recurrent unemployment. GDR featherbedding was a "social luxury" that such a less productive economy could ill afford, paying persons who did not render any services, and it would have to go if the GDR were ever to attract new investments and catch up with the West. A purely economic point of view, however,

---

5. See Kommers, "The Basic Law of the FRG After Forty Years," in Merkl, ed., *The Federal Republic of Germany at Forty*, pp. 133–159, esp. 142–143. See also the list of amendments in *Grundgesetz für die BRD* (Bonn: Deutscher Bundestag 1989), pp. 94–96, spanning the years from 1951 to the 1980s.

6. This should not be confused with American "right to work" campaigns against trade unions and job control by the unions. In the European version, a "right to work" refers to state guarantees against being dismissed without due cause and to state measures for providing jobs.

7. See, for example, *Berliner Zeitung* (East Berlin), Feb. 1, 1990. GDR labor law (the *Arbeitsgesetzbuch*) was in the process of being revised.

ignores the psychological and social importance of being meaningfully and remuneratively employed, part of a comradely work force even if the work was sporadic, inefficient, and only intermittent—from one *Materialpause* to the next. The expectation of massive unemployment in the immediate future of East Germany[8] inspired efforts by the trade unions and others to push for unemployment insurance and state employment services like the ones in West Germany, although the few employment offices were soon overrun with applicants and it took a while to add new ones. Unemployment insurance had been dropped in 1978 but was now revived in the form of social assistance.[9] Also suggested was the insertion of a "right to work" into the new constitution for a united Germany. The Basic Law so far had only a right to choose a career freely and protection against being forced to work, aside from prison sentences (art. 12) and beyond the public duties imposed on everybody—for example, to scatter sand on icy sidewalks in front of one's property in order to avoid accidents.

Another concern was the preservation of the right to political asylum which the framers of the Basic Law had inserted (art. 16), remembering the plight of German political refugees, not to mention the politically and racially persecuted, in the days of the Third Reich. In the immediate postwar years, there had been further immense streams of political refugees, many of them ethnic Germans expelled from various parts of Eastern Europe, and large numbers of displaced persons such as East European refugees from communist regimes. There were also a great many—including East European workers who had been recruited by the German occupation authority to slave in armaments factories in wartime Germany—who refused to go back to their native lands for fear of the new communist rulers.[10] Back in those early years, West Germany offered at least temporary safety, if not physical comfort or a thriving economy except for various forms of black market and postwar racketeering.

8. Unemployment among the academically trained, in particular university graduates in the humanities and social sciences—communist-style—had already crested early in 1990, before the March elections. The Modrow government tried to slim down the work force by permitting retirements at 70% of the last annual salary, or a minimum of 500 East marks, and up to five years or less before a person reached retirement age.

9. The Modrow cabinet also passed ordinances to provide for retraining of workers (February 8, 1990) as well as the laws to enlarge employment services and unemployment assistance. *Das Parlament*, no. 15, Apr. 6, 1990, p. 7.

10. The problems of the postwar refugees were so diverse as to defy generalization. In the worst-case scenario, some of them were sent back forcibly (e.g., Operation Keelhaul) to a perilous fate at the request of wartime ally Stalin, who called them "profascist traitors." In the best case, they eventually found new homes in various Western countries, including West Germany.

After the immediate postwar flood had ebbed, in the fifties, came the guest-worker schemes of the sixties which brought millions of willing workers and families from Yugoslavia (600,000), the Iberian Peninsula (144,000), and Turkey (1.5 million), not to mention immigrants from within the Common Market, such as Italians (550,000) and Greeks (200,000), to slake the thirst of the booming West German economy for labor. The guest workers mostly came for several years at a time, on the basis of state treaties with their countries of origin which included various social benefits and wage guarantees. By now, many of these foreign workers and their families have been in Germany for a decade (70%) or two—in some cases, their children were born or grew up there, obviously strangers to the countries of their parents, yet not really accepted in Germany either—but they have not been permitted to acquire German citizenship on demand.[11] Strained intercultural relations have developed particularly between Germans and Turks but also in regard to other immigrants from the wide world beyond Western Europe and North America. Occasional proposals to enable these longtime foreign residents to vote at least in their local communities were rarely successful.

Finally, when two SPD-governed *Länder*, Hamburg and Schleswig-Holstein, decided to introduce communal suffrage for foreign residents, in February 1989, the CSU-governed state of Bavaria and the CDU/CSU in parliament challenged this action before the Federal Constitutional Court. As they argued before the court when the case came up, in mid-1990, the right to vote could not be separated from the granting of citizenship, "least of all now when citizenship is the legal foundation of the [new] unity of Germany." Attorneys for the defendants argued that the granting of local suffrage was meant as a "signal of openness" and that it was likely to be perceived as a good sign by neighboring countries wary of a united Germany. They pointed out that foreign workers already had the right to vote in local elections in the GDR—hardly the most convincing example of democratic voting rights until that time—and a representative of the Danish minority in the Schleswig-Holstein diet added a plea not to refuse resident Danes the right to vote. But in the

11. Although 70% of West Germans welcome the right to asylum, just as many would like to grant it only to some (58%) or to no applicants at all (14%). See Institut für praxisorientierte Sozialforschung (IPOS), *Einstellungen zu aktuellen Fragen der Innenpolitik in der BRD und in der DDR* (Mannheim: 1990), pp. 42–43. The survey involved a representative adult male sample in mid-May of 1990. The definition of citizenship and its acquisition is quite narrow (art. 116). It includes the ethnic German refugees of the 1940s and persons whom the Nazis deprived of citizenship for political, racial, or religious reasons.

end, the court ruled, unanimously and in favor of the plaintiffs, that only German citizens had the right to vote.[12]

As a postlude to this decision, the State Court of *Land* Bremen, in mid-June 1991, invalidated an attempt by the dominant coalition of SPD, FDP, and Greens in that small state to let resident foreigners vote in the elections to the advisory district councils (*Stadtteilbeiräte*) of the city. The motion was brought by twenty-five CDU members of the Bremen Bürgerschaft (Landtag), and the court ruled that such a law would violate both the state constitution and the Basic Law. "Even communal district advisory bodies have to conform to the principles of democratic legitimation and organization," the court said. "Only the citizenry, that is the Germans residing in the district and defined by the Basic Law" could by their votes give legitimacy to the exercise of state power.

The West German boom of the eighties coincided with bad times in many parts of the world and loosed an avalanche of refugees who wanted to settle down in the Federal Republic. "Our right of political asylum is the Statue of Liberty of our constitution," according to Bundestag Deputy Burkhard Hirsch (FDP). This beacon of well-being—not just political freedom—attracted about 80,000 ethnic German refugees in 1987, 202,000 in 1988, 377,000 in 1989, and 400,000 in 1990. Also in 1990, other refugees applied for political asylum, including 22,100 Turks and Kurds, 22,000 Yugoslavs, 35,350 Romanians, and 9,200 Poles (down from 26,000 in 1989); also 12,000 Lebanese, 5,000 Palestinians, 6,000 Iranians, and 3,500 Afghanis.[13] Another 5,500 applied from

12. The court followed public sentiment: 80% of adult West Germans were against voting rights without citizenship (vs. 20% in favor). See IPOS/BRD, May–June 1990, p. 42. The Hamburg bill would have granted local suffrage to all foreigners after eight years of residence. Schleswig-Holstein had planned to accord it to residents of Scandinavian, Dutch, Irish, and Swiss nationality. The Greens in the Bundestag said the court ruling bore out "a nationalist and chauvinist view of democracy." *Göttinger Tageblatt*, June 27, 1990, p. 2; *Rheinische Post*, Nov. 1, 1990. See also the arguments of Berlin Senator of Justice Jutta Limbach in *Der Tagesspiegel* (Berlin), Jul. 3, 1991, regarding the elections of foreigners to the Berlin district assemblies (*Bezirksverordnetenversammlungen*). Limbach, who is a member of the Bundestag Committee on Constitutional Reform, advocates dual citizenship for longtime foreign residents but envisions a division between purely local and national questions: the latter should be reserved for German citizens, whereas the legitimate interest of foreigners in local concerns ought to give them local rights of representation.

13. An application for political asylum involves the following steps. The applicant is taken to a foreign resident office, where a file is opened on the person and forwarded to the Federal Office for Recognition of Foreign Refugees, in Zirndorf, Bavaria, which also has representatives in the foreign resident offices. In the meantime, the authorities must decide whether the applicant and family are indeed persecuted at home. There are interviews and additional questions for the applicant, but it is not a long, drawn-out process; the official

Vietnam and 2,500 from Sri Lanka. In 1985, as many as 30% of the applicants were permitted to stay, but today it is only 4–5%. All others are considered "economic refugees" and can stay only if they convince reluctant authorities that they are refugees from civil wars or ethnic conflicts or that they fall under the definition of the U.N. Refugee Convention of 1951.

The issue of what to do with the large number of asylum seekers seemed never more pressing than in the summer and fall of 1991, when the government decided to house them in "collection camps"—critics speak of barbed wire and concentration camps—and to speed up the deportation process. By this time, an estimated new 200,000 asylum seekers from Eastern Europe and the Middle East—Poles, Czechs, Turks, Gypsies, and Kurds—had joined the 300,000 already present and being screened at great expense. Only about 7% were expected to be granted asylum after a year-long procedure costing about 5 billion marks. The bulk will be deported as "economic refugees." The Kohl government hoped to reduce the influx by changing the Constitution, but the coalition FDP sided with the opposition on this matter. The government hopes that the camps will both minimize the attraction of Germany to the refugee stream and permit better protection of the refugees from a rash of physical and firebomb attacks in 1991 by neo-Nazis, "skinheads," and rowdy youths. One of the worst of these incidents occurred in a small East German coal-mining town, Hoyerswerda, where a series of neo-Nazi and skinhead fire attacks on the apartment buildings inhabited by Vietnamese and Mozambicans caused deaths and injuries and led to streetfighting brawls between right-wing and left-wing radicals from out of town.

In practice, there are two tiers of refugees and two levels of treatment, of which the lower level, for the non-German refugees, has so far given— a foreign resident law is in preparation[14]—local and regional authorities an unusual amount of discretion. Requiring visas and fining airlines for bringing in refugees without a visa is supposed to head them off before embarkation in Sri Lanka, Iran, Iraq, Lebanon, and other countries. But the GDR for years let them come in at the East Berlin airport and, via the S-bahn to West Berlin, permitted their arrival by the thousands in the

answer may take from a week to three months. Negative findings come faster and lead to speedy expulsion, which was the fate of 98% of 150,000 applicants in 1990.

14. The treatment of asylum applicants has worsened in recent years as a result of the 1987 Asylum Process Law and court decisions which reduced, for example, the percentage of Eritrean applicants accepted from 87% in 1987 to 4.5% in 1990 while the civil war situation in their country had hardly changed.

West. Not allowing them gainful employment or housing outside the West German camps was not sufficient discouragement either.

The year 1989/90, like the banner years of 1980 and 1986, has meant large numbers of refugees demanding political asylum and, considering the ethnic upheaval in Eastern Europe and the Soviet Union alone, there is no end in sight. Among others, a wave of Gypsies uprooted by ethnic strife has recently arrived in West Germany from Romania and other East European areas and has become a target of hostile local authorities and right-wing skinhead gangs.[15] Their numbers are not yet clear, but estimates range from 12,000 to 20,000 Roma. There are now also 3,000 Albanians who sought refuge in the German Embassy in Tirana. Another new category of refugees are Russian Jews threatened by the new waves of anti-Semitism and ethnic conflict in the Soviet Union. German authorities estimate that they have received about 10,000 Russian requests for immigration so far, and there has been considerable controversy over the reluctance of German authorities simply to admit them *en bloc*—immigration authorities have claimed that Russian-Jewish emigrants should be encouraged to immigrate instead to Israel, where they are wanted badly.[16] The most recent new category of persecuted refugees are some of the Soviet soldiers stationed in East Germany and mandated to return soon. Ethnic persecution, fanned to a deadly white glow by *glasnost*, had long found its way into an army long known for hazing deaths and incidents. There were also some among the 340,000 still stationed in the former GDR who feared returning to their homes and families, where unemployment and new social conflicts awaited them.

According to current statistics, 4.85 million foreigners already live in West Germany (one-third Turks) and another 120,000 in East Germany (one-third Vietnamese), making up about 7% of the population. The new streams of non-German refugees have brought forth defenders of the right to political asylum as well as people bent on eliminating it from the Constitution. The former included the coalition FDP, certain prominent government figures (Süssmuth, Schäuble), and the opposition SPD and Greens, while the latter have the support of the CDU/CSU and of certain *Länder* governments in the south, particularly Bavaria. There is also a widespread fear that united Germany's entire border with hungry East European nations will become like the U.S.-Mexican border—far too long and porous to keep out illegal immigrants and job seekers. And

15. Gypsies have endured centuries of persecution in Germany, culminating in their inclusion in Nazi concentration camps and the holocaust in which an estimated 200,000–400,000 of them died. See also *Der Spiegel* 44, no. 36, Sept. 3, 1990, pp. 34–57.

16. See *Die Zeit*, no. 37, Sept. 14, 1990, pp. 6 and 16, and *Nürnberger Nachrichten*, Oct. 24, 1990. Estimates of a first wave of Soviet emigrants range from 5 to 9 million.

there may be the same sort of collusion between employers needing cheap and willing labor (rather than the choosy West Germans) and the huddled masses yearning to be free, or at least to be well fed.[17] Even a prominent CDU politician like Stuttgart Mayor Manfred Rommel, who otherwise would prefer immigration quotas for asylum seekers, suggested lines of work for them that are not popular with the shrinking numbers of German workers, such as working as nurses in hospitals and old folks' homes.[18] SPD chancellor candidate Lafontaine wanted to amend the asylum article of the Basic Law with a law that would specify countries from which no refugee could claim political persecution. The low German birthrate suggests a future need for guest workers (and their families), especially by the year 2010, although in 1990 the number of births in the old FRG exceeded the number of deaths for the first time in twenty years, and the number of marriages topped that of any year since 1972. In the old GDR, by the same token, and after ten years of a consistent birth surplus (1979–1988), the births were fewer than the deaths. This response, however, was neither in keeping with the historical (especially British and French) notion of political asylum nor likely to hide the crude prejudices that already colored administrative denials of requests for asylum from some such nationalities as East Europeans, Africans, and Asians.[19]

The Issue of Abortion Law

The biggest losers in German unification were East German working women (90% of the adult female population), whose status the previous

17. Before 1989, Poles and other East European refugees were received with open arms as refugees from communist oppression. Once the borders were opened, however, the "East bloc privilege" was dropped and Polish refugees, for example, were consigned to the asylum procedure. Since April 1991, Polish visitors and transit travelers no longer needed a visa to enter Germany.

18. There was no lack of rationalizing images for those who would like to limit the language of article 16 or eliminate it altogether. "Why should we be the refuge of former Securitate men, retired Palestinian and other terrorists, and other undesirables," went the argument. See Kuno Kruse, "Politisch Verfolgte geniessen Asylrecht," Die Zeit, no. 37, Sept. 14, 1990, pp. 7–8.

19. The U.N. Refugee Convention of 1951 certainly never meant to exclude any nationality from the claim to asylum on the grounds of political persecution. Early in October 1990, a motion to limit the right of asylum was brought before the Bundesrat by Baden-Württemberg and found some sympathy even with the delegations from SPD-governed Länder such as North Rhine Westphalia. The number of asylum seekers for 1990 reached nearly 200,000, whereas "only" 120,000 came in 1989. See Der Spiegel 44, no. 42, Oct. 15, 1990, pp. 31–36, and no. 45, Nov. 5, 1990, pp. 36–44.

regime had supported with equal pay and opportunity, child care for one- to three-year-olds and kindergartens for older preschoolers, a birth premium of 1,000 marks, up to ten weeks' leave to tend sick children, and (since 1972) legal abortions during the first three months of pregnancy. The result was that, unlike capitalist West Germany, where only two-thirds of women choose motherhood and only one-half are gainfully employed (80% would like to have a job), 92% of East German women could afford to have children. One-fifth of East German families, in fact, got on well with only one parent, usually the mother. To be sure, everything was not all roses for GDR women, and a *Frauenreport '90* [Women's Report 1990] quickly revealed the ideological shallowness of socialist emancipation; but there could be no doubt about the results or the contrast to the West where, in spite of pious assertions about the rights of the unborn, live children are still a luxury that requires either wealth or an acceptance of relative poverty in the midst of an affluent society. In any case, the economic impact of German unification on East German women was far worse than that on men. Many enterprises in dire straits closed their child care centers, forcing working mothers to quit. In the huge wave of dismissals, furthermore, women were usually selected as the first to be fired.

In August 1990, a major disagreement before the Bonn parliament grew from the fact that GDR law permitted abortion on demand within the first twelve weeks of pregnancy, whereas West German law during the same period required that an abortion be justified on medical, eugenic, ethical (rape), or social (economic) grounds.[20] There was agreement among the parties—but not with the women's organizations, which would prefer to apply the East German regulation in the West, too—that the existing laws should remain in force for two years following unification. The CDU/CSU not only balked at accepting the exemption of the East German *Länder* from the abortion laws of the West in the long run, but insisted that women be governed during the interim by the laws valid in their area of residence.[21] This meant that West German women

20. On West German abortion law, see Merkl, "West German Women: A Long Way From Kinder, Küche, Kirche," in Lynne Iglitzin and Ruth Ross, eds., *Women in the World: The Women's Decade 1975–1985* (Santa Barbara, Calif.: ABC-Clio, 1986), pp. 27–52, and the supplement to *Das Parlament*, B14/90, March 30, 1990, where various abortion issues are discussed, including the role of doctors and the constitutional controversy before the Federal Constitutional Court in the seventies.

21. This was decided in early summer between the ministries of justice in East Berlin and Bonn. There was an assumption that the deplorable state of the GDR clinics would probably not attract "abortion tourism" as did those of the Netherlands and that, after the two years were over, all of Germany would have to live under West German regulations of

terminating their pregnancies in East Germany would be criminally liable for not following West German restrictions. Or, in the words of Berlin women senators (magistrates) of the SPD and the Alternative List (AL-Greens), West and East German women lying in adjoining hospital beds of Berlin's maternity wards would not be equal before the law.

The CDU/CSU coalition partner in Bonn, the FDP, spent four or five hours of coalition negotiations on this subject alone with its Christian Democratic partners. Since the CDU/CSU did not have a majority without the FDP, the latter party's position was crucial to the outcome. The opposition parties and women's organizations favored a "scene of the crime" approach, which simply made the different laws apply to where the abortions were performed. The FDP Presidium finally reaffirmed that the party would not do anything that might lead to criminal prosecutions of West German women in the former GDR. The FDP deputy chair, Irmgard Adam-Schwätzer, and CDU Bundestag President Rita Süssmuth finally attempted to launch a compromise that might serve both East and West Germany in the future. The compromise would simply have required pregnant women to seek counseling and think things over for three days before proceeding with an abortion. Abiding by this procedure would make the decision a "matter of conscience," which is constitutionally protected from prosecution. But the new effort at opening up discussion did not produce an all-German compromise, but a split in the FDP.[22] The pro-choice faction had to settle for the earlier agreement (on the basis of a woman's residence) until a newly elected all-German parliament might get around to the subject.

The SPD felt strongly enough about this issue to threaten withholding its consent to the final unification treaty[23] which required a two-thirds vote, but in the end did not do so. Süssmuth's compromise formula at the time was neither acceptable to her own party—least of all to the Bavarian CSU, which heads a bloc of ninety-nine CDU/CSU hard-liners on the subject—nor to the pro-choice Pro Familia organization or the Greens who saw it in a revival of the already defeated legislation on

---

abortion. Since nearly 90% of West German abortions are authorized upon claims of socioeconomic necessity (social indication), the practice in East and West has not differed as much as the theory.

22. Bonn Minister of Justice Engelhard (FDP) sided with the CDU/CSU position, but his successor, Kinkel (FDP), helped FDP, SPD, Green, Bündnis 90, and PDS deputies to form another coalition along the lines of the Süssmuth–Adam-Schwätzer proposal. See *Der Spiegel* 45, no. 20, May 13, 1991, pp. 18–31.

23. A failure to approve the treaty, however, would not have stopped unification on schedule. The treaty would have been replaced with a simple law on such matters as finance, education, and property which would have required only a simple majority. See *Der Spiegel* 44, no. 31, Jul. 30, 1990, pp. 23–25.

abortion counseling. There was also a CDU women's proposal to establish a special Bundestag subcommittee on abortion reform.

Prominent voices, including East German CDU Premier de Maizière and *Der Spiegel* publisher Rudolf Augstein, wanted to do away with the criminal law article on abortion (art. 218) altogether.[24] A bill before the Bundestag on protection of embryos, on the other hand, laid the ground for future political battles by defining embryos as "beginning with the fertilized human ovum." No wonder Chancellor Kohl's preference was to keep the entire "emotionalized issue of art. 218" out of the election campaign for an all-German parliament. The opinions expressed by most German women's organizations and the liberal news media indeed promise a battle royal on the subject of abortion.[25] In public opinion polls by *Quick* magazine, three-fourths of German adult women favored freeing pregnant women's choice during the first three months of all restrictions—only 19% favored the West German law—and the same solution was adopted eleven to three by a federal state conference of *Länder* ministers and deputies of women's affairs, in May 1991, which also called for special support for families and for single mothers or fathers. There are other unification issues of particular relevance to women, beginning with the differential impact of mass unemployment, the loss of part-time positions, and the long-term loss of the ample East German child care facilities which Bonn agreed to finance until the end of 1991. The difference in the availability of child care for all working

24. See Augstein's plea for abolition of article 218 (ibid., p. 24) which, among other points, argues that Catholics and the Catholic church (which was girding up for the mother of political battles) should not be permitted to impose their values on everybody else. The new Baden-Württemberg minister president, Erwin Teufel (CDU), spelled out what it would take to encourage a positive attitude among young Germans toward having children: educational aid (scholarships) and leave for young parents, real opportunities for women to return to their careers, pension credit for staying home to raise children, tax relief and other subsidies for families, and sufficient child care places. See *Süddeutsche Zeitung*, Apr. 20 and 21, 1991.

25. The ZDF *Politbarometer* for May 1991 showed the different response of German adults in East and West. About one-third of all respondents insisted there be no punishment for abortion in the first trimester. Another third of West Germans and half the East Germans favored a requirement for consultation but leaving it in principle to the woman to decide. Thus, two-thirds of West Germans and three-fourths of East Germans would support the Süssmuth–Adam-Schwätzer formula. One in ten East and West Germans was dead set against abortions, and one in four West Germans would have forbidden them but with "exceptions," presumably the current list of "indications." The embryo law bans all changes of human genes, surrogate mothers, and trade or experimentation with human embryos. There were notable objections to the ban on medical research. See *Süddeutsche Zeitung*, Oct. 24, 1990. On the abortion issue, see also Margit Gerste, "Gleichheit für die Frauen," *Die Zeit*, no. 37, Sept. 14, 1990, p. 1, and the dialogue between Süssmuth and Helga Schubert in *Die Zeit*, no. 43, Oct. 26, 1990, pp. 18–20.

women—91% of East German women were gainfully employed, which was both a regime-intended necessity because of low wage levels and a source of female independence—had been one of the true social advantages of the GDR over the Federal Republic, although it did not escape criticism in 1989/90.[26] The vaunted equality of women in the GDR, furthermore, did not translate into shared child-rearing and household chores any more than it has in the West.

There is no end to the agenda for further constitutional changes favored by various parties and groups. For example, there is considerable support, for inserting a provision for initiatives and referenda into the Basic Law, whose framers were so diffident concerning the people's will that they made a point of leaving initiatives and referenda out (except in the case of territorial change).[27] Many Germans, West and East, would like the Constitution to declare environmental protection a solemn goal and obligation of the country. The Free Democrats hope to broaden the federal powers over education, which is still a subject of *Länder* jurisdiction. SPD chancellor candidate Lafontaine favors a right to housing, an idea related to the housing shortage of both West and East and its role during the great exodus of refugees in 1989/90.[28] Chancellor Kohl promised the Western allies that he would try to change the Constitution to permit the deployment of German troops overseas (e.g., in the Persian Gulf). Public opinion polls, however, have been running heavily against sending German soldiers abroad for any purpose other than the defense of Germany and German interests. The newly elected Bundestag may still tackle some of these items on the constitutional agenda in 1991, or at least air them before the united German public.[29]

The demise of a whole system shot through with political repression and favoritism raises large questions of law and justice which have been highlighted by the Soviet-aided escape of Erich Honecker to Moscow and

26. Child care facilities and personnel often shared the run-down fate and neglect of the East German infrastructure, and some West Germans claimed also that children in the GDR state's care suffered disproportionately from respiratory and other illnesses.

27. On a number of occasions—e.g., with respect to German rearmament in the fifties and the modernization of NATO missiles in the early eighties—initiatives were called for but held to be illegal.

28. *Rheinischer Merkur/Christ and Welt*, Oct. 12, 1990. By 1995, 1.5 million East Germans are expected to have immigrated into crowded West German cities, where the total of the homeless is already estimated at 1 million by one association concerned about their fate (BAGNH).

29. Other issues involved the unification of educational systems, driving while under the influence of alcohol—in the GDR there was a zero-tolerance policy, while in the West a blood alcohol level of .8 per mill was the limit—and purging and reorganizing the public service.

the arrest of several other former GDR leaders—among them Willi Stoph and ex-Defense Minister Kessler—on charges of complicity in the shooting of more than two hundred East German refugees at the Wall and elsewhere along the inner-German border. It certainly makes more sense to try and convict those who made the big decisions rather than to focus on a handful of all-too-obedient guards who carried out the deadly—and repeatedly and officially denied—orders to shoot to kill. Further crimes by the minions of the communist state were committed against captured escapees, whose right to leave the country had been acknowledged in the Helsinki Agreements and who were frequently "wounded while trying to escape," injured, or tortured after capture. Worst of all, the children of escapees and of other "politically unreliable" persons were frequently taken away and stuck into juvenile homes or given to "politically reliable" parents for forcible adoption. As with its version of denazification, West German justice has not been able to accept the principle of personal responsibility in regard to the main figures of a grim dictatorship, only violations of positive and possibly unjust laws, so that monstrous deeds may still be held legally unassailable. The question of compensation of the victims for physical injury, unjustified detention and maltreatment, lost years, and destroyed careers is likely to be in limbo for many years to come, and at niggardly levels at that. After forty years of dictatorship, our knowledge of what exactly went on in the GDR and who was responsible for it is still in its beginning phase. And the peculiar mixture of force and grasping cooperation, of entrapment and blackmail in the octopus arms of the Stasi, often obscures the nature of individual responsibility behind the mortal coils of human affairs.

The Changing Property Constitution

At the heart of the communist economy is a concept of property and of governmental powers over private property in the hands of the State Planning Commission and the party agencies that amounts to a profoundly different order of property (or *Eigentumsverfassung*) than what prevailed in the Federal Republic and other Western, capitalist states. We need to examine these changing concepts of property, and the transfers from collective to private ownership, together with the work of the Trust Agency for the People's Property (Treuhandanstalt für Volkseigentum) in order to understand this important aspect of constitutional change in East Germany. Nearly all productive enterprises in the GDR were "people's own firms" (*Volkseigene Betriebe*, or VEBs), often grouped into large *Kombinate*. Privatization, return to former owners, or sale of such enterprises, not to mention "joint ventures" with foreign firms, all involve disentangling the complexities of the old forms of collective property in the GDR.

Since the vast majority of capital assets like factories, cooperative farms, and apartment houses in the GDR belonged to the state and other public bodies, it was only logical to look to this large reserve as a source of capital to bail out the failing economy, settle debts, and provide collateral for credits. As it turned out, however, things were not that simple. To begin with, there were the distinctions between state, cooperative, semistatal, and private property, of which state and semistatal property amounted to 80.7%, cooperative property to 14.7%, and private property to a mere 4.7% of all assets at the time of the March elections. "Socialist property," as defined by the GDR Constitution, included the considerable property of the communist SED,[30] other "bloc parties," and state mass organizations such as the trade unions (FDGB) or communist youth (FDJ)—such things as vacation homes and printing facilities. State property, or "people's property"—the GDR always preferred juristically dubious or hazy definitions—included mines, power plants, factories or the land on which they were, banks and insurance companies, whole states, and the transport and communications equipment of the railroads and postal service. Cooperative property belonged mostly to agricultural (LPGs), handicraft (PGMs), or housing cooperatives (AWGs) and included tools, machinery, livestock, buildings, and the yield of these operations.

This left little private property and few people independently employed. In 1988, only 2% of the gainfully employed were independent (down from 20% in 1955): 81,700 in the trades, 39,200 in commerce, and 27,000 service operators.[31] Their property included shops, business lots, retail stores, and even manufacturing equipment, also the members' land used by agricultural and other cooperatives (originally contributed when a person joined the cooperative), as well as church property and

30. Some PDS/SED functionaries obviously had their own idea of socialist property when in October 1990 they attempted to flee to the Soviet Union with 107 million marks ($70 million) of party property in cash and were caught. Further, secret bank accounts of the state party have been found since, and the issue of such dubious wealth in a poor country—the SED property alone is believed to add up to 3 billion marks—looms large in the public mind. The PDS leaders, in particular Gregor Gysi, have denied knowing about the financial shenanigans of their functionaries.

31. There were also 18,000 building contractors or subcontractors, 8,000 in transport, 5,900 in agriculture and forestry, and 1,500 other independents. See *Die Zeit*, no. 12, March 16, 1990, pp. 20–22.

the assets of refugees who had fled the GDR in earlier years and whose property was then taken over by trustees. Cooperatives did not permit members to withdraw their assets, nor could they sell them except within the cooperative. GDR law also speaks of "personal property," such as family residences, weekend dachas, residential lots, and garages, with the state reserving a first right of purchase and of approval for all property transactions.

The Soviet occupation had begun the first round of expropriations when, beginning on October 30, 1945, it took away the property of "war criminals" and Nazi activists; houses, furniture, real estate, and industrial plants were all to be placed under communal trusteeship.[32] By 1948, 3,843 firms had been expropriated without compensation, and 676 of them (including 213 large enterprises) were dismantled and transported to the Soviet Union as reparations, leaving 61% of East German industrial capacity in state (or Soviet) hands.[33] A "democratic land reform" of the Soviet occupation also expropriated all estates over 100 hectares (250 acres) for the purpose of "punishing and taking away the power of Junkers and large landowners," also without compensation and without any regard to the past political conduct of the owners. The expropriated land was transferred to a Land Fund and in large part was handed out in lots of 20–22 acres to small peasants and landless agricultural workers, tradesmen, and ethnic German refugees from Eastern Europe and the Oder-Neisse area—altogether about half a million persons, frequently new to farming. They were not allowed to sell or lease their properties. A total area of about 8 million acres was expropriated in this fashion—not including lands beyond the Oder-Neisse line or in East Prussia—and about 2.5 million of this was eventually turned into state farms.[34]

Under the East German state constitutions of the occupation years, coal and metals mining, iron and steel production, energy-supply monopolies, natural resources, and banks and insurance firms were also turned over to the state, this time however with a compensation determined, without further recourse, by the counties (*Kreise*). In 1990, after long

32. Order no. 124 of the Soviet Military Administration in Germany (SMAD), pursuant to the Potsdam Agreements and Allied Control Council Law no. 10. See also Gregory W. Sandford, *From Hitler to Ulbricht: The Communist Reconstruction of Eastern Germany, 1945–46* (Princeton, N.J.: Princeton University Press, 1983), chap. 3.

33. This was accomplished also by a 1946 plebiscite in Saxony which expropriated those assets already seized without compensation and transferred them to state property. SMAD Order no. 64, on April 17, 1948, completed this phase and declared the "people's property" inviolable. See Sandford, *From Hitler to Ulbricht*, chap. 5.

34. See Sandford, *From Hitler to Ulbricht*, pp. 85–118, for an account of the land reform campaign and its implementation. The Modrow government and the Soviet Union insisted that the 1945–1949 expropriations not be undone but simply accepted.

discussions within both the East German cabinet and the parliament, it was decided not to reopen the question of returning property or offering compensation for it if the property had been taken under the Soviet occupation. However, plaintiffs brought suit and the Federal Constitutional Court decided to uphold the agreement with the Soviet government under the "two-plus-four" negotiations: "An assessment of what could be gotten out of the negotiations," the court said with remarkable judicial self-restraint, "was up to the judgment of the federal government and cannot be reassessed by a constitutional court." The plaintiffs spoke for more than 10,000 expropriated parties and had attacked the enshrinement of the expropriation in article 143 of the Basic Law—not invoked was the Basic Law guarantee of private property which dates back only to 1949. Their claim was reduced to a theoretical right to compensation commensurate to "the desolate situation of the new *Länder*" at the time of unification. Like the land ceded to Poland or the Soviet Union and to the great relief of East German farmers, the loss was not to be treated like similar losses after 1949.

Once the GDR was established in 1949, it was also given the authority to determine its own policy of nationalization. Deliberate economic discrimination—e.g., in allocating skilled labor and supplies—had already reduced the share of private industrial enterprises between 1948 and 1952 from 60% to a mere 19%. In 1955/56, the SED Central Committee began to "offer" some of the remaining private firms state participation, and in 1959 a wave of semistatal enterprises resulted whose now partial owners were made chief managers but who were also personally liable for debts or failure. In 1972, the GDR Council of Ministers transferred all remaining industrial and construction firms and cooperatives to "people's property" and froze compensation for this confiscation in a form that permitted only limited annual withdrawals, an action that resulted in 11,000 new VEBs.[35]

In agriculture, the great wave of collectivization began in 1952/53, when "abandoned or improperly maintained farms" (meaning mostly those of GDR refugees to the West) were given to the counties to administer. Refugees from the GDR were promised that they could have their property back if they returned. But in practice they could not extract them from the agricultural LPGs being created in the big campaigns of the mid-fifties[36] which put farmers under great pressure to join the

35. In early 1990 the Modrow government reversed the trend and encouraged the creation of new private enterprises, permitting also the repurchase of firms taken away since 1972.

36. There were three types of these cooperative farms, one including only the arable land (I), another including this as well as machinery and draft animals (II), and the third including everything (III). In 1957, the share of refugee properties among the LPGs

"voluntary" LPG cooperatives. Some farmers also lost their farms because they happened to be located along the boundary with West Germany. Their complaints were ignored as they were hauled away against their will to a grim factory job. LPG members retained property rights in their land but could sell that land only to the LPG or to other LPG members. By 1967, with further concentration, there were 9,000 LPGs, averaging 1,500 acres and encompassing 95% of the agricultural production of the GDR. We shall return to the resulting agrifactories and their problems in Chapter Six.

The GDR constitutions of 1949 and 1968 did set forth a legal procedure for expropriations, but the large number of accepted reasons for it and the preference for "socialist" over private property held out little hope for the property owner. Expropriation was permissible in "barred areas," in border zones, and for tearing down buildings in bad repair—this alone could be applied easily to three-fourths of the country in 1990. Providing housing, urban renewal, or the need for workers or large families to build their own homes was considered sufficient reason to nationalize a house. Today very few East German families own their houses or condominiums, only 25% as compared to 39% in the FRG and 64% in the United States. Those who do often owe this privilege to past political favoritism or clout. Those who retained rental housing as their property found themselves beset by the double impact of incredibly low rents and the obligation to keep up repairs. Most of them ended up donating their apartment house to municipal housing authorities, and often they had to pay the authorities to accept it. But now the wave of the expropriated of forty years of the GDR is coming back with a vengeance: half a million former East German refugees want their property returned or at least fair compensation for it if, in the meantime, it has become too transformed or entangled in common institutions to be returned.[37] Compensation is likely to cost over 100 billion marks even if, as currently estimated, it is limited to 5–20% of today's market value.

A good deal of public criticism has already focused on the policy of letting a claimant demand the property rather than compensation because, in many cities, this ties up valuable business properties that could

amounted to 57% of the arable acreage. At that time, nearly a million farmers had been collectivized, and a similar number followed by 1960. See Henry Krisch, *The German Democratic Republic: The Search for Identity* (Boulder, Colo.: Westview Press, 1985), pp. 103–108.

37. There was some resistance to returning the property itself. Prime Minister de Maizière and others favored compensation in all cases, but were overruled. *Stuttgarter Zeitung*, June 18, 1990. Observers also fear that windfall appreciation of some properties will favor some owners.

otherwise be attracting investors. The new GDR government insisted that the present renters, users, and cooperative partners should also have certain protected rights. Unfortunately, in 1990 the entire GDR had only about 700 "independent" attorneys—West Berlin alone had 2,000—and almost no trained assessors of property or land registry personnel to straighten out all the legal complications. The courts will be busy for many years to come. West German law is quite different and knows neither "people's property" nor the ins and outs of the user's rights of, for example, 1 million private dachas built on people's property. Outside investors and joint-venture partners also have a right to know the property status of what they wish to acquire. A simple takeover of West German law in this matter could create nightmares for many East Germans.

Expropriating the Expropriators

A growing number of court cases has already revealed weak areas in resolving disputes over the property of refugees. There are thousands of cases involving former SED or NVA functionaries, perhaps even Stasi operatives who acquired attractive properties cheap before the currency union. They sometimes managed to destroy or remove all public records of the previous ownership—presumably the same friends who helped make the records disappear also assisted with the dubious acquisition of the refugee's house—and the lot was converted to "people's property." Present local officials who may be with the PDS often did their best to interfere with efforts to reestablish the claim of the refugee. All the while the PDS daily, *Neues Deutschland*, trumpeted headlines about the "great raid" of rich West Germans on East German real estate. The Unification Treaty of October 3, 1990, is full of formulations inviting claims—the deadline for residential property was October 13 and for business, September 16, 1990—even from those who donated their apartment houses to local authorities, but it is also full of loopholes that set up hurdles for the claimants. It is rarely easy after many years to demonstrate the chicanery of corrupt communist officials and their party friends. Public use of a property for building residential housing, parks, or sports facilities, moreover, revives the old GDR laws regarding the priority of public property over its restoration to a previous owner. Compensation depends on the "value at the point of expropriation," and there is bound to be controversy about real-estate values of years ago and in the absence of a market. The properties were also overloaded with GDR government mortgages (which have to be serviced) and are likely to be as run-down and neglected as can be.[38] Title records are so poor that even the communist cities and towns have difficulties documenting their own property titles (e.g., in East Berlin). Since private ownership of land was undesirable in communist Germany, some land registry records were lost, destroyed, or not maintained beginning in the late forties. Whatever new records ensued often did not match the old ones and were not based on accurate measurements or boundaries. The new land registry personnel can hardly keep up with new transactions, let alone clear up the old ones.

The Round Table of the winter of 1989/90 drew attention to the extraordinary complexity of these questions, and one of its prominent members (later a minister without portfolio), Wolfgang Ullmann of Democracy Now, proposed a Trust Agency (Treuhandanstalt) for maintaining the share of GDR citizens in the people's property, a daring attempt to make the average citizen a shareholder in "GDR, Inc."[39] Thanks to his efforts, though probably many years down the road, the average GDR citizen may yet receive such a share from forty years of communist management, albeit small compensation for decades of repression. The newly formed Democratic Peasant party (DBP) had meanwhile tried to pass a bill in the old GDR parliament (before the March elections) to convert land owned by the LPG cooperatives from "people's property" into their private property, to be sold or leased if desired.[40] Ullmann stopped this raid on the people's property, just as he had to with the trust agencies of various *Kombinate* and housing authorities that were ready to sell the public assets as if they were theirs alone. The legal tangles resulting from old expropriations under duress and from the corrupt shenanigans of former GDR power brokers and profiteers, however, must not be confused with major legal enactments such as the

38. For details of the Unification Treaty, see below, or the West German government's *Bulletin*, no. 104, Sept. 6, 1990, and the Basic Law, articles 14 and 135a. See also *Der Spiegel* 44, no. 41, Oct. 8, 1990, pp. 46–77. By this time, estimates spoke of more than 1 million claimants. Among the claims being processed are also claims by some victims of expropriation during the Third Reich. Some of those who lost their property under the Soviet occupation, 1945–1949, are also suing to overturn those clauses of the treaty which have legalized such expropriations.

39. Ullmann, a theologian and church historian, viewed the privatization campaign and refugee claims with some misgivings and proposed a periodization which would separate claims stemming from pre-Wall flight from claims pertaining to post-1961 properties in question, which he appreciated more. See *Die Zeit*, no. 12, March 16, 1990, pp. 18–22.

40. Many LPG members showed little desire to pull out of their respective cooperative agribusinesses because, among other reasons, the original farm and the conditions making it viable had long disappeared. For the same reason, many refugees saw little point in reclaiming farms whose soil had been depleted and polluted and whose other assets had been ruined by years of LPG operations.

democratic land reform and legal expropriation procedures against
individuals for stated reasons. The victims and the Bonn government, on
the other hand, may hesitate to accept the "socialist legality" of these
transactions. In March 1991, a law was passed facilitating at least the
process of determining ownership, compensation, and transfer to new
owners; despite some flaws, it was a milestone on the way to a clearer
"property constitution" in the former GDR.

The First State Treaty on the currency unification had special provisions
(supp. 9) to ensure that enterprises could acquire full title in a property
and promised that the GDR would make available plenty of suitable
commercial and manufacturing lots. Even the people's own land under
the VEBs in transformation was to be deeded to them as their private
property, but with the proviso that the purchase price could be settled
only later, when there might be a functioning market that would allow
its determination. Once the purchase prices have been collected, the
resulting sum will be the basis for the shares of the GDR citizens. There
is some doubt, however, whether this solution was sufficiently reassuring
to new buyers, investors, or entrepreneurs. The end of communist
economic management on July 1, 1990, also put an end to the recurrent
annual bleeding, for the benefit of the state, of some 200 billion East
marks from the VEBs' production, promised new investment subsidies,
and exchanged both the credits and the liabilities of the VEBs at the rate
of 2:1, a noticeable break for enterprises on the way toward a market
economy.[41]

The Trust Agency for the People's Property

The problems of reconciling collective property and privatization were
finally placed into the hands of a Trust Agency for the People's Property
(Treuhandgesellschaft), a public holding company to watch over the 8,000
VEBs and *Kombinate* as well as the people's own estates and forests of
the GDR. Established by the Law for the Privatization and Reorganiza-

41. The inalienability of about 50% of the land had also been a major obstacle for the
600 joint ventures set up by June 1990. Moreover, there was no lack of West German
speculators and real-estate men with few scruples traveling up and down the GDR in search
of bargains and opportunities amidst all this legal confusion. See *Der Spiegel* 44, no. 13,
March 26, 1990, pp. 140–142. See also *Rheinischer Merkur/Christ und Welt*, May 11,
1990; *Göttinger Tageszeitung*, May 10, 1990; and *Stuttgarter Zeitung*, June 18, 1990, on
the property questions. See also the account in *Der Spiegel* 44, no. 44, Oct. 29, 1990,
pp. 16–27, which details incidents of massive fraud and racketeering.

tion of the People's Own Property (July 1, 1990), the Trust Agency was
to decide the following: a) which GDR firms would be bailed out and
with how much money; b) which firms could invite outside partners and
under what conditions; c) the conditions for outright sales of VEB firms;
d) the future of the *Kombinate* and the people's own estates and forests;
and e) the use of the profits generated by these firms. Popularly called
Treuhand, this agency was inauspiciously housed in Nazi Air Minister
Hermann Göring's old Aviation Ministry building in Berlin. It is the
largest enterprise in the world if we count the assets and employees under
its command. It has also attracted never-ending criticism, attacks, and
public demonstrations because of the painful nature of its decisions. The
most spectacular expression of hostility to the Treuhand was the assassination on April 1, 1991, of its activist chief, Detlev Karsten Rohwedder,
by the terrorist RAF.

The Trust Agency was originally responsible to the GDR prime minister and cabinet, who in turn were accountable to the People's Chamber,
with whom they appointed an Administrative Council for the Trust
Agency. The new agency had a council composed of West German
business leaders and experts and East German CEOs,[42] but no representatives of small or medium-size business or of the trade unions. The Trust
Agency furthermore established five trust stock companies (Treuhand-
AGs) to oversee their charges—one for the people's forests and estates
and the others for all the VEBs—and their transformation into private
joint-stock companies. Each VEB had to produce a plan for this purpose
and a certified opening balance by October 13, 1990. It had to complete
the process or face automatic dissolution on July 1, 1991. The Trust
Agency gave liquidity loans to VEBs for the first three months so that
they could meet their payrolls and other obligations after the currency
reform of July 1, 1990.[43]

The evolution of this difficult task can be followed by perusal of the
relevant enactments between June 17 (the date the treaty on the currency
union was completed) and mid-September 1990. Upon insistence of the
SPD in the People's Chamber, residential properties were allocated to
municipal authorities that also control people's own property required
for local services. The original Organic Law for the Privatization and
Reorganization of the People's Own Property of June 17 set the following
goals for the Trust Agency:

42. See *Die Zeit*, no. 26, June 22, 1990, p. 29, and no. 29, Jul. 13, 1990, p. 21.
43. See Heinz Suhr, *Was kostet uns die DDR?* (Frankfurt: Eichborn, 1990), pp. 14–
21, and *Die Zeit*, no. 29, Jul. 13, 1990, p. 21.

1. the speedy reduction of state entrepreneurial activity by privatization,
2. establishing and securing competitiveness as quickly as possible,
3. making real estate available for economic purposes,
4. giving holders of savings accounts which were exchanged on July 2 at reduced rates [i.e., beyond the amounts exchanged 1:1] certified shares in the people's property that can be redeemed at a later date. Such shares can be determined only after a survey of the people's own property and its productivity and after other priorities have been set for its use in restructuring the economy and consolidating the state budget.[44]

The Trust Agency became the holder of the capital shares of the people's own companies (VEBs) that were restructured or in the process of reorganization (para. 1, sec. 4 of the Trust Agency law) until the creation of the trust joint stock companies (para. 7). This was clarified further with a resolution of the de Maizière cabinet, which gave the Trust Agency a statute in mid-July and added further specifics about its legal rights in an executive ordinance in mid-August.[45] A second ordinance a week later regulated the privatization of the considerable land, buildings, and other assets of the East German military (NVA) and the Ministry for Disarmament and Defense, hopefully for nonmilitary production. A third ordinance gave the Trust Agency control over the people's own estates, fisheries and fish ponds, horse ranches, state-owned forestry operations, and the Kombinat Animal Products. A fourth and fifth ordinance, on September 12, 1990, turned over the considerable real property of the Stasi Ministry (MfS/AfNS) to the agency and determined the specifics of its takeover of Stasi commercial real estate.[46] In a report to the East German People's Chamber a day later, Trust Agency President Detlev Rohwedder announced that instead of the trust joint-stock companies decided earlier, regional trust agencies should be established which would each guide about 250–350 small and medium-size VEB enterprises. This

44. *Gesetz zur Privatisierung und Reorganisierung des volkseigenen Vermögens (Treuhandgesetz) vom 17. Juni 1990*, effective from July 1. See also article 25 of the Unification Treaty of October 3, 1990.

45. *Beschluss des Ministerrates über die Satzung der Treuhandanstalt vom 18. Juli 1990 und Erste Durchführungsverordnung zum Treuhandgesetz vom 15. August 1990*.

46. *Vierte und Fünfte Durchführungsverordnung zum Treuhandgesetz vom 12. Sept. 1990*. The Stasi alone owned more than 2,000 buildings, apartments, and recreation facilities, not to mention its military arsenal. The extensive property of the PDS/SED and of the other bloc parties was also to become part of the assets at the disposal of the Trust Agency.

decentralization of the mammoth responsibilities of the Trust Agency, it was hoped, would benefit the growth of the East German market economy.

By this time, the text of the Unification Treaty was already firm: article 25 determined details of organization and capital for the Trust Agency. It subordinated the agency to the federal minister of finance together with the economy minister and whatever other ministers might be involved in particular cases. The statute of the Trust Agency henceforth (October 3) could be changed only with the consent of the federal cabinet. Article 25 also added representatives of each of the new *Länder* to the administrative council, dropping the Volkskammer representatives and increasing the council representatives ultimately to twenty, which had to be appointed by the federal cabinet, as did the chair. It pledged that the people's own property would be used and sold only for the benefit of the Eastern areas, also in accordance with the First State Treaty (arts. 26[4] and 27[3]). It authorized the Trust Agency to assist with clearing the debts of agricultural LPGs and to issue guarantees and other pledges. It raised its capital from 17 to 25 billion marks and specified that the credits granted by it should be repaid "as a rule" by the end of 1995. Finally, it repeated the promise to indemnify the holders of savings accounts which exceeded the ceiling for an exchange rate of 1:1 at some future date.

By the time of Rohwedder's death, a preliminary balance sheet showed that only about 300 VEBs had been privatized, securing about 300,000 jobs and generating 55 billion marks in promised investment by the new owners over several years. Only 4 billion marks had been collected for these sales while the Treuhand agency already expected to exceed its 1991 budget by 21 billion marks, including 12 billion in assumed VEB interest payments, 4 billion for environmental cleanups, 9 billion for rehabilitating run-down or inefficient VEBs, 2.5 billion to aid exports to Eastern Europe, 3.5 billion to ensure liquidity, and 2 billion to close down some 330 VEBs, causing a loss of 80,000 jobs. In the end, the Treuhand expected to pay out some 35 billion marks while gaining only 14 billion marks in sales, a substantial deficit to add to the cost of German unification.

The Trust Agency also experienced problems of personnel and leadership almost from the beginning. By August the agency had already lost its first director, Reiner Gohlke, a railroad executive, and it went through a management shake-up a month later. Upon Gohlke's resignation, the board chairman of the agency, Rohwedder, took over and set the agenda for a series of privatizations.[47] Premier de Maizière's candidates for the

---

47. Rohwedder, who once served as a state secretary in the Ministry of the Economy

administrative council were not only inexperienced in regard to market
economics and capital, but they were all former SED activists and some
may even have been Stasi agents. Until 1990 no one was likely to become an economic manager in the GDR without a significant career in
the communist state party. Their West German replacements had all the
necessary experience, but some had conflicts of interest. The subsidies of
the Trust Agency for the 8,000 VEBs in its care were the target of massive
requests totaling 20 billion marks in the first month after the currency
union took effect. Rather than investigating each claim, the agency simply
decided to give each applicant 40% of what had been asked for. Rohwedder's proved to be a strong and prudent management that, after replacing
all the East German regional trust directors with West Germans or East
German refugees with Western experience, stood up to such West German takeover schemes as the one by the luxury Steigenberger Hotels,
which sought to buy all thirty-four Interhotel branches, and the one by
Lufthansa, which wanted to acquire a controlling interest in the East
German Interflug. Nevertheless, there was a chorus of critics, ranging
from workers facing unemployment to Western business managers complaining about the bureaucratic complications and slow pace of the
agency. Its biggest problem by far was an inability to attract the thousands of top Western executives whom Rohwedder had hoped to enlist,
like himself, in the difficult management of the transition.[48] The agency's
estimated needs were in the range of 12,000 CEOs and 30,000 board
members for all the VEBs.

Moreover, there were differences of opinion regarding the best policy
for the difficult journey toward a market economy. The Modrow government had planned only to turn the 8,000 VEBs into public stock
companies which would operate within a market context, not to privatize
them as Treuhand intended to do. Should the agency try to sell the old
VEBs as quickly as possible, or should it attempt to help rehabilitate the
East German enterprises regardless of the mounting cost? After lengthy
deliberation, a new set of guidelines opting for the second policy choice
was sent out to the regional trust offices in late October, although

for the Schmidt administration, was the very successful chairman of the Hoesch steel group,
which had earlier required rescue from the brink of oblivion. One of his East German
decisions involved Pentacon, the makers of Praktica cameras, of which three-fourths used
to go abroad at big discounts in order to attract foreign currency funds. With a work force
of 5,600, Pentacon was considered unsalvageable even after dismissing two-thirds of its
employees unless the agency would pump 160 million marks into its operation. Rohwedder
decided to liquidate the firm. See *The Economist*, Aug. 25 and Oct. 20, 1990.
    48. See *Der Spiegel* 44, no. 42, Oct. 15, 1990, pp. 40–45. Rohwedder served as head
of the Trust Agency at a considerable loss in salary and signed a four-year renewal contract.

reasonable purchase offers were by no means refused—unfortunately, such offers had become the exception. The new policy considered most VEBs to be capable of successful restructuring and particularly favored those which were still exporting to their old COMECON partners (e.g., the Trabant factory in Zwickau and the truck factory in Ludwigsfelde), even though such exports are heavily in need of subsidies.[49] Such a course of action at least bought time for the transition and, to hear the opposition SPD tell it, it also bought CDU/CSU votes on December 2, 1990, especially the votes of many who would have been unemployed sooner rather than later. Yet, the agency was also the butt of bitter criticism from such heavyweights as the director of the Kiel Institute for World Economics, from the Saxonian Minister President, Kurt Biedenkopf (CDU), and from former CDU General Secretary Heiner Geissler. Some critics considered the restructuring of communist enterprises by the agency, rather than by a new owner, an impossibility; others picked on Rohwedder himself; and a third line of attack was aimed at the agency's alleged centralism. The director offered his critics a self-confident answer: "The Trust Agency is a piece of machinery, which has barely been started, for the purpose of decommunizing 40 years of communist economics. This is a unique undertaking that cannot be found in any of the other former socialist countries in the process of reform. . . . There are no models for our task."[50]

Eventually, Biedenkopf joined the agency's administrative council, and Rohwedder was acclaimed "Manager of the Year 1990" by *Industriemagazin*, a prominent business journal. Business organizations such as DIHT and the Employers' Associations (BDA) began to endorse the agency and its desire for more autonomy with respect to deciding the privatization of particular VEBs and for less interference from the new *Länder* governments. A spinoff, the Trust Agency for the Privatization of Retail Business put up 8,500 retail stores and 2,500 restaurants for sale in November 1990. Economy Minister Helmut Haussmann (FDP) wanted to speed up the disassembly and reassembly of the *Kombinate* in order to make the new pieces more attractive for buyers. Haussmann

49. Ibid., no. 44, Oct. 29, 1990, pp. 146–149. There are conflicting estimates of the market value of the East German industrial enterprises. Modrow's government had estimated these at 750 billion East marks; Rohwedder casually mentioned a figure of 600 billion marks.

50. Ibid., no. 46, Nov. 12, 1990, pp. 154–55; *Die Zeit*, no. 46, Nov. 16, 1990, p. 7. Decentralization has been substantial and has, for example, put 3,500 of the 8,000 VEBs under the regional offices; another 2,000 are expected to be run by municipalities, leaving only about 1,000–1,500 VEBs under the central office. About 1,000 were expected to fold, and some 500 agricultural processing firms were also to become municipal.

considered the remuneration of VEB employees on short hours (90% of
salary) not low enough to encourage their looking for another job. At the
same time, everyone feared that the East-to-West drain of qualified labor,
given the wage differentials, would undermine the viability of the VEBs.
Upon his death, Rohwedder's second-in-command, the energetic and
very able Birgit Breuel, former Lower Saxonian finance minister, was
entrusted with the directorship and promised to continue along similar
lines.

The claim of uniqueness for the Trust Agency is true enough. In
Eastern Europe, the process of privatizing a communist economy has
been compared to trying to turn fish soup into an aquarium of live fish—
a process of change that is more easily accomplished in the opposite
direction. (Milton) Friedmanesque economic preferences would militate
against the adoption of a public superagency like the Treuhand which, to
East Europeans, has overtones of the old state planning commissions.
But that option is not free from criticism either. The pace of transformation alone has split East European experts between advocacy of dramatic
and sweeping privatization measures, on the one hand, and the gradual-
ism currently in vogue (given the painful upheavals of bankruptcy and
mass unemployment associated with the former), on the other hand. In
Hungary, which has attracted more foreign investors and has been at it
the longest, there have been charges that public enterprises are being sold
too cheap, as in the case of the Ibusz Travel Company, whose shares sold
like hotcakes on the stock exchanges of Budapest and Vienna, doubling
their price within a week of sale. The newly elected government of July
1990 took firm control of the process and prepared a big sale of state
shops, restaurants, and retail businesses in 1991.

In Poland, where the Finance Ministry handled privatizations at a
snail's pace, the IMF finally lit a fire under the government, demanding
that one-half of the state-owned enterprises be sold off within three years.
The government responded in a panic and reminded everyone how, in the
Weimar Republic, mass unemployment had generated political crisis and
instability. Poland's modest progress had already produced 12% unemployment and a 20% plunge in output. The 1991 Star truck factory
strike—here, too, the automobile workers are an aristocracy, but their
product has lost its international competitiveness—led to a Pyrrhic
victory over the government: the Star workers were given a "new" truck
model to develop, but they lost workers and ended up with four-day
workweeks. On the other hand, the *zloty* has become a freely convertible
currency, and so now German merchants are flooding Poland trying to
sell their wares instead of the other way around. Although Poland has
sold off only a couple of hundred of about two thousand state-owned

companies, among its early successes were sales of large enterprises to the workers for cash and "citizens' vouchers" issued as shares in the enterprises to be privatized. Polish state monopolies in the transition were frequently accused of exploiting their position to increase prices, cut output, and fuel inflation. A "shock privatization plan" was launched in the winter of 1990/91 to turn several hundred state enterprises into joint-stock companies so that provincial and local governments could sell them off in order to raise revenues for the benefit of hospitals and other local services. Foreign investors stayed away or backed out of deals because of ambiguities in Polish law and privatization policies.

In early 1992 Czechoslovakia made big news when it readied a sale of vouchers, or shares, on 1,200 state-owned firms for sale to its citizenry— soon to be followed by similarly massive auctions. The sale was a rousing success for Finance and now Prime Minister Vaclav Klaus, the driving force behind the idea; indeed, he won a big majority in the June elections even though the effects of voucher privatization are still far from clear. Unfortunately, the voucher plan for rapid privatization, at about a week's wage (1,035 *koruna*, or $300) per unit, turned out to be as alarming to the gradualist Slovaks as it was popular among the Czechs. The Slovak economy is rather typically communist: a rural society with very large state industrial enterprises and little of the small and medium development in between that the Czechs share with many a Western neighbor. Slovaks fearing drastic privatization joined with other nationalist discontents, under the leadership of Vladimir Meciar, and brought the country to the edge of the eventual breakup. Before the voucher plan, Czechoslovakia had passed a law on "small company privatization" (October 1990), but it still faced great difficulties with large factories and enterprises which, like the East German *Kombinate*, have to prepare their own plans for privatization. The country has a separate Ministry of Privatization, headed by Tomas Jezek, but its staff consists of only a dozen officials.[51]

Why do East Europeans shy away from the Treuhand way of privatizing publicly owned enterprises? Aside from its resemblance to the old state planning commissions, the financial and socioeconomic costs are an important reason. A June 1991 symposium at the Eastern Europe Institute of the Free University of Berlin addressed this question and obtained some answers. Hungary's first privatization law, an economist from Hungary pointed out, at first applied to only 200 large, state-owned companies and used Western consultants. Employing thousands of bureaucrats, as the Trust Agency does, seems extravagant to the Hungarian

51. *The Economist*, Nov. 17, 1990, p. 88.

government. A second stage was aimed at the Hungarian service sector, especially hotels and restaurants. The third stage, involving small and medium-size enterprises of fewer than 300 employees was just beginning in mid-1991—again with consultants who were entitled to a commission on each sale. The annual Treuhand budget of 17–25 billion marks and the vast sums flowing from Bonn into the five new *Länder*—these are far beyond the capacity of the East European states, which clearly found a gradual changeover of the legal framework preferable to the East German plunge to a market economy. East Europeans have particularly preferred joint ventures and arrangements that limit liability and offer tax breaks. Partnerships for manufacturing usually pair the Western investor's role of supplying technical know-how and marketability with the Eastern partner's ability to get along with the local authorities. Multinational investors even contract with the appropriate local ministries in order to operate and plan on a large-scale basis. In this fashion, nevertheless, Hungary and Poland have already gone three-fourths of the way toward free-market institutions—property, contract, commercial, tax and social security law—and toward a free market in goods and labor. Hungary, moreover, has developed its capital market (banking and stock exchange systems) fully half the way, a step barely begun in Poland and the other East European countries. The Soviet Union had gone only one-fourth of the way toward a market economy in its institutions and its exchange of goods, as had Czechoslovakia. But the Soviet labor market was also half emancipated in 1991, a process that had only just begun in the Czecho-Slovak Federal Republic (CSFR). The rest of the East Europeans still had nearly all the great changes before them.[52]

The Role of the Volkskammer

The process of unification gathered a momentum of its own from the day a new People's Chamber was chosen in free elections. The old, communist-dominated People's Chamber had already cleared the way in February with a series of resolutions and laws guaranteeing freedom of speech and press, arranging for the elections, and setting forth the new rules regarding a pluralistic system of parties and groups. Premier Modrow brought no fewer than sixteen of the cabinet members in his new "government of national responsibility" to Bonn, including eight opposition figures of the Round Table which had commissioned him to ask for a "solidarity

52. See *Tagesspiegel*, June 11 and 25, 1991.

contribution" of 10–15 billion marks (February 13 and 14). Kohl declined but, in a counteroffer, proposed the currency and economic union, leaving the details to be determined by a commission of experts.

As the parliamentary source both of the new "government of national responsibility" and of the legislation for its own democratic legitimation, the People's Chamber thus became an important central institution of the GDR, anticipating the process about to unfold.[53] Under the GDR Constitution of 1974, the chamber had been merely a vessel for the "rule of the working class and its Marxist-Leninist party" (art. 1), at best the nominally highest state organ (art. 48) and in practice anything but the center of power in the GDR system. With the progressive disintegration of SED rule, and in particular with the formal disestablishment of the SED's monopoly of power (early December 1989), the Volkskammer found itself in a position of unaccustomed authority[54] and in the middle of insistent demands for reform. It responded, in its eleventh session (November 13, 1989)—some said at the eleventh hour—by reconstituting some of its organs and by feebly challenging the government in the manner of a parliamentary opposition. A parliamentary investigating committee was appointed (November 22) to look into charges of abuse of authority and personal corruption, and two more commissions were delegated to propose constitutional changes and to work out the new electoral law (December 7 and 8). It was not a bad start considering that the SED and its repressive apparatus still dominated the 500 chamber deputies until the March elections and that they owed their nomination and "election" strictly to this same source of authority. The competition of the mass demonstrations and, from December 7, 1989, the Round

53. For a description of the Modrow visit to Bonn, see especially Johannes Kuppe, "Modrow in Bonn" (and documentation), in *Deutschland Archiv* 23, no. 3 (March 1990), 337–340, 474–480. The proposal of a currency union was first broached on February 7, and Kohl's refusal concerning the 10–15 billion marks was widely criticized by the opposition in Bonn. For the text of the relevant legislation and constitutional amendments, see the reprinted versions in *Zeitschrift für Parlamentsfragen* 21, no. 1 (April 1990), 38–69. But also see the last-minute attempt to secure a "social charter" for East Germany after unification, with the right to a job, to training without gender discrimination, and to health care and housing. This social charter originated with the last Round Table and was passed by the old Volkskammer to serve as a basis for the economic and social union. For the text, see *Frankfurter Rundschau*, March 15, 1990, p. 16.

54. Even the nature of the proceedings changed profoundly with the fall of Honecker: all of a sudden, there were real debates and contentious clashes such as had never been witnessed before. For details, see Peter Joachim Lapp, *Die Volkskammer der DDR*, (Opladen: Westdeutscher Verlag, 1975). Like most parliaments in communist states, the old People's Chamber held infrequent sessions and its deputies served on an honorary basis, albeit with per diem compensation. See Lapp's account in *Zeitschrift für Parlamentsfragen* 21, no. 1 (April 1990), 115–125, on the dramatic changes.

Table—which started its own investigating committees and proposals—must have stiffened their backs.

The continued strength of the SED regime until mid-January, despite appearances to the contrary, can be gauged from the dominant role of Hans Modrow and his efforts to prepare for riding out the crisis. Billed like the Romanian leader Ion Iliescu as a quasi-dissident, long-repressed SED reformer, Modrow commanded a level of popularity that testifies to the gullibility of East Germans and outside observers alike. In reality, he was still busy rescuing the Stasi—by turning it into an innocuous-sounding national security agency—hiding SED assets of any kind, obliterating incriminating documents about himself and his friends, and playing the role of the closet democrat and reasonable communist leader to the hilt. Only when the massive demonstrations turned on the Stasi headquarters and offices, in mid-January 1990, did the last bubble of deception burst. In rapid succession, then, mass organizations like the communist youth (FDJ) collapsed, and public life in the GDR became pluralistic. Reform sentiment in the SED had already led to a mass exodus of party members and now pressed upon the Modrow regime. Gorbachev's refusal, in Moscow, to shore up the moribund regime in the GDR with the Soviet military stationed there administered the *coup de grâce*.

As it turned out, the democratically elected Volkskammer of March 18, 1990, served only half a year until it decided on its own dissolution,[55] along with the official completion of the unification process, on October 3, 1990. During this brief span, however, that body tightened the reins which would soon turn the "inner-German" relationship between two states into the constitutional development of one united German state. In a way, the moment of unification had already been anticipated by the demonstrators of the previous December with their slogans of "We are one people" and "Germany, united fatherland," and by the express if step-by-step commitment of the Modrow government to German unification, which culminated in Modrow's February 1 proposal of steps

55. A transitional law of August 14 had proposed that 144 People's Chamber deputies, in exact proportion to their strength in the chamber, become full-fledged Bundestag deputies until the first all-German elections. On August 22, 1990, a two-thirds majority of the People's Chamber accepted the Election Treaty, which at this point still featured a uniform electoral law that was later modified by the Federal Constitutional Court. A day later, the chamber surprised the GDR government by calling a session at which a majority of 294 CDU/DA, DSU, FDP, and SPD deputies, against 62 PDS and Bündnis 90 votes and 6 abstentions, voted to accede immediately to the West German Federal Republic. *Deutschland Archiv* 22, no. 10 (Oct. 1990), 148.

toward a "German federation" with one parliament, one constitution, and one government whose seat would be in Berlin.[56] While Modrow and most Western and Eastern leaders probably did not envision the accelerating pace of the process—and set up hurdles and obstacles that would have to be cleared first—economic deterioration and mass flight from the GDR forced their hand. The very thought of joint or coordinated measures to stop or cope with the exodus of East German refugees to the West also reflects a sense of shared management, if not of common institutions for that purpose.

The election of a democratically legitimated People's Chamber, of course, at first consolidated the preunification sovereignty of the GDR.[57] But there soon appeared a web of intra-German commissions and committees to negotiate differences and prepare the currency, economic, and social unity of Germany. Joint committees of experts from both governments had been at work since January. Bonn had formed a Cabinet Committee on German Unity in early February. A first proposal for the currency union became a matter of public knowledge (and an object of heated debate) a mere two weeks after the March elections, when it kindled a counterstatement by the new East German coalition government of the CDU Alliance, the FDP, and the SPD insisting on an exchange rate of 1:1 (April 12). On April 24, Kohl and de Maizière agreed on a target date of July 1 for both the currency union and the union of social insurance systems. From April 25 on, the expert groups of both governments once more were in negotiations, and there was a showdown in which the Bonn government rejected a series of East and West German SPD demands for modifying the agreements (May 3). On May 12 the GDR government asked that the property questions be left out of the treaty text as publicized two days later.[58]

56. Cf. Ilse Spittmann, author of the authoritative *Die DDR unter Honecker* (Cologne: Wissenschaft & Politik, 1990) and other writings on the GDR, who prefers to set the opening date of all the borders (November 9) as the key date "by which the Krenz leadership, presumably without knowing or wanting it, set the train toward unification in motion, as an emergency measure against mass flight via the CSR." Dr. Spittmann also mentions the January 30 agreement in principle of General Secretary Gorbachev, to the effect that German unification was inevitable, and describes the evolution of thinking on the Soviet side. Spittmann, "Deutschland einig Vaterland," *Deutschland Archiv* 22, no. 2 (Feb. 1990), 187–190.

57. It is worth recalling how West German officialdom for the first two decades of the GDR tended to treat the East German state as if it were still "*die Zone*," a Soviet-occupied colony, or as an illegitimate government of totalitarian usurpers who maintained themselves only by brute force.

58. See *Das Parlament*, nos. 23–24, June 1–8, 1990, p. 11, where the first joint session of the Bundestag Committee on German Unity and the corresponding People's Chamber

The First State Treaty

The resulting First State Treaty clearly authorized the Bundesbank as the first common institution having the sweeping powers over the currency that we associate with a central bank (art. 12). Pledging both parties to a common economic and legal order (arts. 2–6), it also established an arbitral tribunal for disputes (art. 7) and a Common Governing Committee composed of representatives from both governments (art. 8).[59] The Common Governing Committee was authorized to resolve disputes in the first instance, after which a dissatisfied party could appeal to the arbiters. Further articles spelled out details of the economic and social order that was to obtain: trade, restructuring of GDR economic enterprises, agriculture, environmental protection, labor law (arts. 11–16), social insurance (arts. 17–24: pensions, health care, unemployment, and accident insurance), funding of social insurance—pledging Bonn to initial financing (art. 25) of the unemployment insurance and pension rights—and, finally, the West German system of public insurance and budgetary law (arts. 26–28, 30–31, 34). As agreed with the GDR government, the treaty was remarkably vague about the problems of privatizing property, although it did mention "people's own property," economic restructuring, and the selling of "property held in trust" (*Treuhandvermögen*) in a cursory way. It also gave the West German finance minister special powers to limit the amount of credit given to public bodies of the GDR (art. 27).[60]

There were spirited debates in the West German and East German parliaments over details of the treaty, and the controversies continued among the parties and in state elections.[61] The West German and East German finance ministers had signed the state treaty on May 18, along with a codicil that was meant to clarify some of the details—for example,

---

Committee (May 23) is described. The opposition parties, among other demands, also called for a plebiscite on German unification.

59. The Independent Arbitral Tribunal (Schiedsgericht) consisted of a president and four members to be appointed, for two years, with each government proposing candidates and alternates (app. VIII). If the appointments were not completed within a month of the treaty taking effect, the president of the EC Court was authorized to make the appropriate appointments.

60. For an authoritative text, see "Vertrag über die Schaffung einer Währungs-, Wirtschafts- und Sozialunion," *Bulletin* of the West German Press and Information Office, no. 63, May 18, 1990; or, in English, *Treaty Between the FRG and the GDR Establishing a Monetary, Economic, and Social Union* (German Information Center, n.d.).

61. The Bundestag debates began in mid-April, a month before the treaty was even signed in its final form. They were part of the acrimonious public discussions over the East mark–deutschmark exchange rate. See *Das Parlament* 40, nos. 16–17, April 13–20, 1990,

that the GDR would grant equal treatment with West German individuals and enterprises to the nationals and firms of all EC member states.[62] In statements accompanying the signing of the treaty, Chancellor Kohl called it the "first decisive step on the way to unity" and "a clear indication of intra-German solidarity" because, through it, "the fates of the Germans in the FRG and the GDR become inseparably linked." GDR Prime Minister de Maizière added that "this was not a case of foreign states negotiating but of compatriots and friends who refuse to be estranged any longer."[63] There were wry press commentaries on the vanishing unification—and deutschmark—euphoria. East Germans soberly contemplated the difficult transition ahead, while their West German compatriots began to anticipate the high cost of unity that they more than anyone would have to bear in one way or another.

A week before the currency and social union, the Volkskammer formally approved the First State Treaty by 302 to 82 votes.[64] The West German Bundestag likewise approved it 445 to 60, with the Greens and some SPD deputies voting no. In the upper house, the Bundesrat, only the delegations of the Saar (Lafontaine's *Land*) and Lower Saxony[65] voted against the currency, economic, and social union. The challenge by Lafontaine, the SPD chancellor candidate, to slow down and modify the economic and social union had failed, though not without exposing him to a great deal of criticism, especially among East Germans but also from among the older generation of Social Democrats in the West. Behind the negative votes there often stood profound ambiguities and the sudden realization that the pace of the unification process had become uncontrollable.

On June 17, both parliaments met in East Berlin to commemorate what West Germans for three and a half decades had called the Day of

---

and nos. 23–24, June 1–8, 1990, for the West German parliamentary debates, including the objections of the SPD *Länder* delegations of the Bundesrat.

62. For the text, see *Documents on German Unity*, a *German Tribune* supplement (Hamburg: Reinecke, 1990).

63. Kohl also tried to meet popular objections by reminding his countrymen that "for forty years the people in the GDR were forcibly prevented from living the kind of life we enjoyed here in the FRG," and telling the people in the GDR that "the prosperity of the FRG is the result of much hard work": "We must not place excessive demands upon one another." Ibid., pp. 2–3. De Maizière obliged with a similar exhortation to his fellow citizens. Ibid., pp. 3–4.

64. The opposition came from the PDS and from among the several groups of the old democratic opposition, such as Bündnis 90 and the Greens/Independent Women.

65. Oskar Lafontaine is the minister president of the Saar and had recently scored an impressive election victory there. The Lower Saxonian state elections of mid-May had brought a Red-Green (SPD-Greens) coalition into power under Minister President Gerhard Schröder, a follower of Lafontaine.

German Unity, the anniversary of the 1953 workers' uprising in the GDR. In the Volkskammer earlier in the day, to nearly everyone's surprise, an unlikely alliance of two representatives of Bündnis 90/New Forum[66] and the right-wing German Social Union (DSU) had submitted a motion for the immediate accession of East Germany to the Federal Republic under article 23 of the Basic Law. After a two-hour debate, with Chancellor Kohl and other Bonn visitors watching the proceedings from the balcony, the chamber voted with a large majority for this resolution, although many deputies shared the desire of Premier Minister Lothar de Maizière to couple their commitment to the West German Basic Law with further, careful discussion of details as well as scrutiny by the appropriate legislative committees. In the end, the premature motion was indeed diverted toward the committees of the chamber. The *Berliner Zeitung*, which was close to the PDS, commented in mock despair: "Some people are utterly sick and tired of the GDR in its present form. . . . [O]thers are worried that GDR citizens may lose their rights in the wake of . . . subordination to the intra-German treaty. . . . We may all long for a return to some semblance of order. But does it have to be the order that prevails in the FRG?" The respected Hamburg weekly *Die Zeit* spoke of the unification process as "in a state of free-fall," when even the people's representatives of the GDR—the Gradually Disappearing Republic— would have to "do their work under the sword of Damocles, the threat of instant self-dissolution."[67]

Indeed, with the fateful date of the currency union, the GDR irretriev- ably lost its sovereign power to determine its own taxes, its monetary circulation, its economic, social and environmental policies, and even its exclusive right to pursue federal police investigations of the Bundesbank, the West German parliament, and the government in Bonn—and all this without the leverage of its own representation. The Volkskammer was no longer able to veto decisions made in Bonn about its constituents. How could one tolerate regulation and taxation without representation short of an East Berlin equivalent of the Boston Tea Party? All hopes therefore began to focus on the day when East German representatives might receive seats and voting rights in the Bundestag and Bundesrat in Bonn.

66. The two, Wolfgang Ullmann and Konrad Weiss, later withdrew their sponsorship in evident embarrassment. A convention of Greens and Bündnis 90 (June 8–10) in Dortmund had just resolved to reject the First State Treaty and demanded instead a constitutional convention and popular ratification of the resulting constitutional draft. See the documentation in *Das Parlament*, no. 26, June 22, 1990, p. 10. The parliamentary groups of both parties combined their resolution with a strong denunciation of the "hastened pace of unification."
67. Robert Leicht, "Vereinigung im freien Fall," *Die Zeit*, no. 26, June 22, 1990, p. 1.

In spite of its proudly maintained pretensions, the GDR at this point was a mere shadow of a state. As Robert Leicht observed trenchantly, the GDR had proclaimed itself to be a state of law (*Rechtsstaat*) and yet lacked the trained personnel to live up to this billing. It had declared its ambition to become a Western-style welfare state and, again, had neither the personnel nor the structures for the required fiscal, labor, and social security administration. By now it had no choice but to collapse into the reluctant arms of the West German republic, provided the international obstacles could be overcome. The alternative of a gradual unification would have demanded the presence of two well-founded states with staying power. The parlous condition of the GDR gave the FRG a trusteeship role and made the First State Treaty—and any further state treaties—into a testament to be carried out by the FRG government, leaving the helpless GDR government with an impossible burden.[68]

It has become fashionable meanwhile to suggest or imply that German unification should have proceeded more gradually than it did. Usually such suggestions are not accompanied with any details of exactly how such gradual progress should have been accomplished or exactly how this would have caused the East Germans—who did vote overwhelmingly for fast unification via the overpriced currency union—less pain. Unification in "free-fall," to be sure, was not likely to permit an orderly, planned transition. In the meantime, however, a new argument has surfaced, as presented by both Soviet Foreign Minister Eduard Shevardnadze and Chancellor Kohl: namely, that there was a window of opportunity of only two weeks or so at the time the Soviet Politbureau was reconstituted with 90% new members, in mid-July 1990, in which to get Soviet consent for German unification. If this is true, it is indeed worth contemplating what might have happened if the Soviets had denied their blessing at that point and if their massive army in East Germany, in line with the wishes of Moscow military and KGB conservatives, had kept the GDR as the keystone in the arch of Soviet domination over the East European satellite empire. Such a *nyet* at the crucial moment after the currency union and related measures had been started would have had extraordinary consequences for the West European economies, the European Community, and the already severely ailing American economy. We would not go far wrong to characterize such an impasse as a disaster

68. Ibid. Leicht frowned on any attempt by the GDR leadership to escape their burden by asking for the completion of unification now, much as he could see the West German politicians' interest in getting on with the business of the first all-German electoral race. Instead, he expressed the hope that the other Western powers and the Soviet Union would help the Germans to complete the task. See also the review of the internal politics in Bonn in the same issue (pp. 6–7).

on the magnitude of the Great Depression, especially if we added the
likely revival of the Cold War upon such a show of Soviet military
hostility. The German unifiers obviously were taking an enormous chance
and, considering the risk, must consider themselves very lucky today,
regardless of the economic and cultural pains they have had to endure
since.

The Return of the East German Länder

The ink of the formal signatures on the First State Treaty was not quite
dry when the negotiators and expert commissions of Bonn and East
Berlin were already plotting and drafting the next steps toward complete
unification. There was no secret about the acceleration of the process
amidst all the television coverage of East Germans lining up at bank
windows to get their new deutschmarks and all the discussions in the
press of what should be the name and the national hymn of the new
united Germany. There was also no secret about the readiness of the East
German government to fall into the arms of the FRG: Premier de
Maizière hinted as much during his visit to Washington and so did his
second-in-command in East Berlin, Günter Krause (CDU), the chief
negotiator of the First State Treaty on the Eastern side. But the most
pressing constitutional assignment after the date of the currency union
was the reestablishment of the East German *Länder*. Unification via
article 23 of the Basic Law required that the GDR join the FRG *Land* by
Land, and not as a whole, although the still-valid GDR Constitution
might suggest a modified version of this procedure, such as a simultane-
ous accession of the reconstituted *Länder*, plebiscites in the GDR, or a
temporary suspension of parts of the Basic Law for the purpose of
accession, if conditions should so warrant.[69] The Federal Republic, according to constitutional law authorities, was obliged to accept "any
other parts of Germany" without any conditions if they chose to accede
(art. 23).

Between 1945 and 1952, East Germany had already been composed of
Länder, which derived their configuration from pre-1933 antecedents
that had been adjusted after the imposition of the Oder-Neisse line and
the zonal boundaries toward the west and south. Today's Mecklenburg-

69. This modus of unification, rather than union via a constituent assembly and a new
constitution (art. 146), also implied in principle that the old GDR as an internationally
recognized state (and all its treaty obligations) would lapse. See the constitutional debates
in *Das Parlament*, no. 15, Apr. 6, 1990, p. 12, and nos. 16–17, Apr. 13–20, p. 8.

Vorpommern is the old Grand Duchy of Mecklenburg augmented with what was left of Pomerania west of the Oder River. Both had been Prussian provinces, although plans of territorial reorganization from 1928 to 1944 proposed making them *Länder* in their own right.[70] Saxony, the most populous of the new *Länder*, is the old kingdom and state bordering now on the Neisse River. Brandenburg, between these two, also had its historical antecedent, except that now, in 1945, the area of Greater Berlin was separated out (and divided into four occupation zones) in a fashion likewise anticipated on various maps since Hugo Preuss presented his proposal for the Weimar Constitution.[71] There is a move afoot to merge Berlin with Brandenburg in 1992 or 1993, a kind of revival of Small Prussia. The three Western zones of Berlin were the embattled Western enclave, while East Berlin eventually became the GDR capital. To the west of Saxony, the consolidated old Thuringian states in 1945 formed a *Land* similar to—if somewhat smaller and less populated than[72]—the Weimar *Land* of that name. *Land* Saxony-Anhalt, finally, consists of the former Prussian province of Saxony and the ministate of Anhalt.

These five *Länder* of the 1945 Soviet Zone of Occupation (except for Greater Berlin) were largely identical with those reconstituted in 1990. In the early years of the GDR, they constituted the states of a federal system and enjoyed representation in a weak Länderkammer, comparable with the Weimar Reichsrat and the West German Bundesrat. The Länderkammer played a minor role in the initiation of legislation and survived in obscurity until its abolition in 1958. The *Länder* and their governments were abolished in mid-1952 and replaced by fourteen regions (*Bezirke*) which in the interim sent delegates to the Länderkammer.[73] When the reestablishment of the five *Länder* first became a likely choice for unification via article 23, there was a flurry of suggestions for redrawing *Länder* boundaries in the GDR and also in the old FRG, where article 29 of the Basic Law had always offered this route for correcting inequities

70. See the maps of the *Länderkonferenz* of 1928 and of the conspirators of July 20, 1944, in *Die Bundesländer. Beiträge zur Neugliederung der Bundesrepublik* (Frankfurt: Institut zur Förderung öffentlicher Angelegenheiten, 1950).

71. Ibid. Preuss, however, had combined Brandenburg with underpopulated Pomerania, and a 1949 proposal of W. Münchheimer combined it with Mecklenburg-Vorpommern.

72. Its 1945 expansion added some formerly Prussian enclaves and border areas, particularly Erfurt and Mühlhausen, and it absorbed considerable numbers of Eastern refugees. For a list of territorial changes, see P. J. Lapp in *Deutschland Archiv* 22, no. 9 (Sept. 1990), 1315.

73. The Länderkammer showed a great deal less life than even the Volkskammer, which in those days met only six to fourteen days a year. See David Childs, *The GDR: Moscow's German Ally* (London: Allen & Unwin, 1983), pp. 118–119.

and imbalances in the original, postwar configuration of member states of the West German federation. As in West Germany, however, hardly anything came of these public discussions, and the 1946–1952 East German *Länder* were simply reconstituted in their earlier configuration for the purpose of *Land* elections in October.[74] There was also some controversy about the capital of Mecklenburg-Vorpommern—should it be Rostock or Schwerin?—and about that of Saxony-Anhalt: should it be Magdeburg, Halle, or even Dessau?

In this form the People's Chamber passed the law for the reintroduction of the *Länder* (July 22) which was to take effect when the Second State Treaty entered into force on October 3. The chamber also formally passed the accession of the entire GDR (August 23) to the Federal Republic with a two-thirds majority of 294 to 62. On August 31, the treaty itself was signed solemnly by the West German Minister of the Interior, Wolfgang Schäuble, and the East German State Secretary, Günter Krause, in the former Crown Prince Palace Unter den Linden in East Berlin. Three weeks later, the Volkskammer approved the Second State Treaty, again with the required two-thirds majority (299–80) against the votes of the PDS and parts of the Bündnis 90. The treaty also passed the Bundestag on the same day (September 20) with the necessary two-thirds majority (442–47) against the Greens and a handful of CDU/ CSU deputies—eight of whom had unsuccessfully brought their objections to recognizing the Oder-Neisse line before the Federal Constitutional Court. All these laws and treaties—including the one whereby the four victorious powers of World War II and the two Germanys restored full international sovereignty to a united Germany—were to take effect on German Unity Day, October 3, when the GDR would disappear as an entity.[75] The five new *Länder* would remain and, on October 14, elections

74. The earlier West German concern had been particularly about the artificial nature of some new "hyphenated states" such as Rhineland-Palatinate. See especially Bundesminister des Innern, *Die Neugliederung des Bundesgebietes, Gutachten* (Bonn and Cologne: Heymann, 1955) or the Bundestag proceedings for December 12, 1957. In 1990, the proposed changes were very minor, including such items as the transfer of some Thuringian territory to Bavaria. The GDR government established a Commission for Administrative Reform in December 1989. The roundtables of various East German districts also set up joint commissions to discuss possible modifications—e.g., dividing Saxony-Anhalt between Brandenburg and Saxony or creating small additional *Länder*, such as Vorpommern and Lausitz, an area inhabited by the Sorbic minority. See also P. J. Lapp in *Das Parlament*, no. 15, Apr. 6, 1990, p. 7.

75. The Volkskammer and GDR cabinet, too, disbanded while 144 chamber deputies, in proportion to the political parties represented there, joined the Bundestag. Five GDR cabinet members including Premier de Maizière were taken as ministers without portfolio into the Bonn cabinet.

for their respective diets (*Landtage*) would each in turn establish a parliamentary *Land* government headed by a minister president just as in the West German *Länder*.[76] The new *Landtage* and *Land* cabinets would then send instructed *Land* delegations to the enlarged German upper house, the Bundesrat, each to take their seats and vote *en bloc* alongside the *Land* delegations of Hamburg, Bavaria, and the other West German states.

The Politics of the New Federalism

The formation of the five new-old *Länder* was accompanied by a revival of regional and local sentiment beginning with the original upheaval of 1989, when the old state colors and flags began to appear in demonstrations in Leipzig, Dresden, Halle, Erfurt, Magdeburg, Potsdam, and Schwerin. "We are the people" and other protest slogans seemed more effective when sported on a local and regional background, asserting traditional identities against the increasingly artificial one of centralized, communist rule, a longtime source of the GDR's "history of frustrations." Awareness of the impending demise of the GDR state and of their coming inclusion as states in a larger German federal union revived memories of that brief postwar moment when each had a democratic constitution, although the federal character of the 1949 GDR Constitution had been weak and was no match for the determination of the SED state in East Berlin to wield untrammeled power.[77] "The Germans in the east have extra reasons to be keen federalists," wrote *The Economist*. "After decades of rule by communists from the center, they want the same local control that the western states enjoy over the police, cultural affairs, and finance. . . . The reemerging *Länder* . . . offer people a sense of stability, of *Heimat* (homeland), at a time of disorientation."[78]

76. East Berliners did not participate in these state elections but had to wait until the all-German elections, when both East and West Berlin were to elect a common *Senat*, forming a sixteenth *Land* with representation in the Bundesrat. In the intervening months, some of their Volkskammer deputies became members of the Bundestag.

77. See Peter Joachim Lapp, "Fünf plus eins: Länder statt DDR," *Deutschland Archiv* 23, no. 7 (Jul. 1990), 1079–1084. The relatively small size of most of the new *Länder* encouraged plans for mergers, including some joining Berlin to Brandenburg and some reducing the resultant united Germany to seven instead of sixteen states. See also *Frankfurter Allgemeine Zeitung*, Apr. 19, 1990, p. 5, and *Neues Deutschland*, March 10–11 and Apr. 28/29, 1990.

78. *The Economist*, Oct. 6, 1990, pp. 54–55. The revival of East German federalism coincided with heightened interest in strengthening the *Länder* in West German federalism. See Uwe Thaysen, "Die 'Eckpunkte' der Bundesländer für den Föderalismus im vereinigten

A look at the *Länder* of the united country (Table 5.1 and map) shows
the relative smallness of the populations of all but highly industrialized
Saxony. North Rhine Westphalia alone is the equal, in population, of the
entire GDR. The anemic financial and administrative capacities of the five
new *Länder* make them no match even for the well-established city-states
of Hamburg and Bremen or the Saar, all three of which had been objects
of West German merger plans (Münchmeyer) at one time. Their representation in the upper house—a cornerstone of all federal systems—reflects
the adjustments of 1990, which not only changed the range from three
seats for the smallest states up to five seats for the biggest to a ratio of
3:6 but, thereby, also modified the subtle arithmetic of the political
equation of federalism. Now each of the four largest states has twice the
clout of each of the three smallest—all SPD-ruled *Länder* at this time—
although the increased number of states makes it more difficult to

Table 5.1.   Population and Bundesrat Seats of German *Länder,* 1991

	Population (millions)	Seats (1991)	(pre-1991)
North Rhine Westphalia	16.7	6	5
Bavaria	10.9	6	5
Baden-Württemberg	9.3	6	5
Lower Saxony	7.2	6	5
Hesse	5.5	4	4
Saxony	5.0	4	
Rhineland-Palatinate	3.6	4	4
Berlin	3.3	4	(4)*
Saxony-Anhalt	3.0	4	
Brandenburg	2.7	4	
Schleswig-Holstein	2.6	4	4
Thuringia	2.5	4	
Mecklenburg–West Pomerania	2.1	3	
Hamburg	1.6	3	3
Saarland	1.1	3	3
Bremen	0.7	3	3
TOTAL	77.7	68	45

SOURCE: As reported in all the German newspapers.

*West Berlin sent delegations both to the Bundesrat and the Bundestag before 1991, but
without voting rights.

Deutschland," *Zeitschrift für Parlamentsfragen* 21, no. 3 (Oct. 1990), 461–463, and the
recommendations of the *Enquête* Commission on Constitutional Reform, *Bundestag
Drucksache* 7/5924 (1976).

Fig. 5.1. The German States. (Courtesy German Information Center, New York)

assemble majorities, especially constitution-changing two-thirds majorities. The short-lived SPD majority of May through October of 1990 turned into a comfortable majority of CDU/CSU-dominated state governments,[79] thirty-nine to twenty-nine.[80] In the first months of 1991, however, the SPD regained its edge in the Bundesrat with victories in Hamburg, Hesse, and Rhineland-Palatinate, for a new balance of thirty-seven against thirty-one votes from CDU/CSU states. Forty-six is the two-thirds majority that can amend the Basic Law. The five new *Länder* of East Germany, with their nineteen votes, cannot even block changes in the Constitution which they so trustingly adopted—East German Berlin has no Bundesrat representation except as part of the unified *Land* Berlin of which the Western parts make up the majority.

The elections in the five new *Länder* brought ample confirmation for the preeminent position of the CDU/CSU-dominated Alliance that had swept the Volkskammer elections of March 18 and that suffered little erosion in the communal elections of May. Even though the electoral turnout shrank by almost one-fourth and the CDU-oriented parties reshuffled their alliances in ways that differed somewhat from state to state,[81] it is fair to say that the CDU held its ground with 45% and, in fact, swept to power in four of the five *Länder*, not to mention two months later in Berlin (see Table 5.2).

Its old chief antagonist, the SPD (with nearly 26%, including the East Berlin vote of the following December) did noticeably better than it had in the Volkskammer elections of March when it polled a disappointing 21.8%. The reform communist PDS lost about as much as the SPD gained, falling from 16.9% in March to 12.9% in October/December.[82]

79. Since the state delegations have to vote *en bloc*, partisan majorities are accumulated by adding the delegations of state governments dominated by one or the other of the two major parties. But the varying state party coalitions and the cumbersome procedure tend to weaken the hold of partisanship on the Bundesrat.

80. In the West German round of state elections during the first half of 1990, Lower Saxony changed hands, giving the SPD a majority of twenty-three of the forty-one votes (without Berlin). After October 14, the CDU/CSU *Land* delegations were augmented with four of the five East German *Länder* and, after December 2, with the votes of the new *Land* of Berlin, while the SPD gained only the four votes of Brandenburg. In early 1991, the SPD gained (and the CDU lost) four votes each for winning in Hesse and Rhineland-Palatinate.

81. The CDU, for example, merged with the Farmers' party (DBD), the DSU, and Democratic Start (DA) in Mecklenburg-Vorpommern, Brandenburg, Saxony-Anhalt and Thuringia, but not in Saxony. There were also some smaller groups such as Christian right-to-life parties (Christian List) and the Beer Drinkers' Union (DBU). The elements of the democratic opposition of 1989 had not all merged into Bündnis 90. The list of competing groups, however, had shrunk considerably from the two dozen of March.

82. With the drop in turnout from 93.4% in March to about 70% in October/November, the significance of such shifts is lessened so long as we cannot be sure how the drop is distributed.

Table 5.2. Land Elections in East Germany, Second Ballot, October 1990 (in %)

	CDU/CSU	Liberals	SPD	Bündnis 90	PDS
Mecklenburg-Vorpommern	40.4	5.7	27.0	2.2[a]	15.7
Brandenburg	30.4	6.6	38.3	6.4[b]	13.4
Saxony-Anhalt	40.7	13.5	26.0	5.3[c]	12.0[d]
Saxony	53.8	5.3	19.1	5.6[e]	10.2
Thuringia	48.7	9.3	22.8	6.5[f]	9.7
Berlin (Dec. 2)	40.4	7.1	30.4	9.4[g]	9.2
East Berlin	(25.0)	(5.6)	(32.1)	(11.5)	(23.6)

SOURCES: Forschungsgruppe Wahlen, Mannheim, *Wahl in den Neuen Bundesländern. Eine Analyse der Landtagswahlen vom 14. Oktober 1990*, p. 10; *Bundestagswahl 1990*, p. 15; *Wahl in Berlin. Eine Analyse der Wahl zum Abgeordnetenhaus vom 2. Dezember 1990*, p. 7.

[a]Also on the ballot were Greens (4.2%) and the New Forum (2.9%).

[b]Also Greens (2.8%) and Forum party (DFP) (0.1%).

[c]Under the name Greens/New Forum.

[d]Also USPD (Unabhängige Sozialistische Partei Deutschlands) (0.1%).

[e]Under the name New Forum.

[f]Under the name New Forum/Greens/Democracy Now (NFGRDJ).

[g]Alternative List/Greens (West Berlin) plus Bündnis 90 (East Berlin).

The various groups associated with the democratic opposition of 1989, despite a continuing lag in organizational unity, received a heartening 7.2% of the popular vote, nearly twice their March showing and well above the 5% clause of the electoral law.[83]

The formation of the new *Land* governments was remarkable also for the determined entry of West German politicians into the race for the new top positions. Not that they had not been present in earlier East German campaigns during the year, but at that time they still tended to withdraw discreetly and let the East Germans form their own governments.[84] This time, there were prominent "Westimports" among the ten

83. Unlike in March, the electoral law for the *Land* elections had been the one valid in most West German *Länder*: a modified version of proportional representation with a minimum 5% of the popular vote required for representation. There are two votes to be cast, one for a candidate in a single-member plurality constituency and one for a party. The legislature is composed of two halves, one half elected on the single-member plurality vote and the other half by party list. The second vote is also used to ensure proportionality of partisan composition of the legislature to the popular vote.

84. There are exceptions, such as the Leipzig mayor who originally was a prominent figure in Hannover politics.

major-party candidates for the position of minister president (premier) in each of the five new *Länder*. In Mecklenburg-Vorpommern, for instance, the SPD nominated the former justice minister of the neighboring *Land* Schleswig-Holstein to run against a native, Alfred Gomolka (CDU), who won the position. In Thuringia, the SPD fielded a North Rhine Westphalian; and in Saxony, the SPD Party Secretary, Anke Fuchs, lost the contest against Kurt Biedenkopf (CDU), a former CDU general secretary and a veteran of the leadership struggles in Bonn and in Düsseldorf. Being the premier of one of the new *Länder* was obviously very attractive to West German politicos, who hoped to secure for themselves a place in history, though no great riches. The high visibility of the minister presidency also encouraged the parties to pick candidates with great care, as in the case of Manfred Stolpe, who had been a prominent church official (Konsistorialrat) and candidate for cabinet office under Modrow before the SPD recruited him as Brandenburgian premier[85] and head of a cabinet of ten, including four "Westimports."

Aside from Saxony, there were some difficulties with the establishment of parliamentary coalition cabinets and with the government seats. In Mecklenburg-Vorpommern, the 33 seats (of 66) of the CDU-FDP coalition fell short by one vote, and it took a convert from the SPD and two more secret supporters to give Minister President Alfred Gomolka a decent margin. The city of Schwerin was designated the state capital with a majority of 40 (of 66). Stolpe assembled a "traffic light coalition"—Red-Yellow-Green—of SPD, FDP, and Bündnis 90 deputies (58 of 88) in Potsdam (Brandenburg). In Saxony-Anhalt, Magdeburg narrowly won the contest for capital over Halle (the capital from 1946 to 1952) and Dessau, which were given some ministries as consolation. Minister President Friedhelm Farthmann (CDU) formed a CDU-FDP coalition with an ample margin. In Erfurt (Thuringia), Minister President Josef Duchac (CDU) formed the same kind of coalition, after narrowly missing a majority for the CDU, with 44 of 88 seats. In Dresden (Saxony), Kurt Biedenkopf (CDU) needed no coalition party; in fact, he was installed in office by an enthusiastic vote of 120 (of 152) diet members, far more than the 92 votes of his own parliamentary party.[86]

85. Modrow, in his effort to grasp at straws of legitimacy for a moribund regime, reportedly wanted to make Stolpe a minister of foreign or, at least, church affairs. See *Die Zeit*, no. 42, Oct. 19, 1990, p. 5. The SPD made spectacular gains over its March poll in Brandenburg, where it replaced the CDU as a front-runner.

86. See Peter J. Lapp, "Fünf neue Bundesländer—Stärkung des Föderalismus," *Deutschland Archiv* 22, no. 11 (Nov. 1990), 1659–1661. Lapp attributes the CDU's failure to triumph over the SPD in Brandenburg to the candidacy of Peter-Michael Diestel (CDU) for the minister presidency. A DSU minister of the interior under de Maizière, Diestel had attracted a lot of criticism with his handling of the Stasi legacy.

The Question of Berlin

"The capital of Germany is Berlin," says article 2 of the Second State Treaty. "The seat of Parliament and Government are to be decided after the restoration of the unity of Germany," presumably by the newly elected parliament and its government. The clarification of the first sentence by its successor serves to remind us that the question of the German capital, despite the relevant clause of the treaty, was not exactly settled. There has been considerable controversy over it, indeed, including the exchange between former Lord Mayor Walter Momper (SPD) and his party colleague, North Rhine Westphalia Minister President Johannes Rau (SPD), who like most *Länder* chiefs and organized interests in the West would have preferred to keep the capital in Bonn.

The West German Bundestag, in fact, has long been on record with its own position, beginning soon after the birth of the West German republic, on September 30, 1949, when West Berlin found itself intentionally kept out of the construction of the FRG by the Western allies. West Berlin was an endangered and crisis-prone appendage, placed strictly under occupation status while other West Germans enjoyed building their democratic traditions and self-sustaining prosperity. All four allies always insisted on keeping West Berlin separate, denying its representatives voting powers in Bonn and frowning on Bonn's gestures to establish a symbolic linkage with Berlin. Nevertheless, the Bundestag, in September 1949, called the city a "democratic outpost" of the country and pledged its word to keep the city as part of the Federal Republic *and its capital*.[87] The Bundestag also established a committee to assess the suitability of Bonn versus Frankfurt as provisional capital of the FRG.[88] On November 3, 1949, the lower house confirmed the choice of Bonn as a "provisional capital" by Konrad Adenauer and the Parliamentary Council, which

87. This was the final punch of an SPD bill of September 30, 1949, which survived amendments by the Bavaria party (BP) and by Franz-Josef Strauss (CSU), who wanted to use this opportunity to depose the hated old capital of the country once and for all. The current Bavarian premier, Max Streibl, suggested a more contemporary angle when he argued that "Berlin could not possibly be the German capital as long as there were Soviet troops in the former GDR"—in other words, not before 1994.

88. The committee reported on November 14, 1949, and there was a vote of 176 against 200 to move the capital to Frankfurt. Three abstained and eleven turned in invalid ballots. Thus the provisional capital remained in Bonn. See "Frankfurt? Coburg? What About Bonn? Die Hauptstadtfrage nach 1945," in *Forschungen* (DFG), no. 2 (1991), 15–18, whose author emphasizes the disinclination of the French, British, and Soviet occupation to perpetuate Berlin's status as the German capital. Even Dwight D. Eisenhower saw in it merely a "geographic point," while the Soviets were at least ready to use it for extending their control over the rest of Germany. In the end, it was by no means only Konrad

drew up the Basic Law in the city. SPD efforts to transplant the Parliamentary Council to West Berlin and to locate the FRG capital there had been squelched by the Western occupying powers in May 1949, when they reminded the constitutional convention that Berlin was not to be a part of the FRG and would be permitted only nonvoting representatives in the West German parliament (as, indeed, it had on the Parliamentary Council). But the Bundestag also resolved that "the leading federal institutions will move to Berlin as soon as general, free, equal, secret and direct elections are carried out in all of Berlin and in the Soviet Occupation Zone. Thereupon the Bundestag will meet in Berlin."[89]

The separation of Berlin from the FRG continued to rankle, and there were further debates on the subject in the Bundestag. In fact, the recurring Berlin crises were frequently triggered by West German attempts to have a Bundestag committee or the electoral college for the election of the FRG president meet there.[90] In June 1955, there was an unsuccessful proposal to move the Bonn Ministry of All-German Affairs to Berlin and, in the debate, it was revealed that the palace of Bellevue was being readied as "a second seat of office" for the federal president. Both moves were likely to stir up major protests from the GDR and the Soviets. Again, in December 1956—after the Soviet invasion of Hungary—the Bundestag voted almost unanimously for a resolution that stated simply: "Berlin is the capital of Germany." In the years following the vote, however, the interest of the Bundestag seemed to slacken, even though there were a few more mentions of the old capital and some reiterations of the principles stated above.[91]

While these statements are not exactly a commitment to Berlin, they mirror its dominance over West German thinking. The Basic Law clearly gives the chief constitutional organs—Bundestag, Bundesrat, and Federal

---

Adenauer but also the British and American occupation and eight of eleven state premiers who opted for Bonn.

89. See Merkl, *The Origin of the West German Republic*, pp. 63–64. The West German communists (KPD) had moved on November 1 that parliament and the leading federal institutions be moved to Berlin, and the SPD added the condition of free democratic elections in East Berlin and the Soviet-occupied zone. See also the collection of documents and commentary on the Berlin policy of the GDR by Gerd Langguth, ed., *Die Berlin-Politik der DDR*, KAS Deutschland-Report no. 3 (Melle: Knoth, 1987).

90. The federal president is chosen by the Federal Assembly, an electoral body which consists of the lower house of the West German parliament and a like number of Landtag deputies selected in proportion to their partisan representation in the Bundestag (Basic Law, art. 54).

91. See especially Ulrich Rephewitz, "Berlin: Hauptstadt der BRD und eines vereinigten Deutschlands? Rechtliche Aspekte der Hauptstadtfrage," *Zeitschrift für Parlamentsfragen* 21, no. 3 (Oct. 1990), 505–515.

Cabinet—the right to determine their own organization, their procedure within its specifications, and presumably also their seat;[92] the other organs have no such rights. Each newly elected Bundestag, however, has a new mandate unencumbered by decisions of its predecessors and, hence, even the last resolution of the FRG Bundestag of February 13, 1990, "that Berlin must become the capital again" has no binding force over the Bundestag elected for a united Germany on December 2, 1990. The new Bundestag, moreover, can take its time reopening the question of determining its seat of operations and can wait until such temporary obstacles as the unsettled state of barely reunited Berlin permit rational planning. The current condition of the old capital—with a big open slash in its center where the Wall stood and where a wide strip of buildings was razed to the east, with its massive urban problems of overburdened transport and other services, and with the expectation of overwhelming immigration and growth problems for the foreseeable future—may suggest caution at precisely the point when Berliners hope to finance solutions to their many problems by becoming the capital again.[93]

Over the forty years of the FRG, West Berlin remained occupied territory under the three Western allies while East Berlin was the 15th district (since 1952) and capital of the GDR, which consented to a prominent Soviet presence in the city.[94] When the Western military governors issued their Letter of Approval for the Basic Law (May 12, 1949), they specifically exempted West Berlin from the valid effects of this new West German constitution and from acts of the new federal parliament and government. They had no objection, in practice, to the voluntary adoption by the West Berlin German authorities of most West

92. Articles 40(1), 52(3), and 64(4). The federal president also has such privileges in West German constitutional law commentaries. According to the Federal Constitutional Court decision of October 23, 1952, the old Reich did not disappear as a legal entity by capitulating and being divided in May 1945, but lived on with the FRG. But since the territory of the latter did not include Berlin, the status of the Reich capital did not endure.

93. The history of Berlin in Prussia offers several earlier situations where the city was able to cope with its problems of economic stagnation and poverty only when the Brandenburg rulers were willing to maintain residence there.

94. In early 1947, the quadripartite Allied Control Council for Occupied Germany had still agreed in principle and upon Soviet insistence that steps should be taken to rebuild German central-government institutions, presumably in Berlin, and this Allied action followed the formal dissolution of the Prussian state, which had been "the clamp holding the Reich together." By the end of that year, however, the London Conference of Foreign Ministers began to chart a separate course of consolidation for the Western zones which in the end created the FRG, leaving West Berlin an island in the middle of the Soviet Zone of Occupation. The breakup of the quadripartite Allied *Komandatura* of Berlin and its division followed and was perpetuated after the Soviet blockade (1948/49) and the Allied airlift to the city. See Merkl, *The Origin of the West German Republic*, pp. 17–19, 63–64.

German laws and court decisions, a procedure that retained certain significant differences in Berlin law. The West German conscription laws, for example, did not apply to West Berlin, with the result that the city became a haven for young men seeking to avoid the draft. The Western Allied *Komandatura* concluded an agreement with the city modeled on that between the FRG and the Western high commissioners and having the same Allied reservations plus a clause retaining such occupation powers as were necessary "to ensure the security, the good order, and financial and economic stability of the city."[95] The Allied High Commission had a special committee for the affairs of the *Komandatura* in West Berlin, and High Commission laws were generally applicable in the city unless waived. Even the West Berlin Constitution, adopted in 1950, resembled those of the Hamburg and Bremen city-states in the West. The Bonn government took it upon itself, with direct subsidies and generous tax write-offs, as well as recurring symbolic actions, to maintain close ties with West Berlin.[96]

The Western allies repeated their injunction against any organic link between Berlin and the FRG in the treaties of 1952 and 1954, which formed the basis of West German sovereignty and NATO membership. But they had no objections to the location of more than fifty West German government agencies in West Berlin, nor to frequent public functions such as the election of the federal president or West German party meetings there. They refused a Soviet offer to make the city an unoccupied "free city" with guaranteed access. They endured recurrent Berlin crises, including the construction of the Wall (August 13, 1961), always hewing to the defense of the three essentials enunciated by President John F. Kennedy in his *"Ich bin ein Berliner"* (I am a Berliner) speech: Allied occupation rights, access to the city from the West, and the viability of life in West Berlin.[97]

The issue of access from the West became the focus of the dramatic *Ostpolitik* initiatives of 1969 when the former Lord Mayor of West Berlin, Chancellor Willy Brandt, cleverly tied the future of "his" city to the ratification of the mutual-renunciation-of-force treaties between Bonn

95. Ibid., pp. 125, 173–175.

96. The subsidy involved about half the city's budget, the occupation costs, and tax concessions to West German businesses willing to maintain branches in Berlin. See the list of Bonn's gestures to maintain its ties to the beleaguered city in Willy Brandt, *Von Bonn nach Berlin* (Berlin: Arain, 1957), pp. 14–79. Also see W. P. Davison, *The Berlin Blockade: A Study in Cold War Politics* (Princeton, N.J.: Princeton University Press, 1958) and Hans Speier, *Divided Berlin* (New York: Praeger, 1962).

97. See also Gerd Langguth, ed., *Berlin. Vom Brennpunkt der Teilung zur Brücke der Einheit* (Cologne: Wissenschaft & Politik, 1990).

and Moscow, Warsaw, and Prague. Brandt succeeded in getting the representatives of the four victorious powers together for a long series of meetings, and in 1971 they finally agreed to a four-power treaty, the Berlin Agreement, which

1. recognized the reserved rights of all four powers, and by which they pledged not to change the status quo unilaterally or by threat of force;
2. guaranteed unimpeded traffic between the FRG and West Berlin across GDR territory, with some details left to inter-German agreements;
3. reaffirmed Bonn–West Berlin ties, provided that the political organs of the FRG not be convened in Berlin and the latter not become part of the FRG;
4. granted West Berliners the same visiting rights in East Germany that had hitherto been enjoyed by West Germans and foreigners, who had been accorded access upon acquisition of visas, payment of transit fees, and obligatory exchange of a considerable sum of deutschmarks for East marks at the official exchange rate of 1:1; and
5. permitted West Berliners consular representation abroad by West German representatives and established a Soviet Consulate in West Berlin.

The Significance of the Choice of Berlin

Allied agreement securing the status of West Berlin removed the "birth defect" of unsecured Western rights of access and, in particular, returned responsibility for the status of the city from East German hands to those of the Soviets, who were developing a warm relationship with the SPD leaders in power in Bonn.[98] The East German government, under Walter Ulbricht, struggled in vain against this collusion by Bonn and Moscow which threatened the GDR's legitimacy and even challenged its right to appropriate East Berlin—a part of quadripartite occupied Berlin—as its capital and 15th district.[99] Eventually inter-German negotiations calmed

98. See Merkl, *German Foreign Policies, West and East* (Santa Barbara, Calif.: ABC-Clio, 1974), pp. 156–165.
99. To quote *Neues Deutschland*, the official SED organ: "There is only Berlin, the capital of the GDR, and the independent political unit West Berlin, which is in the middle of and *on the territory of the GDR*" (Nov. 13, 1970; emphasis added).

the fears of the East German government, and Ulbricht's successor, Erich Honecker, established a *modus vivendi* with the West German governments of Willy Brandt and Helmut Schmidt. But despite the breakdown of the Wall, the separation of West Berlin from the FRG continued until, in June 1990, the three Western powers lifted at least the injunction against direct election of West Berlin deputies to the Bundestag and granted voting rights for them and for Berlin delegates to the Bundesrat. At the same time, they reaffirmed that "these Western sectors continue *not* to be a constituent part of the FRG and *not* to be governed by the latter."[100] The allied reservations regarding the status of West Berlin and, hence, the final obstacle to the reunification of the city were lifted only with the entry into force of the Second State Treaty of October 3, which also proclaimed that "the capital of Germany is Berlin" (art. 2[1]) and asserted that "the twenty-three districts of Berlin form the *Land* Berlin" (art. 1[2]).

Until the final resolution of the capital question in June 1991, the choice of Berlin versus any other capital was argued with considerable passion.[101] A bevy of notables and former Berlin mayors, including Federal President Richard von Weizsäcker (CDU), Walter Momper (SPD), Hans-Jochen Vogel, Willy Brandt, and countless Berlin and East German spokespersons weighed in with a strong appeal to restore the reunited city to its "historic place" as the German capital—actually, it played such a role only from 1871 to 1945.[102] East Germans in particular, alienated by their current situation, pleaded to make "our capital" that of unified Germany and pointed to the availability not only of the old Reichstag building for the Bundestag but of the Volkskammer as quarters for the Bundesrat, and of office space for the deputies in the SED Central Committee building. Indeed, the Berlin city government had been busy preparing plans for housing government and parliament as well as federal civil servants and their families—the calculations included large amounts of housing made available by the expected departure of the allied troops and their families. Unfortunately, as of this writing, large amounts of

100. See *Bundesgesetzblatt* I, 1068, June 12, 1990.

101. See, for example, Jörg-Detlef Kühne, "Replik in Sachen Hauptstadt: Nicht nur Papier und Sonntagsreden," *Zeitschrift für Parlamentsfragen* 12, no. 3 (Oct. 1990), 515–524. Among the features of the emotional campaign to select Berlin were the following: a delegation of thirty Berlin women bringing each Bundestag deputy a rose and a knotted handkerchief; a petition with 4,000 signatures; a lifelike bear costume; demonstrations; and advertisements with pictures of such notables as Kurt Masur, the Leipzig Gewandhaus Orchestra director.

102. Weizsäcker came under a great deal of criticism for his stand from many quarters, including the Bonn SPD deputy and vice-chair of his parliamentary party, Horst Ehmke, who felt that the president had no business taking sides in this question.

asbestos were discovered in the Reichstag which, engineers suggest, might require eight years of reconstruction to be made safe. There are also massive equipment, personnel, and logistics deficits that need to be overcome in order to meet the requirements of the Bundestag and federal government, which are accustomed to a level of efficiency and service that may be hard to come by for Berlin.[103]

A major role in the dispute naturally fell to the question of how much it would cost to move government and parliament from Bonn to Berlin—no other possible sites had a chance against the powerful lobbies for Bonn and Berlin. The Federal Ministries of the Interior, Finance, and Housing prepared calculations for the Bundestag decision which suggested a figure of 6 billion marks, not including compensation for the considerable losses of the Bonn area, where 42,000 jobs were said to be dependent on the presence of the capital. SPD finance expert Ingrid Matthäus-Maier estimated the expense in two-digit billions, of which, according to a Prognos survey, about 20 billion marks would be required just to move the public institutions. When Chancellor Kohl, in an emotional appeal, supported the choice of Berlin "in ten to fifteen years," Finance Minister Waigel (CSU)—probably distraught about the astronomical cost of German unification—opined that there was no money available for such "symbolic exercises."

The Berlin lobby, for its part, pointed out that Bonn had during the last several years engaged in vast building projects for the government (1.5 billion marks), and especially for the Bundestag (655 million), for which the money had evidently been made available. Berliner Bank, to top it all off, presented a study according to which the federal government would stand to gain a surplus of 2.4 billion marks within ten years as a result of the move. The bank embroidered this bit of creative financing by adding that the move of the capital to Berlin might serve to "trigger the economic 'take-off' of East Germany." This argument that Berlin as the capital of the united country would "send a signal to East Germany" was a favorite of all Berlin boosters, as if a new federal district, say in Thuringia, could not have had the same effect. For the present and near future, unfortunately, the dominant Berlin tune calls for the continuation of massive federal subsidies for the city—originally, these Berlin subsidies were expected to foot a large part of the bill for German unification—which cannot even tolerate a reduction for 1992 from 14.5 to 13.1 billion marks, not to mention halving it, and which runs annual deficits

103. Several extensive features in *Der Spiegel* discuss the facilities and problems of Berlin as a revived German capital. See, for example, no. 17, Apr. 22, 1991, pp. 34–77, and the issues for Apr. 29, 1991, pp. 140–162, and May 5, 1991.

of 3–6 billion marks to meet its own extraordinary challenges of unification between East and West Berlin.[104]

On the other side, that of Bonn as the capital, the minister presidents of such important *Länder* as North Rhine Westphalia, Hesse, and Bavaria spoke for many West and South German businessmen and *Land* politicians when they praised the West German capital—the *Bundesdorf* (federal village)—precisely for its low profile and small-town character, and most of all for its proven democratic leadership over four decades of German history. Berlin, said Bavarian Minister President Max Streibl, was often "under pressure of street mobs, left and right, against parliamentary decisions," a potential "Kreuzberg as capital"—in reference to the alternative, "autonomous," and often violent subculture of that part of the city.

Indeed, German federalism was not likely to benefit from a resurgence of the centralized bureaucracy and society of the megalopolis Berlin, whose towering size alone would soon be three times greater than the next-largest city in Germany, Hamburg. Berliners have little concept of federalism, having lived outside the FRG for the last forty years and without federalism since 1933. The local press kept emphasizing the megapolitan size and splendor of Berlin—to rival Paris and London in the unitary states of France and Britain—if this were an asset for a federal capital. There are indeed several examples of federations—the United States, Canada, Australia—that have chosen to separate their capital from their largest metropolitan aggregation. Foreign observers, too, watched the choice of Berlin with a wary eye, given its historical record as the capital of Germany at its worst: under the Kaiser, under Hitler, and under the communist dictatorship. They also viewed the eastward shift, to within less than an hour of Poland and the lost Oder-Neisse and East Prussian territories, as an omen of a great shift toward an East European geopolitical fulcrum for German hegemony over all of Europe. There were favorable comments from across Eastern Europe, where people wanted to adopt Berlin as their regional capital, too. In spite of statements to the contrary collected avidly by Berlin boosters, the undercurrent of diplomatic and press opinion in France and Britain was one of alarm: the German cat was out of the bag after all, and it did not look like the proven democratic partner of the last forty years.[105]

104. See *Der Tagesspiegel*, May 14, 1991, and June 7, 17, and 19, 1991; Joachim Nawrocki, "Die 60-Milliarden-Legende," *Die Zeit*, May 20 and 25, 1991. Also *Süddeutsche Zeitung*, Apr. 27–28, 1991.
105. See *The Economist*, Jul. 28, 1990, p. 14, and *Der Spiegel* 44, no. 32, Aug. 6, 1990, pp. 39–41. See also the reaction to the actual decision in *Le Figaro*, June 20, 1991, pp. 6–7, and June 22–23, 1991, pp. 1–2. *Washington Post* correspondent Marc Fisher even

The debate over the capital was also reflected in public opinion polls that seesawed back and forth since the first excitement of fall 1989, when even Bonn Mayor Hans Daniels had said that his city "was serving in the role of capital only in lieu of Berlin." If anyone doubted the significance of generational distinctions for the politics of German national unification, for example, there was the public opinion poll by Infratest, in June 1990, regarding the choice of a capital for a united Germany. This poll was widely reported in the news media, along with the general debate on this subject.[106] Back in February, in the heady rush toward union, a reported 70% of West Germans had still opted for Berlin as the once and future German capital, and a month later there was still a majority of 60%. By June 1990, however, this Berlin majority had dwindled to 32.3%, while nearly half the respondents (48.7%) wanted Bonn to remain capital of the united country. The pedestrian capital found its majorities not only among Rhinelanders and Southerners but among women. Four out of five of all respondents agreed readily that Bonn had served creditably as the capital of West German democracy. Most tellingly for our generational analysis, clear majorities of young West Germans wanted to retain Bonn as the united German capital. Only among those born before 1940—in other words, in the first postwar and older political generations—did a majority favor Berlin. Perhaps we tend to overinterpret the survey commissioned by a Bonn newspaper—which may also have injected a bias—if we suggest that a vote for Berlin conjured up ghosts of the pursuit of national power and prestige, but the generational division on nationalism is clear.

Later *Politbarometer* polls in West Germany gave Bonn 52.4% (Berlin 41.7%) in October and 55.8% (Berlin 37.6%) in November 1990. After the all-German elections, Bonn continued to be the popular choice: 50% vs. 45% in March 1991, 55% vs. 45% in April. By November 1990, many national politicians, including Chancellor Kohl, had already cooled noticeably in their earlier ardor for Berlin. In the November *Politbarometer* poll, furthermore, a mere 23.8% of West Germans wanted the Bundestag to meet only in Berlin. Another 26.7% wanted it to stay in

---

credited the new capital with "some of the best . . . cuisine in Europe." *San Francisco Chronicle*, June 21, 1991. Cf. Daniel Vernet in *Die Zeit*, no. 19, May 3, 1991, p. 39.

106. The Infratest poll was commissioned by the Bonn *General-Anzeiger*, the principal local newspaper of Bonn. The respondents were a sample of adult West Germans and West Berliners. East Germans, who probably would have opted for Berlin, were not consulted. There might have been an even split if they had been. In May, an IPOS poll in West Germany had given Berlin 55% over 43% for Bonn, versus a May/June result of 91% for Berlin over 7% for Bonn in East Germany. IPOS/BRD, May–June 1990, p. 73.

Bonn, and nearly half (45.8%) liked the idea that the parliament could alternate between Bonn and Berlin.[107] There were also polls that indicated a desire to see the federal executive reside in Berlin (75% vs. 23%) while the Bundestag might alternate (41.4%) or be either in Berlin (44.4%) or in Bonn (12.5%).

As the self-imposed deadline neared for the Bundestag to make the decision (June 20, 1991), public debate intensified between the two lobbies while the politicians became notably more nervous. One way out of making an unpopular decision was the "organ bank" idea: that is, to divide up the various federal organs of government, especially executive agencies or levels thereof, between the contending cities. Another obvious solution was to postpone the decision until the next Bundestag elections, in 1994. A third dodge, advocated by the SPD and opposed by the CDU/ CSU, was to have a plebiscite rather than a decision by the Bundestag. In the end, all of these were rejected and, after a twelve-hour, heated debate, the Bundestag voted 338 to 320 for Berlin. Chancellor Kohl, who had endorsed the choice of Berlin, indicated that the actual transfer was likely to take six to twelve years and cost between 34 and 41 billion marks.

No sooner had the Bundestag surprised itself and most observers with this decision, than the pendulum swung in the opposite direction. The narrow majority, less than 3% of the Bundestag, for such an important decision provided an example of how politicians should not act unless they want to court disaster. The Bonn lobby received immediate reinforcement from the federal bureaucracy, which was most reluctant to move from institutional and residential quarters to the uncertain vagaries of a metropolis in turmoil and beset by exploding real-estate prices, not to mention the poor services and backward service traditions of Berlin. Kohl soon moved to regulate the transfer with two legislative enactments, to be passed in late 1992, in order to ensure financial compensation for the Bonn area and, presumably, to contain the runaway costs of the development of Berlin.[108] Since the vote obliged only the "core administration" to move, efforts were taken up again to keep the Bundesrat and

107. FGW, *Politbarometer*, nos. 714 and 710, Nov. 1990, p. 50.
108. During the debate, according to an early count by *Le Figaro*, the CDU/CSU split 107 for Berlin, 181 for Bonn; the FDP of Genscher—who had already picked out a handsome building for his foreign minister's residence—45–32 for Berlin; and the SPD 127–94 for Bonn. The PDS voted 15–1 and the Greens 6–2 for Berlin. These figures do not quite add up to the final tally, but they do suggest that the decisive influence came from the small parties and from the advocacy of prominent figures such as Kohl and the former West Berlin mayors. See *Der Tagesspiegel*, June 6, 1991, and *Le Figaro*, June 20 and 22–23, 1991. The Ministry of the Interior developed a series of compensations for federal civil servants who would have to swap Bonn residences for overpriced quarters in Berlin. See *Der Spiegel* 45, no. 27, Jul. 1, 1991, pp. 36–37.

the middle and lower levels of the ministries—most of which are only head offices without field administrations—and entire ministries such as Telecommunications, Scientific Research, and Foreign Economic Aid in Bonn.

Berliners responded with anger to such plans and delays. Ever anxious to argue against all other claimants for federal money—including further economic aid to Russia and Eastern Europe, according to press accounts—Berlin also hopes to increase its revenues from a vast influx of private capital and by becoming the site of the Olympics in 2000. The hopes of Bonn to become a center of European Community institutions instead of the German capital fizzled at an early point in the debate. Its only hope lay in delaying the transfer until Berlin was "really ready"— that is to say, far beyond the four years agreed upon. This was to be accomplished by, among other things, the coordinated inertia of Housing Minister and Bonn booster Irmgard Adam-Schwätzer (FDP), the Federal Construction Administration (Bundesbaudirektion)—which claimed to be employed to capacity—and the chancellery, and this even though the federal government owns more real estate in Berlin than anywhere else. Aside from the alleged asbestos problem with the Reichstag building, the planners actually found within less than a mile no fewer than twenty buildings that could be refurbished in six years to suit the needs of the federal government by 1997, at a cost of under 2 billion marks. An alternative plan would take advantage of the empty areas nearby that had been occupied by the Wall and the death strip behind it. The politicians who had voted for Berlin were further discouraged by the August *Politbarometer* polls, which asked for the voters' opinion of their "hasty pudding" decision of June: a substantial majority (55.9%) answered that they had made the wrong decision; only two of five (39.8%) agreed with it. Only a bare majority (50.1%) was drawn among CDU/CSU supporters. The FDP, SPD, and Green adherents replied three to five against it.

The Unification Treaty

At midnight, October 2, as champagne corks were popping all over Germany to celebrate German unification, the Second State Treaty, or Unification Treaty (*EV*), went into effect along with the Two-Plus-Four Treaty, the reestablishment of the five new *Länder* and Berlin, and the admission of the GDR (August 23) to the Federal Republic of the West. The Unification Treaty, in addition to tying the historic knot, also contributed in several essential ways to the integration of the former

GDR into the fabric of the new Federal Republic of Germany. The treaty itself looks forbidding with its 1,000-plus pages, three supplements, and appended protocol notes;[109] but its most significant contributions are found in supplements I and II, where the adaptation of East German law to West German law is attempted. Ministry by ministry, supplements I and II systematically catalogue which areas of East German law are exempt and which are changed, augmented, or require additional arrangements. Under the heading of the Foreign Office, for example, there is a long list of treaties (between the FRG and the Western powers regarding the stationing of troops of the latter) which are not to apply to the five new East German *Länder*. Under the Ministry of the Interior, the maintenance of Stasi records on East and West Germans is entrusted to a special federal deputy until the newly elected Bundestag can regulate the matter by law, and the latter is urged to consider a relevant Volkskammer law of August 24, 1990, for this purpose. Criminal prosecutions and investigations regarding civil service appointments were granted access to the Stasi files.[110]

A great deal of dismay was expressed among the vast numbers of former public employees of the GDR communist bureaucracy when the treaty confirmed that they would not simply be taken over into the civil service of the new German state, with its *Beamten* tenure and privileges and immunities, but might have to be screened and, quite possibly, not reemployed (*EV* art. 20 and Basic Law art. 33). During the long "screening loop" (*Warteschleife*) of six to nine months on reduced pay, public employees were neither employed nor assured of being rehired in the end. At GDR universities, for example, the process involved reapplying for one's old job in competition with West Germans of often better qualifications—especially in the social sciences, for instance, where the GDR's compulsory Marxist-Leninist indoctrination courses had taken the place of Western sociology and political science—and no incriminating past. The Federal Constitutional Court, in April 1991, confirmed the legality of the "screening loop" and the *de facto* dismissal of large numbers of GDR judges and the like. But the court also insisted that academic employees could not simply be *"abgewickelt"* (dropped) unless their

109. A complete edition is *Der Einigungsvertrag. Vertrag zwischen der BRD und der DDR über die Herstellung der Einheit Deutschlands* (Munich: Goldmann/Bertelsmann, 1990), hereafter referred to as *EV* with number of article, protocol note to article, or supplement).

110. The Volkskammer law in question meant to keep these records in the Eastern *Länder* and barred the West German Constitutional Protection Service from access to them. *EV* supp. I, chap. 2B (paras. 1 and 2), and amendment to the Federal Archive Law of Jan. 6, 1988.

entire college, department, or institute was eliminated. This decision was observed with great interest by such East German universities as Humboldt University (Berlin), which was fearful of a West German "takeover" and had already brought suit before the highest administrative court of the new state of Berlin.[111] Administrations, educational and cultural institutions, and public radio and television were either turned over to the new *Länder* or, if they were within federal jurisdiction, subordinated to West German federal offices (*EV* arts. 13–15).

Supplement II of the Unification Treaty specified which legal subjects regulated by GDR law were to remain in force in their entirety or with what changes and adjustments. Since the agreements regarding the property constitution (see above) had been incorporated into the treaty only in the form of general principles enunciated in a June 15 joint declaration of both governments,[112] four laws drawn up by the Bonn Ministry of Justice without discussion by Bundestag and Volkskammer were inserted by the negotiators into supplement II.[113] One of these laws provides for the right of public bodies to sell "people's own" properties—even if they are the subject of lawsuits for restitution—if such a sale is for investment for such purposes as securing or creating needed employment, housing, or infrastructure. The claimants, of course, are entitled to appropriate compensation. Another law of thirty-four lengthy paragraphs regulated the question of compensation in great detail.[114] The Trust Agency for the People's Property was mentioned five times—in article 21 (administrative property), article 22 (public properties), article 23 (public debts), article 24 (foreign debt), and article 25 (trust properties)—as well as in notes

111. The forty-page court decision was greeted with relief by large numbers of other people in the "screening loop" who welcomed the affirmation of such social rights as apply to single mothers, the handicapped, and "older" public GDR employees as well as their protection from dismissal without due process (i.e., retraining and possibilities for reemployment). In East Berlin alone, some 35,000 former public employees were in the limbo of the *Warteschleife* in 1991. The court also invalidated the government's argument that the labor contracts of such employees had lapsed along with the demise of the GDR government, the original employer. The federation and new *Länder* were the legal successors of the GDR, the ruling went, but this did not keep them from terminating the contracts so long as the holdover employees were not considered tenured civil servants.

112. *EV* supp. III, pp. 1110–1120.

113. The effect of this procedure was that these laws not only could not be amended by the legislatures but, as part of a treaty, had to be accepted or rejected *in toto* and are now in the treaty at the level of the Basic Law itself, a status which represents in a manner of speaking the survival of a contracting partner, the GDR, that no longer exists.

114. For the text of both laws, see *EV* supp. II, pp. 1071–1077. Also see *Der Vertrag zur deutschen Einheit. Ausgewählte Texte*, with commentary by Günther Bannas et al. (Frankfurt and Leipzig: Insel & Nomos, 1990), pp. 35–40 and 105–134. See, too, *EV* art. 41.

on these articles (article 25 contains details about the organization of the Trust Agency) contained in a memorandum appended to the treaty.[115]

The New Constitutional Order

In principle, the constitutional order of the old FRG, and especially its "inviolable principles" of federalism and the bill of rights (Basic Law arts. 1–20, 79[3]) is now that of the new Federal Republic of Germany. East German laws that, according to the functional division between *Länder* and federation, are within *Land* jurisdiction remain valid, unless they violate the Basic Law itself. Federal-level laws, however, are superseded by West German law (*EV* arts. 8 and 9). The new state also took over the financial constitution (i.e., the fiscal system), albeit with some delayed effects regarding the distribution of revenue (Basic Law art. 106) and its equalization among the five new *Länder* (BL art. 107), which instead will receive transfers from the Fund for German Unity pledged by the West German *Länder* (*EV* art. 17). The preamble of the new Basic Law no longer speaks of the desire "to maintain German national and state unity," nor of "a transitional period" and "those Germans who were denied the opportunity to participate." It no longer "challenges the German people to complete the unity and freedom of Germany," but announces that the Germans in the enumerated *Länder* have "in free self-determination completed unity and freedom" (*EV* art. 4).

The article 23 under which the five new *Länder* were admitted to the FRG was simply dropped, thus addressing the apprehensions in some quarters that future territorial ambitions could be accommodated with its invitation that the Basic Law "is to be put into force in other parts of Germany on their accession." After all, the Sudetenland of the Czechoslovak republic might at some point in the future ask to be admitted as a new *Land* of Germany, to give an example. The Second State Treaty also took the old disclaimer of the Basic Law to honor only in part or not at all the debt of the old German Reich (art. 135a) and applied it to the debts of the GDR. The application of the laws of the FRG to the territory of the former GDR, however, can be suspended only until December 31, 1992 (*EV* art. 4[5] and new BL art. 143)—which means, for example, the final legal demise of abortion on demand during the first trimester,

---

115. Administrative property includes that of the Stasi ministry. See *EV* pp. xii–xiv. The treaty also declared that all judicial and administrative decisions would continue in force unless specifically countermanded or appealed under laws of restitution and relief that were still to be passed (*EV* art. 17–19).

unless the old West German law is amended.[116] The treaty also urges parliament to take up the following subjects within two years of unification (*EV* art. 5): 1) *Land*–federal relations as discussed earlier (July 5) among the Western minister presidents; 2) a territorial reorganization of the borders of Berlin and Brandenburg;[117] 3) the possible addition of goals of the state—so far, the Basic Law simply calls the Federal Republic "a democratic and social[-welfare] federation" and enjoins government to abide by the laws and by the Constitution (Basic Law art. 20)—and 4) possible adoption of a new or rewritten constitution under article 146 of the Basic Law and with the benefit of popular ratification. Indeed, the Basic Law, now valid for nearly 80 million people, has never been submitted for their approval.[118]

The discussion about whether to change the Basic Law in a fundamental way was revived in the spring of 1991 when the government coalition of CDU/CSU and FDP proposed a commission to consider constitutional amendments. It was to be composed of sixteen Bundestag and sixteen Bundesrat representatives and to be presided over by the constitutional law professor Rupert Scholz. The government rejected the plan of the SPD opposition to call a constitutional council of 120 members, including nonpoliticians, in order to undertake a total revision and to ready the resulting document for popular ratification on the theory that "the ever more complicated problems of a society characterized by the division of labor did not lend themselves to simple yes-or-no formulations." The government did approve of such amendments as making environmental protection a "goal of the state," privatization of aviation control, and states rights within European integration. The Bundesrat became the first to form a constitutional commission—thirty-two representatives, two from each *Land*—headed by an acting chair, Minister President Max

116. See also *EV* pp. v–vi (of the memorandum). For certain financial regulations, postponement is permitted until the end of 1995 at the latest. The treaty also changed the number of seats given the larger *Länder* in the Bundesrat (Basic Law art. 51).

117. The reference appears to be directed not to a merger, but rather to an adjustment of borders in line with the priorities of regional planning. The article permits the *Land* governments involved to negotiate without the restrictions of Basic Law article 29, which demands plebiscites for territorial changes. There are negotiations afoot for a complete merger, however, which would create a state of at least 6 million residents and facilitate planning for the expected megapolitan growth of Berlin.

118. Another article of the treaty (*EV* 6) specifically suspended *"vorerst"* (for the time being) any application to East Germans of the controversial article 131 of the Basic Law, by which the Adenauer government had granted reinstatement and pension rights to large numbers of low-level Nazi civil servants. The East and West German governments thus ducked both the financial obligations and a possible rollback of Soviet and East German denazification measures.

Streibl (CSU), who claimed that there was a "broad nonpartisan consensus" among the *Länder* chiefs.[119] The Bundestag obliged with a commission of similar size—the total of sixty-four being meant as a compromise with the SPD—and the Federal Minister of the Interior, Wolfgang Schäuble (CDU), specifically rejected such SPD concerns as prohibiting industrial lockouts and arms exports to nonallied countries or giving specifics to the constitutionally prescribed gender equality. He had no objection to a prohibition of ABC weapons, recommended EC-wide solutions to the problems of migrant foreigners, and supported political asylum. He called the police surveillance of the PDS, as practiced in Bavaria, "not yet indicated at the federal level" because he considered the outlawing of political parties under the Basic Law "an extreme measure."[120]

Another bellwether of the constitutional trends was the debate about the new East German *Länder* constitutions and their details—most of them were still being written in mid-1991. The now defunct East Berlin Constitution of July 1990, for example, protected the environment, the right to housing, privacy rights in data processing, first-trimester abortions, and local suffrage for foreigners. Brandenburg hoped to adopt "the most modern constitution" in 1992, if the CDU and PDS would go along, a document alive with the spirit of the democratic upheaval of 1989 and the work of the Round Table. Among other things, it contained the possibility of popular initiatives (requiring only 20,000 signatures), the referendum, the protection of minorities (including gay couples), an obligation of government and individuals to protect the environment, prohibition of nuclear energy and storage of ABC weapons, the right to work, housing, education and public information (as "goals of the state"), as well as the right to counseling and social assistance, and no criminal punishment—even the CDU agreed—for abortion during the first trimester. The draft was made available to a wide audience, even though some political details (electoral law, second chamber) were still controversial. Saxonians were similarly invited to debate a conservative draft by a group of lawyers from the town of Gohrisch. In Mecklenburg-Vorpommern, a commission of experts was still deliberating over a draft by two Schleswig-Holstein jurists, while Saxony-Anhalt preferred to leave out of its constitutional draft all mention of goals, civil rights, plebiscites,

119. Among the SPD minister presidents, only Johannes Rau (North Rhine Westphalia), Henning Voscherau (Hamburg), and Gerhard Schröder (Lower Saxony) mentioned as their agenda territorial reorganization (art. 29), nuclear energy, rights to work and to housing, local suffrage for foreigners, the introduction of plebiscites, or specification of when or under what circumstances German troops might be involved in an ally's war. See *Der Tagesspiegel*, April 20–21, 1991, and Jul. 3, 1991, as well as the "Deutsches Haus" series in *Die Zeit*, March 22, Apr. 12, and May 10, 1991.
120. Quoted in *Süddeutsche Zeitung*, May 25–26, 1991, pp. 2 and 12.

or the popular demand for a citizens' advocate (ombudsman). Its draft was not only stripped to the organizational bare bones but lacked even the Brandenburgian injunction for the *Land* government to disclose all its activities to the Landtag. Conservative Thuringia also showed little enthusiasm for direct democracy, a feature present even in the Saxonian draft, where 40,000 signatures (of 5 million residents) will authorize an initiative and half the registered voters (in Brandenburg only one-fourth) must go to the polls to make a majority vote stick. Mecklenburg-Vorpommern's draft contains the same regulation. Both Saxony and Brandenburg favor establishing a constitutional court and a citizen's right to all environmental data known to the government. Finally, the Brandenburg draft specifically recognizes citizen initiatives—the old Basic Law speaks only of parties—and would lower the electoral minimum for representation in Landtag and city councils to 3% (from 5%).[121]

A very significant innovation in view of the expanding and solidifying European Community, moreover, was the expansion of European Community law as well as other international treaties and agreements with Western powers to the former GDR (*EV* arts. 10 and 11). The Second State Treaty was less open to recognition of the international treaty obligations of the old GDR except where such recognition might enhance trust (in a united Germany), meet mutual interests, and not run counter to existing West German obligations (*EV* art. 12). East German membership in multilateral organizations to which the FRG did not belong, such as the Warsaw Pact or CMEA (both of which have since lapsed), required negotiations with the old East German partners as well as with competing Western organizations. The competing diplomatic representations of both states with many countries, and with organizations such as the United Nations and the World Health Organization, were simply reduced in favor of the West German diplomats and embassies (*EV* art. 24). The obligations of the GDR also included foreign debts incurred until July 1, 1990, for which the new Federal Republic took qualified responsibility.[122] Economic, social, cultural, and environmental regulations, especially those concerning the promotion of economic development and the restructuring of the GDR institutions of higher education and research,[123] rounded out the provisions of the treaty (*EV* arts. 28–39).

121. See *Der Tagesspiegel* and *Berliner Zeitung* for Jul. 1, 1991.

122. By this time, instances of fraud at the time of the currency union had become known: some GDR foreign trade officials had siphoned off several hundred million marks, using fraudulent foreign claims. There were also the antiquated assets of the East German railroads and postal service which, as properties about to be transferred to West German railroads and postal service, required assessment (*EV* arts. 26 and 27).

123. The federal government was expected to play a major role in financing and directing the development of universities, university medical clinics, and various research activities.

The Unification Treaty also had a preamble, which related the completion of the process to the several themes that were on the minds of the contracting parties: 1) becoming an equal member of the community of nations in peace, freedom, and self-determination; 2) living together in peace and freedom in a state of law (*Rechtsstaat*) and in a democratic and social-welfare state; 3) gratitude toward those who peacefully helped to free the GDR and those who persisted in completing the unification process; 4) awareness of the continuity of German history and the special responsibility for a democratic development mindful of human rights and the maintenance of peace; 5) the desire to contribute to European unification and to a European order of peace in which all European nations could live together; and 6) an emphasis on the inviolability of borders and on the territorial integrity and sovereignty of all European states as an elementary prerequisite of peace. This was the basis upon which the German people wished to found their united commonwealth.

The usual fifty-fifty financing in the Western *Länder* was considered inadequate in the East German *Länder*, which lack the economic capacity found in the West. See *Der Vertrag zur deutschen Einheit*, p. 26.

Chapter SIX

The Economic Problems of Union

Throughout the euphoria and the disillusionment of the first year after the currency union, there was no greater bone of contention than the question of how much the unification would cost in the end. In September 1990, 85% of West German and 72% of East German adults pointed to the costs of union as the most frequently discussed subject. Was there not a less expensive or at least a less painful alternative to the path chosen by the Kohl government? Who would pay for it all? Chancellor Kohl's government had always insisted that the cost would simply be borne from the added revenues of economic growth and would not require raising taxes. But his principal challenger, Oskar Lafontaine (SPD), and other critics bitterly complained that the government was not forthcoming about the actual costs and that it offered deliberate mystifications about the subject. The astronomical cost would probably be borne not by those who profited most from the union, but by ordinary people who would suffer from the painful adjustments and sacrifices that were the result of a lack of forethought and planning, and of Kohl's unseemly haste. The critics hinted, in particular, that slowing down the process of unification and somehow shielding East Germany from the immediate consequences of unification would have helped, but without offering a concrete alternative plan that might have found the support of German voters East and West. Even by the end of the year of unification, 1990/91, as the reader will see, there was still no clear idea of the true costs of restructuring and integrating East Germany into West Germany—the peculiar nature of the communist economy of the GDR is at the heart of the problem. The questions of cost and of how to achieve unification in the least painful way, in fact, extend into the foreseeable future, the next five or ten years, and we may not know anything but charges and countercharges for quite a long time.

In the meantime, the issue of the excessive cost of unification continued to fester and to embarrass the Kohl government. In November 1990, when asked if they thought that unification could be financed *without tax increases*, two-thirds of West German respondents still expressed their belief that tax increases would indeed be necessary, and such increases were opposed by only a narrow majority (52.7% vs. 45.6% in favor).[1] Two months later, during the state elections in Hesse, which the CDU/CSU lost, a majority of the respondents agreed that Chancellor Kohl had been guilty of a *"Steuerlüge"* (lie about taxes), a deliberate "fraud upon the voters." And when the details of proposed tax increases became known, later in January 1991, nearly two-thirds agreed with the charge of "fraud," and a similar majority directed its ire at the new gasoline tax, which had raised the price of gas by nearly a dollar a gallon to more than three dollars. At the national level, meanwhile, the public was less vindictive: the *Politbarometer* for January still gave Kohl 51% (vs. 48.3%) in favor of his tax raise, and only 40.3% (vs. 49.3%) concurred in the fraud charge,[2] and all this in the shadow of the aerial bombardment of Iraq which was likely to add further to the German tax load. By April 1991, after a three-month slump for the Kohl government in the opinion

1. Only 30.8% literally believed Kohl's line of "no new taxes," while 65.9% saw it as a white lie. Even among CDU/CSU adherents, 52.8% thought it was a lie and, among the coalition FDP, 74.2%. A narrow majority among the CDU/CSU supported the tax increase—two-thirds among FDP supporters—while the opposition SPD opposed it by a margin of three to two. A month earlier, a narrow majority of 50.2% of all respondents (vs. 47.5%) had still supported the increase and 77.2% said they knew that taxes had to be raised. See *Politbarometer*, Nov. 1990, p. 49.

2. The support level for raising taxes to finance German unification remained at 53.2% "against" vs. 45.5% "for," but 51.6% (vs. 36.7%) agreed with the charge of fraud in a highly partisan response. FGW, *Blitzumfrage zur Landtagswahl in Hessen*, Jan. 14–16, 1991, p. 162ff. A week later, the reaction to raising specifically the income tax (*Lohnsteuer*) was in the same range, 54.4% "against" vs. 42.4% "for," but on the gas tax, it was 61.7% vs. 35% and on the fraud charge 62.8% vs. 31.8%, as even the adherents of the coalition FDP now called it a "fraud" by 53.9% to 35.5%. See the exit polls in *Wahltagsbefragung Landtagswahl in Hessen*, Jan. 20, 1991, pp. 185–189, and *Politbarometer*, Jan. 1991, pp. 51, 55.

polls and in three state elections, the segment of West Germans who thought the charge of the "tax lie" justified had risen to 69% (vs. 27%) nationwide, even though half the respondents (49% vs. 49%) still considered the increased income taxes reasonable. The East Germans, for whose benefit the taxes were being raised, were no consolation to the hapless chancellor: 72% of them opposed the tax increases for unification (vs. 27%), evidently embarrassed by the situation and confused by the mendacious ways of Western politicians. In a May survey, many expressed the feeling that even to discuss tax increases was a breach of the electoral promises made by the federal government they had helped to reelect. Some 90% thought that this turn of events placed the cost of unification squarely upon the backs of ordinary people. Obviously, their previous rulers had produced a more satisfying mix of lies—and no discussions.[3]

The Most Prosperous and Economically Efficient State

As communist economies went—Westerners never learned more about communism than they did from its disintegration—the GDR was long regarded as the soundest until the opening of the Wall revealed its glaring weaknesses for all to see. "Since the 1960s," the jacket copy for Jonathan Steele's *Inside East Germany* (1977) proclaimed, "the country has become the most prosperous and economically efficient state in Eastern Europe, with a higher per capita income than Britain's." Similar laudatory comparisons by Western observers have continued until quite recently, often glossing over even the technical difficulties of comparing communist and capitalist economies, and generally placing the GDR among the top twenty—or even the top ten—industrialized countries of the world.[4] In late 1990, however, the *EC Bulletin* dryly noted the vital

3. See *Politbarometer*, Apr. 1991, pp. 52–53, 87, and *Berliner Morgenpost*, May 3, 1991. By this time, 84% of West Germans said they knew the taxes would have to go up because of German unification. Finance Minister Waigel (CSU), in a March 1991 interview, still claimed that "without the Gulf war expenses of 1990/91 and the expenditures connected with Eastern and Central Europe, we would not have had to raise taxes in 1991." *Der Spiegel* 45, no. 12, March 18, 1991, p. 24. He claimed that the decision for the tax increase came as late as the end of January 1991, after the Eastern CMEA market collapsed and after the beginning of the Gulf war.

4. Günter Mittag, for example, indicated in 1982 that the GDR ranked first in the production of potash fertilizer and lignite coal, sixth in cement, synthetic fiber and beer, and twelfth in electrical energy. *Neues Deutschland*, Dec. 5, 1982, p. 5. For earlier

statistics of the state of the GDR economy. After commenting on the high level of labor force participation, 50% more than in the old FRG, and on its relatively high level of professional qualification, it mentioned "shortcomings" among economists, lawyers, and administrators and the need for "considerable adaptation to new Western technology" among skilled workers. "Moreover, a crucial condition for successful integration of the East German economy into the Western market economy will be the regeneration of entrepreneurship and market-oriented management methods." Comparing the GDR living standard with that of other European countries, the *EC Bulletin* suggested that it was "undoubtedly the highest in Eastern Europe" and "probably higher than in Ireland, Greece and Portugal, but lower than in Spain." It also pointed to the low degree of industrial specialization, owing in part to autarky and a lack of foreign currency, and noted that the GDR economic structures had "changed relatively little over the past few decades." Labor productivity was, generally, only about one-third that of the old FRG, owing to centralized bureaucratic planning, lack of incentives, and outdated technology and capital stock—the last-named suffering particularly from lagging investment in the 1980s. The static CMEA (COMECON) market never made up for the lack of integration into the world market.

Sector by sector, the economic situation was bleak. GDR energy production concentrated on soft coal (lignite), and the nuclear plants (10% of energy needs) were below Western safety standards. Steel production was inefficient and expensive, chemical industries of pre-1939 vintage, and synthetics production "far behind Western standards." Machine tools, once an area of East German strength, were behind their importance in the FRG, though still capable of being made competitive on the world market. The machinery suffered from a need for the electronic control mechanisms embargoed by the Western Cocom list of items not to be sold to communist states. Cars and trucks, a major part of most Western economies, were not even an important export to Eastern Europe. Microelectronics swallowed up vast sums of GDR investment in the hope of building up a monopoly on computers in Eastern Europe, but the results were far from gratifying except for a considerable capacity for software production.[5] In precision engineering

comparisons, see also Deutsches Institut für Wirtschaftsforschung, Berlin, *DDR-Wirtschaft: Eine Bestandsaufnahme* (Frankfurt: Fischer, 1974), pp. 262–269, which suggested, with many qualifications, that GDR living standards in 1972 were well ahead of all communist states and at about half the West German level.

5. There are nasty jokes about the Robotron *Kombinat* that used to be the chief producer of East German computers, such as the story about the Japanese visitor who is asked at the conclusion of a thoroughgoing tour what he liked best in the GDR. His answer was "the museums, Pergamon [the famous antiquities museum] and Robotron." Robotron

and optics, two traditional East German fortes, the GDR was "relatively well-prepared for international competition." The construction industry boasted advanced techniques of prefabricated housing construction, but the demand was for small housing units and for modernizing the decrepit older housing, not for more of the ugly *Plattenbau* suburbs that already dotted the environs of the run-down cities. Textile production was based mostly on pre-1939 capital stock, without automation, and no match for the competition of the NICs (newly industrialized countries) and developing nations, at least for the mass market. Food production was of poor quality and little variety, no match for high-quality imports and an example of particularly low labor productivity and shorter working hours in comparison to West Germany. The *EC Bulletin* also highlighted infrastructural and environmental problems as "a major impediment to private investment." The chief transportation medium, the railroad network, needed repair and modernization. The state of the roads was "far below West German standards" and was not up to the expected increases in traffic and car ownership. Telecommunications were "very bad." The telephone system was overburdened, antiquated, and had too few connections:[6] "Modernization will probably mean the complete rebuilding of the communications system . . . [which will] introduce the most advanced technology." Sewerage modernization would also require major investment, as only half of the system was connected to purification plants. Many rivers were polluted, forests were damaged—with sulfur dioxide emissions eight times as high per inhabitant as in the old FRG—and safe drinking water was scarce.[7]

From all indications, the economic decline of the GDR appears to have started before the early eighties, perhaps following the impact of the energy crises of the seventies (1973 and 1979), which also had a disastrous impact on other East European economies.[8] There is abundant

---

also made personal computers, but in quality and price never came even close to its American, Japanese, or other European competitors.

6. In mid-1991, it was still nearly impossible to make a phone call from West Berlin to East Berlin—the first all-Berlin telephone directory had just come out—or to any other place in East Germany. The central interchange of Leipzig's telephone trunk lines featured underground installations and equipment dating back to the early 1920s.

7. "The European Community and German Unification," *Bulletin of the European Communities*, supp. 4/90, pp. 30–33.

8. In many cases, the rise in energy costs, despite oil deliveries from the Soviet Union (which, in any case were increasingly smaller and more expensive), led to crippling shortages, a drying up of the exchange of goods for lack of hard currency, and the accumulation of horrendous foreign debt by most East European countries. See Paul Marer, "The Economies and Trade of Eastern Europe," in William E. Griffith, ed., *Central and Eastern Europe: The Opening Curtain* (Boulder, Colo.: Westview, 1989) and Andrzej Korbonski, "The Politics of Economic Reform in Eastern Europe: The Last Thirty Years,"

evidence that, in the eighties, the GDR was unable to keep up its economic development in many areas, especially in regard to the development of automation and high-tech industries,[9] but also in regard to utilization of those resources still available to the moribund system. Where West Germany and other Western systems were able to adapt to the economic realities of the eighties, the GDR tended to retreat into a shell of autarky and self-delusion, blissfully ignoring its economic problems and squeezing the last ounce from shrinking natural resources such as lignite, regardless of the environmental and other costs. During that decade, however, the Honecker regime did respond politically by securing more trade, larger loans (1983), and statements of common interest in peace, denuclearization, and even a common past and future (*Schicksalsgemeinschaft*) from the West German government and its opposition. Furthermore, as the dissident economist Rudolf Bahro claimed in a television discussion early in 1991, it was not centralized planning per se but the constant dumping of valuable goods for hard currency on the world market that was the ruin of the GDR. For intra-German trade, of course, the East Germans neither needed hard currency nor were they handicapped by the EC customs border.

The Five-Year Plan of 1981–1985 still set unrealistic goals for increasing the production of soft coal and natural gas, as well as for electricity from nuclear plants of Russian design. Until 1989, the official statements and statistics of the GDR still painted a rosy picture which claimed that the net material product—the net domestic product without certain parts of the service sector—had been "rising at an annual rate of 4% in 1980–1988." Net investment during the same period was said to have grown 2% a year, and the real disposable income per capita at 4.5% a year. The International Monetary Fund (IMF) in 1990 characterized the actual economic performance as "much worse" and attributed the problems to

1. the inflexibility of an increasingly centralized system that could not adjust to the external shocks of the seventies and eighties;
2. the emergence of new technologies and consumer tastes;
3. the lack of integration into the world economy, insulating the GDR from external competition;

Soviet Studies 41, no. 1 (1989). Also see the East German literature, for example, Hans-Georg Haupt et al., eds., *Die sozialistische Gemeinschaft. Interessen–Zusammenarbeit–Wirtschaftswachstum* (East Berlin: VEB, 1985), and *Neues Deutschland*, Nov. 11–12, 1986.

9. The turning away from the short-lived cybernetics movement in the seventies (Chapter Three) was only a part of the problem, just as energy and other shortages were only contributing factors in the "arterial hardening" of the administrative system (see Chapter Three) and in the defensive attitudes which hid a dying, quasi-religious faith.

4. the concentration of investment in a few technology-intensive areas[10] and at the expense of the deterioration of capital stock elsewhere, in particular in infrastructure and the consumer durables industry;
5. the increased reliance on pollution-prone soft coal for energy;
6. the rigid and excessively egalitarian labor market, which lacked mobility and appropriate wage incentives; and
7. the declining morale of workers in the face of the well-known superiority of West German living standards and the harsh rejection of any reform and criticism by the GDR regime.[11]

The upshot was a productivity gap between the GDR and the old FRG estimated variously at 40–50% of the West German level.[12] As we shall see, these details and figures still fall considerably short of describing life in the pre-1990 GDR.

The realization that their country was economically in trouble, government lies notwithstanding, must have hit GDR citizens very hard in 1989/90, perhaps as hard as the military collapse of the German army in late 1918, after years of government lies. Then, as now, many Germans took an inordinate pride in their prowess—in fact, they were ready to accept the new lie that the German army had been "stabbed in the back" by traitors and revolutionaries—and they may well take their East German economic defeat today just as hard. Imagine the drop in esteem, both abroad and among its own hard-pressed citizens, since Western journalists, politicians, and entrepreneurs began to take a closer look early in 1990 with a view toward economic union with the booming West German market economy. This is a major challenge to international political-economic theory, in particular to the theories of dependency. Does development within the communist orbit actually "underdevelop" a country? Are the gigantic and nearly useless pig farms and industrial

10. The selection of microelectronics by the 10th SED Congress (1981) is the best example. For "optimistic" statistics, see *Statistisches Jahrbuch der DDR* (East Berlin: 1989).

11. See Thomas Mayer and Günther Thumann, "German Democratic Republic: Background and Plans for Reform," in *German Unification: Economic Issues*, ed. Leslie Lipschitz and Donogh McDonald (Washington, D.C.: IMF, Dec. 1990), pp. 49–70, esp. 52–53.

12. In 1987, the *Materialien zum Bericht zur Lage der Nation* of the Bundestag contained an estimate of 50% for the industrial sector of the GDR economy, a figure based on research by DIW (Deutsches Institut für Wirtschaftsforschung). The DIW *Wochenbericht* 26/90, June 28, 1990, however, suggested a GDP level of 40% for all employed persons in the GDR. Statistical comparisons between capitalist and communist economies are notably unreliable.

white elephants of the GDR, for whose products there is almost no demand today, merely the result of a communist *comprador* system beholden more to the Soviet empire than to the countries which were made utterly dependent on that empire and which were not allowed to achieve real autonomy in the world? Or did the GDR economy in the eighties suffer a set of economic crises similar to those outlined by the director of the Budapest Institute for Economic Planning, Bela Kádár: namely, foreign and domestic deficits, and crises of economic growth and economic planning?[13] What share of GDR enterprises before 1989 was really producing no profits or hefty losses? In Hungary, it was 30% even after a decade or more of economic liberalization under János Kádár. Without prices set by a domestic market and international marketability measured by a convertible currency, it seemed impossible to determine profitability.[14] The London *Economist* attributes the drop in self-esteem, at least inside East Germany, to the dramatically different West German wage levels and consumer choices that East German visitors and refugees were able to glimpse in the last quarter of 1989. Otherwise, the all-too-visible hand of the state, rather than the invisible one of the marketplace, tended to obscure a deteriorating situation that was caused by the rigid structures of communist economic policy.

The First Moments of Truth

At the level of the individual worker and consumer, and within individual enterprises, however, neither East nor West Germans were long in the dark about the real state of the GDR economy of 1989/90. An East German public opinion poll, commissioned in the first half of December 1989, disclosed that at least 82% of the population considered their

13. See Gabor Révész, *Perestroika in Eastern Europe: Hungary's Economic Transformation, 1945–1988* (Boulder, Colo.: Westview, 1990) and Miklós Losoncz, "Ungarische Liberalisierung," *Politische Meinung 35*, no. 249 (March/Apr. 1990), 63–67. Structural weaknesses of the Hungarian economy, in particular the shrinking share of certain Hungarian industries in the changing world market (e.g., mining, steel and iron, "heavy chemistry") but also the country's total production, were causing the deficits and the lagging growth. Also see Judy Batt, *Economic Reform and Political Change in Eastern Europe: A Comparison of the Czechoslovak and Hungarian Experience* (New York: St. Martin's Press, 1988).
14. See *The Economist* for Dec. 15, 1989, pp. 11–12, 47–48, and for Jan. 19, 1990, pp. 21–26. In Hungary, where the early seventies had brought economic liberalization and expansion, growth began to slow down by the end of that decade and, again, as the external demand from the Soviet Union and other COMECON countries declined. Hungarian foreign trade began to look for customers and suppliers in the West.

economy to be in a "bad" or "very bad" state. This level of negative self-assessment remained steady for the next two years.[15] In 1989, 98% wanted "the functionaries responsible for the crises in the GDR sent up before a judge," with the remaining 2% presumably afraid that they themselves might be personally accused.[16] An amazing 82% of the respondents already claimed to have visited West Germany or West Berlin since the borders opened, probably getting their first glimpse of consumer heaven, albeit (for them) at mostly unaffordable prices. Gorbachev proved even more popular in the GDR than in the Federal Republic, but he was still no match for the extraordinary popularity of communist Premier Hans Modrow, who received a high rating from 91% of the sample.[17]

It was not long after the opening of the borders that the West Germans got their first glimpse of the economic weaknesses of the GDR. By the second half of November 1989, *Der Spiegel* published the first impressions of its reporters. They noted the exorbitant profits made by West German and West Berlin retailers from eager East German shoppers—even the Frankfurt Stock Exchange registered an extraordinary surge in the stocks of retail chains—the antiquated GDR automobile engines and telephone system, and the street rate for ostmarks against deutschmarks (1:10 and even 1:20). More important, they noted that many of East German foreign trade products had long been traded in Eastern Europe below cost, just to get rid of them, and that the volume of industrial machinery—a leader of East German industry for nearly a century—sold to Western industrial countries was now one-fourth what the GDR had sold in 1973. There had been desperate attempts to maintain certain prestige products and especially Robotron, the flagship of East Germany's giant companies—but at the expense of all other industry, where obsolescence, mushrooming repair costs, and production breakdowns

15. See *Der Spiegel* 43, no. 51, Dec. 18, 1989, pp. 86–89. Fully 98% of the respondents also felt that there were "pressing environmental problems" in the GDR, but 71% at that time still wanted to retain the sovereignty of their country (vs. 27% opting for German unification). In November 1990, 78% of all German respondents (1.6% said "good" and 18.6% "partly good, partly bad") still considered the East German economy "bad"—the most negative rating came from PDS adherents (92.5% "bad"). See *Politbarometer*, Nov. 1990, p. 90.

16. At that moment, 43% of East German adults blamed "most of the higher-ups in party and state," 41% blamed many of them, and 9% felt that "only a few . . . had abused their authority." A year later, 84.2% of East Germans (including 65.3% of PDS adherents) blamed "the former SED" for the current economic problems. *Politbarometer*, Nov. 1990, p. 71.

17. By comparison, Günter Maleuda of the Democratic Peasant party (DBD), Wolfgang Berghofer (SED), and the new president of the State Council, Manfred Gerlach (LDPD) received the approval of 50–75%; all the opposition leaders were well under 50%, beginning with Bärbel Bohley (45%).

weighed heavily upon the low average level of productivity.[18] The infamous *Materialpause*, a production break caused by the unavailability or delayed arrival of critical supplies, kept East German enterprises at a mere fraction of their already low capacity (compared to West German firms). Even the Soviets, who in the past had received up to 40% of East German trade, were returning unsatisfactory goods by the wagon load.

The magazine also interviewed experts. The chief of the German McKinsey agency said that more than one-half of all East German firms were either beyond salvage or in need of drastic surgery. Alfred Herrhausen, the head of one of the three major West German banks, thought it would take five to ten years for the GDR to build a market economy. He indicated that West German employers and large firms were "ready to assist," but he questioned the desire of East German leaders to accept such help (on terms acceptable to the donors). Herrhausen believed a mix of a planned and a market economy for the GDR to be "unthinkable." While distinguishing the property structures from the decision structures, he did not exclude the possibility that such East German state enterprises as the huge *Kombinate* might work with the market. They would, of course, have to compete fairly and "stop acting like sleepy monopolies." Private foreign investors were quite likely to come in, provided the GDR offered 1) a solid legal basis for joint ventures (as in Poland and in the USSR); 2) a sound price system; 3) a property reform that would allow entrepreneurs to acquire uncontested titles; 4) a currency reform to make the East mark convertible; and 5) political democratization.[19] West German public investment should properly be directed toward the East German infrastructures, such as transportation, telecommunications and telephones, and public health. But "premature generosity" on the part of the Kohl government would be counterproductive in that it would reduce the "healthy democratic pressure" on the GDR to reform itself root and branch. The banker expected a fairly quick response by the East German economy to the pressure of total reform, albeit also some unemployment and inflation.

18. Comparative calculations of unit value cost suggested that a unit cost of 2.50 East marks per deutschmark in the early eighties had now deteriorated (or become inflated) to 4.40 by the end of the decade. *Der Spiegel* 43, no. 47, Nov. 20, 1989, pp. 20–23. Industrial production itself began to drop in October 1989, with the decline reaching 40% in July 1990. Heinz Suhr, *Was kostet uns die ehemalige DDR?* (Frankfurt: Eichborn, 1990), p. 10. See also Gernot Schneider, *Wirtschaftswunder DDR. Anspruch und Realität*, 2nd ed. (Berlin: Bundverlag, 1990).

19. Interview in *Der Spiegel* 43, no. 47, Nov. 20, 1989, pp. 26, 28–30.

Early Concrete Proposals

Around the end of 1989 and in the first weeks of 1990, while East German politics became committed to democratic reform, Germans East and West also began to consider concrete economic reforms. To borrow Bela Kádár's terminology of internal and external imbalance, the East German internal debt was estimated at 130 billion East marks and the foreign debt at 34 billion East marks, or 8.8% of its gross domestic product. This was only about a third of the foreign debt (in % GDP) of Hungary, Yugoslavia, or Poland, to be sure, but about double the amount owed by Czechoslovakia or by Romania—where the dictator Ceauşescu had squeezed the country's debt payments from the living flesh of its citizenry.

The GDR had long received fairly accurate reports about the parlous state of the economy from such knowledgeable experts as the former head of the state planning commission, Gerhard Schürer, and the ex-Minister of Finance, Ernst Höfner, but the SED leaders paid no attention to such bad news. Instead they spoke of wanting a "better socialism" and "market-oriented reforms," but not of scrapping the planned economy. The new SED leader Gregor Gysi, in an interview, declared his interest in joint ventures and in permitting private enterprises outside the key industries, but he was adamant about maintaining the sovereignty of the GDR.[20] The democratic opposition generally said the same. The New Forum spoke vaguely of "socialism with a human face" and other old utopian dreams. The new Social Democrats (SDP) advocated "an ecologically oriented social market economy with mixed economic structures and varied forms of property." Democratic Start (DA) voiced its concern about a sellout to the "big money" of the West and an "economic Niedervereinigung" (downward unification), a wordplay on Wiedervereinigung (reunification).

With the exception of the banker Alfred Herrhausen, West German leaders at first were hardly ready with plans for economic union, except to say, "Whatever we do, let us not stabilize the GDR," a statement attributed to both Count Lambsdorff (FDP) and Finance Minister Waigel (CSU). Two-thirds of the West German public, however, did approve of the "welcome money" of 100 marks extended to each East German refugee. Some 74% also endorsed aid to East Germany, provided it would not require raising West German taxes—only 22% were prepared to do so if it would raise their taxes. Chancellor Kohl and a chorus of

20. Der Spiegel 43, no. 51, Dec. 18, 1989, pp. 26–29.

politicians and businessmen to the right of center began to insist that German unification could be financed entirely with the economic growth expected from a booming West German economy. The West German public greeted his rosy optimism with notable skepticism, and opposition leaders such as Oskar Lafontaine (SPD) promptly seized upon this issue of credibility.[21] Behind this skeptical response to government assurances, most probably, lay the concerns of many voters about the drawbacks likely to accompany hundreds of thousands of East German and other Eastern refugees. Some 350,000 East German and other Eastern refugees had already arrived by January 1990, and at least another 100,000 were expected, straining to the very limit the West German capacity to absorb them.

The government parties made a valiant effort to ignore the negative clamor while considering concrete steps to be taken in the event either of a looser "confederation" or a genuine federal union. Kohl's ten-point program, as he explained, had envisaged "common institutions for economic, traffic, environmental . . . and health policies," to be negotiated by topical joint committees under a "confederative arrangement," an approach not all that different from the subministerial cooperation of the two states under the Basic Treaty of the seventies.[22] East Germany's Premier Modrow, in an interview with *Der Spiegel*, advocated a move toward "more self-administration" of the big companies rather than reliance on state direction. He spoke of a combination of public, mixed, and private ownership, joint ventures, and an emphasis on quality, competitiveness, and profitability. But he staunchly rejected the idea of unification and pleaded for time to carry out appropriate reforms, while dodging all questions about price reform and subsidies for housing and food. He even showed a willingness to pare down the ubiquitous East German bureaucracy to only half its former size.[23]

21. In November 1990, two-thirds of West German adult respondents, including over half of the CDU adherents and three-fourths of the coalition FDP, expected higher taxes. *Politbarometer*, Nov. 1990, p. 49. The SPD also prepared an "Emergency Program for the GDR" at its party conference of December 18–20, promising firm exchange rates and support for the East German infrastructure, especially the environment, transportation, and tourism.
22. Because Kohl brought the question of whether to "dampen the enthusiasm for unification" or "give the Germans a vision of a united future" to a parliamentary debate, there were also numerous positive statements from SPD leaders such as Johannes Rau, Willy Brandt, and Karsten Voigt about the economic aspects. Pensioners' organizations and labor market experts, on the other hand, worried with Oskar Lafontaine and his partisans about how to keep the East German refugees from being attracted by and siphoning off West German welfare benefits.
23. *Der Spiegel* 43, no. 49, Dec. 4, 1989, pp. 34–35.

The months before the decisive East German parliamentary elections on March 18 focused the planned steps toward a likely economic union. West German economists and political leaders made preliminary macroeconomic assessments of the GDR economy, and there were even early estimates of what economic unification might cost the Federal Republic. The 1989 East German GDP per capita was estimated to be only 40% of West Germany's, and GDR manufacturing was about 30% and services about 20% below the West German levels—all prior to the impact of the great exodus! Federal Economics Minister Helmut Haussmann developed a three-step plan for tackling economic unification. The first stage involved the abolition of trade barriers and the creation of a suitable legal framework for direct investment and capital participation in East German firms. A second stage would aim at company-to-company cooperation, such as was already developing between Volkswagen and the manufacturers of the Trabant. The third stage would take place only after the elections had swept the communist government out of office: it would be aimed at strengthening the East German infrastructure through appropriate measures and Western aid. The economics minister made clear the need for basic structural reforms, especially a reduction of central planning, in order to encourage among other things a broad new private sector with many small and medium-size enterprises. There would have to be investment guarantees—through a revived European Recovery Program (Marshall Plan)—and major efforts at technological modernization in the GDR. Haussmann also advocated the creation of joint economic commissions, GDR employer's associations, chambers of commerce, and links with Western credit institutions. But his plan for economic and monetary union called for the introduction of deutschmarks in the GDR only at the end of 1992, and even this was considered too ambitious at first.

In the ensuing debate, some of the East German fears about the coming of capitalism came to the fore. Well-nurtured communist propaganda images of the Western capitalist "jungle society" or "elbow society," where presumably the stronger elbow out their competitors, came to the surface and were linked to the anticipated high levels of unemployment. And yet, about 2,000 East German refugees a day were still entering that capitalist jungle—one reason Kohl and Modrow agreed to advance the election date—although the economic system that greeted them must have seemed like something out of Charlie Chaplin's *Modern Times*.[24] West Germans, by the same token, worried about the likelihood of higher

24. *The Economist*, Feb. 16, 1990, p. 47. There were indeed complaints by early arrivals about the relentless pace of West German assembly lines.

interest rates and inflation caused by major West German investment in the GDR, both public and private, and by West German refinancing of East German social security. Particular attention was also lavished on a possible currency union and on exchange rates between deutschmarks and East marks, especially as they might apply to some 160–170 billion East marks held by East Germans in savings accounts. A currency union, moreover, implies control by a central bank (i.e., the Bundesbank).[25] Another major focus of debate concerned the low productivity of the overstaffed and underworked industrial economy of the GDR. Still another problem involved the pressing need to clarify the ubiquitous claims by an estimated 500,000 former East German refugees for property taken away by the communist state. None of these questions was resolved before the elections, thus giving rise to bitter recriminations afterward over the precise nature of election promises made and perhaps not kept.[26]

Opportunities Betwixt and Between

As the day of the election drew near, the great wave of East German consumer purchases in the West—also by West German visitors looking for bargains in the East—reached a new fever pitch. Perhaps anticipating supply shortages or what a currency reform might do to their accumulated savings, East Germans spent their money as if there were no tomorrow—after all, there had been little around to spend it on before. Coverage by West German news also began to shift notably toward describing the abuses of the interim period between opening the borders and real economic union: there were many stories about people paying subsidized apartment rents and living on subsidized food in East Germany while working at West German wages just across the border.[27] The system of GDR government subsidies indeed opens Western eyes to a

25. The West German Bundesbank had its doubts about taking over money management in the GDR even as soon as the end of 1990, because the huge state subsidies and lack of a private banking system and capital market would have to be resolved first.

26. No other subject, perhaps, raised such uncertainties as the question of whether Chancellor Kohl had or had not promised the East Germans that each of their East marks would be honored with one deutschmark in exchange. See below.

27. See The Economist, Feb. 24, 1990, pp. 49–50. The GDR government unwittingly increased the uncertainty when it announced the end of the annual subsidy on food and then reinstated it until after the elections. At the border and in Berlin, East Germans often found unregistered West German jobs at substandard wages (say, $5 per hour) which they could increase dramatically at street exchange rates.

major aspect of communist thinking. The GDR drastically lowered the real cost of housing, food staples, postage, and a host of other goods and services (e.g., medicine) to the consumer while paying them wages pegged at such a low level that wives and adolescents out of school had little choice but to work full-time. The extremely low rents made it impossible for landlords of older housing to repair or renovate—even if they were somehow able to obtain the extremely scarce materials.[28]

As in the Soviet Union, the price of bread was subsidized so much that farmers used it to feed the chickens and other livestock. Curiously, the GDR also subsidized cake and cut flowers, perhaps in order to provide any necessary bourgeois gloss that beer and other vulgar spirits, likewise subsidized, had not already furnished to a drab, gray proletarian existence. Tickets for cultural events such as theater and opera, as well as more plebeian recreational pursuits, were likewise subsidized to round out an evening in the GDR. The communist government also subsidized postage stamps and public transportation. With annual subsidies of 33 billion East marks for food staples, including 15 billion for meat alone and 50 billion for postage, transport, and other services, the GDR had also created captive markets for its meat production and for beer, bread, and other staples; yet, people still had to stand in line all the time, and there was never enough of everything in the stores. As to the transformation into a market economy, moreover, the subsidy system left a vexing legacy: rents, bread, and services naturally had to rise to a market level at some point, and the transition was bound to hurt those who could least afford the increased cost. East German pensioners and large families, in particular, would find market capitalism harder to bear than the preceding regime, even though their benefits would become much larger.

Some of the stories about fraud or abuse at the border were so extreme as to cry out for a way to establish just how representative such cases may have been. For German newspapers often repeat urban legends that fulfill popular expectations, such as the horror stories regarding "welfare fraud by Turkish guest workers." There were rumors of East German refugee families that collected 250 marks in welcome money, checked into one of the refugee shelters, and then disappeared, presumably returning to the GDR with the money. Others told of children being brought in twice for the welcome money, once by Dad and once by Mom. One urban legend told of a West German man's second wife or mistress

28. East German urban housing, especially in the older sections of towns and cities, was in an unbelievably desolate condition and was hardly habitable in 1989/90. Instead, communist housing plans built new satellite cities of prefabricated *Plattenbau*, Russian-style tenements.

in East Germany who had always been kept away from the first wife in West Germany by the Iron Curtain, while he evidently was able to cross over periodically. The opening of the borders pulled away the veil of his deception.[29] While there were many stories of fraud perpetrated on East German consumers, there were also the stories of the Kreuzberg[30] taverns that accepted the despised ostmark 1:1 or gave free beer to East Berliners. Kreuzberg's "autonomous" residents (anarchists) and representatives of the "alternative scene" took a dim view of German unification, and there was even a Kurfürstendamm demonstration of about a thousand Kreuzbergers. They carried banners attacking Kohl and national unification, some bearing the inscription "Your [East German] freedom is that of the Deutsche Bank." But the East Germans ridiculed their slogans and told them, "Why don't you go to the GDR yourselves if you like it so well."[31]

29. Another story is about an East German fellow on the make: "I'm from over there," he tells a casual female acquaintance. "Can I sleep at your place tonight?" See *Der Stern*, May 7, 1990, pp. 262–266.

30. Kreuzberg is a district of West Berlin once typical of working-class tenements and more recently inhabited by Turkish families and the counterculture.

31. One of the more amusing vignettes of the imminent West German "takeover" of the East German economy was its description as a "leveraged buyout" in the London *Economist*. The author declared that the initial cost to the corporate raider, the Bonn government, would "probably exceed the current record" of $25 billion (the R. J. Reynolds buyout) when one added the cost of merging currencies, pensioners and unemployment benefits, and cleaning up the East German environment. But "Helmut, the stripper" might realize a lot more by selling off most government buildings, persuading the Getty Foundation to acquire the Pergamon antiquities museum for its Malibu museum, and offering the Brandenburg Gate and part of Unter den Linden to the "great symbols of foreign culture" collection of Mitsubishi trust, along with Rockefeller Center. Another $7.5 billion could be realized from the sale of the fifteen giant *Kombinate*, each worth at least half a billion dollars, including those making Meissen porcelain and the two-stroke Trabant car (which might have a bright future in oil-poor times and areas). Finally, the author proposed to sell off the old Junker estates—no doubt for junker bonds—and to sell government-owned housing to the occupants in return for the money they had been hiding under the bed. *The Economist*, March 2, 1990, p. 16.

A Berkeley law professor, Franklin E. Zimring, soon topped this vision by relating his dream that Michael Milken, the junk bond king, had fled to the GDR and arranged for his safety there by offering the following advice. The GDR is to announce a leveraged buyout of the Federal Republic by offering each West German 250,000 marks, in bonds to be issued by the new government, which would threaten to hold a West German referendum on this plan with the slogan "Each family a millionaire." In the ensuing takeover battle, Bonn in desperation offers each East German 300,000 marks at 8% interest over fifteen years in exchange for a "standstill" provision and forswearing of future raids until the year 2020, thus giving East Germany the highest per capita income in Europe. Zimring's dream ends with swarms of West German poor relations flooding into the GDR, which develops a case of cold feet about German unification. There is even a suggestion to build a new Berlin Wall, but this time to keep out the West Germans. "Greenmail Goes Transnational," *Los Angeles Times*, Jul. 28, 1990.

The Aftermath of the Deutschmark Elections

"The winner [of the March election] is the D-mark," crowed the cover of the popular weekly magazine *Der Stern*, which credited Chancellor Kohl and his promise of speedy economic and currency union for the victory of the CDU Alliance. The magazine criticized Kohl and his advisers for still not knowing the real cost of that union and then made some quick calculations of its own. If each of the 16.8 million East Germans could exchange 2,000 East marks at the rate of 1:1,[32] that alone would cost Bonn more than 32 billion marks, not to mention the question of how to handle the remainder of the East German savings—another 120 billion or more East marks. Because of the low productivity of East German services and manufacturing, *Der Stern* quoted a Düsseldorf consulting firm, Axel Boje, to the effect that it would take 900 billion marks (about $500 billion) over the "medium term" to bring East Germany up to the West German standard. A former SPD Bundestag deputy and member of the Budget Committee, Heinz Suhr, estimated that the total cost of unification to the state would be at least 1.034 trillion marks by the year 2000—and 2.3 trillion in order to bring East Germany up to the West German level—including 200 billion marks each for urban renewal, environmental cleanup, and transport and up to 100 billion marks each for unemployment, health and old-age insurance, energy supplies, and agriculture. On the credit side, Suhr listed 310 billion marks in additional revenue and the German Unity Fund of 95 billion marks. Small wonder that the *Stern* article also raised dire warning about the inflationary impact and likely high interest rates resulting from such massive expenditures, not to mention the likelihood of substantial tax raises rather than the promised cuts.[33] And these horrendous costs did not even account for needed private investment in East German business—maybe 2.8 trillion marks—or for possible reparation payments to the victors or other

32. Some East Germans with large savings were also said to have spread their money around among several local banks, 2,000 East marks at a time, in a manner reminiscent of the American savings and loan shenanigans, where some wealthy customers milked the federal loan insurance system by having savings insured up to the $100,000 limit several times, using several accounts. The GDR government tried to meet this challenge by careful checking and by backdating the exchange to the status of January 1, 1990.

33. Chancellor Kohl had earlier promised to cut business taxes by 25 billion marks. Higher interest rates were likely to result from the enormous demand for credit on the part of new and surviving enterprises in the GDR, trying to meet their first payrolls after the date of the currency union. See "Die Kohl(e) Wahl," *Der Stern* 43, no. 13, March 22–28, 1990, pp. 20–41. Also see Suhr, *Was kostet uns die ehemalige DDR?* pp. 38–94, esp. p. 92. Suhr's shocking estimates were surprisingly close to the IMF assessment of the following December, which projected that a net investment of 1.5–1.9 trillion marks would

antagonists in World War II, such as Poland[34] and the Soviet Union, not to mention a hundred other participants in the war. Also to be considered are the foreign debt and trade obligations of the GDR toward Eastern countries, including 7 billion deutschmarks for nondelivery of nuclear plants to the Soviet Union.

"No serious government . . . could have put a price tag on the cost of unification," the former SPD Mayor of Hamburg, Klaus von Dohnanyi, wrote in his serialized book *The German Wager*, "But it is possible to determine the probable financial demands of the GDR region . . . more precisely than the finance minister and the chancellor have done so far."[35] With a sidelong glance at the profits to accrue to West German businesses and the gains for consumers and tax collection expected from East German demand in the first years, Dohnanyi began by separating the current social expenditures—unemployment and social security—from the cost of investments in infrastructure and industrial modernization (leaving the last-mentioned largely to self-financing from profits). For the communication and transport network, he estimated the cost at about 300 billion marks; for housing, urban renewal, and historic preservation another 300 billion marks; and for public health and environmental protection, 400 billion marks—all this to help the former GDR to approximate West German levels over a span of fifteen years. The West German levels, he did not forget to point out, also have their low spots of neglect and environmental problems. The SPD politician was well aware of estimates that were half the size of his own, but he felt that, with the addition of public education, science, culture, and recreation, a total public investment well over 1 trillion marks was a fair guess. Add the private investment needed to renew about three-fourths of the capital stock of East German industry by the year 2000: about 1.5 trillion marks. Thus, the estimated capital needs for modernizing the GDR come to 2–2.5 trillion marks,[36] corresponding to the entire 1989 GNP of the

---

be needed by the year 2001 to bring East German per capita output up to West German 1990 levels, and that just to reach 80% of the West German level of 1990 would require 1–1.3 trillion marks. Donogh McDonald and Günther Thumann, "Investment Needs in East Germany," in *German Unification: Economic Issues*, pp. 71–77.

34. Kohl himself brought up the possible Polish demands of 537 billion marks for reparations and, in March 1990, insisted that a Polish quitclaim be connected with his government's agreement to the validity of the Oder-Neisse border. See also *Der Spiegel* 44, no. 11, March 12, 1990, pp. 174–182, which details the history of German reparations paid and demanded since 1919 and after 1945.

35. *Das deutsche Wagnis* (Munich: Drömersche Verlagsanstalt, 1990), serialized in *Der Spiegel* 44, nos. 39–42 (1990). The quoted passage appears in no. 42, Oct. 15, 1990, p. 239.

36. Arthur Janke of the Rheinisch-Westphalian Institute for Economic Research has

Federal Republic, or five to six times its own annual investment rate. So Dohnanyi did not expect the GDR region to catch up with the West until twenty or thirty years hence, not in a decade.[37] How much money would have to come from West Germany depended on many unpredictable factors of the restructuring process, such as the development of wages and salaries, unemployment, and the liquidity of VEBs in the hands of the Trust Agency. But certainly the German Unity Fund would be quite inadequate to the task which, according to a British consulting firm, requires 140–160 billion marks a year for public investments alone.[38] Dohnanyi concludes that the effort demanded of a united Germany is clearly "the greatest economic effort undertaken by [this country] since 1945" and a risky venture involving massive additional public indebtedness. The gigantic volume of investment might be compared, in a manner of speaking, to war reparations Germany is paying to itself, Dohnanyi believes, and the great effort may not be worth it.[39] (See Table 6.1.)

The environmental degradation of parts of the GDR bore an awesome price tag, both in human health and in what it would cost to clean up the results of decades of communist industrial and agricultural abuse. Visible damage to East German forests ranges from one-fourth to one-half the wooded area and is far worse than in West Germany, particularly in Saxony-Anhalt and Mecklenburg-Vorpommern. A comparison of mortality rates between the Federal Republic and the GDR shows East German men and women dying in numbers more than 20% higher than West Germans. The parade of regional environmental horrors ranged from open-pit uranium mining carried on by the Soviets in the south—which left many square miles of irradiated soil behind and, it is now believed, will require billions of marks to clean up—to the sulfur dioxide emissions of soft coal processing in the southeast, worst of all in Bitterfeld, where such emissions reduce adult life expectancy by nine years and stunt the growth of children, burden their blood capacity, and make them less responsive to common immunizations and medicines. Bitterfeld's chil-

---

estimated that the capital stock needed by GDR industry to reach West German levels would be about 2 trillion marks.

37. CDU and FDP politicians aside, more optimistic predictions can be found—for example, from Roland Berger, whose business consulting firm is involved in the restructuring of many industrial *Kombinate*. He expected the economic disparities to even out by the year 2000, though only after a wave of bankruptcies and unemployment at the 3.2 million level. See *Süddeutsche Zeitung*, Sept. 28, 1990.

38. Dohnanyi refers to estimates made by David C. Roche of Morgan, Stanley consultants in London. The annual estimate assumes a total infrastructural-investment requirement of 800–1,100 billion marks. See *Der Spiegel* 44, no. 42, Oct. 15, 1990, pp. 241, 244.

39. Dohnanyi fears a loss of international competitiveness and questions the advantage of gaining a larger national market in a world of Western integration. Ibid., p. 247.

Table 6.1. Estimated Public Costs of Integrating the GDR into the FRG, 1990–2000 (in Billions of Deutschmarks)

	Various Estimates	Minimum Level (Suhr)	West German Level (Suhr)	Dohnanyi (15 Years)
Debits				
Social union[a]	50[b]	126.5	336.5	...
Environmental cleanup	100	200.0	410.0	400
Energy supply and management	100	85.0	180.0	...
Transport and communications[c]	250	230.0	345.0	300
Urban renewal	100	200.0	800.0	300
Agricultural restructuring	30	70.0	110.0	...
Industrial restructuring	40	40.0	40.0	...
Foreign obligations[d]	41–57			...
Old state obligations[e]	161–217	31.0	31.0	...
TOTAL	872–944	982.5	2,252.5	1,000–1,500
Credits				
Additional tax revenues	300	310	310	
German Unity Fund (5 years)	95	95	95	
Savings on Berlin and border zone subsidies, etc.	200–300	...	...	...
Gasoline tax	200–250	...	...	...
Savings on business tax cut	250–300	...	...	...
VAT increase by 2–4%	250–450	...	...	...
TOTAL	1,295–1,695			

SOURCES: Calculated from Heinz Suhr, *Was kostet uns die ehemalige DDR?* (Frankfurt: Eichborn, 1990); *Der Spiegel* 44, nos. 39–42 (1990); and other estimates cited in the present chapter.

[a] Pensions, medical and unemployment insurance, retraining, education.

[b] The East German ministerial planner Werner Obst suggested that the pension system alone would require 100 billion deutschmarks to upgrade.

[c] Roads, bridges, railroads, the mails, telegraph and telephone, data transmission.

[d] Trade obligations and the cost of removing Soviet troops.

[e] Exchange funds for GDR banks; state insurance debt.

dren are also liable to experience neurological disorders and retardation of psychomotor functions. The chemical industry, especially near Halle, has poured toxic wastes and carcinogenic dust into the atmosphere and water courses, not to mention the groundwater, producing three to four times the skin cancer rate of the rest of the GDR and twenty times the incidence of asthma. Again, it is particularly among the children living near chemical plants (especially plastics) that respiratory disease and eczema have been endemic and other syndromes of dysfunction and discomfort have been found. Adults have suffered leukemia and other cancerous afflictions at several times the GDR rate, particularly in all the metropolitan areas: Gera, Halle, Erfurt, Leipzig, Chemnitz, Dresden, and East Berlin. The drinking water of nearly half the East German population (7.6 million) was not safe. Sulfur dioxide emissions for the GDR were 313 kilograms per annum per resident, three times the average West European level. Pollution with heavy metals, a major carcinogen, was typical of many East German industrial plants. Poisoning by cadmium, lead, chromium, and dioxin (especially in copper processing) has been common among workers.

In the past, the East German government kept all reports of these unhealthy conditions a state secret, fearing that their disclosure might touch off a massive flight from industrial areas.[40] There is not much that can be done to reverse the damaged health and shortened lives of many East Germans. Bonn's Minister for the Environment, Klaus Töpfer, took a trip to see the environmental degradation for himself. A billion marks were made available for an initial seventeen projects of environmental control and amelioration—notably an official measurement of various kinds of pollution—but Töpfer's ministry has received little cooperation from GDR firms. Poor recordkeeping and sloppy East German managers—also, perhaps, embarrassed and hence uncooperative old bosses—at first hampered and delayed any action. There was also the recognition, in some cases, that it would be far better simply to close down the worst polluters and their obsolete equipment and to build something new. Even

40. The first "environmental refugees" from Bitterfeld had appeared in the West by April 1990. There is a parallel here to Soviet policies regarding nuclear plant accidents. See the report on the 1989 cover-up of an environmental assessment by members of the GDR Academy of Sciences in *Sachsenspiegel*, Nov. 23, 1990, p. 16. See also *Der Spiegel* 44, no. 2, Jan. 8, 1990, and no. 12, March 19, 1990, pp. 134–135, as well as no. 15, Apr. 9, 1990, pp. 31–32. There was also considerable controversy about GDR nuclear plants built on the Chernobyl model (i.e., without a protective shell in case of meltdowns). After a good deal of criticism, the Bonn government decided to shut down the last of the four reactors at Greifswald. Also see Suhr, *Was kostet uns die ehemalige DDR?* pp. 53–66, on the environmental problems, including the uranium mines of the Soviet German Wismut Co., which since 1948 has supplied material for Soviet atom bombs.

a GDR government commission looking over the Bitterfeld area thought so, and recommended an end to fifteen industrial plants, whose products ranged from cellulose to sulphur yellow dyes. The cost of actually cleaning up the polluted soil and water in this area was estimated to be in the neighborhood of 50 billion marks, and it was not surprising that the successors to the firm of IG Farben, which once ran the Leuna, Buna, and Mansfeld enterprises in the area—among other things, making synthetic gasoline for the war effort—have been reluctant to reclaim this property and the poisons slumbering in its soil.

The Currency Reform

Since currency reform was mostly a rather temporary solution to the long-range problems of the GDR, an unusually controversial role in the wrangling over East German economic reform fell to the details of a currency union to be achieved "some time during 1990" or "as soon as possible." Originally, at his February meeting with Modrow, Kohl had intended his proposal of a currency union to stem the flow of East German refugees who were still coming to the West at the rate of from 2,000 to 3,000 a day. To the hopeful and apprehensive East Germans, evidently nothing sounded quite so promising in the siren song of the CDU Alliance and in Chancellor Kohl's election rhetoric as the introduction of the coveted deutschmark to their country. Once the elections had given the Alliance a mandate, however, there was a strong suspicion among the inexperienced GDR electorate that "those slick West German politicians" had promised a lot more than they were willing to deliver. The East mark–deutschmark exchange rate, in particular, became the focus of acrimonious recriminations. Many East German voters, and especially the communist PDS politicians—quick to seize upon embarrassing moments for their democratic rivals—insisted that Kohl and other West German politicians had promised to exchange all East mark holdings at an exchange rate of 1:1 into deutschmarks. Foreign observers were quick to point out the folly of such an exchange with a currency that at the time, on the free market, traded at a rate of 1 mark to 6 or 7 East marks. They added up the vast expense of such an undertaking in hundreds of billions of marks, inflation, and deterioration of West German wages and savings.[41] No less an authority than the head of the

41. See, for example, *The Economist*, March 3, 1990, pp. 13–14. The author assumed that "unity bonds" might be issued to tie up East German savings for several years and pointed out that an additional 80 billion marks paid by the Bundesbank for the currency

Bundesbank weighed in and pronounced the 1:1 ratio unrealistic, proposing instead 1:2. Some West German cabinet members agreed and insisted that a rate of 1:2 "would not hurt East German pensions or wages." Even European voices, such as French Gaullists (RPR), chided Bonn for considering a more generous exchange rate because it would be paid in the end by the other members of the European Community as well.

Most West German economists, including the bankers of the Bundesbank, had advised against a speedy currency union in the first place and were critical of Kohl's coalition and others for suggesting it—however, the West German trade unions (DGB), in a Resolution on German Unity (March 7), advocated going ahead with it after proposing a unification fund of their own. Most economists believed that the basis for the future well-being of the GDR was to be found in higher economic productivity by its enterprises. To this end some suggested 1) to let the East mark float to find an appropriate level, 2) to accept the Bundesbank proposal of 2:1, provided the bank receive real control over the level of expenditures East and West, or 3) to follow the Austrian example and let the GDR struggle for convertibility with appropriate wage, monetary, and fiscal policies. This approach would achieve its goal only very gradually and might require high interest rates to reward investors—and also would involve a continued mass exodus to the west. A fourth proposal (by R. Pohl of the Berlin Institute for Empirical Economic Research) called for issuance by the Bundesbank of a new East mark currency, of limited convertibility, to protect the GDR economy from Western competition until it was ready for the real currency union, presumably years down the road. A fifth proposal would have postponed the German currency union until the EC currency union was achieved, although this would have prevented the Bundesbank from tight control over the possible "monetary solution of deficits" (i.e., printing more money). The GDR government and electorate obviously would not have found any of these alternatives acceptable, nor would they have kept the continuing exodus from ruining the economy.[42] The deutschmark cat was out of the bag, and it made more sense to look into the pros and cons of the inevitable.

---

union would amount to 19% of the M_1 money supply, or 6.5% of M_3. See also *The Economist* for March 10, 1990, pp. 13–14.

42. The new GDR government was most unlikely to settle for any postponement or a reduced rate of exchange. A double currency might prolong and double the misery of taking the plunge. A "more realistic" exchange rate of 1:3 or 1:2 would have been extremely depressing and would no doubt have encouraged further migration from East to West. As for the EC currency union, perhaps the German union might even facilitate that of Western Europe. See *Bundestag Report* 2/90, Apr. 12, 1990, pp. 1–2, and *Das Parlament*, Apr. 13–20, 1990, pp. 1–7, for the partisan debates on the currency reform.

The advantages of a speedy currency union at 1:1 were many. Its real incentives would facilitate economic renewal and start-up activities in the GDR. It would end the two-currency system with its inequalities and abuses and, perhaps, help keep the East Germans at home. To be sure, there would be glaring wage differentials, but those would be even bigger with the other solutions. After their shopping forays into the West, most East Germans knew all too well the score on East and West German wage and price differentials. A speedy union would also facilitate capital transfers (investments), lower the risks to outside investors, and facilitate the modernization of East German firms. There would be no more *Materialpause*, or waiting for supplies, because they would be readily available in the West. All of this would improve productivity, which should also increase with the intensification of the division of labor and the breakup of the *Kombinate*, with technology transfers, profit and merit increases, and with the ready availability of Western patents and licenses.[43]

Given the backward state of the East German economy, economists expected the multiplier effect of investment/new jobs to be nearly five times as great as in the Federal Republic: 1 million marks = 23 new jobs (vs. only 5 in the FRG). The unemployment caused by structural changes in the GDR would peak quickly and last only a few years, while about 650,000 new independent entrepreneurs—the new Marshall Plan (ERP) funds of 6 billion marks were finding many interested takers—would generate an estimated 2.6 million new jobs. The economists had little fear of inflation in East Germany because, unlike in other Eastern countries, GDR prices would find natural limits in the price levels of West Germany.[44] They also thought the idea of protecting the GDR with

43. See G. Nötzold in *Handelsblatt*, March 23, 1990, who expected a 30% productivity increase within the first year. The Bonn Ministry of the Economy also predicted two-digit economic growth for the GDR (March 30–31, 1990) in the same time frame and reminded its readers of the dramatic West German growth that occurred in the first six months after the 1948 currency reform. See also the discussion of the implications of a currency union by Mayer and Thumann, "German Democratic Republic," pp. 58–59, and in the *EC Bulletin*, supp. 4/90, pp. 33–34.

44. The exchange of East German savings at a rate of 1:1, on the other hand, would outrun the potential increase in productivity so drastically that it might have an inflationary impact. The wage costs in the GDR, according to the Berlin German Institute for Economic Research (DIW), were likely to remain a mere 42.5% of the West German level—even after the addition of the employers' share of their social security and cost-of-living increases in order to make up for an end to subsidies and for price increases. At a rate of 2:1, wage costs would have been even lower: 21.3%. For the implications of the exchange rate, see Garry J. Schinasi, Leslie Lipschitz, and Donogh McDonald, "Monetary and Financial

customs barriers to be counterproductive, believing in the benefits of a free circulation of goods, services, capital, and even foreign workers.

On the other hand, it might be a good idea to keep down possible East German buying sprees after the currency union of July 1, perhaps by freezing portions of the savings accounts or permitting their use only for the purchase of state-owned property. The very low nominal wages, East marks or deutschmarks, would severely restrict East German appetites. Regarding the debts of VEBs to the GDR State Bank—about 260 billion East marks—at least some economists close to the DGB agreed that they should be discounted 5:1 or forgiven altogether so as not to make it impossible to modernize outdated production methods.[45] In view of the antiquated infrastructure—transport and communications, machinery, energy industry—and the environmental problems that so many feared, the reforms needed to be broadened and accelerated, flanked with the abolition of central planning and the availability of private bank credit, and aided by the freeing of private enterprise. Early retirement and unemployment insurance (abolished in 1978), along with pension re- form, would have to cushion the wave of temporary mass unemployment expected in the immediate future. The specter of unemployment, indeed, was likely to be moderated by the "voluntary" dropping out of much of the female labor force—83% of East German adult women were gain- fully employed—the continued migration to West Germany, and by early retirement programs.[46]

Issues in German Unification," in Leslie Lipschitz and Donogh McDonald, eds., *German Unification: Economic Issues*, pp. 147–149.

45. Hartmut Küchle and Gernot Müller, "Währungsunion zwischen BRD und DDR," *WSI Mitteilungen* 43, no. 5 (May 1990), 256–265. See also E. Lüdenmann, "Zur öko- nomischen Situation der DDR am Beginn der Erneuerung," *IPW Berichte* 2 (1990), arguing in favor of speeding up rather than slowing down the economic reform over several years by means of an exchange mechanism.

46. On female unemployment, see Gerd Grözinger, *Teures Deutschland: Was kostet uns die DDR?* (Berlin: Rotbuch, 1990), pp. 22–29. Further, Küchle and Müller, "Wäh- rungsunion," pp. 263–265. The economists also offered a rough estimate of both the cost of economic union and ways to finance it. On the debit side, they suggested 150 billion marks for railroads and roads, and 100 billion each for telecommunications, energy supplies and the environment, as well as funds for other infrastructural development over fifteen years. The GDR could not be expected to absorb more than 30–35 billion marks a year for the infrastructure. Bonn would save on the united foreign currency fund, on East German refugees, and on subsidies for West Berlin and the depressed zonal border areas, easily amounting to 20 billion marks a year and substantially more while the economic growth rate was so high. Add a raise in the gasoline tax of 20 pfennigs a liter (17 billion marks) and drop the business tax cut (25 billion marks), they said, and the books would be balanced.

A Political Decision

Faced with public pressure and well-argued advice, and after some public vacillation and disclaimers of earlier promises, Chancellor Kohl finally agreed that 1:1 should indeed be the basic exchange rate for wages and for savings accounts up to a certain level (4,000 East marks), after which a ratio of 2:1 might apply (the same ratio for business savings). But there was to be no future wage adjustment for price increases or for the pensions that were to be raised along with the wages. This solution seemed to please even the opposition SPD, which had complained that the West German parliament had been excluded from the negotiations. Together with the new East German government of Lothar de Maizière (CDU), the SPD called for a plebiscite on the state treaty regarding the currency union. Bundesbank President Karl Otto Pöhl, on the other hand, called the 1:1 ratio "a political decision" and the German stock market reacted with notable jitters.[47] The Green party, however, still spoke of "cheating the people of the GDR," while West German Finance Minister Theo Waigel (CSU) warned that "the limit of fiscal tolerance" had been reached.

Unlike the secrecy surrounding the preparation of the West German currency reform of 1948,[48] the introduction of the deutschmark to the GDR was debated furiously under the full glare of publicity. Massive demonstrations erupted again in East Germany—100,000 strong in East Berlin, 70,000 in Dresden—carrying banners against Kohl and his alleged electoral fraud of offering an exchange rate of less than 1:1. He was assailed not only by the opposition candidate for chancellor, Lafontaine (SPD), but by Count Lambsdorff (FDP) of his coalition partners and by the head of the East German CDU, de Maizière. Even the East German state trade unions (FDGB) showed unaccustomed initiative and threatened to go on strike.

The disagreement between Bundesbank President Pöhl and the East Germans was based, among other things, on an assessment of the balance sheet of the GDR State Bank which showed the clash of communist

47. The DIHT also called the decision "risky." At the bankers' conference in Cologne, Pöhl suggested raising taxes in order to balance the added expense. *Frankfurter Allgemeine Zeitung*, April 26, 1990. See also Schinasi et al., "Monetary and Financial Issues," pp. 144–147, 149–157.

48. The surprise introduction of a dollar-based deutschmark in mid-1948 was prepared by eight experts locked up under military guard for six weeks. It phased out the old reichsmark, gave individuals and firms barely enough to make it through the next payday, and froze the rest of West German savings. It was the first significant step toward the West German "economic miracle" of the fifties.

public finance with Western methods. According to its own records, the bank had credits of 200 billion East marks with firms, all of it noncollectible and at low interest because of the communist method of using such "credits" to centrally steer production.[49] A balance of 34 billion East marks in foreign debt to noncommunist countries (payable with 35–49 billion marks) was simply passed on to a reluctant Bundesbank by the East German negotiators drawing up the formal state treaty on the currency and economic union. Exchanging all of the East German private bank accounts 1:1, as Pöhl explained, added at least 130 billion marks to the national debt and cost 10 billion marks annually in interest. Anxious to contain this fiscal hemorrhage, the Central Bank Council initially proposed limiting the 1:1 rate to the first 2,000 East marks and to apply a lesser rate thereafter. Worse, they suggested that wages and pensions be at the 2:1 rate, which would have resulted in lowering the modest East German industrial wage levels (1,300 East marks) to an average of 650 marks a month—one-fourth of comparable West German wages—and reducing many pensioners (average industrial pension, 450 East marks) to welfare cases.[50]

It was symptomatic that the East German understanding of the problems of the exchange rate followed dirigistic lines—a decision to be made by the central planners—and that it considered neither the viability of their own workplaces under increased wage obligations nor the likely future upward development of wages, not to mention the likelihood of unemployment. Viable enterprises would soon have to pay better wages, and in some cases the workers would do well to settle for less now in order to enable their firm to survive the transition. On the other hand, a comparison of GDR and FRG consumer prices, measured in work hours as of early April 1990 (Table 6.2), dramatizes the marginality of an average wage of 650 marks a month and its vulnerability to the removal of subsidies for food staples and rents. Wages also varied by a factor of one to ten from the bottom to the top salaries. Food staples would probably rise to the West German level, and rents would go from the

49. There was a consensus between East and West German negotiators that the accounts of East German firms with the State Bank could not be exchanged at a rate better than 2:1; it was feared, however, that the VEBs might not be able to meet their first deutschmark payrolls. See *Die Zeit*, no. 15, Apr. 6, 1990, pp. 1, 4, 27–28.

50. See "DDR-BRD Perspektiven," *WSI Mitteilungen*, no. 5 (Wirtschafts- und Sozialwissenschaftliches Institut, 1990). A draft by the West German economics and finance ministers indeed proposed a 2:1 ratio, which they expected would not burden East German firms to the point of bankruptcy even though they also would have obliged the firms to pay unemployment, health, and retirement insurance, thus raising the average wage to about 800 marks. A rival plan from Labor Minister Norbert Blüm featured an average wage of 1,050 marks on the basis of 1:1.

Table 6.2. Comparing GDR and FRG Purchasing Power, April 1, 1990 (in Hours of Work by an Average Industrial Worker)

Item	GDR	FRG
Color television	739 hrs.	84 hrs.
Washing machine	347 hrs.	53 hrs. 13 min.
Refrigerator	215 hrs.	30 hrs.
Rent (monthly)	11 hrs. 19 min.	22 hrs. 18 min.
Coffee (1 kg.)	10 hrs. 32 min.	1 hr.
Brandy (.750 l.)	2 hrs. 11 min.	48 min.
Cheese (1 kg.)	1 hr. 25 min.	39 min.
Beef (1 kg.)	52 min.	32 min.
Butter (1 kg.)	5 hrs. 48 min.	28 min.
Bread (1 kg.)	5 min.	10 min.
Potatoes (2.5 kg.)	4 min.	8 min.
Sugar (1 kg.)	14 min.	6 min.
Pork cutlet (1 kg.)	1 hr. 12 min.	35 min.
Eggs (1 doz.)	36 min.	12 min.
Beer (1 l.)	14 min.	6 min.
Postage (domestic letter)	2 min.	3 min.

SOURCE: Statistical offices of the GDR and the FRG, spring 1990.

NOTE: The hourly industrial wage for the GDR was 6.63 East marks; for the FRG, 18.43 deutschmarks.

present one-twentieth or less of one's salary to more than half[51] (see Table 6.3).

There were many critical voices, in particular from the East German democratic opposition and the West German DGB and SPD, complaining that the "social union" of the currency treaty was insufficiently provided for. The union was likely to amount to a "social-political colonization" of the GDR which was based on one-sided reforms in the GDR and no attempt by the FRG at meeting East Germany even halfway. "Everything in the GDR is to be questioned, but nothing in the FRG." The Bonn "colonizers," the argument went, had already sidelined the Social Charter

51. On GDR salaries, see Henry Krisch, *The GDR: The Search for Identity* (Boulder, Colo.: Westview Press, 1985), p. 99. West German rents (at an average 850 marks) vary greatly between metropolitan and rural or small-town areas. In cities like West Berlin, Hamburg, or Munich they are often comparable to rents in the metropolitan United States. East German rents, on the other hand, have been extremely low, frequently well under 100 ostmarks a month, although housing quality has ranged from very poor to mediocre. The average apartment (70 sq. meters, or 778 sq. feet) cost 63 East marks, which was expected to rise in three stages to 147, 224, and finally 378 deutschmarks beginning January 1991. The bad conditions in the GDR inevitably forced the government to postpone these stages in 1991/92.

Table 6.3. Average Monthly Household Expenditures in GDR (East marks) and FRG (Deutschmarks)

Category	GDR	FRG
Food	524	679
Industrial products	522	852
Clothing, shoes	289	231
Tobacco, coffee, tea, alcohol	189	157
Repairs and services	175	539
Rent and utilities	85	901
Insurance, licensing fees	228	444
Savings, debt service	295	311
TOTAL	2,308	4,115

SOURCE: Statistical offices of the GDR and the FRG, spring 1990.

NOTE: Four-person households.

passed at the Round Table and by the old Volkskammer (People's Chamber), as well as the constitutional draft of the newly elected People's Chamber which, among other things, tried to protect employees with a "right to work" law against arbitrary firings.[52] The critics expected women to be hardest hit by unemployment and, as GDR Minister of Labor Regine Hildebrandt (SPD) feared, not to put up a fight against dismissals.[53] A former member of Democracy Now, the labor minister expressed great concern that a cowed GDR population might not know how to stand up for its rights. Massive retraining programs in existing VEBs ought to ease the way into the future. West German Labor Minister Norbert Blüm (CDU) agreed to cooperate in this and in early retirement programs—for women at age fifty-five and men at sixty. Despite their partisan differences, each was similarly concerned about the fate of East German pensions after the reform.[54]

Tables 6.2 and 6.3 reflect not only the subsidized rents and prices of

52. Gerhard Bäcker and Johannes Steffen, "Sozialunion—Was soll wie vereinigt werden?" *WSI Mitteilungen* 43, no. 5 (May 1990), 265–269.

53. See Hildegard M. Nickel, "Frauen in der DDR," *Das Parlament*, supp., April 13, 1990, and "Erwerbstätigkeit und Einkommen von Frauen in der DDR," *DIW Wochenbericht*, no. 19 (1990). Single mothers especially, according to Labor Minister Hildebrandt, were meek targets of early dismissals. The worst situation could be found in the textile, shoe, electronics, food, and related industries whose products were simply refused by the retail chains. Dr. Hildebrandt, a biochemist, hoped that, after the currency reform, East German deutschmark savings might serve to raise capital for structural reforms. By the end of 1990, in fact, the East Germans were reported still to have, or to have accumulated again, 80 billion deutschmarks in savings.

54. See the interview in *Der Spiegel* 44, no. 20, May 14, 1990, pp. 123–126.

bread and potatoes—which East Germans have consumed a lot more of than the diet-conscious West Germans—but also the inflated prices of such "luxury goods" as refrigerators, coffee, and butter. Not shown, of course, is the difference in quality which has made East Germans so eager to shop for Western products to the exclusion of their own. The end of subsidies would affect pensioners especially and—since the East Germans were expected to take over the West German welfare state's "social net," which ties pensions and unemployment benefits to the wage level—it appeared that not only a 1:1 ratio for both wages and benefits would be required, but a substantial further upgrading as well. Labor Minister Blüm hoped to bring the average East German pensioner from a monthly pension of 450 East marks up to about 700 marks and to set unemployment benefits at about 65% of net wages. But the Bonn negotiators refused the demand for setting a minimal level for East German pensions and dismissed all hopes for later concessions on this subject.[55] The 8.6 million persons gainfully employed in the GDR, at least before the onset of mass unemployment, were expected to balance income and expenditures of the social security system—there are 2.7 million pensioners—almost from the start. But Bonn would have to pay not only start-up costs (about 5 billion marks for pensions), but also the burden of benefits for East German refugees in the West and the dues for students and soldiers not yet paying into the social security fund. The expected mass unemployment insurance (start-up cost, another 5 billion marks) and need for welfare aid—unemployment in the GDR was expected to top 1.4 million plus 1.8 million on "short hours" in 1991— was likely to strain the West German social budget to the limit.[56]

In the meantime, East and West German negotiators were working on the State Treaty establishing the monetary, economic, and social union and were taking cognizance of the various opinions expressed. Chapter II of the treaty flatly applied the 1:1 ratio to "wages, salaries, grants, pensions, rents, leases, and other recurring payments." All other claims and East mark liabilities were to be exchanged 2:1, except for private

55. The West German social security system promises a worker 70% of the net wage as a pension; unemployed persons get 63–68% of their net wages, depending on family status.

56. There were administrative problems with the collection of contributions for social security in East Germany from July through December 1990, and Bonn had to advance funds from the beginning. The West German pension fund, however, was reported to be 28 billion marks in the black, which the labor minister hoped to use for the transition. From January 1991, an increase of 15% of the pension level required an additional 4 billion marks. The relative youth of most East German refugees also helped to maintain the balance between social security income and expenditures.

bank accounts of which a "free amount," depending on the age of the account holder, would be exchanged 1:1, as follows: for GDR residents age fourteen or under (as of July 1, 1990), up to 2,000 East marks; for those between fifteen and fifty-nine, up to 4,000 East marks; and for those older than that, up to 6,000 East marks. Nonresidents with GDR bank accounts dating from January 1, 1990, or later were to receive a rate of only 3:1.[57] This agreement was hammered out in the midst of the West German state elections of May 15 in Lower Saxony and North Rhine Westphalia which resulted in modest, if significant, losses for Kohl's coalition in Bonn.

Under a lot of criticism, the state treaty was initialed on May 18 by representatives of the two governments and was scheduled for consideration first by joint committees of both legislatures and then by the two parliaments. Major challenges were mounted by Oskar Lafontaine, who wanted to show the new SPD leverage in the upper house, the Bundesrat, with a complex maneuver in both houses involving the state treaty. Older SPD leaders and the Bundestag SPD members refused to go along with him, or he might have forced a unification slowdown upon the government at this point. The West German public, in opinion polls, continued to say that they were not prepared to make any financial sacrifices for German reunification (71%)—only 28% were ready to do so by the end of May.[58] But at least there was a two-thirds majority in the GDR (68%) who expressed satisfaction with the very details of the currency union that struck their West German compatriots as too generous by far.[59] It would appear that the majority of East Germans, far from the alleged confusion of inexperience, was quite consistent in its opinion on the course and pace of economic unification. From the March elections

57. *Treaty Between the FRG and the GDR, Establishing a Monetary, Economic and Social Union*, chap. II and ann. I, art. 6. Debts were to be paid at a rate of 2:1, except for salaries and wages applicable on May 1, 1990, and grants, pensions, rents, and leases due after July 1 (art. 7).

58. By October, three-fourths of West German adults assumed that they would have to accept tax increases—despite government statements to the contrary—and 50.2% were reconciled to them (47.2% were not). *Politbarometer*, Nov. 1990, p. 49. For the earlier poll, see *Der Spiegel* 44, no. 17, Apr. 23, 1990, pp. 14–17. Some 60% of West Germans rejected an exchange rate of 1:1; at the same time, GDR citizens were not only for it, but three-fourths of them had assumed all along that this had already been settled. More than two-thirds thought they heard Kohl promising exactly that during the campaign (pp. 100–103).

59. See *Der Spiegel* 44, no. 22, May 28, 1990, pp. 34–44. This *Spiegel* poll saw Kohl at his nadir and Lafontaine ahead, but not for long (Lafontaine dropped a full ten points by the next monthly poll). This was the same poll that found the West Germans preferring nine other issues by huge margins over the unification measures, which were endorsed by only 26–28%.

through polls taken in September and at the all-German elections in December, more or less the same conservative majority opted for the course proposed by Kohl's government.

Reassessment After One Year

The controversy over the rightness or wrongness of the monetary union (and economic and social union) still had not died down a full year after July 1, 1990, when the last East German borders fell and people received the coveted deutschmark. Chancellor Kohl, for one, defended the timing in retrospect and insisted that the changeover had not destabilized the currency, although "naturally we would not do everything the same way today." Although he claimed that the coming of the deutschmark to the GDR had encouraged personal savings, opened new career opportunities, and let the Ossis experience economic freedom, Kohl also admitted that he had underestimated the problems involved in the economic rehabilitation of East Germany and had made mistakes in the disbursement of funds of the new *Länder*. He cited, in particular, the unresolved property questions as a hindrance to economic reconstruction. West German banking and business, at first skeptical, now praised the "bold step" in retrospect. The Federation of German Banks (BDB) proclaimed that its fears of an East German "buying frenzy" and a softening of the currency had not materialized. The Federation of German Industry (BDI) added that West Germans should accept their increased taxes in a spirit of solidarity: after all, East German demand had brought about a West German boom. Another bank association representative (DSGV) claimed that, in view of the massive exodus of refugees, there had been no alternative to "throwing the GDR economy into the cold waters of the world market," sink or swim. The entrepreneurial DIHT, too, now regarded July 1, 1990, as the "right day" and the introduction of the deutschmark as a success, but it criticized the trade unions for their "excessive wage concessions" won in the East which East German enterprises had to absorb at the same time they lost their East European markets.[60] The bankers also suggested that the concentration of effort on small and medium-size enterprises may have impeded more effective

60. The "premature" wage increases gained by many trade-union-organized East German workers were said to have accelerated the bankruptcies of many firms, or at least to have taken away their low-wage attraction for customers and potential buyers, according to the BDI, Count Lambsdorff, and many others. *Tagesspiegel*, June 19 and 28, 1991. Individual banks that went to the East also expressed great satisfaction with their profits.

measures. In their end effect, the billions flowing to the former GDR were a major cause of the West German boom.

The positive assessments were matched in spades by the critics.[61] Kohl's SPD antagonist, Saarland Premier Lafontaine, countered on the radio that "it was a mistake to subject the Eastern economy overnight to competition on the world markets." The hasty union, he felt, had deepened the abyss between the wealthy West and the underdeveloped East. Rising unemployment in the East was the result, and it would take a major effort by everyone to prevent a recession for all of Germany. The currency union had amounted to a "gigantic program for a West German boom." CDU Interior Minister Schäuble, the chief West German negotiator on the unification treaties, wrote in his book[62] about his fears that Lafontaine might get the upper hand and that the union might turn from a national into a social-welfare enterprise. In contrast to his chancellor's innocence about the likely consequences, furthermore, Schäuble said that "Lother de Maizière, Hans Tietmeyer, and I realized clearly that the introduction of the Western currency would overnight put the GDR enterprises out of competition." The last GDR Finance Minister, Walter Romberg (SPD), was made to resign when he spoke out of turn, telling whoever wanted to listen how expensive this route to unification would be. As he pointed out in May 1991, at Humboldt University (East Berlin), the West German leadership simply failed to understand that the GDR's Stalinist economic structures would not yield to standard West German economic policies. As late as the early summer of 1990, he explained, the planners expected a two-year process of separate economic systems on a basis of partnership, not an accelerating "subjection to the laws and mechanisms of the capitalist world," triggered by the currency union.[63] He hoped that the GDR could salvage and bring to the union "that which grew up with us and was worth contributing."

Bundesbank President Pöhl was no less critical in March 1991 about the currency union than he had been in early 1990. Speaking before the Economics and Currency Committee of the European Parliament, he used the German monetary union as "a drastic illustration" of the

61. SPD finance expert Ingrid Matthäus-Maier criticized, in particular, such decisions as denying debt forgiveness to Eastern companies and insufficient promotion of investment, although she thought the timing of the currency union was "right and necessary."

62. *Der Vertrag. Wie ich über die deutsche Einheit verhandelte* (Stuttgart: Deutsche Verlagsanstalt, 1991). See also *Der Spiegel* 45, no. 29, Jul. 15, 1991, pp. 40–45.

63. Romberg was one of the signatories of the treaty on the currency union in mid-May 1990. *Tagesspiegel*, May 21, 1991. He particularly regretted that the disposition of the property questions had been so hasty and without careful preparation, a "victory of mindless capitalist ideology," in his opinion.

mistakes to be avoided with the preparation of the European currency union. The German union was "too hasty, . . . without preparation, and at the wrong exchange rate," and it resulted in "a catastrophe which did not surprise me in the least, in contrast to many politicians." He conceded that the political decision to form a common currency area at that date may have been "unavoidable," but East Germany was then no longer able to compete, and the wrong goods were produced for the wrong markets at the wrong time—a warning to the European Community not to force discipline on countries with weaker economies.[64] Ex-Chancellor Helmut Schmidt, who had originally appointed the distinguished Pöhl, also weighed in with criticisms during an appearance before an audience of the SPD-linked Friedrich Ebert Foundation. He had no quarrel with Kohl's timing nor, in disagreement with Lafontaine, with the commitment to unification regardless of cost—he belongs to the World War II generation—but he did accuse the government of "objectionable naiveté" and "bad mistakes" in expecting the introduction of the deutschmark to bring about an economic miracle like the West German one after the currency reform of 1948; after all, the GDR economy had been protected for years from foreign competition. Schmidt warned West Germans about the drop in East German morale and drew a parallel between the levels of unemployment in the GDR and in the last years of the Weimar Republic.[65]

The Kohl government and the big industrial associations finally reacted to this barrage and to the drastic downturn in the East German economy by defending themselves with vigor, egged on also by people like retiring State Secretary of the Economy Otto Schlecht, a lifelong admirer of Ludwig Erhard and a wry observer of the bumbling politicians in this crisis. Schlecht had said he could easily imagine how Erhard would have attacked this situation, by jawboning the East and West German public

64. Pöhl also criticized the level of the public debt—150 billion deutschmarks—but only after the all-German elections and in an interview for an illustrated magazine. One result of his criticism was the drop in value of the deutschmark on the international market. See *Die Zeit*, no. 13, March 29, 1991, and no. 11, March 17, 1991. He announced his imminent resignation a short time afterward.

65. *Tagesspiegel*, May 17, 1991. See also his eight-point program in "Uns Deutsche kann der Teufel holen," *Die Zeit*, no. 21, May 17, 1991, p. 3. Pöhl had served under Economy Minister Schiller (1970), Chancellor Brandt (1971), and Chancellor Schmidt before becoming a vice-president (1977) and later president (1980) of the Bundesbank. His successor Helmut Schlesinger is "a rigid monetarist" (James Baker) who is likely to second Pöhl's concerns about weakening the mark. He once called the currency union "a birth by dropping (*Sturzgeburt*) which we Germans can't afford to go through again" with the European Community. *Die Zeit*, no. 22, May 24, 1991, p. 20.

tirelessly on the hustings, exuding optimism and spreading the word about his faith in free enterprise and the right economic order.[66] There were some not very successful efforts to launch bipartisan committees—neither the SPD nor the CDU/CSU was united behind this cooperative attempt, not to mention the carping of the FDP—and summit chats between Kohl and the SPD leader, Hans-Jochen Vogel. Finally, the top associations and government representatives launched the committee on *Aufschwung-Ost* (Eastern recovery), which strove to coordinate business and labor actions, investment, and trade initiatives somewhat as Karl Schiller's neocorporatist Concerted Action had done twenty-five years earlier.

Government and business circles also began to trumpet the increasing signs of economic progress in the East: 600,000 new jobs since July 1990, a crash program of telecommunication improvements for 1991, retraining opportunities, exemplary private investments, and the like. Obviously, the jawboning had to address West German business more than anyone—foreign and especially EC investors were also solicited—because it had held back its Eastern commitments.[67] Kohl and his government team took to periodic, well-publicized visits to East German cities and *Länder* to show their concern and listen to the local complaints. He hoped to regain momentum after a string of defeats in Western *Länder* elections and after the ominous turning away of East Germans (in the polls) from his Eastern CDU and FDP allies, the discredited "bloc parties" of the old regime.

A series of CDU party conventions in each Eastern *Land* began in Weimar—still a secure outpost of Christian Democrats—and the last convention was scheduled for December in Saxony, where the CDU held a majority. At Weimar, the chancellor defended himself vigorously,

66. The economic policymakers in Bonn, indeed, had taken Erhard's *ordo* liberalism—an economic philosophy that insists on establishing the right order before market forces are unleashed—as their philosophy but neglected to make the joyful noises about it that his contemporaries associated with the rotund, cigar-smoking architect of the West German economic miracle. See Thomas Mayer, "The Role of Fiscal and Structural Policies in German Unification: Lessons from the Past," in *German Unification: Economic Issues*, pp. 165–171.

67. See, for example, *Tagesspiegel*, June 5, 1991, for a report on the activities of *Aufschwung-Ost*. The Danish newspaper *Jyllands-Posten*, June 3, 1991, put it well when it blamed "Kohl's return to his pre-1990 habit of merely reacting to crises and preferring empty phrases to concrete proposals and clear policy lines" after his election victory of December 2, 1990. Perhaps it should have added the paralyzing and divisive impact of the Gulf War on German politics and the character of the leadership of the East German CDU and FDP.

admitting that he had made some mistakes in the unification process, but also pounding the SPD and its failure to support German unification in 1990, or even since.[68] A seven-point Declaration of Weimar Toward Internal Unity was issued, representing the CDU position, although it gingerly tiptoed around the East German demand that West Germans would have to come up with more money for East German recovery. At the heart of the declaration was the call to "bring about equal living standards in all of Germany," which echoes a clause of the Basic Law and once more revealed more political than economic thinking.[69] It appealed to all Germans to overcome their internal division, and to East Germans to adapt themselves to the great changes in their lives. The depths of the economic trough were still some distance in the future. Kohl also called upon the CDU rank and file, which was known to be extremely demoralized, to go out and "sell the achievements of the party," not just to expect the CDU leaders to do so. The deepening crisis of the CDU appeared to be largely of a subjective character, haunted by signals of the possible defection of the coalition partner, the FDP,[70] while the SPD was reaping the rewards, in state elections, of the economic boom generated by the unification policies, right or wrong, of the CDU/CSU.

East German Industry for Sale

It was not easy to account for the economic attractions to buyers of East German industry amidst a crumbling infrastructure, featherbedding and inefficiency, obsolete equipment, and environmental degradation. There was a virtual stampede of West German businesses into joint ventures

68. Kohl, of course, did not neglect the historical setting and, among other symbolic signals, went to Buchenwald and paid homage both to the 56,000 victims of the Nazi dictatorship and to the 13,000 killed there under the Soviet occupation, 1945–1949, and up to 1952. *Tagesspiegel*, June 11, 1991.

69. West Germans seem to forget that their own "economic miracle" of the fifties was never fueled by a desire to catch up to any neighbor's living standards. Economic growth then featured all kinds of gross inequalities. It is the exaggerated expectations of East Germans that make their recovery subjectively so painful.

70. While there have been some heated disagreements between the coalition partners, especially about the abortion law and involving also the restlessness of the Bavarian CSU leadership, a defection seems unlikely at this writing. To quote Count Lambsdorff, the FDP chief, "the party likes to rattle the cage of its coalition commitment only when elections are far off; when they approach we come to understand that a coalition commitment on the federal level is a good idea." *Frankfurter Allgemeine Zeitung*, Jul. 18, 1991, p. 5.

with East German industry, banks, even publishing houses, before the legal and property structures were in place, following the March elections. Was it the expectation of 16.8 million new customers and their pent-up demand, the attraction of a large pool of cheap and relatively skilled labor, or the struggle to secure shares of the new market? The biannual Leipzig Trade Fair opened the doors of opportunity wide when some 9,000 exhibitors from sixty nations—an increase of one-fifth over the preceding year—offered their wares while West German bankers and businessmen crowded East German hotels from the Baltic to the Bavarian border offering their services and making deals. Among the better-known companies involved in joint ventures and sales agreements were the three big automobile manufacturers Volkswagen,[71] Opel, and Daimler-Benz. Lufthansa airlines offered to buy 26% of Interflug, the East German state airline, while Siemens announced agreements with three East German partners.[72] The giant Robotron *Kombinat* found many West German partners for cooperative undertakings. The three biggest West German banks—Deutsche Bank, Dresdner Bank, and Commerzbank—were likewise moving in, as were book and periodical publishers.

Now West German specialists could at last examine each of the East German giant *Kombinate* and assess their stock in machinery, buildings, and supplies to create the basic accounts for the currency reform to come (see Table 6.4). Even at an exchange rate of 1 East mark for 1 deutschmark, and after being turned into joint-stock companies and capitalized perhaps with outside investments, some were unlikely to survive. In most cases, dismantling the oversized *Kombinat* would be desirable because it made little economic sense to continue to combine all the services and manufacture of products and parts that the poorly functioning supply networks of the communist economy of the past had made necessary. Breaking off the suppliers of various parts and services also promised to create opportunities for the large numbers of independent, small and medium-size enterprises favored by Bonn. There were many East Germans eager to seize the chance of being independent.

71. Volkswagen bought into the Ifa Kombinat, the makers of the Trabant, with plans to manufacture 250,000 VW Polos a year. The agreement involved about $2.9 billion and, in the course of modernization, would entail the layoff of half the East German workers by the end of 1990. Opel announced plans to go into full production of the Opel Kadett by 1994.

72. Lufthansa's plans of acquiring a share of East German flying rights also involved access to Berlin which, under the Western occupation, had been limited to allied carriers such as British European Airways (BEA) and Pan Am. Meanwhile, however, BEA has surprised observers with a bid to buy a significant share of Interflug as well, while Pan Am abandoned its position in Berlin.

Table 6.4. The Largest GDR *Kombinate* and Their Products, 1989

	Location	Product	No. Employees (in thousands)
Baumwolle	Karl-Marx-Stadt	textiles	70
Carl Zeiss	Jena	optics	70
Robotron	Dresden	computers, office machinery	69
Mikroelektronik	Erfurt	microelectronics	59
Fortschritt Landmaschinen	Neustadt/S.	agricultural machinery	58
Schiffbau	Rostock	shipbuilding	58
Automatisierungs- anlagenbau	East Berlin	automation equipment	56
Braunkohlenbau Senftenberg	Brieske Ost	soft coal	55
Ifa Kombinat Nutzkraftwagen	Ludwigsfelde	trucks	55
Ifa Kombinat Pkw	Karl-Marx-Stadt	passenger cars	55
Trikotagen	Karl-Marx-Stadt	lingerie	54
Braunkohlenkombinat	Bitterfeld	soft coal	53
Wilhelm Pieck	Eisleben	nonferrous metals	47
Schuhe	Weissenfels	shoes	45
Kraftwerks- anlagenbau	East Berlin	power plants, energy	41
Takraf	Leipzig	machinery	40
Wolle & Seide	Meerana	textiles	39
Nachrichten- elektronik	Leipzig	communications equipment	39

SOURCES: Various German newspaper accounts in 1989/1990.

The first of the *Kombinate* announcing its transformation into a joint-stock company was Electronic Building Supplies, Teltow, with 28,000 employees, which anticipated its capitalist transformation as early as May or June 1989. The foreign trade sections of several *Kombinate* had already made the transition at the time of the March elections, rather to the dismay of their creditors, because their joint-stock offshoots were extremely undercapitalized. West German banks assumed, however, that the GDR would provide the security for their unmet obligations. The result of the West German audit of each *Kombinat* was to determine not only its entry into the market but also its status for and after the currency reform. Previous management had often engaged in deliberate overassessment of assets and in other practices that created an unrealistic picture of a *Kombinat*'s vitality and chances of survival in a free market. A considerable number of production lines were incapable of producing competitive products and would have to be closed down.

The restructuring of East European markets for some East German products—two-thirds of East German trade—also introduced considerable uncertainties among the rest of the manufacturing industry. COMECON trade had not exactly been a free market either, and the former flow of exports was likely to dry up. About 65% of East German trade was with CMEA countries, including the Soviet Union (40%) as compared to 8% intra-German trade, 12% with other Western countries, and 5% with developing countries—which explains the crucial role of the decline of the CMEA. To be sure, these CMEA ties were often more political than economic, and yet this may be precisely the reason for united Germany to continue them if possible.

Transitional Pains

In the past, the East German *Kombinate* had not been permitted to retain their "profits," if any, but had to turn them over to the state, which in turn decided whether to permit them to use *its* funds for repairs and for research and development. This also deprived them of the opportunity to build up reserves with which to meet obligations to creditors or to make the transition to their new status as private enterprises. This may explain the eloquent plea of the manager of Robotron at the Leipzig Trade Fair to connect the currency reform with a cancellation of all East German company debts. Even the better-invested *Kombinate* (e.g., Carl Zeiss and Mikroelektronik) were not sure the West German banks would regard them as creditworthy.[73]

The mandate of the March elections indeed put an end to talk about proceeding gradually, not to mention following a "third way" between the market and a planned, centralized economy. Just as in Poland, Czechoslovakia, and Hungary, the East Germans had decided to go for a market economy by the straightest route and regardless of the pain. The principles of a centrally planned economy, enshrined in articles 9–12 of the East German Constitution, were a dead letter now. The time had come to place the 200-odd state *Kombinate* that governed some 3,500 "people's own companies" (VEBs) into a competitive market situation

73. See *Süddeutsche Zeitung*, March 19, 1990.

and to remove the crippling restrictions from some 80,000 small, private trade and manufacturing firms. Once all the fetters of planning and the limits on production, size, and location had fallen, market forces would assert themselves. The Modrow administration had already taken the first steps in this direction in order to attract foreign investors.

The elimination of subsidies, though hardly painless, would give prices a chance to become the chief market mechanism to determine what was to be produced and by whom, and what a product was worth on the market. The introduction of the deutschmark in the GDR—proposed by Bonn on February 7—also implied that the GDR would lose autonomy over its monetary and currency policy to the West German Bundesbank, although it would regain some participation in the near future when one or two *Land* central bank presidents (after the reestablishment of *Länder* in the GDR) might be on the council of the Bundesbank. Another problem, often overlooked in discussions about the currency exchange rate of ostmark savings accounts, was the existing bank and credit system and the immense debts of East German enterprises. The GDR state planning commission had granted billions in credit to enterprises that would never have been so favored in a market economy.[74] Since most East German enterprises would be unable to service these debts after the currency reform, the East German banks involved would go bankrupt and the only recourse would be Bonn—probably to the tune of over 100 billion marks. As of March 1990, East German enterprises owed a total of 260 billion East marks, of which 31 billion were new indebtedness dating from 1989. The imminent need for drastic restructuring of most industries was likely to make it impossible for them to carry the interest now in deutschmarks, not to mention repaying the principal.[75] Eventually there was talk of Bonn having to take on a burden as high as 300 billion marks.

74. With the exception, of course, of the American savings and loan institutions of the Reagan era which made huge loans (and "nonrepayable" loans) for friends and for dubious undertakings, and which did so on the basis of FDIC guarantees of deposits up to $100,000. The similarities are far from accidental—socialism for the rich—although the GDR loans at least were concentrated on bottlenecks of supply and industrial activity rather than on conspicuous consumption.

75. The East German state banking system bears only a superficial resemblance to the West German banks and cannot be reformed by deregulation alone or decentralization of the GDR State Bank. The prevailing system forced enterprises to finance 60–70% of their capital investment with State Bank credit as a means to steer their development. See "Banken in Not," by Bernard Blohm and Peter Christ, in *Die Zeit*, no. 13, March 23, 1990, p. 29, and the interview with an East German banker, Edgar Most of the private German Credit Bank, on the following page. See also *Frankfurter Allgemeine Zeitung*, no. 70, March 23, 1990, p. 19, on the obligations of the State Bank.

In addition to the creation of an autonomous banking system, including competition among the banks and with foreign banks, the GDR would also need a new system of taxation. The old one imposed tax rates up to 98% on state enterprises (VEBs), but very little on individuals except for independent professions and small entrepreneurs; very little also on consumption—except for gasoline and automobiles—because prices were artificial in any case and the supplies under tight control. The new tax system, however, could not simply be the exceedingly complex one of the Federal Republic and, even though a value-added tax (VAT) was inevitable, the tax burdens must not scare away outside investors. Six months after the March elections, FRG Economy Minister Haussmann proposed that the whole GDR be made an area of significant tax incentives in the hope of attracting the West German investors who had still not come through by that time, three months after the currency reform. West German business and its chief organizations, the Federation of German Industry (BDI) and the German Diet of Industry and Trade (DIHT) were delighted, but critics expressed the suspicion that this was merely the opening gambit of controversial government plans to lower business taxes all over Germany.[76] Bonn could hardly afford to give away 25–30 billion marks at this time of financial strain, they felt.

Last but not least, the economic union required the introduction and financing of unemployment insurance and employment offices that could organize the retraining and redirection of redundant personnel. The social security system of the GDR offered pension levels far below those of the Federal Republic—again, we have to remember its heavily subsidized food, rents, and services, not to mention its progressive family and health laws and its protection of renters against eviction and employees against dismissal—namely, an average level of 377 East marks versus 1,073 deutschmarks in the West.[77]

Light and Shadow

The first wave of West German businesses in the GDR naturally aroused some fears of an economic "takeover" and of the establishment of West

76. Spokespersons for German business claimed that their tax burden was higher than that in other industrial countries, thus giving foreign competition an unfair advantage. See Klaus-Peter Schmid, "Nicht mehr als eine Fata Morgana," *Die Zeit*, no. 39, Sept. 28, 1990, p. 10.

77. See Suhr, *Was kostet uns die ehemalige DDR?* pp. 27–29, and Grözinger, *Teures Deutschland*, pp. 30–57. Also see Klaus-Peter Schmid, "Der lange Weg zum Markt," *Die Zeit*, no. 13, March 23, 1990, pp. 25–26. GDR Economy Minister candidate Elmar Pieroth estimated the cost of pension increases, health subsidies, and unemployment insurance to the FRG—presumably, Bonn would only pay start-up costs—at 50 billion marks.

German monopolies and hegemonies over the East German economy. A case in point, critics argued, was the new partnership between West Germany's largest insurance company, Allianz (Munich), and the State Insurance Company of the GDR which promised to give Allianz a market share of 20% in a united Germany. Any acquisition of a former GDR state monopoly firm by a powerful West German firm ought to have rung alarm bells in the Federal Cartel Office in West Berlin. The new government of the GDR would have to curb a potential "sellout" by intervening into such mergers in a continuation of the anticartel initiatives begun under Modrow. Similar fears were raised when the West German Preussag-Salzgitter and the equivalent of General Electric, AEG, began to negotiate a merger with the *Kombinat* Rail Vehicles (Schienenfahrzeugbau), which promised to bring its seventeen plants and 23,000 employees into a new giant railroad car conglomerate, Deutsche Waggonbau AG. The Krupp company was looking for East German opportunities to manufacture diesel engines, Klöckner-Humboldt-Deutz was interested in tractors, and the West German industrial giants Mannesmann and Thyssen were also reportedly wheeling and dealing at the Leipzig Trade Fair. By the end of the year, the Trabant Works in Zwickau could be just another VW plant, the Wartburg production in Eisenach another Opel factory,[78] and Daimler-Benz might be manufacturing trucks in the Ifa Nutzkraftwagen facility at Ludwigsfelde. March was still too early for the complete sale of these *Kombinate* to Western bidders—current law then permitting only joint ventures and capital participation—but Western managers were already preparing the contracts for complete acquisition—rusty lock, obsolete stock, and rotten barrel—for the day after economic union. The long-range goal was to grab market share in East Germany and, perhaps, in Eastern Europe as well.

The West Berlin Senator for the Economy and candidate for the GDR Economy Ministry, Elmar Pieroth, on the other hand, had been preaching the need for small and medium-size entrepreneurs and for practical solutions to their supply and credit problems since late 1989. If the West German ratio of small and medium-size to large entrepreneurs could be

---

78. As it turned out, the occasion was most solemn, even sad, when the last Trabi rolled off the assembly line in spring of 1991. The unpretentious automobile had a history going back to the Horch Co. in 1909, the DKW of the thirties, and the first plastic car of the fifties. It went into production with a 500-cc., 18-horsepower engine in 1958, and by 1974 had its first million cars on the pre-1939 Autobahn of the GDR. Customers with the necessary 13,000 East marks (1989) had to wait as long as thirteen years for delivery. In 1989, before the market for them dried up, Zwickau still built 144,000 Trabis. The closing down of the Wartburg plant, a little later, witnessed considerable hostility by the Wartburg work force toward Opel, for whom they seemed reluctant to work.

realized in the East, the former West Berlin senator argued, the GDR would have nearly 4 million new jobs to make up for the anticipated wave of 2 or 3 million unemployed. In the trades alone, 1.3 million handicraft jobs ought to be added to replicate their share in the West, where their numbers are still notoriously short of the demand for their services. The charismatic Pieroth was more concerned about the future of the bloated *Kombinate* than about the ability of new small-scale entrepreneurs to find the gaps in the service and in the supply needs of production.[79]

Forty years of communist social and economic management had not wiped out the resilience of the East German bourgeois middle class. In mid-May, just as the currency union was initialed in Bonn and East Berlin, the West German state governments set up their Germany Fund of 115 billion marks for the development of East Germany from 1991 to 1994. Advice and potential cooperation for the new entrepreneurial class also came from promotional offices and activities of West German state governments. The *Land* Baden-Württemberg established offices for economic and technical cooperation in Leipzig and Karl-Marx-Stadt (Chemnitz). North Rhine Westphalia set up a liaison service in East Berlin. Rhineland-Palatinate opened a bureau in Erfurt, and Schleswig-Holstein planned "little embassies" in Rostock, Schwerin, and Neubrandenburg. Saxony attracted the entrepreneurial attention of both Bavaria and Baden-Württemberg. Arrangements between such sister cities as Hamburg and Dresden—which also benefited from the attention of sister cities Strasbourg, Rotterdam, and Salzburg—were not far behind in bringing together West and East German entrepreneurs.[80]

Inevitably, the future of the *Kombinate* did not always result in a West German takeover or partial sellout, whatever one may think of such transactions. A number of *Kombinate* instead suffered the fate of Nordag Company (part of the *Kombinat* Agriculture Technic [Landtechnik]), which had employed about 600 workers making large farm machinery for the highly mechanized East German agricultural sector. By mid-August, barely six weeks after the currency union, the company had lost all its markets and income, and there was no West German or other outside partner in sight. Even its East European markets had dried up as a result of their respective political upheavals and shortages of foreign

79. See Grözinger, *Teures Deutschland*, pp. 71–103, and Joachim Nawrocki, "Erbetene Einmischung," *Die Zeit*, no. 13, March 23, 1990, pp. 26–28. See also *Die Zeit*, no. 15, Apr. 6, 1990, p. 28, on the invasion by West German publishers.

80. See *Der Spiegel* 44, no. 12, March 19, 1990, pp. 80 and 136–143 and 148–149, and Grözinger, *Teures Deutschland*, pp. 95–103, on the West German bids for the more attractive *Kombinate*, especially in automobile manufacturing and in the production of beer.

currency. All the bright plans of the weeks following the March elections, when this "people's own company" was converted into a private joint-stock firm, had failed in the face of its domestic customers' inability to pay in deutschmarks. The accustomed heavy export subsidies likewise disappeared with the old COMECON (CMEA) relationships. Bank credits were unavailable as long as the future of Nordag seemed so uncertain. Potential partners were waiting for the firm to declare bankruptcy so that its debts would not burden a new owner. They were also reluctant to be the ones to fire redundant workers, often as many as half the employees.

Another example is the lightbulb company Narwa, which likewise lost its markets when East German retailers stopped stocking Narwa bulbs on the day of the currency union and East European customers similarly disappeared. A large bill was still unpaid by the Soviet Union, which had to husband its own reserves and had lost most of its own export markets in the GDR. Like other spinoffs of the old *Kombinat* Electric Equipment (Elektro-Apparate), this VEB faced a grim future unless the West German lightbulb giant Osram would condescend to buy into Narwa (which had originated from an East German, prewar Osram antecedent). Narwa could not even get credit against its industrial real estate because the latter is "people's property," controlled by the Trust Agency.[81]

The Role of the Treuhand Trust

We have already encountered the Trust Agency (Chapter Five) but still need to assess its success as a means to turn the communist "fish soup" of centrally directed, publicly owned enterprises into a free market "aquarium" of private, autonomous fish. How representative were the cases of Nordag and Narwa? In mid-May 1990, GDR State Secretary Günter Krause (CDU) already expected about one-eighth of the VEBs to go bankrupt, and another three-eighths to need a lot of recapitalization to remain afloat. These 1,080 larger companies would throw 2.5 million people out of work if they failed. Less than a third of all the VEBs appeared to be viable enterprises. In mid-August *Der Spiegel* quoted a prominent economic consultant as expecting about 40–50% of East German firms to go bankrupt. Another 20–30% might make the transi-

81. The same Trust Agency also collected the 1.6 million East marks in profits that Nordag still had in the last month before the currency union (June) and that was supposed to help the company survive. Evidently the Trust Agency was not willing to give Nordag an early start. See *Der Spiegel* 44, no. 33, Aug. 13, 1990, pp. 77 and 85–92.

tion, if "with great difficulties." Only 20–30% appeared to be internationally competitive and therefore good prospects for partnerships.[82] As a sign of the changing requirements, the Trust Agency had to revise its earlier estimate of 7 billion marks in order to ensure liquidity in the second half of 1990 after the East German firms sent in requests totaling 22–25 billion marks. As many as three-fourths of all East German workers might sooner or later have to look for a new job, which might be found especially in public infrastructural employment (e.g., road construction, railroads, and telecommunications—as many as 3–4 million jobs) and in services, which alone should provide 2 million new jobs if services come to play a role equal to that in the West German economy.

When *Der Spiegel* magazine commissioned a survey in March 1991, one year after the crucial GDR elections, one of the questions was "Why are so many enterprises of the former GDR at the end of their tether (*am Ende*)?" Some 51% of East Germans replied, "because the Trust Agency is so slow about (*verschleppt*) privatizing the economy."[83] This is strong criticism for an agency that, at its very start in early March 1990, under the Modrow government, was really meant to preserve the "people's property" rather than to reorganize or privatize it. Only in July of that year was its new mission "to privatize, rehabilitate and, if necessary, liquidate the GDR *Kombinate*" spelled out.[84] As industrial production dropped dramatically (as much as 40%), the tourism sector collapsed— neither West nor East German tourists were keen on flocking to the substandard facilities—and mass unemployment threatened; never-ending storms of criticism began to howl about the agency from every side, most notably from the trade unions. Franz Steinkühler, for instance, the head of the powerful metal workers' union IG Metall, proposed a state holding company along Italian, French, Spanish, or Belgian lines to take over the two-thirds of GDR enterprises that were candidates neither for a quick sale nor for closing down in the near future. But the Treuhand

82. The consultant, Herbert Henzler of the American McKinsey agency in Germany, also emphasized the need for East German firms to concentrate on their core activities and to leave all sidelines and unproductive services such as vacation homes and kindergartens to contractors. Henzler also pinpointed the need to develop markets for East German products in the West and to recruit more management personnel there to make up for critical shortages. *Der Spiegel* 44, no. 20, May 14, 1990, pp. 122 and 87–88.

83. Only one in four West Germans shared this assessment, which was one of the strongest responses among the Ossis, outdone only by "decades of SED mismanagement of the economy" (53%) and followed by the complaint that "the old [SED] management is still there" (50%), a concern shared passionately by many East Germans. *Der Spiegel* 45, no. 12, March 18, 1991, p. 55.

84. See *Deutschland Archiv* 23 (Sept. 1990), 1333–1335. For critical comments, see also *Der Spiegel* 45, no. 10, March 4, 1991, pp. 126–131.

stuck by its guns under Detlev Rohwedder and, after his assassination, Birgit Breuel (age fifty-three), a banker's daughter who had been economy minister and then finance minister of Lower Saxony (1978–1990). Her motto for the activities of the Trust Agency has been "Privatize quickly, rehabilitate resolutely"—primarily to make units salable—"and, if necessary, close 'em down with care." This did not stop the attacks from the Left, and the SPD's Bundestag speaker on economic policy, Wolfgang Roth, even asserted that "so far, she has not demonstrated the necessary social sensitivity and ability to relate to the fate of millions of workers."[85] Breuel is on record with her strong free-enterprise convictions, but she also has been credited with sound administrative skills which, for example, clarified the division of labor between the central agency and its regional offices, thus facilitating the sale of 500 of the firms under the latter's care in February and March of 1991 alone.[86]

The critical confrontations of the escalating East German unemployment and bankruptcies of spring 1991 had a noticeable impact on both Mrs. Breuel and the policies of the agencies. The Treuhand president experienced, like her martyred predecessor, the existential fear of the workers in the doomed enterprises for whom even the elemental freedoms won in 1989/90—travel, speech, and free elections—had begun to pale before their angst. By the end of May, when she was interviewed by the weekly Die Zeit, she was ready to concede "several years" of subsidized transition to East German enterprises and took pride in having saved 31,000 of 76,000 jobs by salvaging parts of over 400 companies in the process of being closed down. By this time, more than one in eight individual VEB firms had already been privatized, many by turning them over to their own managers for a management buyout, or MBO. Still, 1,150 companies had failed to provide an opening deutschmark balance as mandated by law, possibly because the management was afraid to show the Trust Agency the accounts, or because they were unable to develop a clear business concept relating their enterprise to the market, or were reluctant to restructure the white elephants of the Red past.[87] The

85. Quoted in Die Zeit, no. 17, Apr. 19, 1991, p. 21. Both Roth and Kohl evidently would have preferred an experienced CEO of a large company in this position, but there is a Treuhand vice-president of such background at her side, Hero Brahms, who had already been Rohwedder's assistant at the Hoesch steelworks and who is slated to head the industrial holding operation within the agency.

86. Breuel is also a veteran of the attempts to privatize the Volkswagen company, but the failure of those attempts did not keep her from justifying a continued 20% share of the state of Lower Saxony in VW stock. See Der Spiegel 45, no. 16, Apr. 15, 1991, pp. 118–119.

87. Interested buyers usually have to agree to further investment and to retain a specified labor force. Only 5% of privatized firms went to foreign entrepreneurs, even though expressions of interest have been frequent among other EC countries. See Die Zeit,

agency also prepared a marketing plan to approach investors abroad and, at the trade fairs in Leipzig and Hannover in spring 1991, organized an *Unternehmensbörse* (enterprise market). An estimated 2,500 further interested parties showed up at the Leipzig event, and the data bank of Treuhand information at the Cebit fair in Hannover attracted even larger numbers. There is the expectation that the Treuhand will put itself out of business in a few more years, possibly having a few unsalable but important *Kombinate* left to be taken over by the states, communes, or the federal government.

The enormity of the problems of privatization somehow seems more intelligible when we focus on the *Kombinate*. Toward the end of 1990, for example, the Treuhand made ready to privatize retail businesses, about 11,000 of them, including many small stores and restaurants of the HO chain under the aegis of its trust agency for privatizing retail trade (Gesellschaft zur Privatisierung des Handels).[88] Buyers were to obtain only users' rights. Upon conclusion, this undertaking brought the total of HO businesses sold to private concessionaires to 23,000 out of the original 29,000. The rest had been spoken for by big West German chains such as Rewe, Edeka, Spar, or Tengelmann which also ended up employing about half of the 154,000-strong HO sales force of 1989. Among newly independent owners, however, the attrition rate was very high, probably in four digits, as many of them closed their doors within a few weeks, defeated by the exorbitant store rents charged by some communes or by liquidity and marketing problems.

Fortunately, the Treuhand had worked out elaborate "social plans" with the appropriate trade unions for ex-employees of HO stores—some 26,000 in the second half of 1990—guaranteeing them a percentage of their last salary. The failing stores, however, left particularly rural areas and nonmotorized customers without retail services, a situation that has its parallel in West Germany. Independent tradesmen and handicraft

---

no. 22, May 24, 1991, pp. 19–20; on the MBO wave, see Judith Reicherzer, "Em-bi-ou im VEB," ibid., p. 21. There had already been hundreds of MBOs in West Germany and the MBO May congress for 750 interested East German managers was mobbed by another 500 it could not accommodate. By 1993, there may be as many as 3,000–4,000 East German MBOs, particularly firms unattractive to Western investors. The Treuhand has become more receptive to MBO proposals and by May 1991 had permitted 150 of them. There is some fear that MBOs may be viewed as a panacea, even though they are not immune to most of the pitfalls of other new privately owned businesses, such as their inability to purchase, or even know the final price of, the real estate on which they are located, and the survival of the old communist managers and their collusion, much as elsewhere in Eastern Europe.

88. An earlier offering had to be stopped because of irregularities. The once very important consumers' cooperatives had already shrunk to a mere 110,000 employees, but the Treuhand strove to encourage cooperation between them and the West German chains.

shops of, on the average, three employees have found the going rough, too, in spite of the emphasis in Bonn on promoting small and medium-size enterprises. The Trust Agency, by the way, was not as generous with most retirement social plans of moribund companies unless their promised severance pay was within the capacity of the company to pay.[89] According to the Social Pact negotiated in April 1991 between the Treuhand and the big trade unions, DGB and DAG (white collar), however, even employees of VEBs that cannot afford the standard four months' salary as severance pay may expect a lump sum of 5,000 marks from the Treuhand itself.[90]

The change of command of the Trust Agency to Birgit Breuel also brought a summary assessment of its work during the first nine months after the currency reform. In this short period, the agency had privatized one-eighth of the productive industry, sold all 14 warehouses, 70% of all restaurants and retail stores (15,200), and half of the state-owned pharmacies (951) to private operators. In the first quarter of 1991 alone, 150,000 jobs had been guaranteed and 8 billion marks pledged in investments, for a grand total of 344,000 jobs and 50 billion marks in pledges, including 30 billion marks in the energy industry. A total of 1,261 enterprises had been privatized (including 883 small and medium-size firms), and this, since February, at an accelerating clip of 300 or so a month. Not quite 6 billion marks had been realized from the sales, but 34 billion marks were spent to rehabilitate the firms, including subsidies for export and debts. For 1991, the Trust Agency expected a deficit of 21 billion marks on top of an authorized 25 billion marks for the whole year. So far, 40% of the privatized firms were in the machine and vehicle construction industry, 28% in the food industry, 17% in electronics, and 12% in the chemical and rubber industry. Another 3,000 enterprises expropriated in 1972 were reprivatized. There were 2,100 serious offers on the table; 432 concepts for rehabilitation or privatization had been

89. West German labor law prescribes severance payments but leaves the amount open to negotiation and the ability of the employer to pay. See Der Spiegel 45, no. 10, March 4, 1991, pp. 124–125, and the New York Times, March 12, 1991, where the difficulties of competition with West German rivals are described for a Leipzig brewery that, for forty years, had enjoyed a captive market.

90. There are other feature stories, such as the privatization of Kombinat Jenoptik Carl Zeiss by a merger with the South-West German Zeiss Co. which cost the Trust Agency nearly 4 billion marks; or the Treuhand concept for shoring up the entire East German shipbuilding industry, at a comparable cost, on the argument that closing it down would cost just as much—much of the cost stems from the loss of Eastern and Soviet orders. One of the most controversial actions was the sale of ten SED regional newspapers to Western press tycoons. It was contested in court by the SPD, which claimed property rights stemming from its postwar takeover in 1946 by the SED.

approved, and another 300 were under scrutiny. In addition, 333 enterprises had to be closed down, involving 87,500 workers, some with new jobs elsewhere by now.[91] The Treuhand also turned over 58 enterprises to cities and townships and considered applications to communalize 151 other businesses. Finally, there were 33,000 applications by communes for restitution of land, of which one-third involved the Treuhand, as well as the acquisition of Rostock Harbor (three-fourths of the stock) by the city and of Meissen Porcelain by the *Land* government of Saxony.

East Germans Refuse Their Own Products

In late April 1990, a shocking glimpse of the problems of East German agriculture in selling its products appeared on West German television screens: East German farmers could be seen killing unsalable piglets by brutally dashing them against stone walls. Before 1990, pig production by East German LPGs took place on a monstrous scale, involving huge pork production cooperative farms that annually produced from 120,000 to 160,000 pigs.[92] A large part of the pork problem also had to do with the fact that East German producers had not satisfied the stringent rules of EC producers. Lagging sales, as in all kinds of East German agricultural enterprise, as well as insufficient capacity to slaughter their vast production of pigs had already produced, among other things, a *Schweineberg* (mountain of pork) in analogy to the West German "milk lake" and "butter mountain," all the result of subsidized overproduction. GDR planning had failed to make available enough feed or enough slaughterhouse facilities for the pigs, while all along East German butcher shops frequently have had no meat for days on end, owing to a notably underdeveloped distribution and marketing system.

We have already encountered the collectivization of GDR agriculture (Chapter Five) by 1960 and the subsequent development of large-scale

91. A famous example is Interflug, whose privatization failed because, among other reasons, the Federal Cartel Office blocked its acquisition by Lufthansa. The Treuhand finally closed it down and helped at least one-third of its 2,900 employees to secure other employment. *Frankfurter Allgemeine Zeitung*, Apr. 15, 1991, pp. 13–15.

92. See Suhr, *Was kostet uns die ehemalige DDR?* pp. 71–77, who also describes the structural problems of the LPGs and the impact of their surpluses on West German agriculture in 1990. A typical pork LPG that raised 160,000 is the VEB SZM Neustadt/Orla, which was described in *Der Spiegel* 44, no. 17, Apr. 23, 1990, pp. 42–47. The demonstrative action certainly got West German attention when hundreds of irate parents of traumatized children called the television network offices. *Monitor* television magazine, Apr. 24, 1990.

and highly mechanized agribusiness in place of the old East German family farm and the traditional East Elbian estates.[93] The LPGs, divided since 1972 into animal-producing and produce-growing units, had run into increasing problems with efficiency, capital, and marketability in recent years which greatly contrasts with the relatively successful West German agriculture and its emphasis on quality products and specialization. Among other problems of East German agribusiness, the LPGs have suffered from a reckless disregard for environmental pollution. Soil depletion owing to monoculture, contamination of ground and drinking water—particularly with vast quantities of pig *Gülle* (urine and feces), which also defoliate trees and bushes for miles around—chemical pollutants in live streams and lakes, and other environmental sins of enduring consequence have made East German agriculture a chamber of horrors.[94] On top of their economic and environmental problems, the present LPG officers also tend to be former SED and often present-day PDS functionaries, and not infrequently with a Stasi background as well.

Article 15 of the State Treaty on the currency union mentioned agricultural price supports and external protection within the EC market, as well as setting producer prices at the West German level, but there is no clue as to the future form of landholding. There is a bare consensus that the East is unlikely to revert to its precommunist patterns but that it will not adopt a family farm system similar to that of West Germany any time soon—pre-1945 East German farming was always on a larger scale than in the West.[95] By May 1991, there were only 6,000 independent

93. See C. Bradley Scharf, *Politics and Change in East Germany: An Evaluation of Socialist Democracy* (Boulder, Colo.: Westview, 1984), pp. 88–89. Also see Joachim Hosnag, "Boden und Besitz," *Die politische Meinung* 35, no. 251 (Jul./Aug. 1990), 19–25, on the problems of agricultural reform in the GDR. The agriculturally employed, as a percentage of total employed population, were more than twice as numerous as their counterparts in the FRG, and LPG staff per hectare was more than three times as large as staff in a comparable FRG enterprise. In 1980, agriculture in the GDR accounted for 13.7% of the GNP, as compared to 16.1% for the Czechoslovak Socialist Republic and 24.4% for Poland. West Germany, and also the United States, had a farm percentage of only 2.8% of the GNP. Scharf, *Politics and Change*, p. 83.

94. The annual *Gülle* output of the pig production unit at Neustadt/Orla alone compares with the sewage produced annually by Leipzig's half-million residents. It has already devastated 1,500 acres of forestland and is expected to do the same to another 4,000 acres in ten years' time. *Gülle* and poultry wastes also appear to be sources of serious human medical problems, not to mention the offensive odor. See *Der Spiegel* 45, no. 24, Jul. 1, 1991, pp. 66–68.

95. Prime Minister de Maizière, in his government's opening speech, specifically sanctioned the "democratic land reform" of the Soviets, but declared also that the various forms of East German agricultural ownership should be on an equal level. This last-mentioned equality is included in the Agricultural Adjustment Law of July 1990, which the People's Chamber passed after a wave of GDR farmer demonstrations, blockades, and

farmers in the five new *Länder*, and Federal Agriculture Minister Ignaz Kiechle blamed the high capital needs and lack of experience as much as the communist legacy for this low rate of privatization. One should remember also that GDR agriculture was a leader among communist bloc countries, producing nearly all (93%) of the country's needs and surpluses in meat, milk and eggs, animal fat, potatoes, even though its role in GDR exports had been declining for decades. There were shortages only in vegetable oils, fruit, vegetables, and grain. At full capacity, GDR agriculture could produce huge surpluses, though at excessive cost and poor levels of productivity[96] and quality when compared to West German and most EC levels. The number of agricultural jobs is expected to decline by more than half by the end of 1991. The quality and diversity of East German food products and their retail distribution had always been bad and will require modernization capital and know-how from the West. The new awareness of product quality among East German consumers has led to a rejection of vast amounts of Eastern pork, eggs, yogurt, and milk. Instead, these consumers bought West German alternatives, frequently at inflated prices—in many cases, nonetheless, the better West German product also cost less in West German stores.[97] According to an East Berlin market research institute, even LPG workers spurned their own agricultural and dairy products. Perhaps the brand names, packaging, and indication of origin needed to be changed to get East German consumers to buy East German products again. East Germans living close to the old border routinely did their shopping on Saturday mornings in the West (the stores there are closed for the rest of the weekend).

The LPGs had to store their products and explore possibilities of exporting them to Eastern Europe—that is to say, in competition with

---

attacks with eggs and tomatoes upon East and West German politicians. To embarrass floundering LPG management further, there have also appeared a few energetic "Wessi" farmers who leased East German farmland and showed how a successful farm can be managed.

96. See *DDR Handbuch*, 3rd ed. (Cologne: Wissenschaft & Politik, 1985), vol. 1, pp. 126–129 and 785–801. Pre-1990 productivity in agriculture has been estimated to be about 20–30% below West German levels, an astonishing triumph of the modern family farm over the highly mechanized, overfertilized, and pesticide-ridden LPG with its large number of laborers and specialized functions and equipment. See Antonius John, "Neue Landwirtschaft," *Die politische Meinung* 35, no. 251 (Jul./Aug. 1990), 27–32. The exodus of East German refugees has also affected the specialist personnel of the LPGs.

97. See *Rheinischer Merkur/Christ und Welt*, Sept. 28, 1990. The subsidies for such staples as meat and potatoes also hid the actual cost of production: when a consumer paid only 12.90 East marks for 220 pounds of potatoes, that was because the GDR government had added another 51.40 marks in subsidies to the LPGs.

the local producers and with other priorities for the use of hard currency by East European governments. The cozy old deals of COMECON (CMEA) agricultural markets are almost gone. The governments of East and West Germany, moreover, were in agreement from the start about restricting agricultural imports from the West to East German territory for a transition period of three to five years. During this period, East German agriculture is supposed to modernize and rationalize opera- tions—laying off vast numbers of people and shrinking its present scale— and to adapt to the conditions of the EC market. The end of most subsidies on July 1, 1990, had already raised consumer prices by 20% while producer prices dropped by more than 50%. Obviously the agri- cultural transition cannot squeeze its unsubsidized margins simply out of mass-produced pigs but will have to turn out highly refined pork products such as constitute the quality advantage of the West. The same goes for milk, bread, and a whole range of other unrefined products that will still be protected by the import restrictions of the "green border" for a while.[98] Restrictions did not stop "small imports" (under 1,000 deutsch- marks), though, nor did they keep East German raw products from being shipped to and refined in the West.

In April 1991, the Bundestag passed a law to facilitate the difficult process of breaking up and privatizing the LPGs, revising the year-old Volkskammer law and forcing the pace of the process, which might now be completed by the end of 1991. The new law set forth the conditions for the return of cooperative farm property to individual families and even assigned them quotas of milk and sugar beet production based on those of their old LPG. The deliberate shrinkage of the LPGs also took the form of stopping farming altogether on about 1.5 million acres of farmland, more than in all the EC countries over the decades. In fall 1991, the LPG cooperatives would be dissolved altogether unless sold off by then, an unlikely prospect with many because of their high indebted- ness. The Treuhand also sold off 86 of the 307 food-processing enter- prises to entrepreneurs who pledged to invest 3 billion marks in their modernization. A portion of the agricultural acreage was also sold to industry, which paid 130 million marks and pledged to invest about 10 billion marks, creating 31,000 new jobs. The example of the LPGs of *Land* Brandenburg illustrates their problems. By mid-June 1991, three-

98. In September 1990, the East German agriculture minister decided to increase aid to agriculture in 1990/91 to 3 billion marks, which amounts to a subsidy of 2,900 marks per worker in full-time employment. But such a subsidy cannot go on forever. A total of 4.9 billion marks went to East German agriculture in 1990, and the 1.4 billion marks budgeted for 1991—plus 1.2 billion marks in liquidity credits—were likely to be exceeded by far. *Tagesspiegel*, May 29, 1991.

fourths of them, according to a well-guarded survey, were facing bank-ruptcy. Their work force had declined from 180,000 in 1989 to between 30,000 and 40,000 by the end of 1991. A good 84% of respondents in the work force had not even heard of any retraining opportunities. LPG governing boards were resigning left and right because they had received no assurance regarding their liability and the LPG debts. Most farmers and farm politicians tended to blame the new agricultural law for their plight.[99]

Where do East German consumer preferences come in, however? And what about all the retail chains which, if we are to believe farmers and workers, were conspiring to keep East German goods off their shelves? At least some of the problem lay with East German retail organizations, which first had to be decentralized and, of course, privatized. Some of it also resulted from the poor attitudes of the old personnel toward the consumer, although the lack of "consumer-friendliness" can be observed just as much in West Berlin—it is a regional specialty, in other words, not just a legacy of communism. A consumer survey, conducted by Infratest in both Germanys in September 1990, showed that not only foods but also clothing, furniture, toys, and cosmetics produced in East Germany received poor marks from the population there. Cars and electrical products were regarded with contempt. Only the local beer, liquor, wine, and sausages did well. In more than two-thirds of the forty most important product groups, according to a study by the Nielsen market research company of Frankfurt, Western brand names were dominant, presumably benefiting from West German television advertise-ments and carefully perfected product images.

It would be an understatement to say that in 1989/90 West German retailers were eager to invade the GDR markets by buying into the state-run HO chain of stores and restaurants or in any other way possible. Indeed, a veritable invasion and takeover did take place and was reflected in the extraordinary 10.8% increase of West German retail turnover in 1990. This was composed of a 16.9% increase in German mail order volume, a 10.9% jump in supermarket sales, and 10.6% in specialized (*Fachgeschäfte*) retail sales in an economic sector that throughout the eighties averaged less than 3% annual growth.[100] Early in 1990, one of the West German grocery chains,

99. The total indebtedness of the LPGs amounted to 6.5 billion deutschmarks, of which a large part will have to be forgiven. See *Der Tagesspiegel*, Apr. 26 and June 7, 12 and 19, 1991. The Treuhand also seeks to privatize or return 130 of the 460 state estates and the "people's own estates" (VEGs). See especially *Der Spiegel* 45, no. 19, May 6, 1991, pp. 70–80, for an account of the desperate efforts by LPG managers, the Red Barons of the past, to fight off more efficient competitors and to feather their nests from the collapse.

100. Business had already picked up in late 1989, when the Ossis began to go West and buy West German goods at exchange rates between 1:7 and 1:20. Discount stores and

Spar ("Save"), had already announced plans to open a string of thirty supermarkets at the time of the March elections. Eventually, the Rewe, Edeka, and Tengelmann chains followed. The department store chain Karstadt went East, too, and the multinational department store chains Horten (50% owned by Britain's BAT Industries) promised to open a "hypermarket" in the GDR. A newly founded East German small business association already had 20,000 members at the time, including many new small entrepreneurs. In early May, in the midst of an invasion of West German dairy and meat wholesalers, Prime Minister de Maizière felt compelled to appeal to his countrymen to buy their own products: "Our merchandise is not inferior; it just does not look as pretty [as the West German imports]."[101] By this time, some GDR consumer-goods VEBs were already in deep trouble. VEB Stern-Radio, the sole East German manufacturer of cassette recorders, was unable to sell its products any more and was denied bank credit. Shoe factory workers conducted a "warning strike," expecting government assistance or at least consumer sympathy. East Berlin's candy factory Elfe found itself unable to compete with the Western chocolate bars and other sweets.

The VEBs affected by the consumer switch to lower prices and better quality desperately looked for Western partners and often found that their Western competitors were interested only in the East German markets and not in coproduction or investment in VEB modernization. Depending on their own expansive capacity to produce for an additional market of 16.8 million, Western companies might have little reason to get into a production partnership.[102] But quality and cost clearly were the chief burdens of East German producers of consumer goods. Plastics-makers like Plaste & Elaste in Schkopau and the color-negative film company Orwo in Wolfen/Bitterfeld had hopelessly antiquated and environmentally damaging equipment. The fishing Kombinat in Rostock, on the Baltic, used ancient trawlers and obsolete canning equipment, not to mention one-third more workers than the Western competition, which resulted in noncompetitive prices for every can of fish.

At the center of the consumer dreams of East Germans, however, stood the automobile or, rather, exchanging their trusty old Trabi for a West German car, even a used one. By a year after the currency reform, not

department stores also boasted increases between 7% and 9% in 1990. See Die Zeit, no. 24, June 7, 1991.

101. Der Spiegel 44, no. 19, May 7, 1990, pp. 18–26.

102. The relatively small market precludes, for example, making automobiles, personal computers, or cassette recorders just for the GDR. In the case of beer breweries, it was the existing concentration in the FRG that made it unlikely that all but a few of the 108 small GDR breweries would survive, and soft drink production faced the importation by truck of multinational Coca-Cola, Pepsi, and Fanta.

only were East German forests and ditches full of junked Trabis—along with vast amounts of other dumped debris—but the total number of cars on the road had jumped from 3.8 million in 1989 to 4.5 million in 1990 and on to an estimated 5.6 million for 1991. All the West German used car lots had sold their last "lemons" at jacked-up prices, and some were importing used cars from other EC countries to satisfy the East German demand. East Germany's pre-1945 road system filled up with this flood of vehicles, and *Staus* (miles-long traffic tie-ups) became an everyday feature of East German life. West German used car dealers, and dealers in color televisions and video recorders, must have become rich from all this demand. Factories expanded production, sales organizations expanded, and West German unemployment shrank in spite of all the refugees and immigrants. An economic minimiracle had indeed resulted from German unification—but in West Germany, not in the East.

The feeble government response from Bonn and East Berlin was a system of import quotas, permitting in the third quarter of 1990, for example, the importation into the GDR of only 300 tons of honey, 6,000 tons of ice cream, 14,000 tons of baked goods and 10,000 tons of sweets, 1,200 million liters of beer and soft drinks, and 2.5 million liters of champagne in order to give domestic production a little breathing space.[103] There was no attempt to curb the West German retail takeover beyond this, nor any noticeable effort to require the Western chains to stock East German goods. The GDR government imposed a heavy import duty of 11% on Western textiles, bicycles, and electrical appliances. The effect of such restraints was to make the Western merchandise more expensive and to absorb some of the hard-earned East German wages. With rare exceptions, there was clearly a fear of introducing new subsidies that would be likely to create patterns of long-range dependency among East German producers.

Only in spring 1991, apparently, after many East German enterprises were at the end of their tether for lack of customers, did the Ossis think of demanding East German–made produce and merchandise. A survey of the DIHT business and trade organization in May disclosed that, by then, over 30% of food items, over 25% of beverages, over 20% of paper goods, office supplies, household supplies and furniture, and over 15% of drugstore items in East German stores were actually East German–made. East German textiles constituted over 10% of the total, but electronic gadgets comprised only between 5% and 10% of the items stocked.[104] Sometimes it took considerable persuasion to get East Ger-

103. See *Der Spiegel* 44, no. 22, May 28, 1990, pp. 106–110.
104. The survey did not disclose what share of these percentages the West German chains in the East absorbed, as compared to stores owned or operated by East Germans. *Süddeutsche Zeitung*, May 13, 1991. The *Berliner Zeitung*, however, reported in early April

man producers to make an effort to supply willing chains like Spar with
a large quantity of goods of dependable quality. Spar was pleased to
announce that 95% of the meat and sausage products on its 2,000-
market meat counters in the Eastern *Länder* were from the East. At the
same time, new Eastern marketing groups such as the Central Marketing
Society of German Agriculture and the Working Group *Ostgemachtes*
(Eastern-produced food) made renewed efforts to introduce their wares
to the West German market. Among other activities, they prepared an
East Berlin July fair with the name "*Ostgemachtes*—A Good Piece of
Germany" to introduce their products to a wider public.[105] Perhaps, in
the end, the marketplace will make up for the retail hiatus caused by
counterproductive East German buying and West German greed.

The East German Disaster

Even without considering the subjective feelings of the average East German,
the objective dimensions of their economic "disaster," to speak with Bundesbank President Pöhl, are easily sketched. The manufacturing product in the
former GDR dropped 46.5% in the second half of 1990 (as compared to the
same period a year earlier) and 51.1% in the first half of 1991 (Table 6.5).
Agriculture and forestry shrank by similar amounts—and this on top of an
initial drop of 25% in the first half of 1990, before the currency reform.
Altogether, the gross domestic product was down 31.8% in the second half
of 1990 (plus 5.2% from before the currency union) and 30.7% in the first
half of 1991. An internal memorandum of the Federal Ministry of Finance
called this "deindustrialization" and a kind of "*mezzogiorno* effect" turning
East Germany into the South of Italy, or into a developing country in relation
to West Germany. The unemployment resulting from this structural disaster
was nearly as dramatic.[106]

In March 1991, this meant 800,000 officially unemployed plus 2

---

that "the larger chain stores," presumably Western-owned, had very few such goods and
that "some smaller markets" were specializing in East German goods. Among them was a
Berlin chain of Park Markets and, by June, some of the larger supermarket chains and
gourmet sections of Berlin department stores were even advertising East German delicacies.

105. One of the problems of East German producers, oddly enough, is the lack of
capacity to fill the big orders, perhaps also a lack of marketing and advertising experience.
Earlier efforts to sell goods to West German stores in the West were not rejected, although
East German promoters complained that their products ended up poorly placed on the
shelves of the West German markets unless they paid kickbacks.

106. The figures are from the DIW prognosis cited in *Der Spiegel* 45, no. 16, Apr. 15,
1991.

Table 6.5. Mass Unemployment and Deindustrialization in the Former GDR, 1990–1991 (in %)

	Time Period	
	I	II
Decline in product		
Manufacturing	−46.5	−51.1
Agriculture and forestry	−35.7	−21.0
Commerce and services	−40.8	−32.9
GDP	−31.8	−30.7
B. Decline in employment		
Manufacturing	−20.3	−36.7
Agriculture and forestry	−21.2	−28.1
Commerce	−12.6	−22.2
Public and private services	−3.6	−7.7

SOURCE: Various German newspaper and television accounts.

NOTE: Period I = July–December 1990; Period II = January–June 1991.

million on "short hours," frequently "zero hours"—about 22% of employables—and, by the end of 1991, 3–4 million Ossis were expected to be out of work.[107] Tongue-clucking news commentators compared this state of affairs—rather unfavorably—to the darkest days of the Great Depression (when 17% were out of work) and noted the deep demoralization and misery of those days, usually without offering any concrete alternative policies to avoid a repetition. One analysis compared the GDR per gainfully employed East German in 1991 to that of West Germany in 1950. Chancellor Kohl and his partners in *Aufschwung-Ost* promised that the East would catch up in three to five years; some said five to ten years. Either version was a far more modest if still optimistic statement than the chancellor's rhetoric of early 1990: "No one will be any worse off than they are today, and many will do better."[108] The East German pensioners, at least according to Social Welfare Minister Norbert Blüm, did receive two consecutive boosts that lifted their pensions up to the

107. On July 1, 1991, hundreds of thousands lost their jobs as the contractual protection against dismissal in the metalworking and electronics industries and the "screening loop" (*Warteschleife*) of civil servants expired.

108. *Der Spiegel* magazine blamed the currency reform, which had suddenly made "the optical lenses of Zeiss, the plastic of Buna, and the Ifa trucks four times as expensive" as before, "assuming that anyone wanted them at all," and added as further errors an "underestimation of the importance of having a functioning administration" and the fixation of West German investors on real control of property, which stymied renovation and investment opportunities. *Der Spiegel* 45, no. 16, Apr. 15, 1991, pp. 124–136.

West German level—at the expense of 8–10 billion marks a year until 1995 from the pockets of West German workers and employers.

Mass demonstrations once more broke out in the former GDR: 80,000 people in Leipzig alone on a Monday night (March 12, 1991) and tens of thousands marching elsewhere against the federal government and the Treuhand, with posters dramatizing unemployment and demanding "No more layoffs this year" and "Rehabilitation of firms, not blind privatization." Even though it was hardly unexpected, massive unemployment seemed to awaken existential anxieties deep within, where former citizens of the "workers-and-peasants state," and perhaps many other Germans, had been socialized to a belief in grace through dedicated work habits. The organizers were trade unions, citizen and church groups, pacifists, and SPD and PDS operatives; speakers called East Germany the "poorhouse of the country." Again there was the unspoken assumption either that the East Germans had a prosperous past of which they had been robbed or that the SPD and PDS had alternative solutions other than massive public works programs or a return to communist dictatorship and economic mismanagement on a colossal scale. As Interior Minister Schäuble wrote in a magazine article, it was "like blaming the doctor for the disease." The demonstrations continued into April, but with notably fewer participants. The trade unions (DGB), especially IG Metall, had aggravated the crisis with major efforts to raise East German wages in spite of the low productivity there: wages rose from an average of 1,350 marks a month to 1,700 marks. Now they pressured state governments and the Treuhand into vastly expanding the employment agencies and public work programs (ABM) in anticipation of the great wave of layoffs to come in July. The London *Economist* compared German woes with those of Poland, where "output has fallen by far less than in eastern Germany," even though the former GDR has vast advantages over Poland, such as West German financial help, political and economic institutions, a legal framework, and a skilled work force of its own.

The Economist neglected to point out that East German wage and social support levels were infinitely higher than those of the Poles or any other East Europeans, if only the Ossis would not compare themselves exclusively to their Western countrymen. It pointed out quite rightly that Poland devalued the *zloty* to remain internationally competitive, whereas East Germany became chained to a common deutschmark which robbed *its* goods of that competitiveness. The currency reform at the rate of 1:1 was not far from the real levels of productivity, since the administered GDR wages had been pegged at nominal levels of about a third of West German wages. However, they did not stay there for long, the London magazine explained, but began to follow "the irresistible pressure for wage convergence in a single country, as workers were free to migrate from east to west." Wages rose between 50% and 80% and might reach two-thirds of the West German level by the end of 1991, without any gain in productivity, thus wiping out the advantage of cheap labor in a capitalist economy.[109] *The Economist* also pointed out that it is very common for wage levels to vary within countries—textile wages in Saarland, for example, being 26% lower than those in Hamburg—and quoted the IMF paper on German unification, to the effect that continued low productivity and lagging investment would keep unemployment above 10% into the twenty-first century and would produce a continuing stream of migration of 150,000 a year. Indeed, *The Economist* predicted a worse outcome: a vicious cycle of rising unit wage costs that would deter investments. It proposed a temporary wage subsidy to halt migration without discouraging investors. This might be cheaper than unemployment benefits.

Franz Steinkühler, the head of the largest and most aggressive of the all-German trade unions, IG Metall, described the state of mind of the East German workers in late April 1991 like this: "They are insecure and want to know what is going to happen now. They can see no future for themselves. There is a deep resignation . . . and an unfocused rage rising every day." He blamed the unwillingness of West German workers to make sacrifices for German unification on the Kohl government's insistence in 1990 that no sacrifices would be needed.[110] The continuing motivation of young East Germans to follow the wage differential and migrate West is well documented by surveys and statistics: 111,000 moved in the second half of 1990, 520 a day and 16,000 a month, according to government estimates. According to an EMNID survey in March 1991, 5% of the population of the former GDR will still "probably" make the change, 1% "with certainty." Among East Germans under

109. A lower exchange rate would not have stopped the pressure toward wage convergence. Hopes for increasing productivity by shedding redundant workers at a rate of 20–30% could not keep step with the impact of the obsolescence of East German capital stock under conditions of rising wages. Heavy capital investment which could have boosted productivity did not materialize because of other problems, such as property rights and bottlenecks in the infrastructure. *The Economist*, Apr. 9, 1991, p. 63.

110. Steinkühler denied any connection between the 10% wage increase his union demanded in the West and the employers' reluctance or inability to invest in the East, but not between price increases "caused by government measures" and wage demands. Neither was he worried that the wage increases might choke off the West German boom in the midst of the great unification effort. He did advocate that the West German investments in the East be tied to conditions, such as a "local contents" requirement, that would truly benefit Eastern reconstruction and not just Western sales. *Der Spiegel* 45, no. 18, Apr. 29, 1991, pp. 34–37.

thirty, fewer than half said they would stick it out for certain; 11% want to leave, which will damage an already blighted society even further. At the time, 82% (67% in an earlier poll) considered the state of the East German economy "bad" or "very bad," only 44% (58% earlier) were "sure" or "rather sure" of keeping their job, and 50% (49% earlier) were worried about losing their jobs.

The pollsters also asked a question indirectly, fearing that otherwise they would not get a straight answer from East Germans: "How many ex-GDR citizens, do you suppose, wish today there had never been a reunification?"—in lieu of "Do *you* wish so?" The answer was "almost everybody" (1%), "most people" (10%), or "a large number" (46%). Some 4% said "almost nobody," and 38% "only a few." Their regrets may not mirror a realistic appreciation of, say, the Polish option of poverty or, even less, a desire for their old repressive system, but the respondents certainly mourn their secure jobs and the subsidized living of old. Ossis, moreover, tended to blame the Wessis or West German–dominated institutions for their plight—i.e., the Treuhand agency, the Bonn government, or West German firms—whereas the Wessis blamed SED mismanagement, obsolete equipment, workers who are not used to Western competition, the old SED managers still being in control, and counterproductive East German buying habits.[111] East German disappointment in 1991 was also reflected in a lurch toward the SPD in the polls. The CDU and FDP, the government parties in Bonn and in four of the five new *Länder*, lost their majority in the East—the CDU slipped from 41.8% in the December 1990 elections to a mere 34%, which now tied it with the SPD (only 24.3% in December). Kohl's popularity, which had been higher in the East than in the West as recently as January 1991, soon took a nosedive, a steeper decline than that of any other politician.

Not all East Germans actually took such a dim view of the situation or lacked vision beyond the immediate pain of the transition. In April 1991, after the renewed demonstrations had begun to taper off again, 41% of Easterners agreed that German unification had gone *as expected*,

111. The poll was commissioned by *Der Spiegel* and printed in vol. 45, no. 12, March 18, 1991, pp. 50–57. See also FGW, *Blitzumfrage zur Landtagswahl in Rheinland-Pfalz*, Apr. 16–18, 1991, p. 192, 194, where only 27.6% of the respondents in Rhineland-Palatinate believed that East German discontents were justified (68% did not) and only 27.3% agreed that the Bonn government was not doing enough to raise the East to the Western level. Another 58.3% thought Bonn was "doing just right," and 10.2% thought it was doing "too much." Union members were more sympathetic (36.8% said "not enough"). In April, West Germans in general grew more exasperated with East German discontents—64% thought they were *not justified* (up from 55% in March)—just as East Germans began to complain less than in February and March. *Politbarometer*, Apr. 1991, p. 55.

and 12% even thought "better than expected," leaving slightly less than half acutely disappointed.[112] And, while 73% still called their economy "bad" (down from 82% in March) and 75% blamed Bonn policies, 39% expected the economic situation to improve within a year (60% did the previous December!) and 28% considered their own economic situation "good" (up from 22% in March). Another 57% thought it was "partly good, partly bad," and only 16% regarded it as "bad" (down from 21% in March); 30% said it had improved, and 46% that it was the same as one year earlier, right after the fateful elections of March 1990. This is hardly a picture of explosive economic discontent. Even more revealing, 56% of East Germans agreed that "it was better to have low wages if this meant more jobs," and only 34% shared Steinkühler's view that rising wages were the top priority regardless of the maintenance of jobs.[113]

A Flexible Balance Sheet

"Whoever would predict today how much German unity will cost in the end," Bonn Finance Minister Theo Waigel said in May 1990, "is either a con man or a psychic."[114] The international fears of a huge financial

112. At the same time, 52% still claimed that their expectations had "not been fulfilled," but they may have included their expectations for national solidarity and brotherhood, a theme they often expressed, along with economic discontents. *Politbarometer*, Apr. 1991, pp. v, 51, 89, and 91. Some 51% of West Germans thought that unification had gone as expected; 40%, worse than expected.

113. Ibid., pp. 55, 90–91, 100. Earlier polls drew fine distinctions. In January 1991, for example, 20.6% of East German respondents (29.2% among CDU supporters) thought economic development in their area since the turnabout (March 1990) to have been "rather successful," and 59.8% said the arrival of the deutschmark had fulfilled their personal expectations (73.2% of CDU supporters) while 37.2% (62.2% of PDS supporters, the only negative majority) insisted it had not. *Politbarometer*, Jan. 1991, p. 81. CDU supporters must have done well in 1990. An INFAS poll commissioned by *Berliner Zeitung* in June also confirmed that 30% of East Germans felt they could afford more in mid-1991 than at the time of the currency union: 39% said "just as much"; 13% said "just as little," a sign of the subjectivity of the responses; and 15% said "less" than a year earlier. *Berliner Zeitung*, Jul. 1, 1991, p. 3.

114. Of course, he himself then produced a position paper on the subject. There is also more than a hint of partisanship in this statement, the "con man" probably referring to the opposition candidate, Oskar Lafontaine, who never tired of assailing the fiscal recklessness of the government's unification policy and of warning about the huge debts resulting from it for generations to come. Lafontaine's criticism was aimed both at the rising public indebtedness and the likely recourse to the money markets of the world. See Nikolaus Piper, "Einheit auf Pump," *Die Zeit*, no. 21, May 18, 1990, pp. 23–25. Also see Suhr, *Was kostet uns die ehemalige DDR?* pp. 17–22, for more details.

gamble were hardly relieved when the Bonn correspondent of the London *Financial Times*, David Marsh, mentioned on page one of his newspaper that the Bonn government was considering issuing unity bonds aimed at foreign investors, particularly the Japanese. Indeed, this might add American deficit managers—who heavily rely on international money markets to help pay for U.S. deficits until the day when future generations of Americans will inherit the obligations from the profligate eighties and the early nineties—to the long list of people understandably concerned about *who* will pay for German unification. The list includes West German voters and the opposition SPD and Greens, the *Länder* and communal governments who were asked to share their resources,[115] German businesses forgoing a tax cut of 25–30 billion marks and being expected to invest 70 billion marks a year, EC partners (most notably the French and Belgians, each for different reasons), all worried about the impact of German expenditures on their budgets and on European unification, and of course the East Germans themselves who will pay in so many ways.[116]

In the face of the worsening situation of the East German economy in 1991, West Germans still wondered about the total cost of unification and how it would be paid. The government had given them, at best, only partial clues. In mid-September 1990, Finance Minister Waigel released the "final figures" on the July 16 agreement between Chancellor Kohl and President Gorbachev: Bonn would pay 15 billion marks ($8 billion) for the phased withdrawal of Soviet troops from East Germany, 12 billion marks alone to go toward building housing in the Soviet Union for the returning soldiers and a loan of 3 billion marks toward the cost of stationing the troops in Germany.[117] The Soviets also agreed to import 1 billion marks in East German farm produce—a German-Soviet trade treaty has meanwhile spelled out the details—paying only 200 million marks in hard currency and the rest in "transferable rubles," the accounting unit customary between the Soviets and the GDR. There may be

---

115. One proposal required the state and local level to share more of the proceeds of the turnover (mostly sales) tax that they usually get to keep. The *Länder* and the federal government have already set up the German Unity Fund of 115 billion marks, of which only 20 billion marks were promised by Bonn.

116. See the interview with GDR Finance Minister Romberg (SPD) in *Die Zeit*, no. 20, May 11, 1990, pp. 41–42, and his plea for securing minimal incomes and for additional measures of aid after the State Treaty of July 1. Romberg had his disagreements with Waigel and eventually resigned. Suhr, *Was kostet uns die ehemalige DDR?* pp. 22–31.

117. This is only a portion of German financial commitments to the Soviets. There are also the costs, billions of marks, relating to the wasteland left behind by Soviet bases and, incidentally, also by American bases; neither the Soviets nor the Americans bothered to dispose of their toxic wastes and other material in an orderly fashion. *Der Spiegel* 44, no. 40, Oct. 1, 1990, pp. 110–121.

further such external obligations of the defunct GDR toward third parties for Bonn to pay.[118]

During the Bundestag election campaign, in late November 1990, the CDU/CSU had still published advertisements in newspapers reading:

> We stick with it: No increases in taxes for German unity. Kohl alone can give you this assurance because only our policy guarantees economic strength . . . by economic growth, savings, redistribution of burdens, reduction of subsidies. . . . All the SPD ever thinks of is raising taxes. It did so seventeen times during its turn in government. The last four years it presented 48 tax-raising proposals. We instead lowered the taxes: In 1990 the people are paying DM 50 billion less than in 1985. Give your . . . vote to the chancellor."[119]

Unfortunately, Chancellor Kohl is neither a very good liar nor a great communicator, and the long morning after his electoral triumph was brutal—not the least reason for which being the outbreak of the hot phase of the Gulf War with its external demands upon the German treasury. In the weeks following the introduction of the new cabinet— January 18, two days after the bombs began to fall on Iraq—a painful debate set in, not about *whether* to raise taxes, but how much and which taxes to raise.

In the midst of the debate, Finance Minister Waigel (CSU) performed his juggler's trick of "savings, redistribution of burdens, reduction of subsidies" to make it look as if the 1991 budget deficit could be kept under 70 billion marks.[120] The interest on these deficits alone is expected to rise from an annual share of 9% of the budget to about 17%, and the

118. See *Hannoversche Allgemeine*, Sept. 15, 1990. Soviet trade was about 30% of GDR foreign trade in 1989, and the exchange of GDR machinery for Soviet oil and raw materials may well continue in the future.

119. *Tagesspiegel*, Nov. 24, 1990. Interestingly, the Federal Ministry of Finance by this time had already put out a release on what it had cost for Germany not to be united, 407 billion marks, in obvious anticipation of the coming *dénouement*. That sum comprised 205 billion marks in federal aid to Berlin, 144 billion for Berlin economic promotion, 35 billion for depressed zonal border aid (along the Iron Curtain), 10 billion for ransoming GDR political prisoners, 9 billion for transit facilities, and 2 billion each for flight subsidies and improvements of the Autobahn to Berlin.

120. For details on some 35 billion marks in budget savings, see especially Wilfried Hanke, "Zu sparsam beim Sparen," *Die Zeit*, no. 4, Jan. 25, 1991, p. 9. For all three levels of government—federation, *Länder*, and communes—an annual deficit of 140 billion marks is projected until 1994, when the deficit is supposed to drop below 10 billion. Also see ibid., p. 10, and nos. 5–6, Feb. 1 and 8, 1991, pp. 12 and 11, respectively.

dependence on capital markets will keep interest rates high even though Germany's European and transatlantic allies kept pleading for Germany to keep the lid on such a development. Particularly the United States and Great Britain, the chief victims of the worldwide recession, wanted interest rates lowered so as to cope better with their problems. The opposition also complained about the fact that Waigel's "savings" mostly came from the pockets of the working class and the retired: raising unemployment insurance fees, telephone surcharges, and still unspecified burdens.

The contribution demanded by the United States for the Gulf War, 5.5 billion marks, not counting payments to other states (Turkey, Egypt, Israel), finally became Bonn's excuse to raise taxes in a big way. Obvious targets were gasoline taxes and the value-added tax, a popular source of revenue among most European countries, many of which charged a higher percentage on sales transactions than Germany (14%)[121] (which even had a reduced rate (7%) for food items, books, and urban transport). Raising the VAT to 15% and 7.5%, respectively, would bring an extra 14 billion marks (one-third goes to the *Länder*). Like most sales taxes, a VAT is regressive and hits a greater share of the disposable income of the less well heeled even though the reduced rate moderates its regressiveness. The idea of a surtax on taxable incomes above 30,000 marks (single) or 60,000 marks (married) per annum would yield nearly 10 billion marks for every 5% of surtax and would affect about 9 million taxpayers, mostly West Germans. Aiming at the better heeled by doubling the income threshold to 60,000/120,000 marks would yield about 5 billion marks for a 5% surtax and would target about 1.5 million taxpayers.[122] On the projected-expenditure side for 1991 were 80 billion marks and an expected statutory welfare start-up cost in the five new *Länder* in the neighborhood of 14 billion marks from the federation and 30 billion marks from the German Unity Fund.

Little is to be expected from direct East German tax revenues because,

121. Denmark (22%) and Ireland (21%) have the highest VAT, followed by Italy and Belgium (19%), France, the Netherlands, and Greece (18–18.6%), and Great Britain (17.5%). The gasoline tax used to be at the level of 2.28 marks (about $1.25) a gallon for regular until a recent small increase to 2.40 marks. It is the lion's share of the mineral oil tax, which also includes natural gas and light heating oil, and customers also pay VAT on their gas purchases.
122. A threshold of 100,000/200,000 marks (about $55,000/110,000) would yield 3.6 billion marks with every 5% surtax. The surtax has precedents in 1968–1974 and was rejected as a means to balance the books in 1981 and 1984. See Klaus-Peter Schmid, "Waigel hat die Wahl," *Die Zeit*, no. 6, Feb. 8, 1991, p. 11, and *Süddeutsche Zeitung*, Feb. 22, 1991.

first of all, there was no effort to introduce a uniform all-German tax system with the currency reform. East Germans, in fact, have lived under no fewer than three totally different tax systems in the twelve months since the Wall came down: the old communist system; Modrow's transitional measures; and the none-too-tidy situation after the state treaty on the currency reform, when the property situation and the effective dates of various revenue-related laws[123] were still rather uncertain. There was also the question of whether the continuing or renewed flight of East Germans to West Germany might not reduce the base population of East Germany before long to far fewer than the 16.8 million we have taken for granted.[124] We know that nearly 600,000 had left by the end of 1990 and that, if the polls quoted earlier are any indication, another 6% of the 1991 population may leave. This would reduce the East German (without East Berlin) population of the five new *Länder* to about 13.6 million, of whom a disproportionate number are retired and not contributing to the productive enterprise. Since interest rates on all debts and mortgages were bound to go up, this too would involve all consumers.[125]

The moment of budgetary truth arrived at midyear 1991, and not without critical voices which claimed that it was not the final truth or that Waigel and the ambitious new Economy Minister, Jürgen Möllemann, were still playing games. Möllemann had insisted he would resign if additional cuts of government subsidies in the West, in the amount of 10 billion marks, were not made by a certain date (July 10), triggering protest demonstrations among West German coal miners and other

123. The State Treaty articles of this description were, for example, article 15(1) concerning levies on EC-regulated agricultural produce, article 18(1–5) on social insurance contributions, article 19 on unemployment insurance contributions, article 20 on pension plan payments, article 21 on health, and article 23 on accident insurance. See also articles 26, 28, 30 and 31 and annex IV. Concerning the introduction of the West German tax system, see *Der Spiegel* 44, no. 24, June 11, 1990, pp. 92–95.

124. A monthly·number of 15,000–20,000 people were still migrating to the West in the winter of 1990/91. Given the modest wage levels, even the unemployment dole at 68% of wages was not enough to sustain a family. Social assistance, especially for families with children, might be preferred by the unemployed. Estimating the GDR population even for the immediate future is very complex, considering the present drop in the birthrate and likely inflows of West Germans and foreign workers. See Gerhard K. Heiling, Thomas Büttner, and Wolfgang Lutz, *Germany's Population: Turbulent Past, Uncertain Future* (Washington, D.C.: Population Bulletin, 1991).

125. A number of vocal critics such as Bundesbank President Karl-Otto Pöhl and Rüdiger Pohl, an economist and member of the five-man panel of advisers to the federal government, have warned against letting the interest rates go much beyond the present 10%. To quote Eberhard Martini, the president-elect of the German Banking Association, "higher taxes would be better than overburdening the capital market."

subsidized interests, such as agriculture, shipbuilding, the federal railroads, aviation—a total of 130 billion marks annually has gone for such
subsidies.[126] Within the three years 1992, 1993, and 1994—when GDR
debts, foreign obligations, and State Bank debts have to be accounted
against the federal credits (*Sondervermögen*) with the Treuhand and the
new Länder, at a level of about 300 billion marks[127]—33 billion marks
in subsidies are projected to be cut. The tax revenues for the year (651
billion marks), moreover, were 17.8 billion above the winter projections,
and there were further savings in sight.[128]

The budget was also waylaid by the SPD opposition, which used its
leverage in the upper house, the Bundesrat, to object to a surtax on any
but the better-off (a 7.5% surcharge on the taxes of people earning
60,000/120,000 marks per annum) and to help the new *Länder* acquire
a direct share of the gasoline tax increase. When it was all over, the VAT
had also been increased to 15% (as of 1993) and the federal government
had to borrow 66.4 billion marks for 1991[129]—a level that Waigel
promised to reduce to a "mere 25 billion" by 1995. The surtax, too, is
limited to its duration. Almost one-fourth of the new budget, nearly 100
billion marks, was meant for the five new *Länder*, 65 billion marks for
public investment alone.[130] The budget of the Ministry of Labor and
Social Welfare increased 27% to a level of 88.1 billion marks, a reflection

126. Some 30 billion were earmarked for agriculture, 15–30 billion for housing (construction and rent subsidies), and 11 billion for mining—which brought the actual cost of
producing a ton of coal to 257 marks as compared to a world market price of 100 marks—
not to mention the subsidies for shipbuilding, coastal fishing, space and aviation. Even beer
and the cigarette industry benefited from well-lobbied subsidies which were now projected
to shrink 50% by 1991.

127. See *Frankfurter Rundschau*, June 25, 1991, and *Süddeutsche Zeitung* for the same
date. The Bundestag committee on the Treuhand agency calculated the total from interest
payments on the GDR debt (25 billion marks each year) and the additional burdens of 1994
and recommended that each company's obligations be separately examined. Until the end
of June, the Treuhand had raised only 9.5 billion marks by selling off 2,140 firms.

128. After a sharp-eyed search for possible savings, the East German *Länder* were
discovered to have some budgetary fat for trimming in spite of their constant pleas for help.
Among other things, they had 5 billion marks in central bank accounts, about 5.5 billion
marks in redundant public employees, and 5 billion marks in trimmable price subsidies,
and they had estimated their investment needs at 21.5 billion marks where 14 billion
seemed adequate—for a grand total well in excess of 20 billion marks. *Die Zeit*, no. 9,
March 1, 1991, p. 10.

129. This has to be compared to net borrowing of 46.7 billion marks in 1990 and 19.2
billion in 1989. Among the subsidies experiencing cuts was that to Berlin (1.3 billion cut).

130. In addition to the 18 billion marks in increased revenues, the federal government
also put 12 billion marks for *Aufschwung-Ost* into the budget. The budget contains 50.5
billion marks to service the national debt. The deficit of all three levels of government, 160
billion marks, amounts to 5.5% of GNP.

of the needs of the East Germans. The Economy Ministry, also heavily involved in Eastern reconstruction, more than doubled its budget; the Postal Ministry added two-thirds; and the Ministry of Transportation, a good one-third. For the next year, 1992, government and opposition agreed, the deficit might rise to 185–190 billion marks, and this would approach the limit of what the German economy could take. Bundesbank chief Pöhl echoed the sentiment and hinted that the East German burden might begin to erode the stability of the West German economy.

Expert estimates of the need to raise more funds on the capital markets spoke of 40–80 billion deutschmarks for 1990 and more for 1991. The first German Unity bonds, similar to U.S. Treasury bonds and promising a fixed interest rate for ten years, were issued in July 1990 in issues of several billion marks at a time, and were bought by a consortium of banks and bank groups. This is the financial base of the German Unity Fund of 95 billion marks—which opposition finance expert Ingrid Matthäus-Maier (SPD) says "will end up costing 275 billion marks, with all the interest." The banks, of course, sell their government bonds to individual investors, mutual funds, and insurance companies in 100-deutschmark units. West Germans save and invest 280 billion marks a year, including 120 billion marks abroad, and the volume of trade on the German bond market was 1,232 billion marks in 1989. The interest offered by German Unity bonds will have to be attractive enough to compete with many other bonds, including those expected from East European countries and, of course, from the ever-hungry U.S. deficit economy and other deficit Western economies. Nevertheless, to quote President Richard von Weizsäcker's speech on German Unity Day (October 3) at the Berlin Philharmonic Hall, "the end of the German division could never be financed by borrowing alone."[131]

Was German Unification Good Business?

Unless we jump to the conclusion that unification is simply the result of recondite German nationalism, we also ought to look into the question of who benefited—*cui bono*? We have already seen how West German retail stores near the border and their suppliers enjoyed windfall profits, benefiting from the patronage of millions of East German customers as well as East Europeans since the collapse of the Wall. West German exports to the GDR more than doubled (121% above 1989) in the first

131. See *Die Zeit*, June 15, 1990, and *Süddeutsche Zeitung*, Oct. 4, 1990.

half of 1990 alone. By September 1990, West German deliveries to East Germany, according to official statistics, were approaching four times the level of September 1989, including sixteen times the level of food and other groceries. Food and agricultural exports from East to West also ran at a respectable four- to fivefold increase. Even the large foreign trade surplus of the FRG—in 1990 it still headed the world's list as champion exporter, ahead of the United States and Japan—mysteriously disappeared by early summer of 1991 as East German demand drew in imports from West Germany and from other EC countries like a black hole among the stars. It was as if Japan had become the fifty-first state of the United States and its trade surplus vanished.

Industrial production in West Germany was straining near full capacity (89.9%) at the very moment that a slowdown of the international market would lead one to expect something different. As the five big West German economic research institutes put it in their joint annual assessment of the nation's economic situation:[132] "Just as foreign demand for West German goods was slackening [because of the worldwide slowdown], and West German demand was held back by the rising interest rates, East German demand picked up the slack with an enormous appetite for consumer goods and machinery." Indeed, East Germans reportedly have bought up every used car on the West German lots and quite a few new cars as well, easily 2 million vehicles in 1990/91. Also, unemployment in the Federal Republic has been dropping, which leaves the country with an unemployed rate of only 6.6% (down from over 10% in 1983). Even before the currency union, the West German institutes of economic research uniformly predicted that "strong impulses on economic growth and employment" in the FRG would come from unification. A vice-president of the Bundesbank and Pöhl's eventual successor, Helmut Schlesinger, pointed to the effects of continuing high demand from East Germany as harbingers of the 10% growth in production to be expected in both Germanys. Considering this expansion, he was not particularly concerned that the increased money supply caused by the currency union would contribute to inflation.[133] If part of German

132. Quoted by Klaus-Peter Schmid, "Schöne Aussichten," Die Zeit, Apr. 13, 1991, p. 24. The institutes painted a rather rosy scenario of the future of East German development, including a much lower level of cost than most projections.

133. He was pleased that the actual rate of exchange for East mark savings into deutschmarks, while not 2:1, came to an average of 1.83:1, not all that far from the proposed rate of the Bundesbank. He was less enthusiastic about the 1:1 rate in wages and salaries, given the still extremely low productivity of East German firms. See the interview in Süddeutsche Zeitung, no. 142, June 23–24, 1990, p. 34. The money supply in Germany actually has grown well beyond the 20% increase projected, and there will probably soon be an inflation rate of 4.2% in that inflation-wary country. It may wipe out a growth rate of the same order.

capital exports (investment abroad) could be shifted more toward East Germany, he felt (still before the currency reform), even the temporarily high West and East German public deficits would not necessarily lead to tax increases. Total German investments at home and abroad were about 500 billion marks in 1990 and would be 570 billion marks the following year—West German industry was expected to increase domestic investment by 12% in 1991. East Germany could probably attract enough of this to modernize from top to bottom in a few years.

The Cologne Institute of the German Economy even prognosticated a considerable "unification bonus": its economists expected the tax revenues from unification until the year 2000 to exceed the estimated costs by more than 100 billion marks.[134] A Swiss economic consultant, Nicholas G. Hayek, suggested in May 1990 that the temporarily lower wage levels in the GDR and in Eastern Europe could help entrepreneurs to revive mass production of consumer items that Europe had lost to Japan and the newly industrialized countries of East Asia decades ago. The availability of highly skilled labor in the GDR particularly favored such a policy, in Mr. Hayek's opinion, until East German wages caught up with West German levels.[135] Needless to say, East Germans did not feel flattered at being considered a *Billiglohnland* (land of cheap wages)— and the PDS will undoubtedly use this for its propaganda—but, as Hayek suggests, this image is precisely what could have enabled them in short order to work their way up to a more prosperous future. In fact, the present inflated wage level—in terms of productivity—was a major factor in the arguments cited by West German companies for *not* investing in East Germany,[136] especially after the first post–currency reform round of collective bargaining raised wages between 15% and 72% from their 1:1 East mark exchange level, shortened the workweek, and granted longer,

134. The Working Group on Tax Estimates, which includes the Bundesbank, the Federal Statistical Office, and the German economic research institutes, estimated total 1990 tax revenues to be 545 billion marks, up 1.8% over 1989 and, for the period 1990–1993, 115 billion marks more than the official estimates. This not only exceeds the intended borrowing of the German Unity Fund but would enable the German capital markets to handle its bonds with ease and at a rate of 8.5–9%.

135. *Die Zeit*, no. 22, May 25, 1990, p. 30; see also no. 29, June 29, 1990, pp. 23–25. East German reactions to this way of thinking were probably behind the big railroad strike of the East German Reichsbahn from November 26 to 29, when all but local commuter trains were stopped by the railroad workers' union (GdED), which sought to raise wages from about 46% to 65% of West German Bundesbahn levels.

136. The German Diet of Industry and Trade (DIHT) listed fifteen reasons for not investing, ranging from uncertain property status to liability for ecological damage done by prospective East German partners. See *Die Zeit*, no. 42, Oct. 19, 1990, p. 8. Another oft-cited reason was the ponderousness of the bureaucracy. *Rheinischer Merkur/Christ und Welt*, Sept. 28, 1990.

paid annual vacations. The new unions (DGB) that had taken over from the communist state union (FDGB) understandably cited as reasons for raises the end of the subsidies on food and the new social security and income taxes, and pointed to the fact that their newly independent employers would now be spared the vast payments once exacted from them by the state—easily 100 billion East marks a year. They were caught on the horns of a dilemma: if wages were "too low," the workers would go West, if "too high," bankruptcies and unemployment would result.

Regarding the shrinking foreign trade surplus, economists were quick to point out that this was also a result of the weakness of the yen and the dollar, and of other international shifts that make German exports comparatively more expensive to foreign buyers. The European currency relations of the Federal Republic had not changed much; in fact, the level of imports into Germany, West and East, had risen appreciably. The French railroads, for example, were pleased to be invited to participate in planning for the greatly expanded intercity train service to East Germany for the summer of 1991, complete with dining cars featuring French chefs and cuisine. There are concrete hopes that German unification may spur economic growth and expansion throughout the entire European Community. But there is also apprehension that the Germans may be picking up the profligate habits of other EC nations, as the Governor of the Bank of France Jacques de Larosière protested recently, and thus burden the planned EC central bank with vast public debts.

By the end of the first year after the currency reform, there were numerous signs that economic activity in the former GDR was picking up, if not yet in a major way. After early complaints that East German communal officials were not taking advantage of the newly available grant and loan programs, State Secretary of the Interior Horst Waffenschmidt (CDU) announced that counties and communes in the new *Länder* had indeed applied for and obtained 10.7 billion of the 15 billion marks made available in the *Kommunalkreditprogramm* for public local investments. Along with 5 billion marks from *Aufschwung-Ost*,[137] local communities became so busy with construction projects that, by the fall of 1991, they ran out of local construction teams. They also started a "personnel exchange" in order to solicit West German local specialists. This office soon had more than enough offers and began to forward applications from the West to a similar office in Berlin. East German communes were particularly anxious to hire young lawyers to help them

---

137. The *Gemeinschaftswerk Aufschwung-Ost* is raising about 100 billion marks for East German reconstruction. See *Tagesspiegel*, May 1, 1991, p. 4, for complaints about communes not applying for available funds.

put their real-estate records in order. More than 10,000 West German administrators had already gone East, although there has been sharp criticism of the monetary incentives they were offered. Management consultant Roland Berger also claimed to see a turn for the better, coming after the second half of 1991. He expected to see, by 1996, specific changes that would make the former GDR more like the FRG, among them the lowering of the high rate of labor participation to West German levels, which certainly is a new way of viewing rising unemployment. He also pointed to the 400,000 newly independent entrepreneurial families and to the increase of independent professionals from 8,000 to 30,000.[138] Finally, plans and good advice were now forthcoming from many quarters as to the best way to carry out East German reconstruction. Many of the new proposals of 1991 seemed worthy of further consideration.[139]

138. *Tagesspiegel*, Jul. 18, 1991.
139. See, for example, Fritz Homann, "Strategie für die wirtschaftliche Erholung in den neuen Bundesländern," *Deutschland Archiv* 24, no. 6 (June 1991), 608–617.

Chapter SEVEN

German Unity, Europe, and the World

German unification in the nineteenth century, the reader will recall (Chapter One), was never a matter for the Germans to decide by themselves. Their "middle location" among at least eight nations—France, Belgium, the Netherlands, Denmark, Russia, Austria-Hungary, Italy, Switzerland—and uncertain boundaries all around the would-be German nation-state made the original German unification of 1871 a destabilizing landslide for most of Europe and a matter of deep concern for the offshore international power of Great Britain. It took Otto von Bismarck three wars of unification to disentangle his Small German (Prussian-dominated) nation-state from the fetters of its European environment, if only for a while. An unsettled border toward the east and unredeemed nationalities under four empires (Prussia, Hapsburg, Russia, and Turkey) fatally drew this Bismarckian creation into the tumult of World War I, a death knell for all four empires and the occasion for Germany's bitter defeat by a global grand alliance that brought in the United States to settle the balance in Europe.

The deeply felt humiliation of defeat and the Versailles Peace Treaty combined with a desire to recover lost territory and to reassert ethnic dominance, giving birth to a nationalistic movement of revenge and reconquest (of eastern territories) that was led, rather appropriately, by an Austrian: Adolf Hitler. The Nazi leader succeeded in marshaling the industrial and military might of Germany in ruthless pursuit of a German racial empire over allegedly inferior breeds. Barely two decades after the end of the First World War, a Second World War engulfed Europe and decisively thrust the United States into the middle of the postwar order about to be born in Europe and the world, a political order based on collective security under the aegis of the United Nations. Long before U.S. public opinion soured on the United Nations,[1] that organization was one of the great American contributions toward a peaceful postwar world. Unlike the earlier League of Nations, which had been created and then abandoned by the United States, the United Nations was given real "teeth" for enforcing peace against aggressors: namely, the Security Council and its five permanent members—the United States, the USSR, Britain, France, and China. The aggressor nations originally envisaged for possible enforcement action were the fascist powers of World War II, in particular Germany, in the event of a revival of the power politics of the thirties. Unfortunately, the outbreak of the Cold War and Soviet vetoes soon stalemated the Security Council and prevented U.N. action on a wide range of issues relevant to the conflict between East and West.[2]

A Product of the Cold War

Nowhere was the Cold War manifested more dramatically than in the center of continental Europe when, within little more than a year after the end of World War II, relations between the Soviets and the Western allies began to deteriorate. As the "Iron Curtain" (Winston Churchill) began to descend upon Europe, it turned liberated East European coun-

1. In large part, the American public became disenchanted with the United Nations when the rising number of Third World nations in it began to form a voting bloc, whose superior numbers deprived the United States of the control it had once exercised over the U.N. General Assembly by means of a coterie of allies and client states. The ever-present isolationist and right-wing opposition to "one-world government" became a potent force against the United Nations only with the Reagan administration which, among other things, refused to make the usual annual support payments to the organization.

2. The U.N. organization still accomplished its goals in some areas, but the conflict extended even to the question of U.N. personnel and to allegations of abuse of diplomatic privilege by communist nations for purposes of espionage against the United States. On the other hand, there were occasions such as the outbreak of the Korean War (1950) when the Soviet Union by accident failed to veto a General Assembly resolution authorizing enforcement. The Soviet representatives had walked out in protest before the vote occurred.

tries into "captive nations" and democratic coalition governments into Stalinist dictatorships. The borderline between the Western Occupation Zones of Germany and the Soviet Zone became impassable, a line of division between two hostile worlds. The insular location of the Western sectors of Berlin in the midst of communist territory—and without guaranteed land access—became the setting for more than twenty years of repeated Berlin crises, beginning with the Soviet blockade of 1948. The West German zones and West Berlin became the strategic geopolitical toehold of the Western powers in a tug-of-war over Europe with an expansive Soviet empire. It was here that the West encouraged economic reconstruction in a setting of European cooperation, under the Marshall Plan, and here that the allies authorized the creation of a West German rump state,[3] the old Federal Republic (FRG), from the three Western Zones of Occupation. Thus the old FRG—and its East German counterpiece, the GDR—were clearly products of the Cold War. This is not to deny the eager cooperation of West German politicians such as the first West German Chancellor, Konrad Adenauer, nor the fact that the allies had the good sense to let the West Germans arrange their own government and the details of economic and military cooperation more or less as the latter preferred.[4]

German rearmament and integration into NATO is perhaps the most telling example of the changing relationship between the Western allies and their erstwhile enemy. NATO had evolved from the Brussels Treaty Organization of 1947, a defensive alliance against the possible resurgence of a German military threat at a time when a Soviet threat to West European peace was not yet a primary concern. The heating up of the Cold War—the communist coups in Czechoslovakia during 1948 and the division of Germany between the hostile blocs—suggested the necessity of rearming a rehabilitated West Germany and converting it and its territory into a strategic anticommunist fortress. This was at first attempted through the creation of a European Defense Community (EDC)

3. The changing international situation also explains the substantial modifications in the policies of industrial reparations and denazification which ensued along with the Cold War.

4. There is still a surprising amount of controversy on this point. Many left-wing critics insist that the Basic Law of the FRG was the result of allied interventions and preferences, and that the West German government did not undertake its treaties and contractual obligations to the Western allies and NATO of its own free will. These critics conveniently ignore the ample popular majorities that supported Adenauer and his government throughout the fifties. Except for small numbers of ideological opponents of a pro-Western course, the West German electorate was as unlikely to pass up such unique opportunities for economic and political rehabilitation under the protection of the Western alliance as the East German electorate was in 1990.

with the same membership as the European Coal and Steel Community (ECSC), a forerunner of the Common Market and, among other things, an attempt to bring the coal and steel resources that had supported the German war effort in two world wars permanently under international control. When the EDC failed to come off,[5] a substitute defense organization, the Western European Union (WEU), was designed that included Great Britain to strengthen the other West European nations against the weight of a rearmed West Germany. But the best solution of the problem was the North Atlantic Treaty Organization, headed by the United States, which with the waning of British power had become the new extracontinental maintainer of the balance in Europe against the Soviet challenge. The new West German army was integrated completely and at all levels into the NATO forces, so that German officers, soldiers, and equipment were available to hold off the Soviet threat without forming a national army under German command. Again, this was quite acceptable to the Adenauer government, which shared the apprehensions of Germany's Western neighbors about a resurgence of German aggressive nationalism. NATO was the perfect device, in the words of a British NATO general secretary, "to keep the Russians out, the Americans in, and the Germans down."

If the old Federal Republic for the forty-one years of its existence was largely a product of the East-West conflict, this was no less true of the German Democratic Republic, the Soviets' client state and military base in the heart of Central Europe. Just as the Americans were not quite sure of French and Italian support for the anti-Soviet alliance at the outset of the Cold War—large communist parties had emerged in both countries at the end of World War II—and for this reason had to rely more emphatically on the development of a strategic base in West Germany, the Soviets could not be sure in the long run of their East European satellites, Poland, Czechoslovakia, and Hungary, not to mention Tito's Yugoslavia. They had to rely even more heavily on a rearmed East Germany as the keystone of their arch of captive nations, held in place by externally buttressed communist dictatorships and the Warsaw Treaty Organization (WTO). And, as the reader will recall (Chapter Two), there were recurrent crises in East Germany (1953), Hungary (1956), Czechoslovakia (1968), and Poland (1956, 1980) when brutal military force, or the threat of it, appeared to be the only way to keep the Soviet empire together.

5. The EDC Treaty failed to be ratified in the French National Assembly, where fear of a remilitarized West Germany won out over the advocates of a new Franco-German partnership. French security concerns could be overcome only by adding Britain to the original six members of the ECSC and planned EDC.

Soviet Policy Toward Germany

These memories of the international realities of yesterday must have gone through the minds of many a German newspaper reader in April 1991 when parts of a press interview with ex-Foreign Minister Eduard Shevardnadze[6] sent chills up the spines of many Germans and East Europeans. The retired comrade-in-arms of President Gorbachev identified himself as an early (1986) advocate of German reunification. He mentioned to reporters that, toward the end of the eventful year 1989 and in the midst of the final unraveling of communist power throughout Eastern Europe, there had been enormous pressure on Gorbachev, presumably by the hard-liners in the Soviet army and the CPSU (and by the East European dictatorships), using "the psychology of great-power politics and empire," to stop all reforms and revolutions "in the manner of 1953, 1956, and 1968." The hard-liners accused Gorbachev of having brought on the escalating collapse of communist regimes with his *perestroika*. They urged him to use armed force along the lines of a revived Brezhnev Doctrine to beat down all popular protest and, presumably, to thwart any movement in the direction of German unification "with troops and border barricades, and by starting up the engines of the tanks." Indeed, losing the GDR to German unification removed the keystone of Soviet empire. Henceforth, resurgent Polish, Czechoslovak, Hungarian, Bulgarian, and Romanian nationalisms would each slip away in different directions, pushing what was left of Soviet power back to Soviet borders and, in some cases, perhaps even beyond those borders. Gorbachev and Shevardnadze did not buckle under the pressure of the hard-liners in 1989, however, and indeed countermanded any inclination in Leipzig, Prague, or Bucharest to crush insurrection, Beijing-style, with brute force.[7]

In 1985 Mikhail Gorbachev became general secretary of the CPSU, the position once occupied by Joseph Stalin, and at the 27th CPSU Congress (1986), he described the gathering internal crisis of the Soviet Union in detail. This was also the twenty-fifth anniversary of the erection of the Berlin Wall. A military parade of 8,000 East German soldiers marched

---

6. *Literaturnaya Gazeta*, Apr. 10, 1991, reported the interview, and from there it made most major European newspapers. See *Berliner Morgenpost*, Apr. 11, 1991, pp. 1–2, and *Der Spiegel* 45, no. 16, Apr. 15, 1991, p. 41. Shevardnadze was opposed, in particular, by the Foreign Ministry and by ex-Ambassador Valentin Falin, who regarded the GDR as the Soviet victory prize of World War II.

7. As recently as April 1989, the Soviet establishment still stood firmly against any thought of reconsidering the German situation, and it was unlikely to yield until about 90% of the old Politbureau membership changed in July 1990.

down Karl-Marx-Allee in East Berlin while Erich Honecker, in his address of commemoration, called the Wall "a historical deed that laid the foundation for sustained prosperity in East Germany." Meanwhile, West Berliners were laying wreaths at the many markers along the Wall that to this day recall the East German refugees killed there, and Chancellor Kohl said in the old Reichstag auditorium next to the Wall: "As long as there is a wall, barbed wire, and orders to shoot, there can be no talk of normality in Germany." A year later, President Reagan made his appearance at the Wall and challenged Gorbachev, in one of his more felicitous German photo opportunities, to "tear down this wall" if he really meant to be serious about winding down the Cold War.

The Soviet leader was indeed serious about *perestroika* but was hardly prepared to give his blessing to German unification, either in 1986 or in 1989. In July 1987, on the occasion of an official visit to the Kremlin, West German Federal President Richard von Weizsäcker had broached the German question and received a telling earful from Gorbachev himself. The Soviet general secretary told him, as reported by TASS: "There are two German states with different social systems. Each of them learned its lesson from history and they can each make their contributions to the cause of Europe and of peace. History will decide what may happen a hundred years from now. We cannot accept any other position and, if anyone would pursue a different path, there will be very serious consequences."[8]

Relations between Bonn and Moscow had been chilly since the breakdown of negotiations over intermediate-range missiles several years earlier—in fact, so frigid that even the GDR government of Erich Honecker made great efforts to shield the German-German relationship from the climate of East-West confrontations.[9] Soviet dogma on the German question remained well entrenched in the form in which the late Foreign Minister Andrei Gromyko had formulated and reiterated it again and again during his long tenure. The "aggressive circles of the U.S." were blamed for the failure of the Potsdam resolutions, for West German

8. Quoted from *Pravda*, Jul. 8, 1987, by Hans-Peter Riese, "Die Geschichte hat sich ans Werk gemacht. Der Wandel der sowjetischen Position zur deutschen Frage," *Europa Archiv*, no. 4 (Feb. 15, 1990), 117. See also Gerhard Wettig, "Stadien der sowjetischen Deutschlandpolitik," *Deutschland Archiv* 23, no. 7 (Jul. 1990), 1070–1078, and the sources cited there. Wettig describes the Soviet acquiescence as an on-again, off-again process in which the Soviet government's attitude softened in January/February only to harden again.

9. There had also been a flap when Kohl, in a press interview, compared Gorbachev with the Nazi propaganda chief Josef Goebbels. See Stephen F. Larrabee, "The View from Moscow," in Stephen F. Larrabee, ed., *The Two German States and European Security* (New York: St. Martin's Press, 1989), pp. 183–205.

rearmament in NATO, and for "the inclusion of the FRG in the crusade against the socialist countries" (a reference to President Reagan's campaign against the "evil empire"). These same forces now advocated "overcoming the division of Germany," but what they really meant was the "takeover of the GDR by the capitalist FRG" and the "step-by-step liquidation of the socialist order of other East European states." Any such attempt would mean war, and the Bonn pledges to achieve change "by peaceful means" were sheer deception. Similarly deceptive, according to Gromyko, were Bonn statements calling the (pre-1989) borders "provisional" and reserving their determination for a future peace conference, as well as all the talk about an "unsolved German question."[10] And although relations between Gorbachev and Honecker deteriorated in the late eighties—*perestroika* being quite unwelcome in East Berlin—the Soviet leader again told Chancellor Kohl during a visit in Moscow, in October 1988, that[11] "the current situation is the result of history. Attempts to change what is created, or unrealistic policies to force change raise incalculable and even dangerous risks."

History on the Brink of Decision

There is still much speculation about exactly how and when the Soviet government changed its mind about letting the Germans unite. One view raises speculations in retrospect about subtle changes of wording in Gorbachev's statements in 1989 leading up to his East Berlin visit of October 7, the fortieth anniversary of the GDR, when he said, "Life itself will punish those who come too late."[12] There had been pronouncements, such as the mention of the "principle of freedom of choice" before the United Nations (December 1988), that appeared to give a green light to the other East European satellites even if they too were slow to recognize it. In February and again in June of 1989, the Soviet leader clearly abandoned the Brezhnev Doctrine of armed intervention,[13] but even this

10. Quoted from *Sovietskaya Rossiya*, Jul. 17, 1985, by Riese, "Die Geschichte hat sich ans Werk gemacht," p. 91.

11. See Hannes Adomeit, "Gorbachev and German Unification: Revision of Thinking, Realignment of Power," *Problems of Communism* 39 (Jul./Aug. 1990), 1–23.

12. See, for example, the review of Gorbachev's statements by Riese, "Die Geschichte hat sich ans Werk gemacht," pp. 91–93. This and other phrases, at least with the benefit of hindsight, look like a warning of the change to come. See also Boris Meissner. "Das neue Denken Gorbatschows und die deutsche Frage," in Wjatscheslaw Daschitschew and Carl-Gustaf Ströhm, eds., *Die Neuordnung Mitteleuropas* (Mainz: Hase & Köhler, 1991), pp. 15–32, and his essay in *Aussenpolitik*, no. 2 (1989).

13. See Adomeit's survey, "Gorbachev and German Unification," pp. 4–5. The joint

did not necessarily apply to the GDR in quite the same way as it encouraged reformers in Poland and Hungary. The strategic importance of East Germany to Soviet defense and the 360,000 Soviet soldiers there gave the hard-line stance of the otherwise not very popular Honecker a significance not unlike that of Gibraltar for an otherwise decolonized British empire. This may well have been the ultimate dilemma of Gorbachev and Shevardnadze in the rapidly disintegrating East German situation of October/November 1989, when they refused to give in to the furious reaction of army generals and diplomats in Moscow who wanted to "send in an army a million strong to close the border" (Falin in East Berlin, November 1989). At the July 1990 party conference of the CPSU, an angry Yegor Ligachev and his party conservatives once more called for armed intervention—half a million soldiers—to secure the Soviet hold on the GDR, but it was too late. The East German cat was out of the bag, not to mention the other East European felines, and German unification had been sanctioned both internally and externally.[14]

The most plausible explanation still appears to be that the rapid acceleration of events, the very "history" to which Gorbachev likes to attribute so much, forced his hand and, after some confusing signals, forced him to accept gracefully a change he had not intended. The great exodus of refugees, the fall of the hated Honecker, the unexpected opening of the Berlin Wall, the disintegration of the SED state party, and the deterioration of the East German economy foreclosed what was undoubtedly Gorbachev's preferred choice: a reform communist GDR independent of West Germany. Even on December 3, 1989, just before the Malta summit, therefore, Gorbachev reiterated that

> as a result of many international treaties, including the Helsinki Agreements, there are two German states today, the FRG and the GDR, both members of the U.N., with full diplomatic relations,

declaration by Bonn and Moscow (June 1989) is cited as the proof that Gorbachev meant to let the GDR go, although he continued to object to unification for months to come.

14. By that time, following the currency and economic union and several rounds of agreement at the "two-plus-four" meetings, a Soviet resort to strong-arm methods might indeed have precipitated war between East and West, a threat (by Shevardnadze) that had been less plausible in late 1989. Half a year later, in January 1991, if the Soviets had attempted a strong-arm coup in the absence of U.S. and some other NATO forces, it might have succeeded in the event but would have been even more of an outrage, for by then the internal union of Germany had been formally completed and the Two-Plus-Four Treaty ratified by all except the Soviets (who signed it in March 1991). The abortive military coup of August 1991 apparently was careful to leave international implications alone for the time being. The Soviet Army Group West in East Germany, in particular, showed no sign of rebellion or unrest.

sovereign states. . . . We have an interest in what is going to happen with these two states, with the world, with Europe, with our civilization. Time will tell, history will decide. But to raise the question of reunification today would not be legitimate; it would make the situation worse. . . . But the changes in the FRG and GDR do open up possibilities of cooperation, and of the development of relations and of human contacts so that all this can follow a normal procedure. Let history decide. One should not artificially trigger or accelerate processes that have not yet reached maturity.[15]

Two and a half weeks later, in a speech before the Political Committee of the EC Parliament in Brussels, Eduard Shevardnadze dotted the i's and crossed the t's of the Soviet change of position when he qualified the principle of "self-determination" by the two German states with an "application only in the context of the norms and principles of international law, the peculiar status of both German states, and their responsibility before the nations of Europe and the world never to permit another war to start from German soil." He added, in the form of questions, the following "conditions":[16]

1. What guarantees of a political, legal, or material sort can protect the security and peace of other European states from the consequences of German unity?
2. Would such a unified Germany really accept the existing borders in Europe and drop all territorial claims (for the return of lost German land)?
3. What role would such a German nation-state play in the existing military-political structures?
4. What would be its military potential? Would it be prepared to accept demilitarization, neutrality, and a mandate to restructure Eastern Europe economically and otherwise?
5. How would it act toward the presence of allied troops on German soil and with regard to the allied liaison missions and the Four-Power Agreements of 1971 (on Berlin)?
6. How would it fit into the CSCE (Helsinki) process? Would it help to overcome the division of Europe and to create a cohesive,

15. Quoted from *Pravda*, Dec. 3, 1989, by Riese, "Die Geschichte hat sich ans Werk gemacht," p. 94.
16. The formula "never to permit another war to start from German soil" repeats the formulations of previous joint statements by the SPD and the SED, as well as statements by Green pacifists. See also Riese, ibid., pp. 95–97, for the statement.

       nondiscriminatory legal, economic, environmental, and cultural
       European union, without any discrimination?
   7. Would the two German states be prepared, upon reunification, to
       seek collective solutions agreeable to the other European states,
       including a European peace settlement?

As a world power, one of the major allies of World War II, and a nation
that lost 27 million dead to the German war machine, the Soviet Union
believed it had a right to raise these questions.

By the end of January 1990, the dynamics of the economic and political
crisis of the GDR left no doubt that the situation had reached "maturity."
Upon the visit of GDR Premier Hans Modrow and, ten days later,
Helmut Kohl, General Secretary Gorbachev made clear the Soviet agreement in principle to German unification. Kohl returned in triumph from
Moscow, proclaiming he held the "key to German unification" in his
hand. Gorbachev, however, still proposed conditions for his specific
assent to German unification: Soviet interests must not be irreversibly
damaged by German union and, consequently, Shevardnadze's list of
searching questions still represented the particular concerns of Moscow,
including a desire to demilitarize and neutralize the emerging popular
and economic giant in the middle of Europe. The entire fabric of the
Soviet empire in Eastern Europe had changed profoundly by January
1990, and the Soviet Union itself was hardly in the pink of health. Years
of *perestroika* had failed to bring economic prosperity and modernization. Instead, nationalist movements and ethnic violence tore at the very
fabric of the Soviet Union in the Baltic states, Moldavia, and in the south
and southeast.

It would be simplistic, however, to assume that such weakness and
preoccupation with problems close to home would incline a great power
to yield to its long-standing antagonists. To the contrary, the Soviets'
problems and weaknesses made them less willing to give away their
strategic position to NATO. Fortunately, the bullying of the Reagan
administration had ceased anyway and, in the crucial period from late
1989 to mid-1990, Americans, West Europeans, and especially the West
Germans treated the Soviet reluctance to release East Germany or a
united Germany to NATO with patience and understanding. West German Foreign Minister Hans-Dietrich Genscher, in particular, presented
an agreeable compromise: West Germany would remain with NATO,
which was in a process of change anyway, setting lower force levels and
lower levels of readiness for combat. East Germany would leave the
Warsaw Pact and join the Federal Republic economically and politically,
but would not be part of NATO territory. It would be demilitarized,

barred from the stationing of NATO troops, and have its own limited territorial defense forces. The 360,000 Soviet troops stationed in the GDR, finally, would remain there for the next few years.

With such gentle persuasion, by mid-1990, the Soviet government eventually came to accept the reasoning that—since the neutralization of a united Germany was quite unacceptable to the Western powers—NATO would offer sufficient guarantees to keep a possible German military threat to the East under control. After all, the containment of a resurgent Germany had always been a second major purpose of NATO, next to containing Soviet expansion, and there was a broad consensus among all powers that Germany should not have a national army of its own and under its own command. The Kohl government itself was emphatic in its desire not to be isolated from its European neighbors on both sides and to be seen as a friendly government by the USSR.

On July 16, during Kohl's visit to Zhelezdnovodsk, near Gorbachev's old haunts—only days after the stormy 28th Congress of the CPSU— Gorbachev agreed that a unified Germany could belong to NATO. This was the great break facilitated by the changeover of most of the Politbureau membership. Kohl in turn accepted a cap on German troop strength of 370,000, about half the size of the West and East German forces at the time, and pledged again that Germany would possess neither nuclear, biological, nor chemical weapons. Kohl also promised 13 billion marks toward paying and supplying the Soviet troops on German soil and toward their repatriation and housing in the Soviet Union which was to be completed in 1994.[17] At this moment, the process of German unification had turned the international corner, and soon the Two-Plus-Four Treaty sealed the deal. This was the moment Chancellor Kohl later referred to when he claimed, "I only had two or three weeks in which German unification became a possibility, internationally speaking."

Some observers have suggested that the agreement in the Caucasus merely reflected the existing economic ties between West Germany and the Soviet Union. It is true that East German trade with the Soviets had all along amounted to about 10–12%—two-thirds of East German foreign trade—and West German trade to another 4–5% of Soviet trade, but the Soviet Union had not played a major role in the West German economy. Nevertheless, Gorbachev's economic modernization program

17. Until the currency union, when the West German government took on the expense in deutschmarks, the GDR had paid close to 3 billion East marks annually for the Soviet stationing cost. See *Der Spiegel* 44, nos. 29 and 31, July 16 and Aug. 20, 1990. Total payments to the Soviet Union were said to be close to 50 billion marks, including trade obligations of the GDR (17 billion marks), export credits (15 billion marks), and future credit backing (5–20 billion marks). See *The Economist*, June 29, 1991, p. 43.

for the Soviet Union strategically depended on technology and high-quality imports—to the extent that they were not embargoed by the Cocom list which the Germans were insistent on revising. Germany might profit from an expansion of oil and natural gas imports from the Soviet Union to close its gap in energy supplies. West German bank credits and loans (3 billion marks in 1988) were another crucial resource for Soviet modernization. East German exports to the Soviet Union were at a high before German economic unification, at least until the deutsch-mark came to the GDR. After that point, continued Soviet purchases required West German hard currency loans which might never be repaid, and which increased Soviet indebtedness to Germany to great heights. As of April 1991, Germany also had more joint ventures in the Soviet Union (244, with an investment of nearly $300 million) than any other Western state. In June 1991, moreover, a new 5 billion marks credit was agreed on and, after Zhelezdnovodsk, the German financial commitment grew tenfold. Studies from the Berlin Institute of German Economic Research (DIW) predicted a tripling of Soviet trade, of which Germany might get the lion's share.

Following Zhelezdnovodsk and the Two-Plus-Four Treaty granting complete sovereignty to a united Germany, the new Soviet-German entente reached a landmark with the signing (November 9, 1990)—one year after the collapse of the Wall—and eventual ratification (April/May 1991) of the "good neighbor" treaties between the two governments. The treaties passed the Bundestag in a rare show of unanimity. The first treaty states that it is of primary importance to "finally be done with the past, and to use understanding and reconciliation to . . . overcome Europe's division." The twenty-year friendship treaties aimed at expanding bilat-eral ties and building greater trust, especially by renouncing all territorial claims and providing a framework for economic-technical cooperation and political consultation—one summit and at least two foreign minis-terial meetings a year—as well as assistance in setting up the new Soviet social security system. The agreements, dubbed the Treaty on Good Neighborliness, Partnership, and Cooperation, also assured the Soviet troops of German respect and guaranteed cultural and language rights to the German-speaking minority in the Soviet Union, about 2.5 million people whose roots go back centuries and who were stripped of their Volga German Republic and dispersed by Stalin in 1945. Even though substantial numbers of German-Russians (400,000) have already mi-grated to Germany or are prepared to do so, the Soviet parliament has promised to reestablish the Volga German Republic, and a German-Russian deputy, Alexander Bier, has proposed a plebiscite to ascertain the wishes of the population of the Saratov and Volgograd areas in that regard.

Attitudes of Germany's Western Allies

While West Germany's allies were at first reluctant to disentangle the German state from its international treaty and occupation status prior to 1989, the public response in most allied nations was very encouraging from the start. One month after the fall of the Wall, a *New York Times/CBS* poll ascertained that two-thirds of the American adult respondents (67%) supported a reunification of the FRG and the GDR (16% feared a united Germany might try to dominate the world). A *Business Week* and Lou Harris poll found 76% for and 16% against German unification.[18] A *Los Angeles Times/Economist* poll in January 1990—when unification had become likely—however, gave a more thoughtful response. It confirmed the American level of support at 61% and added 61% among the French, but only 45% in Britain and 41% in Poland. No less than 53% of Britons feared a return of German fascism, and 38% of the French echoed this fear. But only 30% of Britons were actually opposed to German unification, and a large majority expected it to come about anyway.[19]

The outpouring of sentiment from average people was not quite matched at the level of the news media (see Introduction) or of official government policies—except perhaps among American politicians, where outright opposition was rare. Even the Polish-American Congress, which might have been expected to share the apprehension of the Polish government about Chancellor Kohl's prevarications regarding the Oder-Neisse line, combined its mild reminder on this issue with a clear endorsement of the German right to self-determination. Coverage of the East German scene and of the steps toward economic union was unusually strong and consistent among the U.S. news media.[20] The attitude in Congress and

18. See the *New York Times*, Dec. 12, 1989, and *Business Week*, Nov. 27, 1989. An earlier poll in October ascertained the support of 71% of the French, 70% of the British, 83% of the Italians, and 56% of the West Germans (!) for German unification. Cited by Richard Davy, "Grossbritannien und die deutsche Frage," *Europa Archiv*, no. 4 (Feb. 15, 1990), 139–144.

19. See *The Economist*, Jan. 27, 1990, p. 48.

20. See especially Michael H. Haltzel, "Amerikanische Einstellungen zur deutschen Wiedervereinigung," *Europa Archiv*, no. 4 (Feb. 15, 1990), 127–132. See also Karl Kaiser, *Deutschlands Vereinigung. Die internationalen Aspekte* (Bergisch-Gladbach: Lübbe-Bastei, 1991), pp. 21–25 and 49–58, who pays particular tribute to American support.

the White House toward German reunification, ever since the 1952 agreements (amended in 1954) which turned West Germany from an occupied country into a NATO partner with few remaining allied reservations, had always supported German aspirations on paper. This included, if in a rather halfhearted way, Bonn's insistence on leaving the final settlement of reparations and border questions to a peace treaty. Washington was certainly not reluctant to accept the solemn West German pledges of 1971 and 1975 not to contest the eastern borders by force.

When the Wall fell and German unification actually became a likely prospect, however, the Bush administration was taken by surprise. It reacted with ritual reiteration of formulas that had been used for forty years of the Cold War, formulas that seemed to endorse everything the Germans could want. Eventually, however, it dawned on the Republican establishment that the Cold War was winding down—in spite of continual warnings from conservative voices that Gorbachev was not to be trusted or was about to fall himself—and that a faltering Soviet Union, the emancipation of Eastern Europe, and the unification of Germany were potentially very destabilizing events both for NATO and for European order and peace. The extraordinary pace of events in East Germany alarmed Washington as it alarmed Moscow. We would not be far from the truth to assume that Washington, too, was fearful of any attempt to "artificially trigger or accelerate processes that have not yet reached maturity" (Gorbachev). In this climate, even Kohl's supercautious ten-point program seemed an alarming initiative and there were complaints about our not having been consulted, as there were to be at the time of the Zhelezdnovodsk meeting.

At the Malta summit, President Bush and General Secretary Gorbachev, appropriately tossed together by turbulent seas, agreed that there should be no precipitate measures taken that might endanger the stable order of post–Cold War Europe. At the NATO meeting in Brussels (December 4, 1989), President Bush proposed four principles regarding German unification: 1) leave the outcome of German self-determination and possible form of union open; 2) tie German unification to NATO and to the further integration of the European Community, as well as to the rights and obligations of the allied powers; 3) keep efforts toward union peaceful and gradual in the interest of general stability in Europe; and 4) embrace the principles of the Final Act of Helsinki regarding the question of borders.

A week later, Secretary of State James A. Baker met Prime Minister Modrow in Potsdam and repeated these four principles before the Press Club of West Berlin, where he also spoke of "a new architecture for a new age," consisting of a reformed and broadened NATO, a European Community with new links of American participation, and the Council on Security and Cooperation in Europe (CSCE) of the Helsinki Agreements. The remarks about NATO came as no surprise, for the organization had been open to the discussion of détente and other changes since the days of the Harmel Report of 1967. More novel was the reference to the CSCE, which had long been seen as a Soviet creation and regarded with considerable suspicion in Washington. The U.S. government even signaled its support for another Helsinki summit in late 1990, provided that the Vienna Conference on the Reduction of Conventional Forces in Europe (CFE) had by then produced some results. The CSCE was credited with progress in human rights and freedom of travel in Eastern Europe and, it was hoped, would have an important supporting role in the development of elections and democratic government throughout the newly emancipated states of the region.

In all this, the Bush administration was careful not to weaken Gorbachev's internal position which it had come to embrace. The Soviet leader had initially expressed his opposition to German unification and hinted that it would precipitate his downfall. When Gorbachev came around to accepting a "neutralized" united Germany, Chancellor Kohl immediately objected to German neutrality. Then Genscher devised his compromise plan for neutralizing only East Germany, and the plan was quickly adopted by the United States before most of the details had been clarified. Gorbachev in time accepted it too once he had succeeded in shoring up his support at home.[21] Given the historical precedents of Soviet/Russian cooperation with Germany from the days of Bismarck and earlier (the Rapallo Treaty of Weimar days [1922], the Hitler-Stalin pact of 1939, and of course the forty years of the GDR), the Western fears of a "Stavrapallo"—an allusion to Gorbachev's old home grounds in Stavropol—form a natural part of the difficult choices confronting American policymakers. German neutrality would be only one step removed from the tradition of German *Schaukelpolitik* (policy of the swing) between East and West, and from collusion with the East against the West.

German policymakers and public opinion have credited the Bush administration, and especially the president himself and his secretary, Baker, with a major role supporting German unification through its

21. There had been considerable speculation about whether the United States could really have stopped the Germans from a neutralized, pro-Soviet, or "equidistant" course between the powers. See Rowland Evans and Robert Novak, "Will Bush 'Lose' Germany?" *Washington Post*, Dec. 27, 1989. An election mandate of this direction in the March elections of the GDR and a neutralist turn in West German opinion might have put the United States in an awkward position.

difficult first year. Only Gorbachev and Shevardnadze have been perceived as supporters in similar, glowing terms. On the other hand, German public opinion has also been aware of the frequently critical voices in the American press against whom the Bush administration pursued its German policy.

Great Britain and France

If Washington was able to rally to a consistent and supportive policy because the changes in the Soviet Union, Eastern Europe, and the reunification of Germany, if unexpected, corresponded more or less to long-established goals of American foreign policy, this was hardly true of France, Great Britain, and Germany's other neighbors in Europe. France and Britain, in particular, faced the prospect of a considerable shift in their respective weight in the European Community and Western alliance and, worst yet, little leverage in influencing the specific course which developments might take. For France, in particular, the option of exercising leverage through NATO—a crucial lever that was used particularly by the United States—was not available since France had left NATO in the early years of de Gaulle's presidency. France was reduced to emphasizing the leverage through the European Community which, at this point, was still mostly an economic and not a political union. Britain, by the same logic, could not use its EC leverage because the Thatcher administration was in the middle of a major rearguard battle against the EC program to "deepen" European integration after 1992, a battle in which the fear of losing British sovereignty to a European political union, currency, and central bank were joined with age-old prejudices against the French—"the poodles of the Germans" (Nicholas Ridley)—and the World War I and II animosity against the Germans. Margaret Thatcher and half her cabinet, as well as President Mitterrand, were of a generation that could vividly recall the German assault in the Second World War and that, therefore, reacted with great alarm at the prospect of revived German might and, half a year later, at the renewed entente of Zhelezdnovodsk. The two countries could have combined forces and, at the very least, delayed German unification beyond its narrow window of opportunity in mid-1990, had they been able to overcome their mutual distrust and had not the victorious superpower of the West—also led by a war generation president, but a veteran of the Pacific theater—confidently steered the Western alliance along a path of East-West reconciliation and German unification.

France, Germany's most important continental partner in Western Europe until then, was as surprised by the dramatic turn of events in 1989 as anyone. The great upheaval in Eastern Europe captured the popular imagination and, as noted above, ample majorities supported German self-determination and unification as well. Perhaps, the bicentennial of the French Revolution also helped to awaken French sympathies for the demonstrators of Leipzig who eventually brought down the communist dictatorship. On the other hand, the French commemorated the fiftieth anniversary of the German invasion of their country (May 10, 1940) with many a bitter editorial and reminiscence, with appropriate comments on the *"incertitudes allemandes,"* and the *"grosse Allemagne"* of past and future. But in November 1989, the Mitterrand government had emphasized the role of the four allies in any change of status of the two Germanys, when pressed by journalists who had also questioned the Soviet leader. A month later in another press interview, Mitterrand said he could not imagine that the Germans would want to sacrifice European unity to their own, but there were many voices in his administration and in the French press who could indeed.[22] Worse yet, whereas the French stressed West German commitment to a "deepening" of the European Community in its present borders, the British promoted precisely the broader, East European reference points for a solution of the German question that the French feared.

Mitterrand also insisted on the democratic and peaceful nature of any progress in this direction and mentioned the need to persuade not only the four wartime allies but also the GDR, which at the time was still known to oppose unification. Perhaps he could have "guided the course of German unification," as *Le Figaro* editor Franz-Olivier Giesbert put it in his biography of Mitterrand but, instead, he just let it happen as something inevitable. French policy had long accepted the survival of the GDR as a guarantee of European stability and of the presence of the Soviet power in the midst of Europe, keeping the Federal Republic in the Western alliance. France had been the only Western ally to exchange visits at the highest level with the GDR, in early 1988, and Mitterrand chose to visit the Modrow government, after several postponements, just ahead of Kohl the week before Christmas 1989.[23] France was quite happy

22. *Nouvel Observateur*, Jul. 27, 1989. He also doubted that the Soviet Union would ever accept German unification. On French reactions to German unification, see especially Ingo Kolboom, *Vom geteilten zum vereinigten Deutschland. Deutschland-Bilder in Frankreich* (Bonn: Europa Union, April 1991), pp. 9–12, and the reprinted French magazine covers on pp. 80–106.

23. Concerned about Honecker's refusal to adopt *perestroika* in the GDR, the French government had expressed its apprehensions and had postponed its state visit twice. Mitterrand had also declared ten years earlier, during the European elections of 1979, that

with the division of Europe—despite such slogans as "one Europe from
the Atlantic to the Ural Mountains" (de Gaulle) or "overcoming Yalta"
(Mitterrand). The unity-bent Germans were simply "in too much of a
hurry," said Foreign Minister Roland Dumas in a press interview with
Der Spiegel magazine (June 5, 1990). Dumas (age sixty-seven), whose
father was in the Resistance and was executed by the German occupation
for his activities, is also of the war generation.

The accelerating crisis of the GDR regime knocked most of these
considerations of an East-West balance into a cocked hat and left the
French government mute and helpless. At this point, the close and cordial
relations of the entire postwar period—between Konrad Adenauer and
Robert Schuman, later with Charles de Gaulle, and between Helmut
Schmidt and Giscard d'Estaing, far less between Kohl and Mitterrand—
the Franco-German entente of the European Community, began to collide
with the geopolitical rivalry between France and a prospective, considerably enlarged Germany at the center of Europe. President Mitterrand
(age seventy-three) remembered the war and the Third Reich all too well,
although most of his party leaders and cabinet members belonged to the
two postwar generations. He pointed to the risk of "destabilizing the
existing East-West balance" at a time when that balance had long been
irretrievably lost. Foreign Minister Dumas, on the other hand, insisted on
pressing the agenda for further European integration, which held the
promise of tying down the emerging giant in constructive ways.[24] The
French government was particularly concerned about the German commitment to the maintenance of European borders guaranteed by the
Helsinki Agreements (CSCE), which the Bonn government had signed in
1975. The French government felt that Kohl's ten-point statement (November 28, 1989) should have included a pledge to respect the Oder-
Neisse line and expressed genuine alarm at the flap over the border
question. Like President de Gaulle, thirty years earlier, Mitterrand also
made French assent contingent on the express renunciation of nuclear
arms by Germany. France, however, was still building the atomic Hadés
missile (range: 300 miles), which could reach much of Germany. In the
conservative newspaper *Le Figaro*, moreover, Edouard Balladur raised

German unification was neither likely nor desirable. See Wilfried Loth, *Ost-West Konflikt
und deutsche Frage* (Stuttgart: DTV, 1989), p. 46ff.

24. French public opinion in favor of German unification had been rising since August
and was quite free of the caustic slogans concerning the "rise of a Fourth Reich" (Conor
Cruise O'Brien) which could be heard in Britain at this time. But see the popular
apprehensions expressed by Alain Minc, *La Grande Illusion* (Paris: Grasset, 1989) and
Michel Koriman, *Quand l'Allemagne pensait le monde. Grandeur et décadence d'une
géopolitique* (Paris: Fayard, 1990).

the crucial Eurostrategic question of whether there would emerge a neutral, unified Germany outside of NATO and the Warsaw Pact (WTO), the worst possible scenario in the eyes of France[25] but the obvious preference of the Soviet Union at the time. This disagreement was a major obstacle to a renewal of the old strategic alliance of French and Soviet interests.

In the end, the Mitterrand government decided to combine cautious support for Kohl with an emphasis on European integration, the CSCE (Helsinki) organization, and working out problems on the basis of the occupation rights of the old Allied Control Council for Germany and the treaties and arrangements modifying those rights.[26] As the French saw it, the Kohl government and its predecessors had made a sincere commitment to European integration and could be expected to live up to its pledge within reason. The French public also maintained its generous support for German unification even though the perception of worrisome consequences was widespread. A Sofres poll ascertained that 58% of French adults were "for German reunification," 9% against, and 28% indifferent. But large majorities saw a united Germany as economically (83% yes, 6% no), politically (70% yes, 17% no), and even militarily (44% yes, 35% no)—despite the French *force de frappe*—predominant in Europe. Young Frenchmen and Frenchwomen were significantly more positive about German unity than those over age sixty-five. In another Sofres poll, nearly half the French respondents (43%) feared that German unification would make European unification more difficult—20% thought it would become easier, 25% that it might not make a difference—and nearly that many (37%) believed it would weaken France. Another 62% believed that a united Germany would dominate the European Community. Nevertheless, a large majority of French (67%) and Germans (54%) in October considered themselves "best friends."

British opinion on German politics and culture had long been divided along two opposite strands: a negative syndrome fed by the emotions of two world wars and a sense of competition to the bitter end—in World

25. The U.S. Secretary of State, James Baker, had insisted from the beginning that a united Germany should be in NATO, but the Quai d'Orsay and knowledgeable observers believed this to be an unacceptable choice for the Soviets. See *Le Figaro*, Nov. 16, 1989. The French foreign minister feared that the Soviet Union might offer the Germans a bargain they could hardly refuse: reunification in exchange for neutralization.

26. See "Frankreich angesichts der deutschen Einheit," by Walter Schütze, the general secretary of the Franco-German Study Group of the Institut Français des Relations Internationales (IFRI) (Paris), in *Europa Archiv*, no. 4 (Feb. 15, 1990), 133–138, and the polls reprinted in Kolboom, *Vom geteilten zum vereinigten Deutschland*, pp. 70–79, and in *Das Profil der Deutschen. Was sie vereint, was sie trennt* (Hamburg: Spiegel-Spezial, Jan. 1991), pp. 24–27. The polls range from October 1988 to January 1991.

War I Britain even banned the public performance of Wagnerian music—
and a positive one based on old alliances, shared antagonists (France, the
Hapsburg empire) and considerable cultural influence (e.g., in British
elite education), which generally was abandoned after 1945. The discredit of German cultural influence as a result of Nazi crimes and two
wars, of course, explains why many educated young Britons, but also
young Americans, Scandinavians, and other Europeans after 1945, did
not acquire the familiarity with the German language and German
cultural figures that many of their fathers and mothers still had. As a
factor running contrary to the direct effect of the wartime experience on
pro- and anti-German attitudes, this deserves some emphasis. The postwar generations of Germany's neighbors might lack the well-founded
hostility of their predecessors, but they were also far less familiar with
the postwar Germans. In countries like the Netherlands, Denmark, or
Italy, the negative views of Germany by both old and young tended to
predominate.

The government of Great Britain had signed as many treaties committing it to German reunification as anyone in the alliance, in particular the
Germany Treaty of 1952/54 and later agreements. Under the combative
Thatcher administration, which next to Mrs. Thatcher (age sixty-four)
included many members of the World War II generation, however, the
sudden prospect of unification was received with a belligerent attitude
worthy of a threat of renewed German attack on the British isles. One
British observer, Richard Davy of Oxford, suggested three specifically
British elements behind the strong reaction, all relating to World War II
and the British reluctance to become involved with the continent. Great
Britain was never conquered and occupied by the Germans and, for that
reason, never experienced the many forms of collaboration and proximity
that have colored most of the other continental neighbors' feelings about
the Germans for the last fifty years. Distance and late entry into the
European Community also gave Great Britain an outsider status among
continentals and a marginal position vis-à-vis the Franco-German duo-
poly. Finally, Davy mentioned the mythology in public opinion and
television concerning the Second World War as a high point of British
history after which economic decline and the erosion of British influence
in the world are seen to have occurred.[27] The rise of defeated Germany to
prosperity and power was perceived as the counterpoint to the humbling
of British imperial pride, even though the latter had very little to do with
the former. To be sure, there had been earlier German challenges to

27. Richard Davy, "Grossbritannien und die deutsche Frage," *Europa Archiv*, no. 4
(Feb. 15, 1990), 139–144.

British dominance in the twentieth century, especially in 1914 and 1939, but Great Britain had always won the contest. If Britons now felt subjectively they were the losers vis-à-vis their German competitors, moreover, it could only be a matter of economic prowess and not of military posture or the "return of German fascism," as a majority of Britons said they feared. The Gulf War finally deflated the myth of a German military threat to Great Britain, argued so passionately by Nicholas Ridley and Conor Cruise O'Brien, and turned the issue into British complaints about German cowardice and unwillingness to fight.

The warnings of O'Brien in the London *Times* (Oct. 31) and of Lord Rees-Mogg in *The Independent* (Dec. 4) were extreme enough to generate a reaction. O'Brien had predicted the rise of a Fourth Reich that might "rehabilitate racial theories" and erect a monument to Hitler in every town. Or, as he added as an afterthought in the *Times* (Nov. 17), it would at least resemble the empire of Bismarck and the Hohenzollerns. Rees-Mogg conjured up the rise of a "German Age" but expressed the hope that it would not be characterized by the swastika and by concentration camps. A number of notable journalists and politicians such as ex–Prime Minister James Callahan (Labour) pointed out the democratic record of forty years of West German government or pleaded to give the Germans a chance to show what they would actually do.[28] The extreme contrasts between these alternative futures, in any case, tended to obscure the real issues relevant to British options in regard to future cooperation with Germany and the European Community. The wild speculations about the presumable intent of future German governments and their supporters also obstructed any realistic discussion of the real problem of German unification for the European allies: the size of the German population and economy.

The younger generations and British businessmen had long suffered under the Thatcherite reluctance to become involved with the continent and continental nations like the French and the Germans. Like the younger generations on the continent, they exhibit far less pride in the British nation and empire than that which still motivates their elders of the Ridley and Thatcher generation. They have little fear of the measures for further integration of the European Community and are anxious not to be left out when European economic opportunities resulting from these measures beckon. They tend to view the European Community as promising a tide of prosperity that will raise their ships as well.[29]

28. See Bernard Levin in *The Times* (London), Nov. 2, 1989, and James Callahan, ibid., Jan. 5, 1990. Also see *The Economist*, Jan. 27, 1990, and Peter Jenkins in *The Independent*, Feb. 1, 1990.
29. With Prime Minister Thatcher, the transitional thinking of Manchesterism and

The Thatcher administration reacted at first with anger to Kohl's ten points of November 28, 1989, reading a curiously patronizing interpretation of the "responsibility of the allies for German reunification" into the appropriate clause (art. 7) of the Germany Treaty of 1952/54: "Until the final regulation in a peace treaty, the signatory states will work peacefully towards the realization of their common goal: a reunified Germany with a liberal democratic constitution like that of the FRG and integrated into the European community of nations." There was a strong feeling that the allies should have been consulted, and even Egon Krenz did not escape criticism for "having opened the Wall" without consulting the Soviets. Better counsel soon prevailed, however, as events escalated during the following two months. By February 1990, when even the Kremlin had approved unification in principle, Foreign Secretary Douglas Hurd was ready to spell out a more pragmatic approach—the secret Thatcher seminar of experts on Germany was meant to brief Mrs. Thatcher on German "national attributes" for an impending Kohl visit—which concentrated on *how* and no longer on *whether* unification would take place. A "confederative arrangement" between the FRG and the GDR might slow down the process by which Thatcherite England felt it was being pulled into European integration. Slowing it down and reinforcing the status quo by leaving some Soviet troops in the GDR would "force us to appraise the current situation correctly," she said in an interview with *Der Spiegel* magazine (March 27, 1990). A closer relationship between Germany and the Soviet Union, on the other hand, was an alarming development and needed to be avoided. The CSCE, NATO, and even the Warsaw Pact might provide sea anchors in the approaching storm, calming the effect of the forces of change on the status quo.

The replacement of Mrs. Thatcher with John Major in the fall of 1990 put an end not only to her campaign against further European integration—it was preceded by the Venice EC summit at which she had pretended to be a victim, surrounded by malevolent continentals scheming to take advantage of British sovereignty—but also to the official hostility to the Kohl government and to German unification.[30] Her

---

imperial pride seemed to be combined with a personal dislike for Germans and for Chancellor Kohl in particular. Her tendency to orient her international policies toward the superpowers, moreover, has inspired both a kind of jealousy in regard to the growth of a special relationship between Washington and Bonn and an exaggerated desire to support Gorbachev by avoiding steps that might embarrass him. In a January 1990 interview with the *Wall Street Journal*, Mrs. Thatcher somehow connected the possible disequilibrium in the European Community, resulting from German unification, with dire consequences for Gorbachev himself.

30. In some circles, British-German backbiting had taken on amazing forms. In a curious counterpoint to the Chequers seminar on German national "characteristics," West German

successor by no means abandoned Britain's reservations about the European financial and economic plans, but preferred early and active involvement to a defensive rearguard battle. By means of visits to various European leaders, particularly Chancellor Kohl, Prime Minister Major set out to take a direct hand in shaping the anticipated EC measures and, in the process, discovered some of the commonly held interests of Britons and Germans. His initiative was gratefully received in Bonn where the German policymakers had really been at a loss regarding well-considered responses to British hostility.[31]

Canadian opinion on German unification did not differ notably from that in the United States. In Italy and the Benelux countries there was a mixture of supportive and very critical comments. Some voices in the Italian press, in particular, expressed great apprehension of the political and economic power of a united Germany. In the ensuing discussion of which countries among the numerous World War II belligerents ought to participate in the final peace settlement, the Italian government also tried to put in a claim, presumably on the basis of the argument that it, too, fell under hostile German occupation in the last year of war, lost 40,000 casualties to Nazi occupation, and ought to ask for reparations from its erstwhile Axis ally. This claim was not accepted by the powers of the "two-plus-four" group.

One of the first governments to raise objections to possible German unification plans was the Likud government of Israel, whose Prime Minister Itzak Shamir, already in November 1989, had remarked on American television that "a strong and united Germany might again try to annihilate the Jewish people." He was soon echoed by former Defense Minister Ariel Sharon: "We must not forget what the Germans did to us when they were united." Nobel Prize winner Elie Wiesel added, in *Der Spiegel* magazine early in 1991, that "we Jews cannot consider a unification of Germany. We have to think twice about the implications." These opinions, however, were soon contradicted by other Jewish voices, such as the Israel-born Munich historian Michael Wolffsohn who, in his book

---

business managers were at one point reported discussing publicly the alleged inferiority of the British "business culture" or entrepreneurial climate, with predictable consequences of mutual recrimination and countercharges.

31. Chancellor Kohl's first response to the disclosures about Ridley's statements and the Chequers seminar was appropriate but not particularly constructive. He was reported to have called them, with a chuckle, "rather silly." See also the discussion of various top-level Anglo-German relationships, from the warmth between Chancellor Brandt and Edward Heath to the new entente of Kohl and Major, in *The Economist*, March 9, 1991, pp. 51–52. The same issue also describes the contribution of British television to the anti-German stereotypes of the nation.

No Need to Fear Germany [Keine Angst vor Deutschland], criticized German intellectuals Günter Grass and Walter Jens who use Auschwitz as a "political means of buying souls against reunification." Wolffsohn argued that the German division was the result of the "rivalries of power politics and ideology," and not of a moral judgment, and that there is no logical nexus connecting Auschwitz and reunification. There were other voices on both sides, including sober accounts of the forty-year history of Bonn's efforts to give restitution both to individual survivors and to the state of Israel—which has resulted in the "special relationship" of the two peoples, if not without some flaws, breakdowns, and misunderstandings on both sides.

The prospect of German unification even lit a fire under the last communist premier of the GDR, Hans Modrow, to reverse decades of anti-Zionism, nonrecognition of Israel, and support for Arab terrorist groups. Since early February 1990, representatives of the GDR and of Israel had been at work in Copenhagen, preparing the ground for diplomatic relations. Israel insisted that the GDR must recognize, for the GDR population, the German responsibility for the holocaust and agree to restitution for the victims. In mid-February, then, the GDR premier wrote President E. Bronfman of the Jewish World Congress that "the GDR accepts the responsibility of the whole German people for the past . . . crimes against the Jewish people" and indicated "a willingness to grant solidary material support to former Nazi victims of persecution of Jewish origin." This completed the German acknowledgment of the responsibility for the holocaust—the newly elected government of Lothar de Maizière followed suit—and reinforced the German-Israeli relationship in time for the actual measures of the unification that had so troubled some Jewish observers. A poll of 1,200 Israelis conducted by Hebrew University of Jerusalem in May 1990—on the twenty-fifth anniversary of the establishment of West German–Israeli diplomatic relations—revealed that two-thirds of Israelis considered the German-Israeli relationship "normal." Eight years earlier, only one-third of Israeli adults had said so. Even more significant was the finding that a substantial majority, 57% (it had been only 40% in 1982) of Israelis no longer held "today's Germans" responsible for the holocaust. This was, of course, not the end of critical voices, which would be heard again at the time of the Zhelezdnovodsk meeting, along with Nicholas Ridley, when Britain's Chief Rabbi, Lord Jacobovits made a public appeal for international guarantees to prevent "a resurgence of German militarism" and to ensure that never again would "hate propaganda, religious oppression, or the persecution of minorities be tolerated, or excused by the claim, as used by the Nazis, that these were purely German matters."[32]

The Hapsburg Spell Without the Empire

While it was a matter of first priority to look at the policies and attitudes of the great powers and West European leaders toward German unification, that only explains the past and is hardly enough to gauge the future role of a united Germany, now that the unification has taken place. The drastic changes in Eastern Europe, and increasingly in parts of the Soviet Union, constitute an extraordinary opportunity for German economic power (and, perhaps also, political influence) to expand into the great vacuum and willy-nilly to develop a hegemonic position in the East. Such a shift of politicoeconomic power from the old FRG to the East—possibly implied also by the choice of Berlin as the capital—would increase German leverage in the European Community and in the Western alliance far beyond the effect of simply adding the old GDR to the FRG. To assess the likelihood of such a development, however, we first need to understand the present and historical attitudes of the various East European neighbors toward the Germans, and German efforts to woo them. Second, we must assume that as the economic recovery of a united Germany or, rather, of the former GDR, proceeds on schedule, the eventual result will be an economically strong Germany, say at the pre-1990 level of the old FRG. And, third, we must assume that German–East European relations in the future will be cooperative and not inhibited by a possible German relapse into imperialism or an East European turn toward dictatorship and autarky.

The aspect that raises the greatest problem is the geopolitical configuration of the great changes in Eastern and Central Europe and in German-Austrian, -Polish, -Czech, -Yugoslav, and -Hungarian relations. It was here, after all, that Hapsburg rule and the other pre-1914 empires began to unravel more than a hundred years ago amid the stirring

---

32. Wolffsohn's book was published in 1990 by Straube of Erlangen, Bonn, and Vienna. See also Rainer Zitelmann in *Süddeutsche Zeitung*, Nov. 27, 1990, as well as the historical review of German-Israeli relations by Jitzhak Ben-Ari, "Israel und die Bundesrepublik. Eine Bilanz besonderer Beziehungen," *Das Parlament*, supp. B15/90, Apr. 6, 1990, pp. 3–7, and Niels Hansen, "Verbindungen in die Zukunft, 25 Jahre diplomatische Beziehungen zwischen Deutschland und Israel," ibid., pp. 8–18. Lord Jacobovits is quoted in *Manchester Guardian Weekly*, Jul. 29, 1990.

Fig. 7.1. Central Europe before 1914.

nationalisms of Eastern Europe. It was here also that German expansion-
ism throughout modern history was directed—the *Drang nach dem
Osten* (desire to go east) which motivated early German settlers, crusaders, and colonizers centuries ago, as well as the latter-day crusaders of
World Wars I and II.

The reactions to the collapse of East European communism and to the
prospect of German unification were felt nowhere more keenly than in
Austria, where "the abruptly reemerging German question raised the
question of Austrian identity more promptly than it had ever been raised
since 1945."[33] As the last heir of the Hapsburg empire over many

33. Otto Schneider, "Wien und die deutsche Wiedervereinigung," *Europa Archiv*, no. 4
(Feb. 15, 1990), 145.

awakening nationalities, the Austrian republic had been reeling from the terminal crisis of that empire in 1918 through civil war and dictatorship into the arms of the Third Reich, courtesy of the Austrian-born Adolf Hitler, only to be swept along and defeated once more in World War II. Pretending to be merely another victim of Nazi aggression, it had the good fortune of being saved from the great Cold War schism by its enforced neutrality under the State Treaty of 1955 and to stand aloof from the confrontations between East and West, as well as between Bonn and East Berlin, while sharing Western culture and prosperity. For Austria, neutrality meant a break with its imperial past, acceptance of the role of a small state, and a new identity, at least until the end of the eighties when the Kurt Waldheim debacle, the meltdown of the communist empire, and its own readiness to join the European Community broke the spell. While it lasted, Austria in fact was able to play an important, mediating role between West and East—and, in the East, the role of keeping doors open and offering shelter to dissidents and refugees from conflict and communist repression.

The great upheaval of 1989 found the country in a new position, having labored hard to arrive at the consensus needed for an application for EC admission, which made Austrian neutrality irrelevant just as the government had learned to derive maximum advantage from it.[34] The application was not intended to end Austrian neutrality but was motivated mostly by anticipation of the EC Single Market after 1992 which Austria—two-thirds of its foreign trade has been with EC countries, especially with Germany, and its currency is tied to the deutschmark—could hardly afford to miss. Neutrality also helped to keep both the GDR and Bonn at arm's length, an important requirement for a state struggling to establish its own identity separate from the Germans: in the thirty-odd years since 1956, Austrians identifying with an Austrian national identity have grown from 49% to 86% while those identifying with Germany dropped below one in ten.[35] On the other hand, as the historian Gerhard

34. It was a difficult decision because both major parties viewed the European Community with suspicion, the Socialists (SPÖ) as a capitalist cartel and the People's party (ÖVP) as a threat to its corporatist mode of operation (*Ständestaat*). The prospect of being in a European Community dominated by a united Germany must be worse than all these fears. There were also Soviet pressures against joining the European Community, and the present EC members would not consider its application until after 1992. See Anton Pelinka, "The Politics of Neutrality," *German Politics and Society* 21 (Fall 1990), 19–32. Unlike Switzerland, Austria belonged to the United Nations, the Council of Europe, and the European Free-Trade Association. Only NATO and EC membership had been a taboo.

35. See Felix Kreissler, *Der Österreicher und seine Nation. Ein Lernprozess mit Hindernissen* (Vienna: Braumüller, 1984). See also Gerhard Botz, "Will Unification Bring the 'German Question' to an End?" *German Politics and Society* 21 (Fall 1990), 1–19, esp. 9–13.

Botz has pointed out, the majority People's party (ÖVP) and supporters of President Kurt Waldheim apparently still agreed with his argument that Austrian Wehrmacht soldiers "had to do their duty" to the German Nazi state to the bitter end. The upheaval in Eastern Europe had been preceded in 1988/89 by an upturn of Austrian trade with Poland (55% increase) and with Hungary (35%), thus presenting Austria with a new set of challenges and opportunities unrivaled since 1914. Memories of the pre–World War I era, unfortunately, are ominously replete with the Hapsburg struggle against growing economic dependency on Germany, from 1906, and against German plans for a *Mitteleuropa* that proved unacceptable to the awakening East European nationalities. Perhaps the little Austrian republic would succeed in a consensual way where the jackboot of imperial and Nazi Germany failed dismally, in winning the confidence and patronage of Eastern Europe, now that the reasons for the Iron Curtain of forty years, the military blocs, the juxtaposition between communist dictatorships and democracy, and the striving for economic autarky were all melting away.

While the union of the FRG and GDR was no cause for celebration in Vienna, Austria suddenly found itself very popular among most of the newly emancipated East European states, especially those which had once been part of the Hapsburg empire and its sphere of influence: Poland, Czechoslovakia, Hungary, Yugoslavia, even Italy. In February 1990, the leaders of the first three of these states met in Budapest, where they formed a Triple Alliance to reinforce their mutual contacts and cooperation in anticipation of the eventual disintegration of the Warsaw Pact—they sealed their pact in Visegrad Castle, the site of a similar meeting of the kings of Bohemia, Poland, and Hungary six and a half centuries earlier. The Italian Foreign Minister Gianni De Michelis also spoke about a bloc of five nations (including Austria and Yugoslavia but not Poland), a *pentagonale*, that might constitute a trading area or common market of its own. Some municipalities and counties in these nations had been cooperating for some time in an Alpen-Adria association oriented toward certain shared economic concerns. There was talk of a Danube Federation, possibly including Romania and even Bulgaria, for the same purpose, and perhaps with Austria as a link to the West and to the European Community. Once more, the Austrian Germans found themselves forgiven or not even associated with the bitter memories of World War II, while the "ugly West and East Germans"—and now the sheer size and power of a united Germany—continued to raise hackles and apprehensions all over Eastern Europe, as much as it might need German economic aid.

Even though the Cold War is over, furthermore, a mediating role continues to be a real choice for Austria, which is linked, at least in theory, to the CSCE (Helsinki) process and to the various efforts at disarmament and arms limitation that are going on in Vienna. If future East European developments make it possible, an all-embracing European security system might well find its center and fulcrum in Vienna rather than in more Western areas which are still widely seen, in Eastern Europe, as linked with the old NATO and Western powers. For nearly half a century, Vienna has been oriented toward Western Europe rather than toward its more traditional focus down the Danube River. But this state of affairs is changing profoundly, and the old *Mitteleuropa* leverage may be restored, once the instability and hectic transformation in Eastern Europe (including the former GDR) have diminished. The new identity of Austria may then be rather like the old one of the centuries before 1914.[36]

Hungary, Czechoslovakia, and Poland are greatly interested in the economic power of the European Community and, with Austrian encouragement, might in time apply for full membership. Except for Hungary, however, their current economic weakness suggests great caution. The European Community, in turn, has developed aid programs for Eastern Europe. East European interest in eventual EC membership, of course, supplies one more reason for Austria to apply. Austria can also offer unique advantages to multinational corporations interested in Eastern Europe and has high hopes for a great boost for its depressed northern and eastern border regions from economic cooperation with the CSFR and Hungary.[37]

The postneutral future of Austria in foreign and defense policy looks less rosy than the economic one. There is little apprehension in Vienna of being drawn into another power play by Germany, and knowledgeable observers have long excluded any likely desire for *Anschluss* (German annexation). At the same time, Austrians are watching for a revival in Germany of nationalist and radical-right agitation to recover the "lost Eastern territories" and for an increase of Pan-German and pro-German sentiment in Austria, where the Austrian Freedom party (FPÖ) scored considerable gains in the eighties. Its leader, Jörg Haider, until recently was governor (*Landeshauptmann*) of Carinthia, a state with a consider-

36. See Otto Schulmeister, *Die Zukunft Österreichs* (Vienna: Molden, 1967), pp. 145–148. See also Ludek Pachman, "Konföderation Mitteleuropa—Unsere Zukunft," in Daschitschew and Ströhm, eds., *Die Neuordnung Mitteleuropas*, pp. 51–58, as well as the discussion on pp. 59–82.
37. Eastern trade and EC membership will probably benefit Austrian industry at the price of depressing agriculture and the trades. See especially Brigitte Unger, "Possibilities and Constraints for National Economic Policies in Small Countries: The Case of Austria," *German Politics and Society* 21 (Fall 1991), 63–77.

able Slovenian minority and, hence, a pronounced sense of German (not Austrian) identity. Far more likely than a merger is a rivalry between little Austria and the economic giant of Germany, which may consider under-developed East-Central and Southeastern Europe as its "backyard." Austria is already economically dependent on Germany, and there is every reason to expect the rest of Eastern Europe to become so, too.

The Yugoslav civil war, which has pitted the Yugoslav Federal Army, led mostly by Serbian communists, against the breakaway republics of Slovenia next door and Croatia—both within the Hapsburg sphere of yesteryear—certainly demonstrated the need for a buildup of Austrian defenses against small conventional wars in Eastern Europe. While it did not at first recognize the independence of the secessionist republics, Austria cannot tolerate violations of its territory or view with indiffer-ence the thrusts of Serbian "tank communism" at its borders.[38] A worse scenario would have been the success of a conservative military coup in the Soviet Union which might have reestablished authoritarian rule there and, possibly, supplied a basis for Soviet intervention and influence in the former satellite countries of Eastern Europe. The impact on Austria of such a revived Soviet hegemony over Eastern Europe would not have been quite as direct as that on Poland, the CSFR, or Hungary, and the actual demise of the Soviet Union in late 1991 seems to have calmed Austrian apprehensions. Since Austria dropped its shield of neutrality, however, the uncertainties of such a situation drive it to seek protection from NATO and the West, including Germany. Hence, whatever the future holds, German hegemony appears to be an unavoidable part of Austria's future.

The response to German self-determination and unification in Czecho-slovakia and Hungary, old core areas of the Hapsburg empire, was decidedly more positive than in Austria, although the generous support of President Vaclav Havel may not represent the feelings of all Czechs: "A democratic system and democratic awareness [in Germany] are more important than the number of inhabitants of a reunited Germany," he said. "We don't have to be afraid of a peaceful and democratic state."

---

38. The mostly Serbian and communist officer corps has tried to stop Slovenian succession with its tanks and, as of this writing, is supporting Serbian nationalists in a campaign of secession in eastern Croatia, Bosnia-Herzegovina, and the rest of what used to be Yugoslavia. How these or other breakaway mini–nation-states might fit into the new order has not yet even been discussed widely in Austria or the West. But see the discussion of South-Central Europe in Daschitschew and Ströhm, eds., *Die Neuordnung Mitteleuro-pas*, pp. 93–116, among knowledgeable people from some of the countries involved, most of them advocates of a *Mitteleuropa* confederacy which could give Slovenia and Croatia a larger framework free from Serbian imperialism.

There is still considerable anti-German feeling in the CSFR and it should not have surprised anyone that Czech authorities indignantly rejected German attempts to claim damages or compensation for the losses suffered by the Sudeten Germans when they were expelled after World War II. However, as Hungarian President Arpad Göncz was to do, President Havel issued a formal apology to these German expellees for their sufferings, a gesture that was as much resented by many Czechs as it was gratefully accepted by the Germans.[39] Both governments at least seemed in agreement on a "zero solution"—that is to say, a mutual cancellation of obligations including possible reparation claims. The German news media also revealed that a substantial minority of Sudeten Germans still live in the CSFR. Havel's thinking about the German question was spelled out further in his address to the U.S. Congress on February 21, 1990, when he put in a good word for a second summit conference of the Helsinki (CSCE) members. He expressed the hope that Helsinki II might become "a European Peace Conference that . . . would put a formal end to the Second World War and its consequences (among other things), officially bringing a future democratic Germany—in the process of unification—into a pan-European structure that could determine its own security system." He also mentioned the border questions and the desirability of giving legal sanction to them by means of a common treaty. He hoped that "borders in Europe would become far less important than in the years of the Cold War," but noted that they would first require firm and reliable guarantees.

The initiatives toward Czech-German rapprochement have to be seen against the lobbying of the Sudeten German refugee associations in Germany, which continue to agitate for compensation for property losses and damage dating from the terrible years of 1945–1948, when the government of Edvard Beneš and Klement Gottwald persecuted Germans as well as Hungarians and gave away the property of expellees to Czechs and Slovaks who are now fearful of claims for restitution. As the association's spokesman, Franz Neubauer, has made clear, a "zero solution" was not acceptable to the refugees, who would prefer the creation of a neutral claims commission to a settlement within the Czech-German friendship treaty under discussion.[40] The Sudeten Germans have also

39. At the official level, the CSFR had already been a difficult partner at the time of the *Ostpolitik* treaties in the early seventies, and it proved so again with the Framework Agreement between the two nations in 1991. In both cases, the difficulties had to do with questions of property and damage claims arising from the expulsion of Germans and with German rights following the takeover under the 1938 Munich Agreements, which ceded the Sudetenland to Germany.

40. Among the legalistic quibbles presented is the Sudeten German argument that the Potsdam Agreement did not really apply to them because, at the outbreak of the war in

mobilized the support of the state of Bavaria—where many of them are living and which has assured them of its protection—for their claims. The roots of this dissension lie deep in the history of Bohemia, which was a very successful cultural union of Czechs and Germans until the Hussite wars of the fifteenth century.[41] The fall of the house of Hapsburg in 1918 created a Czechoslovak republic inhabited by, in addition to 6 million Czechs and 3 million Slovaks taken away from Hungary, 3.5 million Sudeten Germans whose attempt to join their Sudetenland to Weimar Germany was vetoed by the victorious allies. Twenty years later, Adolf Hitler took advantage of the ethnic tensions in this area to seize first the Sudetenland—with reluctant French and British consent—and then the rest of Czechoslovakia. The Nazi takeover resulted in the death of hundreds of thousands of Czech intellectuals, politicians, Jews, and many others.

The collapse of the Third Reich led inevitably to the violent expulsion of all but about 200,000 of the Sudeten Germans. Some 241,000 of the original population lost their lives, and many of the expellees reported physical violence directed against them. Another 70,000 Sudeten Germans emigrated in the fifties and sixties. The GDR officially recognized the expulsion of the Sudeten Germans in 1950. West Germany, where most of the expellees are living, was slower to oblige, although the successive governments of Chancellors Kiesinger (1966) and Brandt (1973) declared the Munich Agreements of 1938 to be invalid.

Whatever may have been the tenor of past relations, the postcommunist government of President Havel and Foreign Minister Jiri Dienstbier in Prague developed a good relationship with their German counterparts in the context of Czech desires for greater involvement with Western Europe. At the same time, they sought a kind of associate status with NATO—Romania and Poland had already expressed similar interests— which NATO was unable to grant for fear of the Soviet reaction to such a step.[42] The abortive 1991 military coup in the Soviet Union demon-

---

1939, the CSFR had already ceased to exist in international law, having been annexed by Greater Germany, and therefore could not have been "at war" with the German Reich. On the other side, the flames of ethnic friction were fanned particularly by *Rudé Právo*, the daily newspaper of the Czech communist party, which hoped to destabilize postcommunist politics with chauvinistic passions and to spread fears that there was a Sudeten campaign under way to expropriate Czech property and punish Czechs for long-forgotten deeds.

41. At its height, the old kingdom of Bohemia encompassed many areas later considered German, including the first German university (Prague, founded 1348), and played a major role in the Holy Roman Empire. The Hussite wars—two decades of vengeful Czech nationalist and religious campaigns in German territories—were triggered by the trial and execution of the Prague religious reformer Jan Hus by the Catholic church.

42. Addressing a NATO delegates' meeting in Brussels (March 1991), President Havel acknowledged the inadvisability of NATO membership at that time, although "our coun-

strated the potential need for NATO protection of the CSFR and other former Soviet satellites. In any case, the CSCE (Helsinki) organization was a more likely vehicle for ensuring European security, as President Havel pointed out in his welcoming address to a NATO gathering in Prague (April 25, 1991) and according to a memorandum prepared by Foreign Minister Dienstbier on the "European peace order." As Dienstbier explained in an interview with the Berlin *Tagesspiegel*, CSCE was a forum that like NATO included the United States, but it was not yet sufficiently institutionalized. Otherwise, a network of bilateral security treaties with West European countries would be needed to create "a stable ring of security" instead of regional uncertainties in the shadow of instability in the Soviet Union.

The decline of Soviet orders for Czechoslovak and Hungarian industrial goods, furthermore, made the Hungarian plans for a Hungarian-Czech-Polish free-trade zone very attractive, among other reasons, because they would prepare the CSFR for eventual membership in the European Community.[43] The return of the CSFR into the community of European and North American nations was celebrated appropriately with the awarding of the Charlemagne Prize to Vaclav Havel in Aachen, in the presence of King Juan Carlos, German dignitaries, and President Mitterrand, who glowingly spoke of the stages of European unification to come, presumably including also Eastern Europe. The Czechs still had a serious minority problem: namely, the Slovaks, who were part of pre–World War I Hungary and who formed a Nazi puppet state during World War II. Slovakia was restive in regard to Prague, although it lacks the economic strength to be an independent state and is frightened of the prospects of privatization.

Poland Between the Powers

The historical relationship of Soviet and Russian influence to the fellow Slavic peoples in Poland and the CSFR also helps to define the relations

---

tries are dangerously sliding into a certain political, economic, and security vacuum," but he did ask for "a lasting system" of cooperation and support from NATO for the former Warsaw Pact countries. *Los Angeles Times*, March 22, 1991.

43. *Tagesspiegel*, Apr. 11, 1991, p. 3. The severity of Czechoslovak foreign trade problems is highlighted by their determination once again, in the spring of 1991, to sell arms to the Middle East for hard currency. Slovakia is home to much of this arms industry which, unlike the Czech areas, was built up there to create industrial employment for a largely rural society. Czech industry is older and far more diversified than Slovakia's, which also accounts for its greater willingness to be privatized.

of the Poles and Czechs with today's Germans. The allure of Pan-slavism has been much stronger for the Czechs, who had lived under the Hapsburg empire, well assimilated over many centuries, than it has been for the Poles, whose historical memories were formed mostly by Russian domination in the nineteenth century and after 1945.[44] As a result of World War II, however, postcommunist Poland today is as fearful of a resurgent Germany—having received the Oder-Neisse area in 1945 as compensation for eastern Poland, which Stalin had annexed in 1939 and would not return in 1945—as it is of Soviet power next door. There is in fact a long tradition of Polish uprisings against Russian domination ever since Poland became a proud, Catholic nation-state in the eighteenth century, adopted the first European written constitution in 1791, and sent prominent military figures (Tadeusz Kościuszko for one) to fight for American independence. There were revolts in 1794, 1830/31, 1846, 1863/64, and 1905, not to mention General Józef Pilsudski's successful struggle to secure the Polish border against the Soviet Union in the 1920s.[45]

The recurring resistance and unrest under the communist regime of Poland has always had Catholic and anti-Russian overtones, and this never stronger than with the Solidarity movement in the 1980s. Even the carefully cultivated memories of German aggression and wartime atrocities—which led to an estimated 6 million Polish Catholic and Polish Jewish deaths—were often associated with a Soviet desire to maintain the Polish fear of a "revanchist Germany in league with Western imperialist forces." The Bonn government, furthermore, had signaled its readiness to accept the Oder-Neisse line twice in the seventies, once in connection with the Mutual Renunciation of Force Treaty of the early seventies and again by signing the 1975 Helsinki Agreements, which sanctioned all existing borders in Europe. Nevertheless, the final approval was left to a peace conference on Germany since, for forty-five years, no formal peace treaty had been signed. The era of good feelings in the wake

44. Poland was divided out of existence by surrounding empires, but the religious differences with and domination by orthodox, backward Russia seems to have left a deeper scar than did Prussian and Austrian rule in the west and south. Betrayed and divided once again by the Hitler-Stalin pact of 1939, eastern Poland was reabsorbed into Soviet Russia while western Poland and the Oder-Neisse area became a Soviet satellite. See Michael Ludwig, *Polen und die deutsche Frage* (Bonn: Europa Union, 1991), pp. 6–9, and Eberhard Schulz, *Die deutsche Frage und die Nachbarn im Osten* (Munich: R. Oldenbourg, 1989), pp. 145–154.

45. While Poland strove to hold off the Russians in the 1920s, the Russophile foreign minister of newly created Czechoslovakia, Edvard Beneš, sought friendly contacts with the equally new Soviet state. Suspicion of Soviet motives has established itself in the CSFR only since 1968, when the Warsaw Pact invasion taught the Czechs an unforgettable lesson.

of the treaties of the 1970s, unfortunately, went through a cooling-off period with the martial law regime of the 1980s in Poland.

The seeds of the historical tragedy of German-Polish relations were sown in the post–World War I clashes and intrigues involving the determination of national borders between the Weimar Republic and the new Polish state. Questionable applications of the principle of national self-determination, plebiscites, and quasi-military forays by German and Polish nationalists and irregular army units—with the connivance of the regular army and governments on both sides—had set the stage. Even while pursuing a "policy of fulfillment" of allied demands and recognition of the borders in the West, Weimar governments wanted to keep their eastern frontiers open toward such "successor states" as Poland. They played a waiting game, keeping their eastern neighbors destabilized and hoping for their eventual recapture, if necessary with the help of the Soviets.

Once Germany was sufficiently rearmed, under the Nazi regime, to overcome the resistance of a strong Poland, the stage was set for the 1939 division of Poland under the Hitler-Stalin pact. The Soviet Union grabbed the part of Poland east of the old Curzon line[46] while a Nazi *Blitzkrieg* was launched on the western half on the pretext that the Poles had been mistreating the sizable German minorities within their borders. Great Britain had guaranteed the existence of Poland and hence entered the war against Germany. A Polish government-in-exile, moreover, spent the war years in London while the Soviets were grooming the rival Lublin Committee of Polish communists for the time after the war. Already in late 1943 at Teheran, while German armies were holding both halves of Poland and vast Russian territories, British leaders proposed to Stalin how the Polish western and eastern borders could both be moved westward. The Polish exile government was keen on more favorable borders with Germany, possibly including East Prussia, Gdansk (Danzig), and Upper Silesia, but not at the price of governing 8–10 million Germans.[47] At the Yalta Conference in February 1945, after Stalin's armies had pushed the German forces out of most of Poland, the three allies announced that Poland must be augmented in territory toward the north

46. Named after Lord Curzon, this line was drawn by the Western powers as an ethnic frontier between the Polish-majority areas to the west and areas to the east where Poles were in the minority among Ukrainian and Byelorussian majorities. The new Polish state conquered these latter areas during the hostilities with the Soviet Union in 1920/21. An estimated 10.6 million ethnic Poles lived there in 1931.

47. Soviet policies toward the recaptured Polish areas in 1939–1941, such as the mass execution of Polish officers in the Katyn forest and similar actions, had also intensified Polish fears concerning Soviet postwar rule over them.

and west, but they left the final border to be drawn with the peace treaty.[48] By the end of the war, however, the Soviets had already turned over all areas east of the rivers Oder and (western) Neisse *de facto* to Poland, thus starting the exodus of millions of German refugees toward the rest of Germany. At Potsdam (July 1945), according to British documents that have become available recently, conflicting positions of the Soviet, American, and British delegations were reconciled with Polish demands for the industrial areas of Upper and Lower Silesia and the harbor of Szczecin (Stettin), as well as for land for the millions of Polish refugees from beyond the Curzon line and abroad.[49]

No sooner had the deal been struck among the allies than Winston Churchill—who had been its early architect—began to have second thoughts which, by March 1946, in Fulton, Missouri, led him to warn of an "Iron Curtain" that had descended across Europe from Szczecin to Trieste. Half a year later, the U.S. Secretary of State James F. Byrnes also threw the Oder-Neisse line into question in his Stuttgart speech of September 6, 1946, in which he left the extent of the German territories to be ceded to Poland to final determination at some future point. While there was little regard for the Germans who fled or were expelled from the area, the progressive Sovietization of Poland and other East European countries focused the emerging Cold War tensions upon the Oder-Neisse line and made it an object of renewed Western demands. The American military government in Germany even drew up several new border plans,[50] beginning in November 1946, and the new Secretary of State, George C. Marshall, on the occasion of his Moscow visit (April 9, 1947) insisted on a revision of the borderline in favor of Germany. Together with British Foreign Secretary, Sir Ernest Bevin, he proposed returning much of the agricultural area of Pomerania and Silesia (up to the eastern Neisse River) to Germany, which had just survived the hungry winter of

48. The Western delegations favored border versions considerably east of the Oder and along the eastern (Glatzer) Neisse, but yielded the point to the Soviets for concessions on the question of reparations from the Western parts of Germany. See Hansjakob Stehle and Karl-Heinz Janssen, "Oder-Neisse Grenze," *Die Zeit*, no. 26, June 22, 1990, pp. 49–50.

49. The Potsdam Agreements speak of "former German territories" now "under Polish administration" until the final determination of their status by a peace settlement.

50. The three plans proposed various solutions based on the prewar borders, but generally they agreed to give Poland a large part of eastern Pomerania and Upper Silesia as well as Gdansk and East Prussia, leaving the bulk of the Oder-Neisse area (including Lower Silesia) with Germany. See the various maps reprinted in Daschitschew and Ströhm, eds., *Die Neuordnung Mitteleuropas*, pp. 83–97. Naturally, the refugee associations seized upon this unexpected encouragement by the Western allies to claim that the border was still up for revision.

1946/47, and bringing industrial Upper Silesia under international control.

The proposal was, of course, rejected by the Soviets, who sanctimoniously said it would be "intolerably cruel" to resettle several million Poles and Germans yet again. The position of the Polish government was predictable, while the noncommunist Poles must have felt utterly dependent upon their great protector to the east. By 1948/49, the Cold War alignment had settled in around the new Polish-German border, determining the tenor of most public reactions for at least the next forty years.[51] Thus, in 1950, the new GDR government under Minister President Otto Grotewohl concluded an agreement with Poland regarding the Oder-Neisse border between the two communist countries, solemnly proclaiming that hereby "a final concluding line had been drawn under the past." The West German Bundestag responded with a strong joint resolution read by Silesia-born Paul Löbe (SPD): "No one has the right to give up [German] land and people based on his own alleged power to do so (*Machtvollkommenheit*)." Meanwhile the German refugee organizations proclaimed their "right to their homeland" in a dramatic rally at Stuttgart. The first steps toward West German acceptance and reconciliation with Poland were still more than a decade away.

Suddenly, the fall of the Berlin Wall and the reunification likely to follow revived Polish fears of a united Germany at the precise moment when the Hungarians and Czechs had come to applaud it. A substantial majority of Polish adults in a poll opposed German unification, although younger Poles, as in other neighboring countries, tended to accept it. One reason was the determined assertion of the claims of German refugees from the Oder-Neisse area, particularly from Silesia but also from the part of East Prussia in Polish (rather than Russian) hands. Mindful of the weakness of his CDU/CSU on the right[52] and of the recent CSU defections

51. In 1949, GDR President Wilhelm Pieck (SED) wrote Polish President Boleslaw Bierut that "anyone suggesting a revision of the Oder-Neisse border was an enemy of both the German and the Polish people," a dramatic reversal of the nationalistic 1946 SED position that the border was "merely provisional in character." West German Chancellor Adenauer, for his part, rejected the cession of these territories in his government's official 1949 declaration of policy, although CDU politicians (Jakob Kaiser) and SPD leader Kurt Schumacher had both shown a willingness to accept considerable Polish augmentations of territory in 1946/47 (though perhaps less than the total Oder-Neisse area, which amounted to about one-fourth of German prewar land).

52. From the beginning of his national career Kohl has been identified with a more liberal strand of Christian Democracy, close to then Lower Saxonian Governor Albrecht and the FDP, rather than to the conservative mainstream, and hence was less able to contain right-wing opinion than, say, his idolized predecessor Konrad Adenauer or his persistent rival and critic, Franz-Josef Strauss. Adenauer and Strauss both sought to prevent any right-

to the Republicans, Kohl conspicuously balked at simply recognizing the Oder-Neisse line as the eastern border of the new state to be united. To the great shock of the Polish government and cries of dismay from Western leaders, notably Mitterrand—and to the dismay of his own coalition partners in the FDP, not to mention the opposition—Kohl then refused to retract his earlier statements and rejected a proposal by Bundestag President Rita Süssmuth (CDU) that the two German states should issue a joint declaration endorsing the present border (December 29, 1989).[53] The newly elected East German Volkskammer was happy to oblige with a resolution recognizing the border once more, and without the old legal subterfuge of "leaving the final decision" to a peace conference or "a duly elected all-German parliament," formulas preferred by the Federal Constitutional Court of the FRG and by Kohl and the conservatives.

In a maneuver reminiscent of the bad-cop, good-cop routine, and hardly reassuring to the Poles, President Weizsäcker and Foreign Minister Genscher then promptly issued personal statements supporting the border, and Genscher even added that there was "no dissent" between him and the chancellor. The Polish press followed all of these contradictory statements with rising alarm. Prime Minister Tadeusz Mazowiecki, who had until this time had a reputation of favoring reconciliation with Germany, launched a major initiative in response to this challenge. Referring to the story that, at Teheran in 1943, Churchill and Stalin had worked out the swap of eastern Poland for the Oder-Neisse area, he declared that there should not be "another Yalta Conference" and that "never again must there be decisions about our fate without our participation." Mazowiecki demanded that Poland be included in the "two-plus-four" negotiations to protect its borders and also to help determine the future European security arrangements. He also countermanded the earlier Polish government position that the Soviet troops stationed in Poland be withdrawn, as indeed they had been in Hungary and the CSFR. They should stay a while longer, Mazowiecki now thought, a decision

wing party from flourishing among the voters and thereby preserved the political stability of the FRG.

53. Aside from his statement that Poland owed an apology to the German expellees, Kohl's excuse for finding the Süssmuth proposal "not acceptable" was that the GDR did not yet have a freely elected, legitimate government; he added that there had been a Bundestag resolution accepting the present border by "a great majority" as recently as November 8, 1989, the day before the Wall fell. "No one need fear that we will follow the injustice of expulsion [of the Germans there] with further expulsions," he explained somewhat ominously. See also the account of German ethnic reactions in Poland in the *Manchester Guardian Weekly*, Nov. 19, 1989, p. 11.

that Poland came to rue before long, certainly after the resignation of
Soviet Foreign Minister Eduard Shevardnadze and at the time of the
August 1991 coup attempt in Moscow, when 50,000 Soviet troops were
still in Poland and another 300,000 in East Germany, whence they might
have tried to trek home through Poland and the CSFR. Since Kohl
suddenly (in mid-1990) appeared to give in, the Polish role in the "two-
plus-four" group produced a satisfactory declaration that was solemnly
endorsed by all seven powers, including West and East Germany. Kohl's
maneuver thus shifted responsibility for acceptance of the Oder-Neisse
line from himself and his party to the four World War II powers in order
to dodge the recriminations of the refugees.[54]

Public opinion and the Polish press had become similarly apprehensive
and turned a jaundiced eye upon the German minority still inside Poland,
especially those in Silesia, remembering all too well the "Hitlerists,"
"Goebbels people," and "werewolves" of Germany during the harsh
German wartime occupation of their country. Poles had long been less
than enthusiastic about the Germans of the GDR and their peculiar blend
of Prussian authoritarianism and communism, even though Poland was
as aware as France that its security depended on the continued presence
of the GDR. Now, as the barriers to their travel to East Germany were
removed, they became aware of a rising tide of aggressive East German
xenophobia directed especially against them.[55] Unlike the sixties and
seventies when there had been mutual gestures of reconciliation—by the
Catholic bishops in the mid-sixties, by Chancellor Brandt in the early
seventies, and by the dissident Opposition for (Polish) Independence
(PPN) in the late seventies—German-Polish relations were hardly propi-
tious for a new beginning. Kohl's shameless insistence that the Poles

54. The Polish demands were spelled out in an April 27, 1990, document and commu-
nicated to all six countries. Former Polish Prime Minister Mieczyslaw Rakowski viewed the
situation with philosophical detachment: he was glad that Kohl's remark had called forth
the combined insistence of the old allies on this point, even though he had no doubt about
the continued popular majorities in Germany supporting the Oder-Neisse border. In a
survey by the British *Independent*, the attitudes of Polish respondents reflected the new
apprehensions at German unification: while 51% of Soviet and 68% of Hungarian
respondents welcomed German unification, only 26% of the Poles shared this opinion;
64% of the Poles were wholly or in part opposed to it. Cited in *Die Zeit*, no. 15, Apr. 6,
1990, p. 5.

55. German nationalist hostility and contempt for Poles and "Polish [economic] conditions" are hardly new, but the flames of popular prejudice were fanned anew by large
numbers of Polish visitors buying up scarce East German merchandise or setting up their
own street markets in places such as West Berlin's Kantstrasse. In spring of 1991, when the
last visa requirements for entry into or transit through Germany were lifted, some Polish
visitors even had to endure physical assaults and humiliation by neo-Nazi skinheads and
East German hooligans.

should apologize to the German expellees and his wooing of the latter
and of the Polish-German minority were most unlikely to calm popular
fears in Poland. On the other hand, politically aware Poles understood
that they would have to wake up from their postcommunist and postdic-
tatorial provincialism and overcome their instinctive fear of their German
neighbors in order to be ready for European partnership and integration.[56]

The West German Bundestag also rose to the occasion with a resolution (March 8, 1990) that once more repeated its determination to
guarantee the thrice-recognized borders and added its desire to back up
its good intentions with a Polish-German friendship treaty.[57] President
Weizsäcker and others, moreover, pleaded for a massive effort to aid
Poland economically—reminiscent of the aid packages organized by the
Protestant German churches in the eighties—beginning with a reduction
of the Polish foreign debt to the German government, a necessity for the
success of Polish economic recovery.[58] A 50% reduction of the 8.9 billion
marks owed was agreed upon. Toward the end of 1990, furthermore,
after the challenge of the Republicans had clearly subsided, Chancellor
Kohl had an amicable four-hour meeting with Premier Mazowiecki in the
border town of Frankfurt on the Oder River. There the two reached
agreement in principle on the friendship treaty to come, on lifting the
visa requirement for Poles,[59] and on the treatment of an ethnic German
minority population of some 300,000—the refugee association claims
1.1 million, the Red Cross 80,000; the German "circles of friends"

56. Mazowiecki repeated his emphasis on reconciliation with the Germans and Russians
on the occasion of the Solidarity Congress, but he was unable to counteract the public
reaction to Kohl's earlier visit and subsequent statements. See the interview in *Die Zeit*, no.
19, May 4, 1990, p. 3, and Ludwig, *Polen*, pp. 9–21, who presents a new conciliatory
Polish policy line toward Germany: Poland needs to get on good terms both with the
Soviets and the Germans and, to that end, should accept German unification and seek
participation in "the German economic potential" for restructuring the Polish economy,
while remaining adamant about the Oder-Neisse line.

57. See the popular Polish press as well as *Rzecpospolita* for the years 1989–1990.
Mazowiecki and others—e.g., the Polish bishops in the mid-seventies—have paid tribute to
the sufferings of the German expellees in 1945 on repeated occasions, but they were not
prepared to make a grand public apology in a climate of German nationalistic agitation as
demanded by Kohl and the expellee chief Herbert Czaja.

58. Among other Polish concerns, there was the question of reimbursement of the
involuntary Polish labor force requisitioned by the Third Reich. See also the *Spiegel*
interviews with Weizsäcker and Rakowski. *Der Spiegel* 45, no. 18, Apr. 29, 1991, pp. 37–
48, 169–170.

59. The announcement that Poles would be free to enter was greeted with dismay and
apprehension in some German quarters, especially by local police. But the anticipated
difficulties and disturbances in Germany never developed. The need to open more border
crossings also was acknowledged and led to promises on both sides.

collected about 300,000 signatures, which is also the estimate of reputable researchers—still living in Poland. The treaty negotiations, however, ran into major interference when the German refugee associations used their leverage with the Bavarian CSU to insist on a series of additional concessions to the German minority in Poland.

The Christian Democratic Crisis Over the Friendship Treaties

The long-standing coalition between the Bavarian CSU and the CDU of all the other *Länder* had already been in crisis since the last government coalition was formed with the FDP in Bonn (January 1991). For the first time in forty-one years, the CSU had found that its parliamentary votes in the Bundestag were no longer needed. The CDU and FDP could afford to ignore its protests since German unification had greatly reduced its relative share of the national vote, and an effort to establish itself through the DSU in the new *Länder* had failed. There were renewed CSU attacks on its old rival, the FDP, angry confrontations with Kohl, and threats to withdraw from the government[60] at the very moment when Poland, for one, had agreed to a satisfactory package of guarantees for the German minority there, along the lines envisaged by the CSCE (Helsinki) meeting in Copenhagen (1989).

By this time, the long-discriminated-against minority had been permitted to reintroduce German instruction in hundreds of schools—although there were still severe shortages of teachers and books—and, in many Silesian communities, were enjoying German church services. German minority associations ("friendship circles") were organized in numerous communities. In the latest Polish local elections, in fact, German slates of candidates were presented in thirty-six communes and won majorities in twenty-six of them, mostly around Oppeln (Silesia). The new Polish Premier, Jan Krzystof Bielecki, and the chair of the *Sejm* committee on national minorities, Jerzy Wuttke, met in Gogolin (Silesia) with representatives of the German friendship circles (DFK), which by then were about 200,000 strong, and discussed mutual concerns, such as the German

60. The hostility focused, inevitably, on Foreign Minister Genscher, who had been instrumental in preparing the ground for a new *Ostpolitik* toward postcommunist Poland and the CSFR. CSU chair Waigel also complained that he, personally, had come under attack for his part in the financing of German unification, was pilloried for having been less than candid about the need to raise taxes for that purpose, and had been left "standing in the rain" by Chancellor Kohl.

insistence on dual citizenship for refugees who would like to return to their Polish home areas. Poland has been tolerant of such returnees but is apprehensive of large numbers and of formal agreements sanctioning their return. There is also some concern that the exuberant minority might go overboard with changes of street and place names—to re-Germanize those which were Polonized in 1945—and with the removal of Polish symbols and coats of arms.

The Polish public has not been unreasonable toward the German minority, even though, according to a March 1990 poll, a majority (51%) expected ethnic conflicts and tensions. A good 82% agreed that their ethnic German fellow citizens ought to have the same rights as other Polish minorities: Ukrainians, White Russians, and Jews. A majority of Polish adults also recognized the minority right to German schools and religious services. After six negotiating sessions, the Polish-German friendship treaty—now named the Good Neighborhood and Cooperation Treaty—was signed in draft form by representatives of both governments toward the end of April 1991. It was at this point that the CSU intervened with a series of eight objections and demands regarding the German minority in Poland and participation by the refugee associations in negotiating details—the government had kept the exact wording of the draft treaty secret up to this point.[61] The CSU particularly insisted on legal guarantees for the use of the German language, dual citizenship, dual place names, a "right to the homeland," rights to confiscated property, and the establishment of arbitral tribunals and autonomous administrative agencies for the minority. It remained for Foreign Minister Genscher to negotiate with the CSU, and he finally proposed that the Bundestag put its remaining concerns into the form of an explanatory resolution, which admittedly does not have the obligatory force of treaties and international law, even though it may be transmitted to Poland along with the treaty.[62] The Federation of Refugees (BdV) President, Herbert

61. At a meeting of East Prussian refugees, in Düsseldorf, they also received political support from the chair of the Bundestag CDU, Alfred Dregger, who is known for his conservative views. At a meeting of Sudeten Germans in Nuremberg, CSU leader and Federal Finance Minister Waigel, after calling the Sudeten Germans "the fourth tribe of Bavaria [after the Old Bavarians, Franconians, and Swabians]," called for Sudeten German participation in the negotiations and a similar friendship treaty with the CSFR, and he promised the direct backing of the Bavarian state government for this purpose.

62. As *Rzeczpospolita* commented in late May 1991, the CSU maneuver was demanded by domestic politics and a CSU fear of losing face. In the end, the more extreme demands such as regional autonomy for Silesia were quietly dropped, and the concerns were reduced to only two points: bilingual place names and a "right to return" for refugees. The issue of dual citizenship was also abandoned because there is *de facto* toleration of all such claims. See also *Zycie Warszawy* for the same period.

Czaja, rejected the compromise, which allegedly violated no fewer than twenty-two constitutional rights of Silesians and other groups, by dint of principles—applicable also to Poles in Germany—such as that minority members were enjoined "to conduct themselves loyally, like any other citizens, toward their respective state." Czaja claimed that the draft treaty "was a stumbling block on the way to a more progressive CSCE code of ethnic group rights," that there was not enough German instruction, and that the Polish government barred minority groups from cooperation with BdV projects. He hinted that his organization might take the treaty to the Federal Constitutional Court. The treaty also provided a common youth authority, an environmental council, and a joint border commission, and it offered Poles residing in Germany the same privileges as were given to the Germans in Poland. Germany also agreed to do its best to get Poland into the European Community and spoke of establishing "common security structures."

For the Pentecost holidays (May 19–20, 1991), the German Silesians in Poland held a festival on the Annaberg—a site of the armed struggle between German and Polish irregulars and paramilitaries in the early 1920s—and there were 25,000 foreign visitors, mostly Germans. In early July 1991, at their annual convention in Nuremberg, Silesia Association President Herbert Hupka (CDU), sharply attacked the government for "selling out Silesia." In vain, the seventy-five-year-old refugee politician assailed the Polish-German Reconciliation and Friendship Treaty and, before an audience of 120,000, demanded a role in the shaping of such agreements for the refugee associations. At the same time, the Sudeten Germans had a meeting of 100,000 from Germany, Austria, and the CSFR in Nuremberg at which, among others, Federal Interior Minister Wolfgang Schäuble (CDU) set forth the point of view of the Kohl government. The main objective of Bonn, he said, was "to improve the lives of Germans in their old home area so that they would have a secure future there." He rejected all talk of territorial claims, "for it was impossible to reconcile the borders of states and nationalities in East-Central Europe." The inability of the refugee association to prevail brought about serious internal splits and brought on a leadership crisis in the BdV over Poland.

Sudeten German spokesperson Franz Neubauer criticized the Bonn government for a "lack of strong support" for his group and for the attempt "to draw a bottom line (*Schlusstrich*) under the Sudeten German question," an allusion to Genscher's comments about "not adding new injustice to the old injustice." But there was no doubt about the resolve of the government to avoid rekindling the old fires of national conflict even while lending the refugees a sympathetic ear. As the *Süddeutsche*

Zeitung editorialized in a critical column, "should we really burden the reconciliation with our Eastern neighbors with a new mortgage just because the grandchildren insist on compensation for granddad's farmhouse in the Bohemian Forest? Financial compensation now would put an intolerable load on the fragile economies of Poland and the CSFR . . . [and would keep them from] entering the European Community. Only in a united Europe that is free from distrust can the refugees hope to fulfill their dream of a return to their old home."[63]

The Significance of Eastern Opportunities for Germany

What is the significance of the opportunities opening up in Eastern Europe vis-à-vis German initiatives? For openers, it is important to distinguish the old nationalist, territorially based conceptions of power and influence that once made multinational Eastern Europe such a powder keg for world wars—especially after the decline and fall of the great empires of the region (Hapsburg, Russian, Ottoman, and Prussian, not to mention earlier or smaller (Hungarian, Serbian, Bulgarian) and other imperialisms—from today's versions of economic power projection. Lenin (or J. A. Hobson) was mistaken in assuming that investment abroad sooner or later had to be followed by the flag or by the establishment of colonial rule. Latter-day imperialists, from Nazi Germany to the Japanese military in the thirties, were even more misguided in their primitive quest for unskilled slave labor from conquered lands as a route to prosperity at home, although the Germans, of course, were drawn in the imperialistic direction by the sizable and restive ethnic German minorities in the East. Today's German entrepreneurs and bankers do not have to conquer and establish territorial dominion over a client area any more than the multinational corporations in various countries of the First and Third World need colonies. They can live with reasonably stable self-government, and autonomous states with them, by working out agreements to share the wealth that is to be produced by bringing together foreign capital and skilled local workers and consumers.[64]

63. Quoted in *Tagesspiegel* (Berlin), May 22, 1991, and in *Süddeutsche Zeitung*, May 21, 1991. Both Schäuble and representatives of Bavaria's CSU government, however, promised that the refugee association could "participate in the reconciliation with the East European reform states" but did not specifically endorse refugee claims for compensation of properties confiscated in 1945.

64. At least from a scientific or economic point of view, this writer finds most theories

To be sure, there are a number of preconditions, especially in the case of Germany in Eastern Europe—and, for that matter, Japan in Asia—that have to prevail for optimal results. One is, obviously, the German departure from old nationalist notions of empire, and from notions concerning the defense of ethnic German minorities along the old territorial lines, that once led Germany down the garden path into World War II and that still rankle among the ethnic German refugees of 1945 and the radical right. By the same token, the East European nations would have to cooperate willingly, whether they develop into stable democracies, relapse into authoritarian regimes, or settle into a more-or-less stable system somewhere between the two poles. Naturally, historical memories and resentments may frustrate such patterns of cooperation either directly or indirectly—for example, when competitors try to win out by playing up the old themes of hatred and conflict, or when one of several nationalities tries to hide its imperial (or reactionary communist) ambitions by accusing the other(s) of being once more in cahoots with alleged German imperialism. This latter scenario was presented by the Serbian "tank communists"—and was promptly believed by some American journalists[65]—who blamed Slovenian democratic separatism and, more plausibly, that of neodemocratic Croatia, once the old *ustasha* puppet state of the Axis, on German imperial ambitions in the Balkans. On the other hand, the memories of past German nationalism and imperialism are likely to be a major control on German conduct in the future: German governments and businesses cannot afford any relapse because it would destroy their profits and profitable relationships.

How do the various East European peoples view Germany and the changing status of their region? In May 1991, a comprehensive Times-Mirror survey, *The Pulse of Europe*, which included comparative polls in Eastern Europe, confirmed many of our speculations. After asking the respondents for reactions to various aspects of their social, political, and economic future, the pollsters asked, "And what about the following countries, how would you rate the kind of influence they are having on the way things are going in [your country]?" Asked about Germany's impact on Poland, 41% of adult Poles replied positively and 32% negatively, the least positive response of any East European nation

---

of international dependency rather incomplete as explanations for understanding Eastern Europe, although they obviously can serve a political purpose, as they did within the old communist empire.

65. It was picked up eagerly by the *New York Times* and the *Los Angeles Times*, neither of which could explain exactly why the presumable German conspirators would undertake such a cloak-and-dagger mission, unprecedented for the democratic German governments after 1949.

(between 7% and 28% of East Europeans said "both negative and positive" or "neither"). The positive responses were 78% among Hungarians, 53% among Czechoslovakians, 52% among Russians, 60% in the Ukraine, and 46% in Lithuania. Only the United States was looked upon with more hope, especially in Poland where 77% responded positively. Austria's influence was viewed positively by 60% of the Czechs and 79% of Hungarians; the Poles were not asked this question. The Soviet Union received negative majorities in Poland (58%) and Hungary (56%), and nearly that (44%) in the CSFR. The Czechs, by the way, gave the German minority in the CSFR quite a positive rating (66%), ahead of all other minorities, and the Hungarians took a similarly kind view of their German minority (73%). The Poles, on the other hand, divided almost evenly on their German minority: 39% favorable and 45% unfavorable, and in their eastern regions dislike for Germans was at 53%. Poles also felt that they did not "have much in common with other ethnic groups and races" (73% yes) in far larger numbers than any of the other thirteen nations polled. Finally, asked what they thought of Chancellor Kohl—who was often pictured in the American press as the great threat to the Oder-Neisse line and to European peace—two-thirds of the Poles (65%) and the Russians (61%), and three-fourths of the Czechs (76%) and Hungarians (77%), turned out to view him favorably. That was much better than what the chancellor could command in his own country (48%), and much better also than Mikhail Gorbachev did in Poland (48%) and Hungary (64%—the Czechs gave him 75%). The Times-Mirror survey also concluded that "all [East Europeans] believe that parts of neighboring territory belong to them," are militaristic (especially Poland and Bulgaria), are xenophobic, and are worried about political instability in their region. They put their security hopes in bilateral defense treaties, regional pacts (especially Hungary and the CSFR), and NATO (especially Poland), but hardly at all in the CSCE.[66]

The likely future scenarios of German economic influence in Eastern Europe range across a considerable spectrum and will most probably feature a competitive environment in which other EC members, Austria, the United States, and Japan, not to mention other East European states including the successor states of the Soviet Union,[67] will play an increas-

66. *The Pulse of Europe: A Survey of Political and Social Values and Attitudes* (Washington, D.C.: Times-Mirror Center for the People and the Press, 1991), pp. 199 and 207 and the tables on pp. 59–60, 74–76, and 128–129.

67. The competition over the construction of housing for returning Russian soldiers, financed with 13 billion marks from Bonn, is a case in point. To the surprise of German business, Turkish entrepreneurs had seized the building contracts—maybe it was the Soviet construction Mafia—and the German government had to exert determined political pressure

ing role. Germany has a head start, thanks to its economic prowess and geographic location, although the technology of modern transport and communications has reduced the old geographic advantage a great deal. The present size of the Germany economy and the extent of its financial power will dwarf or match most European competitors (e.g., Austria) but not the United States or Japan. Austria and some of the East European countries may form a trading bloc or even a closer union to make up for their disadvantages of size. Unlike East Germany, which had only one-fourth of the population of the FRG, the potential market for unified Germany involves at least one and a half times as many eager customers as there are Germans. If we add a further "concentric circle," to speak with Jacques Delors of the EC Commission, there will be two and a half times as many customers—by including those in the westernmost break-away Soviet republics. Add the Russian Federation, and the figure would be four and a half times. At this writing, Germany had already pledged more than half the funds, $32 billion of $55 billion, that the West promised the Soviet Union, and it has campaigned indefatigably among the Group of 7 to raise more. This policy course is clearly meant to reap future rewards and not just to accumulate points in heaven for altruism. The short-run payoff from unification with the poor but hungry East German consumers was a dramatic boost for West German manufacturing, services, and retail. The equally poor or poorer East Europeans have already started importing cars and other goods in quantity from the West.

It remains to be seen, of course, how well Germany's economic interests will penetrate this large market against its competitors and pockets of resistance. There are likely to be limiting factors such as reform communism, holdouts for autarky—perhaps Romania and Bulgaria—and occurrences of civil war and other forms of unrest. Areas of untrammeled free enterprise may be restricted once the East European love affair with Milton Friedman gives way to a sober reappraisal. But it is also possible to do business with interventionist governments and dictatorships—up to a point. Even a Soviet military coup and regional hegemony might not be the end, so long as economic reconstruction continues. Ethnic conflicts and, in particular, historically founded resentments against Germans may play a large role, especially if German entrepreneurs are not extremely sensitive about how they may be perceived, rightly or wrongly. Not the least of the incentives for Germany and other prosperous Western countries to invest in Eastern Europe and

---

in order to rescue at least a portion of the contracts for German construction firms, especially East German ones.

the Soviet Union is the threat of massive migration, legal or illegal, across the long, unguarded frontier between East and West. Just as in the spring of 1990, when the East Germans were saying "If the D-mark does not come to us, we will go to the D-mark"—and they did—East Europeans will come to the West in droves unless the West takes action soon to improve opportunities where they are now.[68]

In the best-case scenario, there will be a vast and moving soup of restless nationalities, from the Baltic states to Poland and down to Albania and the Bulgarian Turks, living tolerantly side by side in self-governing ethnic communities under more-encompassing federal or confederate umbrella states and larger trade blocs. Some of the lumps in this soup will be larger, but none may take advantage of the smaller ones, who can appeal to the CSCE Council and its human rights guarantees. Some (e.g., the Poles) may be too suspicious at first of German economic wheeling and dealing, but eventually they will notice that their German neighbors are mostly out to make a profit in Eastern countries and that they, too, can share in such wealth-creating activities—most foreign investment in Poland is German, and individually many Poles have already been traveling and doing business in the West since the borders opened up.[69] Today's Germans are rather unlikely to nurse thoughts of territorial conquest and dominion in Eastern Europe—for the simple reason that they have to compete on the open market against all their competitors and must do so before a suspicious clientele and among rivals from the United States, Soviet successor states, and EC countries who would be the first to cry foul. Why would today's German entrepreneurs be so stupid as to spoil their successful business by frightening away their customers and giving their competition good reason to denounce them? On the other hand, the German head start and its likely economic consequences will undoubtedly tilt the balance within the

68. According to Bundestag Deputy Peter Conradi, this is true even of the ethnic Germans who once had a homeland in the Volga German Republic and who are about to return there after forty-five years of dispersion and punishment at Stalin's hand. Unless investments make life worthwhile there, they will come to live in Germany, as many have already done. An alternative plan was to settle them in the Soviet half of what used to be East Prussia. See Daschitschew in Daschitschew and Ströhm, eds., *Die Neuordnung Mitteleuropas*, p. 47.

69. The Vienna correspondent of the conservative daily *Die Welt*, Carl-Gustaf Ströhm, described the massive daily influx of "up to 40,000 Polish cars with black marketeers who offer their wares for sale in Vienna" and of hundreds of thousands of Czechs, Slovaks and, before them, Hungarians buying up everything in Viennese supermarkets. Ibid., p. 114. At a conservative and Christian Democratic meeting in Weikersheim, Ströhm objected to the delight expressed by the former premier of Baden-Württemberg, Lothar Späth, at the thought of "open borders."

European Community—at least in its current composition—even further toward German economic dominance. Economic weight may also produce increased political influence, as indeed it should, but hardly territorial dominion. Last but not least, there will be larger powers about, such as the United States, the Commonwealth of Independent States, perhaps even a *Mitteleuropa* confederacy around Austria, that would be unlikely to tolerate any German attempt at aggrandizement. The times for territorial empires in Europe are long past.

Chapter EIGHT

The Quest for European Security

We appear to have gotten a little ahead of our story about the international context of German unification, but for a reason: it would be rather misleading to describe the structures of European security before a full awareness of the profoundly different context that is to be served by the German and other European security policies is established. In the chronology of German unification, nevertheless, we do have to begin with the structures of yesteryear that, by now, have registered the extraordinary changes of 1989–1991. In the beginning, the great shock of the collapse of the Berlin Wall and the opening of the inner-German borders, as will be remembered, caused such a reaction among some of Germany's Western allies that they invoked long-forgotten—at least by the German public, which believed that the occupation had ended and that West Germany had regained sovereignty back in 1955—occupation rights. The Germany Treaty of 1952 (art. 11) between the Adenauer government and the three Western allies had indeed provided for the abrogation of the Occupation Statute of 1949 and the end of the Allied High Commission for Germany, and the intended "transfer of sovereignty" had occurred after some delay with the admission of the FRG to NATO on May 5, 1955. But there had been allied reservations from the beginning, "regarding the allied rights and responsibilities" with respect to "Berlin and to Germany as a whole," including German reunification and a final settlement in a peace treaty. The ratification of the Germany Treaty triggered prolonged debates over German rearmament and the constitutional obstacles to it and, in the FRG, it was not completed until 1953, long after the treaty had been accepted by the appropriate authorities in Great Britain and the United States.

French agreement was even harder to obtain. In fact, the whole enterprise faltered when the French National Assembly, on August 30, 1954, rejected the European Defense Community (EDC), which would have placed the German military forces into the same six-nation framework that had been created for the European Coal and Steel Community and would soon form the Common Market. In place of the EDC, which did not include Great Britain, a seven-nation group including Britain was devised at the Fall 1954 Foreign Ministers' Conference in London and was called the Western European Union (WEU). The Paris treaties finally completed German accession to NATO and thereby put the Germany Treaty into effect.

The allies had also reserved the right to station military forces and to provide for possible emergencies regarding the protection of those forces—a provision (art. 5[2]) that lapsed when the FRG adopted its own emergency legislation in 1968. Article 7 of the Germany Treaty also pledged the FRG to abide by the principles of the United Nations and the Council of Europe, and obliged all signatories to work toward the "common goal of German reunification in freedom" and toward the conclusion of a peace treaty for all of Germany.[1] West German membership in NATO meant that the FRG made considerable forces available to Western defense against a possible Soviet or Warsaw Pact attack. These forces, however, up to the highest command levels, were completely integrated into the multinational NATO structure so as to avoid leaving a German army under German command to pursue German objectives— such as liberating East Germany or the Oder-Neisse area. West German defense ministers and generals participated regularly in the meetings of the NATO Council, its Military Committee, and in the integrated command structure. German membership in WEU overcame French fears of West German rearmament and facilitated acceptance of German entry into NATO by exacting certain pledges of arms control from the FRG, such as the one against the production of nuclear, biological, or chemical (ABC) weapons in the FRG.[2]

---

1. Additional treaties between the FRG and the three Western allies regulated the further stationing of allied troops, the West German contribution toward their maintenance, and other matters resulting from war and occupation.

2. See Helga Haftendorn and Lothar Wilker, "Die Sicherheitspolitik der beiden

When the Thatcher cabinet and the Mitterrand administration in their first reaction to the collapse of the Wall resurrected the notion of reserved rights, better counsel soon prevailed in Washington. The presidential advisers and the U.S. State Department evidently took the long-range view that such a stance would make for dissension within NATO and might push the Germans into the neutralist camp if not into collusion with the Soviets at this extraordinary moment in history. American policymakers also saw in Bonn a reliable partner within the establishment of a free and unified European Community of the future, which might possibly extend far into Eastern Europe.[3] As President Bush reported at the NATO summit in late 1989, the United States was prepared to endorse a possible German unification, provided that Germany remain in NATO and be part of the intensified European Community, that the allied rights and responsibilities be respected, and that the unification process be peaceful and gradual and not challenge the postwar boundaries in Europe (such as the Polish and Czech borders with Germany). The Bush administration envisaged the final liquidation of allied occupation rights and the establishment of full German sovereignty, including a free choice of alliances—Kohl had left no doubt as to how his government would respond, and the American line further strengthened his resolve against Soviet insistence on German neutrality. The American policy was also designed to soften the impact on German and international opinion of the ambassadorial-level meeting of the quadripartite Allied Control Council (December 11, 1989) that had been called by the Soviets to reassert the residual occupation rights.

The Two-Plus-Four Negotiations

At the "open skies" meeting of the Conference on Security and Cooperation in Europe (CSCE) in Ottawa (February 13, 1990), after months of persuading the French and the British to go along, a series of "two-plus-four" meetings among the two German governments and the four wartime allies was launched to deal with the "external aspects" of German unification. The "internal unification" would be left to the two German states, the allied foreign ministers decided. While "internal unification"

---

deutschen Staaten," in *Deutschland Handbuch. Eine doppelte Bilanz 1949–1989* (Munich: Hanser, 1989), pp. 605–620.

3. See Elizabeth Pond, *After the Wall: American Policy Towards Germany* (New York: Priority Press, 1990), chaps. 4–6, and Karl Kaiser, *Deutschlands Vereinigung: Die internationalen Aspekte* (Bergisch-Gladbach: Bastei-Lübbe, 1991), pp. 49–58.

proceeded at its own speed, the two-plus-four group met subsequently in Bonn (May 5), East Berlin (June 22), Paris (July 17), and finally Moscow (September 12), where the final agreement was signed. The meetings involved considerable conflict over timing and such questions as borders, new European security arrangements, the status of occupied Berlin, and various Soviet proposals.[4] After the Bonn meeting, for example, the West Germans expressed their alarm at the Soviet emphasis on separating the "internal" and "external" aspects, with Moscow evidently wishing to postpone the latter and thus deny the Germans the self-determination they wanted. At the Paris meeting, Polish Foreign Minister Skubiszevski was also invited, and the Oder-Neisse line was fixed in a Five-Point Declaration pledging the Germans to recognize this border in a treaty following the completion of unification. The earlier Western emphasis on the containment of Soviet power softened as soon as the Soviets dropped their opposition to united German NATO membership—that is to say, when President Gorbachev met with Kohl in Zhelezdnovodsk in mid-July. Frequent meetings between the Soviet, American, and West German foreign ministers did much to prepare the ground for the sudden agreement in July[5] and the subsequent Treaty on German Sovereignty (Two-Plus-Four) of September 12, 1990. The unexpected acquiescence of the Soviet Union—and the revelation of Nicholas Ridley's views—helped to overcome the last resistance of the British government as well. The final treaty was accompanied by a letter to the wartime allies, in particular the Soviet government, signed by both German representatives. This letter assured the Soviets that a) the East German expropriations of 1945–1949 (under Soviet occupation) would not be rescinded and b) the territory of the former GDR would not see NATO maneuvers or have non-German NATO troops stationed there.

The treaty itself once more guaranteed all the German borders and linked them with the peaceful future European order. The two Germanys, and united Germany, pledged to forswear any territorial claims and promised to eliminate all wording to the contrary (for instance, arts. 23[2] and 146) from the Basic Law.[6] The two German governments,

4. At the meeting in East Berlin, for example, Soviet Foreign Minister Eduard Shevardnadze proposed to limit German troops to 250,000 (half of the West German contribution to NATO) and to provide a five-year period during which all treaties of either Germany and especially those regarding their membership in NATO and the Warsaw Pact were to continue in force. The proposal was defeated.

5. See especially Wilhelm Bruns, "Die Regelung der äusseren Aspekte der deutschen Einigung," *Deutschland Archiv* 22, no. 11 (Nov. 1990), 1726–1728.

6. These articles, which had of course been meant for German unification only, were viewed as possible openings for German imperialistic expansion (e.g., if German Oder-Neisse or Sudeten refugees should appeal to them as a basis for "admission" of their Eastern territories to the FRG).

furthermore, confirmed their earlier declaration "that [from now on] only peace will emanate from German soil" and that any actions disturbing peaceful relations between nations, particularly "preparing for aggressive war," would be proscribed by German law and the Constitution. German arms, the two governments pledged, would never be used again except under these constitutional restrictions and according to the U.N. Charter. The treaty also repeated the German renunciation of the "manufacture, possession, and control" of ABC weapons and reiterated Kohl's promise at Zhelezdnovodsk, and the West German statement at the Conventional Forces in Europe (CFE) negotiations in Vienna two weeks earlier, placing a cap of 370,000 soldiers on German land, air, and naval forces (345,000 in the army and air force). The treaty also provided for the removal of Soviet troops from German soil by the end of 1994 and stipulated that, until that time, the Germans could only station territorial defense troops there that did not belong to NATO or other military alliances. The Western allied troops stationed in Berlin before the conclusion of the treaty were permitted to remain there until the final withdrawal of the Soviet army. After 1994, foreign troops and nuclear delivery systems could no longer be in the former GDR—only German conventional troops. In other words, the East German area would become a neutral and nuclear-free zone.

The treaty specifically left "the rest of united Germany" free to belong to any military alliance. It also terminated all remaining rights of the four powers with respect to Berlin and "Germany as a whole" and any practices or quadripartite agreements pertaining thereto: "united Germany shall have accordingly full sovereignty over its internal and external affairs."[7] As the late Wilhelm Bruns pointed out, the "two-plus-four" negotiators were quite successful in resolving most of the pressing questions of the international context of German unification, except for showing the way to a new security system. There was, however, a concern that Soviet consent to this settlement might be no more reliable than Gorbachev's and Shevardnadze's stay in office. The Soviet leaders had not consulted their opposition—influential opponents such as Yegor Ligachev and Valentin Falin—and had neglected to persuade the wider Soviet public and its representatives that the agreements between Kohl and the Soviet president were in the best long-term interest of the Soviet Union.[8]

7. For the German text, see Kaiser, *Deutschlands Vereinigung*, pp. 260–268. The letters of Genscher and de Maizière, on the German side, and an exchange between Genscher and Secretary of State Baker follow (pp. 269–273), regarding property claims of U.S. citizens in East Germany. There is also Shevardnadze's statement of September 20, 1990, before the Foreign Affairs Committee of the Supreme Soviet, together with the official Soviet interpretation of what had transpired.
8. Bruns, "Die Regelung," pp. 1730–1732. Bruns still had his doubts about whether

Foreign Minister Genscher, in a concluding statement evidently aimed at Germany's smaller European neighbors—which had been excluded from the "two-plus-four" meeting and which at one point had clamored for participation—still promised to present this "final settlement" to the CSCE Foreign Ministers' Conference in New York early in October and to the CSCE summit meeting to follow so that "every CSCE participant will recognize that the final settlement is wholly consistent with CSCE principles."

The treaty and the full sovereignty of united Germany were to enter into force as soon as the treaty was ratified by all six signatories. Such agreement was quite likely to be forthcoming so long as the process of bilateral contacts and multilateral meetings and agreements continued apace. The Soviet Union and united Germany were already working on their Good Neighbor, Partnership, and Cooperation Treaty—which reiterated the basic ideas of the Kohl-Gorbachev statement of June 13, 1989. In a remarkable passage (art. 3), it obliged the Germans "not to give any military assistance or aid to any attacker" of the Soviet Union (or vice versa) but to resolve the conflict under the rules of the United Nations or other collective security organizations; this was signed on September 13, 1990, by Genscher and Shevardnadze. There were two further agreements on the conditions of Soviet troop withdrawal and German financial support for this action (October 9 and 12). The Two-Plus-Four (Moscow) Treaty was ratified within a few months by the three Western allies and united Germany and, after some acrimonious debates, by the Supreme Soviet in early March 1991 (at which time it became effective).

It bears repeating that, contrary to German apprehensions, the Western allies made practically no painful demands on Germany—the recognition of borders, the limitation of German forces and ABC armaments, and the German preference for membership in NATO were never really a matter of dispute among the governments involved. The U.S. government, in fact, was instrumental in calming British and French fears and in turning a quadripartite decisionmaking process *about* Germany into reasonably consensual discussions *with* the two German governments. The Germans were also fortunate to be spared the long-threatened peace conference with all their wartime enemies—which probably would have been a time-consuming and expensive process—and the Moscow Treaty became the final peace treaty. The Soviet (and Polish) demands, while perhaps more painful, had already been conceded in bilateral contacts such as the Zhelezdnovodsk meeting before the final session by the German government.[9] To the Soviets under Gorbachev, it would seem,

the still-inexperienced decisionmaking process of the Supreme Soviet would bring this matter to a conclusion, since the German question probably paled before other policy necessities in Soviet eyes.

9. Polish concerns regarding the Oder-Neisse line were laid to rest at the Paris meeting.

the great attraction of German cooperation was that it promised Soviet access to Europe and the West, economic aid for *perestroika*, and a key to the "European house." Hence, forty-five years to the day after the beginning of the Potsdam Conference, on July 17, 1990, the extraordinary new understanding of Zhelezdnovodsk between Germany and the Soviet Union[10] had at least the potential of, say, close economic cooperation between Japan and China, between an economic locomotive and an endless train of resources. This potential, which of course is still uncertain of realization at this moment—especially in view of the centrifugal forces tearing at the Soviet Union—was bound to raise uneasy reflections in London and Paris, even though no one at the time questioned the Western democratic character and loyalties of the Federal Republic. The source of European apprehension, as before, appeared to be not the discernible intentions or even the military power of united Germany, but the magnitude of the emerging economic colossus.[11]

At the Security Crossroads in Europe

In the preamble of the Two-Plus-Four Treaty, there are several clauses referring to European security needs in the midst of the breakup of the prior system of three decades of détente and deterrence between NATO

German and other European press reactions echoed the profound significance of the Zhelezdnovodsk meeting between President Gorbachev and Chancellor Kohl, who probably also owes his December election victory to it. See *Der Spiegel* 44, no. 30, Jul. 23, 1990, pp. 16–27, and *Le Monde*, *Le Quotidien de Paris*, *The Economist*, and *Frankfurter Allgemeine Zeitung* for the dates following July 17, 1990.

10. Former French Foreign Minister Jean-François Poncet, after a rather positive assessment in a *Spiegel* interview, added: "It is possible that some people in Moscow are thinking of a German-Russian double hegemony over Europe—an outdated, nonmodern, Little European idea." *Der Spiegel* 45, no. 30, Jul. 23, 1991, p. 23. The *Neue Zürcher Zeitung* of the week after Zhelezdnovodsk was quite typical in its suspicious reactions to the restoration of German sovereignty. The editorials reflected the difficulty of conceiving of a sovereign nation-state of the size of Germany which did not hanker for nuclear weapons and power politics. See also the *Daily Telegraph* and Sweden's *Dagens Nyheter* for that date.

11. Bonn's negotiating strategies were sorely challenged by Moscow's earlier suggestions that perhaps all European nations should vote on German unification and, later, when Shevardnadze first proposed to postpone the resolution of the "external aspects" of unification in a move seemingly designed to foil united German NATO membership (May 5). Genscher's counterstrategy was to reinforce the CSCE, thereby giving the Soviet Union an institutionalized role in European security, to submit German arms reductions to the CFE negotiations in Vienna, and to offer a non-NATO former GDR—all *before* the Soviets could feel too isolated and cornered to respond to Kohl's offer of financial aid and economic cooperation.

and the Warsaw Pact: There is mention of the U.N. "principle of equal rights and self-determination of peoples," of the principles of the Final Act of the CSCE (Helsinki Agreements), of "a just and lasting peaceful order in Europe," and of taking "account of everyone's security interests." The contracting governments, moreover, proclaimed their readiness to adopt "effective arms control, disarmament, and confidence-building measures" and to set up "appropriate institutional arrangements within the framework of the CSCE." But there was no mistaking the great uncertainties on nearly everyone's mind that came with the passing of the Cold War. What would take the place of the East-West stalemate, the face-off at Checkpoint Charlie—which was dismantled and shipped to the Smithsonian Institution—or at the Fulda Gap, through which the tanks of the Warsaw Pact had been expected to cross the German mountain ranges for more than three long decades?[12]

Already in late 1989, a secret intelligence report from the U.S. Defense Department had disclosed that "for the past several years" the Soviet Union and its Warsaw Pact allies had been incapable of quickly launching a massive attack—however much the "slanting" rhetoric of the "evil empire" may have demanded it for the domestic purposes of the Reagan administration. The rationale for Western strategy and troop deployment was long out of date. Back in mid-1990, the Warsaw Treaty Organization (WTO) had not yet been dissolved, although most of its smaller members could no longer be counted upon. Still, there was the mighty Soviet military, and most observers took it for granted that the two main defense organizations, East and West, would continue to exist, albeit with intensified and progressive measures of disarmament and détente. A second possible scenario would have joined the two together in a permanent common security conference that would ensure that the steps of disarmament would be mutually balanced and verified. This was greatly facilitated by the "open skies" agreements disclosed at the NATO summit in mid-December 1989 and confirmed at Ottawa in mid-February 1990: a kind of *glasnost* of disarmament, the agreement permitted military inspection by overflight so that major troop movements and deployments could be observed by the other side. A third scenario foresaw the replacement of both defense organizations with a new, all-inclusive system of European collective security such as the CSCE, which included

12. See especially the pre-1990 literature, such as Stephen F. Larrabee, ed., *The Two German States and European Security* (New York: St. Martin's, 1989); Mary Kaldor, Gerard Holden, and Richard Falk, eds., *The New Détente: Rethinking East-West Relations* (London and Tokyo: Verso and the U.N. University, 1989); and James R. Golden et al., eds., *NATO at Forty: Change, Continuity, and Prospects* (Boulder, Colo.: Westview, 1989). Also see Wolfram Hanrieder, *Deutschland, Europa, Amerika* (Munich/Vienna/Zurich: Schöningh, 1991), chap. 4.

all thirty-four (with Albania, thirty-five) of the interested nations, includ-ing two superpowers.[13]

After some passage of time, it became clear that the WTO would collapse and, in fact, that the entire Soviet empire had for many years already been much too weak to mount the kind of attack for which the American taxpayer had wasted billions of dollars. As Wolfram Hanrieder has suggested, the fading of the chief object of NATO's "double contain-ment," the Soviet threat, put the onus of justification on those who continued to impose the containment on the other object, Germany. By fall of 1991, the Soviet Union was clearly unraveling as an empire with respect to some of its own union republics, not to mention former East European satellites, and had disappeared before the year was out. In March 1990, before this point had been reached, the foreign ministers of most East European governments made it clear to their Soviet WTO partners that they were far more afraid of a neutral Germany between the blocs, even a disarmed one, than they were of a united Germany under the double containment of NATO. In fact, some of them (especially Poland) began to explore—to the great surprise of the Soviets—whether they might join NATO themselves, or at least become associated with it. The point was that NATO continued to be strong while the WTO and the Soviet Union were no longer able to function as a significant counter-weight. The Soviet decision to come to terms at Zhelezdnovodsk signaled a wholesale Soviet retreat from East-Central Europe. The Moscow Treaty, once ratified, terminated all Soviet military agreements with the GDR, began the gigantic Soviet troop withdrawal, and permitted the East German army to be absorbed by the West. After a while there were even some authoritative Soviet voices, such as the historian Vyacheslav Dashichev, an adviser of Mikhail Gorbachev, who also thought German NATO membership was preferable to neutrality, or the status of a "loose cannon" between the blocs.[14]

13. See the internal discussion in the Soviet Union reported by Wolfgang Pfeiler, *Die Viermächteoption als Instrument sowjetischer Deutschlandpolitik*, Interne Studie no. 25 (St. Augustin: Konrad Adenauer Stiftung, 1991), pp. 58–70. The basic Soviet position had been to seek a neutralized Germany between the blocs or, alternatively, a neutral and drastically disarmed Germany—solutions viewed with alarm for different reasons by East and West Europeans, not to mention the Germans. Soviet and WTO resistance to NATO membership for a united Germany ranged from the idea of linking reunification with the dissolution of NATO, to German "dual membership"(!) for at least five years, to arrange-ments of mere "association" with NATO, perhaps analogous to the "French solution" of political but not military association. One proposal aimed at further maintenance of Soviet troops in East Germany, or continued four-power control of the former GDR while permitting "internal unification," or even joint NATO-WTO troop contingents stationed there.

14. See Pfeiler, *Die Viermächteoption*, pp. 64–67. Hanrieder's argument appears in *Deutschland, Europa, Amerika*, pp. 446–448.

As the Soviets gradually came around to their new position of accepting German NATO membership, they also adopted an increasingly more positive image of Germany. Still, the Soviets and all the East and West Europeans—except for the Thatcher government in Britain—assumed that NATO, too, would change profoundly from "its old confrontational stance and its policy of putting weapons of mass destruction into German hands" into a more political structure.[15] The East European desire to find reassurance with NATO continued unabated through the first half of 1991, if always mindful not to antagonize the Soviets by seeming too eager. Each of the Eastern nations made its own ambassador to Belgium simultaneously a diplomatic liaison with NATO and its committees. The "in-between Europeans" also appealed to WEU for security guarantees, their sense of urgency no doubt intensified by the murderous civil war in Yugoslavia. Finally, at their Copenhagen meeting (June 6, 1991), the NATO foreign ministers invited the East European governments *and the Soviet Union* to intensify their contacts with NATO, particularly at the higher levels of the officer corps (pointedly including the Soviet Union) but short of actual association. The abortive Soviet military coup of August 1991 witnessed even closer collaboration when the Polish and Czechoslovak military leadership traded intelligence with NATO about whether or not the remaining 300,000 Soviet troops in East Germany, especially in the eastern border regions, threatened to fight among each other or would bolt and battle their way home through Poland or the CSFR. NATO also considered setting up a NATO Cooperation Council for purposes of institutionalized consultation with the East Europeans and the Soviets, all of whom would be members. East Europeans have been among the most ardent supporters of NATO and of the U.S. role in Europe which they have viewed as a counterweight against Soviet power and against destabilization from within. They were hoping for some NATO action to oppose ethnic violence in Yugoslavia and elsewhere,[16] although this was not an option acceptable to France, which (not being a NATO member) would prefer to leave such actions to the European Community or WEU.

15. The quote comes from an interview given by Evgeniy Primakov, another Gorbachev adviser and spokesman, on June 19, 1990, in Pfeiler, *Die Viermächteoption*, p. 68. The Thatcher government, after a week of bitter recrimination, finally applauded the decisions of Zhelezdnovodsk for the sake of NATO but feared it would speed up the pace of European union.

16. Hungarian dignitaries still tell about the attempt by former Soviet Defense Minister Dimitri T. Yazov, early in 1991, to blackmail the Hungarian government into signing a "friendship treaty" that would have forsworn any Western alliance, on pain of the last troops the Soviets had in Hungary not being withdrawn. Hungary also permitted NATO aircraft to cross its territory on the way to the Gulf.

Adjusting NATO to the New Requirements

The role of NATO indeed began to change by its own lights at the Turnberry (Scotland) meeting of the NATO Council on June 7–8, 1990, when the assembled defense ministers agreed to address directly their WTO colleagues, who were simultaneously gathering in Moscow, hoping to turn their military pact into a political union. The "message of Turnberry" was a hand of friendship and cooperation extended to the Soviet Union and the East European nations. The same message was repeated at the NATO summit in London (June 6), where a number of proposals were made for restructuring NATO. Among other things, it was proposed that both NATO and the WTO states issue a joint declaration renouncing armed aggression, and the Soviets and other WTO states were invited to address the NATO Council and to maintain diplomatic relations with it. The London summit also suggested a revision of NATO strategy, aiming at the reduction of nuclear arms and abandonment of the strategy of forward defense.[17]

To understand the altogether positive reactions to this "turning point"—not counting the groans from the military-industrial complexes on both sides[18]—we need only recall that, as recently as May 1990, NATO had canceled a huge force maneuver simulating its response to a Warsaw Pact ground attack. There had been small, combat-readiness maneuvers on both sides all the while that the negotiations in Vienna and Geneva were dragging on. Still under arms were 4.1 million men in East and West Germany (only about one-sixth of them Germans), 13,000 tanks, 1,200 fighter planes, and substantial numbers of short-range and tactical nuclear weapons. On the other hand, some NATO defense experts were already calling for unilateral force reductions—e.g. to fewer than 100,000 in the case of American troops (U.S. Senator Sam Nunn)—and for a phasing out of short-range and tactical nuclear arms, over which the West German government had been in conflict with Great Britain and

17. See Kaiser, *Deutschlands Vereinigung*, pp. 77–80, and Hanrieder, *Deutschland, Europa, Amerika*, pp. 446–447. In the end, both sides also agreed to withdraw their troops some distance from the old combat zone in order to minimize accidental encounters and provocation. The "message of Turnberry" is reprinted in German in Kaiser, pp. 225–226; the London Declaration is reprinted in *Europa Archiv*, no. 17 (Sept. 1, 1990), D456–460.

18. The negative reactions were just as strong in the Soviet army and defense industry as in their Western counterparts. In the CPSU, in particular, the conservative forces were rallying for their all-out assault on Gorbachev at the imminent 28th CPSU Congress. With Boris Yeltsin's election as president of the Russian Federation, and the declaration of sovereignty by the latter, the conservatives believed Gorbachev to be vulnerable.

the United States only a year earlier.[19] Understandably, Soviet and WTO generals found the pace of change rather overwhelming and pleaded for guarantees of Soviet security and limits on German freedom. As Shevard-nadze replied to them, in an interview with *Pravda* (June 26, 1990), "the time has come to understand that neither socialism nor friendship, good neighborly relations, and respect can be built on bayonets, tanks, and bloodshed."[20]

By this time, Foreign Minister Genscher had made great and continuous efforts to tie together the Soviet and East European security interests manifested through CSCE with the repeated assertion of the future *political purposes* of NATO. It is true that the United States and Great Britain at first viewed CSCE and Genscher's promotion of it with considerable suspicion, particularly his apparent earlier assumption that in time CSCE would take over NATO's security function in Europe. But he gradually changed his mind back to principal reliance on NATO, and there can be no doubt that the Soviets felt greatly reassured during the crucial months of February through June of 1990 by the German emphasis on the CSCE. In fact, it may well have been this reassurance that persuaded them in July to drop their hard-line resistance to permit-ting a united Germany to stay in NATO—and, by implication, to let the GDR leave the WTO and be absorbed, with some restrictions, into the Western alliance.

The political purposes or goals that would sustain NATO in the future—after its military character was scaled down as a result of the reduction of forces committed to by its members—had been spelled out before in repeated statements emphasizing the North Atlantic community of Western, democratic nations and its interest in arms control, disar-mament, and the peaceful resolution of international conflict.[21] Most

19. In April 1990, American forces had barely started to bring back eight of the sixty-four cruise missiles of the INF missiles the United States had agreed to scrap. The Soviets also had gotten rid of the first INF missiles they had promised to eliminate under an agreement that dated back two years. The decision to modernize the next-smaller nuclear missiles had precipitated determined opposition from the Kohl government in April 1989. In spring of 1990, NATO, or rather the United States and Britain, finally gave in to the Germans on this account and, in 1991, decided to phase out the short-range and tactical nuclear weapons as well.

20. Reprinted in Kaiser, *Deutschlands Vereinigung*, pp. 239–241. The Soviet foreign minister sought the solution in drastic arms reductions, especially of the united Germany, and in a strengthened CSCE process.

21. See especially the Harmel report of 1967. But there were similar statements through-out the forty-year history of the organization. By June 1990, Chancellor Kohl admitted freely that CSCE would not replace NATO, but he still thought CSCE was a most important process linking the North American and European governments with the construction of the future Europe.

recently, the Brussels summit of the heads of NATO governments, in May 1989, had spoken of the goal of an international community, "based on the rule of law in which all nations join together to reduce world tensions, settle disputes peacefully, and search for solutions to issues of global concern, including poverty, social injustice and environmental burdens, on which our common fate depends." At the London Summit Declaration of July 6, 1990, the heads of the sixteen NATO governments proposed to the WTO member states a joint declaration that would include[22]

- an assurance not to consider each other adversaries
- a commitment to nonaggression
- a reaffirmation of the intention to refrain from the use or threat of force against the territorial integrity or political independence of any state.

Finally, we can find some of the political role also in President Bush's definition of the global "new world order," in his speech to the U.N. General Assembly and in a toast to retiring General Secretary Javier Pérez de Cuellar in which he pointed out that the Cold War and East-West ideological rivalry had dominated and poisoned U.N. debates for decades:

> But the passing of this rivalry has enabled the U.N. to assume its proper role on the world stage. . . . Where institutions of freedom have lain dormant, the U.N. can offer them new life . . . [since they] play a crucial role in our quest for a new world order, an order in which no nation must surrender an iota of its own sovereignty, an order characterized by the rule of law rather than the resort to force; the cooperative settlement of disputes, rather than anarchy and bloodshed, and an unstinting belief in human rights.

Among other things, Bush referred to the peaceful settlement of border disputes and to the ethnic rivalries and hostilities that sprang up after the demise of communism. The president's speech was evocative of the hopes expressed for the League of Nations by President Woodrow Wilson in 1918 and by Harry S. Truman in 1945 for the United Nations, and

---

22. *Report on Arms Control and Disarmament and on Changes in the Balance of Military Power 1989/1990 (1 July 1989–30 June 1990)* (Bonn: Federal Republic of Germany, Press and Information Office, March 1991), pp. 12–13.

perhaps of his own dreams when he was the American U.N. ambassador under President Nixon.

While these pronouncements fall short of a clarion call into the political future of NATO, they have to be set within the context of the other processes of East-West reconciliation and the existing organizations of the European Community—particularly the latter, since the dramatic changes had so far been confined almost entirely to the East-West confrontation in Europe, and there was some irritation in Washington at the European insistence that there was a distinctive "European security interest" separate from the global security interests of the United States and the United Nations. In the first eight months of the unification process alone (November–July), there were four bilateral meetings between President Bush and Chancellor Kohl, three between Kohl and Gorbachev, eleven between Secretary of State Baker and Genscher, eight between Baker and Shevardnadze, three between Baker and Gorbachev and, of course, two summit meetings between the presidents of the United States and the Soviet Union. For years there had also been the negotiations on conventional arms reduction (CFE) and confidence- and security-building measures (CSBM) in Vienna, the direct negotiations between the United States and the Soviet Union about strategic nuclear arms (START) and shorter-range missiles, and the Geneva Conference on Disarmament (CD) as well as U.N. debates and special commissions (UNDC) on the appropriate subjects. But the process was slow and the current readiness for solutions considerably ahead of the schedules of conferences and subjects such as nuclear test bans, the elimination of chemical and biological weapons, and nuclear nonproliferation.[23] Progress at the various disarmament meetings often awaited breakthroughs in bilateral contacts and might have taken years more if the unraveling of Soviet control in the East and enlightened responses in Washington had not pushed things along.

By the same token, bold steps in bilateral negotiations were frequently not forthcoming because the intelligence-gathering process was slanted— as revealed, for example, during the Senate hearings on the nomination of Robert Gates for CIA director and probably replicated often on the Soviet side—or because the glacial progress in Geneva or Vienna discouraged them.[24] On the other hand, well-planned summit meetings of world

23. Ibid., pt. 2.
24. As late as May 10, 1990, at a meeting of the Nuclear Planning Group at Kananaskis, Canada, Defense Secretary Richard Cheney still would not consider the disintegration of WTO sufficient reason for abandoning the basic nuclear deterrence strategy of the West. Other defense ministers, notably the German minister of defense, were ready to scrap the short-range missiles. In the meantime, Hungary and Czechoslovakia were pressing for the dissolution of the WTO at a mid-June meeting in Moscow.

leaders such as Gorbachev and Bush often served as deadlines for achieving definite disarmament agreements ready to sign on the appointed day. The pressures against the reluctance of the military-industrial complexes to scale back the high cost of continuing engagement also built up quickly on all sides. In the United States, for instance, where Senator Sam Nunn and Representative Patricia Schroeder have estimated the annual cost of maintaining the American commitment in Europe at $160 billion a year—there has always been a concern that the West Europeans have not borne their share—there was Nunn's proposal to scale back American forces to 75,000–100,000 soldiers and not just to the 195,000 set by the administration. The 400,000 allied troops and 200,000 dependents had also been costing the German treasury a considerable amount.[25] The American budget deficit naturally makes the large sums at issue a great attraction to budget cutters and to popular forces clamoring for a "peace dividend." To quote Democratic Senator Kent Conrad (North Dakota), "the West Germans are paying to keep Soviet troops in East Germany at the very time we are paying to keep our troops in West Germany to protect them against Soviet troops in East Germany. That makes no sense." He was speaking while the Senate was voting to save the B-2 bomber and two battleships from the budget axe.

Again, this scenario was likely to be replayed a hundredfold in the Soviet Union, in cases of resistance both from the military establishment and from the defense industry. Soviet resistance, for example, nearly scuttled the Two-Plus-Four Treaty, German unification, and the great CFE disarmament agreements of October 3, 1990, when the military argued that the CFE pact might prevent the Soviets from countering the U.S. military buildup in the Gulf, only 700 miles away, by concentrating Soviet forces in southern Russia. Fortunately, its objections were overcome and the Gulf War eventually revealed itself not to be an American feint for a knockout blow and invasion of the Soviet Union, after all.[26]

25. Involved were land and base facilities with a real-estate value of $28 billion and an annual rental value of $800 million. Some $500 million a year were needed to keep up the allied forces in Berlin as well as another 120 million marks a year to pay for maneuver damage—not to mention the $550 million needed to maintain the Soviet troops for five years in a united Germany, or the sums that had been paid by the GDR to the Soviets for this purpose (2.8 billion East marks a year). See the *Washington Post* (national weekly edition), Jul. 23–29, 1990, p. 16.

26. The disarmament meeting in New York between Secretary Baker and his Soviet colleague Shevardnadze (October 3, 1990) capped seventeen years of CFE negotiations. It resulted in the scrapping of 2,900 NATO tanks, 23,000 WTO tanks, and 26,900 WTO artillery pieces in order to reach levels of 20,000 tanks, 30,000 armored vehicles, and 20,000 artillery pieces on each side. The United States had insisted on this agreement before the December CSCE summit could occur. It is worth mentioning that, notwithstanding some press voices, statements by key Democratic politicians in Congress, as well as popular

On the other hand, as Henry Kissinger pointed out, the remaining strategic nuclear arsenal of the Soviet Union after a START agreement would still be ten times the size of the British and French nuclear forces combined and not necessarily subject to the same handicap that continuing domestic turmoil has placed upon Soviet conventional forces.[27]

The noble competition between Bush and Gorbachev in slashing conventional and nuclear arms in a big way, as announced at the time of this writing, should go a long way toward resolving the financial problems of both superpowers.[28] In the meantime, of course, the possible division of some Soviet nuclear arms among several independent union republics—the Ukraine, Kazakhstan, and others—has further complicated the situation. The question of how the West could prepare itself for all eventualities, including the possible resurgence of Russian military might under a post-Yeltsin military dictatorship, is no cause for complacency either. The failed military coup and the subsequent disintegration of the Soviet Union forced the United States and NATO to take cognizance of the fading of a familiar enemy and of the diminished capacity and will of its remnants to invade the West. The Russian President, Boris Yeltsin, even hopes to rid his federation of nuclear weapons, in the long run, although Russian missiles were still aimed at the United States in October 1992, according to Marshall Yevgeny I. Shaposhnikov, the CIS military commander. What mission does this leave for NATO? Unfortunately, at this point, a baker's dozen of Third World countries, beginning with Iraq, stand at the threshold of nuclear armament, poised to be the next deadly challenge to their neighbors and the West. How can we close the barn door of nuclear proliferation again, or stop the raging bulls that have escaped?

To round out the discussion, nevertheless, we need to consider also the

---

rumblings, the White House has not taken umbrage at the new German financial assertiveness in supplying Soviet aid as a *quid pro quo* for removing the last obstacles to German unification. Nor did President Bush have any objection to the Japanese renewal of its pre-Tiananmen loan program to China ($5.8 billion).

27. See Kissinger's article in the *Los Angeles Times*, Jul. 22, 1990. He was also concerned that the German renunciation of nuclear arms might, in case of Soviet attack, once again place responsibility for bailing out a nuclear-free Germany on the United States, which would have to risk the nuclear devastation the Germans escaped by means of their renunciation. See also Werner Weidenfeld and Josef Janning, eds., *Global Responsibilities: Europe in Tomorrow's World* (Gütersloh: Bertelsmann Foundation, 1991), pp. 96–111 and 161–195.

28. The WTO's tanks and artillery were divided in such a way as to leave about two-thirds with the Soviet Union, between 7% and 9% each with Poland, Bulgaria, the CSFR, and Romania, and about 4% with Hungary.

optimistic view of European security which was expressed late in 1990, to the embarrassment of the British government, first by the British Minister of Defense Procurement, Alan Clark, and then by the retiring director of the Royal Institute of International Affairs (RIIA), Admiral Sir James Eberle, a former NATO commander, who said in his valedictory address:[29] "Having accomplished its aim of bringing the division of Europe to a peaceful end, there remains one final task for NATO, that would lead to the fulfillment of the political ideals of its founding fathers . . . namely to create the conditions for its own dissolution."

Eberle's statement was said to be much closer to the position taken then by France, Italy, and united Germany in preparation for the EC summit late in 1990 and focused on the creation of a West European defense organization (WEA) grafted onto the European Community's WEU. The former RIIA director believed that NATO had outlived its usefulness and that its defense-planning functions should be progressively turned over to WEU and the European Community. Whereas the British government believed that NATO alone could guarantee transatlantic cooperation in defense, Eberle thought that the United States would continue to be involved in European stability simply because of its major economic interests there. To that end, he pictured WEU as an integral part of the EC structure and not just a NATO auxiliary.

This differed, if only by degree and tendency, from the evolving American point of view as expressed, for example, at an American Assembly gathering in Harriman, New York, on May 30, 1991. As reported in advance of publication of the papers[30] presented there, NATO structures should be revised and not reinforced, but "the U.S. should support a European defense structure as a complement to NATO, perhaps the WEU, which might, in due course, become the focal point for European contributions to actions outside Europe." CSCE was viewed as a useful "complement" to NATO that might "build military transparency," monitor human rights, and resolve or mediate regional conflicts.

---

29. *Manchester Guardian Weekly*, Dec. 23, 1990. It should be noted that this innocent view of European security was evidently expressed well before the impact of the Gulf War had sunk in. The Gulf War dramatized the issue of Third World dictators acquiring ABC weapons and blackmailing the Western industrial nations.

30. *Rethinking America's Security: U.S. Interests in the 1990s*, 79th American Assembly (New York: Council on Foreign Relations, 1991), pp. 11–13, and Graham Allison and Gregory Treverton, eds., *Rethinking American Security: Beyond Cold War to New York Order* (New York: Norton, 1992). The report called nuclear proliferation "a major threat" and called for a test ban and for outlawing the possession of ABC weapons outside the nuclear club.

NATO and WEU

A brief summary might help to guide the reader through the political
maze of European security questions after the great changes of 1990/91
in the Soviet Union and in Eastern Europe, after Zhelezdnovodsk and
German unification, after the CFE pact of October 1990, and after the
dramatic events of 1991. The core of NATO strategy, forward defense
along the old Iron Curtain, lost its German locale and its *raison d'être*.
The Soviet Union lost much of its capability for constituting a threat—in
particular, its capacity for a quick strike and, eventually, its very cohesion.
On the other hand, even if only the Russian Federation under a reactionary regime were left, a possible renewal of the threat cannot entirely be
excluded. Its nuclear might still makes it the dominant military force in
Europe and the only power capable of destroying the United States,[31]
although the CFE pact, by putting East and West on an even level, put an
end to decades of WTO conventional superiority over NATO. The mutual
de-escalation decided in the fall of 1991 will make the military threat
quite tame by about 1995. Since the final demise of WTO, moreover,
Eastern Europe has become a denuclearized buffer zone between NATO
and what remains of the Soviet Union. Eastern Europe is particularly in
need of the stabilizing effects of the NATO presence without which its
democratic and economic development—to which the European Community, CSCE, and individual investors are expected to contribute—
might be engulfed in ethnic conflict and domestic coups.

Given the range of social and economic problems in Europe, NATO as
a military organization lacks the required capacity for problem-solving
and will require help from WEU, the European Community, CSCE, or a
combination of these to address the problems of Europe effectively. One
feasible option would be to combine CSCE as a broader, problem-solving
organization—its tasks are still to be clarified—with NATO, which
would engage in crisis management, conflict resolution, collective security, maintenance of existing borders, and prevention of wars both within
the larger European area and with respect to outside threats, such as
instability in Eastern Europe or Iraq's aggressive designs. To that end, it

31. In the words of the American Assembly report (p. 11): "if increasing economic
disruption and disintegration results in civil war, frightening questions arise whether
centralized command and control of 30,000 nuclear weapons spread over half a dozen
republics can be maintained." There is also the "risk of nuclear artillery shells or advanced
conventional weapons finding their way into the international arms bazaar."

would seem, NATO would require a new political mission,[32] but also a well-equipped, well-organized core of conventional troops, including some for rapid deployment at trouble spots within and on the periphery of Europe in order to counter hostile troop concentrations with superior force. The plans for a NATO rapid reaction force—which could also serve WEU, as France and the Europeans at Brussels contend—envisage four mobile divisions of about 70,000 troops each, under a British commander, and equipped with American combat helicopters and fighter planes. The rest of NATO forces in Europe might be scaled down from twenty-three to sixteen divisions in seven army corps, including six of multinational composition stationed in Central Europe. One division will be purely German and under German command, stationed (as agreed with the Soviets) in Potsdam, East Germany. One will be British and another, in Southern Europe, might be under Italian leadership.

The Gulf War and the Yugoslavian imbroglio dramatized the problems of linkage between U.S. and regional European security interests, problems that could not be solved by establishing a "Eurogroup" within NATO (of which France and Spain are not members) or by "refunctioning" WEU, as proposed by the Dutch, for intervention in the Yugoslav civil war. Tying U.S. nuclear power into the European security system—keeping the Americans "in"—seems as important and continuing a goal as "tying down" the military potential of a united Germany. The latter goal, in fact, requires the former. Since the Russians have already gone "out" of Central Europe of their own accord, the old goal of "keeping them out" seems redundant now and could be replaced, up to a point, by aid, cooperation, and even joint action against third parties that threaten peace in the region. Finally, in place of a strategy of flexible response, with its tactics of "direct defense" and "deliberate escalation," it might be better to return to using nuclear arms—especially with the as yet uncoordinated French and British forces—but only as a last resort.

The impact of the Gulf War on rethinking European security strategy produced unexpected results not only because of Germany's constitutional doubts and the widely shared conviction that NATO's mission could not simply be broadened to deploy its military forces outside the NATO area. For a while, attention shifted to the nine-member WEU—Ireland, Denmark, and Greece are the three EC members that do not

32. The early call for a newly formulated political mission for NATO came particularly from the NATO General Secretary and former West German Defense Minister Manfred Wörner. See *Die Welt*, Jan. 13, 1989. Wörner's critics, however, argue that NATO has always been political and that its networks of consultation keep it so.

belong to WEU, but it does include non-NATO France. The long years of inactivity and minuscule staff support made WEU's willingness to organize Europe's response in the Gulf "something of a joke," to quote a NATO specialist, even though it was widely credited with one notable contribution: coordinating naval operations. In mid-1991, in any event, the British government still supported a strong role for WEU, if not as a stand-in for NATO or as a duplication of the rapid reaction force (RRF) agreed on for NATO. With some Italian support, the British proposal envisaged WEU as a link between the European Community and NATO, subordinate to but "autonomous" from the latter, as their "Atlanticist" contribution to the Maastricht summit on the future of the European Community. It was a solution sure to please Washington and those EC members who were hesitant to deepen the Community in this respect.

But the Germans and the French seized the initiative for a defense force to result from European political union—in fact, following up article 1 of the draft treaty for a new European Community which defines its objective as "the assertion of European identity in the world, in particular by implementing a common foreign and security policy which will ultimately include a common defense." Their proposal reiterated their intent, expressed in a joint letter to the European Community a year earlier, to make WEU "an integral part of the European union process" by entrusting it with "full or part responsibility for working out decisions and measures concerning the Union's defense and security" (as their draft article 2 put it and which could of course be amended). The European Community and WEU, moreover, were to be brought closer together by moving WEU headquarters from London to Brussels and establishing closer cooperation and consultation between them. Initially, the Germans had thought to mediate between the two camps, while the French seemed intent on pushing the United States entirely out of Europe, just as the British strove to keep America engaged there. The Franco-German initiative immediately won the support of Italy, Spain, and Belgium, as well as that of EC Commission President Jacques Delors, but not that of Denmark and the Netherlands. From the British point of view, the European Community is itself in the process of considering applications from neutralist Sweden and Switzerland for future membership, and is a less likely choice because of its preoccupation with the process of "widening" or "deepening" European economic integration in the near future. Such a plan was more within the mandate of CSCE, but the sheer size of that thirty-five-member organization makes it difficult to generate a consensus for action. To overcome this impasse, also, the United Nations could be enlisted in support of sanctions and even military action to counter Iraqi aggression against neighboring Arab states—an option which was greatly preferred by the Europeans and which was, after all, within the original mandate of the world organization. After the Gulf War and the Soviet postcoup evolution of 1991, however, the tendencies toward a pulling away from American hegemonic control among the West European EC nations, the East European and Soviet republics, Japan, China, and the U.N. members in general were greater than ever.[33]

The exaggerated hopes raised by the Gulf War, or more likely by the publicity put out about it, soon gave way to European pessimism about extinguishing the smoldering fires of nationalism and ethnic hatred in Yugoslavia and elsewhere in Eastern Europe. The German reaction to the Gulf War is in a number of respects more significant than their reaction to the nationality conflict in Yugoslavia where, the *New York Times* editorials notwithstanding, the German government had attempted to mediate between Serbs and Croats in the same ineffectual way as the other EC countries.[34]

The Gulf action, on the other hand, did not only land the Kohl government between angry pacifist reaction at home and pressure to participate from the allies; more significantly, it confronted the German government with questions of German national identity, an economic rather than a military mission,[35] and the future of Germany. How would it have looked to Germany's suspicious neighbors and the world if the first major action of the united country had been a military foray involving massive killing of Third World (Iraqi) soldiers? Unlike Ameri-

33. On the Franco-German proposal, see Jacques Amalric and Jean-Pierre Langellier in *Le Monde*, Oct. 17, 1991, and the editorial in the *Manchester Guardian Weekly*, Oct. 27, 1991, p. 12. The Franco-German initiative also invited non–WEU members Denmark, Ireland, and Greece to join, and took the trouble to inform Washington of its new proposals. See also the in-depth feature on the subject in "Defense," *The Economist*, Sept. 1, 1990, pp. 1–18. The latter spelled out the situation in mid-1990, as seen by British opinion, including London's skepticism about a "new, all-European security order" (p. 16) and the CSCE's capacity for decisive action within the unpredictable world at the time—in short, the need to keep America involved and the Germans tied down, and to worry about developments in the former Soviet Union (pp. 17–18).

34. Again, Genscher and others hoped the CSCE might be able to live up to its collective security and conflict-resolving mission, but the organization was still too unwieldy and this particular issue was very difficult to decide: repeated truces arranged by the European Community and its emissaries were broken by both sides, again and again.

35. Another in-depth feature in *The Economist*, Sept. 28, 1991, pp. 21–24, an assessment of the "new world order" after the Gulf War and the postcoup developments in the former Soviet Union, approvingly quotes Edward Luttwak to the effect that world economic competition, after the patriotic celebrations of victory in the Gulf, is once more taking the place of the politico-military struggle for supremacy: "the pursuit of adversarial goals with commercial means." The failure of American negotiators in the GATT negotiations, consequently, signaled the growing independence of the EC nations.

can and British reactions to the deeds of their own troops, German public opinion would have mercilessly exposed and been revolted by the brutality of war, and Germany's neighbors would have crucified the German government and its troops. Also very important was the likely reception of a German military participation by the Soviet public and by Soviet hard-liners who, as mentioned earlier, suspected the Western Gulf troops to be planning a major attack on an enfeebled Soviet Union. Given Soviet memories of the allied invasion of 1918 and the German assault of 1941/42, it would have been a huge blunder for the German government to send troops to the Gulf at this precise moment, when the Soviet Union had not even ratified the Two-Plus-Four and the Soviet Troop Repatriation treaties. Ratification by the Supreme Soviet took place only in March and in the first days of April 1991, having been held up by the objections of suspicious hard-liners in Moscow.[36]

The Role of the CSCE

The question still remains: How does the Conference on Security and Cooperation in Europe (CSCE), the Helsinki organization better known for its assertion of human rights and promotion of social and cultural cooperation, fit into the European security scenario? Is it, as German Foreign Minister Genscher put it in his address to the U.N. General Assembly on September 25, 1991, just a matter of "expanded responsibilities" to be given CSCE to render it "capable of action"? Or did he already prejudge the question, on this occasion, by calling on the U.N. Security Council to "adopt a clear, unequivocal position so that the fighting can be stopped" in Yugoslavia? Genscher also paid tribute to the "continued efforts of the Western alliance [NATO] to ensure stability throughout Europe," and he promised that the German Constitution would be changed so that, in future, united Germany could fulfill its security obligations under the U.N. Charter.[37] Even Secretary Baker is on

36. Furthermore, aside from the more superficial criticisms of German "cowardice" and "disloyalty" to the Western alliance, the thought may well have crossed some minds among the irreconcilable critics of German unification that this would be the perfect way to push the Germans into making bullies of themselves again, a self-fulfilling prophecy of the first water.

37. Genscher's promise was received critically in the German press, which promptly reminded him that such a constitutional change required qualified majorities in the Bundestag—that is to say, SPD cooperation, which the government was unlikely to obtain. See *Mainzer Allgemeine Zeitung*, Sept. 26, 1991, for example.

record with a "joint statement" with Genscher (May 12, 1991), proposing, as he had done in December 1989, that closer relations between
NATO and East European governments be organized through CSCE:
"NATO will support the CSCE in meeting security demands in Europe,"
read their finalized proposal, in which a "North Atlantic Cooperative
Council" of regular meetings between NATO and the "liaison nations"
in Eastern Europe was specified (October 2, 1991). Indeed, most continental nations, West and East, set great store by the "CSCE process,"
but it appears to be a slow, cumulative process of building up the all-
European (and North American) house brick by brick, rather than a
quick, prefabricated building project designed for imminent functions
such as keeping the peace or protecting national minorities.[38]

This is not to deny that the CSCE has been a major factor behind the
multilateral development of political freedom and cooperation in Eastern
Europe since its inception with the 1975 Final Act of Helsinki. For the
GDR, in particular, the CSCE's emphasis on international contacts and
cooperation along with the promotion of human rights and quasi-
democratic discussion subtly began to undermine Honecker's restrictive
system and to trigger acute conflicts over the gaps between constitutional
promise and performance.[39] A state that rigidly isolated its citizens from
the outside world could not but be continually embarrassed by discussions of *Rechtsstaat* (government of law) and international law, or of free
mobility in other socialist states (e.g., in 1973)—not to mention the
contacts with Western countries and organizations such as the European
Community, NATO, WEU, CFE, and the Council of Europe, even in the
early years (1969–1975). In the seventies, the CSCE played an important
role in advancing East-West détente against a background of tentative
cooperation between Leonid Brezhnev and Richard Nixon, thus permitting Willy Brandt's *Ostpolitik* to bring about a rapprochement between
Bonn and the main WTO governments—most of all the Soviet Union,
which paid a high price in concessions at Helsinki (1975) and at later
meetings in Belgrade (1977) and Madrid (1988).[40]

38. See the account and documents of the early years of CSCE in *Sicherheit und
Zusammenarbeit in Europa (KSZE). Analyse und Dokumentation 1965–1972*, and the
follow-up volume for 1973–1978, both edited by Hans-Adolf Jacobsen, Wolfgang Mallmann, and Christian Meier (Cologne: Wissenschaft & Politik, 1973 and 1978).

39. Rolf Reissig, "Der Umbruch in der DDR und der Niedergang realsozialistischer
Systeme," *Biss Public* 1 (Jan. 1991), 35–64, esp. 41. See also the chronology of CSCE
activities in *Sicherheit und Zusammenarbeit*, vol. 2, pp. 977–1001, which details themes
and contacts with EC and other Western organizations, and the six-language "phraseology"
of the Helsinki, Belgrade, and Madrid meetings in *KSZE–KVAE* (Bonn: Auswärtiges Amt,
1987).

40. See Hanrieder, *Deutschland, Europa, Amerika*, pp. 237–254, and Robert Tucker,
The Nuclear Debate: Deterrence and the Lapse of Faith (New York: Holmes & Meier,

As the security structures of the East-West conflict began to decline—notwithstanding the "evil empire" rhetoric in Washington during the years until 1987—the CSCE process became more important than ever, defusing moments of confrontation, sponsoring "confidence-building" measures, and eventually making German unification possible. In 1989/90, its protean role was to provide major assistance in everything but force to the evolving new democratic systems of Eastern Europe—for example, with its Conferences on the Human Dimension (the "third basket" of Helsinki) in June 1989 and June 1990, opening up visions of a Europe of democracy and political pluralism with common institutions.

The CSCE Conference on Economic Cooperation in Europe (Bonn, March/April 1990) not only championed cooperation in industry, commerce, science, and technology but agreed on the practical steps of cooperation as well as a shared orientation toward a market economy; it also expressed hopes of avoiding a permanent East-West division between the poor and the rich.[41] An earlier CSCE meeting in Sofia (October/November 1989) also set common goals of cooperation in environmental protection—before most people were fully aware of the gigantic environmental problems of the GDR, Poland, and the CSFR. In the field of security policy, CSCE held a seminar on military doctrines and strategy in Vienna (January/February 1990) and helped the CFE negotiations along with a joint statement by the foreign ministers of France and West Germany to the CSCE plenary session in Vienna (January 25, 1990) in favor of completing the big CFE agreement toward the end of that year.

Three months later, the Franco-German Defense and Security Council advocated extensive defense cooperation between France and Germany, thus reviving the process that, in mid-October 1991, was to lead Mitterrand and Kohl to call for the development of a "genuine European security and defense identity" and a Franco-German WEU defense force. In early 1990, Chancellor Kohl also emphasized the importance of utilizing the increasing common ground of values and consensus to establish "an interlocking CSCE security structure for the whole of Europe."[42] Because of the comprehensive membership of the CSCE, all

---

1985). See also the report of a November 1989 meeting on the impact of the CSCE process on the GDR in *Deutschland Archiv* 23, no. 3 (March 1990), 438–439, and Stephan Lehne, *The Vienna Meeting of the CSCE, 1986–1989: A Turning Point in East-West Relations* (Boulder, Colo.: Westview, 1991), which also goes into the background of CSCE. But see also François Heisbourg, "From a Common European Home to a European Security System," in Gregory F. Treverton, ed., *The Shape of the New Europe* (New York: Council on Foreign Relations, 1992), pp. 48–50.

41. See the document in the *Report on Arms Control and Disarmament and on Changes in the Balance of Military Power 1989/1990*, pp. 79–81. The conference also emphasized the link between a democratic multiparty system and economic development.

42. See ibid., pp. 14–17. In an interview with *Der Spiegel* magazine, Genscher suggested

arms control, disarmament, and confidence-building measures somehow redound to the credit of the organization while overall setbacks or periods of stagnation seem to inflict no permanent harm.

Formal unification having been completed, the united German government and the four wartime allies presented the result of the "two-plus-four" negotiations first to the CSCE foreign ministers meeting at New York (October 1–2) and then to the Paris summit of CSCE (November 19–21, 1990) to assure everyone that German unification would create no new problems for Europe but, rather, would "increase our hopes of a better future" there. The Soviets pointedly disavowed their superpower and adversary role of four decades and proclaimed themselves "a European power," eager to take its place in the "common European home." This momentous move also underscored the position of the new Germany between Western Europe and the Soviets. The long-awaited Paris summit, as expected, came to agree on annual ministerial consultations, biennial review conferences to assess "progress towards a Europe whole and free," the establishment of a CSCE Secretariat in Prague, and an agency in Warsaw to monitor elections in CSCE countries—especially in the new democracies of Eastern Europe. It also agreed on a CSCE Conflict Resolution Center in Vienna, to assist with contacts among the military and for the conciliation of disputes among member states, and on a CSCE parliamentary body, the Assembly of Europe, which was to be based on the existing twenty-one-member Parliamentary Assembly of the Council of Europe.[43]

The Paris summit also involved the solemn proclamation of a CSCE Charter for a New Europe, dubbed "a post–Cold War Magna Charta" by outgoing British Prime Minister Thatcher, which proclaimed everyone's "right to participate in free and fair elections, to own property . . . and to exercise individual enterprise." While the American and British press still expressed doubts about an organization that gave the same voice (and a veto) to superpowers, NATO or WTO members, and to

"institutionalizing the CSCE process" with a crisis avoidance and resolution center and an arms control verification agency. *Der Spiegel* 44, no. 20, May 15, 1990, p. 30. He stressed the great interest of the Soviets in "deepening and elaborating the CSCE process." There was also the Czech proposal of a European Security Commission (modeled on the U.N. Security Council) in Prague. The American interest in CSCE had always been focused on human rights complaints against the East rather than on the security and economic cooperation in which the Europeans were primarily interested.

43. The Council of Europe includes all but the WTO and transatlantic nations and some ministates. The CFE Treaty regarding balanced disarmament was also supposed to be linked to the Paris CSCE summit. See the report in *Deutschland Archiv* 23, no. 8 (Aug. 1990), 1154–1156. The Prague Secretariat has the function of organizing the annual foreign ministers' and biennial summit meetings.

neutrals and ministates like Liechtenstein, Malta, or San Marino, continental European leaders and the press solemnly declared the Cold War to be over and an "age of democracy, peace, and unity" to be at hand in Europe. The signatories pledged peaceful cooperation and forswore the military approach to the resolution of conflict. President Bush welcomed the disappearance of the old divisions, but warned also—seconded by Gorbachev—against a "Lebanonization of whole regions of Europe," presumably those torn by nationality conflicts.[44] With the Soviet Union now a "European power," it was important for the United States to continue its role in Europe. Chancellor Kohl also emphasized the CSCE role of the United States and Canada along with transatlantic solidarity at the same time that he expressed his pleasure at the institutional evolution of the organization[45] and looked forward to Germans hosting the next foreign ministers' meeting in Berlin.

The indeterminate nature of the CSCE process continued to confuse observers who had been most impressed by its contribution to the evolving East-West European consensus on democracy, human rights, and economic development during the difficult transition. Even senior statesmen such as Foreign Minister Genscher, not to mention less experienced contemporaries, thought that a CSCE structure might defuse the Middle East crisis of 1990/91 or lead to "a Middle Eastern peace order"—or they hoped to apply the same magic to the Yugoslavian conflict—all to no avail. The Berlin meeting of foreign ministers still drew acerbic comments in the American press, even though the institutionalization of CSCE had grown apace. The Conflict Prevention Center in Vienna, for example, gave birth to a separate Conflict Resolution Center which prepared emergency measures for crisis management: short-cut measures were devised, such as speedy convocation of the foreign ministers and applications requiring the consent of only a dozen foreign ministers for action. The fears of the Soviet Union regarding its Baltic minority, of Turkey regarding Armenians, or of the Czechs with respect to the Slovaks are a considerable hindrance to relying on any enforcement—so long as the damage does not seem serious enough to call for determined remedies.[46] The impending waves of East-West migration and

44. Michael Mandelbaum also called it "the peace conference of the Cold War" and compared it to the 1815 Congress of Vienna or the 1919 peace conference at Versailles. *Los Angeles Times*, Nov. 17, 1990.

45. See his government declaration of policy before the Bundestag, in Presse- und Informationsamt, *Bulletin* no. 136, Nov. 23, 1990, p. 1405. The text of the Paris Charter is in *Bulletin* no. 137, Nov. 24, 1990, p. 1409. Among other statements, it welcomes the Two-Plus-Four (Moscow) Treaty of September 12, 1990, and Germany unity and commitment to the Helsinki principles.

46. See *Der Spiegel* 45, no. 26, June 25, 1991. In late April 1991, the Soviet Union

the gradual withdrawal of nearly all foreign troops will sooner or later have their effects as well: they will make weak governments look even weaker.

The Berlin meeting (June 19–20, 1991) of the CSCE Council of Foreign Ministers found the CSCE process once more at full flow—though some observers claimed it had already run out of things to do after overcoming the East-West division—and representatives were engaged in loose preliminary discussions about the nature of the CSCE parliament[47] and about the principle of federalism or confederacy to underlie its organization. There was even idle talk of locating the organization in Bonn, once the German government had moved to the new capital. The indefatigable Genscher still hosted Soviet Foreign Minister Alexander Bessmertnykh in Bonn, among other reasons in order to inquire whether there were any nuclear arms left with the Soviet troops in East Germany. Chancellor Kohl, in his opening address, welcomed the establishment of a parliament and called for "permanent political consultation on a wider scale" as well as for "new mechanisms for settling conflicts and disputes" and ratification of the big CFE agreement of the previous fall.

One day earlier, Secretary James Baker had spoken of a "transatlantic community from Vancouver to Vladivostok" to complete the European democratic "architecture," clearly inviting the Soviet Union into the charmed circle of Western democracies, a "commonwealth of freedom." He repeated the buzzwords "a just and stable European peace order"—he called it the traditional NATO goal—and a "cooperative security system" for all of free Europe without giving further details. He also made the by-now-customary welcoming sounds toward the new East European democracies, their economic integration by the European Community, the *pentagonale*, and the new CSCE institutions.[48] Having admit-

---

apparently stopped expecting European security to come through CSCE—offering its erstwhile WTO partners bilateral defense treaties instead. But Kohl continued (e.g., on May 20, 1991, in Washington, D.C.) to call for further institutionalization of CSCE.

47. The hosts of a previous meeting in Madrid (April 1, 1991) proposed a representative assembly of "very simple structure" and one annual meeting of three to five days to review the progress of the CSCE and fulfillment of its principles. The meeting could be hosted in turn by various national parliaments of the member states. In mid-April, Genscher and the Czechoslovak Foreign Minister Dienstbier also presented the ten-point Prague Postulates, which called for the further expansion and deepening of CSCE.

48. See *Tagesspiegel*, June 19, 1991, pp. 1–5. The three Baltic states also sent representatives who participated as guests of the Scandinavian and Belgian delegations since they could not be accredited officially to CSCE. A Slovenian representative was included in the Austrian delegation. Three months later, the Baltic states also became CSCE members with full rights of representation.

ted Albania as the thirty-fifth member, the conference declared the opening of a "new, operative phase" to make the organization the core of a comprehensive system of European collective security, presumably by establishing a mechanism of conflict resolution guided by a committee of high civil servants to prepare the decisionmaking of the foreign ministers. Preferably, this mechanism would be so designed that the alleged troublemaker in a crisis could not stall the proceedings. The conferees, naturally, were concerned about the conflict in Yugoslavia, but were still inclined at the time to preserve the Yugoslav union at all cost.

The site of the conference of the thirty-five CSCE ministers, the old Reichstag building next to the scar left by the removal of the Berlin Wall, "where the Germans and Americans first began their struggle for freedom" together (Baker), was most evocative and so was Kohl's opening address. The chancellor warned the European conferees against a relapse into nationalism and ideological intolerance—forces that could tear apart the larger European community that the CSCE process was building. This process is admittedly slow, but most go on voluntarily and on many small stages of the larger European theater in order to be effective in building a political consensus after half a century of hot and cold war and polarization. It is indeed effective in the long run, though perhaps not as satisfying as a lightning strike against alleged evildoers. The "all-European (and North American) security structures" envisaged by CSCE still require the threat of military enforcement by NATO or by a WEU force (or harmonious cooperation by several of these) as well as a transatlantic consensus. Secretary Baker, speaking for his government, was quite prepared to endorse a "European security identity" so long as the Western alliance remained strong.

The Europeanization of Germany

"We want to commit united Germany to Europe, not to the nation-state ideal," Foreign Minister Genscher said in mid-1991 in a television interview. He was obviously referring to the European Community which, by the end of 1992, was expected to reach another milestone on its long path toward European integration and likely further expansion. For Americans looking warily at such a consolidation of the European trade market—whose customs barriers and policies toward outsiders might some day begin to treat the United States as they have Japan—the situation may become more comprehensible by thinking back to the origins of integration, to the Marshall Plan of 1947/48, which demanded

European economic cooperation as a condition for American aid. There is no need here to go over the evolution of cooperation among the original six members in any detail, except to explain the extraordinary opportunities this offered, in particular, to West Germans (and far beyond the economic aspects). In the immediate postwar years, the Germans were a deeply dispirited nation—today's East Germans are only a pale copy of the political and cultural disillusionment of most postwar Germans, to the extent that everyday problems of food and shelter even left them with the energy to contemplate their disastrous failure as a nation and nation-state.[49]

In this spiritual vacuum of a failed and flawed national identity, the new Pan-European identity (at first limited to the six countries of the European Coal and Steel Community of 1951) offered itself as a kind of salvation and was avidly embraced by the bourgeois and liberal-conservative forces that had been most beholden to the German national idea, the German *Sonderweg* or Manifest Destiny—it was less popular with the Left, which came to accept it only in the sixties. A European identity was at first a ticket back to respectability from the well-deserved hatred and contempt of Germany's wartime neighbors and enemies. It could be connected to the common religious and cultural heritage of Europe, and it opened the door to acceptance of the Adenauer government, in particular, among the Christian Democratic parties of Italy, France (MRP), and the Benelux countries.

Public opinion polls reflected the new European fixation of the Germans from 1946/47 on, when a U.S. Occupation Zone sample of German community leaders favored a "central government for all European countries" (82% for), and when a survey of the adult population in West Berlin and the American Zone showed majority support for a "United States of Europe" by including in it every one of twenty-three European nations except the Soviet Union, which received the support of "only" 38%.[50] By March 1948, growing majorities in the American Zone expressed themselves in favor of West European political unification. But

49. See Merkl, *The Origin of the West German Republic* (New York: Oxford University Press, 1963), pp. 20–38.

50. Anna J. Merritt and Richard L. Merritt, eds., *Public Opinion in Occupied Germany: The OMGUS Surveys, 1945–1949* (Urbana: University of Illinois Press, 1970), pp. 139, 172–173, and 216–218, 223. The first poll was taken in late 1946, before the Marshall Plan was announced. The second poll of 3,450 adults in the American Zone and West Berlin was carried out in August 1947. Some 47% of the respondents claimed to have heard of the Marshall Plan and, after it was explained to them, large majorities expressed approval, although it is unlikely that they understood the plan's European implications at that point.

when the first institutions of European integration appeared—ECSC (1951), the EDC (1952), WEU (1954), and the Common Market (EEC, 1957), even the more inclusive Council of Europe (1949)—they all mirrored the same divisions which had divided Germany.

To be sure, there were also economic wellsprings feeding the West German enthusiasm for European integration, some stemming from the traditional, prewar German patterns of trade with lost East European markets which had to be replaced, some from the general discredit of Germany as a supplier which was hard to overcome. European economic integration at least helped German business to get a new start in the EC area which, even in the eighties, accounted for most of the exports and imports of the West German economy, an economy that is strongly export-oriented. With the establishment and growth of the European Economic Community (EEC) during the sixties, this economic emphasis became particularly pronounced, especially after the initial failure of the Franco-German (de Gaulle–Adenauer) plan for a more politically oriented European union under French or Franco-German leadership. In the sixties, the reaction to the Franco-German initiative helped to align the other EEC members and German "Atlanticists," with their ties to Great Britain and the United States, against the French and German Gaullists, although it would be an exaggeration to claim that this was ever a threat to the Atlantic alliance.

It is true, on the other hand, that a large part of West Germany's crucial export market was and is outside the original EEC area, and even outside the enlarged European Community. In particular, the trade in goods and services between the United States and Germany brings with it considerable economic interdependence that German business and government would be most reluctant to sacrifice in search of other markets.[51] For the Americans, this is a guarantee of sorts that the United States will not be shut out of the European Community either. The Franco-German entente was revived in the seventies, especially under Chancellor Schmidt (1974–1982), and has surfaced repeatedly in the form of proposals for a Franco-German defense force—not to replace but to supplement NATO with a strong and purely European defense function. Chancellor Kohl and President Mitterrand also supported the establishment of the Franco-German Council on Security and Deter-

51. There are massive capital investments in both directions, diversified commercial and banking activities, and other forms of exchange and coordination. See especially Sidney L. Jones, "The Integration and Divergence of German and American Economic Interest," in James A. Cooney, Gordon A. Craig, Hans Peter Schwarz, and Fritz Stern, eds., *The Federal Republic of Germany and the United States: Changing Political, Social, and Economic Relations* (Boulder, Colo.: Westview, 1984), pp. 109–129.

rence and a Franco-German brigade (1988) or, later, a WEU strike force of 50,000 troops (1991) as the nucleus of a European army.[52]

A third dimension of German EC policy—after the transatlantic/global one and that of Franco-German dual hegemony[53]—has been the concern that Germany often ends up paying the bills for the less productive EC regions. This European *Zahlmeister* (paymaster) syndrome had been gathering steam in the sixties and began to draw German anger especially with the energy and financial problems of the seventies, when it culminated in a German refusal to agree to the European Regional Development fund.[54] German unification may yet reduce these fears in German minds, since East Germany is now receiving substantial EC aid and has been warmly accepted as a part of the European Community while Poland and other hungry East European countries are kept waiting outside the door.

In any case, the West German opinion polls on the European Community during the seventies hardly reflected the growing pragmatism of the German public, except for a gradual decline of the expectation that respondents would "live to see the day when the Western European countries join together to form the United States of Europe": from 41% saying yes in 1953 (vs. 29% who said no), the optimistic responses drifted down gradually to 31% in 1979 (vs. 47%) in a development reminiscent of the growing skepticism about German reunification. In 1979, in fact, the two expectations were pitted against each other, and

52. The size of such a force would be puny compared to the 5-million-strong NATO force and even the French non-NATO force of 554,000, but the proposal drew a good deal of British criticism for "trying to substitute itself for NATO" at a time when NATO forces were to be reduced drastically and NATO nuclear weapons were to be cut by 80%. See the *Los Angeles Times*, Oct. 17, 1991, and the *Manchester Guardian Weekly*, Oct. 13, 1991.

53. Taking its cue from the potent argument of de Gaulle that the United States just "might not be willing to risk America cities for Berlin," the Institut für Demoskopie asked West German adults in 1965, 1966, and 1980 to weigh the American security guarantee against Franco-German cooperation "to make Europe strong." In 1965 and 1980, the U.S. guarantee won 45–48% versus 19–20% for France, but in 1966—after the Erhard administration had fallen, owing to its inability to get Washington to ease the cost of U.S. troops stationed in Germany—the two options were tied, 29% and 29%. The questions had an emotional tinge in order to bring out gut reactions. See Elisabeth Noelle-Neumann, ed., *The Germans: Public Opinion Polls, 1967–1980*, rev. ed. (Westport, Conn.: Greenwood Press, 1981), p. 456. In 1968, 22% expressed "strong faith" and another 40% "not so strong a faith" in de Gaulle, while 24% had "no faith at all" in him. See also Peter Schmidt, "West Germany and France: Convergent or Divergent Perspectives on European Security Cooperation?" in Reinhard Rummel, ed., *The Evolution of an International Actor: Western Europe's New Assertiveness* (Boulder, Colo.: Westview, 1990), pp. 161–178, esp. the sources cited in n. 1, p. 161.

54. Simon Bulmer and William E. Paterson, *The Federal Republic of Germany and the European Community* (London: Allen & Unwin, 1987), chap. 9.

69% agreed that "all energies should . . . be channelled into creating a United Europe," as long as German reunification seemed unattainable. Only 12% thought that European unification might jeopardize the chances for German reunification. Throughout the seventies, 68–73% of West German adults were in favor of turning the European Community into "a political community—a United Europe" while only one in ten was opposed.[55]

There can be little doubt that West Germans have been among the most enthusiastic advocates of European integration throughout the seventies and the eighties, as compared to other EC nations. In 1973, with 49% "very much in favor of European unification" and 29% "somewhat in favor of European unification," they were ahead of everyone, though followed at varying intervals by the people of Luxembourg, the Netherlands, Italy, France, and Belgium. Only 6% among the West Germans were against European integration, a figure to be compared with 30% of British and 32% of Danish respondents at the time. By the end of 1986, France, Italy, and the Benelux countries were as strong or even stronger than the Germans in their support for European unification—France 86% and Italy 91% versus 82% of Germans—and many more Britons (68% as compared to 37% in 1973) now were also in favor of European integration.[56]

The *Euro-Barometer* for 1982–1985 also revealed an amazing 75% of West Germans who said that they "often" (25%) or "sometimes" (50%) feel like citizens of Europe rather than like West Germans. Except for Luxembourg, no EC nation could rival this sentiment. In fact, the 18% of West Germans who said they "never" felt that way should be compared to 72% of Britons, 53–57% of the Danes, Belgians, and Dutch, 41% of Italians, and 37% of the French who "never" felt that way.[57] The glaring difference between West German "Euro-enthusiasm" and the average for the European Community (43–44% of EC Europeans felt like "Euro-

55. Noelle-Neumann, *The Germans*, pp. 440–445. During the seventies, also, the proportion of West Germans willing to accept a European government responsible for common foreign, defense, and economic policies dropped from 56% (vs. 20%) to 45% (vs. 31%), even though, in 1979, 64% (vs. 17%) still expected EC membership to make the FRG militarily more secure.

56. In 1973, only 14% of Britons were "very much" and 23% "somewhat" for European integration, but by late 1986 these figures had risen—26% "very much" and 43% "somewhat"—while only 19% agreed with the negative views of Prime Minister Thatcher. *Euro-Barometer* 22 (1984) and 26 (1986).

57. *Euro-Barometer* 24 (1985), p. 54. Here are the 1982 figures, which had changed only a little by 1985: the West Germans then had 64% *pro* and 27% *contra*, while the French and Italians had more respondents who "often" felt that way and fewer who "sometimes" felt that way.

citizens" and 42–43% "never" did) raises the question of why the West Germans in particular should feel this way. Why did they even write into their Constitution (art. 24) the possible transfer to an international authority of their national sovereignty, that good which is treasured so highly by most other nations? The answer has to do with the flawed and truncated identity of the West German republic.[58] One day, perhaps, a unified Germany, reconciled at last with its neighbors and former enemies and victims, will be as possessive of its national sovereignty as Britain and France; or, alternatively, British and French youth may be as disdainful of the nationalism and sovereignty games of their elders and political leaders as many Germans, especially young ones, appear to be today.

German and European Unification

"Until now," the French manager and journalist Alain Minc said in an April 1990 interview with *Die Zeit*, "the French believed that the Germans had only one foreign policy goal, to build [a united] Europe, and that they were always prepared to accept French superiority in the Franco-German relationship." Minc related the disturbing reversal in this relationship and French fears of a united Germany to the great changes of 1989/90. He expected French business to benefit from German unification, perhaps gaining some independence from the weak American economy, and was looking forward to a weakened deutschmark caused by high spending for German unification with the German "*mezzogiorno*," the GDR, "where no one but people from Turin are working."[59]

Minc also foresaw a strengthening of the European Monetary System—but without the German willingness to be *Zahlmeister*—at the same time that Germany, despite all protestations by the Kohl government to the contrary, might in the end refuse to adopt the European currency projected by the EC gatherings. In October 1990, however, the German representative at the EC meeting in Rome still voted with the other

58. See my argument in "Politico-Cultural Restraints on West German Foreign Policy," in *Comparative Political Studies* 3, no. 4 (Jan. 1971), 443–467, esp. 450–453.
59. Minc is the CEO of a Franco-Italian holding company and the author of the influential book *The German Challenge* (1988). He believes that European markets are "only a training ground" for German industry, which has global aspirations. See *Die Zeit*, Apr. 27, 1990, pp. 35–36. Minc also viewed West Germany as a protectionist economy that made it difficult for French industry to break in.

members for a common currency—against Prime Minister Thatcher, who opposed it along with the idea of a European central bank and European political union. A year later, however, at a meeting of EC finance ministers at Luxembourg, German Finance Minister Waigel proved Minc right by arguing against a currency union "without the necessary strict budget discipline," a position bitterly resisted by Italy, Belgium, and Greece. Germany was supported in turn by France, the Netherlands, Spain, and Portugal who proposed that punitive sanctions should be imposed against nations with "excessive government debts," a standard that could be gauged as a percentage of the gross domestic product.[60]

We can read these conflicting reports as a reflection of the inexorable progress of European integration—or as a painful adjustment process by the Kohl and Genscher government still trying to please two of the major powers, France and Great Britain with *de facto* vetoes over German unification—or as the calculated pursuit of German long-term and short-term interests in Europe. Upon the fall of the Berlin Wall in mid-November 1989, the Paris meeting of the twelve EC heads of government had sought to agree on a common attitude toward the dramatic changes in Central and Eastern Europe and resolved to make aid contingent upon democratic reforms while studiously avoiding the subject of German unification. Prime Minister Thatcher opposed a French proposal for an East European development bank. President Mitterrand sought to step up the pace of EC integration in tandem with the upheaval in the East, and he wanted an at first noncommittal Kohl to back up his initiative. At the follow-up EC meeting of foreign ministers in Strasbourg (December 8, 1989), after Kohl had surprised the Western allies with his ten-point program of "confederative" arrangements with a sovereign GDR,[61] his well-known reluctance to commit Germany to a schedule for European economic and monetary union caved in—or, rather, it was traded, along with his apparent resistance to recognizing the Oder-Neisse border, for EC endorsement of the German right of self-determination "within the framework of East-West dialogue and cooperation" and in lockstep with

60. In 1988, the five highest annual budget deficits ranged from Italy's 5.7% and Britain's 9.7% of GDP to Portugal's 12.9% and Greece's 17.9% Low-deficit countries were the preunification FRG (2.3%), the Benelux countries (2.2–3.4%), Denmark (2.4%), and France (3%). The German budget deficit in 1990 and 1991 was between 4.5% and 5%.

61. A cartoon by Plantin in *Le Monde* showed Chancellor Kohl at dinner with the other heads of state, saying "I could eat enough for two." *Le Monde*, Nov. 21, 1989. The GDR and other East European states had put out feelers for EC assistance. On the preunification background history, see also Jochen Thies and Wolfgang Wagner, eds., *Auf dem Weg zum Binnenmarkt. Europäische Integration und deutscher Föderalismus* (Bonn: Verlag für internationale Politik, 1989), a collection of articles from *Europa Archiv*, 1986–1988.

EC integration. Mrs. Thatcher found herself in isolation, as Kohl spoke out strongly in favor of Mitterrand's proposed EC summit for December 1990 which would begin revising the original Rome treaties that set up the Common Market in 1957. This was a giant step forward on the road to European economic and monetary union, the adoption of a social charter, and the completion of the EC single market by the end of 1992, all part of the Delors Plan and all anathema to the Thatcher government.[62]

The Delors Plan put economic and monetary union before further strides toward a political union. The need to decide on a central bank (Euro-Fed) and treasury to issue a common currency provoked enormous controversy, not to mention a great deal of jealousy among national politicians and bank leaders such as those of the West German Bundesbank. The latter not only insisted on a largely independent central bank, but also resisted any outside control over their own decisions. The power of the Bundesbank was the West German equivalent to the British national sovereignty, it seems, the last inalienable piece of German nationhood not to be surrendered lightly.[63] The impetus toward monetary union had originally been the reaction of EC Commission President Roy Jenkins (1977) to the experience with floating exchange rates (the "snake") during the seventies. In an approximation of a single European currency, Jenkins's European Monetary System (EMS) was based on the European currency unit, the ECU, which was derived from a basket of various European currencies. At its 1985 Luxembourg meeting, the EC Council agreed to bring monetary matters under EC control. Among contending proposals for monetary union was a British plan for a "hard ECU" and a Hard ECU Bank (HEB). A Spanish compromise between the Delors Plan and the HEB would move toward the hard ECU—and toward a ban on financing national debt by printing more money—over a period of four to five years, beginning in 1994. There was also some dissension over the timetable of the Delors Plan. The Bundesbank came out against fixed interest rates, EC monetary management, and rigid deadlines. It preferred instead that the single European market should be completed first, inflation brought down, and current-account deficits reduced. It proposed to proceed in two tiers: at a faster speed for the "richer ECU nations," particularly the so-called "D-mark club" (France, Germany,

62. The French plan for a supranational Bank of Europe was not rejected outright by the Thatcher government, but there was determined British opposition to French and German attempts to give a bigger role to the elected European Parliament vis-à-vis the Council of Ministers. See *Le Monde*, Dec. 10–11, 1989, and the *Manchester Guardian Weekly*, Dec. 17, 1989, p. 6.

63. See Anne Daltrop, *Politics and the European Community*, 2nd ed. (Essex: Longman, 1986), pp. 168–171.

the Benelux countries, and possibly Denmark); and at a slower pace for those which, for internal reasons, could not begin right away. Bundesbank President Karl Otto Pöhl drafted a statute for the European Central Bank on this basis, with Finance Minister Waigel's approval, although they frowned upon French attempts to water down the scheme by letting some of the national banks that are dependent on their respective finance ministries survive. Those outside the club were resentful—notably the British, who feared that they were once again missing the European boat.[64]

When the December 1990 EC summit on economic and monetary union was still more than half a year away, a second Mitterrand-Kohl initiative grabbed the headlines by proposing a second December 1990 EC conference to advance the long-dormant cause of European political union. European political coordination, of course, was the objective from the beginning, but it had been driven back again and again in the sixties (Fouchet Plan) and the seventies (Davignon Plan) by various forces. Upon the adoption of the Single European Act (1986), the European Parliament noted with evident regret that the "Community Institutions' influence over political cooperation remains very slight" and expressed its own aspirations for a more direct role, "in particular by means of periodic progress reports submitted to Parliament by the Ministers."[65] However true this self-image of the European Parliament may be, it has already attracted scores of full-time lobbyists, of which about two hundred were counted by the London *Economist* in late 1990. This is hardly a sign of obscurity and impotence.

The decision at the 1990 EC summit in Dublin to take up the subject of political union by the beginning of 1993 was coupled with EC approval for the integration of a united Germany, including the GDR, into the Community. This was not a simple matter when we consider the nonconforming CMEA trade ties, agricultural production, and other

64. See the compelling arguments in Rolf H. Hasse, *The European Central Bank: Perspectives for a Development of the European Monetary System* (Gütersloh: Bertelsmann, 1990), pp. 11–13, 19–25, and 114–153, and Jean-Victor Louis, *From EMS to Monetary Union* (Luxembourg: EC Publications, 1990).

65. See, for example, the excellent history by Derek Urwin, *The Community of Europe: A History of European Integration Since 1945* (London and New York: Longman, 1991), pp. 135–139, 146–154, and 212–228, and the documents collected in *European Political Cooperation*, 5th ed. (Bonn: West German Federal Press and Information Office, 1988) for the years from the 1969 Hague summit to 1987, especially the documents reflecting the coordination of foreign policies in the eighties (pp. 93–307 and 396–397). The goal had always been the institutionalization of consultations among the heads of state (European Council) or the foreign ministers, two or three times a year, and with thorough preparation of the meetings.

obligations of the GDR. Normally, the European Community requires of its members a commitment to forsake all others and, in this case, transitional periods had to be agreed upon. The EC conference of April 1990 did not yet consider a special package for the GDR, but its response was widely considered a triumph for Chancellor Kohl and his program of German unification. Still, there was no lack of voices that called the renewed slogan of "political union" at this point a transparent ploy to ingratiate a sulking Mitterrand or to prepare a continental "horse and rider" scenario, with Kohl as the heavyset horse and Mitterrand as the clever little jockey (London *Times*).

Aside from British resistance, however, there was wide acceptance among EC member states of the idea that the old EC institutional structure needed to be tightened and democratized. The European Parliament, according to a Belgian proposal, ought to have the right to elect the president of the hitherto rather independent European Commission (Parliament can dismiss the commission as a whole) which could advance the organization toward functioning more like a European government with the authority to compel compliance. The Parliament ought to be able to initiate and pass its own laws. The all-powerful Council of Ministers could move from the requirement of unanimity to majority decisions, at least on some subjects, and introduce more transparency into its process of making decisions. The area of common foreign and security policy, in particular, could be placed more and more into the hands of the periodic foreign ministerial meetings.[66] The movement for reform received particular support from Italian representatives, especially in the form of a proposal for a full-blown federal union by Emilio Colombo, as well as from the Germans, whose country is so far the only federal state in the Community and who believe that their type of Bundesrat federalism is much closer, than other federal systems, to the actual EC structure and its potential for organic reform.[67]

66. See the discussion in *Der Spiegel* 44, no. 19, May 9, 1990, pp. 185–186. Until drastic reforms occurred, the European Parliament, though popularly elected since 1979, could only debate drafts from the European Commission and express its opinion; it could not veto the final decisions. Also see *The Economist*, Feb. 24, 1990, pp. 45–46. A member of the European Parliament, David Martin (Labour, Scotland) added the demand to expand the Parliament's powers of "co-decision" with the council, of a veto over legislation (unless the commission agrees, only the Community budget has been subject to a parliamentary veto so far), and of the ratification of treaties, trade agreements, and EC constitutional reforms. Jacques Delors preferred to cut the number of commissioners, currently seventeen, and to reduce the role of the council in the work of the many topical committees that determine and slow down the commission's work.

67. See *The Economist*, Nov. 10, 1990, pp. 55–56. Since the introduction of the Single European Act, as *The Economist* pointed out, more than half (1,052) of the Parliament's 1,724 amendments of single-market laws have actually been accepted by the commission,

The German Point of View Regarding Europe

In this frame of mind, the twelve EC governments assembled two parallel conferences, in mid-December 1990, to work on the new draft treaties of Rome. There was a lot of talk about a "confederation of Europe" (Mitterrand) and rather more emphasis on a presidential regime along French lines than on a strengthened European Parliament.[68] Again during 1991, in the horse race between the economic and the political union, the former inched ahead and produced enough consensus, if not progress, for the single market to start in 1993. The Euro-Fed Bank was to open in 1994, but its function would only be to "coordinate" the twelve currencies and, perhaps, to stop the reckless printing of money by some countries. A common currency might be in place in 1997, but then again maybe not.[69] The economic union envisaged in the 1985 EC White Paper, on the other hand—a single open market with stable prices, growth, employment, and environmental protection—was readily accepted, confirming the incipient trends, such as a bias against state assistance to national industries. The elimination of border controls was avidly awaited by business and travelers. A strong start had already been made with the Schengen Agreement, which abolished such controls among France, the Benelux countries, and Germany; Italy, Spain, and Portugal were soon to follow suit. Adjustment of industrial standards and, after a bad start, VAT taxes might be next on the agenda.

While the details of the Rome treaties were being worked out, the year 1991 brought at least clarification of the united German point of view.

---

and 719 of those were adopted by the council, too. We might add, though, that the present structure has permitted widespread noncompliance with EC decisions and court rulings (often hand in hand with undiminished enthusiasm for European integration in the same noncomplying countries).

68. See Thomas Läufer, 22 *Fragen zu Europa. Europäische Gemeinschaft und Europäisches Parlament.*(Bonn: Europa Union, 1990) and Michael Garthe, *Weichenstellung zur Europäischen Union? Der Verfassungsentwurf des Europäischen Parlaments und sein Beitrag zur Überwindung der EG-Krise* (Bonn: Europa Union, 1989). Also see *The Economist*, Dec. 8 and 15, 1990, and *Frankfurter Allgemeine Zeitung*, Dec. 17, 1990.

69. See Dieter Biehl and Gero Pfennig, eds., *Zur Reform der EG-Finanzverfassung. Beiträge zur wissenschaftlichen und politischen Debatte* (Bonn: Europa Union, 1990). The draft Economic and Monetary Union (EMU) Treaty reflected some acceptance by Delors of the British view in that it limited itself to a) banning deficit-financing by printing money, b) authorizing that conditions be attached to EC assistance, and c) pillorying "excessive government deficits." He accepted the British contention that EMU did not require *a priori* central control of the national budgets. After 1994, the "second phase" of the original plans would start, whereupon the commission and the Euro-Fed Council would report to the "Ecofin" Council. *Manchester Guardian Weekly*, Nov. 4, 1990.

At an EC finance ministers' meeting in Brussels (February 25, 1991), after the Gulf War cease-fire, the Germans fell in line with the Dutch, the Britons, and Spain—but in opposition to French policy—on postponing the establishment of the Central Bank; there was "no need for it" during the transitional (second) phase beginning in 1994. The German delegation was willing to accept the date of 1994, but the EC partners should first have "achieved sufficient and lasting progress in the convergence of their economies, in particular in price stability and the organization of [their] public finances." In May 1991, this decision was confirmed, and the date for the beginning of a common currency and the Central Bank, 1997, was made contingent on a determination "as to whether the prerequisites for the final stage existed or not." However, without stringent budgetary self-discipline, neither the countries of Southern Europe nor Great Britain would satisfy those prerequisites.[70] Finally, toward October 1991, at an informal meeting of EC finance ministers and heads of central banks in Apeldoorn (Netherlands), there was agreement that the economically stronger EC countries could soon establish their common currency (the "hard ECU") while the others could participate in the process of deciding what economic performance was needed to gain entrance to the club. A currency union agreement might be ready to be signed by the time of the Maastricht (Netherlands) summit in December 1991, provided that political union had sufficiently advanced by that date.

Maastricht did indeed result in some decisions, although there was no lack of critics concerning particular aspects of the new draft treaties—they still needed to be ratified by the various national parliaments—or concerning the sweep or pace of the integration proposed. Some members thought the pace of union too fast, others thought it too slow, and some criticized the evasion of conflicts and issues in the draft. To mention one of the more striking contradictions, a resolution to develop an EC social charter proclaiming such workers' rights as a maximum forty-eight-hour workweek(!) led to an agreement exempting post-Thatcherite Britain from its provisions in order to meet Prime Minister Major's objections that the Community was forcing the welfare state upon the British. On the other hand, a consultative Danish referendum on the treaties half a year later led to their defeat by a narrow margin because, reportedly,

70. According to a report in *Die Welt*, May 11, 1991, the question of sanctions for fiscal irresponsibility was also rejected by the South Europeans. France, Italy, and Belgium were still for a "strong central bank," although details of its structure and functions had not been clarified. The German government and, presumably, the Bundesbank at first suggested a council of the presidents of the national central banks with little authority, not unlike the German Central Bank Council that oversees the Bundesbank.

many Danes (especially women) feared that the European Community might diminish their treasured welfare rights.[71] On the subject of the currency union, the Maastricht meeting adopted the German preference for a deadline between 1997 and 1999—again with Britain reserving the right to stay out of the union. Curiously, recent *Euro-Barometer* polls have disclosed that the German population is now the least open among all the EC member states to the adoption of the new ECU in place of the deutschmark. In 1992, 63% opposed and only 24% favored the ECU in Germany, as compared to 27% *contra* and 50% *pro* only two years earlier.[72] The meeting also made a vague commitment to the plans for closer political union, once more emphasizing structures and the consultation process rather than pledging a strong will to produce common foreign, defense, and other policies: in place of the European Political Cooperation (EPC), a Common Foreign and Security Policy (CFSP) process is to begin, but there still will not be a common defense policy.

If the willingness to "deepen" the union seemed at best tentative, the "widening" perspective certainly received its due. With the admission in the near future of a number of economically puissant West European countries—Sweden, Finland, Norway, Iceland, Austria, Switzerland, and Liechtenstein—a European Economic Area (EEA) of nineteen members and 377 million prosperous people will be created. The further addition of ten East European nations, including the Baltic states and Slovenia and Croatia, in the more distant future seems far more problematic. In a way, the problems posed by the weaker EC members might reflect those which would be brought in by the "widening" process of admitting further members to the Community, especially from Eastern Europe or Turkey. While the first batch of applicants, the rest of the European Free Trade Association (EFTA) members, such as Austria and Sweden,[73] may have no problems with the EC economic hierarchy, Turkey, Cyprus,

71. The Danish government, which strongly favored adoption of the treaties, had flooded the country with free copies of the treaty texts, a voluminous document. So we cannot simply blame the "democratic deficit," or even voter ignorance, for the popular verdict. In the French plebiscite on the treaty, three months later, the government also passed out copies of the document and it was approved by a narrow margin, 51% to 49%.

72. The poll showed similar levels of rejection only in Denmark (60%) and Britain (58%), while seven of the remaining nine EC members gave majority support. Reported in the *Los Angeles Times*, June 9, 1992.

73. Since Finland, Norway, Iceland, Switzerland, and Liechtenstein are potential members, some of them would like to participate in decisions shaping the European Community, now, before their admission. Some, like Norway with its fishing industry, have special interests to protect. All of them will face enormous adjustments to make up for the decades of standardization that the older EC members have experienced. Sweden, Norway, and Finland have just begun to tie their respective currencies to the ECU.

Malta, and former CMEA countries surely will, once they have overcome an apprenticeship as associate members. Their eventual accession is already a cause of jealousy among the Mediterranean members, owing to limited EC assistance resources. For the existing membership, the options of "widening" versus "deepening" EC may well seem incompatible. An opponent of "deepening," or intensifying the association, like Great Britain, may well use a drastic widening of the Community as a way of slowing down the whole process of European integration. The German government believes that "widening" is bound to "deepen" the European Community. It would probably welcome most comers, including the Baltic states and an independent Slovenia and Croatia, and especially Germany's Eastern neighbors. France, on the other hand, is committed to deepening the Community into a federation and fears that all these new members would be a major obstacle to a more perfect union. Some of the smaller EC members (e.g., Portugal) are apprehensive about the Maastricht attempt to introduce majority rule into EC decisions because it would lessen their autonomy.

The German approach to European integration thus emerged clearly and early in the year 1991. While Kohl's negotiators were known to be rather pragmatic about the details, the basic thrust was a desire for concessions from others on political union in exchange for giving up so much German financial autonomy to help bring about European monetary union.[74] "The chancellor is prepared to sign away the D-mark and see it replaced by a Euro-currency, but only if the treaty on political union gives the European parliament lots more power," as *The Economist* put it, with a chuckle about such "curious idealism." As compared to the pursuit of more obvious national interests by other EC members, this may indeed seem odd—except that the chancellor and his generation of German leaders are in fact aiming at the institutional consolidation of a strong United States of Europe as a valid alternative to the flawed German national identity of the past.

If they have their way, a Europeanized Germany may indeed dissolve eventually into the larger Europe, committing its heart, soul and, last but not least, its pocketbook to the common enterprise. In so doing they can count on substantial support among the German public which, in Sep-

74. Premature centralization of banking in the form of Euro-Fed authority over the Bundesbank, the German argument goes, might lead to the erosion of the EMS itself. *The Economist*, March 9, 1991. A major flap also arose when a Dutch draft on political union proposed a more centralized system—with central power over the members' foreign and defense policies—than countries like Britain could possibly accept. The premature demarche was defeated 10 votes to 2 and may have set back the cause of political union, except that Britain seemed far more inclined now to accept the earlier Luxembourg draft.

tember 1990 and again in mid-1991, endorsed European unification with nearly nine out of ten responses, according to polls by the Konrad Adenauer Foundation: about half of the respondents—a good majority (56%) in East Germany—expected, "after the unification of Germany, [that] the importance of European unification" would be "even greater," and another four out of ten that it would be "just as great." This policy course of the Kohl administration also lays out a constructive solution of the German question before Germany's suspicious European neighbors, who are still uneasy about the German past and about the sheer size of a united Germany in Europe. Its success, however, still depends on the resolution of the conflict between Britain and France over the role of NATO and the "European security identity," possibly with WEU as the European pillar of NATO. The Germans are not eager to choose among the three poles of their international existence: their transatlantic U.S./ NATO ties, their European EC and French partnership, and their re-emerging trade and cultural linkages to Eastern Europe. Britain has never completely committed itself to a European future as France has. With the degree of economic integration envisaged at Maastricht, there would no longer be any real likelihood of German domination. There would be a Europeanized Germany, no longer an isolated and consolidated power tempted to dominate others.[75]

75. See "A German Idea of Europe," *The Economist*, Jul. 27, 1991, p. 50, which laces its factual reporting with British preferences regarding the European Community, a tendency familiar from American reporting on the same subject. Kohl has also proposed a new European agency to handle common policies on visas, political asylum, and immigration. Both Germany and France would like the goal of a common European defense policy written into the Political Union Treaty, with provisions for a review of the defense arrangements planned in 1996. In this, too, the German public endorsed the Community's responsibility for common defense, with a good two-thirds in support. The public opinion data are all cited in a paper by Hans-Joachim Veen, "The Europeanization of German Politics," presented at the German Studies Association conference in Los Angeles, Sept. 26–29, 1991.

Conclusion: Whither Germany?

The time has come to look back upon the vast and greatly changed panorama of Europe, and on the likely future role of united Germany in this new world. We have charted the path of Germany in Europe—from the old German question, via the confrontational and self-destructive *Sonderweg* (and its catastrophic consequences for Europe), through the postwar years of German and European division, the bitter confrontations of the Cold War, and the extraordinary and peaceful upheaval of the year and a half after the collapse of the Berlin Wall. It is a dramatic story full of crises and problems, ambitions and frustrations, forward movement and the inertia and resistance of the larger international context. The German achievement of national unity was only a small, if central, part of an evolving larger scene: namely, the breakup of the Soviet empire over its client states and, in particular, the unraveling of communist rule in the GDR in 1989/90 and earlier. The impetus for the collapse of GDR communism certainly did not come from Bonn, which to a considerable extent was merely reacting to the astounding changes in the East and to what they seemed to require of the reluctant West Germans. As we have already seen and will pursue further in this conclusion, the Germans themselves are not particularly elated by their unification and can hardly wait to give away their national sovereignty to a united Europe about to be born.

The bulk of our attention has been focused on analyzing the transformation of West and East German politics from 1989 to the united Germany of the first half of 1991—and this especially in regard to the elections and party system, the constitutional fabric, and the economics of East German rehabilitation. As the reader will recall, our principal finding was that the East German imput has confused and destabilized the old West German party system. Not only have East German voters proven fickle, but evidently they are still not identifiable by class and occupation. Unlike in the West, for example, the CDU voters are predominantly working-class, the communist PDS voters white-collar and civil service. The East German democratic opposition which won the revolution failed to catch on in the East German elections throughout 1990 until the all-German elections of December. These parliamentary elections routed the Greens (at least temporarily) and greatly diminished the SPD following, but they also ushered in a prolonged crisis for the Kohl administration. Finally, there is a confused neo-Nazi element, many of them the "brown sons of red fathers." Nevertheless, the electoral future seems to point to equal strength between the SPD and the CDU/CSU in the united political system, provided the embattled chancellor can ride out the fiscal crisis.

Regarding the constitutional system, we found that unification has brought a new federalism, greater power (and blame) to the chancellor, extraordinary economic leverage to the Treuhand agency amidst a complex mix of property law and relationships, a new capital in Berlin, and a different support base for such causes as first-trimester abortions and political asylum. It will take several years of adjustment before the institutional system can settle down, quite possibly only after major constitutional reform. Economically, we found that the fervently desired currency union at a rate of 1:1 had a disastrous impact on the East German industrial economy (on top of the many flaws and liabilities of the latter); indeed, the exorbitant cost of rehabilitation, privatizing, and modernizing East Germany may yet topple Chancellor Kohl and keep West Germany from fulfilling its role as the economic locomotive of European integration and East European economic growth. Kohl and the unifiers, to be sure, had little choice in the matter of the currency reform.

The Stature of Chancellor Kohl

Helmut Kohl, the chancellor of German unification, had to work very hard to make any headway against the resistance of his political opposition, and against his own people. Germans like to heap abuse upon their chancellors—they did it to the now-idolized Adenauer and to Ludwig Erhard, to Willy Brandt, and certainly to Helmut Schmidt—and in the case of Kohl they have always received able assistance from outside their country as well. Perhaps this custom is rooted in a reaction to the last time they were enthusiastic about a newly elected chancellor, in 1933. The most unfair criticism of Kohl is one that could be found across the spectrum of German newspapers and magazines in connection with unification, especially when the long-awaited, long-denied tax increases came, in early 1991: namely, that he had failed to make an honest, timely appeal to his fellow citizens for the necessary support. Why did he tell us, in 1990, that unification would not cost us anything; why couldn't he have appealed to our patriotic sense of sacrifice and told us the truth to begin with? The answer is that the Kohl administration was surely aware of the polls which indicated that the West German public in 1989/90 was *not* willing to pay increased taxes for any aspect of unification, or for aid to East Germany, until they were faced with accomplished facts, say from mid-1990 onward, and even then only with a recurring show of ill will. Since Kohl and his team evidently thought they were doing the right and responsible thing—and were probably rather in the dark as to the enormous real costs—they simply went ahead and plotted unification without a specific tax authorization by the voters as best they could, repeating their "no new taxes" formula all the way to the December elections. According to the *Politbarometer* polls, almost four-fifths of the West German voters knew that unification would require tax increases, and a narrow majority, by October 1990, found such increases acceptable. But when the painful tax bills finally arrived, in the midst of several contentious *Länder* elections, up to two-thirds turned on Kohl and called him a *Steuerlügner* (tax liar).[1]

It was not that Helmut Kohl began this quest as a knight in shining armor. Being identified with German unification undoubtedly helped Chancellor Kohl to recover from what looked like a fatal slump in popularity in the mid-eighties and after the 1987 elections. His recovery was not exactly instantaneous either, as will be remembered; indeed, it

1. In October, it was 77.2% who knew it would require a tax increase (65.9% in November), and 50.2% approved it anyway (45.6% in November, when the opposition to such an increase rose to 52.7%). Party supporters tended to divide more along their respective party lines. See *Politbarometer*, Nov. 1990, p. 49. By the time of the April elections in Rhineland-Palatinate, 62.8% of the voters there supported the "tax lie" charge. See FGW, *Blitzumfrage zur Landtagswahl 1991 in Rheinland-Pfalz* (Mannheim: FGW, 1991), p. 189. In the *Politbarometer* survey of April 1991, 69% of West Germans called the charge "true" (vs. 27% who did not), up from 66% vs. 30% in March (p. 53).

took until the middle of 1990 for him to emerge from the contest with his arch-rival, Oskar Lafontaine. But his stand did help him win the first all-German elections to take place in fifty-seven years, after which his star began to decline again and the opposition SPD made a miraculous recovery from its debacle in the elections, particularly in East Germany.[2] Very likely it will be only after he leaves office, and perhaps only posthumously, that Kohl will be appreciated by his countrymen and -women for steering the country through the shoals of unification, European integration, and German-Soviet/Russian rapprochement. So far, he enjoyed a more balanced treatment in the German press on only two occasions: his sixtieth birthday (April 3, 1990) and right after Zhelezdnovodsk when even his longtime critic, *Der Spiegel* publisher Rudolf Augstein, paid tribute to the man who in his magazine is usually either ridiculed as a bumbling provincial politician or attacked as a cross between Niccolò Machiavelli and a spineless sycophant of American presidents.

Kohl's influence upon his age also includes the shaping of some of the international structures within which Germany was unified and will live henceforth. While Hans-Dietrich Genscher's hand molded in particular the "two-plus-four" relationships, Kohl had his principal impact upon the structures of the evolving European Community at the Maastricht threshold, stimulating both "deepening" and "widening" processes of great force and consequence. He may not succeed in Europeanizing Germany far beyond the preferences of the bankers and deutschmark lovers in his own country. His mediating position between the Anglo-American NATO nexus and the Franco-German defense identity may well hold together the Western alliance. As in other international relationships, the united German government would obviously prefer a compromise. Its defense needs could hardly be expected to be safeguarded by CSCE, which has otherwise performed magnificently in overcoming the European division by patiently building the consensus for a European house. NATO and the transatlantic ties with the United States, on the other hand, promise to maintain Germany's links with a wider, global market and community.

A Sense of National Pride?

With all these pieces to fit together in a mosaic, we still cannot quite answer Nicholas Ridley's question about where the Germans might be

2. See *Politbarometer*, Aug. 1991, pp. i–iii and 10–11. Among prominent politicians on a list, he was tenth in popularity, far behind his coalition partner Genscher and three other CDU figures as well as five SPD politicians.

headed fifteen, twenty years from now. Perhaps, without recourse to a crystal ball, we cannot answer such a question satisfactorily in regard to any nation. If we knew, however, how the Germans, East or West, young or old, viewed themselves and where they thought they were going, say, in the next ten years, we would be much closer to answering Ridley's riddle. The reader will recall how West German hopes for reunification had gradually died down by the 1980s (Chapter Four) and how the desire for reunification had become a disembodied issue of no policy content whatsoever just when it actually began to happen. As a symbolic issue, asserting the desire for reunification became mostly a distinguishing mark between CDU/CSU supporters, on the one hand, and SPD and the Greens, who scoffed at it, on the other. Even the voices and movements of the radical Right were at best half-hearted in using such a "dead issue" for their agitation.[3] Did this mean that most Germans no longer harbored the old nationalist syndrome that had ravaged the continent for thirty years (1914–1945)? We know that the West German response to unification, when it did occur, was still rather tepid, full of qualifications and conditions imposed by the SPD opposition, and more concerned with what it might cost than with the glory of the fatherland (see Chapter Four). Only the Ossis were behaving a little more in the nationalist character attributed to the Germans by their critics.[4]

Do Germans today even perceive themselves as "a people"? When forty-year-old novelist Patrick Süskind heard Berlin Mayor Walter Momper say, in a radio interview at the time of the Berlin Wall's collapse, that "tonight the German people are the happiest people on earth," he responded with a question:

> Whom could he mean by "the German people," the FRG or the GDR citizens? The East and West Berliners? All of them together? . . . Maybe even me? . . . And how can a people, assuming there is such a thing as *the* German people, be happy?

Süskind was appalled by the favorable press reaction to Momper's turn of phrase, and at the many prounity statements of such prominent figures

3. *Jahrbuch der öffentlichen Meinung* (Allensbach: Institut für Demoskopie, 1968–1973), pp. 505–506. See also Gebhard Schweigler, *Nationalbewusstsein in der BRD und der DDR* (Düsseldorf: Bertelsmann, 1973), pp. 121–140, where the complex reactions of West Germans to the questions of German unification were expertly dissected against a setting of *Ostpolitik* initiatives.

4. While nearly all (94%) of Ossis endorsed unification in mid-1990, the three-fourths of Wessis who did were composed of only 25% who were "very much for it" and 23% each who were simply "in favor" or "somewhat in favor," hardly a manifestation of raving nationalism (EMNID poll, September 1990).

as Willy Brandt, or the toast offered "to Germany" by a triumphant Chancellor Kohl returning from Moscow in February 1990. "And, of all countries in the world [to drink to], why Germany with . . . which the Great War and Auschwitz are irrevocably linked?"[5] Unlike Brandt, Kohl, Genscher, and many others, Süskind identified with the "68er" generation, for whom Western and Southern Europe always seemed closer than "such dubious territories as Saxony, Thuringia . . ." etc.

A rather obvious way to determine a nation's sense of identity has always been the extent to which its citizens exhibit pride in their nationality and identify with such national symbols as the flag. In the German case, of course, the succession of recent regimes, each with a different sense of identity and flags, complicates such assessments. The Weimar Republic, the Third Reich, the FRG, and the GDR in this respect differ profoundly from one another; the last two, in fact, were diametrical opposites in many respects. Some studies have therefore preferred to avoid direct reference to Germany or the Germans and have concentrated instead on West German pride in the country's institutions. The "civic culture" survey of 1959, for example, asked respondents in five countries about "which aspect of their nation" they were proud of. The researchers discovered that Germans had a much lower level of appreciation for their own political institutions and social legislation than, say, Britons. In 1959, only 7% of West German adults were proud of their democratic institutions (85% in the United States, 46% in Britain), whereas 33% took pride in their economic system (23% United States, 10% Britain) and 36% in their national character (7% United States, 18% Britain).[6] How they viewed themselves as a nation was revealed in a series of questions asked by the Institut für Demoskopie between 1955 and 1980, concerning "whether Germany would ever again be a great power." In 1954, 38% said yes and 41% no; in 1965, it was 17% yes and 52% no; in 1975, 18% yes and 62% no; and in 1980, 22% yes and 59% no.[7]

Fortunately, German confidence and pride in their political institutions grew prodigiously over the years, and never more dramatically than when

5. Quoted in *Der Spiegel* 43, no. 38, Sept. 17, 1990, pp. 116–117, from Ulrich Wickert, ed., *Angst vor Deutschland* (New York and Hamburg: Hoffman & Campe, 1990). Süskind also comments on the lively interest of the fifty-five- to sixty-five-year-olds and the ardor of "the political and cultural oldsters" of the war and prewar generations in German unification (pp. 123–125).

6. Gabriel A. Almond and Sidney Verba, *The Civic Culture: Political Attitudes and Democracy in Five Nations* (Princeton, N.J.: Princeton University Press, 1963), p. 102.

7. *Jahrbuch der öffentlichen Meinung* (Allensbach: Institut für Demoskopie, 1957, 1964, 1966) and Elisabeth Noelle-Neumann, ed., *The Germans: Public Opinion Polls, 1967–1980*, rev. ed. (Westport, Conn.: Greenwood Press, 1981).

confronted with a communist GDR in dissolution. Between mid-1989 and May 1990, West German "satisfaction with our democracy" rose from 73% "satisfied" citizens to 85%, a considerable jump.[8] A year later, satisfaction was back to 64% versus 34% who were critical, although this included the more critical Ossis (49% and 49%). In December 1989, nine out of ten East Germans also "esteemed democracy as in the FRG"—either "greatly" or had "some respect for it"—although their response to another question, raised by the communists and some leaders of the democratic opposition—might give one pause. East Germans were asked whether they thought the GDR was being "taken over" (*vereinnahmt*) by the economically superior FRG. Only a narrow majority rejected such an interpretation; 45% agreed with it, although one in four of them regarded such a "takeover" as "a good thing."[9] Respondents over age sixty particularly stood out with this double-barreled reaction.

The same survey also asked East Germans whether they considered themselves "Germans" or "GDR citizens" and received a response of three-fifths who identified themselves as "Germans." Half a year later, in May 1990, they were asked whether they were glad whenever they saw the West German flag(!): half of them responded yes (43% expressed indifference), which was nearly as high as the West German reaction to their own flag. On this occasion, GDR citizens were also polled about whether they were "proud to be German": 79% said yes (8% said no), a level considerably ahead of that in the old FRG, where in 1990—a year earlier, before the onset of all the changes—only 70% agreed that they were "proud" (13% said no). When we recall the internationalist indoctrination of the East Germans in schools and mass organizations, such a high degree of national identification comes as a surprise.[10]

In the old FRG, German national pride has always been a point of great debate and partisan division because of Germany's past. Even after forty years of nonaggressive, democratic behavior, German nationalism in the eighties has been more subdued than elsewhere in Europe—witness the 86% in 1985 who indicated their belief that "exaggerated nationalism is bad, but a healthy national identification is worth striving for."[11] In

8. Institut für praxisorientierte Sozialforschung (IPOS), *Einstellungen zu aktuellen Fragen der Innenpolitik in der BRD 1989* (Mannheim: 1989), pp. 48–49; IPOS, May–June 1990 (including GDR), pp. 21–23; *Politbarometer*, Aug. 1991, pp. 12 and 99.

9. Forschungsgruppe Wahlen (FGW), *Meinungen der Bürger der DDR*, December 1989, pp. 1, 122–123, 126.

10. IPOS, May–June 1990, pp. 74–76.

11. See Harro Honolka, *Schwarzrotgrün. Die BRD auf der Suche nach ihrer Identität* (Munich: Beck, 1987), p. 199. Also see Merkl, *German Foreign Policies, West and East* (Santa Barbara, Calif.: ABC-Clio, 1974), pp. 26–35.

1970, for example, only 38% of West Germans pronounced themselves "very proud to be German," as compared to 66% of French and 62% of Italian respondents and an EC average of 55%. Another 33% of West Germans (EC average: 27%) were "rather proud," while 23% were "not very proud" or "not at all proud" (cf. an EC average of 13%). In the early eighties, after a decade of declining confidence in political institutions in most Western countries, the proportion of "very proud" West Germans (22%) could be compared with 56% among the British and 76% among the Greeks (EC average: 37%). During the years of the great peace demonstrations against the deployment of new missiles, the "very proud" percentage among the Germans—but not elsewhere—drifted even lower, to 17–20%, while the "not very proud" and "not at all proud" rose to 30–33%.[12] Polls by the Konrad Adenauer Foundation from 1985 on add yet another angle: from a level of around 70% in both East and West, it seems, the responses of "very proud" and "rather proud" drifted down to 65% in September 1990 and then dropped to 58% in mid-1991 (only 50% in East Germany), as if to say "Enough of the national excitement."[13]

The upshot of all this for the current German sense of identity appears to be that, aside from the confusion over whether national pride refers to both Germanys or just one, contrary trends seem to have stabilized the responses. On the one hand, since 1949 there has been growing identification with the old FRG and its institutions, which now include also those of the united Germany. On the other hand, deliberate moderation and the postindustrial attitudes of younger Germans have kept national pride and confidence in institutions at a comparatively low level, far from the flag-waving patriotism of the United States and Great Britain. There is also a geographic reason for confusion about whether the old GDR and the old FRG were "two states in one nation"—the underlying principle of Brandt's *Ostpolitik*—or separate nations. A good 70% still spoke of one nation in 1974, whereas 29% denied that the Germans of East and West belonged to the same nation. By 1984, a majority of 53% held the latter view while only 42% still thought of Germans as "one nation." This gives us an idea of the situation just before the two Germanys were actually merged. To complicate the reference point of national identity still further with geographic details, an Allensbach poll asked West Germans in 1981 and 1986 what they meant by "the German

12. *Euro-Barometer* (1971), (1981), and (1985), p. 21.
13. See Hans-Joachim Veen, "The Europeanization of German Politics," a paper presented at the German Studies Association conference in Los Angeles, Sept. 26–29, 1991, table 1 and pp. 3–4, where the drop in national pride is attributed to disillusionment.

nation today," or by "German culture." The 1981 answer was as follows: the old FRG, 43%; the two Germanys, 32%; the two plus ethnic German areas in the East, 12%; all German-speaking areas, 7%. The 1986 answers were very similar.[14] It will be many years before the two populations of the GDR and the old FRG really grow together and share a national identity that is not confused by the geographic legacy of recent history.

German-Russian Reconciliation

In the week of June 22, 1991, a number of joint German-Soviet photographic exhibitions—e.g., "Topography of War" in Berlin—television features, and historians' conferences marked the fiftieth anniversary of the unprovoked Nazi German invasion of the Soviet Union. Operation Barbarossa started off as a savage campaign to wrest *Lebensraum* (living space) in the East from its "subhuman" population, to destroy the alleged Jewish-Bolshevik conspiracy, and to force World War II to an early conclusion favorable to the Third Reich. It ended with immense suffering on all sides, first visited on millions of Soviet soldiers, prisoners of war, and civilians—with genocidal mania against Jews and Gypsies, but also other Soviets—and with plans to starve another 30 million to death. An estimated 27 million Soviet citizens died, including 8.5 million soldiers. Then, as the fortunes of the war turned, Soviet vengeance was wrought on German soldiers and civilians, prisoners of war, refugees, and conquered villages—and on millions of Soviet citizens, especially those captured by the Germans, those suspected of collaboration, even the forced Soviet laborers that the German army had pressed into service in Germany.

For the German side, historians at these conferences clearly established that the responsibility for all this killing and brutality was by no means limited to special SS units, but involved the entire Wehrmacht in the East which had been penetrated by racist beliefs and Nazi ideology. Millions of officers and soldiers had known, witnessed, participated in, and lied about it to their families back home. The burden of guilt of this "second holocaust" of the war generation was heaped upon that of the first one. But instead of trading bitter recriminations, German and Soviet representatives now assured each other of their sincere desire not to allow the

14. *Emnid-Informationen*, nos. 3–4 (1984), 8; *Jahrbuch der öffentlichen Meinung* (1981); *IFD-Umfrage* 4076 (1986).

horrors of the past to intrude on cooperation and friendship between the new generations.

It is perhaps too early to gauge the extent to which the friendly feelings of the new era have penetrated the Soviet population where, rather than playing cowboys and Indians, boys in their make-believe battles are likely to fight Germans. For forty-five years, the communist regime made sure that its schoolchildren and adults never forgot the German invasion, and that the victorious Soviet army would always be proud of having humbled and defeated the Nazi juggernaut. Today, official German opinion views the Soviet troops remaining until 1994 in East Germany as "guests" under the Troop Repatriation Treaty, and the German Bundeswehr tries to maintain friendly contacts with them. While there have been expressions of unforgotten hard feelings, especially among members of the Soviet war generation, which is not easily mollified by German care packages and aid, there have also been the new Times-Mirror polls of mid-1991 which asked Russians and Ukrainians what they thought of "the kind of influence Germany is having on the way things are going in their countries." Russian adults responded that the influence was "very good" (9%) or "mostly good" (43%), and Ukrainians responded even better (9% and 51%, respectively). Germans were asked about the Soviet influence on German developments, and they replied "very good" (9%) and "mostly good" (46%).[15]

The Haunting Memories of the Past

The great upheaval in the Soviet Union, particularly the step-by-step disintegration since the abortive military coup of August 1991, has complicated the process of reconciliation both on a collective—e.g., the treaties and agreements between Kohl and Gorbachev—and on an individual basis to an extraordinary degree. Soviet military historians are

15. To these figures we should add 16% (Russia), 19% (Ukraine), and 15% (Germany) who said "both good and bad" or "neither good nor bad." While 19% of the Germans believed the Soviet influence to be "bad" for Germany, there were few Germanophobes in the Soviet Union (5–8%). See *The Pulse of Europe: A Survey of Political and Social Values and Attitudes* (Washington, D.C.: Times-Mirror Center for the People and the Press, 1991), table section, p. 59. Regarding Soviet "vengeance" on German POWs and civilians in 1945, there has also been a revival of charges—e.g., in the recent book *Other Losses*, by a Canadian, James Bacque—that the American forces under General Eisenhower allowed huge numbers of POWs to die of disease and starvation in the camps, and that tens of thousands were turned over to the French for years of forced labor, all in violation of the Geneva Convention.

currently more preoccupied with the egregious miscalculations of Stalin in 1939 and 1941 than with the German aggression against the Soviets. The second German-Soviet Forum of October 1991 brought together official representatives from the two governments and societies: it was a genuinely German-Russian forum and was imbued with Russian hopes that NATO and the European Community might stem the threat of ethnic anarchy and civil war among the Soviet successor republics. The first forum, organized by the Society for German Foreign Policy in 1989, had been between representatives of the FRG and Soviet delegates selected by the Soviet Academy of Sciences. The German 1991 delegates (representing the administration, parliament, business, and the academic community) were profoundly confused by all this, including by the warnings about "profascist tendencies among some 40 million Soviet unemployed," disputed borders between successor republics, "ambitious demagogues" (historian Yuri Davidov), and the Russian belief that political stabilization must come before the satisfaction of the obvious economic needs in the former Soviet Union. There was not only talk of Russia and other former Soviet states joining NATO and the European Community, but of a two-tier NATO, or "bicameral NATO," of which an "Eastern offshoot" composed of "newly independent East European and Soviet republics"—or the CSCE—would be expected to "guarantee the status quo for the democratic regimes of the area" against foreign and domestic threats. The German representatives were deeply troubled by this shift of their German-Soviet entente away from Britain and France and toward Eastern ways of life from which they had been sheltered for so long by the Iron Curtain. They were pained by Russian suggestions that, as in the days of Peter the Great, foreigners should be sent to help develop Russia—their first response was: Why don't you colonize yourselves?—and appalled to hear from a German banker that 80% of the German aid sent in winter of 1990/91 had been kept or misdirected by the Russian clergy on whose assistance the Germans had relied. Under present conditions, there seemed to be little hope of rendering effective economic assistance to most of the former Soviet areas.[16]

Given the cataclysmic history of Germany over the last hundred years, it should not surprise us that historical events and their current interpretations play a major role in how Germans see themselves. Having fought and lost two world wars and having lived through a murderous, totalitar-

16. See especially the report on the Freiburg Military History Conference—among other things, for the probable connection between the German attack on the Soviet Union and the holocaust of European Jews—in *Frankfurter Allgemeine Zeitung*, Oct. 14, 1991, and the report on the German-Soviet Forum at Moscow, in *Süddeutsche Zeitung*, Oct. 14, 1991.

ian dictatorship which enjoyed their enthusiastic support has left a confusing array of memories, guilt feelings, and nostalgic distortions differentiated by partisanship and distinctive generations in their sense of identity. Partisan views range from the communists (associated with the GDR and the Greens) to the guilt-ridden left (i.e., the moderate antifascist and anticommunist Social Democrats (SPD)—and the broad range of the bourgeois and conservative Free Democrats (FDP) and Christian Democrats (CDU/CSU)—to the ever-changing gaggle of neofascist, radical-right groups, such as the NPD and Republicans, which still orient themselves in spite of everything by the lodestar of the Third Reich.

The range of generational views concerning the Nazi past begins with the World War II and Nazi generation—defined according to when its members were in their formative years, between about fifteen and twenty-five years of age—and older generations, all over age sixty-five today and therefore including only about one in five Germans. It is important to remember that the broad brush of generational analysis accounts only for the bulk of a given generation and, in this case, misses the many victims and opponents of the Third Reich who, of course, share little of the rest of their generation's attitudes then or now. After all, are not Willy Brandt (age seventy-eight), Helmut Schmidt (seventy-three), Richard von Weizsäcker (seventy-one), and Hans-Dietrich Genscher (sixty-four) also members of the war generation as we have defined it here?

After the war and Nazi generation, the reader will recall (Chapter One), there are three or four postwar generations beginning with the birth cohorts of about 1927/28. The first of these is the democratic, antifascist, and anticommunist generation of Chancellor Kohl who, in his controversial phrase, thanked the Lord for having been "born too late (*die Gnade der späten Geburt*)" to have become involved in the deeds of the Nazis and soldiers of his generational predecessors. The second postwar generation are the students and other rebels of 1968 (born between about 1940 and 1955) who shared a completely different outlook on social life and politics from Kohl's generation, the fifty- to sixty-five-year olds. The "68er" generation is between thirty-five and fifty today and is beginning to move into leadership positions throughout German society. In fact, there have been major problems of generational renewal in some German organizations, such as Kohl's CDU/CSU, where the ascent of younger talent has been lagging among the party leadership. Finally, there is a younger generation, perhaps even two, who grew up during the energy crises of the seventies and the pacifist agitation of the early eighties and the Gulf War. Maybe the banner year of 1989 will define the formative experience of the latter generation. All of these generations, by reason of their different birth cohorts and formative periods, perceive German history in very different ways.

Over the forty years of the FRG, the dying off of the older generations and the maturing of new generations can account for most of the changes in political opinion. Thus, for example, West German attitudes regarding "Who is to blame for World War II?" have changed dramatically since the early fifties when the adult population of the FRG belonged almost exclusively to the war generation, whose aggressive nationalist and imperialist views and participation in the war may have hardened their hearts against the victims and antagonists. In 1951, only six years after the end of the war, therefore, one out of four in a representative adult sample responded that "the others" were to blame, 18% said "both sides," and a mere 32% admitted it was Germany's fault. By 1967, twenty-two years later, enough people of the next generation had attained adulthood and sufficient older cohorts had died off to raise the admission of German responsibility gradually to 62%, while only 8% claimed the war had been the fault of "the others" and another 8% said "both sides."[17] Of course, it is not easy for adults to admit guilt or that they have been wrong, and Germans are no exception.

In the same way, West Germans changed their minds about the restoration of monarchy—probably dear only to members of the pre–World War I and World War I generations, who still remembered the Kaiser— from one-third for it in 1951 to a mere 11% in 1965, while the opposition rose from 36% to 66%. An appreciation of Adolf Hitler as "one of Germany's greatest statesmen" similarly declined from nearly 50% in 1955 (vs. 36% opposed) to 31% in 1978 (vs. 56% opposed), even though young neo-Nazi groups and opinions were replacing some of the earlier, dying supporters. In early 1989, on the ten-point scale of a *Spiegel* poll, only 14% gave Hitler a positive vote as a historical figure, scattering their marks over a range of 1–5 points. Fully 74% rated him negatively, including 36% as the "worst" (-5 on the scale) and 27% as the "next to worst" choice.[18] In 1951, people favoring one-party rule still made up 25% of the respondents, even though a majority of 53% championed multiparty politics. But by 1978, the pluralistic majority had grown to 92%, leaving a mere 5% to dream of one-party rule as in the Third Reich.[19] Obviously, it took the coming and going of generational cohorts to facilitate the learning process by which the FRG became a stable democracy, the younger generations being a far better bet than their elders to make pluralist democracy work in Germany.

17. *Jahrbuch der öffentlichen Meinung* (1967), p. 146.
18. *Der Spiegel* 43, no. 15, Apr. 10, 1989, pp. 150–160.
19. David Conradt, *The German Polity*, 3rd ed. (New York: Longman, 1986), p. 54.

Can one tell what members of the war generation may have learned from their experience after forty years? A bellwether issue is recognition of the finality of the loss of the once-German Oder-Neisse area to Poland which was officially accepted by the Brandt administration in the early seventies, after a quarter of a century of West German denials and after furious resistance on the part of German refugees who had been expelled from there in 1945. In 1951, 80% of West Germans agreed (8% did not) that "we should *not* reconcile ourselves to the Oder-Neisse border"; two years later, confronted by the Soviet colossus—West Germany had not yet been brought into NATO and felt itself at the mercy of the power politics between East and West—two-thirds insisted that, some day, "Pomerania, Silesia, and East Prussia would once again belong to Germany" and "not be lost forever."[20] This was mostly the war generation talking, including some 10 million German refugees, a majority from the Oder-Neisse area and Poland. By 1962, the percentages had changed dramatically, as half of the West Germans agreed (26% did not) that Germans should resign themselves to the Oder-Neisse line, thus preparing the ground for Chancellor Brandt's *Ostpolitik* of the early seventies. The GDR government had recognized the new Polish border in 1950, right after its own establishment by the Soviets.

In winter 1989/90, the collapse of the communist regime in the GDR and the prospect of a united Germany bordering on Poland revived the Oder-Neisse issue as Chancellor Kohl and other CDU/CSU politicians once again tried to pacify the refugee organizations with a feigned reluctance to accept the borderline. The mass of Germans, at any rate, have long been on record with their opinions: in 1990, 81% of West Germans accepted the Oder-Neisse line (17% did not), as did 91% of East Germans (only 7% were still opposed). The differences in East and West reflected, among other things, the larger numbers of refugees and members of the older generation in the FRG. For those over age sixty, however, the rates of rejection were 25% in the West and 15% in the GDR. In other words, even among the older West Germans in 1990 (who were twenty years and older in 1951) at least two-thirds had come to accept the inevitable. The large numbers of refugees from the Oder-Neisse to the old FRG made it possible to separate responses by people who themselves had fled from the Oder-Neisse area or who were the children or grandchildren of such refugees. Of the war generation respondents who personally experienced the hardships and brutality of the expulsion, only 56% were prepared to recognize the Oder-Neisse line

20. *Jahrbuch der öffentlichen Meinung* (1955), p. 313; ibid. (1964), pp. 482–483, 504–505.

created by the war; 43% were opposed. Among the children and grand-children of these refugees, 24–28% opposed recognition, evidently reflecting some family indoctrination or loyalty, while 72–75% accepted the new border, really not all that different from the general averages.[21]

The Third Reich Generation

Let us take a closer look at the German generation that corresponds to that of Thatcher and Ridley and to the many older Britons, French, and Russians who remember the war all too well and who therefore have difficulty accepting the new, united Germany. "Born after a [world] war that later was dubbed the first. Raised for an even crueler second world war," reads the caption under a picture of a row of milk-faced thirteen-year-old boys in the winter uniforms of the Jungvolk (Junior Hitler Youth), gathered around their flag in a book on German Gymnasium graduates of 1939, from the Dreikönigschule for boys in Dresden. Born in 1920/21, all but one of this class of fifty-four boys served in the war, twenty-three fell in battle, two died from their injuries right after the war, and a few more somewhat later. Quite a few returned to the ruins of their hometown, Dresden, where Allied bombers had killed and incinerated at least 40,000—some estimates suggest five times that many—over a few days in mid-February 1945. One slashed his wrists upon seeing the ruins of his parents' house. Twenty-three of the survivors were interviewed by the author, Helga Gotschlich, now the director of the Berlin Institute for Contemporary Historical Youth Research, who sought to fathom the great urge of German youth to kill and be killed in World War II.[22] What she found was the legacy of the "great patriotic war" of 1914–1918, passed on to immature boys in the twenties and thirties by their parents and older siblings (often World War I veterans), teachers, schools dominated by the prewar patriotic Right, memoirs of war heroes, youth groups such as the bourgeois *Bündische* Youth, the old bureaucratic and military establishment and, of course, by the Nazi party, once it was in power, through its hydra-headed propaganda machine. This particular cohort had reached the age when youth is most directly impressed by dramatic political events just in time for the great wave of popular pro-Nazi enthusiasm, 1933–1939. Joseph Goebbels's propa-

21. IPOS, May–June 1990, p. 87.
22. Gotschlich, *Reifezeugnis für den Krieg. Abiturienten des Jahrgangs 1939 erinnern sich* (Berlin: Verlag der Nation, 1990), pp. 7–11, 32.

ganda hydra spewed its militaristic poison at them from every snakehead mouth: schools, Hitler Youth, newsprint, radio, books, movies, the party and Nazi-subverted organizations, and public festivals of every kind, not to mention the role of the patriotic parents.[23]

It was the crest of a generational wave of enthusiasm for renewing the 1914–1918 German struggle for European hegemony to which both younger—by 1945, the Nazi government had drafted all birth cohorts down to the birth year 1928, and even younger males were pressed into service to assist the antiaircraft (flak) brigades—as well as older men and many women rallied. After all, the parents of the birth cohorts from 1920 to 1928 had already been enthusiastic nationalists. The crucible of terrors of World War II, both those they suffered and those they visited upon others, bound them together until the bitter end.

But even catastrophic defeat and the disclosure of their monstrous deeds at the war crimes trials in Nuremberg—the holocaust of 5–6 million European Jews, the deaths of an estimated 25–29 million Soviet citizens and millions more of Poles, Yugoslavs, and many others—did not exactly break the nationalist attitudes of the survivors, witness the American Occupation Zone (OMGUS) surveys of 1945–1947. Despite the war crimes trials and denazification, the views of the adult respondents then were not much different from those in the Nazi period. One-third held racist views regarding Jews, blacks, and Poles, justifying deadly persecution with the claim that "it was necessary for the security of the Germans"; one-half insisted that "Danzig, the Sudetenland, and Austria should be part of Germany proper." Another 15–29% expressed authoritarian views extolling dictatorship and the suppression of dissent, and 12–19% attributed stories of German atrocities and even the war itself to foreign conspiracies and propaganda. In 1945, half of the respondents also characterized national socialism as "a good idea badly carried out," and this percentage rose to 55% in 1947 and 66% in the fifties—only the maturing of new generations in the sixties finally lowered it drastically. The war generation had learned little. But in spite of an appallingly high level of anti-Semitism, three-fifths of the respondents in the late forties also agreed about *what was carried out so badly*: the persecution of the Jews and other minorities.[24] There have since been many polls to measure the popular assessment of the Nazi regime—for example, asking the question of whether or not it was "a criminal regime." In 1964, 54% already thought so (28% did not), and by 1978 it was 71% (21% did not).

23. Ibid., pp. 129–144.
24. See Anna J. Merritt and Richard Merritt, eds., *Public Opinion in Occupied Germany: The OMGUS Surveys, 1945–1949* (Urbana: University of Illinois Press, 1970), pp. 146–148, and Noelle-Neumann, ed., *The Germans*, p. 113.

In 1991, the birth cohort of 1920 was seventy-one years old, and the entire war generation (born before 1928) was over sixty-four. This cohort amounted to about 20% of the voting population over age eighteen, and two-thirds of these potential voters were women. Our opinion polls distinguish only the group of Germans over age sixty, but they set them off from the younger cohorts in significant ways. In 1989, for example, 85% of this group in the FRG (as compared to an average of 70%) professed to be "proud to be German," and only 4% said they were not (average: 12.1%)—both values are similar to the 86.6% and 6.2%, respectively, of today's Republicans. In fact, ten years earlier (1980), 91% of the same people (then seniors over fifty-nine) had expressed national pride—two-thirds were "absolutely proud to be German"— while only 4% were not.[25] This was indeed the crest of the nationalist generational wave behind the war mania and the slaughter of the inno- cent. In 1989, they also differed from today's average, with similar margins, in their rate of approval at hearing the national anthem and seeing the national flag.[26] As we shall see, there is a striking contrast in this respect between the seniors and the youngest generation of today's voters, those under age twenty-five.

Since these percentages vary rather continuously, if not evenly, from one age cohort to the next, it is worth noting that respondents in their fifties (i.e., Kohl's generation) are much closer to those over age sixty than they are to their juniors (in their forties), whom we have dubbed the "68er" generation. Süskind said the same thing, just from his subjective impressions. Some scholars have dubbed Kohl's generation the "Hitler Youth generation," those who were exposed to the contagion but too young to serve in the war.[27] But we need to consider that the formative years (ages fifteen to twenty-five) of the fifty-something cohort were the years of catastrophic defeat, of the division of the country (1945–1949)— and, following this, years of painful and slow rebuilding. Kohl's genera- tion grew up politically in mortal fear of the Soviet threat which, of course, also offered many of the old nationalists a new object for displacement, communism, just as the "fascist" FRG was the displace- ment target for the GDR. The formative experiences of the first decade after the war were likely to produce a tougher, more conservative, and

25. Sibylle Hübner-Funk, "Nationale Identität—Neubeginn und Kontinuität," in Deutsches Jugendinstitut e.V. (DJI), *Immer diese Jugend. Ein zeitgeschichtliches Mosaik* (Munich: Kösel, 1985), p. 495 and IPOS, 1989, p. 141.

26. IPOS, 1989, pp. 137–140.

27. Sibylle Hübner-Funk, "Die Hitlerjugendgeneration. Umstrittenes Objekt und streit- bares subjekt der deutschen Zeitgeschichte," *Prokla* 20, no. 3 (1990), 84–98.

more defensive pattern of political and social attitudes than the years of prosperity after 1955.

Whither German Youth?

At the opposite end of the age scale when the drama of 1989/90 began were the youngest West German voters, between eighteen and twenty-four years. Among this group, only 42% expressed national pride—half the rate of the seniors—30% were indifferent (vs. 4.3% of seniors) and 28.1% "did not know" (vs. 10.7% of seniors). Even fewer (35.8% of the young) "liked" to see the flag (57% did not) or hear the national anthem (38% yes, 50% no). A year later, after the most important decisions on German unification had been made, national pride among West Germans under age twenty-five had risen to a level of 56%.[28] This did not keep the young voters from being substantially more dissatisfied with their own political institutions than the seniors. Still more revealing was their indifference in regard to German unification: whereas the seniors were heavily for it (84%), followed closely by Kohl's generation (81%), respondents under thirty could muster only 64% in favor as compared to 18% *contra* and 18% indifferent.[29] The younger set also was considerably more accepting of liberal notions, such as suffrage for resident foreigners and the right of political asylum, than were the seniors. They are obviously a far cry from the war generation and its nationalism and prejudices.[30]

Young East Germans, by way of contrast, were considerably prouder to be German than their Western cousins (65% vs. 56%), but also less so than the East German average (79%), not to mention East Germans over age sixty (89%). When asked whether they favored German unification—in May and June of 1990—young East Germans went for it, 89%.

28. IPOS, 1989, pp. 137–141; IPOS, May–June 1990, p. 109.

29. IPOS, May–June 1990, p. 114.

30. The level of prejudice has been notably lower among younger Germans, as revealed in a 1975 poll by the Institut für Demoskopie on "what kind of people a respondent wouldn't mind having among [his or her] closest friends." Among the "kinds" that Germans did *not* want included were Jews (16%) and blacks (26%), but also convinced Nazis (44%) and communists (50%). This level of anti-Semitism, moreover, ranged from "only" 9% among the sixteen- to twenty-nine-year-olds, over 14% of those aged thirty to forty-four (in 1975), to 32% of those over age sixty. Age hardly made a difference with respect to prejudice against the old Nazis (with communists, it did). The "68ers" (born between 1940 and 1955) overlapped the youngest and part of the next older generation in the data for 1975. Noelle-Neumann, ed., *The Germans*, p. 59.

While 95% of the seniors endorsed unification as "very important," however, only one-third of our youngest cohort called it that.[31] Some of this surprising nationalism coming out of communist closets was also mirrored in the prominent upwelling of radical-right groups and xenophobia in the former GDR. The Leipzig-based opinion researcher Walter Friedrich speaks of "a strong right-wing extremist potential with distinct nationalist attitudes" among East German youth, "with national arrogance, worship of authoritarian leaders, ostentatious rituals, xenophobia, anti-Semitism, and aggressiveness toward nonconformists."[32] There has been violence against foreigners, anarchist and "alternative" youth, and gays by young neo-Nazis, skinheads, and hooligans. Some of the manifestations may be reminiscent of the early Nazi party, but lack the clear political purpose and the quasi-military organization and operations of the old stormtroopers.

The East German radical Right is a very disorderly scene of skinheaded, youthful louts swilling beer—to the point of "coma drinking"—and then seeking out brawls with likely victims. The handful of genuine neo-Nazis, often led by West Germans or "Western-trained," are having a hard time organizing the skinhead and hooligan rabble; the Nazi slogans and symbols common among the latter are as deceptive as a swastika on the leather jacket of a Hell's Angel or soccer hooligan.[33] The assaults on visible foreigners such as Vietnamese or Mozambicans—"Fijis" in popular parlance—also grew out of massive youth unemployment and from the demoralization of the East German police. The old communist regime itself, the reader may recall, contributed to the rise of neo-Nazism in the eighties by "leaning on" autonomous groups, usually "punk groups" of young people (see Chapter Three). Another reason for the rise of youthful East German nationalism may be the high rate of participation by East German youth in the big demonstrations of the fall and winter of 1989/ 90. Three out of five East Germans under age twenty-five claimed to have been so involved in October/November, and one out of three admitted to having been associated with one of the new opposition groups. They were also far more impatient than their elders for free elections in the GDR—the survey was taken in the first week of December 1989.[34] A third reason, of course, is the self-perception of East German marginality,

31. IPOS/DDR, May–June 1990, pp. 10, 54, 59.
32. Walter Friedrich and Peter Förster, "Ostdeutsche Jugend 1990," *Deutschland Archiv* 24, no. 4 (Apr. 1991), 349–350.
33. See Merkl, ed., *Political Violence and Terror: Motifs and Motivations* (Berkeley and Los Angeles: University of California Press, 1986), pp. 229–233.
34. FGW, *Meinungen*, pp. 5, 7, 11, 52, 93.

as compared to prosperous, well-ordered West Germany, which compels the Ossis to grasp the cloak of the common national identity.

Between November 1989 and the end of 1990, Friedrich's Leipzig Institute for Youth Research conducted several youth surveys with respondents between fifteen (sometimes eighteen) and twenty-four years of age in order to measure the heady impact of the great changes, new freedoms, and sudden mobility—most of these youths made multiple, often extended, trips to the old FRG and other European countries. He found the young people not all that different from the adults with regard to their approval of German unification but haunted by expectations of unemployment, crime, and violence, including violence from the radical Right. Over half of them feared an "influx of foreigners." Their identification with the GDR began to drop from its highest point of 93% in November 1989 to a level of 75% in February 1990, while their willingness to emigrate to the West rose each month in 1990 to as high as 4–12% of whoever was left. At the same time, their identification with Germany, especially in its more intense expression, also drifted down from a level of 69% who "felt completely like Germans" (plus 26% who felt "rather like Germans") in November 1989 to 48% (44% "rather") by September 1990, just before German Unity Day (October 3).[35] The mellowing from feeling "completely" German to "yes, I do feel rather like a German" also mirrors the high enthusiasm of young people during the great upheaval and demonstrations of late 1989. As the Leipzig researchers have shown, political interest among East German youth rose from a modest level, as late as May 1989, to a peak lasting until the elections of the following spring and then returning again to the old level.[36]

The high level of economic dissatisfaction and pessimism of GDR youth also emerged from a study of fifteen- to sixteen-year-olds in both Germanys in June and July of 1990. East German ninth-graders, of whom three-fourths still had shown strong attachment to "their country" in spring of 1988, now had less than half of their numbers similarly attached to the GDR. Women exhibited surprising differences in both Germanys. Of the women, one-third fewer felt national identification as Germans, compared to the boys; yet, on "postmaterialist issues"—in this case, freedom of speech and more citizen influence on government—they were far stronger than the more "materialistic" boys, who concentrated on economic gains and "law and order." Xenophobia and national pride were substantially higher among East German fifteen- or sixteen-year-

35. Friedrich and Förster, "Ostdeutsche Jugend 1990," pp. 349–360.
36. Ibid., pp. 701–714.

olds than among their Western counterparts: half of the East German boys and one-third of the young women said that "they were bothered by the many foreigners in the GDR."[37] Many of the xenophobes, interestingly, also viewed young Germans from the other half as foreign residents, not as German brothers and sisters. The GDR actually had far fewer foreigners per capita in 1990, only about 150,000 (1%) compared to over 4 million (6.4%) in the West. But GDR teenagers, age sixteen and younger, seem to be affected profoundly by the "collapse of their world of [socialist] values" in school and at home. They are disoriented and confused in their identity.

Regarding German reunification—the polls were taken near the moment of the currency, economic, and social union, July 1, 1990—the fifteen- to sixteen-year-olds reacted much like the young voters aged eighteen to twenty-four. In the FRG, they were lukewarm in their endorsement; only 25% of the boys (plus 32% "rather" for it) and 14% of the young women were "very much for it" (28% "rather" for it). Another 14% of the boys and 11% of the girls were "very much opposed" (totals of 18% and 23%, respectively, opposed it). In the GDR, one-fourth of the young men and one-third of the young women were "very much for it" (totals of 80% and 69%, respectively, supported it). The number of young opponents was negligible. The impact of unification on each individual was seen far more negatively in this age group among the Wessis than among the Ossis.[38] The latter apparently had not yet faced the consequences of the poor state of their economy, which has obsessed the young working-age voters of West Germany.

The ninth-grade study also looked into the historical understanding and political opinions East and West. West German ninth-graders, for example, expressed very high levels of approval for the peace movement (86%)—indeed, many of them were probably demonstrating against the Gulf War—human rights groups (79%), ecologists (93%), and anti–nuclear-power groups (76%). They had little sympathy with the neo-Nazi Republicans (9%) or the skinheads (7%), each of which drew 80% in opposition. West German youths also selected as their most admired historical personages Konrad Adenauer (44%), Otto von Bismarck (30%), and Karl Marx (27%), who naturally led the parade among the Ossis (with 42%) before former GDR President Wilhelm Pieck (26%) and Bismarck (25%). Adolf Hitler registered only 10% in the East (15%

37. DJI, *Deutsche Schüler im Sommer 1990—Skeptische Demokraten auf dem Weg in ein vereintes Deutschland. Deutsch-deutsche Schülerbefragung 1990*, Arbeitspapier 3-019 (1990), pp. 5–19.
38. Ibid., pp. 20–25.

of the boys) and 7% in the West (11% of the boys), but even this is a level well in excess of the popular average. About the same percentages agreed with the old question about whether "national socialism was a good idea but badly carried out"—in both cases, again, with a much stronger endorsement from the boys. A statement that "people our age no longer need to feel ashamed of the national socialist period" found agreement at levels between 29% and 34%. On the other hand, nearly half of the young people, East and West, expressed a fear that national socialism might return.[39]

This excursion into the mentalities of the old Germans from the war and the Third Reich generation and of the youngest group with a full set of political attitudes toward the events of the day, of course, amounts to a way of assessing the past and the future, Germany yesterday (or what is left of it) and tomorrow. The generational cohorts in between have, in a way, already been discussed, for they are the ones who have been determining the tenor of German politics and guiding government policies. Because of German unification and the numerical preponderance of West Germans, however, we still need to account for a distinctive minority that shaped the character of East Germany and that still differs profoundly from the overwhelming West German majority today.

A Dying Faith

We are *the* people.
We are *one* people.
We are one stupid people.
—graffiti on an East German underpass

The GDR, like the FRG, started out as a creation of the Cold War. Both states were tied into rival military blocs, NATO and the Warsaw Pact. But beyond this, and especially after the construction of the Berlin Wall, the communist part of Germany was also the realm of a militant, quasi-religious faith, communism or revolutionary socialism, that ruled for three decades with a combination of indoctrination and coercion under the protection of the Soviet empire. The GDR had been founded by a generation of militant old communists, including many veterans of the communist parties of the twenties and thirties, the Spanish Civil War, Nazi jails and concentration camps, and bitter exile outside Germany,

39. Ibid., pp. 40–46, 53–55.

including in the Soviet Union. These founders believed they were establishing a new German identity far from the feudal oppression, Prussian militarism, and capitalist exploitation of German history. In fact, they rejected most of that history, except for the sixteenth-century peasant wars and the radical democratic traditions of 1848, and oriented themselves instead toward such international guideposts as the French Revolution and the Paris Commune of 1870, communism in the Soviet Union, and Third World liberation movements around the world (see Chapter Three).[40]

Over the years, much of their crusading enthusiasm began to fade in the crucible of everyday realities and, by the seventies, they began to settle for "realistic socialism (*real existierender Sozialismus*)" rather than the dreams in whose name their own acts of oppression and coercion had always been justified and continued to be justified. Gradually, and of course without acknowledgment by the communist (SED) rulers themselves, the system slipped into a somewhat more relaxed mode of "party patrimonialism," based on quasi-feudal party bosses, their sinecures, cronies, and corruption. The communist leaders acted as if they "owned" the whole system—hence the label "patrimonialism"—and began to resist modernization or, God forbid, democratization of their authority, and all this while their great propaganda machine continued to spread the faith in public life and in the schools and in such mass organizations as the communist state youth (FDJ). By the mid-eighties, after a decade of economic crises and reverses, the communist theocracy was showing advanced signs of a dying faith, in particular among younger East Germans who were exposed to the new social movements from the West: ecological and pacifist protest, alternative life-styles, individual autonomy and spontaneity were the new messages, all anathema to communist orthodoxy. The communist regime reacted with punitive repression to stirrings of youthful autonomy, sometimes turning harmless groups of apolitical punkers and noncommunist youth into seething neo-Nazis. But none of this constituted a serious challenge to the regime until the "new thinking" of Mikhail Gorbachev and his friends cut smug satellite regimes like the GDR loose from their Soviet moorings and set them adrift—in the midst of new streams of exodus and popular rebellion—in the last quarter of 1989. For the GDR, where even the small civil rights and democracy movements still identified emphatically with a "socialist" future, the alternative was unification with the much larger and more powerful FRG, which hitherto (in the communist vocabulary) had been the capitalist and monopolistic class enemy, the spearhead of "aggressive

40. See also *Der Spiegel 45*, Apr. 22, 1991, pp. 146–164.

West German revanchism" and Western imperialism—in short, the old German identity from which the communists had wanted to depart.

At this point, the East German revolution began to unfold along the lines of the (Albert O.) Hirschman thesis concerning alternative paths for rebelling against any oppressive or exploitative organizations—whether a state, an association, or an economic network—via "exit," "voice," or loyalty. East Germans chose to exit *en masse* and then raised their voices in massive protest until they brought down the regime. The shrinking patterns of loyalty and their aftermath are still to be observed. We have already mentioned the aging of the communist elites and their faith. What about the masses? GDR public opinion polls prior to the opening of the borders are few and highly unreliable, but we do have information on the erosion of the faith from that time on. For example, in early December 1989, the Mannheim polling group asked East German adults whether they "thought a great deal of" or "set some store by" socialism, or "thought hardly anything" or "nothing" of the political faith that was the old identity of the GDR. Some 30.1% said "a great deal" and 41.2% "set some store by socialism," for a positive total of nearly 75%. One-fourth of the respondents thought little or nothing of it. By the time of the March elections in East Germany, the positive total was a bare majority while the scoffers added up to 45.2% of the respondents.[41] As might be expected, a three-fourths majority of supporters of the communist PDS thought "a great deal" of socialism while up to two-thirds of the adherents of the CDU-led Alliance for Germany and a majority of Free Democrats regarded it with disdain. The Alliance and FDP then went on to capture a majority of the popular vote in the GDR elections while the PDS received only 16.4%. Its membership had already lost eight of every ten members.

The change in East German mass opinion from the defense of the old system to its surrender to the majorities of the capitalist FRG (i.e., reunification) also emerges clearly from a set of GDR surveys conducted in November 1989, in January/February 1990, and in February/March of 1990. In November, after the opening of the Wall, a majority of 52% was still "rather" or "completely" against surrender to the class enemy, while 16% were "completely" and 32% "rather for" unification. Toward the end of January, after massive demonstrations had first championed unification and then attacked Stasi headquarters, those "completely for" unification had risen to 40% and the total majority in favor of unification had risen to 79%. On the other hand, only 21% now opposed it, and by February/March they, too, were down to 16%, while the eager supporters

41. FW, *Meinungen*, pp. 122–123, 126, 287.

rose to 44% and their combined majority rose to 84% of all East Germans over fifteen years of age (Chapter Three). The great change in the East German sense of identity had evidently occurred during December and January—still before Gorbachev indicated to GDR Premier Hans Modrow that he accepted unification "in principle."

Thus, the East Germans accepted the West German sense of identity but it left a painful hangover, a sense of void, and a nostalgic yearning for the past. Was it a naive illusion that the coming of the deutschmark and of Western-style capitalism would cure all the ills of the East German economy and society overnight? Was it the depressing thought that, after having been robbed of forty years of their lives by communist deceptions, they would now have to wait another five or ten years in order to catch up with West Germany? Or was it the difficult transition from a collectivist ethos to the individual pursuit of happiness? Traveling Americans are often struck by the difference between what appears to be the cheerful pluckiness of the Poles and Czechs—who cannot expect annual subsidies of $60 billion to come in from West Germany—as compared to the East Germans' sullen and downcast mood.[42] Why are the Ossis always comparing themselves to the West Germans rather than to the Poles and other East Europeans who are satisfied, for the time being, with a much lower living standard than what the Ossis so bitterly complain about?

Then again, perhaps we have tended to overemphasize economic interpretations of what is really a psychological and social-psychological problem—the collapse of the old GDR identity, of a world of values that crumbled all the way down to the nurseries and kindergartens. Where once there were fortified walls and death strips patrolled by snarling German shepherd dogs and trigger-happy border guards—richly rewarded by the regime for shooting some poor wretch trying to escape the communist utopia—there is now an "inner wall" dividing people. Even within families or in the youth scene of East and West Berlin they have not "grown together again," as old Willy Brandt had prophesied. The Ossis complain of feeling exposed and embarrassed. They hate themselves for their "Wessization" and for being *westgeil* (too eager to be embraced by the West). A good 71% of East Germans felt that their country had been "overwhelmed and taken over by West Germany" during the course of unification, they told the Times-Mirror pollsters in 1991 (only 22% did not feel that way). Another 43% resented this "a great deal" (42%

42. It should be pointed out that the comparative 1991 Times-Mirror survey of "expectations for country 5 years from now" differs sharply from the popular impression. That survey credits East Germany with having a higher rate of optimism (76%) than the CSFR (69%), Poland (56%), or Hungary (48%) and certainly more than West Germany (38%). See the tables and graphs appendix of *The Pulse of Europe*, table 5.

"a little bit"), and similar numbers wished "there had been a way of reforming the GDR and maintaining at least some independence from the FRG rather than the complete unification that occurred.[43] Arrogant West Germans, or sometimes just a misunderstanding between different German regional cultures, may make it worse. Mutual recrimination and ridicule aside—now there are East German joke books about the Wessis to match the stupid West German cracks about the Ossis—few things are worse than a *Besserwessi*[44] telling Ossis that they did not know how to work.

From all this has come a profound sense of postunification nostalgia among East Germans, of whom one-third "frequently" finds itself wishing that the "good old days" were back (another third "occasionally" feels that way). There is also a new literature of nostalgia, beginning with old SED bosses such as Egon Krenz or Günther Schabowski writing to justify themselves, but also including East and West German writers— e.g., Günter Grass—and leaders of the democratic opposition of the GDR, like Jens Reich, who coined the phrase *Trotzidentität* (identity of spite) to mourn the passing of a world that could have been reformed to their liking. Some Westerners of the Old or New Left also mourn the passing of their utopia which left behind a dreadful, spiritual hangover. The East German dissident poet Günter Kunert has pointed out the danger in creating a new "myth" of a utopia that never was, a typical German myth cleansed of all the bad aspects, the frauds and the suffering, like the myths of ancestral Germany, of Prussia, of the brave German army of World Wars I and II, of Weimar democracy, or even the Third Reich,[45] not to mention the (German) myth of America. "These myths always stem from . . . a dead yesterday, where they rise, like Count Dracula to delight in the blood of the living . . . and to promise an extraordinary life above the everyday evidence to those who accept their leadership." With many images the poet conjured up the rising myth of life in the GDR, "freed of the last memories of oppression, need, fear and hatred," so that "tears will well up in the eyes of the oldsters."[46] The nostalgic myth of the old GDR aside, it was the past myth of the German

43. Ibid., p. 62 of the tables app.
44. A popular word concoction that blends "Wessi" with the air of being "better" (*besser*) and the German schoolmasterly habit of talking as if one knew everything better (*besser wissen*), making the addressee feel like an idiot.
45. "Mythos Deutschland," in Kunert et al., ed., *Nachdenken über Deutschland* (Berlin: Verlag der Nation, 1991), vol. 4, pp. 43–60, esp. 57–59. The reburial of Frederick II of Prussia, with great pomp and circumstance in the presence of Chancellor Kohl, was a much-criticized example of "myth-servicing."
46. Ibid., pp. 46–54.

nation that "in part turned the traditional ethical norms inside out, and in part suspended them, which in the end made possible the catastrophe of the real, nonmythical Germany." Today's young Germans, we can hope, may have learned to live without such myths.

At this writing, almost all the border fortifications between East and West Germany along the nearly 1,000-mile (1,378-km) border have been removed, and the wide strip once defended by border guards, dogs, and lethal devices is to become a series of nature parks—in Berlin, bucolic bicycle paths run along where East German Border Police vehicles used to patrol the wall. Yet, many of the tall border towers, from which soldiers rushed out with automatic weapons to stop the hapless refugees, are still there to haunt the landscape, reminding people of what once divided them to the extent that refugees were shot or maimed before they could make it through the death strip. Perhaps they should be saved as a monument to the living and a reminder that one person's myth can be another person's dungeon.

Looking Toward the Future

It makes more sense for Germans, East or West, to look forward into the future—say, over the next decade until the year 2000. How do the united Germans envisage their future and their role in the world? We have already mentioned the *Germany 2000* poll by Infratest in which 40% of a representative, adult sample saw their country as another Switzerland and 27% as another Sweden, both known for their peaceful neutrality and prosperity.[47] The Germans' onetime idol, the United States, rated only 6% and this after Italy (10%) and Japan (8%)—a split between *joie de vivre*, economic strength, and military power. There may be a touch of escapism here, but hardly a threat of aggression.

An ample majority of Germans evidently also likes the idea of a future multicultural society, so long as it does not cost much or attract streams of foreign "economic refugees." Half would like to see more tolerance displayed toward foreigners and foreign residents in Germany. But they are only talking about current residents (one-third are satisfied with the current numbers), and a large part of the citizenry would rather stop "economic refugees" (79%)—even ethnic German ones (52%)—and seekers of political asylum (43%) from coming. At least one-third are haunted by the vision of too many foreigners in the year 2000. With

47. *Süddeutsche Zeitung*, Jan. 4, 1991 (supp.).

snowballing incidents of skinhead violence against the shelters which house foreign refugees in East and West Germany, groups of volunteers have formed to protect them—there have also been massive demonstrations and official admonitions against the right-wing violence—for at night and on weekends the police are far too shorthanded to do an effective job. These volunteers are haunted by the German past, by the violent attacks of another day that, for lack of popular resistance, led to the Nazi takeover and the holocaust. Then, too, it all started with large migrations of "different-looking" East Europeans, especially Russian and other East European Jews fleeing the post–World War I upheavals in the East and providing an easily visible displacement target for prejudiced mobs and a society suffering from national humiliation and discredited values.

Unlike the Wessis, who evidently fear the authoritarian state, the Ossis would prefer to see more police, law and order in the streets, and more discipline in the schools by the year 2000. Their concern is evidently motivated by the rise of crime and violence in the five new *Länder*. The Ossis also call for "more respect for state authority" (40% as compared to 22% in the West), a telling manifestation of statism despite their great faith in personal economic success in the GDR. German social life in the year 2000, two-thirds and more of all respondents agree, should be characterized by mutual helpfulness (78%) and respect for the aged (67%). Germans also prize both the courage to speak up and tolerance for nonconformists who do (64% and 63%, respectively).

There can be no future, alas, without some awareness of the past, and 29% of the respondents believe that a sense of "shame about the crimes of fascism" should be an important part of the German future. In East Germany, nearly half do, perhaps a legacy of the carefully nurtured displacement of the old GDR. Yet, 18% of all Germans oppose this attitude (21% in West Germany). One-third, on the other hand, would like the "shame of the crimes of [GDR] socialism" to be kept alive, no doubt including many old Cold Warriors in the West. There are, of course, numerous cases pending against the cruelty and injustice of the old regime—in particular, proceedings against border guards who shot refugees at the Wall or the inner-German border. It is not easy to settle on appropriate compensation or punishment so long as the new governments shy away from considering the entire old regime, or at least some of its decisions, as inhumane and in violation of natural law, and not just its own, dubious, positive law.

Surprisingly, the respondents also broke with some well-established German trends and social patterns, such as sticking to one's calling and a W. C. Fields–like aversion to small children, the *Kinderfeindlichkeit*. In the survey, a majority thought it would be desirable for a person to pursue several careers in succession, and another 9% even feels ready to tackle several careers simultaneously. Up to three-fourths also seem prepared to reverse the long-standing trend away from families with children. They want neighborhoods full of kids, plenty of child care centers—many East German ones have survived the old regime, while, in the West, there is a terrible shortage—and state support for combining motherhood with a career. Two-thirds want to see the man more involved in a couple's household chores (four of five women agree). On the explosive issue of legalizing abortion, a majority of three-fifths favors a woman's free choice, 34% of them during the first trimester, and 24% are for the total elimination of article 218 from the criminal code—even the CDU/CSU supporters endorsed these positions, thereby disagreeing with their conservative representatives in Bonn. Only 28% of the respondents agreed with the old West German law which permitted first-trimester abortion only if certain "indications" are present (dangers to the health of the mother or fetus, cases of rape, and socioeconomic hardship). A mere 13% wish to outlaw abortions altogether.

And what about Germany's role in the world by the year 2000? The German future in the eyes of the respondents is a peaceful one. Fully 75% want the country to stay out of international conflicts—hence the choice of neutral Switzerland and Sweden, rather than superpower America. Only 25% were in favor of getting militarily involved. Their preference for "staying out," of course, was sorely tested within a month of the survey by the hot phase of the Gulf War, whose aerial bombardment triggered vast youthful peace demonstrations, split the German Left, and sparked a spirited debate (aside from bringing back memories for those over fifty of the Allied bombardments of German cities). The pacifist side finally admitted, as the chief German reason for a possible intervention in the Gulf War, its fear that Israel might be drawn into the conflict. Otherwise, they remained adamant about staying out and preferred to pay large sums[48] to buy their way out.

By the year 2000, Germans hope to be part of a European federation. They envisage their country as a "state with open borders, no barriers and no controls" (83%). In their dealings with other nations, the three countries to which Germans would give "priority in good and close relations" were the Soviet Union (59%), the United States (44%), and France (36%). Their friendly feelings toward the Soviets were already demonstrated by the vast sums pledged in aid and credit and by the grand care-package campaign in the fall and winter of 1990/91. The Kohl

48. *Politbarometer*, Jan. 1991, pp. 54–56.

government has spared no effort to enlist other Western countries in aiding Soviet economic reconstruction. To quote President Weizsäcker, "our European humanity and peace depend to an extraordinary degree upon Soviet developments and their impact upon Europe. Gorbachev's most important motive for agreeing to German unification, in my opinion, was the desire not to be left out of the [European house], to overcome the distance. . . . I think we need to respond to that." Neither the fall of Gorbachev nor the disintegration of the Soviet Union has changed the goal of German-Russian reconciliation.

The Germans did respond in a variety of ways, not the least of which were their expressions of deep regret about what German soldiers and administrators had done to ordinary Soviet citizens in their nationalist wartime mania. As simple a human gesture as saying "we are sincerely sorry" has become a landmark of reconciliatory foreign policy style for a country which was once characterized by one of its outstanding psychiatrists, Alexander Mitscherlich, as incorporating a hard-hearted "inability to mourn," to feel sad for its deeds, or to empathize with the feelings of its victims. Konrad Adenauer, in the early fifties, expressed his sorrow to Jewish survivors and the state of Israel, a gesture repeated since by many Germans. Willy Brandt, in 1970, went down on his knees at the Warsaw Ghetto memorial. President Richard von Weizsäcker and others have carried apologies for German aggression to Poland, the CSFR—often with the warmest reciprocal response—and most recently to the city of Coventry, the first target of the Nazi blitz of Hermann Göring. Unfortunately, the British were busy at the time raising a statue of RAF Marshal Arthur Harris ("Bomber" Harris) in London, the man responsible for hundreds of thousands of German civilian deaths with his "carpet-bombing" of nonmilitary German targets in World War II. But would it not be a splendid idea if national representatives would go around instead saying they were sorry—the Spaniards to the Indians of the Americas, historical slavetrading nations to the Africans, onetime colonialists to their former unwilling subjects, bloody-minded religious leaders of every faith to the "infidels" they have persecuted. What a civilized world this could become, say by the year 2000.

Speaking of the simple phrases that can make for a civilized relationship among nations, we should not forget the role that has perhaps not received as much attention as it deserves in this account of German unification in the European context: namely, the role of the U.S. government. Preoccupied as Americans are with the toils of bitter partisan strife and with fatuous discussion about whether or not the United States is in socioeconomic and political decline—instead of rolling up their sleeves to do something about it—most Americans have not even noticed how deeply admired their political system has become throughout Eastern Europe, the former Soviet Union and, yes, in Western Europe as well during these dramatic years. America is admired for its venerable republican Constitution, its working federal system combining central power and home rule—a subject once more of the greatest interest to the builders of a political union in Europe, not to mention the Soviets, Czechs and Slovaks, and Yugoslavs—its presidential–congressional relations and, most of all, its Bill of Rights and regard for the individual, which stand as a beacon to many a nation just emerging from decades of dictatorship.

Europeans, of course, are not blind to America's problems and breakdowns, but they find much to admire in American society—for example, its subjugation of the scourge of nationalism, which threatens peace and survival throughout Eastern Europe and from Bilbao to Belfast. For the Germans, too, America has provided inspiration along many lines, political, economic, and social. Even the criticism issuing from German pens still fits comfortably within the pale of free speech that America helped preserve on this side of Nazi German tyranny and, after 1945, on this side of communist German dictatorship until it could finally flourish even in East Germany (and other former communist states). Chancellor Kohl paid tribute to the American defense of freedom in Europe and to the American presidents of four decades when, in an address at the University of California–Berkeley (September 17, 1991), he invoked memories of a speech by Konrad Adenauer thirty-one years earlier in the same place. "Never before in history," Adenauer said in 1960, "had a victorious nation helped the defeated to such an extent as the American people had aided the Germans." Kohl had come to express his gratitude for America's support for German unification and, with the gift of simplicity that often eludes him, said "Thank you for everything."

Selected Bibliography

Books and Articles

Adomeit, Hannes. "Gorbachev and German Unification: Revision of Thinking, Realignment of Power." *Problems of Communism*, Jul./Aug. 1990, pp. 1–23.

Allison, Graham, and Gregory Treverton, eds. *Rethinking American Security: Beyond Cold War to New World Order.* New York: Norton, 1992.

Almond, Gabriel A., and Sidney Verba. *The Civic Culture: Political Attitudes and Democracy in Five Nations.* Princeton, N.J.: Princeton University Press, 1963.

Arendt, Hannah. *On Revolution.* London: Faber & Faber, 1963.

Auf dem Weg zum Binnenmarkt. Europäische Integration und deutscher Föderalismus. Ed. Jochen Thies and Wolfgang Wagner. Bonn: Verlag für Internationale Politik, 1989.

Auf der Suche nach der Gestalt Europas. Festschrift für Wolfgang Wagner. Bonn: Verlag für Internationale Politik, 1990.

Bäcker, Gerhard, and Johannes Steffen. "Sozialunion—Was soll wie vereinigt werden?" *WSI Mitteilungen* 43, no. 5 (1990), 265–269.

Baker, L. Kendall, Russell J. Dalton, and Kai Hildebrandt. *Germany Transformed: Political Culture and the New Politics.* Cambridge, Mass.: Harvard University Press, 1982.

Baring, Arnulf. *Uprising in East Germany, June 17, 1953.* Ithaca, N.Y.: Cornell University Press, 1972.

Barnes, Samuel H., et al. *Political Action: Mass Participation in Five Western Democracies.* Beverly Hills, Calif.: Sage, 1979.

Batt, Judy. *Economic Reform and Political Change in Eastern Europe: A Comparison of the Czechoslovak and Hungarian Experience.* New York: St. Martin's Press, 1988.

Ben-Ari, Jitzhak. "Israel und die Bundesrepublik. Eine Bilanz besonderer Beziehungen." *Das Parlament,* supp., B 15/90, April 6, 1990, pp. 3–7.

Benz, Wolfgang. *Potsdam 1945. Besatzungsherrschaft und Neuaufbau im Vierzonen-Deutschland.* Munich: DTV, 1986.

Bergsdorf, Wolfgang. "Wer will die deutsche Einheit?" *Die politische Meinung* 35, no. 248 (1990), 13–19.

Biehl, Dieter, and Gero Pfennig, eds. *Zur Reform der EG-Finanzverfassung. Beiträge zur wissenschaftlichen und politischen Debatte.* Bonn: Europa Union, 1990.

Black, Cyril E., and Thomas P. Thornton, eds. *Communism and Revolution: The Strategic Uses of Political Violence.* Princeton, N.J.: Princeton University Press, 1964.

Blacker, Coit D. "The Collapse of Soviet Power in Europe." *Foreign Affairs* 70, no. 1 (1991), 88–102.

Bonvicini, Gianni, et al. *Die EG und die jungen Demokratien in Europa.* Baden-Baden: Nomos, 1991.

Borsdorf, Ulrich, and Lutz Niethammer, eds. *Zwischen Befreiung und Besatzung.* Wuppertal: P. Hammer, 1976.

Botz, Gerhard. "Will Unification Bring the 'German Question' to an End?" *German Politics and Society* 21 (Fall 1990), 1–19.

Brandt, Willy. *Von Bonn nach Berlin,* pp. 14–79. Berlin: Arain, 1957.

———. *"Was zusammengehört." Reden zu Deutschland.* Berlin: Dietz, 1990.

Bruns, Wilhelm. "Die Regelung der äusseren Aspekte der deutschen Einigung." *Deutschland-Archiv* 22, no. 11 (Nov. 1990), 1726–1728.

Bulmer, Simon, and William E. Paterson. *The Federal Republic of Germany and the European Community.* London: Allen & Unwin, 1987.

Bundesminister des Innern. *Die Neugliederung des Bundesgebietes.* Gutachten, Bonn, and Cologne: Heymann, 1955.

Burgess, John P. "Church-State Relations in East Germany: The Church as a Religious and Political Force." *Journal of Church and State* 32 (Winter 1990), 17–35.

Büttner, Thomas, and Wolfgang Lutz. *Germany's Population: Turbulent Past, Uncertain Future.* Washington, D.C.: Population Bulletin, 1991.

Cerny, Karl H. "The Campaign and the 1987 Election Outcome." In Karl H. Cerny, ed., *Germany at the Polls: The Bundestag Elections of the 1980s.* Durham, N.C.: Duke University Press, 1990.

Childs, David. *The GDR: Moscow's German Ally.* London: Allen & Unwin, 1983.

Collier, Irwin I., Jr. "On the First Year of German Monetary, Economic, and Social Union." *Journal of Economic Perspectives* 5, no. 3 (1991).

Collier, Irwin I., Jr., and David H. Papell. "About Two Marks: Refugees and the Exchange Rate Before the Wall." *American Economic Review* 78, no. 3 (1988), 531–542.

———, and Horst Siebert. "The Economic Integration of Post-Wall Germany." *Economic Developments and Prospects* 81, no. 2 (1991), 196–201.

Conradt, David. *The German Polity*. 3rd ed. New York: Longman, 1986.

Council on Foreign Relations, 79th American Assembly. *Rethinking America's Security: U.S. Interests in the 1990s*. Chicago: Council on Foreign Relations, 1983.

Croan, Melvin. "Dilemmas of Ostpolitik." In Peter H. Merkl, ed., *West German Foreign Policy: Dilemmas and Directions*, p. 35ff. Chicago: Council on Foreign Relations, 1983.

Dallin, Alexander, and George Breslauer. *Political Terror in Communist Systems*. Stanford, Calif.: Stanford University Press, 1970.

Dalton, Russel J. *Citizen Politics in Western Democracies*. Chatham, N.J.: Chatham House, 1988.

———, ed. *Germany Votes, 1990: Reunification and the Creation of a New Party System*. New York: Berg, 1992.

Daltrop, Anne. *Politics and the European Community*. 2nd ed. Essex: Longman, 1986.

Daschitschew, Wjatscheslaw, and Carl Gustav Ströhm, eds. *Die Neuordnung Mitteleuropas*. Mainz: Hase & Koehler, 1991.

Davison, W. P. *The Berlin Blockade: A Study in Cold War Politics*. Princeton, N.J.: Princeton University Press, 1958.

Davy, Richard. "Grossbritannien und die deutsche Frage." *Europa-Archiv*, no. 4 (1990), 139–144.

Dehio, Ludwig. *Deutschland und die Weltpolitik im 20. Jahrhundert*. Munich: Oldenbourg, 1955.

Dennis, Mike. *German Democratic Republic: Politics, Economics, and Society*. London: Pinter, 1988.

Desai, Padim. *Perestroika in Perspective: The Design and Dilemmas of Soviet Reform*. Princeton, N.J.: Princeton University Press, 1989.

Dettke, Dieter, ed. *America's Image in Germany and Europe*, pp. 8–33. Washington, D.C.: Friedrich-Ebert-Stiftung, 1985.

Deutsches Institut für Wirtschaftsforschung, Berlin. *DDR-Wirtschaft: Eine Bestandsaufnahme*. Frankfurt: Fischer, 1974.

Dohnanyi, Klaus von. *Das deutsche Wagnis. Europas Schlüssel zum Frieden*. Munich: Drömersche Verlagsanstalt, 1990.

Drühe, Wilhelm. "Beruf Pfarrer." *Die politische Meinung* 35 (March–April 1990), 74–81.

Edinger, Lewis J. *West German Politics*. New York: Columbia University Press, 1986.

Edwards, James R. "The Fall and Rise of East Germany." *Christianity Today*, Apr. 23, 1990, pp. 17–18.

Eith, Ulrich. "Alters- und geschlechtsspezifisches Wahlverhalten." *Der Bürger im Staat* 40, no. 3 (Sept. 1990), 166–170.

Das Ende der Teilung. Der Wandel in Deutschland und Osteuropa. Ed. Jochen Thies and Wolfgang Wagner. Bonn: Verlag für Internationale Politik, 1990.

Fack, Fritz U., K. Fromme, and G. Nonnenmacher, eds. *Das deutsche Modell. Freiheitlicher Rechtsstaat und Soziale Marktwirtschaft*. Cologne: Wirtschaftsverlag, 1990.

Farrar, L. L., Jr. *The Short War Illusion: A Study of German Policy, Strategy, and Domestic Affairs, August–December 1914*. Santa Barbara, Calif.: ABC-Clio, 1973.

Federal Ministry for Inner-German Relations. *DDR Handbuch*. 2 vols. 3rd ed. Cologne: Wissenschaft & Politik, 1984/85.

Fischer, Fritz. *German Aims in the First World War (Griff nach der Weltmacht)*. New York: Norton, 1967.

Friedrich, Carl J. "Denazification." In Carl J. Friedrich, ed., *American Experiences in Military Government in World War II*, pp. 253–275. New York: Rinehart & Co., 1948.

——, ed. *Revolution*. New York: Atherton, 1966.

Friedrich, Walter, and Peter Förster. "Ostdeutsche Jugend 1990." *Deutschland-Archiv* 24, no. 4 (Apr. 1991), 349–350.

Friedrich-Naumann-Stiftung, ed. *German Identity: Forty Years After Zero*. St. Augustin: COMDOK, 1985.

Fritzsch-Bournazel, Renata. *Europa und die deutsche Einheit*. Bonn: Aktuell, 1990.

Garthe, Michael. *Weichenstellung zur Europäischen Union? Der Verfassungsentwurf des Europäischen Parlaments und sein Beitrag zur Überwindung der EG-Krise*. Bonn: Europa Union, 1989.

Gibowski, Wolfgang. "Demokratischer Neubeginn in der DDR. Dokumentation und Analyse der Wahl vom 18. März 1990." *Zeitschrift für Parlamentsfragen* 21, no. 1 (May 1990), 5–22.

Gitelman, Zwi. "The Limits of Organization and Enthusiasm: The Double Failure of the Solidarity Movement and the Polish United Workers' Party." In Kay Lawson and Peter H. Merkl, eds., *When Parties Fail: Emerging Alternative Organizations*, pp. 421–446. Princeton, N.J.: Princeton University Press, 1988.

Glaessner, Gert-Joachim. "Ende der Reformen? Bedingungen und Grenzen der Handlungsfähigkeit sowjet-sozialistischer Systeme am Beispiel der DDR." *Deutschland-Archiv* 15, no. 2 (1982), 700–709.

——. *Herrschaft durch Kader. Leitung der Gesellschaft und Kaderpolitik in der DDR am Beispiel des Staatsapparates*. Opladen: Westdeutscher Verlag, 1977.

——. *Sozialistische Systeme. Einführung in die Kommunismus- und DDR-Forschung*. Opladen: Westdeutscher Verlag, 1983.

Golden, James R., et al., eds. *NATO at Forty: Change, Continuity, and Prospects*. Boulder, Colo.: Westview, 1989.

Gotschlich, Helga. *Reifezeugnis für den Krieg. Abiturienten des Jahrgangs 1939 erinnern sich*. Berlin: Verlag der Nation, 1990.

Grözinger, Gerd. *Teures Deutschland: Was kostet uns die DDR?* Berlin: Rotbuch, 1990.

Habermas, Jürgen. *Die nachholende Revolution*. Frankfurt: Suhrkamp, 1990.

Haftendorn, Helga, and Lothar Wilker. "Die Sicherheitspolitik der beiden deutschen Staaten." In *Deutschland Handbuch. Eine doppelte Bilanz 1949–1989*, pp. 605–620. Munich: Hanser, 1989.

Haltzel, Michael H. "Amerikanische Einstellungen zur deutschen Wiedervereinigung." *Europa-Archiv*, no. 4 (1990), 127–132.

Hanrieder, Wolfram. *Deutschland, Europa, Amerika*. Munich, Vienna, and Zurich: Schöningh, 1991.

Hansen, Niels. "Verbindungen in die Zukunft, 25 Jahre diplomatische Beziehungen zwischen Deutschland und Israel." *Das Parlament*, supp., B 15/90, April 6, 1990, pp. 8–18.

Hasse, Rolf H. *The European Central Bank: Perspectives for a Development of the European Monetary System*. Gütersloh: Bertelsmann, 1990.

Haupt, Hans Georg, et al., eds. *Die sozialistische Gemeinschaft. Interessen—Zusammenarbeit—Wirtschaftswachstum*. East Berlin: VEB, 1985.

Havemann, Robert. *Dialektik ohne Dogma. Naturwissenschaften und Weltanschauung*. Reinbek: Rowohlt, 1964.

Heiling, Gerhard K., Thomas Büttner, and Wolfgang Lutz. *Germany's Population: Turbulent Past, Uncertain Future*. Washington, D.C.: Population Bulletin, 1991.

Heisbourg, François. "From a Common European Home to a European Security System." In Gregory F. Treverton, ed., *The Shape of the New Europe*, pp. 48–50. New York: Council on Foreign Relations, 1992.

Helm, Jutta. "Citizen Lobbies in West Germany." In Peter H. Merkl, ed., *Western European Party Systems: Trends and Prospects*, pp. 576–596. New York: Free Press/Macmillan, 1980.

Herdegen, Gerhard, and Elisabeth Noelle-Neumann. "Protest Howls Belied by Opinion Polls." *Die politische Meinung* 29, no. 212 (1984), 10–15.

Herles, Wolfgang. *Nationalrausch: Szenen aus dem gesamtdeutschen Wahlkampf*. Munich: Kindler, 1990.

Hirsch, Kurt, and Hans Sarkowitz. *Schönhuber, der Politiker und seine Kreise*. Frankfurt: Eichborn, 1989.

Hoffman-Göttig, Joachim. "Die jungen Wähler. Zur Interpretation der Jungwählerdaten der Repräsentativen Wahlstatistik für Bundestag, Landtage und Europaparlament, 1953–1984." Mimeographed. Frankfurt, 1984.

———. *Die Mehrheit steht links—die jungen Wähler in der BRD*. Bonn: SPD-Parteivorstand, 1989.

Holborn, Hajo. *A History of Modern Germany, 1840–1945*. Princeton, N.J.: Princeton University Press, 1969.

Homann, Fritz. "Strategie für die wirtschaftliche Erholung in den neuen Bundesländern." *Deutschland Archiv* 24, no. 6 (June 1991), 608–617.

Honolka, Harro. *Schwarzrotgrün. Die BRD auf der Suche nach ihrer Identität*. Munich: Beck, 1987.

Hosnag, Joachim. "Boden und Besitz." *Die politische Meinung* 35, no. 251 (1990), 19–25.

Hübner-Funk, Sibylle. "Die Hitlerjugendgeneration: Umstrittenes Objekt und streitbares Subjekt der deutschen Zeitgeschichte." *Prokla* 20, no. 3 (1990), 84–98.

———. "Nationale Identität—Neubeginn und Kontinuität." In Deutsches Jugendinstitut e.V. (DJI), *Immer diese Jugend. Ein zeitgeschichtliches Mosaik*. Munich: Kösel, 1985.

Inglehart, Ronald. *The Silent Revolution: Changing Values and Political Styles Among Western Publics*. Princeton, N.J.: Princeton University Press, 1977.

Institut zur Förderung öffentlicher Angelegenheiten. *Die Bundesländer. Beiträge zur Neugliederung der Bundesrepublik*. Frankfurt, 1950.

Jacobsen, Hans-Adolf, Wolfgang Mallmann, and Christian Meier, eds. *Sicherheit und Zusammenarbeit in Europa (KSZE): Analyse und Dokumentation, 1965–1972*. Cologne: Wissenschaft & Politik, 1973.

———. *Sicherheit und Zusammenarbeit in Europa (KSZE). Analyse und Dokumentation, 1973–1978*. Cologne: Wissenschaft & Politik, 1978.

————. *Drei Jahrzehnte Aussenpolitik der DDR.* Munich and Vienna: Oldenbourg, 1979.

James, Harald, and Marla Stone, eds. *When the Wall Came Down: Reactions to German Unification.* New York: Routledge, 1992.

Jesse, Eckhardt, and Armin Mitter, eds. *Die Gestaltung der deutschen Einheit. Geschichte, Politik und Gesellschaft.* Bonn: Bouvier, 1992.

John, Antonius. "Neue Landwirtschaft." *Die politische Meinung* 35, no. 251 (1990), 27–32.

Jones, Sidney L. "The Integration and Divergence of German and American Economic Interests." In James A. Cooney, Gordon A. Craig, Hans Peter Schwarz, and Fritz Stern, eds., *The Federal Republic of Germany and the United States: Changing Political, Social, and Economic Relations,* pp. 109–129. Boulder, Colo.: Westview, 1984.

Kaiser, Karl. *Deutschlands Vereinigung. Die internationalen Aspekte.* Bergisch-Gladbach: Lübbe-Bastei, 1991.

————. "Germany's Unification." *Foreign Affairs* 70, no. 1 (1991), 179–205.

Kaldor, Mary, Gerard Holden, and Richard Falk, eds. *The New Détente: Rethinking East-West Relations.* London and Tokyo: Verso and the U.N. University, 1989.

Kaplan, Lawrence S. *NATO and the United States: The Enduring Alliance.* Boston: Twayne, 1988.

Katzenstein, Peter J. *Policy and Politics in West Germany: The Growth of a Semi-Sovereign State.* Philadelphia: Temple University Press, 1987.

Keller, Dietmar, ed. *Nachdenken über Deutschland.* 4 vols. Berlin: Verlag der Nation, 1990/91.

Kennedy, Paul. *The Rise and Fall of the Great Powers.* New York: Vintage Books, 1987.

Kimmel, Michael S. *Revolution: A Sociological Interpretation.* Cambridge: Polity Press, 1990.

Klaus, Georg. *Kybernetik—Eine neue Universalphilosophie der Gesellschaft?* East Berlin: Akademie-Verlag, 1973.

————. *Kybernetik und Gesellschaft.* East Berlin: Deutscher Verlag der Wissenschaften, 1964 (3rd ed. 1973).

Knapp, Guido, and Ekkehardt Kuhn. *Deutsche Einheit. Traum und Wirklichkeit.* Erlangen: Straube, 1990.

Kolboom, Ingo. *Vom geteilten zum vereinigten Deutschland. Deutschland-Bilder in Frankreich.* Bonn: Europa Union, April 1991.

Kommers, Donald. "The Basic Law of the FRG After Forty Years," in Peter H. Merkl, ed., *The Federal Republic of Germany at Forty,* pp. 133–159. New York: New York University Press, 1989.

Korbonski, Andrzej. "The Politics of Economic Reforms in Eastern Europe: The Last Thirty Years." *Soviet Studies* 41, no. 1 (1989).

Koriman, Michel. *Quand l'Allemagne pensait le monde. Grandeur et décadence d'une géopolitique.* Paris: Fayard, 1990.

Kreissler, Felix. *Der Österreicher und seine Nation. Ein Lernprozess mit Hindernissen.* Vienna: Braumüller, 1984.

Krisch, Henry. *The GDR: The Search for Identity.* Boulder, Colo.: Westview, 1985.

Küchle, Hartmut, and Gernot Müller. "Währungsunion zwischen BRD und DDR." *WSI Mitteilungen* 43, no. 5 (1990), 256–265.

Kühne, Jörg-Detlef. "Replik in Sachen Hauptstadt. Nicht nur Papier und Sonntagsreden." *Zeitschrift für Parlamentsfragen* 12, no. 3 (1990), 515–524.

Kunert, Günther. "Mythos Deutschland." In Günther Kunert et al., eds., *Nachdenken über Deutschland,* vol. 4, pp. 43–60. Berlin: Verlag der Nation, 1991.

Kuppe, Johannes. "Modrow in Bonn." *Deutschland-Archiv* 23, no. 3 (1990), 337–340.

Kuttner, Robert. *The End of Laissez-Faire: National Purpose and the Global Economy After the Cold War.* New York: Knopf, 1990.

Langguth, Gerd, ed. *Die Berlin-Politik der DDR.* KAS Deutschland-Report no. 3. Melle: Knoth, 1987.

———. *Berlin. Vom Brennpunkt der Teilung zur Brücke der Einheit.* Cologne: Wissenschaft & Politik, 1990.

Lapp, Peter Joachim. "Fünf neue Bundesländer—Stärkung des Föderalismus." *Deutschland-Archiv* 22, no. 11 (1990), 1659–1961.

———. *Die Volkskammer der DDR.* Opladen: Westdeutscher Verlag, 1975.

Larrabee, Stephen F. "The View from Moscow." In Stephen F. Larrabee, ed., *The Two German States and European Security,* pp. 183–205. New York: St. Martin's Press, 1989.

Larrabee, Stephen F., ed. *The Two German States and European Security.* New York: St. Martin's Press, 1989.

Läufer, Thomas. *22 Fragen zu Europa. Europäische Gemeinschaft und Europäisches Parlament.* Bonn: Europa Union, 1990.

Leggewie, Claus. *Die Republikaner. Phantombild der Neuen Rechten.* Berlin: Rotbuch, 1989.

Lehne, Stephan. *The Vienna Meeting of the CSCE, 1986–1989: A Turning Point in East-West Relations.* Boulder, Colo.: Westview, 1991.

Leyendecker, Hans, and Richard Rickelmann. *Exporteure des Todes. Deutscher Rüstungsskandal in Nahost.* Göttingen: Steidl Verlag, 1991.

Linz, Juan. "Totalitarian and Authoritarian Regimes." In Nelson Polsby and Fred Greenstein, eds., *Handbook of Political Science,* vol. 3, pp. 175–482. Reading, Mass.: Addison-Wesley, 1975.

Losoncz, Miklós. "Ungarische Liberalisierung." *Politische Meinung* 35, no. 249 (1990), 63–67.

Loth, Wilfried. *Ost-West Konflikt und deutsche Frage.* Munich: DTV, 1989.

Louis, Jean-Victor. *From EMS to Monetary Union.* Luxembourg: EC Publications, 1990.

Lüdenmann, E. "Zur ökonomischen Situation der DDR am Beginn der Erneuerung." *IPW Berichte* 2 (1990).

Ludwig, Michael. *Polen und die deutsche Frage.* Bonn: Europa Union, 1991.

Lundestad, Geir. *East, West, North, South: Major Developments in International Politics, 1945–1986.* Oslo: Norwegian University Press, 1986.

Marer, Paul. "The Economies and Trade of Eastern Europe." In William E. Griffith, ed., *Central and Eastern Europe: The Opening Curtain.* Boulder, Colo.: Westview, 1989.

Markovits, Andrei S. "Anti-Americanism and the Struggle for a West German Identity." In Peter H. Merkl, ed., *The Federal Republic of Germany at Forty,* pp. 35–54. New York: New York University Press, 1989.

Mayer, Thomas, and Günther Thumann. "German Democratic Republic: Background and Plans for Reform." In Leslie Lipschitz and Donogh Mc-

Donald, eds., *German Unification: Economic Issues*, pp. 49–70. Washington, D.C.: IMF, Dec. 1990.
——. "The Role of Fiscal and Structural Policies in German Unification: Lessons from the Past." In Leslie Lipschitz and Donogh McDonald, eds., *German Unification: Economic Issues*, pp. 165–171. Washington, D.C.: IMF, Dec. 1990.
McAdams, A. James. *East Germany and Détente: Building Authority After the Wall.* Cambridge: Cambridge University Press, 1985.
McDonald, Donogh, and Günther Thumann. "Investment Needs in East Germany." In Leslie Lipschitz and Donogh McDonald, eds., *German Unification: Economic Issues*, pp. 71–77. Washington, D.C.: IMF, Dec. 1990.
Meier, Christian. *Deutsche Einheit als Herausforderung. Welche Fundamente für welche Republik?* Munich: Hanser, 1989.
Meinecke, Friedrich. *Weltbürgertum und Nationalstaat.* Munich, 1908.
Meissner, Boris. "Das neue Denken Gorbatschows und die deutsche Frage." In Wjatscheslaw Daschitschew and Carl Gustaf Ströhm, eds., *Die Neuordnung Mitteleuropas*, pp. 15–32. Mainz: Hase & Köhler, 1991.
Menge, Marlies. *Ohne uns läuft nichts mehr. Die Revolution in der DDR.* Stuttgart: DVA, 1990.
Merkl, Peter H. "La Funcion Legitimadora del Lider. Konrad Adenauer, 1949–1976." *Revista de Estudios Politicos*, no. 21 (May–June 1981), 7–25.
——. *German Foreign Policies, West and East.* Santa Barbara, Calif.: ABC-Clio, 1974.
——. *The Making of a Stormtrooper.* Princeton, N.J.: Princeton University Press, 1980.
——. *The Origin of the West German Republic.* New York: Oxford University Press, 1963.
——. "Pacifism in West Germany." *SAIS Review*, no. 4 (Summer 1982), 81–91.
——. "Politico-Cultural Restraints on West German Foreign Policy: Sense of Trust, Identity, and Agency." *Comparative Political Studies* 3, no. 4 (Jan. 1971), 443–467.
——. "The SPD After Brandt: Problems of Integration in an Urban Society." *West European Politics* 11 (Jan. 1988).
——. "West German Public Opinion on Détente Since 1970." In Wolfram F. Hanrieder, ed., *Arms Control, the FRG, and the Future of East-West Relations*, pp. 29–49. Boulder, Colo.: Westview, 1987.
——. "West German Women: A Long Way from Kinder, Küche, Kirche." In Lynne Iglitzin and Ruth Ross, eds., *Women in the World: The Women's Decade 1975–1985*, pp. 27–52. Santa Barbara, Calif.: ABC-Clio, 1986.
Merkl, Peter H., ed. *The Federal Republic of Germany at Forty.* New York: New York University Press, 1989.
——. *Political Violence and Terror: Motifs and Motivations.* Berkeley and Los Angeles: University of California Press, 1986.
——. *Western European Party Systems: Trends and Prospects.* New York: Free Press and Macmillan, 1980.
——. *West German Foreign Policy: Dilemmas and Directions.* Chicago: Council on Foreign Relations, 1983.
Merritt, Anna J., and Richard L. Merritt, eds. *Public Opinion in Occupied Germany: The OMGUS Surveys, 1945–1949.* Urbana: University of Illinois Press, 1970.

————. *Public Opinion in Semisovereign Germany.* Urbana: University of Illinois Press, 1980.

Mertes, Michael, and Norbert J. Prill. "Die deutsche Einheit." *Die politische Meinung* 47, no. 2 (Nov./Dec. 1989), 4–15.

Meuschel, Sigrid. *Legitimation und Parteiherrschaft. Zum Wandel der Legitimitätsansprüche der SED, 1945–1989.* Dissertation, Freie Universität Berlin, 1991.

Minc, Alain. *La grande illusion.* Paris: Grasset, 1989.

Müller-Rommel, Ferdinand. "The Beginning of a New Germany? The GDR Elections of 18 March 1990." *West European Politics* 14, no. 1 (1991), 139–144.

————. "The Social Democratic Party: The Campaigns and Election Outcomes of 1980 and 1987." In Karl H. Cerny, ed., *Germany at the Polls: The Bundestag Elections of the 1980s.* Durham, N.C.: Duke University Press, 1990.

N. N. "DDR-BRD Perspektiven." *WSI Mitteilungen* (Wirtschafts- und Sozialwissenschaftliches Institut), no. 5 (1990).

N. N. "Frankfurt? Coburg? What About Bonn? Die Hauptstadtfrage nach 1945." *Forschungen* (DFG), no. 2 (1991), 15–18.

N. N. "The European Community and German Unification." *Bulletin of the European Communities,* supp. 4/90, pp. 30–33.

Nickel, Hildegard M. "Erwerbstätigkeit und Einkommen von Frauen in der DDR." *DIW Wochenbericht,* no. 19 (1990).

————. "Frauen in der DDR." *Das Parlament,* supp. , April 13, 1990.

Ninkovich, Frank A. *Germany and the United States: The Transformation of the German Question Since 1945.* Boston: Twayne, 1988.

Noelle-Neumann, Elisabeth, ed. *The Germans: Public Opinion Polls, 1967–1980.* Institut für Demoskopie. Westport, Conn.: Greenwood Press, 1981.

Pachman, Ludek. "Konföderation Mitteleuropa—Unsere Zukunft." In Wjatscheslaw Daschitschew and Carl Gustaf Ströhm, eds., *Die Neuordnung Mitteleuropas,* pp. 51–58. Mainz: Hase & Köhler, 1991.

Padgett, Stephen. "British Perspectives on the German Question." *Politics and Society in Germany, Austria, and Switzerland* 3, no. 1 (1990), 22–37.

Pelinka, Anton. "The Politics of Neutrality." *German Politics and Society* 21 (Fall 1990), 19–32.

Pfeiler, Wolfgang. *Die Viermächteoption als Instrument sowjetischer Deutschlandpolitik.* Interne Studie No. 25. St. Augustin: Konrad Adenauer Stiftung, 1991.

Pinson, Koppel S..*Modern Germany: Its History and Civilization.* 2nd ed. New York: Macmillan, 1966.

Pois, Robert A. *Friedrich Meinecke and German Politics in the Twentieth Century.* Berkeley and Los Angeles: University of California Press, 1972.

Pond, Elizabeth. *After the Wall: American Policy Towards Germany.* New York: Priority Press, 1990.

Priewe, Jan, and Rudolf Hickel. *Der Preis der Einheit: Bilanz und Perspektiven der deutschen Vereinigung.* Frankfurt: Fischer, 1991.

Reissig, Rolf. "Der Umbruch in der DDR und der Niedergang realsozialistischer Systeme." *Biss Public* 1 (Jan. 1991), pp. 35–64.

Rephewitz, Ulrich. "Berlin: Hauptstadt der BRD und eines vereinigten Deutschlands? Rechtliche Aspekte der Hauptstadtfrage." *Zeitschrift für Parlamentsfragen* 21, no. 3 (1990), 505–515.

Révész, Gabor. *Perestroika in Eastern Europe: Hungary's Economic Transformation, 1945–1988.* Boulder, Colo.: Westview, 1990.
Riese, Hans-Peter. "Die Geschichte hat sich ans Werk gemacht. Der Wandel der sowjetischen Position zur deutschen Frage." *Europa-Archiv* 4 (1990), 117.
Roth, Dieter. "Der ungeliebte Kanzler." In Reinhard Appel, ed., *Helmut Kohl im Spiegel seiner Macht,* pp. 285–299. Bonn: Aktuell, 1990.
———. "Die Wahlen zur Volkskammer in der DDR." *Politische Vierteljahresschrift* 31, no. 3 (1990), 369–393.
Rummel, Reinhardt, ed. *The Evolution of an International Actor: Western Europe's New Assertiveness.* Boulder, Colo.: Westview, 1990.
Sandford, Gregory W. *From Hitler to Ulbricht: The Communist Reconstruction of Eastern Germany, 1945–1946.* Princeton, N.J.: Princeton University Press, 1983.
Scharf, C. Bradley. *Politics and Change in East Germany: An Evaluation of Socialist Democracy.* Boulder, Colo.: Westview, 1984.
Schäuble, Wolfgang. *Der Vertrag. Wie ich über die deutsche Einheit verhandelte.* Stuttgart: Deutsche Verlagsanstalt, 1991.
Schelsky, Helmut. *Der Mensch in der wissenschaftlichen Zivilisation.* Cologne and Opladen: Westdeutscher Verlag, 1961.
Schinasi, Garry J., Leslie Lipschitz, and Donogh McDonald. "Monetary and Financial Issues in German Unification." In Leslie Lipschitz and Donogh McDonald, eds., *German Unification: Economic Issues,* pp. 147–149. Washington, D.C.: IMF, Dec. 1990.
Schlosser, Horst D. "Ein nur scheinbar bundesdeutscher Wahlkampf." *Deutschland-Archiv* 23, no. 4 (1990), 520–524.
Schmidt, Helmut. *Die Deutschen und ihre Nachbarn.* Stuttgart: Siedler Verlag, 1990.
Schmidt, Peter. "Europeanization of Defense: Prospect of Consensus?" RAND Corporation paper, Dec. 7, 1984.
———. "Public Opinion and Security in West Germany." RAND Corporation paper, Sept. 1984.
———. "West Germany and France: Convergent or Divergent Perspectives on European Security Cooperation?" In Reinhard Rummel, ed., *The Evolution of an International Actor: Western Europe's New Assertiveness,* pp. 161–178. Boulder, Colo.: Westview, 1990.
Schmitt, Rüdiger. "From 'Old Politics' to 'New Politics': Three Decades of Peace Protest in West Germany." In John R. Gibbins, ed., *Contemporary Political Culture: Politics in a Postmodern Age,* pp. 174–198. London: Sage, 1989.
Schneider, Gernot. *Wirtschaftswunder DDR: Anspruch und Realität.* 2nd ed. Berlin: Bundvertrag, 1990.
Schneider, Otto. "Wien und die deutsche Wiedervereinigung." *Europa-Archiv,* no. 4 (Feb. 15, 1990), 145.
Schoessler, Dietmar, ed. *Militär und Politik.* Koblenz: Bernard & Graefe, 1983.
Schoonmaker, Donald. "The Greens and the Federal Elections of 1980 and 1983: Is the Ostpolitik Waxing?" In Karl H. Cerny, ed., *Germany at the Polls: The Bundestag Elections of the 1980s.* Durham, N.C.: Duke University Press, 1990.
Schulmeister, Otto. *Die Zukunft Österreichs.* Vienna: Molden, 1967.
Schulz, Eberhard. *Die deutsche Frage und die Nachbarn im Osten.* Munich: Oldenbourg, 1989.

————. *Die deutsche Nation in Europa.* Bonn: Europa Union, 1982.

Schütze, Walter. "Frankreich angesichts der deutschen Einheit." *Europa Archiv,* no. 4 (Feb. 15, 1990), 133–138.

Schweigler, Gebhard. "Anti-Americanism in German Public Opinion." In Dieter Dettke, ed., *America's Image in Germany and Europe,* pp. 8–33. Washington, D.C.: Friedrich-Ebert-Stiftung, 1985.

————. *Nationalbewusstsein in der BRD und der DDR.* Düsseldorf: Bertelsmann, 1973.

Smith, Gordon, William E. Paterson, and Peter H. Merkl, eds. *Developments in West German Politics.* London: Macmillan, 1989.

Smith, Hedrick. *The New Russians.* New York: Random House, 1990.

Smith, Tom W. "The Polls: American Attitudes Toward the Soviet Union and Communism." *Public Opinion Quarterly* 47 (1983), 277ff.

Smyser, R. W. *The Economy of United Germany.* New York: St. Martin's Press, 1992.

SPD-Parteivorstand. "Die Mehrheit steht links—Die jungen Wähler in der BRD." Mimeographed, 1989.

Speier, Hans. *Divided Berlin.* New York: Praeger, 1962.

Spittman, Ilse. *Die DDR unter Honecker.* Cologne: Wissenschaft & Politik, 1990.

————. "Deutschland einig Vaterland." *Deutschland-Archiv* 22, no. 2 (1990), 187–190.

Steele, Jonathan. *Inside East Germany: The State That Came in from the Cold.* New York: Urizen Books, 1977.

Suhr, Heinz. *Der Treuhandskandal: Wie Ostdeutschland geschlachtet wurde.* Frankfurt: Eichborn, 1991.

————. *Was kostet uns die ehemalige DDR?* Frankfurt: Eichborn, 1990.

Thaysen, Uwe. "Die 'Eckpunkte' der Bundesländer für den Föderalismus im vereinigten Deutschland." *Zeitschrift für Parlamentsfragen* 21, no. 3 (1990), 461–463.

————. "Der runde Tisch. Oder: Wer war das Volk?" *Zeitschrift für Parlamentsfragen* 21, no. 1 (1990), 99–100.

Thies, Jochen, and Wolfgang Wagner, eds. *Auf dem Weg zum Binnenmarkt. Europäische Integration und deutscher Föderalismus.* Bonn: Verlag für Internationale Politik, 1989.

Treverton, Gregory F., ed. *The Shape of the New Europe.* New York: Council on Foreign Relations, 1991.

Tucker, Robert. *The Nuclear Debate: Deterrence and the Lapse of Faith.* New York: Holmes & Meier, 1985.

Unger, Brigitte. "Possibilities and Constraints for National Economic Policies in Small Countries: The Case of Austria." *German Politics and Society* 21 (Fall 1991), 63–77.

Urwin, Derek. *The Community of Europe: A History of European Integration Since 1945.* London and New York: Longman, 1991.

Veen, Hans-Joachim. "The Europeanization of German Politics." Paper presented to the GSA Conference in Los Angeles, Sept. 26–28, 1991.

————. "Die schwankenden Westdeutschen. Ein vorläufiges Meinungsbild zur Einigung." *Die politische Meinung* 35, no. 250 (May/June 1990), 15–22.

Volten, Peter, ed. *Uncertain Futures: Eastern Europe and Democracies.* Boulder, Colo.: Westview, 1990.

Von Beyme, Klaus. *Das politische System der Bundesrepublik Deutschland nach der Vereinigung.* Munich: Piper, 1991.
Wallace, Ian, and Gert-Joachim Glaessner, eds. *The German Revolution of 1989.* New York: Berg, 1992.
Wallach, H. G. Peter, and Ronald A. Francisco. *United Germany: The Past, Politics, Prospects.* New York: Praeger, 1992.
Weber, Max. *Wirtschaft und Gesellschaft. Grundrisse der verstehenden Soziologie.* 5th rev. ed. Tübingen: J. C. B. Mohr, 1972.
Wehler, Ulrich. *The German Empire, 1817–1918.* Lemington Spa/Dover: Berg, 1985.
Weidenfeld, Werner, ed. *Die Identität der Deutschen.* Munich: Hanser, 1983.
———. *Nachdenken über Deutschland: Materialien zur politischen Kultur der deutschen Frage.* Cologne: Wissenschaft & Politik, 1985.
Weidenfeld, Werner, and Josef Janning, eds. *Global Responsibilities: Europe in Tomorrow's World.* Gütersloh: Bertelsmann, 1991.
Weidenfeld, Werner, and Hartmut Zimmermann, eds. *Deutschland Handbuch. Eine doppelte Bilanz, 1949–1989.* Munich: Hanser, 1989.
Wettig, Gerhard. "Stadien der sowjetischen Deutschlandpolitik." *Deutschland-Archiv* 23, no. 7 (Jul. 1990), 1070–1078.
Wickert, Ulrich, ed. *Angst vor Deutschland.* New York and Hamburg: Hoffman & Campe, 1990.
Wissmann, Matthias, ed. *Deutsche Perspektiven: Unser Weg zum Jahr 2000.* Bonn: Universitas, 1990.
Wolffsohn, Michael. *Keine Angst vor Deutschland.* Erlangen and Bonn: Straube, 1990.

Documents and Data

Deutsches Jugendinstitut (DJI). *Deutsche Schüler im Sommer 1990—Skeptische Demokraten auf dem Weg in ein vereintes Deutschland. Deutsch-deutsche Schülerbefragung, 1990.* Arbeitspapier 3-019. DGI, 1990.
Documents on German Unity (a *German Tribune* supplement). Hamburg: Reinecke, 1990.
Der Einigungsvertrag. Vertrag zwischen der BRD und der DDR über die Herstellung der Einheit Deutschlands. Munich: Goldmann (Bertelsmann).
Euro-Barometer, 1971; 1981; 22 (1984); 24 (1985).
Federal Republic of Germany, Press and Information Office. *Report on Arms Control and Disarmament and on Changes in the Balance of Military Power, 1989–1990.* 1 Jul. 1989–30 June 1990. Bonn, March 1991.
Forschungsgruppe Wahlen. *Blitzumfrage zur Landtagswahl 1991 in Hessen.* Jan. 14–16, 1991. Mannheim, 1991.
———. *Meinungen der Bürger der DDR, December 1989.* Mannheim, 1990.
———. *Politbarometer,* November 1990; January 1991; April 1991; May 1991; August 1991.
———. *Vorwahlbericht. Daten zur Bundestagswahl und der Wahl zum Berliner Abgeordnetenhaus am 2. Dezember 1990.* Mannheim, 1991.
———. *Wahltagsbefragung Landtagswahl in Hessen, January 20, 1991.* Mannheim, 1991.

German Foreign Office. *KSZE Dokumentation. KSZE–KVAE, Phraseologie der KSZE und KVAE.* Bonn, 1987.

German Information Center. *Treaty Between the FRG and the GDR: Establishing a Monetary, Economic and Social Union.* New York, 1990.

Institut für Demoskopie. *Jahrbuch der öffentlichen Meinung.* Allensbach, 1947–1955, 1958–1964; 1965–1967, 1968–1973.

Institut für praxisorientierte Sozialforschung (IPOS). *Einstellungen zu aktuellen Fragen der Innenpolitik in der BRD 1989.* Mannheim, 1989.

Institut für praxisorientierte Sozialforschung (IPOS). *Einstellungen zu aktuellen Fragen der Innenpolitik in der BRD und der DDR.* Mannheim, 1990.

Report on Arms Control and Disarmament and on Changes in the Balance of Military Power, 1989–1990.

Statistisches Bundesamt, ed. *Datenreport 1989. Zahlen und Fakten über die BRD.*

Times Mirror Center for the People and the Press. *The Pulse of Europe: A Survey of Political and Social Values and Attitudes.* Washington, D.C., 1991.

Der Vertrag zur deutschen Einheit. Augewählte Texte. Commentary by Günther Bannas et al. Frankfurt and Leipzig: Insel & Nomos, 1990.

West German Federal Press and Information Office, *European Political Cooperation.* Bonn, 1988.

Newspapers and Periodicals

Berliner Morgenpost
Berliner Zeitung
Business Week
Dagens Nyheter
Daily Telegraph
The Economist
Le Figaro
Frankfurter Allgemeine Zeitung
Frankfurter Rundschau
General Anzeiger (Bonn)
Göttinger Tagesblatt
Handelsblatt
Hannoversche Allgemeine
The Independent
Jerusalem Post
Jyllands-Posten
Leipziger Volkszeitung
Los Angeles Times
Mainzer Allgemeine Zeitung
Manchester Guardian Weekly
Le Monde

Neues Deutschland
Neue Zürcher Zeitung
New York Review of Books
New York Times
Nouvel Observateur
Nürnberger Nachrichten
Das Parlament
Rheinische Post
Rheinischer Merkur/Christ und Welt
Rzeczpospolita
Der Spiegel
Der Stern
Stuttgarter Zeitung
Süddeutsche Zeitung
Tagesspiegel
Tageszeitung (taz)
The Times (London)
Washington Post
Die Welt
Die Zeit
Zycie Warszawy

Index